Educational Psychology

BRYCE B. HUDGINS
Washington University

GARY D. PHYE
Iowa State University

CANDACE GARRETT SCHAU
University of New Mexico

GARY L. THEISEN
Ford Foundation

CAROLE AMES
University of Maryland

RUSSELL AMES
University of Maryland

F. E. Peacock Publishers, Inc.
Itasca, Illinois 60143

Contents

Preface

The study of educational psychology should influence the ways a teacher thinks about the instructional process. The purpose of this textbook is to present to the education student some of the most dependable current knowledge about how children develop, how they learn, how groups of people live together in classrooms, and how the instructional process and its outcomes are measured and evaluated.

The approaches to teaching or methods which teachers find successful and with which they can work comfortably vary considerably. The authors of this book believe that teachers can use the findings of educational psychology best by adapting and applying them to the various kinds of educational decisions they must make numerous times each day, rather than following specific teaching methods. In short, we have attempted to produce a book that will help to shape "the ideas in teachers' heads" rather than one that is aimed directly at instruction in particular teaching skills or behaviors.

Originally the intention of the authors was to write each chapter of the book as an exposition of a particular topic. There were to be copious illustrations and examples germane to the point under discussion. The writing was to be as nontechnical as possible. References to and citations of supporting or background research were to be sharply limited. One of the oft-heard student criticisms of educational psychology books is that strings of reference citations interfere with the continuity of the discussion, a point with which we agree.

Though we still regard the initial conception as laudable, we found it extremely difficult to implement, and the finished book departs to a degree from the initial plan. One way is in the use of citations of other work as a basis for documenting conclusions. Deprived of a means to relate a contemporary position or point of view to other work and ideas in the field, the first drafts of several chapters seemed weakened from a scholarly standpoint. In the end it was determined that the authors should have the freedom to build the necessary backgrounds, and so references are cited as needed, to an appropriate extent.

A second way the book departs from the original conception is in the use of textual examples and illustrations. Somewhat to our surprise, early drafts of the chapters seemed to suffer a break in the exposition as a result of the many excellent examples that were given. The problem was solved by the use of the featured boxes, a suggestion offered by Gloria Reardon, F. E. Peacock's development editor. Mrs. Reardon took an active role in the final stages of manuscript editing and preparation and throughout the production phase of the book. The authors owe her a great debt for her many contributions, which we here gladly and publicly acknowledge.

The greatest strength of this book, if I may speak briefly as its senior author and what might be called its "substantive" editor, is the group of co-authors who wrote it. When the publishers, F. E. Peacock and Thomas LaMarre, and I first spoke seriously several years ago about the writing of *Educational Psychology,* it was Ted Peacock's special concern that others who had particular knowledge about and interest in specific areas should be brought into the writing project. Therefore I wrote a statement about the plans and aspirations for the book, named and ordered the chapters that would constitute it, and provided a brief statement about the content of each chapter. In the spring of 1979 Tom LaMarre and I met with each of the co-authors: Gary Phye of Iowa State University; Candace Schau of the University of New Mexico; Gary Theisen, then teaching at the University of Iowa, and now with the Ford Foundation in Indonesia; and Carole and Russell Ames, both of the University of Maryland.

Agreements were reached about the writing responsibilities of each author. Since this is an integrated textbook, not a collection of separate chapters, we agreed that no attribution of authors to chapters was to be made. Chapters were drafted, I read them and offered what suggestions and encouragement I could, and the revision process continued until the manuscript was as clear, accurate, and relevant to our purposes as we could manage.

Although our collective aim was to produce a single, coherent volume, individual authors wrote in their specialized areas, and each of them deserves credit for the chapters that he or she was responsible for. Gary Phye's basic assignment was to write Chapters 2, 3, and 4, all of which deal with human development, and Chapter 5, The Exceptional Learner. Candace Schau assumed responsibility for the discussions of measurement and evaluation that became Chapters 15, 16, 17, and 18. She also wrote Chapter 6 on intelligence. Chapters 13 and 14, devoted to classroom groups and leadership, were undertaken by Gary Theisen. Carole and Russell Ames wrote Chapter 9, on the learning of attitudes and values, and Chapter 11, on motivation. I wrote Chapters 1, 7, 8, 10, and 12.

I wish to acknowledge the contributions made to this book by several other people. Mrs. Joyce Usher and her staff in the Peacock editorial offices worked with us on the initial selection of photographs as well as in many other ways. Tom Fawell provided the line drawings that grace the introduction to each of the four parts of the text and the chapter logos, and his firm, American Graphics, took all but four of the photographs especially for this book. Patricia Simmons typed the manuscript in whole or in part through several revisions, and Robbie Reardon typed the final edited version.

Thanks also go to Therese Herman for her assistance with the instructors' manual. Her work was instrumental in helping the authors achieve their goal of providing instructors with a manual that includes practical suggestions for teaching the course, as well as the usual set of test questions covering the material in each chapter.

Finally a few words of thanks to Tom LaMarre and Ted Peacock must be added. Without both their efforts to help the authors there simply would be no book. Tom LaMarre was intimately involved in the enterprise, from its earliest planning stages until this moment when the book is about to go to press. Whatever doubts and qualms he felt from time to time he admirably kept to himself. The atmosphere of warmth coupled with high standards of performance that characterizes F. E. Peacock Publishers emanates from Ted Peacock. The authors are proud to have our book bear the Peacock label.

Bryce B. Hudgins

St. Louis, Mo.
October 1982

Acknowledgments

Photography and part and chapter opening drawings by Tom Fawell/ American Graphics, Inc.

Additional photographs by:
Jerry Bushey, p. 42
Peggo Cromer, p. 86
William Means, p. 413
David S. Strickler, p. 650

Book design and production by Edit, Inc.

Permission to reprint copyright materials is acknowledged from the following publishers, as a continuation of the copyright page.

BOXES

Chapter 1, Box B: Reprinted from Philip W. Jackson, *Life in Classrooms,* with permission of CBS College Publishing Division. Copyright 1968.

Chapter 8, Box A: Reprinted from B. F. Skinner, "Teaching Machines," *Science,* vol. 128 (October 24, 1958), pp. 969–977, Figures 1 and 2, with permission of the American Association for the Advancement of Science.

Chapter 10, Box A: Reprinted from "Sizing up Assertions," *Elementary School Journal,* vol. 76 (1976), p. 289, by Mary Lee Marksberry, by permission of the University of Chicago Press. © 1976 by the University of Chicago.

Chapter 10, Box C: From pp. 47–48 in *Productive Thinking,* Enl. Edition by Max Wertheimer, Edited by Michael Wertheimer. Copyright 1945, © 1959 by Valentine Wertheimer. By permission of Harper & Row, Publishers, Inc.

Chapter 11, Box C: From pp. 239–241 (text only) in *Learning and Human Abilities,* 4th Edition by Herbert J. Klausmeier and William Goodwin. Copyright © 1961, 1975 by Herbert J. Klausmeier. By permission of Harper & Row, Publishers, Inc.

Chapter 11, Box D: From Richard de Charms, *Enhancing Motivation: Change in the Classroom,* pp. 72–73. Reprinted by permission of Irvington Publishers, Inc., New York.

Chapter 13, Box C: From Willard Waller, *The Sociology of Teaching,* pp. 270–271. Reprinted by permission of John Wiley & Sons, Inc.

Chapter 14, Box A: Reprinted from Thomas J. Cottle, "What Tracking Did to Ollie Taylor," *Social Policy,* July–August 1974, p. 24. © 1974 by Social Policy Corporation.

Chapter 15, Box B: Reprinted from George Borhnstedt and David Knoke, *Statistics for Social Data Analysis,* p. 14, with permission of the authors and F. E. Peacock Publishers, Inc.

TABLES

Table 2.2: Adapted from B. R. McCandless and E. D. Evans, *Children and Youth: Psychosocial Development,* with permission of CBS College Publishing Division. Copyright 1973.

Table 6.1: From "The Development of Intelligence" by Robert S. Siegler and D. Dean Richards, in Robert Sternberg (Ed.), *Handbook of Intelligence Research* to be published by Cambridge University Press. Used with permission of Cambridge University Press.

Tables 9.1 and 9.2: Reprinted with permission of Macmillan Publishing Co., Inc., from *The Nature of Human Values* by Milton Rokeach. Copyright © 1973 by The Free Press, a Division of Macmillan Publishing Co., Inc.

Table 13.3: Adapted from "Effects of the Open Classroom" by Robert Horowitz, in *Educational Environments and Effects* by Herbert Walberg. McCutchan Publishing Corporation, © 1979. Permission granted by the publisher.

Table 17.3: Reprinted from *Teacher's Guide, the Iowa Tests of Basic Skills*, Form 7/8, with permission of Riverside Publishing Company, subsidiary Houghton Mifflin Company.

FIGURES

Figures 6.1 and 6.2: Adapted with permission of Macmillan Publishing Co., Inc., from *Psychological Testing* by Anne Anastasi. Copyright © 1968 by Anne Anastasi.

Figure 6.3: Developed from information in "Organization of Data on Life-Span Development of Human Abilities" by John L. Horn, in L. R. Goulet and Paul B. Baltes, *Life-Span Developmental Psychology*. Used with permission of Academic Press, Inc., and the author.

Figure 6.4: Reprinted from "A Normative Sample of Intelligence and Achievement of Negro Elementary School Children in the Southeastern United States," by W. A. Kennedy, V. Van de Riet, and J. C. White, Jr., in *Monographs of the Society for Research in Child Development*, vol. 28 (1963), Ser. no. 90, with permission of W. A. Kennedy. © the Society for Research in Child Development, Inc.

Figure 8.2: Reprinted from "A Comparison of Students' Studying Behavior Produced by Daily, Weekly and Three-Week Testing Schedules," by V. T. Mawhinney, D. E. Bostow, D. R. Laws, G. J. Blumenfeld, and B. L. Hopkins, with permission of the *Journal of Applied Behavior Analysis*, Department of Human Development, University of Kansas, Lawrence.

Figure 10.1: Adapted from Robert M. Olton and Richard S. Crutchfield, "Developing the Skills of Productive Thinking," in Paul Mussen, Jonas Langer, and Martin V. Covington (Eds.), *Trends and Issues in Developmental Psychology*, with permission of CBS College Publishing Division. Copyright 1969.

Figures 10.2 and 10.3: From "The Origins of Scientific Reasoning" by Robert S. Siegler, in R. S. Siegler (Ed.), *Children's Thinking: What Develops?* Copyright 1978 by Lawrence Erlbaum Associates. Reprinted by permission.

Figure 11.2: Adapted from *Guided Design* by C. E. Wales and R. A. Stager. Used with permission of Charles E. Wales, director, Center for Guided Design, West Virginia University.

Figure 13.2: Reprinted with permission of Macmillan Publishing Co., Inc., from *The Sociometry Reader* by J. L. Moreno. Copyright © 1960 by The Free Press, a Corporation.

QUOTATIONS

P. 314: Reprinted with permission of Macmillan Publishing Co., Inc., from *The Nature of Human Values* by Milton Rokeach. Copyright © 1973 by The Free Press, a Division of Macmillan Publishing Co., Inc.

P. 324: Reprinted from "Stage and Sequence: The Cognitive Developmental Approach to Socialization," by Lawrence Kohlberg, in D. Goslin (Ed.), *Handbook of Socialization Theory and Research*, with permission of Houghton Mifflin Co.

Pp. 362–363: Reprinted from "Sizing up Assertions," Elementary School Journal, vol. 76 (1976), p. 293, by Mary Lee Marksberry, by permission of the University of Chicago Press. © 1976 by the University of Chicago.

Teaching as Social Behavior: An Introduction

This is a book about how teachers teach and students learn. We believe the mysteries of teaching can be explained in terms of everyday social behavior, as limited and defined by the special circumstances of the classroom setting. The transmission of learning is a social act that emerges from and is dependent on the relationship between the teacher and the learner.

The school is recognized by sociologists and social psychologists as second only to the family as an agent of socialization. This is the process whereby children are introduced and indoctrinated into the appropriate behavior expected by members of the society in which they are being reared. The school provides continuing knowledge of the past, vocational skills, and exposure to cultural attitudes and values. Moreover, the effects of the school on personality, through the continual interactions of students with teachers, administrators, and peers, are far-reaching (Williamson, Swingle, & Sargent, 1982). In the school the child learns to behave as a member of a group, to wait for attention, and to tolerate being denied or frustrated. The child is introduced to a more structured evaluation than was provided in the home and must learn to take orders from a more distant authority (Jackson, 1968).

For the teacher, classroom behavior is guided by personal ideas about teaching that have taken hold as a result of the teacher's background of development and interpersonal relations, familiarity with the demands of the subject matter, and professional knowledge and educational expertise. The teacher's specialized knowledge and roles—as group leader, communicator, tutor, and so on—are unique to teaching. Nonetheless, the setting for teaching is a social one, and it is largely conducted through the social medium of language in its numerous forms. The process of teaching, therefore, should be thought of as a type of everyday social interaction, rather than as a distinctive or specialized type of human behavior.

THE CLASSROOM SOCIETY

The social setting for the interactions between teachers and students is the classroom—a busy, confining, verbally demanding, decision oriented, and intense mini society or subculture. Exactly what it is like to be a teacher in a classroom depends on the grade level of the students, the subject matter being taught, and the larger environment in which the school is placed, among other considerations. In the main, however, teachers' classroom experiences have similar characteristics.

All classrooms tend to be busy places. Learning may be easy or difficult, interesting or boring, but it is going on constantly in classrooms. The outward manifestations of this lively interaction are the activities that take place in the classroom: reading, writing, giving demonstrations, conducting and participating in recitations, correcting homework assignments, discussing quiz papers, and all the rest. Both students and teachers are involved in these activities, but in most classrooms, most of the time, the busiest, most involved person in the room is the teacher.

Classrooms and schools are also confining. Students frequently complain about this, especially secondary school students who may have only four or five minutes between classes and a continuous string of classes each day. Teachers have somewhat more freedom, but not much. They can move around in the classroom more easily than students can. A high school teacher will not be given detention for being a few minutes late to class, as a student may be. But school days demand the teacher's presence in the designated place at the designated time. To arrive an hour late or leave an hour early requires special arrangements, and going out to lunch is a rare event in the lives of most teachers. The degree of confinement teachers experience is indicated by the sense of emancipation they feel when an occasional in-service workshop day or teachers' convention breaks the pattern.

Classrooms are also highly verbal settings. Education seems to be transacted mostly through the spoken word, and the principal speaker is the teacher. Beginning teachers, especially, can expect to have sore throats by the end of the school day. There have been reliable estimates that someone is talking about two thirds of the time in the classroom, and two thirds of that time it is the teacher. The talk is not all of the same kind, of course. The teacher gives directions, defines norms, sets expectations, makes assignments, explains ideas, offers reassurance, hears answers to questions, and provides evaluations.

This verbal behavior is one reason the teacher's classroom life is decision oriented. The teacher must decide whether an answer is correct or incorrect, whether to praise or blame a student. She or he must decide whether the classroom's noise level is acceptable, indicating task-oriented hustle and bustle, or whether it is spilling over into disarray and chaos and needs immediate control. The teacher also must make a host of decisions about classroom work. Is too much or too little being expected? Is the pace rapid enough, or too fast? Are homework assignments frequent enough, or too burdensome? Are the teacher's standards too high, or not high enough? Are grading policies too tough or too lenient? The list of decisions the teacher is called on to make is endless.

Finally, there is a moment-to-moment intensity about classroom teaching that denies teachers the luxury of quiet reflection before taking action. That is not true of all aspects of teaching, of course. Teachers have time after school to plan the next day's work, to score tests, and to write helpful notes in the margins of students' papers. But during the interactive phases of teaching, when teachers and students work together those five or six hours of each school day, what teachers say and do, what they permit or disallow, what they accept or reject must ordinarily be decided and acted on quickly—not automatically, but with very little time to ponder and debate. The overall quality of these decisions has a great deal to do with what the students in a teacher's charge learn and how well they learn it. By the same token, it helps to shape the teacher's success.

FACTORS INFLUENCING TEACHING BEHAVIOR

While all teachers have similar experiences in classrooms, an individual's teaching behavior is as distinctive as any other aspect of his or her personality. Basically, we suggest, there are four factors in a teacher's background that influence the kinds of behavior that will be adopted as a vehicle for that teacher's classroom interactions with students. In order of diminishing influence, these factors are:

1. The temperament and disposition of the teacher and the teacher's own cumulative history of social and interpersonal relations.
2. How the teacher was taught.
3. The teacher's acquaintance with the special characteristics of the subject matter being taught.
4. The teacher's professional knowledge about education and teaching, including the applied social science of educational psychology.

Although we place educational psychology within the domain of professional education knowledge and place that category at the bottom of the list of factors that shape teachers' behavior, this does not mean that we consider its function in the teacher's classroom life to be either trivial or irrelevant. We do think such placement is realistic, however, and it may give teachers a clearer understanding of the contribution that educational psychology can make to teaching. Throughout this chapter we will indicate ways in which the study of educational psychology can furnish unique, significant knowledge to be applied in the conduct of education.

As an adult human being, the teacher has a history of social relationships with other people. When teaching is viewed as a matter of social relationships, as it is in this text, the teacher's own cumulative history can be regarded as an influence on teaching because it is transferred to the teacher's relationships with pupils in the classroom. Some teachers, like people in general, are by temperament warm and relaxed in relationships with others, and some are aloof, cool, and distant. A wide range

*As one child tries out the teacher's role with another, how
she "teaches" will be affected by how she has been taught. In
the same way, real-life teachers' behaviors are shaped by the
ideas in their heads about teaching and other factors in
their individual backgrounds.*

of classroom relationships can yield satisfactory results, without providing either a breakdown of necessary discipline or a rebellion against
classroom authority. Each teacher has a characteristic style that is related
to her or his temperament. The teacher is more likely to be comfortable
with this style than trying to alter it to take some recommended approach
to leading a group or working with a class of pupils.

Teachers also are likely to teach as they were themselves taught. This
is understandable, since they were exposed to certain models of teaching
for 14 or 15 years before they started studying teacher education. Unless
a teacher education program offers a highly distinctive approach, its
precepts and methods are likely to be blended with the earlier models
to which the student teacher was exposed.

A third influence on teachers' behavior is the content they are teaching. Content may be more relevant at the secondary level, where its
structure is more differentiated than in the elementary school, in which

virtually all subject matter is reducible to reading. The task of teaching introductory French vocabulary, pronunciation, and grammar to eighth- or ninth-graders, for example, calls for different methods than teaching English literature or American history to the same students.

The effects of these three factors—the teacher's temperament and background, how the teacher was taught, and the demands of the teaching field—are powerful determinants of teacher behavior, and they are virtually independent of any specialized or technical knowledge about teaching. Nevertheless, we think, the study of educational psychology can make a difference in how teachers or others engage in the instructional process. The assumption is that knowledge about the topics of educational psychology becomes integrated into the teacher's views of how teaching is best conducted or how it should or ought to be conducted.

Suppose a recent college graduate who had majored in French but had not studied education or observed teaching in high school classrooms were asked to teach beginning French to a class of high school students. In planning and attempting to teach this course the graduate would soon recognize the need for a conception—we might very informally call it a *theory*—of how people learn. That conception would be heavily influenced by the first three influences on teaching behavior, or variations on them. The novice teacher would bring to the task an idea of how to approach it derived from his background of relationships with others. He would consider by inference what views of learning his various teachers have held, and he would surely make an assessment of any special characteristics the French language has with regard to learning.

Can a teacher whose knowledge about teaching is derived from such personal, unscientific sources succeed in the classroom? Of course. Evidence of such successes is all around us. Teachers in many private or independent schools have received little if any formal study of education. Professors in most departments of colleges and universities have been thoroughly schooled in their disciplines, and not at all in educational psychology or formal teacher education. Some departments attempt to fill this need with seminars which offer practical suggestions and guidelines for teaching various introductory courses. There are many splendid, inspiring teachers who have not studied the specialized content of educational psychology.

Many years ago John Dewey observed that there are teachers with little professional training who succeed, and others who may have abundant knowledge of educational psychology and history and methods of teaching who are not good teachers. In fact, as Stephens (1967) has pointed out, both teaching and learning are general, pervasive forms of human activity. Most people encounter occasions when they must "teach," even if they are not professional teachers. If we had had to wait for the

BOX A   *Teaching:*
A science or an art?

Psychology was introduced to the classroom in the early part of the 20th century when teachers seeking professional status turned to psychologists for help in understanding how the mind works. William James, in *Talks to Teachers on Psychology,* acknowledged their interest but suggested that the science could be of little practical help in the classroom:

. . . you make a great, a very great mistake, if you think that psychology, being the science of the mind's laws, is something from which you can deduce definite programs and schemes and methods of instruction for immediate schoolroom use. Psychology is a science, and teaching is an art; and sciences never generate arts directly out of themselves. An intermediary inventive mind must make the application, by using its originality. . . . A science only lays down lines within which the rules of the art must fall, laws which the follower of the art must not transgress; but what particular thing he shall positively do within those lines is left exclusively to his own genius. . . .
   To know psychology, therefore, is absolutely no guarantee that we shall be good teachers. To advance to that result, we must have an additional endowment altogether, a happy tact and ingenuity to tell us what definite things to say and do when the pupil is before us. That ingenuity in meeting and pursuing the pupil, that tact for the concrete situation, though they are the alpha and omega of the teacher's art, are things to which psychology cannot help us in the least. . . .

Source: William James, *Talks to Teachers on Psychology* (New York: Henry Holt Co., 1920; originally published 1899), p. 24.

development of specialized scientific knowledge about teaching before we could engage in the art, educational progress would have been much different, and definitely slower (see Box A). Like many other activities of mankind, teaching has a certain survival value which ensures its continued existence.

We consider the study of the psychological bases of education, then, as a means of incorporating established social scientific knowledge into the practice of a fundamental, natural form of human activity. It provides a means of rationalizing, clarifying, understanding, and perhaps improving the day-to-day decisions and actions that those cast in the role of teacher are called on to make.

EDUCATIONAL PSYCHOLOGY AS A SCIENCE

Educational psychology is an applied social science whose objective is to provide comprehensive, systematic data about the psychological issues that undergird education. Although these issues cover a vast range of topics, they all usually involve the examination of some variable or variables about learners, the materials of learning, or the outcomes of learning in relation to one another.

EXPANDING THE BODY OF KNOWLEDGE

One function of educational psychology is to conduct scientific inquiry into the issues of teaching and learning. As with any other social science, the objective of inquiry or research in educational psychology is to add to the body of dependable knowledge—in this case, knowledge about some aspect of education.

To illustrate this function we can consider the purposes of a paper selected from the *Journal of Educational Psychology,* a publication of the American Psychological Association which is perhaps the most representative source of educational psychology research in the United States at the present time. The paper, titled "Summarizing Stories After Reading and Listening," by Walter Kintsch and Ely Kominsky, was in the October 1977 issue. From the title you might suppose that the paper deals with how students summarize stories, or even with techniques teachers might use to improve summaries. In fact, it has nothing to do with either topic. Kintsch's interest, of long standing, is the development of a psychological theory of comprehension. In this particular study he and Kominsky compared the lengths and language properties of summaries of easy stories that were produced by a small sample of college students, some of whom read the stories and some of whom heard tape-recorded versions of them.

In their research report, Kintsch and Kominsky expressed surprise that the students' summaries were so similar, since the story media were so different. Otherwise, they observed, their results were not unlike those of earlier studies in which students were asked to engage in free recall of story material or answer questions about the content of stories. This small-scale study, therefore, added an increment of knowledge to Kintsch's developing theory about comprehension.

If you read the Kintsch and Kominsky paper or another from such a journal, you would get an idea of how new knowledge in the field of education is developed. But reading such material would probably not be very helpful in the sense of directly improving your teaching behavior. Its purpose is to contribute to the growing body of applied social science knowledge, not to make direct contact with classroom teaching practice.

SOLVING PROBLEMS IN THE
CLASSROOM CONTEXT

When applied social science is viewed in more global terms than individual research investigations, the larger purpose of the scientific inquiry is to help solve the problems of the field. In this sense educational psychology is an applied social science that tries to provide data, concepts, and theories about human development, learning, motivation, and other topics considered in this text as they function in the context of the classroom. This knowledge is not intended to provide the teacher with answers to the imperative, moment-by-moment questions of "What do I do now?" Rather, it can help fill out the broad conceptual structures—or "theories"—that teachers have about these concepts. The teacher who has a solid base of educational psychology knowledge will have theories to work with that are rooted in established social science principles, and the available alternatives for making decisions will be more dependable than those that are based solely on intuition or folk wisdom.

As an applied social science, educational psychology seeks to find the answers to practical questions, specifically those that pertain to teaching and learning in school-type or other kinds of educational settings. The nature of these settings is becoming increasingly diverse; it now includes hospitals and other medical organizations, the military, business and industry, computer service organizations, and other settings where both teaching and learning go on. In earlier definitions of educational psychology, the province was almost exclusively the schoolroom.

The precepts of social science can help educational problem solvers of all types avoid arriving at hasty or ill-considered answers. The social scientist calls for careful definition of the problem and seeks out the kinds of observations that can provide pertinent information on it. Efforts are made to record observations as carefully and objectively as possible so they can be interpreted unequivocally. Scientific research methods are employed to produce results that are valid and reliable indicators of the probable effects of educational variables in real-life classrooms (see Chapter 15).

A great deal of the best research in educational psychology examines the instructional process. The research is designed to look at the behavior of teachers or of students and teachers in classroom settings, or in settings that make it possible to generalize their results to classrooms. This book is filled with references to such studies. The purpose of such research, however, is not primarily to propose, discover, or recommend particular strategies or techniques of instruction. Rather it is to examine and analyze issues in such a way as to help educational psychologists, and ultimately teachers, to understand the underlying issues that affect educational policies and classroom decisions.

This consideration of research in educational psychology is demonstrated in Chapters 11 and 12. Chapter 11 is a systematic review of theories of motivation, particularly as they apply to education, coupled with an analysis of contemporary programs of training in motivation that have been used in schools or with students in various capacities. Chapter 12 examines certain issues in how empirical knowledge of learning has been brought to focus on classroom approaches to instruction. Despite this practice orientation, these chapters are analytical, however. They stop short of prescribing methods of classroom teaching for specific circumstances.

THE INSTRUCTIONAL PROCESS

The focus of this book is on the instructional process—the procedures by which knowledge or behavior or ways of looking at or thinking about the world are communicated by a teacher to a learner. Our conception of the instructional process stresses the social roles played by the teacher and the learner in this interaction, as we noted at the beginning of this chapter. The content is organized into four major parts or subject areas, each of which influences the process by which instruction is conveyed. These parts are:

> Part I: Development of the Learner—how the learner develops; how the teacher accommodates individual differences in learners.
>
> Part II: Learning, Thinking and Motivation—how the learner learns, thinks, and is motivated; how the teacher's knowledge of these variables influences instructional style.
>
> Part III: The Social Psychology of the Classroom—how the learner functions in classroom groups; the teacher's role as a leader in the classroom and as an agent of socialization in the larger society.
>
> Part IV: Educational Measurement and Evaluation—evaluation of student progress; accountability of the teacher for educational success.

These are the topics that are usually considered in educational psychology, though other texts may place more or less emphasis on certain areas. Our criterion for choosing the content for this book was how each topic fits into our conception of the instructional process as an interaction between teacher and learner.

We also have recognized that while educational psychology has a responsibility to present and integrate psychological knowledge that impinges on the work of teachers, it has something to say to everyone who is interested in education. All teachers do not work in school settings, of course. Our first teachers—perhaps the most important ones in our lives—are our parents. Employers sometimes are teachers, and so are the clergy and other religious leaders, medical professionals, military officers, and others. The list is endless, and it would be impossible to consider all the possibilities in this book. On the contrary, our focus is clearly on children and adolescents as the subjects of instruction, and the teacher we have in mind is the one who teaches in the elementary or secondary schools of the land. Nonetheless, our model of instruction can be applied to these other teaching roles, and the content of the book has relevance for every informed citizen who is concerned with the status of education in our society.

THE INSTRUCTIONAL PROCESS AS COMMUNICATION

When we use the term *instructional process*, we refer to an act of communication between an instructor and a learner. The instructor often is a live teacher, but it may also be a book, film, or other inert medium. Frequently, of course, instruction is delivered by both agents simultaneously; that is, a live teacher guides, mediates, or controls the communication of a specific explanation, the presentation of a mathematical concept, or the interpretation of a poem.

A good description of the interactive and reciprocal nature of the instructional process was provided by B. Othanel Smith (1960), who conceptualized it in terms of teaching cycles. In its simplest form, the teaching cycle consists of an act of teaching and an act of taking instruction. In the teaching act, the teacher does three things in sequence: perceives the state of the learner, diagnoses the learner's level of motivation or comprehension of the subject, and responds to it. The pupil's act of taking instruction is reciprocal; the pupil perceives the behavior of the teacher, diagnoses what is required, and reacts. Teaching cycles can be elaborate and complicated or quite brief and simple, as in the following example from a high school history class discussion:

> *Teacher:* Now, do you know who was the first person to find the
>   Hawaiian Islands? Steve?
> *Steve:* Was it Captain Cook?
> *Teacher:* That's right.
>
> > (Smith & Meux, 1962, p. 15)

Left at this point, the instructional process seems uncomplicated. The teacher's task is to provide instruction; the learner's is to receive it and, implicitly, to take note of and store it. In that way, over time, children become educated. A 19th-century image of education involved "Mark Hopkins" on one end of a log and the student on the other. Presumably Hopkins would explain life and the student would absorb every word and idea.

For better or for worse, however, the process is more complicated than that. The idyll begins to tarnish if we think about it lasting over any period of time. Some teachers, of course, are more knowledgeable and more interesting than others. Even so, suppose that after a while Hopkins, on the far end of the log, talks about ideas that are new to the learner, ideas about which the learner has no background or insufficient intellectual development. The learner becomes confused or intellectually bogged down, or early interest in the topic fades. A bump on the learner's end of the log begins to be irritating, as the spring wildflowers in view grow increasingly enticing. It becomes clear, as teacher educators of the progressive era were fond of putting it, that "teaching is not telling."

In our definition of the instructional process as an act of communication between the instructor or instructive agent and the learner, communication is viewed as a two-way street. The learners are not passive recipients of instruction but will act on it, or react to it, in many ways. The variables that enter into these actions and reactions are considered in the chapters that follow.

THE IDEAS IN TEACHERS' HEADS ABOUT EDUCATION

In the moment-to-moment interactions of the classroom, the sets of beliefs that teachers possess about how teachers learn, what motivates them, the state of their cognitive development, and other such considerations play decisive roles. In any society there are norms and values about what is appropriate or ought to be, as well as how things work, or what is or will be. For example, a man of middle age in American society today probably has a very different view of the role of women than his college-age daughter has. As the behavior of each is played out to express these beliefs, including what each of them says, the other is likely to feel perplexed, alarmed, or angry—or all three. The young woman's behavior may be guided by a general belief that the equality of women has been denied by a male-oriented, male-dominated society, and women's attitudes and behavior must be assertive if they are to realize the equality in all areas that was promised to every American.

The classroom society has its own norms and values, and teachers have ideas in their heads about education. These ideas, cognitive structures, or "theories" are not necessarily very comprehensive or systematic, and it is not unusual for teachers to have competing theories about education that contradict one another.

A teacher may believe that children learn primarily through repetition, for example. A great deal of this teacher's lesson planning, selection of curricular materials, and classroom decisions, therefore, would be influenced by that belief. In this classroom we would expect the recitations to emphasize repetition of facts or the memorization of important text material. Mastery of the finished form of the lesson would be required, but there would probably be little concern with whether learners understood the material or how it relates to anything else in their world.

Another teacher may have a theory that young children require the opportunity to engage in exploratory behavior and manipulative play with concrete objects in order to develop accurate, permanent concepts about the physical world. In this teacher's classroom we would expect to see various children working on somewhat different tasks with concrete objects, since there are differences in the rates at which concept learning occurs.

Where one teacher believes that a group of students must be held in tight control if educational objectives are to be achieved, a different teacher may believe that the emergence of a self-directed group, in which students learn to plan and make decisions, is crucial to their educational development.

Because teaching is essentially everyday social behavior, teaching behavior is guided largely by the "ideas inside teachers' heads." Of the four factors that help shape teacher's behavior in the classroom that were described in the first part of this chapter, only the fourth is concerned with formal analysis of educational issues. The others are powerful because they have an immediate connection with the individual as a teacher and with the subject matter being taught. Because educational psychology is a fundamental part of teacher education, however, it does have a distinctive contribution to make to the teacher's role in the instructional process.

THE CONTRIBUTION
OF EDUCATIONAL PSYCHOLOGY
TO THE INSTRUCTIONAL PROCESS

There are three rather important ways in which teachers' study of educational psychology can contribute to, or modify, the ideas in their heads about education, or their "natural" tendencies to teach in certain ways. These are:

1. The systematic, conceptual nature of educational psychology, in contrast to the limited experience of the individual teacher.

2. The multiple alternatives offered by reference to an applied social science, versus the more confined choices based on personal knowledge.
3. The tentative, hypothetical, and probabalistic nature of educational solutions that emerge from social science reasoning, as opposed to the more concrete and absolute formulations derived from conventional wisdom.

As valuable and as persuasive as personal experience in social relationships is, the direct experience of any one individual is destined to be limited. Reference to an applied social science such as educational psychology can add generality to the teacher's frame of reference. It provides a dimension of cumulative, systematic, and impersonal evidence that bears on a broad range of teacher behaviors.

When teaching decisions must be made, knowledge of educational psychology can suggest broader areas of application and offer alternatives for consideration that fall outside the personal experience of most teachers. Educational psychology also acquaints the teacher with the concept that the principles and generalizations of social science are usually based on probability of occurrence and are not matters of absolute certainty. A teacher who has a social science background can treat classroom decision making as a matter of formulating tentative hypotheses, trying them out in action, checking and correcting the formulation, and once again trying the reformulated hypothesis.

The behavior of teachers in classrooms is only a variation on their normal social behavior. It is different to an extent because of the roles they play in the classroom, and because of their specialized responsibility for the educational development of the learners under their care. But the same forces that ordinarily shape social behavior are at work in the classroom. A knowledge of educational psychology can affect teachers' classroom behavior in positive ways if they will attempt to incorporate its conceptual, general, and hypothetical elements into those ideas in their heads that directly govern the conduct of the instructional process.

AN INTERACTION MODEL OF THE INSTRUCTIONAL PROCESS

Our concept of the educational process as a social interaction or a communication between the teacher and the learner has several dimensions. The first is concerned with the variables that operate in the instructional process in its simplest form, when only an instructional agent and a learner are involved. Even here, the instructor must take account of the long-term development of characteristics as well as the moment-to-moment fluctuations in mood of the individual learner if instruction is to be effective.

The second dimension focuses on what happens to instruction when the interactive relationship between teacher and individual learner is complicated by the usual location of instruction in classrooms. Here the teacher deals not with individual students but with groups of students numbering about 20 or 30. This alters the fundamental instructional relationship between student and teacher in significant ways, and variables that might be trivial in the more basic tutorial relationship take on importance. Basically two changes occur in the teacher's role in this dimension: The teacher must somehow solve instructional problems that are presented by the range of individual differences in the group and also must serve as a manager or leader of the group. The social feedback the teacher receives from group members and the satisfaction students derive from group membership are highly important to the effectiveness of the teacher's classroom instruction.

The third dimension of the interaction model recognizes that teachers teach with a number of invisible visitors looking over their shoulders. The question, "What would the principal, or superintendent, or board of education think about what I am doing?" is not unimportant to many teachers. The questions and challenges of the local and larger communities also condition the classroom instructional process. They may be phrased in terms of "Why doesn't School X have a program for the gifted like my Jimmy?" or "With the support this community gives to its schools, the district's achievement test scores should be a lot higher than they are," or "If the teachers in this school would get back to basics, we'd all be better off."

In a technical sense, this dimension involves the impact of the external system on the events of the classroom. The concerns of the external system are with what is popularly called teacher or school *accountability*. Teachers have to consider whether their actions will meet the multiple expectations held for them. These expectations may be different in different parts of the external system, and none of them may be clearly specified at any point, except after the event. Such conditions can strongly affect what teachers attempt to do instructionally. Moreover, lack of clarity or agreement among members of the external system who control the fate of the classroom teacher can have negative consequences for the instructional process, and therefore for the students who are its targets.

As the following sections will show, our model of the instructional process takes account of the major conceptual and practical issues in the instructional process. One indication of its applicability is that though teachers frequently work with subgroups of students within the larger classroom groups, there is no fundamental difference in the instructional process because of this setting.

THE FIRST DIMENSION: INSTRUCTION
PROVIDED TO THE INDIVIDUAL LEARNER

The first dimension of the instructional process is concerned with situations in which a teacher or other instructional agent is in individual communication with a learner. This kind of communication is at the heart of the process. In this dimension the instructor need not be a manager or a leader of groups, concerned about the complexities of individual differences, or involved in norm-referenced measurements, which compare the accomplishments of an individual to those of groups.

Figure 1.1

First dimension of the instructional process model:
Instruction provided to the individual learner

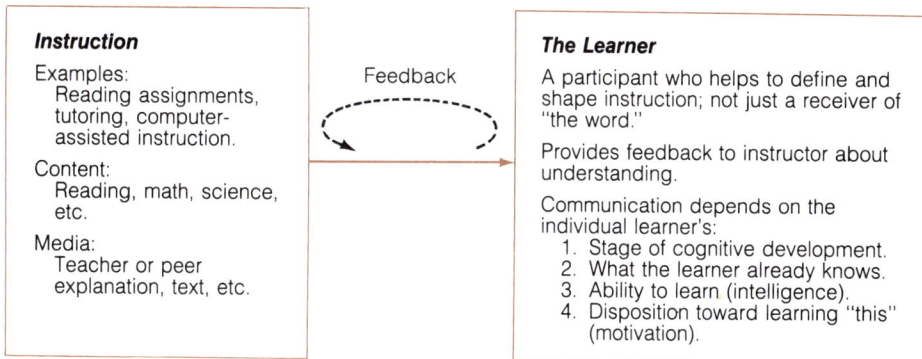

Instruction

Examples:
    Reading assignments,
    tutoring, computer-
    assisted instruction.

Content:
    Reading, math, science,
    etc.

Media:
    Teacher or peer
    explanation, text, etc.

Feedback

The Learner

A participant who helps to define and shape instruction; not just a receiver of "the word."

Provides feedback to instructor about understanding.

Communication depends on the individual learner's:
    1. Stage of cognitive development.
    2. What the learner already knows.
    3. Ability to learn (intelligence).
    4. Disposition toward learning "this" (motivation).

As Figure 1.1 shows, the first dimension of the instructional process depends on several characteristics of the individual learner. One is the learner's stage of cognitive development; the ability to comprehend instruction is dependent on the level of development, and the implications are described in Part I, Development of the Learner, particularly Chapters 2, 3, and 4. Most children in elementary school are probably at the stage of concrete operations, where models or actual objects to be manipulated must be provided in order to enhance comprehension. Somewhat older students probably can think in a formal propositional way and have no such requirement. They are capable of understanding relationships at an abstract or purely verbal level, without the support of the specific examples or materials required by younger brothers and sisters. How learners think and reason is analyzed in Chapter 10, which examines critical and creative thinking as well as thinking that demands reasoning and problem-solving skills.

Similarly, the teacher must be able to make some informed estimate of the state of the learner's knowledge of the topic at hand or related considerations. This can be done in several ways. With individual learners, an informal review may reveal what the child knows, but tests, ranging from those constructed by the classroom teacher to standardized measurement instruments such as achievement batteries and diagnostic tests, also are helpful in that respect. Teachers routinely use tests in their daily work and longer-term planning for instruction, but the ability to construct a valid classroom test, or to select a published test that will provide the needed information and that can be interpreted in terms of furthering the learners' educations, requires professional knowledge. Part IV, Educational Measurement and Evaluation, deals with a host of concepts, issues, and procedures in testing and measuring. For purposes of individual teacher-pupil instruction, Chapters 16 and 17 are the most pertinent.

The teacher's interpretation of the instructional process in the first dimension also must take into consideration the level of intelligence of the individual learner. Chapter 5 describes some of the extremes in levels of intelligence, and Chapter 6 provides answers of several kinds to the question of what intelligence is. The latter chapter examines how intelligence is measured with two of the major available individual tests of intelligence: the Stanford-Binet and the several versions of the Wechsler intelligence scales. Most classroom teachers do not have the specialized training and supervised practice that are required for administering these tests. Nevertheless, knowledge about their construction, the types of tests they include, and the meaning of the intelligence quotients they can yield improve the teacher's understanding of how intelligence is measured.

The teacher also needs some indication of the learner's interest in the material to be learned. An apparent lack of interest in multiplication facts may be a reflection of broader learnings, such as a negative attitude toward mathematics or the study of numbers in general, or a low motive to achieve. Chapter 11 describes how children learn motives, especially those that are related to school achievement, and surveys classroom efforts to encourage students' motivation to learn. The learning of attitudes and values to support these motives, the exploration of feelings, and the consideration of social choices are examined in Chapter 9.

The teacher's task in the first dimension involves integrating the feedback provided by analysis of the individual learner, in terms of cognitive development, intelligence, prior knowledge, and disposition to learn, with the teacher's own knowledge of the particular subject matter at hand. The teacher must organize and present the subject matter in a way that permits meaningful connections to be made with what the

*Individual contact
between teacher and
learner is at the heart
of the instructional
process.*

learner already knows and can comprehend. This is a condition that
cannot be specified in any absolute sense, for what will be meaningful
to an individual learner and fit with her or his existing cognitive structure
and store of knowledge depends precisely on the individual learner.
Chapters 7 and 8 consider classroom learning from two different points
of view; one is cognitive learning and information processing, and the
other is expressed in terms of psychological reinforcement theory, with
special reference to operant conditioning. Each confronts the issue of
teaching from the essential standpoints of content and method. Although
the specifics of the approaches are very different, they both contribute
to the concept that teachers must adapt and organize their knowledge
of the discipline, or of the subject matter to be taught, to fit the psychological state of the learner. To fail to make content contingent in this
way on the state of the learner is to reduce teaching to telling. We would

emphasize that teachers who can adapt the instructional process to fit the learners' characteristics are those who have a deep, well-generalized understanding of the subject matter they are to convey.

THE SECOND DIMENSION: INSTRUCTION PROVIDED TO LEARNERS IN GROUPS

A major variation of the instructional process results from the added dimension when teachers meet learners in groups. This is probably the most common setting for the instructional process, and the basic process is altered in significant ways by this change in the context of instruction. The teacher must perform as a group leader, not just as an instructor for individuals. The behavior of pupils also is altered when they are members of a classroom group and of subgroups within that framework. Each pupil, as well as the teacher, has an enlarged audience for whatever he or she does or does not do.

Factors that affect the teacher's leadership behavior in groups, and the membership roles of students both inside and outside of school, are the fundamental concerns of Part III, The Social Psychology of the Classroom. Chapters 13 and 14 will help the teacher understand the functioning of classroom groups and their own roles within these groups.

In the second dimension, as Figure 1.2 shows, the teacher receives social feedback from the classroom group about how the group itself is functioning, as well as cognitive feedback from individual learners. Since

Figure 1.2

Second dimension of the instructional process model: Instruction provided to learners in groups

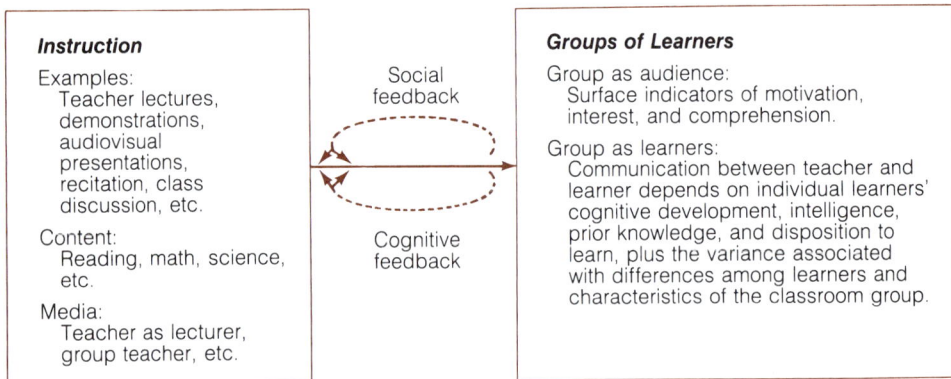

Instruction

Examples:
  Teacher lectures, demonstrations, audiovisual presentations, recitation, class discussion, etc.

Content:
  Reading, math, science, etc.

Media:
  Teacher as lecturer, group teacher, etc.

Social feedback

Cognitive feedback

Groups of Learners

Group as audience:
  Surface indicators of motivation, interest, and comprehension.

Group as learners:
  Communication between teacher and learner depends on individual learners' cognitive development, intelligence, prior knowledge, and disposition to learn, plus the variance associated with differences among learners and characteristics of the classroom group.

learning is contingent on a classroom climate in which students can hear, see, and concentrate on the events of instruction, group-based feedback is important to the teacher. It may not in itself signify that learning is going on, but it can tell the teacher whether the possibility of learning exists.

The two types of feedback in this dimension give the teacher information on the behavior of the group and its members and on the individual or group learning of the pupils. Behavioral cues from the children indicate their response to the classroom activity, and measurable evidence indicates whether or not meaningful learning is taking place (see Box B).

The surface behavior that constitutes social feedback to the teacher may be somewhat misleading about the underlying cognitive activity that leads to subject matter learning, however. Silberman (1963) observed that "Even when the teacher acts like a broadcasting station, it is doubtful that all the pupils are tuned in. A more plausible model is that the teacher is communicating with different individuals for brief sporadic periods and that these pupils are responding to other stimuli the rest of the time." In fact, college students attending lectures reported they spent about 5 percent of their time thinking about themselves (Bloom, 1954).

To determine what the other stimuli might be, Hudgins and Ahlbrand (1969) obtained answers to the question, "What were you thinking about at this point in the lesson?" from junior high students in English classes. In accord with Silberman's assertion that students frequently tune out the teacher, they found that about 47 percent of the responses by the students could be classified as not relevant to the substantive or content issues of the lesson. They devoted slightly more than 25 percent of their thoughts to themselves, perhaps reflecting the special sensitivity to social and personal development that is characteristic of early adolescence. The pupils' comments reveal a wide range of thoughts during lessons that are unrelated to either what the teacher is doing or the sanctioned activities of the class. Examples were: "What I was going to eat for lunch today," "About going ice skating," "Trying to decide what to wear at the Junior Miss Pageant tonight," and many similar statements.

The cognitive feedback to the teacher in this dimension is in large part a reflection of the range of individual differences among the students. When students are instructed in groups, the teacher must be concerned about individual differences in educational achievement within the group, as well as with the cognitive development, intelligence, prior knowledge, and disposition to learn of individual learners, as in the first dimension.

Part I, which deals with the development of children and adolescents, as well as various aspects of intelligence, introduces the concept of individual differences and provides a basis for understanding the wide

BOX B *How am I doing?*

Philip Jackson conducted interviews with teachers who had been recommended as highly effective practitioners of the art of teaching. His general question to them was, "How do you know when you're doing a good job in the classroom?" and their answers described the various types of feedback they received from learners.

An eighth-grade teacher considered the students' expressions and attitudes as a barometer of the success of her efforts:

Interviewer: How can you tell when you're doing a good job?

Teacher: Oh, look at their faces.

Interviewer: Will you tell me more about that?

Teacher: Why sure, they look alert; they look interested; they look questioning—like they're ready to question something. They look like they're anxious to learn more about it. . . . And other times you know you haven't done a good job when they look blah or look disinterested or I-don't-care attitude, well then I feel bad, you know, I've done a bad job. (p. 120)

A first-grade teacher's answer to this question made a distinction between students' liking school and learning from their classroom experiences:

First of all, I think there's a difference between their liking what you're doing and their learning what you're teaching. Sometimes they can like it immensely and not be learning a thing. You can tell when they're enthusiastic but you have to ask a few questions to know whether they're learning or not. In the first grade, if they don't *like* what you're doing, they will usually tell you so. They'll say, "I don't want to do this anymore," or "When are we going home?" or something like this. They're very honest. But if they don't *understand* what you're doing, they usually won't express it verbally. They will climb on the desk or under the chair or make some quiet attempt to escape. They obviously don't want to have anything to do with the whole idea. Or else, if you question them, they'll know the answer, but not be very enthusiastic. They become very passive and usually don't cause you any trouble, but you know that they just aren't paying any attention. (pp. 121–22)

Source: Philip W. Jackson, *Life in Classrooms* (New York: Holt, Rinehart & Winston, 1968).

*Most teaching takes place in classroom groups. The presence
of more than one learner alters the basic instructional
process in significant ways.*

variations in educational achievement which emerge as a special case of
psychological differences. Chapter 5 explores the special considerations
which are needed for exceptional learners of all types. The hereditary
and environmental bases for group differences in intelligence and the
social attempts to intervene in order to accommodate them in the schools,
which will be presented in Chapter 6, are related to both the second and
third dimensions of the model.

Some details about the range of individual differences in achievement
are given in Chapter 12, which contrasts two contemporary, contradictory models for dealing with them. One, called the *mastery learning model,*
is based on the assumption that differences in learning are largely reducible to differences in the amount of time various children need to
learn the same material. It also assumes that, because much school learning is sequential, these differences in learning rate can be markedly
reduced if slow learners are given extra time and help to master the
content in the early stages of learning. They can then confront the next
topic in the sequence together with children who did master the first
topic quickly. If this process is used repeatedly, the range of individual
differences can be shrunk appreciably. Proponents of the model suggest

that virtually all children can master the basics of educational content and skills, instead of only approximately one third to one half of them, as in the usual case. Mastery learning is based on the theoretical work of J. B. Carroll (1963) and Benjamin Bloom (1964), and Bloom's developmental research (1976).

In contrast is a model that traditionally was referred to as *large-group instruction* and today is called *directed teaching*, or *direct instruction*. In this approach, the classroom teacher presents lessons or conducts recitations with the entire group of students in the classroom. Mounting evidence suggests that the best *overall* gains in academic achievement for basic skills learning occur when direct instruction is employed, and the idea is again taking hold after several decades of interest in innovations designed to individualize instruction (the mastery learning model is an example). Methods of teaching that look very much like direct instruction have been used almost universally in classrooms for a long time, and they continue to be used today (Dale & Raths, 1945; Hoetker & Ahlbrand, 1969).

THE THIRD DIMENSION: INSTRUCTION AND THE EXTERNAL ENVIRONMENT

Schools exist, in the ordinary sense of the term, for the purpose of schooling the young or the untutored. The direct beneficiaries of schooling are the students who attend schools day by day and year after year. Less directly, but certainly no less significantly, the society at large also benefits from the outcomes of schooling. Public schools are mandated by the state and supported from tax funds for the good of society. While it is indisputably to Johnny's benefit that he learn how to read, it is also true, as Thomas Jefferson said, that "A nation that expects to be ignorant and free in a state of civilization never was, and never will be." In principle, at least, schools are instruments of the state.

What is taught in schools, and what is not taught there, is regulated in part by the states individually and by community boards of education. Historically in the United States, boards of education, elected directly by the voters of the school district, have been vested with the power to make and execute local educational policy. Many of the functions for which boards of education have responsibility, however, exceed both the technical knowledge of the members and the boards' capability to provide extensive instructional services. Therefore they normally delegate some of their responsibilities to a professionally trained superintendent of schools or superintendent of instruction, one of whose major tasks is to select a staff of teachers and supervise their teaching.

This simplified account of the administration of a school district ignores the many levels of intermediate administrators and supervisory

The instructional process is modified by contacts with the broader society, as when parents and teachers share information about students' progress.

personnel that are employed in most school districts today. Still, the basic points are valid: The superintendent is accountable to the school board for what is taught in the schools, how the teaching is accomplished, and what the outcomes of instruction are, and members of the school board are accountable to the community they represent. Since seats on the school board are elective and are usually renewable, often on a two-year basis, the indirect control of the parents of school children and the community at large over what transpires in the district's schools can be great.

The elements in the third dimension of the instructional process are related to the several sets of norms and expectations in the external environment to which teachers feel they must respond (see Figure 1.3). Chapter 13 explores how teachers' interpretations of their responsibilities affect their relationships in the classroom and the school. The final chapter in the book provides an analysis of issues in the evaluation of teachers, programs, schools, and school districts. In the past such evaluations have usually been informal and unsystematic, and often they

---

Figure 1.3

*Third dimension of the instructional process model:
Instruction and the external environment*

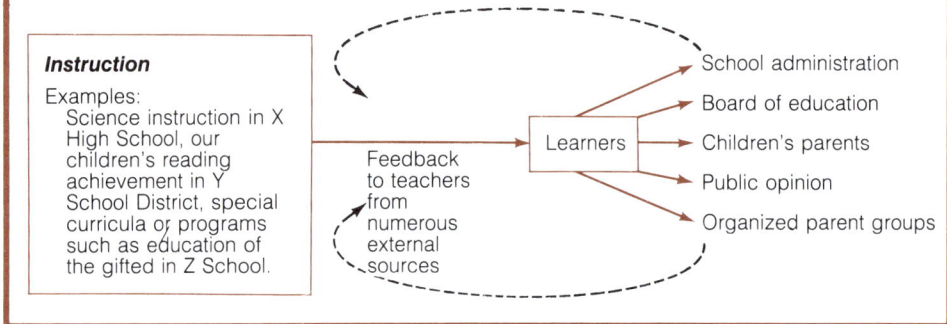

Instruction

Examples:
Science instruction in X
High School, our
children's reading
achievement in Y
School District, special
curricula or programs
such as education of
the gifted in Z School.

Feedback
to teachers
from
numerous
external
sources

Learners

School administration
Board of education
Children's parents
Public opinion
Organized parent groups

---

have not had the power to induce any change in how the system functions. In more recent years, with the development of procedures for the evaluation of faculty by students and of programs and schools by the community, the concept of the accountability of individual teachers and of entire school districts has become more of a reality.

Each of the dimensions of our model of the instructional process plays some role in how teachers construe their professional tasks. Our aim in this book has been to provide for the student of education useful summaries and analyses of the topics that are most directly involved in the instructional process. There will be legitimate questions about why we have not attempted to specify relationships between aspects of instruction and relevant variables, as well as more precise relationships between, say, the students' level of cognitive development and motivation. Or why we have not examined how the teacher's role differs, depending upon the differences in students' levels of prior knowledge or the range of intellectual and educational achievement differences, for example. The basic answer to these questions is that the psychological sciences and their applications in educational psychology are not sufficiently detailed and exact to permit such conclusions or inferences. Furthermore, we do not believe they ever will be. The social act of teaching is dependent on the teacher having specific information about situations that are immediately at hand. Social science generalizations do not provide such information. But they can, and ought to, function as useful knowledge that can be applied to a teacher's instructional strategy. Or, as we expressed it earlier, they can clarify and modify those ideas in the head that are the basis of the teaching experience.

Bloom, Benjamin S. Thought processes of students in discussion. In S. J. French (Ed.), *Accent on Teaching*. New York: Harper, 1954.

Bloom, Benjamin S. *Stability and Change in Human Characteristics*. New York: John Wiley & Sons, 1964.

Bloom, Benjamin S. *Human Characteristics and School Learning*. New York: McGraw-Hill, 1976.

Carroll, J. B. A model of school learning. *Teachers College Record*, 1963, *64*, 723–733.

Dale, Edgar, and Raths, Louis E. Discussion in the secondary school. *Educational Research Bulletin*, 1945, *24*, 1–6.

Hoetker, William J., and Ahlbrand, William P., Jr. The persistence of the recitation. *American Educational Research Journal*, 1969, *6*, 145–167.

Hudgins, Bryce B., and Ahlbrand, William P., Jr. *A Study of Classroom Interaction and Thinking*. St. Louis, Mo.: CEMREL, Inc., 1969.

Jackson, Philip W. *Life in Classrooms*. New York: Holt, Rinehart & Winston, 1968.

Silberman, Harry F. A symposium on current research in classroom behavior of teachers and its implications for teacher education. *Journal of Teacher Education*, 1963, *14*, 235–333.

Smith, B. Othanel. A concept of teaching. *Teachers College Record*, 1960, *61*, 229–241.

Smith, B. Othanel, and Meux, Milton. *A Study of the Logic of Teaching*. Urbana: Bureau of Educational Research, University of Illinois, 1962.

Stephens, John M. *The Process of Schooling*. New York: Holt, Rinehart & Winston, 1967.

Williamson, Robert C., Swingle, Paul G., and Sargent, S. S. *Social Psychology*. Itasca, Ill.: F. E. Peacock Publishers, 1982.

REFERENCES

Development of the Learner

The dual emphases of Part I are on how the learner develops and how the teacher fits instruction to the readiness characteristics or individual differences of the learners in a classroom. The developmental perspective taken in this part applies to both the first and second dimensions of the instructional process model introduced in Chapter 1. Whether learners are considered as individuals or as members of a group, their stage of cognitive development, prior knowledge, level of intelligence, and disposition to learn affect the content and methods teachers can use effectively in presenting the instruction.

In the first and second dimensions of the model, Chapters 2, 3, and 4 detail the development of the learner from early childhood through adolescence in three domains: cognitive-intellectual, social-emotional, and physical-motor. The third dimension of the model is represented in Chapter 5, which examines society's expectations about educating exceptional learners, and Chapter 6, which considers the hereditary and environmental bases for group differences in intelligence and social attempts to intervene in order to accommodate them in the schools.

The Developmental Perspective and Early Childhood

Any attempt at instruction, whether formal or informal, and whether offered by teachers, parents, or anyone else interested in the education of others, must be geared to the developmental level of the learner. A developmental perspective of how students learn takes into consideration their physical, social, and intellectual ability to learn and how their behavior changes over time. A general knowledge of human development, therefore, prepares the teacher to recognize the learners' readiness for new learning experiences and to shape the instructional process accordingly. By continually providing appropriate new learning experiences to students, the teacher challenges their maturational state and ensures their intellectual progress and social growth. The developmental perspective suggests some guidelines on how to promote the change and modification of knowledge or behavior which are the principal aims of instruction, whether the focus is on long-term change throughout the traditional years of schooling or a very short-term change to be achieved by a two-week instructional unit.

INDIVIDUAL DIFFERENCES

An understanding of the kinds of behavioral change that can be expected as a result of the instructional process depends on recognition of the fact that all children do not develop in the same way or at the same speed. Concern with the causes of individual differences and attempts to identify the reason for or source of these differences are part of the nature-nurture, or environment-heredity, controversy, one of the oldest, most persistent, and most frustrating issues in educational psychology. This controversy has important implications for educational practice and theory, though classroom teachers may not spend much time seeking out the theoretical causes of the behaviors they observe in the classroom.

THE NATURE-NURTURE CONTROVERSY

Do human beings develop into whatever it is they are going to become because of the action of their genes, whose development programs are determined at the moment of conception? Or is that newborn child cradled in its adoring mother's or father's arms a soft plastic doll that can be shaped and molded into any form by its life experience? The great behaviorist John B. Watson had no doubts that experience is the key:

> Give me a dozen healthy infants, well formed, and my own specified
> world to bring them up in and I'll guarantee to take any one at random

and train him to become any type of specialist I might select—doctor, lawyer, artist, merchant, chief, and, yes, even beggar-man and thief. (Watson, 1930, p. 104)

Another psychologist who studied how children develop, Arnold Gesell, attributed development much more to their biological nature. According to Gesell, as a child's nervous system grows according to its individual pattern, it establishes the primary forms of behavior. Unlike the behaviorists, Gesell did not believe these forms are determined by experience or stimulation from the outside world. Rather, he maintained, the conditioning patterns have "inner checks which set metes and bounds to the area of conditioning" (Gesell, 1933, pp. 214, 231–32).

The heredity-environment question was the center of lively controversy in the thirties and forties, though many psychologists later came to look on it as a dead issue. According to Anne Anastasi, by the end of the fifties it was generally conceded that both hereditary and environmental factors enter into all behavior. She suggested that the controversy had lingered as a result of the way the problem was being addressed:

In science, as in any logical endeavor, the types of questions asked at the outset, in part, determine the nature of the problem. Historically, scholars grappling with the controversy began by asking *which* type of factor (heredity or environment) accounted for individual differences. A second type of question asked *how much* of the variance was attributed to heredity and how much to environment. A more fruitful approach is to be found in the question "How?" There is still much to be learned about how heredity and environmental factors *operate together* in the development of behavioral differences among individuals. (Anastasi, 1958)

THE INTERACTIONIST POSITION AND EDUCATIONAL DEVELOPMENT

It is the *how* questions that have the most application to the instructional process. These types of questions provide insight to help teachers recognize the individual differences present at the beginning of instruction which are referred to as *student entry* or *readiness characteristics*. These include the individual learner's cognitive development, intelligence, prior knowledge, and disposition to learn, which are part of the first dimension of the model of the instructional process described in Chapter 1. A better understanding of how environment and heredity interact during the course of development provides a more accurate basis for the establishment of short-term instructional objectives and long-term educational goals to guide the process (see Chapter 15 for a discussion of objectives and goals). If instructional objectives are to be effective, they must accurately reflect the ability levels of the learners and the learning to be expected as a result of instruction.

The kinds of educational development parents can anticipate and the effects teachers can expect to have on the different types of students in a typical classroom are related to their ideas of how the learner's development is shaped. All those interested in the education of children tend to agree that features of physical-motor development, such as physical stature or appearance, are relatively fixed by heredity, as reflected in such comments as "What do you expect, her mother is only five feet tall," or "All the boys in that family are big for their age." But they may regard the development of cognitive-intellectual and social-emotional behaviors as completely determined by the environment and uninfluenced by hereditary or biological factors. As a result of these different standards for the various developmental domains (see the next section), the idea has taken hold that application of the right teaching technique or method can bring about almost any change in development.

Instructional programs do influence the course of an individual student's development in school. In a real sense, teaching is an attempt to modify the student's development in a positive direction. The observable, patterned behaviors that are collectively called psychological traits (such as intelligence, personality, and learning) are *indirectly influenced* by heredity. Any hereditary effect on behavior, however, will also be influenced by the context of a supportive, helpful environment. Evidence that environment accounts for some of the variance in children's measured intelligence, for example, has been found in studies of the relationship between the IQs of adopted children and their adoptive parents (see Chapter 6).

The environment or heredity question goes beyond intelligence, as in the case of a specific learning disabilty called *dyslexia*. This disorder of the central nervous system creates a problem in organizing and interpreting numbers and letters for pupils learning to read (see Chapter 5). As a result of this perceptual problem, the learner experiences perceptual distortions like letter reversals or numbers appearing upside down. Dyslexia is known to be transmitted across generations in the same family and appears to be a sex-linked characteristic; males are four to five times more likely to suffer from dyslexia than females. When this inherited disorder is diagnosed early in the primary grades and remediation efforts are introduced in a supportive environment, the child learns to cope with the disorder and may become a good reader. If it is left undiagnosed and untreated, the course of development is not modified, and the dyslexic child becomes a functional illiterate.

A radical position which considers behavior to be either completely fixed and due entirely to heredity, or completely changeable and due

BOX A *Radical environmentalism in the classroom*

The popular idea that "There is no such thing as a poor student, only poor teachers," demonstrates how overemphasis on the environment can lead to misconceptions about teaching and learning. When a group of teachers employed in a small school system requested an in-service workshop, they said they wanted to talk about teacher accountability and individual differences in student achievement. Their underlying reason was that the superintendent had asked each teacher to enter into a behavioral contract whereby the teacher would guarantee that each child in the classroom would be brought up to grade level during the academic year and be ready to work at the appropriate grade level the following year. A sixth-grade teacher, for example, would be expected to provide instruction ensuring that all students in the class would be ready for seventh-grade instruction at the end of the school year.

The teachers pointed out that this would be an unreasonable expectation, because in a sixth-grade classroom, a range in reading ability extending from the third-grade to the ninth-grade levels is not uncommon. It is extremely unlikely that an 11- or 12-year-old sixth-grader who is reading at the third-grade level could make a four-year gain in reading ability in one year.

The problem encountered by the teachers in this system was due to the fact that they worked for an administrator who did not comprehend the interactive effects of heredity and environment on behavioral development. Had the superintendent possessed a better understanding of the modifiability of the learner's development, the problem would not have arisen. The superintendent's apparent belief that cognitive development is influenced only by environmental factors that are readily modified by the teacher led to expectations of dramatic improvements in learning, if the teacher would only come up with the "right" motivator or instructional method.*

* One contemporary approach to the solution of this extremely complex problem is mastery learning, which is described in Chapter 12. The underlying measurement issues are addressed in Part IV.

entirely to the environment (see Box A) ignores the interactive influence of heredity and environment on the course of development. An interactionist position does not specify how the course of development can be modified in all cases. However, it does correct the belief that behavioral differences that have their source in *nature* are unmodifiable, while those that have their source in *nurture* can be readily changed. This means the teacher must develop an awareness that some students will learn swiftly and others will learn slowly. Occasionally a student will not learn, despite the teacher's maximum efforts to tailor the instructional process to meet the needs of the learners.

A TYPOLOGY OF DEVELOPMENTAL DOMAINS

The array of *student entry* or *readiness characteristics,* or the unique abilities and behaviors individual students bring to the classroom as a result of their development, is as vast as the product of all the various differences of class members. As a frame of reference for classifying these myriad differences, we will use a threefold classification scheme based on types of behaviors within developmental domains. In this typology the total behavior a student exhibits is seen as falling within three general areas of development. These are the cognitive-intellectual, social-emotional, and physical-motor domains, as distinguished by McCandless and Evans (1973).

Within the *cognitive-intellectual domain* are the student's level of intelligence, language development, and creative and critical thinking abilities and problem-solving skills. Other skills of a cognitive nature include comprehension, study skills, and information-processing strategies, and academic skills such as reading, mathematics, and writing.

Within the *social-emotional domain* are characteristics related to emotional health and personality development. Specific behaviors include the development of interests, attitudes, norms, values, and moral standards. The social-emotional domain includes student characteristics that may not be evaluated in the classroom but that have effects on those abilities and behaviors that are. Psychosexual development, for example, is an important part of the socialization process that will be considered in this part of the book. It includes such behaviors as adjustment to a biologically defined sex role, attitudes toward sexual behavior, and sexuality in the social sense.

In the *physical-motor domain* are such student characteristics as psychomotor ability and physical traits. Physical traits are related to development in height and weight, for example, and psychomotor abilities include eye-hand coordination, gross and fine motor control, and right-or left-handedness. The physical-motor domain is of greatest interest at the preschool level. The learner's development of fine-motor skills and eye-hand coordination helps determine the instructional process for teaching such skills as holding a pencil, writing, drawing, or using scissors. Similarly, physical education teachers need to consider psycho-motor development in teaching the motor skills needed to participate in such activities. Physical-motor development is also important in special education (see Chapter 5), where information pertaining to physiological and neurological development has extreme value in diagnosing learning problems.

As with any typology, the distinctions between the developmental domains are not definite and can virtually disappear, as in certain areas in the adolescent years (see Chapter 4). Each domain therefore can have a bearing on the others, and so their usefulness in this book is in a classificatory sense rather than a definitive one.

IMPLICATIONS FOR THE INSTRUCTIONAL PROCESS

The typology of developmental domains provides the structure for discussing the various ways learners develop, an essential consideration in the instructional process model introduced in Chapter 1. The teacher must have an understanding of how individual learners in the classroom have developed and their potential for acquiring knowledge and skills. An understanding of individual differences provides the basis for making precise determinations of student characteristics, and an awareness of differing ability levels permits the establishment of more accurate instructional objectives and educational goals (Gagné, 1967). These are necessary bases for the instructional process, whether it is geared to group or individual instruction.

For the teacher who is daily confronted with the need to make lesson plans for a class, the task is akin to problem solving: stating the problem, considering alternatives, and choosing a course of action (Peterson & Clark, 1978). Typically, a group instructional plan is formulated that meets the needs of the majority of students in the class. For the special education teacher, it is a matter of preparing individual educational programs (IEPs) for each student, as described in Chapter 5. In either case, the particular methods of instruction, instructional objectives, and educational goals are determined by an awareness of individual differences in student entry characteristics (see Box B). In this respect, the instructional process is geared to the learner and not vice versa.

BOX B *Teaching-learning interactions:*
It's all in how you look at it

When Wanda Everage, a practicing teacher, was enrolled in an
evening graduate course in educational psychology, she came
to recognize how individual differences affected her perceptions
of her class. In her first month of teaching a mixed group of
black, white, and Mexican-heritage students, she was also
concerned with their perceptions of her:

> The students in my class displayed varying shapes, sizes and
> colors. I thought about how the black students were perceiving me
> as a black person: Whether they considered me as someone who
> felt superior to them because, in their opinion, I had overcome the
> obstacles of being black, or whether I had given up my identity as
> a black person in order to fit into a predominantly white society. . . .
> At the same time, I was wondering whether the white students
> viewed me as incompetent because I was black, . . . or did they
> view me as someone who could protect them from the black
> students and maybe as an exception to the rule. With the Mexican
> students, I pondered whether they viewed me as a rival in the
> sense that we are both fighting for respect and dignity, or whether
> they felt I was very similar to them in that we are all viewed as
> inferior and have to fight a common battle. . . .
>
> There was one fact that I recognized right away—all of my good
> intentions, ideas, techniques, and approaches would take awhile to
> be accepted by some, while others would readily accept me as a
> person who was there to help them develop. I firmly believe that all
> students are capable of learning. Students learn at different paces
> and for different purposes. I knew I would have a meaningful
> teaching experience if I could motivate the unmotivated, challenge
> the unchallenged, continue to inspire those who are eager to learn,
> and help each student see his/her own capabilities and future
> achievements.

SYSTEMS FOR CLASSIFYING DEVELOPMENTAL STAGES

Several systems for classifying various stages within the developmental domains have become accepted as frames of reference for studying the processes involved in the development of the learner. These stage systems are based on the idea that a lower level of development must be attained before a higher one can be reached. Examples are Abraham Maslow's hierarchy of needs (see Chapter 11) and Lawrence Kohlberg's six-stage theory of moral development (see Chapter 9).

The two stage theories that have widest applicability to the developmental domains are Piaget's four stages of intellectual development, in the cognitive-intellectual domain, and Erikson's psychosocial theory, in the social-emotional domain. These are described in this section.

PIAGET'S STAGES OF INTELLECTUAL DEVELOPMENT

The frame of reference that is most often used to classify the stages of intellectual development was created by Jean Piaget, beginning in the 1920s (Piaget & Inhelder, 1969). According to this stage theory, a lower level of cognitive development must be reached before a higher one can follow. Each of the stages of thought integrates the preceding one and prepares for the following one. The emphasis is on the quality of thinking at each stage, from infancy through adolescence (Newman & Newman, 1975).

The *sensorimotor thought* stage, which lasts from birth to about two years of age, is characterized by action and the formation of increasingly complex sensory and motor patterns, or habits. The infant quickly begins to organize the messages received from the environment and so can control it to some extent.

The *preoperational thought* stage begins when the child first uses language to express thought and extends until about age 5 or 6—the end of the early childhood period. The child learns to use words and other symbols to represent things and feelings, and knowledge is largely tied to the child's own direct perceptions of what things are like.

The third stage, *concrete operational thought,* begins where preoperational thought leaves off at about age 5 or 6 and may end in early adolescence, at about 11 or 12, or extend into adulthood. The learner moves things around, physically or by mentally manipulating categories or systems, and makes them fit. Problem solving involves physical objectives and events rather than abstract concepts.

The final stage of cognitive development, according to Piaget, is *formal operational thought,* which may begin in adolescence and persist throughout adulthood. At this stage the level of thinking makes it possible to examine hypothetical propositions. The interactions of many factors can be considered, and systems of rules for solving philosophical or scientific problems can be created.

Criticisms of Piaget's Theory

There is no scholarly agreement that cognitive development proceeds through an invariant sequence of stages, or at uniform ages, as Piaget maintained, however. Gagné (1968), in considering the contributions of learning to human development, proposed a cumulative learning model of development. He maintains that stages, if they exist, are only to be thought of as what the individual learner already knows and what remains to be learned. Stages are not related in any unequivocal way to chronological age, except in the loose sense that learning requires time. They are concerned not with the development or emergence of logical structures but with the accomplishment of a cumulative series of learning tasks.

Specific reservations about the universality of the emergence of Piaget's formal reasoning stage have been stated by Ausubel (1980). With particular reference to students of junior high school age, Ausubel observes that it would be unwise to suppose that all children at that educational level can dispense with concrete props or examples in their learning. He argues that many individuals never make the transition from concrete to abstract levels of cognitive functioning, and the transitions of those who do so may be erratic in the sense that they advance to formal reasoning about some sets of cognitive issues but not others.

The idea of stages of cognitive or intellectual development therefore cannot be thought of as a basis for uniform instruction. On the contrary, variations in the ages at which transitions may occur, or the failure of large segments of the population to reach advanced stages, are evidence of the continuing need for thoughtful individualization of instruction.

Bruner's System of Representation

Piaget's ideas on cognitive development were brought to the awareness of educators in this country by Jerome Bruner in the early 1950s. Bruner (1966) differentiated three systems people use to represent the objects and events they encounter in their environment. These systems are somewhat comparable to Piaget's stages, but Bruner regards language as the key to cognitive development. As children grow and develop they learn to use language to mediate (or to serve an intermediate function) between themselves and their experiences. This allows them to tie one event to another in a causal manner, to link new information with what they already have, and to code objects and events in their thought systems.

Bruner's systems of representation are also sometimes expressed in terms of levels or stages of cognitive growth. In the *enactive stage,* the child understands the world through action. At this stage the meaning of objects is determined by what the child does with them; holding, manipulating, and touching provide information through experience.

At the next cognitive level information is derived from imagery. This is called the *iconic stage,* in which knowledge is largely determined by understandings reached through the child's own perceptions and impressions of objects and events.

Bruner's *symbolic stage* is marked by the use of symbol systems in such areas as language, logic, and mathematics. When the child can translate experience into language and use language as an instrument of thinking, the stage is reached where abstract images can replace action or perceptual understanding in the system of representation.

ERIKSON'S PSYCHOSOCIAL THEORY

Erik Erikson's (1963) developmental theory is concerned with personality development in eight life stages, from infancy to old age. At each of these stages of development, psychological efforts to adjust to the environment produce certain stresses and strains, or *psychosocial crises,* which must be resolved before the person can move to the next stage. The corresponding life stages and psychosocial crises in Erikson's theory are listed in Table 2.1.

According to Erikson, resolution of the psychosocial crisis in infancy occurs when infants learn to trust their surroundings. In very early childhood children begin to exert independence and develop some ability to deal with the environment. The psychosocial crisis of this life stage is resolved when a sense of autonomy (or self-government) is developed.

Table 2.1

Erikson's psychosocial crises in life stages

Life Stage	Psychosocial Crisis
Infancy	Trust vs. mistrust
Early childhood	Autonomy vs. shame and doubt
Middle childhood	Initiative vs. guilt
Later childhood	Industry vs. inferiority
Adolescence	Identity vs. role confusion
Young adulthood	Intimacy vs. isolation
Middle age	Generativity vs. stagnation
Old age	Integrity vs. despair

In the next life stage, middle childhood, children resolve the crisis by taking the initiative in their activities and overcoming feelings of guilt about doing so. In later childhood intellectual curiosity and industriousness help children overcome their feelings of inferiority.

Resolution of the psychosocial crisis in adolescence is concerned with the efforts of teenagers to establish a sense of identity and come to grips with confusion over their social roles. Grounds are laid for resolving the crises of adulthood to allow for intimacy rather than isolation, a concern for the next generation rather than stagnation, and, finally, acceptance rather than despair.

DEVELOPMENT IN EARLY CHILDHOOD: THE YEARS FROM TWO TO SIX

The idea that kindergarten is the first educational experience a child encounters may have been valid 20 or 25 years ago, but it is not accurate today. Many preschool children have participated in some kind of nursery school, day care, or Head Start program, and educationally oriented television shows such as Sesame Street have held the interest of almost all of them from time to time.

Two developments have helped account for the trend toward organized early educational experiences. As more mothers joined the work force, the demand for better provisions for child care increased. And as a result of the civil rights movement, the call for equal educational opportunity led to government-supported programs such as Head Start to place disadvantaged preschoolers on a more equal footing with other students. As Chapter 6 will show, the effects of Head Start have been beneficial to many children, especially when their primary school education includes a follow-through program.

Thus many children begin their formal education much earlier than the conventional entry into kindergarten at the age of five. The interest of teachers and educational psychologists in very young children's development, therefore, is not simply a matter of building a background of knowledge to assist them in understanding the behavior of elementary and secondary school students. An increasing number of teachers are directly engaged in interactions with very young children.

INDIVIDUAL CHARACTERISTICS IN EARLY CHILDHOOD

Early childhood typically refers to the period of development that extends from ages two to six. Many private nursery schools accept children as young as two. Head Start focuses on four-year-olds but will accept three-year-olds who require special services and for whom there are no other available programs, and some participants may stay in the program through age five if they do not seem ready for kindergarten. Most five-year-olds, however, are enrolled in kindergarten. Entrance into the first grade is typically determined by age, with six being the most commonly accepted standard for admission.

While the age range in the early childhood period is only four years, significant changes occur in this period (McCandless & Evans, 1973). Very young children frequently have short attention spans and find it difficult to concentrate on a task, but by age five most kindergarten pupils can work on complicated tasks that may require anywhere from a few minutes to several hours to complete. The behaviors listed in Table 2.2 suggest the differences in behavior exhibited between ages two and six.

The size differences in preschoolers are suggested by a comparison of two- and five-year-olds. At two years the average height is 32–35

Table 2.2

Developmental changes in early childhood

Age	Physical-Motor Domain	Social-Emotional Domain	Cognitive-Intellectual Domain
2–3 yrs.	Jumps off a step Rides a tricycle Throws a small ball 4 or 5 ft. Uses crayons Can walk sideways and backward Builds a 9-10 cube tower Walking rhythm stabilizes True running appears	Fears separation Shows negativistic anger Has a sense of humor Exhibits dependent clinging Is possessive with toys Copies parents' actions Resists parents' demands Cannot make decisions	Starts to use short sentences Controls world with language Uses "I," "me," "you" Identifies parts of body Uses concepts of dog, ball, etc. Obeys simple instructions
5–6 yrs.	Dresses self Has mature motor control Skips Broadjumps 2–3 ft. Can balance on one foot Can catch large ball bounced	Becomes competitive Prefers sex-appropriate activities Shows independence of parents Prefers to play with other children Basic emotions all have appeared	Copies square and triangle Uses adult speech sounds Has mastered basic grammar Knows over 2,000 words Comprehends opposite analogies Comprehends single-digit number concepts (6 yrs.)

Source: Adapted from B. R. McCandless and E. D. Evans, *Children and Youth: Psychosocial Development* (Hinsdale, Ill.: Dryden Press, 1973), pp. 13 and 14.

inches and the average weight is 23–30 pounds, whereas at five years the average preschooler weighs 42–43 pounds and is 43–44 inches tall.

During the preschool years the average boy is slightly taller than the average girl, and other sex differences have also been observed. Beginning at about the age of three, sex differences in aggression are apparent. Research studies have indicated that boys in nursery school are more physically aggressive than girls, behave in more negative, attention-getting ways, and are more negativistic in general. Boys are physically more aggressive than girls during the later stages of early childhood, and girls are more likely to scold and argue (Mussen, Conger, & Kagan, 1974). These developmental trends appear to be reliable, since they have been observed in cultures other than our own, though patterns of aggression vary from one society to another. There have been reliable reports of sex differences in certain types of motor skills, but for the most part height and aggressive behavior are the primary characteristics for which sex differences have been consistently reported in early childhood.

THE PHYSICAL-MOTOR DOMAIN

During early childhood, changes in physical-motor development are highlighted by rapid development of gross and fine motor skills and movements involving large muscles. Structural changes are also occurring. Sex differences emerge in such things as the manner in which the entire body is employed in throwing a ball and other similar tasks. Increased accuracy in hopping is exhibited by girls, for example, while boys' efforts are less coordinated.

Fine motor skills, which underlie many of the academic skills required for successful participation in the interactions of the instructional process, also are being developed (Tanner, 1970). Many preschool programs accordingly encourage these skills. As fine motor control develops during the second year, children attempt to enclose space in circular and spiral patterns, and later they draw squares. During the third and fourth years there is increased intensity in such artistic activities as drawing and coloring. By the end of the fourth year, children typically are able to print several letters and numbers of large size in a jumbled manner on a page. By age five, they start to include animals and trees in the pictures they draw, and most children can print their first names. Six-year-olds can usually draw a recognizable triangle, and about half of them are able to write the numbers from 1 to 20 and the letters of the alphabet.

BODY IMAGE AND BODY AWARENESS

Body image development occurs throughout early childhood. At two, children can typically identify large body parts such as arms, legs, and

To a young child, it's
a long way down.
Situations like this
help children
understand their
limitations, and
running and
jumping aid their
motor skills
development.

hands. By ages three and four, they begin to include a trunk when drawing pictures of themselves. The majority of four-year-olds can identify small body parts such as knees and elbows and can identify facial features with relative ease. By five years children usually begin to identify left and right, but they do so inconsistently. A completely left-right orientation is typically not complete until six years of age.

In addition to being able to identify body parts in pictures and drawings, children develop an awareness of their own bodies during the early childhood period. This starts during infancy with awareness of the elimination of body waste and is brought into focus by the demands of toilet training. Most children become absorbed with examination of the genitals. This perfectly normal aspect of development creates a problem only for the adult caretaker. The problem lies not in the child's activities of exploration and masturbation but the adult's attitudes and reactions to this behavior. Attempts to curtail it should not make the child feel ashamed or guilty; the practice is widespread because it "feels good," and it should not be considered an indication of abnormal development. Special education teachers are more likely to observe this behavior than other early childhood instructors, however.

Between the ages of four and six, the interest in body awareness may also be expressed in play, such as taking the role of doctor or nurse, or appear in the form of curiosity about where babies come from and other questions of this nature. Many children talk about their interest in body awareness when they think no one is listening or peek at suggestive pictures of adults. This behavior also is a normal part of growing up which appears as early as the preschool years.

THE COGNITIVE-INTELLECTUAL DOMAIN

Several characteristics are consistently observed in the thinking patterns of early childhood that set it apart from infancy or later childhood. There is considerable overlap between the physical-motor and cognitive-intellectual domains in infancy, but in the preschool years the distinction becomes clearer. Early childhood roughly corresponds to Piaget's stage of preoperational thinking, a time of preconceptual thought that is characterized by the emergence of symbolic functioning and egocentrism. *Symbolic functioning* is the ability to differentiate between *signifiers* (words, gestures, etc.) and their *referents* (the objects or events that signifiers refer to). For the first time, the child can deal with the future and past as well as the present, due to the development of language and symbolic functioning. These skills provide the ability to use mental images for objects and events that are not present. One of the most clear-cut examples is in play behavior. Children at this stage play "let's pretend," adopting make-believe roles or perhaps pretending that a cardboard box is a boat, a house, or an automobile.

The function of play in the cognitive development of preschoolers is more than the simple pursuit of pleasure. Play provides opportunities to practice solving problems, to assimilate experiences, and to build a repertory of experiences and cognitive skills. The child not only physically manipulates objects but develops an understanding of their functions and relations to one another. This is a time when the child engages in fantasies and plays at adopting adult roles, such as police officer or doctor.

The cognitive aspects of play must be distinguished from games that have a role in the socialization of a preschool child. Socialization, the second important function of play, is described in the next section as an aspect of the social-emotional domain.

COGNITIVE CONCEPTS

Several important concepts begin to develop during early childhood, but they do not reach their final level of development during this period. Among the developing concepts that are important to the instructional process in early childhood are shape, size, time, and numbers. (See, for example, Piaget, 1965; Piaget & Inhelder, 1956; and Piaget & Szesminska, 1964.)

Shape concepts include such forms as squares, circles, and triangles. While children of this age usually can discriminate among such objects as stars, blocks, or balls on the basis of shape ("Point to the one that is round"), the concepts are rather primitive. The more abstract concepts of triangularity, circularity, and squareness await further cognitive development during the concrete operational period of later childhood.

Size concepts also begin to develop, as evidenced by the child's use of labels such as *big, little, small,* and *middle size.* Under normal viewing conditions preschoolers can detect size differences as readily as adults can, but when certain visual cues are limited, they have greater difficulty in making accurate size judgments. These generalizations apply primarily to the size judgments of near objects; the perception of size for distant objects is more complex. For instance, it is not unusual for a five- or six-year-old to think that an object grows larger as it is approached. As a car in which a child of this age is traveling approaches a mountain, for example, the child thinks the mountain is actually getting larger.

Time has very little meaning for children of this age, who have no notion of the duration of time in units such as seconds, minutes, or hours and find it difficult to estimate the length of time required to carry out activities. For preschoolers a day can seem to last forever, particularly around Christmas. College students, in contrast, complain about not having enough time and seem to be always running to catch up. The developmental influences of age on time perception create a situation where time durations are viewed as shorter and shorter as a person grows older.

Number concepts are regarded as an important skill to be acquired in early childhood. As the child's ability to use numbers develops, a difference between counting ability and the ability to comprehend what is being counted typically appears. It is not unusual for a five-year-old to be able to count to 10 or 20, but this ability may reflect rote memory, much like remembering nursery rhymes. A child who counts up to 10 may not be able to withdraw 7 blocks from a pile of 10, for example.

Most children of this age have the ability to count in their heads. The act of counting is revealing because it indicates an ability to formulate a plan or strategy for generating numbers once the basic pattern has been learned. Children of four or five years appear to learn the first 10 or 20 numbers by rote memory, but they soon catch on to the idea that the same names can be repeated with minor variations to form a pattern or grouping. A four-year-old counts up to 19, for example, and then asks for help: "What comes after 19?" When told 20, the child successfully counts from 20 to 29 and then asks, "What's next?" When told 30, the child again successfully counts from 30 to 39, and so on.

Such an episode, which is commonly observed in early childhood, clearly shows that the child has discovered rules. Counting is no longer a simple rote memorization of sounds. Rather, a basic grouping pattern has been learned, and a plan for counting has been formulated by the child.

EGOCENTRISM

The development of these cognitive concepts is influenced by the child's view of the world. This view is unique to early childhood and differs from the view taken by older children, adolescents, or adults. Piaget (1926) refers to the preschooler's view of the world as *egocentric.*

A primary characteristic of the thinking of children in this period is that it is centered on only one perspective, their own. In this perspective, called *egocentrism,* it is impossible to understand a situation from any other point of view. Preschoolers do not realize they are limited in this fashion. They attempt to make the transition between seeing themselves as the center of the universe (which begins in infancy) and more objectively, being aware of others and their own rightful place in the scheme of things. But it is difficult for them to take the other person's point of view. Children at this stage seem to perceive the world as having been made for their exclusive enjoyment.

When egocentrism is the child's frame of reference, restrictions are placed on the ability to think. A young child can form a category of items, but only on the basis of a single attribute (or characteristic). A good example is the three- or four-year-old's inability to take into account simultaneously two attributes of an object, such as height and weight. The child can sort things out on the basis of a single attribute but cannot use two attributes of the same object as the basis of a multidimensional concept or category. A child at this stage would not be able to go to the garden and pick out two groups of tomatoes—big red ones and small green ones—even if accompanied by an understanding parent.

The thoughts of children in early childhood also are heavily influenced by what they see and hear. This creates a situation in which almost everything is taken at face value. At this point in cognitive development, the child tends to relate to particulars. If A is like B in one respect, then A must be like B in all other respects.

Early language development is also influenced by this egocentric perspective. When three- and four-year-old children are playing together in a wading pool, for example, two of them will talk to one another but little real communication results. Both children are so wrapped up in their own thoughts that they engage in parallel monologues rather than an information exchange, such as characterizes adult communication. Each child is his or her own best audience, and reference to self dominates the conversation. Children of this age talk primarily about themselves, their interests, family, or possessions. Toward the end of early childhood, they begin to talk about others as well.

The tendency of young children to criticize others, tattle on playmates, engage in name calling, and complain a lot is also due to the egocentric perspective. The predominance of concern for self and a lack of awareness of others are evident in these behaviors. Complaining is engaged in because of a perceived disadvantage or injustice to the most important thing in the environment—"me." Tattling and criticizing are engaged in because others fail to live up to the child's expectations or demands. Children are said to be honest in their remarks about others, but actually this honesty is a reflection of egocentric speech. They do not tell socially acceptable white lies because they cannot take the perspective of another person. Those who have an egocentric perspective tell it like it is.

As children approach school age they develop the abilities to think in terms of groups, to see relationships, and to deal with number concepts. A gradual departure from the egocentric perspective can be observed during the fifth and sixth years. This transition continues through later childhood until a different form of egocentrism emerges in adolescence.

In this move away from early childhood egocentrism, called *decentration,* children gradually begin to consider more than one aspect of an object or social situation and become aware of alternative points of view.

Decentration is not restricted to the cognitive-intellectual domain, as children of this age also become aware of different ways of reacting to people or social events. In terms of interpersonal behavior, they become more sensitive to the good or bad fortunes of others.

LANGUAGE DEVELOPMENT

Language ability accelerates and rapidly attains an adult quality during the preschool years. At about 24 to 30 months, a two-word sentence form of rudimentary grammar becomes evident. This grammar involves *pivot words* to which other noun forms called *open-class words* are attached. The uniting of a pivot word and an open-class word produces a two-word sentence such as "More milk."

This primitive pivotal grammar is rapidly expanded and differentiated into grammatical classes and rules. As the child's sentence-producing ability becomes more complex, such cases as articles, adjectives, noun phrases, and verb phrases are included. Transformational rules also appear during early childhood, an example being the child's use of morphological rules of tense (past, present, and future). Transformations also include such abilities as negation, as in changing "The boy hit the ball" to "The boy didn't hit the ball."

By the time children have attained school age, they are quite able to generate and comprehend language. Many psychologists believe that language development has an innate biological basis, but some see it as a social habit that is learned like other habits. In either case, *language tutoring* is helpful. Tutors can expand children's grammatical skills, enrich their verbal descriptive systems, or drill them in specific language forms. Lack of tutoring will impair language development.

Language tutoring seems to occur naturally in some families, as parents attempt to expand the sentences their children use. Between two and three years of age the child uses two- and three-word sentences and *telegraphic speech,* which resembles the messages adults construct when sending telegrams. Since words in a telegram cost money, pronouns, articles, adjectives, and so on are eliminated; the words retained are nouns and verbs which contain the most information at the least cost.

When a child uses telegraphic speech, an adult who hears it will frequently interpret the utterance and expand on it. Examples of telegraphic speech and expansions are given in Figure 2.1. It is assumed that expansion efforts provide positive feedback which promotes language acquisition, but the research data are not clear on this point. Efforts to promote language development by expansion are encouraged because they never have been demonstrated to have a negative influence, and it is one form of parent-child interaction that can be engaged in during this important period of development (Brown & Bellugi, 1964).

Figure 2.1

Expansions of children's speech by adults

Child's Sentences	**Adult's Sentences**
Baby chair.	Baby is in the chair.
Tommy milk.	Tommy is drinking milk.
Daddy eat cake.	Daddy is eating his cake.
I want see cow.	Jimmy wants to see the cow.

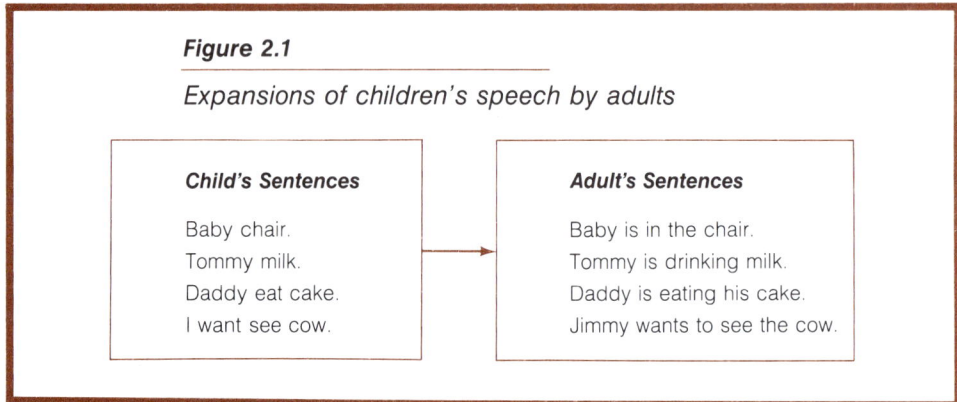

Language development involves five principal factors: grammar, pronunciation, vocabulary, talking rate, and communication style. Communication style, which reflects the type of language environment and the quality of speech model to which the child is exposed, is associated with social class and ethnic group differences. The five factors interact in complex ways and appear to have consequences for later academic development. For example, the language of young children who do not demonstrate satisfactory progress in reading is often marked by unelaborated sentences, a high proportion of short sentences (three or four words), an absence of connectives, and a redundant vocabulary.

COGNITIVE-INTELLECTUAL DEVELOPMENT AND THE INSTRUCTIONAL PROCESS

Teachers of children in the early childhood period must have an awareness of the emergence in their pupils of such abilities as concept learning, number and counting skills, and communication skills. The learning of these abilities signals readiness for structured programming.

A significant shift in the philosophy of preschool programming has occurred recently. The shift is away from the traditional nursery school format, which is rather vague and ill-defined in terms of structure, and toward more specific programming with a sound basis in educational theory.

A structured early childhood education program provides a carefully sequenced pattern of teacher-directed activities. Programs which focus on the tasks of reading, writing, and arithmetic readiness are especially helpful for preschoolers from disadvantaged backgrounds. The emphasis in structured programs is on the development of educational readiness and the attainment of instructional objectives reflecting specific academic tasks. Teaching methods are varied, ranging from social control approaches (loosely defined group activities) to behavioral modification techniques (Bereiter & Engelmann, 1966).

THE SOCIAL-EMOTIONAL DOMAIN

The psychosocial development of early (and middle) childhood includes, according to Erikson, the establishment of a "sense of autonomy vs. a sense of shame and doubt" and a "sense of initiative vs. guilt" (see Table 2.1 above). Between the ages of two and three, children begin to undertake actions with a purpose, such as walking. This activity involves the freedom to make a decision and a choice of "go or not go." Freedom to choose, in turn, provides the basis for a sense of independence or autonomy. Children cannot be allowed total freedom, however, because harmful consequences could result. Adults must maintain enough control to keep them from hurting themselves.

The development of self-control is of extreme importance during early childhood because it can provide the child with a sense of self-esteem. Self-esteem must be acquired before a sense of autonomy, which involves feelings of pride and goodwill, can develop. When a child's attempts at self-control are inspired by threats or fear, however, doubt and shame will result. Doubt arises when the child hesitates to make a decision or exercise freedom of choice, and shame is the eventual consequence of doubt and lack of self-esteem (Erikson, 1963, p. 225).

Four- and five-year-old children who are developing a sense of initiative take an aggressive approach to their environment. Erikson says that children delight in this new feeling of power and derive pleasure from the accomplishment of goals. The danger is that they will act in such an aggressive or coercive manner that they get out of control and then develop a sense of guilt. Successful resolution of the initiative vs. guilt crisis rests on the ability to distinguish between socially approved and disapproved behavior.

EMOTIONAL DEVELOPMENT

Fear, anger, and jealousy are significant emotions in early childhood. The preschool years are a very temperamental age. Fear is inspired by threatening or unfamiliar persons, objects, or events as preschoolers develop cognitively and socially, and they become more aware of their environment and the potential dangers in it. A feeling of vulnerability causes them to experience many fearful episodes, but the nature of the fear undergoes change during this period. While fears are produced by concrete things (animals, people, etc.) at two and three years of age, at four and five children learn to fear distant or imaginary dangers such as ghosts, dragons, or killers. More realistic fears such as being scared of storms, getting hurt, being left alone, the dark, and even death also are part of emotional development in this period.

Anger and temper tantrums appear frequently during early childhood. Any delay of pleasure or failure to meet a need seems to provoke an outburst. Some children get angry for no apparent reason, though closer observation may reveal such underlying factors as frustration at their own ineptness, attention seeking, or simply excessive tiredness.

Jealousy seems to reach a peak around three or four years of age. All children crave attention and affection from adults, and jealousy appears if they think someone else is getting too much attention. Jealousy can be the basis for an anger episode that serves an attention-getting purpose. Instances of jealousy can be minimized if parents and teachers avoid encouraging individual competition, do not make direct comparisons between children, and approach preschoolers as individuals and spend time alone with them.

SOCIALIZATION

Socialization is the process whereby the knowledge, attitudes, values, and social roles that have been developed by a given society or group are passed on to succeeding generations or new members, as we noted in Chapter 1. The agents of socialization provide essential links between the individual and society by means of which children learn the language, skills, attitudes, beliefs, and values that their society accepts. While the family is generally recognized as the most significant agent of socialization, the school is the agency that is formally charged by society with socializing children, weaning them from the home, and preparing them for a productive adulthood.

Forms of Play

In early childhood play is an important means of socialization. Observation of children during this period has revealed three major forms of play activity: solitary, parallel, and cooperative play (Mussen, Conger, & Kagan, 1974). *Solitary play*, at about two years of age, involves onlooker behavior such as watching other children and acknowledging their presence but not playing with them. In *parallel play*, which appears between the ages of three and four, two children in close proximity play by themselves rather than cooperatively with one another. They will play

The play of little girls, all dressed up in their mothers' hats and jewelry, helps them learn traditional social roles. Later they may try out more original roles, like the softball players pictured in Chapter 3.

side by side with similar toys but will not interact or share. *Cooperative play* develops during the later phases of early childhood. Kindergarteners share, work together on a common task, form groups, and play at organized group games. By school age special friendships have developed, and children who have not been included in the peer group can become lonely and unhappy.

The socioeconomic status of the family determines the availability of toys and play equipment and the environment for play. These and other factors influence the patterns of play activities. The interest in toys begins to lessen toward the end of this period, but at approximately three years, children use them as a means of trying out adult roles, as in playing house. Later, toys may be the basis for such make-believe games as doctor or cops and robbers. Play acting serves an important role in the socialization process by giving the child an opportunity to try out adult roles as well as to engage in structured flights of fantasy. Around four or five years of age, children begin to prefer games played with peers, which involve cooperative play. Games requiring cooperation during this period have only a few rules and test such skills as running, skipping, and throwing and catching balls.

Reading activities, which at this level primarily involve the child being read to by an older person, also can be a pattern of play. Some children have favorite books, such as animal stories or fairy tales, that have been read to them so often they can "pretend to read" by holding the book and turning the pages as they tell the story. Some children who play at reading develop a remarkable ability to tell a favorite story in detail and can turn the pages at appropriate points. While playing at reading may not involve the actual reading process, it does help cultivate an appreciation for the reading act as a means of enjoyment and information gathering.

Television appeals to children of this age, and programs such as Captain Kangaroo and Sesame Street are of value. Excessive viewing can create problems, however. Research has suggested that the modeling effects of program violence may encourage children to imitate aggressive acts they see dramatized or stimulate aggression in other forms (Bandura, 1967), though this conclusion has been questioned more recently (see Chapter 3). Excessive television viewing can also hinder the socialization process. A child who sits for hours in front of a television set will be sacrificing peer interactions and thus will miss the valuable socialization lessons that can be gained from cooperative play during the later years of early childhood.

Moral Development

Moral development is an important component of the socialization process which begins during early childhood, though it assumes greater significance later (see Chapter 3). Since the intellectual development of children of these ages has not yet reached the point where they can understand abstract principles of right or wrong, they cannot apply them. And because long-term retention is still poor, they may exhibit inconsistent behavior in terms of conduct, reflecting a tendency to "forget."

Moral development at this point in life involves automatic obedience to adult rules, without applying reason or judgment. Rules are obeyed because an adult in authority says so. The child views right or wrong in terms of consequences; a "wrong" act is followed by punishment. As early childhood draws to an end, most children exhibit an awareness of right and wrong in specific situations. Consistent discipline in the home is helpful for children learning this behavior.

Sextyping

Sextyping, the process of socialization by which socially defined male and female roles are learned, begins as early as infancy, when parents select "boy" or "girl" toys for their baby. Sextyping is a part of the early identification process by which the young child comes to recognize her or his sexual identity or gender, although the female and male roles in our society are not so rigidly defined today as they were previously. While the question of how sextyping is learned during the preschool years is open to several theoretical interpretations, it is generally recognized that sex-role awareness is well established by the school years.

LEARNING TO LEARN IN EARLY CHILDHOOD

The instructional process in early childhood is essentially an interchange between an adult—parent, teacher, or other caregiver—and a young child or group of children. In the ages from two to six, much of the child's significant physical development takes place, and the basics of the intellectual and social skills that are essential for successful learning throughout the school years are acquired.

The principal influence on physical, social, and intellectual development in early childhood remains parents and the family, despite the increasing trend toward early education experience noted above. Family experiences will largely determine how well prepared a child is for formal schooling. Some types of family environments which may lead to behavioral disorders in children are described in Chapter 5.

Happiness in early childhood particularly affects young children's social and emotional outlook as learners in school. Unhappiness is a behavioral condition which is very difficult to modify. Hurlock (1975) has suggested that the family is responsible for seeing that the three A's of happiness are provided for preschoolers: (1) acceptance by others, (2) affection, and (3) acceptance of self through achievement (see Box C).

DECIDING WHAT TO TEACH

For the teacher, deciding what to teach in the preschool or kindergarten is a question of whether to stress the acquisition of skills and knowledge or the process of learning. This need not be an either/or decision. During these years there are opportunities to focus on the acquisition of both—information or facts, and ideas and problem-solving skills. To do less would not be in the best interest of the child.

In some developmental perspectives, the central focus of early childhood education is regarded as the development of general modes of

BOX C *How to get children ready
for school: Make them happy*

Parents can help prepare children for school learning
experiences by providing them with:

- Good health, so they can enjoy whatever they undertake
and carry it out successfully.

- A stimulating environment which gives them opportunities
to use their abilities to the maximum.

- Acceptance of their annoying childish behavior and
guidance to help them learn to behave in a socially
acceptable way.

- A disciplinary policy that is well planned and consistently
adhered to, so they know what is expected and do not
feel they are punished unfairly.

- Appropriate expressions of affection, such as showing
pride in their children's achievements and spending time
doing things they enjoy.

- Guidance of their children's aspirations in accordance with
their abilities, so they will have a reasonable number of
successes and thus develop favorable self-concepts.

- Assurance of acceptance by siblings and playmates
through guidance in how to get along in play situations.

- A general atmosphere of happiness in the home, which
helps children tolerate temporary unpleasantness.

Source: Adapted from Box 5.9 in E. B. Hurlock, *Developmental Psychology*, 4th
ed. (New York: McGraw-Hill, 1975).

information processing, such as rudimentary critical thinking and problem-solving skills. But the development of concepts and principles by which knowledge is structured must also be taken into account, and the social-emotional domain must not be ignored. A central purpose of any preschool or kindergarten program should be the development of an attitude of enjoyment and satisfaction to be derived from products within the school setting. This involves teaching appreciation for the learning of academic skills and the promotion of self-worth as it pertains to academic achievement.

THE SIX-YEAR-OLD LEARNER

The preschool years are brought to an abrupt halt by admittance to kindergarten or the first grade at age five or six. The development of children at this age determines the student entry characteristics teachers of these grades must consider in formulating their instructional plans.

By the time they are six years old, most children are a delight to be around—most of the time, anyway. They may be pleasant and easygoing at one moment and stubborn or headstrong at another. Relationships with friends and family members are variable. Six-year-olds are so competitive they may cheat or break up a game if they foresee failure. Treats must be divided equally, and no one should get an extra turn. They may also depart from the truth and disclaim responsibility; milk gets spilled or chairs get knocked over by mysterious forces or someone else. Nonetheless, they are on the whole delightful companions full of big smiles and hugs.

Six is a restless age. First-graders seem to be in motion most of the time. Even when sitting, there is a lot of wiggling and squirming. Clearly, first-graders have energy to spare. They love to cut, paint, paste, color, make things, finger paint, and write their names. Most can print the numbers to 10, and many can print both their first and last names. Both numbers and letters are frequently reversed (e.g., *M* for *W*, or *b* for *d*), and clumsy-looking efforts to reproduce them are common.

The typical six-year-old likes to talk and talk. Most children of this age can tell you the day and month of their birthday. They can differentiate morning and afternoon and can tell left from right. Learners at this stage of development are eager to please and approach most tasks with enthusiasm. For the most part, they are happy and present few problems for the classroom teacher. Any behavior problems encountered are likely to relate to social-emotional immaturity rather than behaviors in the other domains.

CHAPTER 2 IN RETROSPECT

The developmental perspective recognizes that children do not all develop in the same way or at the same rate. The reasons why are part of the enduring controversy about whether humans develop as they do because of their heredity or their environment. The consensus today is that both affect learning behavior, as expressed in the interactionist position, and their effects on the entry or readiness characteristics of learners must be taken into account in the instructional process.

Our framework for discussing student entry characteristics of different kinds is a threefold typology of developmental domains: cognitive-intellectual, social-emotional, and physical-motor. There are also systems for classifying stages within these domains; the most important are Piaget's four stages of intellectual development and Erikson's psychosocial theory.

During early childhood changes in the physical-motor domain involve rapid development of gross and fine motor skills and the emergence of body image and body awareness. The development of cognitive concepts in regard to size, shape, time, and numbers is related to the child's egocentric view of the world. Language ability improves rapidly, and by the time children are ready for school they can understand and use it quite well. Autonomy and initiative are characteristic of the social-emotional domain in early childhood. The socialization process takes place in the home and the school, with play, moral development, and sextyping as important components.

**QUESTIONS
FOR
DISCUSSION**

1. Preschool programs that focus on the development of early academic skills have proven to be effective. On the basis of information provided under the heading of the cognitive-intellectual domain, develop a set of activities that you could use with a preschool child.
2. In textbooks, authors organize information into meaningful units (e.g, the developmental domains) because this facilitates the learning process. It can lead to misconceptions, however, such as the idea that the behaviors under consideration belong only to single categories. This can be a particular problem in thinking about behaviors within the cognitive-intellectual and social-emotional domains. Analyze this problem and provide instances of behavior during the preschool years where it is necessary to consider the interaction between these domains in order to explain the development of early academic skills.

3. Does the determination of how behavior develops influence what you can do as a teacher or parent to modify the course of development? Take a single academic skill and determine how heredity and environment interact to influence its development.

Anastasi, Anne. *Individual Differences.* New York: John Wiley and Sons, 1965.

One of the classic sources in the area of individual differences, this text focuses on the origin and measurement of individual differences within the cognitive domain. It provides a very readable introduction to the nature-nurture controversy.

Ames, L. B., Gillespie, C., Haines, J., and Ilg, F. L. *The Gesell Institutes Child from One to Six: Evaluating the Behavior of the Preschool Child.* New York: Harper & Row, 1979.

In this valuable guide to development from birth to six, behaviors from the cognitive-intellectual, social-emotional, and physical-motor domains are documented, and the ages at which various behaviors appear are recorded.

Brown, Roger. *A First Language: The Early Stages.* Cambridge, Mass.: Harvard University Press, 1973.

This volume reports developmental psycholinguistic research conducted by Brown and his associates. Although not easy reading, it is considered one of the best single resources on language development.

Thomas, R. Murray. *Comparing Theories of Child Development.* Belmont, Cal.: Wadsworth Publishing Co., 1979.

This comprehensive review of child development theory reviews historical as well as current ideas. In addition to the familiar humanistic, behavioristic, psychodynamic, and cognitive theories, sociobiology is explored in an interesting chapter.

Willerman, Lee. *The Psychology of Individual and Group Differences.* San Francisco: W. H. Freeman & Co., 1979.

In this comprehensive review and interpretation of the research literature on human individual differences, each variable on which human behavior differs is examined from both genetic and environmental points of view. The interest level of the book is high because the author does not attempt to review all the studies in this area, only types that have contributed to a better understanding of the nature and distribution of individual differences.

REFERENCES

Anastasi, Anne. Heredity, environment, and the question "How?" *Psychological Review,* 1958, *65,* 97–208.

Ausubel, David P. Enhancing the acquisition of knowledge. In M. Johnson (Ed.), *Toward Adolescence, The Middle School Years.* 79th Yearbook of the National Society for the Study of Education, Part I. Chicago: University of Chicago Press, 1980.

Bandura, Albert. The role of modeling processes in personality development. In W. W. Hartup and N. L. Smothergill (Eds.), *The Young Child.* Washington, D.C.: National Association for the Education of Young Children, 1967.

Bereiter, C., and Engelmann, S. *Teaching Disadvantaged Children in the Preschool.* Englewood Cliffs, N.J.: Prentice-Hall, 1966.

Brown, Roger, and Bellugi, Ursula. Three processes in the child's acquisition of syntax. *Harvard Educational Review,* 1964, *34,* 133–151.

Bruner, Jerome. *Toward a Theory of Instruction.* Cambridge, Mass.: Harvard University Press, 1966.

Erikson, Erik. *Childhood and Society.* 2nd ed. New York: W. W. Norton, 1963.

Gagné, Robert M. Contributions of learning to human development. *Psychological Review,* 1968, *75,* 177–191.

Gagné, Robert M. *Learning and Individual Differences.* Columbus, Ohio: Charles E. Merrill, 1967.

Gesell, Arnold. Maturation and the patterning of behavior. In C. A. Murcheson (Ed.), *A Handbook of Child Psychology.* Worcester, Mass.: Clark University Press, 1933.

Hurlock, E. B. *Developmental Psychology.* 4th ed. New York: McGraw-Hill, 1975.

McCandless, B. R., and Evans, E. D. *Children and Youth: Psychosocial Development.* Hinsdale, Ill.: Dryden Press, 1973.

Mussen, Paul H., Conger, John J., and Kagan, Jerome. *Child Development and Personality.* 4th ed. New York: Harper & Row, 1974.

Newman, Barbara M., and Newman, Philip R. *Development through Life: A Psychosocial Approach.* Rev. ed. Homewood, Ill.: Dorsey Press, 1979.

Peterson, Penelope L., and Clark, Christopher M. Teachers' reports of their cognitive processes during teaching. *American Educational Research Journal,* 1978, *15,* 555–565.

Piaget, Jean. *The Child's Conception of Number.* New York: W. W. Norton, 1965.

Piaget, Jean. *The Language and Thought of the Child.* London: Routledge & Kegan Paul, 1926.

Piaget, Jean, and Inhelder, Barbel. *The Child's Conception of Space.* London: Routledge, 1956.

Piaget, Jean, and Inhelder, Barbel. *The Psychology of the Child.* New York: Basic Books, 1969.

Piaget, Jean, and Szesminska, A. *The Child's Conception of Geometry.* New York: Harper Torch Books, 1964.

Tanner, J. M. Physical growth. In P. H. Mussen (Ed.), *Carmichael's Manual of Child Psychology.* New York: John Wiley & Sons, 1970.

Watson, John B. *Behaviorism.* Rev. ed. New York: W. W. Norton, 1930.

Willerman, Lee. *The Psychology of Individual and Group Differences.* San Francisco: W. H. Freeman, 1979.

Development in
Later Childhood

From a developmental perspective, the changes in the cognitive-intellectual and social-emotional domains that occur in later childhood, from ages 6 to 12, are probably greater than those taking place in any other phase of a learner's school career. This period extends from about the time the child enters the first grade to the beginning of adolescence. By its end the learner is usually in the seventh grade, which is the first or second year of junior high.

The teacher's relations with the learner in the instructional process also undergo extensive change in this period. In the first grade there is a very highly structured learning environment, and the teacher engages in a great deal of "hands-on," or direct, teaching. Directions, objectives, and so on are presented verbally in a carefully sequenced instruction plan. By the seventh grade, the learner can be expected to assume a large part of the responsibility for reading and comprehending directions, objectives, instructional procedures, and so on.

Physical growth progresses at a slower rate during later childhood than it did earlier. Body changes are less abrupt and physical size increases more slowly, and the slower physical growth is accompanied by a steadier progression of development. On the average, boys are taller and slightly heavier than girls, except during the preadolescent growth spurt at 11 or 12. Boys have more muscle tissue than girls, who have more fat tissue. Muscle growth for both boys and girls is rapid during this period. The skeleton also develops, and calcium and phosphorus are being deposited in cartilage tissue (ossification). In some instances skeletal and muscle development occur at differing rates. A child may appear awkward, gangly, or swaybacked when skeletal development occurs more rapidly than muscle and ligament development.

EDUCATIONAL DEVELOPMENT GEARED TO CHANGE

Since the learner changes a great deal in terms of cognitive and social development in later childhood, the educational curriculum for this period also must be geared to change. The developmental perspective introduced in Chapter 2 involves a set of assumptions about how children come to be educated. If, in fact, curriculum development is an attempt to match learning experiences and educational goals to the learner's level of development, under optimal conditions educational development and learner development would go hand in hand. Nevertheless, the development of the child must lead the educational process.

One critical concern in this concept of an educational process geared to change is setting the general objectives of a successful educational experience. Another is determining the types of entry or readiness characteristics learners must have in order to interact successfully with the teacher in the instructional process. Both are concerned with the learner's capabilities. If the school determines that an 18-year-old should reasonably be expected to be an accomplished reader or solver of everyday math problems, for example, it will specify these accomplishments as educational goals. Then the problem is to decide how the objectives can be achieved in a step-by-step fashion over a twelve-year period (grades 1 through 12). This step-by-step progression through the school career is based on available information about the learners' capabilities and how they develop.

The wedding of learner development and curriculum development is based on psychological principles. A description of the capabilities learners should have at any grade level is available in the literature on child development, and instructional data on the learning tasks underlying school curricula can be analyzed to specify the skills necessary for successful completion of academic tasks at any grade level. In this way, Rohwer (1970) says, "psychological work on cognitive development can provide critical information about the extent to which the capabilities a learner brings to the curriculum mesh with the prerequisites dictated by the nature of the curriculum." Thus the two components, development and curriculum, provide the basis for educational development.

AN EMPHASIS ON MATURATION

In educational development terms, development and change in learners are seen as the result of two factors, maturation and learning. In this chapter the emphasis is on the maturational influence on cognitive development, an idea utilizing the theoretical perspective drawn from the work of Jean Piaget and Jerome Bruner. The distinction between changes in behavior that are brought about by maturation, in which the environment may apply a passive role, and those that are brought about by learning, which are dependent on the learner's *interaction* with the environment, will be made in Chapter 7. It is important to remember, however, that in educational development, learning and maturation are complementary.

Both Bruner (1966) and Piaget (1970) acknowledge that the nature of the learner's sensory systems (vision, hearing, touch, etc.), central nervous system (spinal cord and brain), and motor systems (movement, speech, etc.) determines the limits of the learner's general cognitive development at points in the educational process. While they thus recognize the role of maturation in cognitive development, they also acknowledge the importance of experiences, however. Piaget and Bruner assign considerable importance to the environment as an influence on the nature of cognitive processing in individual learners. In the discussion of language development in Chapter 2, for example, it was noted that any child, regardless of place of birth, will use only simple sentence structure at age two. By age six, however, a child typically has acquired the ability to utter syntactically correct sentences in an adult manner. This is true whether the child grows up speaking English or German or any other language. The language environment of the German culture, for example, will produce a six-year-old who utters adultlike speech patterns that follow German, not English, syntax. Neither English- nor German-speaking learners are able to produce the appropriate adultlike syntax at age two or three.

Most of the curricular material a teacher uses has been closely matched to the learner's maturational level by curriculum experts. Therefore, while readiness is a matter of both prior learning and maturation, in most cases the absence of prior learning rather than a lack of biological maturation is the principal reason a learner may not be *ready* for instruction.

THE PHYSICAL-MOTOR DOMAIN

In later childhood students may experience numerous difficulties in the processing of classroom learning which are due to improper physical-motor development. While the nature of these perceptual or physical difficulties differs, if they can be successfully treated so that no significant educational lag occurs, the learner can operate as a processor of classroom instruction. This view of the learner as a processor of information relates learning and behavioral development to the physical and neurological makeup of the student. It is the basis for the information-processing approach to intelligence to be described in Chapter 6.

A SYSTEMS-PROCESSING PERSPECTIVE

In a systems-processing, or input-process-output perspective, the learner is seen as made up of sensory systems, a central nervous system, and motor systems. The sensory systems are responsible for stimulus input, while the central nervous system processes the information. The motor systems provide the basis for output in the form of observable behaviors such as speech, writing, or marking an answer sheet.

This view of the learner is analogous to the way a hand calculator works. The user has to provide the input (numbers) and designate the operation (i.e., add or subtract). Punching the appropriate operation key sets the circuitry into operation, so the appropriate process is performed.

When processing is complete, the output or answer is flashed on the display panels.

When this perspective is applied to the learner, the emphasis is on physical-neurological capabilities. The learner's organic capabilities provide the basis for the processing of information provided by instruction. Since the learner does not come into the classroom with mature sensory, processing, or motor systems, much instruction must be geared to the development of processing cognitive tasks and skills such as reading, critical thinking, and problem solving, as well as output cognitive tasks and skills like following instructions, writing, and speaking. The development of processing and output tasks and skills is a fundamental, or general, instructional objective (see Chapter 15).

The maturation of the learner's physical-neurological systems influences educational development in two rather significant ways. There must be maturational readiness of the sensory systems, in the form of attention and ability to concentrate, or little or no input will be provided for the learner to process. And there must be maturational readiness of the motor systems for output to develop in the form of abilities like writing, playing a musical instrument, or participating in intramural sports.

For our purposes, readiness of a maturational nature must be viewed as a necessary but not sufficient condition for classroom learning. Maturational readiness is necessary in the sense that the three systems (sensory, central, and motor) must be adequate for the learning task at hand. However, systems that are "ready" are not sufficient in themselves to guarantee learning. A teacher or other instructional medium such as a text or programmed lesson must be available to provide the appropriate experiences in the form of classroom instruction. Instruction provides information, which activates the sensory systems and initiates information-processing activities.

PREREQUISITES FOR THE INSTRUCTIONAL PROCESS

Specific kinds of maturational readiness have educational significance because they are prerequisites to the instructional process. For classroom learning to take place, learners must have adequate capabilities in attention and perception and must be able to control their behavioral tempo.

Attentional Capacity

If communication of the instruction from the teacher to the learner is to succeed, the learner must have the capacity to pay attention. The significance of this prerequisite for the instructional process is attested to by the emphasis on arousing and maintaining attention in most teaching methods. In the absence of attention, it is highly unlikely learning

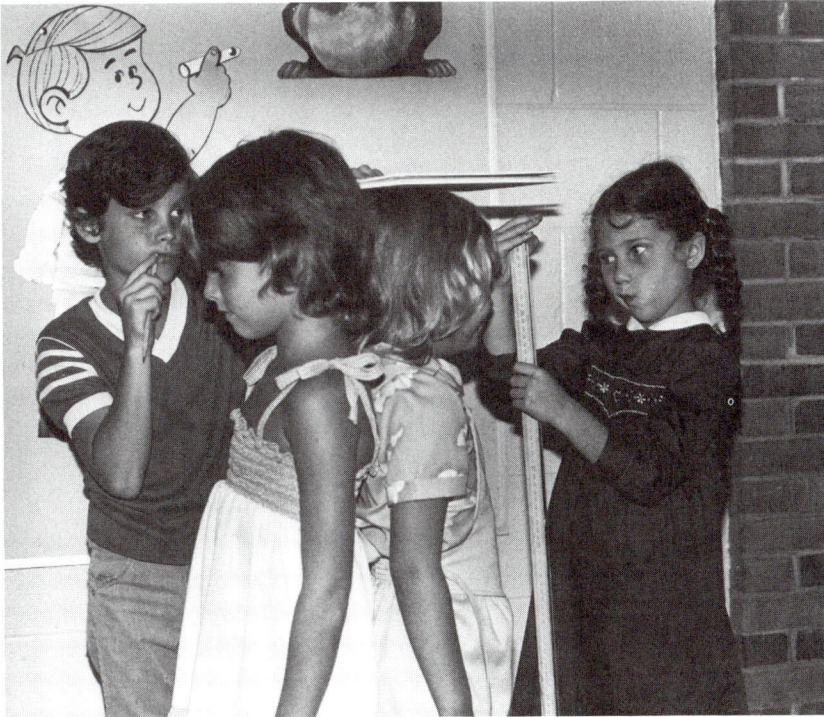

*The look of concentration on the girl doing the measuring
suggests that to children of this age, who is taller than
whom is a momentous consideration.*

will occur. In a classroom where much of the teacher's time must be
taken up with trying to gain the student's attention or attempting to
keep the class from becoming totally disruptive, the noise level is very
high, and it is hard for learners to attend to the instruction. In such a
classroom little or no processing of information can occur, and so learning cannot be expressed in the form of output. The learner must have
the ability to attend to instruction for an appropriate period (or have
an adequate attention span) in order for teaching and learning to
proceed.

Perceptual Capacity

The educational significance of perceptual development is that it serves
as the basis for the discrimination of instructions and information to be

learned. Vision and audition (hearing) are the most important senses for the instructional process because it is through them that information is typically presented.

Perceptual development is an obvious prerequisite for the processing of information about pictures, graphs, diagrams, and mathematical symbols. In the last 20 years or so, however, most educational and psychological research involving perceptual development has focused on the development of reading skills. The significance of perceptual learning in the development of reading skills is now widely recognized.

Perceptual learning ability is needed during the early stages of reading development. In first grade, for example, the learner is asked to discriminate among letters of the alphabet (graphemes) and vocalizations (phonemes). Following discrimination learning, the vocalizations are associated with the appropriate letters of the alphabet. The ability to pair graphemes and phonemes is essential for beginning readers. There is also mounting evidence that emphasis on the teaching of decoding skills (discrimination and analysis) during the first grade benefits the development of skills in not only reading but spelling as well.

Behavioral Tempo

In addition to attentional and perceptual competence, learners must have the maturational ability to modify and control their own behavior. This prerequisite for the educational process can be observed in three rather fundamental ways. The first is the ability to bring overt or observable responses under control upon request, which is one aspect of attentional capacity. In this case, the learner must be able to repress distracting or interfering behavior in order to direct attention to the instruction. The second is the ability to follow one's own instructions, or to make decisions about adopting learning strategies or study methods.

While the ability to attend to others' instructions as well as to one's own relates to input and processing skills, the third instance of behavioral tempo is related to output. The learner must be able to delay responding overtly in order to provide time for the testing or modifying of a response before it is made. This ability is what distinguishes reflective from impulsive learners. Reflective learners respond more slowly but apparently check a response before it is made, because few errors are observed. Impulsive learners respond rapidly but have a high error rate. Research evidence indicates that it is possible to modify an impulsive learner's style to make it more reflective.

The Prerequisites in Teaching Language

One example of how the prerequisites of attention, perception, and behavioral tempo affect the instructional process is in the teaching of language skills. A learner who impulsively responds to a question without thinking may give an answer that is unrelated to the question. When this occurs, the teacher might ask, "What did I say?" If the child responds, "I don't know," it is likely that the question asked was not clarified. An impulsive behavioral tempo or a lack of attention may be the reason a learner runs unrelated ideas together in a single sentence. The child must be taught to pay attention, slow down, and think before responding.

Immature speech patterns, which can result from poor speech models at home, may also reflect a lack of perceptual readiness. For example, inability to discriminate between such sounds as *b* and *d* would reflect a problem with auditory discrimination. Special education teachers can show students how to make such sound discriminations and help them improve their language skills.

In summary, the physical-motor domain, which has its basis in the physiology and biology of the learner, is still important during later childhood. The emphasis on growth of behaviors within the domain has diminished, but the physiological and neurological systems are undergoing continual development. They may not be obvious to the casual observer, but they are significant and necessary conditions for cognitive development.

THE COGNITIVE-INTELLECTUAL DOMAIN

Different study strategies require different types of cognitive skills, and different types of memory processing are required by the various types of items typically found on classroom tests. An awareness of *what* is required in terms of processing skills, plus *how* and *when* to use them, is important for academic success. As we will see, this awareness is not present at the beginning of the school career, nor does it occur automatically. The maturation of cognitive processing skills may be dependent on the growth and development of the central nervous system. However, the ability to know how and when to use these skills must be learned.

COGNITIVE TASKS, SKILLS, AND PROCESSES

Teachers cannot promote the cognitive development of their students unless they can recognize the skills used in the learning process. Figure 3.1 lists some examples of cognitive tasks, skills, and processes. The ordering of tasks, skills, and processes is hierarchical: The successful undertaking of academic tasks depends on the use of cognitive skills that

---

Figure 3.1

Hierarchy of cognitive tasks, skills, and processes

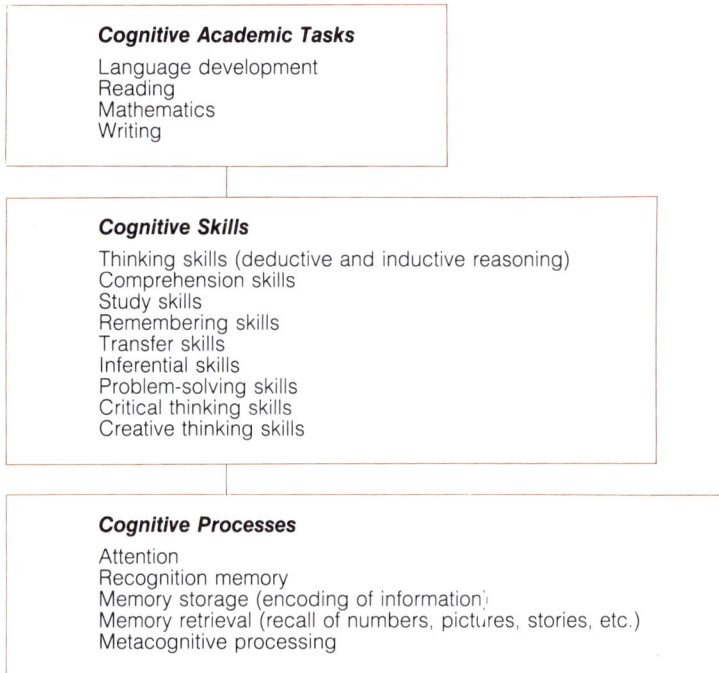

Cognitive Academic Tasks

Language development
Reading
Mathematics
Writing

Cognitive Skills

Thinking skills (deductive and inductive reasoning)
Comprehension skills
Study skills
Remembering skills
Transfer skills
Inferential skills
Problem-solving skills
Critical thinking skills
Creative thinking skills

Cognitive Processes

Attention
Recognition memory
Memory storage (encoding of information)
Memory retrieval (recall of numbers, pictures, stories, etc.)
Metacognitive processing

---

are made up of two or more cognitive processes. Cognitive academic tasks make up the basic subject matter taught in schools, and they are taught in some form throughout the educational experience.

During later childhood the cognitive processes undergo further development, so complex cognitive skills such as problem solving and critical thinking can be taught. Problem solving is a skill that is independent of subject matter, as will be described in Chapter 10, but the ability is frequently taught in mathematics. One way is in the math story problems of the fifth and sixth grades, such as "Jill is taller than Joan; Joan is shorter than Jane; who is shortest?" This type of problem requires a cognitive skill called *deductive reasoning*. Teaching this type of math problem, therefore, will be successful only if the learner has demonstrated the ability to think deductively.

Critical thinking also involves basic cognitive skills (see Chapter 10). There are several aspects of critical thinking, but the ability to recognize an error in an argument or story is basic to reading comprehension. The following type of passage might appear on a test of critical thinking ability:

> A speeding car was stopped by a police officer for traveling 65 miles per hour in a 30-mile zone. The driver explained that the gas tank was almost empty and he wanted to hurry and get home before he ran out of gas. What is foolish about that?

The ability to recognize the error in the speeding driver's logic is typically not learned until about the middle of the concrete operational period (grades 4 or 5). Prior to this, many learners agree that the driver's logic is okay. Our consideration of how these processes develop during later childhood utilizes an excellent review of the development of memory in children by Robert Kail (1979).

TYPES OF COGNITIVE PROCESSES

The cognitive processes listed in Figure 3.1 are of two principal types: attentional and memory processes. Attentional processes are necessary for the input of information, and most other cognitive processes are aspects of memory functioning. More information on memory processes, particularly, will be given in Chapter 7.

Attentional Processes

Attentional processing, which starts with the attentional capacity described above as a prerequisite of the instructional process, is necessary for learning to occur. Two basic aspects of attention are orientation (focusing) and maintenance. The ability of a learner to focus on relevant details and ignore distracting stimuli increases with age. Clear-cut age differences have been demonstrated in comparisons of learners in grades 1, 3, 5, and 7 (Maccoby & Hagen, 1965). Attention is controlled consciously by the learner, but it can be influenced by external factors. It has been determined, for instance, that attention is focused more on persons with high status or competence, a position young children, at least, usually accord their teachers.

Once attention has been focused it must be maintained. This need becomes obvious to practicing teachers, who use a number of techniques to satisfy it. At a personal level, teachers who vary their tone of voice and manner of delivery, in combination with their gestures or actions, are usually rewarded with attention. Audiovisual aids and other instructional media also are designed to help attract and maintain students' attention. In the developmental perspective, the assumption is that as students grow they learn to take increased responsibility for maintaining their attention.

Memory Processes

Memory is not an isolated intellectual skill but consists of the processes involved as the brain proceeds to store and retrieve information and ideas. Kail (1979) suggests that "memory is really a convenient descriptive term for a collection of cognitive processes. Memory development, in turn, is a composite of changes in each of several components of memory" (p. 3). An information-processing view of the memory process is diagrammed in Chapter 7 (Figure 7.2).

Recognition Memory   The ability to determine if a learning input is familiar or new derives from recognition memory. Stimulus inputs, as noted in the preceding section, come from the sensory systems in the form of seeing, hearing, feeling, and so on. In the processing the learner asks, in effect, "Am I familiar with this, or is it a new one for me?" This simple process has implications for more complex memory processing. A learner must have the ability to recognize information, for example, before she or he can retrieve it from memory storage. In other words, learners have to be able to recognize what they know. Otherwise, a great deal of time and effort would be wasted with repetitious learning.

Studies of the development of recognition memory have had interesting results. When children in grades 1, 4, and 7 were asked to recognize previously presented simple paintings, no age differences were noted. Nelson (1971) found that when the stimuli are familiar and simple, first-graders do as well as seventh-graders. With more complex materials, age differences in recognition memory are observed. Newcombe, Rogoff, and Kogen (1977) compared six-year-olds to nine-year-olds and adults on the ability to recognize previously viewed complex scenes as well as simple pictures and found apparent developmental differences. Six-year-olds recognize simple pictures (hat, TV, etc.) with 85 percent accuracy, while nine-year-olds are accurate 90 percent of the time and adults are 98 percent accurate. When materials to be recognized are complex scenes, six-year-olds recognize them at about a chance level (55 percent), nine-year-olds are 80 percent accurate, and adults respond accurately 91 percent of the time.

Two factors account for this developmental trend in recognition memory. One is that younger children (such as first-graders) look at scenes less efficiently than adults do. The other is that older children can make better use of the inherent organization in a complex scene than younger children can.

Memory Storage   The keystone of cognitive skills, memory storage, is essential for the successful completion of academic tasks. A strategy or plan is necessary in order to organize information that is to be remembered. Since some memory strategies are effective and others are not, the ability to select and use one is essential for the learner. The simplest strategy is repetition, but this procedure is rarely used by children of early school age. As children grow older, the likelihood that they will spontaneously use one or more strategies to store information in memory increases.

Two strategies children in the upper elementary grades can use to facilitate memory storage are associative clustering, in which items that are in some way associated are lumped together, and categorizing, which is more precise and requires the use of higher order (superordinate) concepts as organizing principles. For example, if students in a sixth-grade geography class are asked to memorize a list of cities, such as Moscow, Montreal, San Francisco, Lenigrad, New York, and Toronto, a categorizing strategy is helpful. Memorizing these names is easier if the cities are categorized by the country in which they are located.

Children in first grade can be taught to use a categorizing strategy, but they must be told how and when to do so. By the fourth grade, some students will use the categorizing strategy spontaneously. By the end of the later childhood period, most learners will adopt appropriate strategies on their own.

The developmental trend in rehearsal abilities, which enhances memory storage, makes the use of formal study methods possible by the beginning of junior high school. The SQ3R method (Robinson, 1946) has been used for years to improve students' retention of what they read in textbooks. SQ3R stands for a five-step sequence which includes (1) surveying the chapter, (2) asking questions about the material, (3) reading the material, (4) reciting major ideas, and (5) review. Typically, students cannot use such a study strategy to help them organize textbook material until near the end of later childhood.

Memory Retrieval   Both storage and retrieval are involved in the memory retrieval processes. Memory storage is a necessary but not sufficient condition for memory retrieval. The two processes develop in a parallel fashion, and considerable research with both children and adults has indicated that the organizational strategies that enhance memory storage also enhance memory retrieval (Kail, 1979).

The ability to use organization strategies or cues for memory retrieval develops during later childhood. First-graders are unlikely to use retrieval strategies, while sixth- and seventh- graders do so with adultlike skill. If third-graders are asked to memorize the cities listed in the sixth-grade geography class example above, for example, they would probably use the category label of *country* as a retrieval cue but would fail to use it efficiently. Rather than retrieving the two cities in each country, the third-graders would retrieve one at a time (e.g., Russia—Moscow; Canada—Toronto; Russia—Leningrad). By the sixth and seventh grades, students can retrieve both cities under each category before going to the next country (e.g., Russia—Moscow, Leningrad; Canada—Toronto, Montreal).

First-graders can be trained to use retrieval strategies effectively. Why they do not do so spontaneously is an area for further research.

Metacognitive Processing

Metacognition is a cognitive skill which involves not only memory monitoring but the monitoring of comprehension, problem solving, and other cognitive skills listed in Figure 3.1. Students who use metacognitive processing demonstrate an awareness of their own processing abilities. Flavell (1979) suggests that memory monitoring and the monitoring of other cognitive skills can be taught during the primary grades, and "increasing the quantity and quality of children's metacognitive knowledge and monitoring skills through systematic training may be feasible as well as desirable." The teaching of such skills as critical thinking and problem solving can help students to make better real-life decisions, as well as learn and otherwise perform more successfully in the classroom.

COGNITIVE THEORY AND THE INSTRUCTIONAL PROCESS

Two theoretical positions that emphasize how knowledge of cognitive skills development can affect the instructional process in the primary and elementary grades are those of Jean Piaget and Jerome Bruner, which were introduced in Chapter 2. Since both are stage theories, they are based on the assumption that cognitive development during later childhood is different from what takes place either earlier or later. While learners in this period can use symbols and think in simple, logical terms, they are not miniature adults, and the teacher must try to see the world as they do. One way to accomplish this is by becoming familiar with the developmental characteristics of the learner, including cognitive development, intelligence, prior knowledge, and disposition to learn, which are specified in the first dimension of the interaction model of the instructional process introduced in Chapter 1. Both learning and cognitive development are facilitated when the instruction is geared to the capabilities of the learner.

Both Piaget and Bruner suggest that elementary school students learn especially well from working with concrete objects and the use of an inductive approach to instruction. Such learners should be given opportunities to explore and manipulate examples or real objects. Becoming familiar with academic materials enhances the development of concepts, principles, and relationships, and the use of examples as the starting point of instruction provides a basis for an inductive approach to teaching them. Some examples of inductive approaches are described below in the section on Bruner.

Piaget's Concept of Conservation

Although a great deal has been written about Piaget's influences on educational practice, the impact has been more general than specific. The general nature of cognitive development during later childhood can be introduced by examining Piaget's ideas on the relationship between development and learning: "To summarize, learning appears to depend on the mechanisms of development and to become stable only insofar as it utilizes certain aspects of these mechanisms, the instruments of quantification themselves, which would have evolved in the course of spontaneous development" (Piaget, 1970, p. 717). It is the testing of this assumption with conservation tasks for which Piaget is best known. The principle of conservation expresses the idea that the quantity of something stays the same regardless of changes in its mass, weight, or volume. The order in which the conservation of mass, weight, and volume develops is invariant; special training will not alter it. This is taken as evidence that maturation which arises from sources within the learner must precede learning. Other learning psychologists take exception to the assumption that maturation is dependent upon learning; Robert Gagné, for example, argues that learning also makes a definitive contribution to development (see Chapter 7).

Concrete Operations

The concrete operations stage of development, which extends from approximately 7 to 11 years of age, is considered by Piaget to be the beginning of genuine thought. Genuine thought consists of *operations*, or internalized actions which are reversible and are governed by principles that apply to the system as a whole. The process of adding one number to another without using your fingers, or reversing the process and subtracting one number from the total, would be examples.

The term *concrete* is very descriptive of the type of thinking engaged in during this period. Concrete thinking operations are possible only because the learner has concrete (tangible) objects to manipulate, and this serves as a thinking aid during initial learning.

Piaget's concept of an operation is what is usually referred to as *thinking*. Some thinking, however, is nondirected (fantasy or daydreaming), and Piaget considers only thinking that follows a logical structure to be an operation. Four principles provide the structure of thinking and are used in various combinations to perform concrete operations. These *principles of concrete logic* are composition, reversibility, associativity, and identity. Using these principles, a child at the concrete operational stage can engage in thinking operations that involve classification, categorization, and ordering. An example is the classification scheme for the animal kingdom shown in Figure 3.2.

Composition   The principle of composition denotes a superordinate-subordinate relationship within a system. In Figure 3.2, when mammals (A) are combined with fish, birds, and reptiles (A'), they form a new superordinate class called vertebrates (B). This type of grouping principle is the basis for categorizing and also is basic to concept development. For example, a first-grader learns that 26 individual letters make up something called the alphabet, and a particular grouping of letters—*dog*—always means the same thing. Concept development is based on the composition principle. When cats are combined with dogs and goldfish, a new concept—pet—is developed.

Reversibility   Reversibility by the inverse operation is regarded by Piaget as the most significant quality of the concrete operations period. Every combination or composition is seen as being reversible. In mathematics, for example, the inverse of addition is subtraction $(4 + 3 = 7; 7 - 3 = 4)$.

With the principle of reversibility, the inverse of composition can also be performed. In Figure 3.2, for example, when birds, fish, and reptiles (A') are subtracted from vertebrates (B), mammals (A) are left. Reversibility not only indicates use of the composition principle but also the ability to analyze or break down this principle. The analysis procedure (i.e., defining elements) in reversibility is orderly in the sense that it is a mirror image of the additive composition process. The reversibility principle is more complicated than the composition principle because it includes not only the additive operation but the inverse operation as

Figure 3.2

Partial classification scheme for the animal kingdom

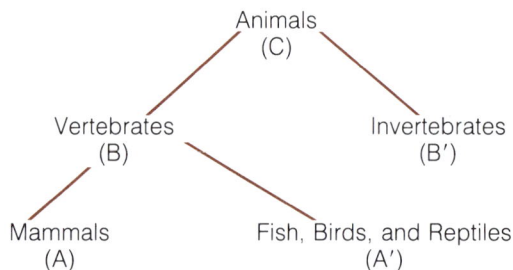

well. Reversibility is basic to development of the math skills of subtraction and division.

Associativity   By associativity Piaget means that in concrete operational thought, detours may be used so that the same end result can be achieved by different methods. In one sense, this may involve nothing more than a *reordering*. Vertebrates (B) plus invertebrates (B') make up the animal (C) kingdom. The order B' + B = C is equally valid. In another sense, the regrouping of elements does not destroy a set. An example from mathematics is equivalent expressions such as (4 + 3) + 5 = 4 + (3 + 5). This principle is basic to all simple algebraic operations, and this type of skill is required to complete many math assignments encountered at the fifth- and sixth-grade levels.

General Identity   The operation of general identity is simply the awareness that nothing has been added or taken away by adding a null class (5 + 0 = 5; 5 − 0 = 5). The concept of identity is very significant in Piagetian theory. In a demonstration of mass conservation, for example, the conserver knows the clay ball remains the same, despite the fact that it changes shape. If the same ball is rolled into a sausage shape, nothing new has been added or taken away. This principle is basic to all math skills learned during the primary grades.

The Learner in the Concrete Operations Stage   The concrete operations period is characterized by the learner's ability to combine two or more principles to form an operation. In this period children become more and more objective in their view of the world. Rather than being fooled by perceptual cues, as younger children can be, the conserver relies on logic. This concrete logic is the systematic application of the principles of composition, reversibility, associativity, and identity described above. As a result of increasing objectivity, the learner exhibits fewer and fewer instances of egocentrism (see Chapter 2). Continued development and learning provide the basis for formal logical thinking operations, which usually begin at adolescence.

Bruner's Symbolic Stage

While Bruner's theory of cognitive development is different from Piaget's, there is little disagreement between them, as was noted in Chapter 2. In Bruner's view, cognitive development occurs in just three stages, enactive, iconic, and symbolic (Bruner, 1966), and the beginning phases of the symbolic stage appear during later childhood. This stage, which continues to be refined as the learner grows into adulthood, is characterized by the use of symbol systems such as those related to language, logic, and mathematics.

For Bruner, language is the instrument of thinking in the symbolic stage. This is one respect in which the two theorists differ. Bruner sees language as the key to cognitive development, while Piaget views it as important but not essential. In Piaget's conceptualization of the sensorimotor stage in infancy, primitive cognitive abilities are already developing, though there has been no prior development of language. Bruner sees language as the basis for communication, which is essential for the teaching act, as described in Chapter 1. A systematic change, via communication, between a learner and a teacher underlies the instructional process. The teacher may be a parent, a peer, or some other member of society, or may even be an inanimate object like a textbook. In any case, language serves as the basis for the teaching that occurs. The emphasis on teaching in the development of cognitive abilities is greatest in Bruner's work.

Teaching strategies based on Bruner's theory, such as the discovery method proposed by Bruner (1960) and the concept attainment method based on Bruner's work by Joyce and Weil (1972), have been characterized as inductive instructional approaches. These approaches are appropriate for young learners in the primary and intermediate grades, when the use of examples in a learning episode coupled with hands-on experiences and the opportunity to ask questions is an effective teaching strategy.

The concept attainment model of instruction is also based on structured learning episodes. If, for example, a primary-grade teacher wants to teach the concept of rectangularity, several sacks, each containing an object of rectangular shape, are placed on a table at the front of the room, along with sacks containing other objects that have other shapes. Students try to identify the contents of each sack by putting a hand in and feeling the objects, without looking. They write down yes if the shape is a rectangle and no if it is not. The topic of concept learning is thoroughly examined in Chapter 7.

LANGUAGE DEVELOPMENT

The preschool child has made remarkable strides in language development by school age, as noted in Chapter 2. In the space of three or four years, the learner has progressed from a producer of two-word sentences to a language user who comprehends most adult communications. Some language skills are yet to be developed, however, and the vocabulary must be greatly expanded.

Language ability in its mature form is composed of a number of distinct but integrated skills related to listening and spelling as well as speaking. For the learner it is a basic educational tool which can be viewed as a necessary skill in the instructional process. Two kinds of language difficulties can hold back learners: immature language skills and use of nonstandard English by students in the classroom.

Immature Language Skills

At each level of development some learners are lagging in language development. Immature language users typically lack style rather than basic ability and so are less well prepared for classroom activities that place a premium on verbal exchanges. They also may not know how to hear or answer questions intelligently, so they erect obstacles to clear communication that may never be overcome, even in adulthood (see Box A).

There has been no clear-cut explanation why some children develop more effective communication patterns than others. Some studies have indicated relationships between general mental ability and social class, as we will note in Chapter 6. Cronbach (1977) found the correlations too small to be of real significance, however, and he suggests some special ability or aptitude may account for the development of language proficiency. In individual cases, the home environment appears to be the most critical factor. An environment that fosters language proficiency is determined primarily by the parents or principal caretakers, a factor which cuts across social class lines. When mothers and fathers interact verbally with their children and provide them opportunities to experiment with communication skills, the children are more likely to have language skills.

The developmental pattern for communication skills has two sides. Listening skills develop rapidly during the primary grades, but the ability to send verbal messages develops more slowly. The ability to send adultlike communications is not even evident prior to junior high, and improvement continues through adolescence and adulthood.

Nonstandard English

It is ordinarily assumed that only a few children who enter school use nonstandard English, but most children use the language with some degree of inexactness. Differences in pronunciation, vocabulary, grammar, or syntax are common in different groups in the United States. These systematic differences may be the result of geographical factors (Northeast vs. Southwest), ethnic background (Italian, Polish), racial background (blacks, Hispanics), or socioeconomic class (middle or lower). The issue for the classroom teacher is whether to build on the language skills the child brings to school or to require that only standard English be used. Current positions on this issue can be stated in terms of the deficit, difference, and bicultural models.

The *deficit model* treats nonstandard speech patterns as deficient. The assumption is that inability to use standard English prevents the devel-

BOX A   *A failure to communicate
in answering questions*

Failure to communicate can occur at the listening level as well
as the sending one. A child who does not answer questions
intelligently has poorly developed communication skills, such as
those listed below.

FAILURE TO CLARIFY THE QUESTION ASKED
The child fails to ask for a restatement of a question that is
unclear and may say something in response that has no bearing
on the question.

POOR ORGANIZATION, POOR SUBORDINATION
The child starts to "free associate" instead of pausing to select
what to say. Unrelated ideas may be run together in the same
sentence, without pause.

UNSUPPORTED CONCLUSIONS
The child lacks critical thinking skills and fails to separate fact
from opinion. To the question, "How do you know John and his
father are good friends?" the reply may be, "Cause that's his
son."

INDEFINITE DESCRIPTIONS
The listener cannot visualize what the child is talking about. In a
discussion of bicycles, the child, asked what a "skinny wheel"
is, replies: "It's a big bike with handbrakes on it. Some of 'em have
handbrakes, some have footbrakes. I like handbrakes; you don't
have to put your feet back."

Source: Adapted from Lee J. Cronbach, *Educational Psychology*, 3rd ed. (New
York: Harcourt Brace Jovanovich, 1977), p. 492.

opment of logical thinking abilities. Thus, the teacher expects that children who use nonstandard English will be unable to develop critical
thinking or problem-solving skills. In this model the learning of basic
standard English language elements, to the exclusion of nonstandard forms, is seen as a necessary step in the sequence of educational
development.

In the *difference model*, the idea is that nonstandard English is as good a language system as standard English. The assumption is that cognitive skills will be developed, regardless of the form of the language. In this model no variation of the English language is considered better than any other. The instructional strategy is to accept the learner's language as the basis for teaching, build on it, and help the learner use the nonstandard forms more efficiently.

The *bicultural model* advocates the use of both nonstandard and standard English (Valentine, 1971). Ethnic and racial groups are seen as being committed to their own cultures as well as to that of the mainstream. This model emphasizes the positive characteristics of both nonstandard and standard English forms. The instructional strategy encourages the use of both forms in teaching, with nonstandard forms used during the early primary grades and successively more emphasis being placed on standard forms throughout the elementary school years. It is assumed that this type of instructional strategy provides the basis for a transition from nonstandard to standard English usage. The long-range educational goal is the development of a proficient user of both nonstandard and standard English.

Implications for Education   Since adults in our society must be able to use standard English, the school's role in teaching it should be clear. To satisfy educational and occupational demands, every adult must have the ability to use standard English. This does not mean that the black urban child, for example, must give up the nonstandard English vernacular. But teaching a child subject matter using nonstandard English without introducing the standard version can be regarded as a type of discriminatory practice. As we will point out in Chapter 6, in the discussion of group differences in intelligence, the language used on an intelligence test and by the test giver has less effect on test scores as the time learners spend in schools that use standard English increases (Jensen, 1980).

THE SOCIAL-EMOTIONAL DOMAIN

In terms of psychological development, later childhood is rather bland compared to early childhood, the critical period for the emergence of social-emotional behavior, and adolescence, generally regarded in our society as a period of storm and stress. Later childhood, sandwiched between these two time frames, plays a functional role in social-emotional development. The learner changes in several ways, but the changes involve either extensions or modifications of prior development. New personality characteristics do not emerge. The learner's principal efforts concern conformity to standards of behavior set by the family, peers, and the school.

Although personality development originates early in life, later childhood provides an opportunity for modifying previous developmental trends. A child who has had few satisfying experiences prior to attending school might find academic success to be a basis for self-esteem, as we will note in the final section of this chapter. Behaviors observed in later childhood for the first time also predict adult behavior. A classic longitudinal (or long-term) study by Kagen and Moss (1962) suggests that the personality characteristics first glimpsed in later childhood are also seen in early childhood.

THE SELF-CONCEPT

In later childhood there are two important aspects of the self-concept: the self as an object and the self as a doer.

Self-as-Object

A sense of bodily self starts in infancy and is very primitive throughout early childhood. When preschoolers are asked who they are, they are likely to supply a very short response. Typically they will give their names and, if pressed for more information, their age and perhaps their gender. Self-control and self-esteem emerge in the social-emotional domain in this period, as we noted in Chapter 2.

The sense of self grows stronger throughout later childhood. The self-as-object develops because the school environment requires students to take a more evaluative look at themselves in comparison to classmates. Schoolchildren share numerous characteristics with peers and are likely to be compared with classmates in such a manner that their own distinguishing features become apparent. They may begin to define themselves objectively in terms of "always in trouble with the teacher," "always willing to share toys," "the best runner," and so forth.

Schoolchildren are also exposed to labels commonly attached to groups of people. These labels, which are expressive of shared stereotypes (or preconceived notions) about others, are widely used by children in later childhood. They may be incorporated into a child's description of self, as when a Hispanic boy describes himself as a he-man or a black girl says she is naturally lazy.

An image of self-as-object is an important aspect of personality development during later childhood. This development grows out of comparisons to others and other groups that are widely made at home, at school, and among peers. The effects of group identifications on the self-concept and academic achievement of students will be examined in Chapter 14.

Self-as-Doer

The second important aspect of the self-concept in later childhood is related to the sense of self as a doer of things. During the first part of this period (ages six, seven, and eight), the learner begins manufacturing things or events. It is the self-as-doer that becomes more distinct as the learner progresses. In addition, the 11- and 12-year-old expresses a system of ideas, attitudes, values, and commitments, as we will note in Chapter 9. Thus learners enter later childhood with a primitive sense of self and emerge as a complex blend of social-emotional characteristics making up a distinctive personality.

The theoretical perspective for the self-as-doer is best summed up in the terms of Erik Erikson's psychosocial theory (see Chapter 2). He sees later childhood as the period of development when the child must develop a sense of industry and overcome a sense of inferiority by winning approval for being productive. This means that the child must acquire the tools of reading, writing, and cooperation with others, because they are the basis for acceptance. When the learner fails to acquire a sense of industry by developing academic skills, there is the danger that a sense of inadequacy will persist.

EMOTIONAL DEVELOPMENT

Emotional maturity is characterized by a change from helplessness to an increased capacity for independence and self-help. The development of self-help skills is reflected in an increase in freedom and a decrease in frustration. At the same time, the learner is becoming more reflective and able to pay attention for longer periods.

During the primary and intermediate grades cognitive decentering continues, and the decrease in egocentrism influences emotional maturity. As a result the learner exhibits an ability to sympathize and empathize with others. *Empathy* is the ability to "walk in the shoes of another," which is one way of referring to the ability to adopt another's frame of reference.

Children's emotions of aggression and fear at this stage have special relevance for the classroom teacher. Under certain circumstances, frustration has been found to produce aggression (Berkowitz, 1969). In school, boys are more frequent offenders than girls, continuing the trend observed in early childhood (see Chapter 2). When aggression occurs in the classroom, it may stem from many different sources. When a child becomes frustrated and angry at another child or even at the teacher, the real source of such aggressive behavior may be the home environment. If the parents are hostile and rejecting, the child may strike out at a teacher who is viewed as a substitute authority figure. Peer leaders can also foster aggressive behavior in the classroom by promoting negative attitudes toward adult authority (the teacher). Such leaders may have success in recruiting followers because they are viewed by classmates as having prestige due to their power or physical attractiveness.

The nature of what children fear undergoes a change during the school years. There is a decrease in fears related to personal safety (dogs, storms, accidents) and an increase in fears related to achievement or social events which may take the form of worry about grades, teachers, or social events.

An intense fear that is sometimes seen in children during the primary grades is school phobia. Parents often fail to understand such a child's problem and are difficult to work with. Chronic school phobia usually begins to appear when school tasks get more demanding and the learner is expected to exhibit greater industry. The age of occurrence varies, but it is most frequent among 10- to 12-year-olds. These children may have unrealistic academic self-concepts; they overestimate their abilities and undervalue their achievements. When their unrealistic academic self-concepts are threatened, they experience extreme anxiety and may refuse to attend school or become physically ill. If such cases are identified and proper treatment is provided, the unrealistic fears can be eliminated.

A sense of competence can and should be a goal of the instructional process. Competence in this case stems from a sense of self-respect that learners derive from their accomplishments in the classroom. The teacher can guide students to success in their schoolwork by providing opportunities for such activities as establishing goals and carrying them to completion, or making up work schedules and holding to them. Many students also need help in developing a sense of quality control. They must learn to apply standards set by the teacher to their own efforts, with minimal supervision.

Difficulty in developing a sense of academic competence frequently leads to school failure, a point we will consider further in Chapter 4. Competency should include the mastery of not only classroom skills but social and recreational skills as well.

The teacher's efforts to help students develop feelings of competence are aided by children's natural curiosity. This provides the basis for exploratory behavior in which the learner attempts to master the classroom environment, as well as to understand the larger world and find out what it is like. The needs to be competent and to know are related to the developing learner's sense of self-worth, as will be noted in Chapter 11. The classroom teacher can offer help in satisfying these needs.

INTRINSIC MOTIVATION

Intrinsic motivation helps ensure academic success because it provides students with activities that appeal to their interests. Intrinsic motives arise from within the individual and cause a person to do something for its own sake. People naturally enjoy intrinsically motivated behavior and do not have to be rewarded in order to stay with it. Students may read simply because they like to, for example, or solve mathematics problems because of the sense of satisfaction it gives them.

Exclusive reliance on intrinsic motivation would be impractical for the classroom teacher. A working knowledge of the typical interests of childhood, however, can facilitate the instructional process. Efforts to become acquainted with the intrinsic interests of students and to build on and expand them give teachers information they can use on a motivational basis. The effectiveness of teaching materials is enhanced when they are related to students' interests. In fact, intrinsic motivation is described as the motivational goal of education in Chapter 11.

While interests are learned and are to some extent an individual matter, those of most children in later childhood are similar enough to permit useful generalizations about them. The list of interests in Box B suggests some topics teachers can use in the classroom to capitalize on students' interests.

MORAL DEVELOPMENT

In later childhood the learner's concept of right and wrong is less narrow and specific than it was earlier. In general, morality in later childhood is fraught with uncertainty. The direct emotional component of morality—guilt feelings—appears in full force. There is, however, an observable developmental trend of morality during this period.

Lawrence Kohlberg (1981) has proposed that humans pass through a series of six stages of moral development in three levels—preconventional, conventional, and postconventional—with a transitional level between the last two. The levels and stages are described in Chapter 9 (Figure 9.3). Kohlberg argues that people's moral development through these stages is in an invariant sequence; that is, it moves without exception from stage 1 through stage 6. Individuals' moral development may pass through the stages at different rates, but none of the stages is ever omitted.

At the beginning of the first grade, children follow rules only when it is in their immediate best interest to do so. What is right is frequently viewed as what is fair. At this time, children expect a reward for doing the right thing. Later, by 9 or 10 years of age, they start to view themselves in relation to other individuals. Living up to what other persons who are important to them expect is viewed as right. Being good is important for its own sake, and children can relate to standards like the Golden Rule.

By the end of later childhood, young adolescents are beginning to view themselves as members of a social system. Right is viewed in terms

BOX B *What interests children most in later childhood*

SCHOOL
Children are usually enthusiastic about school attendance at first. By the end of the second grade negative attitudes often have set in, but they may not extend to nonacademic tasks.

NAMES
A child's own name and those of friends often hold special interest. This interest can be used to show how to look up names and other ways to use reference materials.

FUTURE VOCATIONS
Children's early interests in vocations center on glamorous and exciting jobs. This can be a basis for introducing career education materials.

HUMAN ANATOMY
Since children cannot observe bodily functions (digestion, metabolism, etc.) directly, there is typically a great deal of interest about the body. This may serve as the basis for introducing materials on biology.

SEX
By the fourth grade, most children want to know more about sexual reproduction and the relations between sexes. Often they seek out such information from books or peers. This interest could serve as the basis for introducing sex education programs.

of fulfilling agreed-to duties, and laws are upheld except in extreme cases. Right is also considered in terms of contributing to the group or to society. The learner's conception of self includes a strong moral component. As the end of childhood is reached, the moral code and social behaviors approach adultlike standards.

The family has a strong impact on moral development, with child-rearing practices setting standards and the parents serving as models for morally prescribed behavior. Two other influences are peers (or others belonging to the same groups in society) and television. As childhood progresses, parental influence wanes and peer influence becomes stronger. Peer influence can weaken rather than strengthen the resolve of a person caught up in a moral dilemma.

Children are always influenced by their peers in classroom groups. On the playground, for example, peer pressure can require an attitude of indifference or the rejection of an outsider who is considered "dumb" or "weird." In such an instance, group members are influenced by peer pressure in the form of a group code. Members of the in-group who do not go along risk becoming outsiders themselves. The code of "Don't squeal on your friends" also can require keeping silent about classmates who cheat on exams or homework.

Television is frequently charged with having an impact on long-term moral development. The assumption that television violence affects the development of aggressive behavior in children has been questioned, however. Hoffman (1979) points out that the ability to draw cause-and-effect conclusions is almost impossible when such effects are studied, due to research design limitations. Moreover, the observable effects of television violence on behavior have been largely momentary in nature, with little evidence of long-term influence. Hoffman's conclusions are not meant to imply that there are no effects of television on moral development, and research is continuing on this question. A report by the National Institute for Mental Health issued in May 1982, titled "Television and Behavior: Ten Years of Scientific Progress and Implications for the Eighties," found "overwhelming" evidence that violence on TV leads to aggressive behavior in children and teenagers. The report cites 2,500 studies made since 1970.

SEXTYPING AND SEX-ROLE SEGREGATION

Later childhood is the time when children begin to segregate themselves according to sex. In the process, mannerisms, attitudes, and values the society considers appropriate for a particular gender are adopted. Sex-role identity, which is established in early childhood, is strengthened as the child grows older. An interesting explanation for the segregation

Their team may not be winning today, but these girls are learning traditional masculine sex roles: what it means to compete and to strive for success.

that marks this period is that the developing feminine and masculine identities may be too fragile for excessive mixing.

The pressure toward appropriate sex-role behavior is a very important influence on the preadolescent self-concept. Much of this pressure comes from the child's parents' expectations about appropriate sex-role behaviors. If these expectations are the traditional ones, a male child is strongly encouraged to show aggressive behavior and a female child is socialized to take a more passive role. The child's acquisition of a sex identity is guided in part by observing the behaviors modeled by parents and taking cues from their reactions to the child's behavior. By studying play situations and interviewing parents, Sears, Rau, and Alpert (1965) found that masculinity and femininity were influenced more by the parent's attitudes toward verbal and physical aggression than by any other kind of interaction.

Sextyping involves more than an awareness of the way girls and boys are expected to behave; it influences personality characteristics such as attitudes and beliefs as well as behavior. Some of the differences between boys and girls in behavior or achievement that are observed during the school years are thought to result from sextyping rather than biological or physiological differences. Some boys lack the motivation to master academic skills because they regard such skills as "sissy" and not appropriate, and some girls consider mathematics and the natural sciences unnecessary. Adherence to rigid, socially defined sex-role standards creates differences that have been learned. Concern arises when these learned differences produce adjustment problems or deny equal opportunity for academic achievement or, later, for vocational success.

It has been argued that sex-role stereotyping, which encourages the "little man who never cries" and the "little miss who is all sugar and spice," produces children who have difficulty adjusting to many situations. An appropriate mix of masculine and feminine attitudes and values may be best for both boys and girls. Freeing each to engage in activities traditionally reserved for members of the opposite sex, such as placing boys in cooking and sewing classes and girls in woodworking and shop, provides them with a basis for a stronger self-concept. Males who can express tenderness and females who can be assertive can adjust more easily to the demands of a society that is rapidly changing its views about traditional sex roles and responsibilities. The school should permit wide latitude in sex-role behaviors during childhood, an important aspect of development to be discussed in Chapter 4, on adolescence.

THE PEER GROUP AS A SOCIALIZATION INFLUENCE

Being a member of a peer group and sharing experiences with social equals becomes increasingly important during later childhood. The peer group provides opportunities to develop social skills and learn the value of cooperation. As the needs develop to escape close adult supervision and to interact with others who hold similar views of the world, children seek peer group membership. This membership is not handed out indiscriminately; childhood groups tend to be highly selective. Like other peer groups they base selection criteria on such attributes as similar age, sex, race, and social class.

Popularity within peer groups, which has been studied extensively, appears to be linked to a number of personal traits. Well-accepted, popular children participate in a wide array of activities and have average or better ability in most of them. Because of sextyping, children who do not conform to prevailing ideas about appropriate sex-role behavior will probably be excluded from group membership. Other traits that have been demonstrated to be influences on peer acceptance are physical prowess, friendliness, intelligence, neatness of appearance, and good looks.

There is evidence that children's popularity with peers—or lack of acceptance—influences their overall emotional adjustment. Conformity to peer group pressure in the elementary grades is quite evident for both girls and boys. Generally, however, girls display higher degrees of conformity than boys.

Two special types of peer groups that have play activities as a central focus are the play group and organized team sports. They differ in terms of their structured nature and the amount of adult supervision provided.

Play groups or gangs structure their own play activities. Leadership is typically accorded to a child who is stronger, more extroverted, older, or more intelligent. Belonging to a gang is reflected in members' conformity to dress codes and obvious imitation of one another.

The popularity of team sports for both boys and girls has grown tremendously in recent years. Team sports are highly formal in structure and require extensive adult leadership and supervision. These organized activities help children develop physically and socially and acquire experience with team competition. Well-supervised team sports also can help instill confidence, encourage the use of body and mind, and develop a sense of sportsmanship. Undue emphasis on winning for its own sake, parents with unrealistic expectations, and oversupervision are potential hazards of competition. When team sports are appropriately organized, however, they must be considered an important factor in the socialization process. Properly emphasized competition, cooperation, team spirit, and the idea that games should be fun can make team sports valuable learning experiences.

THE SCHOOL'S ROLE IN PERSONALITY DEVELOPMENT AND SOCIALIZATION

Schools are considered to represent the formal agent of socialization that is most responsible for directing child development to ensure eventual fulfillment of the adult roles society considers proper. Though it is recognized that schools cannot program the personality development of children, to some educators and educational psychologists the primary mission of the school is as a socialization agent.

The teacher's influence on the social-emotional development of students is an acknowledged part of the instructional process. Primary-grade school experiences are considered important factors in social-emotional development because children of these ages spend so much of their waking hours in school, and research has indicated that during later childhood and adolescence, school is one thing most children worry about. Nevertheless, the nature and degree of the school's impact on the long-term personality development of children is frequently over-emphasized.

Theory, research, and common sense all indicate that school experience has an important psychological impact on children. Teachers have an influence on the way children think about themselves, particularly how they think about themselves in school. We have all encountered good and not-so-good feelings about ourselves as students or teachers. The question of impact has to do with *how important* school experiences are compared to other influences on the self-concept, such as experiences on the playground, at home, or in a gang.

The fact that teachers influence learners' self-concepts is not open to question, but answers to the questions of *how much* and *for how long* have not been provided by research. The logic goes something like this: Teachers have an influence on the way children think about themselves. Children's self-concepts, in turn, are related to achievement, which further influences the ways teachers act toward learners, and so on. This is one of those vicious psychological circles—easy to verbalize, easy to relate to, but difficult to interpret and explain.

According to Hamacheck (1971), the possession of a positive self-concept does not by itself *cause* high academic achievement. Rather, it appears to be a necessary but not sufficient condition. An individual student's positive self-concept could be based on nonacademic pursuits such as athletics, popularity with the opposite sex, or extracurricular activities, which would not guarantee academic success. If a student is motivated to do well in a nonacademic area, however, the effects of any lack of academic success on the self-concept are likely to be minimized.

Hamacheck raises the "chicken or the egg" question: What comes first, a positive self-concept, or high achievement? Some children enter school feeling good about themselves and possessing positive self-concepts. Others enter school with low self-confidence and self-regard. For both types of students, a good teacher helps arrange successful academic experiences. Since all learners do not come to the classroom with positive self-concepts, the argument that some of them have low self-concepts because of a lack of academic success should be taken with a grain of salt. The learner has compiled a history of successes and failures prior to coming to school and will continue to add to that history in the arena of life outside the classroom.

For many children, however, the self-concept is affected by academic success, and their appraisal of self-worth will be threatened by poor academic performance. Efforts have been made to develop learning structures for the classroom that are success oriented and reduce such threats (Covington & Beery, 1976). The effects of ability grouping on the self-concept and chances for academic success of low-ability students will be described in Chapter 14.

CHAPTER 3 IN RETROSPECT

Later childhood, which extends approximately from the first grade to adolescence, is the period of greatest developmental growth in the cognitive-intellectual and social-emotional domains. In the physical-motor domain, the nature of the learner's sensory systems, central nervous system, and motor systems determines the limits of educational development and change. In a systems-processing perspective, these systems provide sensory input, information processing, and observable behaviors as output for the instructional process. Maturational readiness in the three systems is essential for learning to take place. The prerequisites include attentional and perceptual capacity and behavioral tempo.

Cognitive development takes place in terms of a hierarchy of tasks, skills, and processes. Successful undertaking of academic tasks depends on the use of cognitive skills that are made up of two or more cognitive processes. These processes are related to attention or to memory, which has several components: recognition, storage, and retrieval.

Knowledge of cognitive skills development has been facilitated by the theoretical work of Piaget and Bruner. Piaget sees concrete operations as the beginning of genuine thought, and Bruner's symbolic stage is based on the idea that language is the instrument of thinking. Some language skills still must be developed in later childhood, and the vocabulary must be greatly expanded. Acceptance and use of nonstandard English in the classroom is a social problem as well as an academic one.

Social-emotional development in later childhood largely consists of extensions or modifications of behaviors established earlier. The principal effort for the learner is to conform to standards set by parents, peers, or the school. A sense of competence develops when the learner can derive self-respect from success in academic activities, and the use of intrinsic motivation by the teacher can help ensure that these activities will appeal to students' interests, thus enhancing their chances for success.

Sextyping, continued from early childhood, takes the form of sex-role segregation. Conformity to the sex roles expected by parents improves students' acceptance by peer groups and other agents of socialization. Among these, the school is the formal agent of society that is most directly responsible for child development. How this is accomplished in the classroom will be explored in Part III, which examines leadership and the functions of groups in terms of the social psychology of the classroom.

1. What type of memory processing is required of a fifth-grader who is asked to fill in the blanks and match the names of capital cities and countries on a geography quiz? What type of study skills would you try to teach the student?
2. Solve the following sixth-grade math problem: $X - 4 = 6$. What principles of concrete logic are required to solve the problem? Using the principles of logic listed below, give in order the logical operations that are necessary to solve the problem:
   a. Composition.
   b. Identity.
   c. Reversibility.
   d. Associativity.
3. During the primary and intermediate grades, the learner must develop a sense of industry. What does this mean within the context of the classroom? How can a teacher help a student learn to be industrious? Develop a set of classroom procedures (for a class you expect to teach) that you feel would achieve this educational goal.

Memory Processes

Kail, Robert. *The Development of Memory in Children.* San Francisco: W. H. Freeman & Co., 1979.

This is an excellent introduction to the manner in which memory processes develop during the preschool and school years. Major topics covered include individual differences, memory and cognition, the development of memory strategies, recognition memory, metamemory, and knowledge development.

Piaget

Wadsworth, B. J. *Piaget for the Classroom Teacher.* New York: Longmans, 1978.

In this readable account of Piagetian theory and its general application to educational practice, Wadsworth does not suggest that Piaget has much to say about specific classroom methods. Rather, a case is made for the role of Piagetian theory as a guide to *general* teaching principles and practices. A section that will appeal to prospective teachers discusses Piagetian theory and reading instruction, the learning of mathematical and science concepts, and learning about society and history.

Self-Concept Development

> Hamacheck, D. E. *Encounters with the Self.* New York: Holt, Rinehart & Winston, 1970.

Although it is a bit dated, this is a valuable resource which is very readable and is slanted toward the teacher's perspective. A major section is devoted to self-concept, academic adjustment, and implications for teaching practices.

> Covington, M. V., and Beery, R. G. *Self-worth and School Learning.* New York: Holt, Rinehart & Winston, 1976.

Self-worth, which is defined as an individual's appraisal of self, is compared to such concepts as self-esteem, self-respect, and personal acceptance. Included are such topics as strategies to avoid failure, attributing causes to success and failure, success-oriented learning, and the teaching of achievement skills.

Personality Development

> Worell, Judith (Ed.). *Psychological Development in the Elementary Years.* New York: Academic Press, 1981.

This is a review of recent research in areas of development that relates to the elementary-age child. Chapters on areas that are both relevant to education and amenable to modification within the school, home, or community were written by authors who are outstanding for their current contributions and willing to develop a conceptual framework for the research area. Research areas include peer relations, sex roles, aggression, self-regulation, achievement motivation, learning processes, cognition, minority group membership, family influences, impact of schools, and learning and behavior problems.

REFERENCES

Berkowitz, Leonard (Ed.). *Roots of Aggression: A Re-examination of the Frustration-Aggression Hypothesis.* New York: Atherton Press, 1969.

Bruner, Jerome S. *The Process of Education.* New York: Vintage Books, 1960.

Bruner, Jerome S. *Toward a Theory of Instruction.* Cambridge, Mass.: Harvard University Press, 1966.

Covington, M. V., and Beery, R. G. *Self-worth and School Learning.* New York: Holt, Rinehart & Winston, 1976.

Cronbach, Lee J. *Educational Psychology.* 3rd ed. New York: Harcourt Brace Jovanovich, 1977.

Flavell, J. H. Metacognitive and cognitive monitoring: A new area of cognitive-developmental inquiry. *American Psychologist,* 1979, *34* (10), 906–911.

Hamacheck, D. E. *Encounters with Self.* New York: Holt, Rinehart & Winston, 1971.

Hoffman, M. L. Development of moral thought, feelings, and behavior. *American Psychologist,* 1979, *34* (10), 958–966.

Jensen, Arthur R. *Bias in Mental Testing.* New York: Free Press, 1980.

Joyce, B. and Weil, M. *Models of Teaching.* Englewood Cliffs, N.J.: Prentice-Hall, 1972.

Kagen, J., & Moss, H. A. *Birth to Maturity.* New York: John Wiley & Sons, 1962.

Kail, R. *The Development of Memory in Children.* San Francisco: W. H. Freeman & Co., 1979.

Kohlberg, Lawrence. *The Philosophy of Moral Development.* New York: Harper & Row, 1981.

Maccoby, E. E., and Hagen, J. W. Effects of distraction upon central versus incidental recall: Developmental trends. *Journal of Experimental Child Psychology,* 1965, *2,* 280–289.

Nelson, K. E. Memory development in children: Evidence from nonverbal tasks. *Psychonomic Science,* 1971, *25,* 346–348.

Newcombe, N. E., Rogoff, B., and Kagan, J. Developmental changes in recognition memory for pictures of objects and scenes. *Developmental Psychology,* 1977, *13,* 337–341.

Piaget, Jean, Piaget's theory. In P. H. Mussen (Ed.), *Carmichael's Manual of Child Psychology.* New York: John Wiley & Sons, 1970.

Robinson, F. P. *Effective Study.* New York: Harper & Bros., 1946.

Rohwer, W. D., Jr. Cognitive development and education. In P. H. Mussen (Ed.), *Carmichael's Manual of Child Psychology.* New York: John Wiley & Sons, 1970.

Sears, R. R., Rau, L., and Alpert, R. *Identification and Child Rearing.* Stanford, Cal.: Stanford University Press, 1965.

Valentine, C. A. Deficit, difference, and bicultural models of Afro-American behavior. *Harvard Educational Review,* 1971, *41,* 137–157.

Development in
Adolescence

Adolescence is often a difficult and trying period of development; certainly this is the case in our own society today. The belief that things are tougher now than they used to be is an easy trap to fall into, but there are several trends that support this idea. It used to be the exceptional teenager who attended secondary school, for example. In the early part of this century, the vast majority of young people left school after the eighth grade or at the age of 16 and began to make their way in the world as adults. Society was in many respects less complex than it is today, and certainly it lacked the technological sophistication that increasingly requires a technical or scientific education. Young men and women could begin their working careers at 16 or 17, and not much later many of them married and began to raise their own families. Standards of living were not what they are at present, but many of today's problems for teenagers—boredom, frustration, and a sense of marking time—were rare. The curriculum of the secondary school was much less differentiated than it is today, but it was probably more adequate to the needs of the students it served.

Adolescents today are growing up within the context of structured secondary schools that often do not provide a good match with their immediate desires and wishes. The captivity of dependence continues to be imposed upon youths at a time when they are physically ready to be on their own, and many of them are also socially and emotionally prepared. When this is coupled with greater freedom in sexual conduct and the easy availability of alcohol and other drugs, it is not surprising that today's adolescents often find society to be confusing, hypocritical, and unrewarding.

ADOLESCENT ATTITUDES TOWARD SCHOOL

Student attitudes toward school shift over time and vary among schools. General trends can be noted, however. The most frequent response to the question, "What's best about school?" is "The friends I have." Few students list activities in the instructional process as the best thing about school.

The evidence is that attitudes toward school change most from junior through senior high. As students move through this educational sequence they become less interested in academics and more interested in social or extracurricular activities. The older the student, the more likely she or he is to view school as a chore to be performed, with boredom an expected outcome. Relief is provided by extracurricular activities, sports, and holidays. The main reason adolescents like school is the social opportunities it provides, not the academic programs.

Most adolescents have specific dislikes about school they are willing to share. In one form or another academic matters, such as the pressure of tests and grades or the selection of appropriate courses, are often mentioned. Students often fail to see the need for certain requirements and dislike coursework they consider irrelevant. This concern is difficult for the school to address because what students consider irrelevant is frequently due to a discrepancy between their view of what they need and the school's educational philosophy. Students who want an educational experience that will fit them for the work force, for example, require a vocational-technical curriculum. If their school concentrates on academics and does not have such a curriculum, they will view its offerings as irrelevant. Students who are academically talented or gifted may also find that a school, program, course, or teacher fails to challenge them.

From the adolescents' point of view, the personality characteristics of teachers with whom they have daily contact is of primary importance in determining what makes a good teacher at the junior and senior high levels. Adolescents consider self-confidence to be a desirable teacher characteristic, because teachers who are self-confident have little or no need to belittle students in order to feel important. Good teachers also are emotionally mature and are not afraid to demonstrate kindness, empathy, and genuine warmth and regard for other people. Students should be able to view teachers as approachable and willing to enter into the student-teacher relationship that is essential in the instructional process. Students also like teachers who are generally happy, pleasant, cheerful people.

Adolescents are undergoing a great deal of social-emotional change, and they need psychologically mature role models. Good teachers can meet this need and still attend to the task of teaching academics. Subject matter competence on the teacher's part is essential; being a pal never makes up for being poorly prepared or not knowing the subject matter.

THE DEVELOPMENTAL DOMAINS IN ADOLESCENCE

The distinctions between the physical-motor, cognitive-intellectual, and social-emotional domains fade more rapidly in the adolescent period of learner development. Cognitive development never occurs in a vacuum, but in adolescence social-emotional development begins to be influenced by cognitive factors. Personal identity is more difficult to attain because adolescents can think hypothetically and thus perceive many choices and alternatives. The ability to understand the views or feelings of others becomes possible as cognitive maturity is reached.

In the physical-motor domain there is a significant biological event—the onset of sexual maturity. Hormonal changes give rise to secondary sexual characteristics, such as facial hair on boys, pubic hair, and breast development in girls. There are growth spurts that produce dramatic increases in height and weight and a change in body proportions. There is no evidence, however, that the human sex drive is a biological imperative. Rather, sex-role development and expressions of the sex drive are elements of learned attitudes and behavior. The social and emotional adjustment problems of adolescents often stem from lack of information about sexual development and behavior. Moreover, sex-related differences in cognitive functioning have been found to be related more to the social environment than to hereditary factors.

Thus there is a significant overlap among the effects of the three domains on the development of the learner in the adolescent years. In this chapter we will describe some aspects of the cognitive-intellectual and social-emotional domains. Consideration of the social and emotional influences on academic adjustment leads to discussion of two issues that consume more time (if not active engagement, then thinking, fantasizing, or worrying about them) than any others confronted during adolescence, including academic achievement and relations with teachers. These issues are casual drug use and sexual development and behavior.

THE COGNITIVE-INTELLECTUAL DOMAIN

The outstanding characteristics of cognitive-intellectual development in adolescence are the emergence of a new kind of egocentrism and the beginnings of the stage of formal operational thought.

ADOLESCENT EGOCENTRISM

The ability to understand the ideas and feelings of others which develops during adolescence is responsible for an interesting characteristic of this period: adolescent egocentrism. The egocentrism of the preschool period, described in Chapter 2, is centered on the child's own view of the world. At that point in their cognitive development children cannot acknowledge the frame of reference of another person. At adolescence, in contrast, egocentrism denotes behavior that is concerned with others' opinions and has been referred to as "being on stage" (see Box A).

In addition to concern for what others think of them, the ability to reason hypothetically which develops at this stage also accounts for adolescent egocentrism. Hypothetical thinking ability provides the basis for creating an imaginary audience for whom the adolescent is always performing. Adolescents are so concerned with their own appearance that they assume others (peers, teachers, etc.) are equally concerned. The tendency toward egocentrism is the result of inability to comprehend that the others also are concerned with their own appearance and actions.

This imaginary audience helps explain some of the behaviors or attitudes that are viewed as adolescent. Self-consciousness is quite evident at this age, for example. The self-critical adolescent assumes that the imaginary audience will also be critical. The desire for privacy and reluctance to discuss feelings and fears may be other reactions to the feeling of being under the scrutiny of a hypothetical audience.

FORMAL OPERATIONAL THOUGHT

It is during secondary school that the Piagetian stage of formal operational thought is reached and the student's capabilities to master problem solving and critical and creative thinking (see Chapter 10) begin to be developed. While formal operations usually become established between the ages of 12 and 15, further development of these operations continues through the teenage years.

Piaget's original thoughts on formal reasoning were later revised. He had hypothesized that the skill of formal reasoning is independent of context or experience, and once formal operational thought has been acquired it could be applied to any subject matter area (mathematics, history, deductive logic). Piaget's mathematical-logical model of reasoning was criticized on this point, and as a result, the present formulation of formal operational thought also considers environmental experiences and opportunities.

Formal operational thought (hypothetical, symbolic, and systematic) represents the crystallization and integration of all past intellectual operations. It is the highest level of cognitive development considered by Piaget, and the greatest degree of retardation may be demonstrated in its formation. If appropriate environmental experiences are not provided during later childhood, the transition from concrete operations to formal operations may be delayed. Children in extremely disadvantaged circumstances may never reach the stage of formal operational thought unless changes in the environment are brought about while development is still possible (see Chapter 6). This is another instance where biological maturation is a necessary but not sufficient condition for normal cognitive development to take place. According to Piaget (1979),

> . . . all *normal* subjects attain the stage of formal operations or structuring if not between 11–12 to 14–15 years, in any case, between 15–20 years. However, they reach this stage in different areas according to their aptitudes and their professional specializations (advanced studies or different types of apprenticeship for the various trades): the way in which these formal structures are used, however, is not necessarily the same in all cases. (p. 207)

GENDER DIFFERENCES IN COGNITIVE FUNCTIONING

Some differences in cognitive abilities have been found to be related to the gender of the learner. These include verbal, visual-spatial, and mathematical abilities (Jacklin, 1979). The size or magnitude of sex-related differences is difficult to estimate, but they are usually found to be very small. Consistent developmental trends are discernible, however.

Girls perform better on tests of verbal ability starting at about junior high. While the verbal ability of both girls and boys continues to improve through the high school years, the rate of improvement for girls seems to be faster. The overall superiority of girls is particularly evident at lower levels of verbal ability. Boys, on average, perform better on tests of mathematics and on spatial visualization, which is thought to underlie mathematical ability. The difference in these abilities also becomes apparent at junior high age, and improvement is noted through high school. In this case, however, boys have a higher rate of improvement.

The causes for such differences in abilities have not been isolated, though the developmental perspective suggests that observed sex-related differences are not related to hereditary biological or constitutional factors. It is likely, therefore, that the differences can be accounted for in the social environment. According to Jacklin, if the number and type of mathematics classes taken by boys and girls are the same, differences in visual-spatial ability disappear. Evidence is also accumulating that this ability can be easily taught, and more girls are enrolling in higher mathematics classes. Differences in verbal ability also appear to be undergoing a change. A 1977 national sample of high school students taking college entrance tests showed no sex-related differences in verbal abilities. Like the times, sex-related differences in cognitive ability may be changing.

IMPLICATIONS FOR THE INSTRUCTIONAL PROCESS IN SECONDARY EDUCATION

Cognitive development during adolescence and its implications for the instructional process have been largely ignored in the United States, but they have received considerable attention in Great Britain, Western Europe, and Australia. A leading figure in this area is E. A. Peel, who has conducted research on the development of adolescent judgment (see Box B). Judgment, in this case, is broadly defined to include concept learning, comprehension, understanding, and critical thinking. According to Peel (1971), the development of understanding during adolescence involves a number of cognitive skills on both sides of the instructional process: the teaching of various subject matters such as math, history, and literature, and the learner's critical thinking and problem-solving efforts in the classroom.

The introduction of a science class to the use of a Bunsen burner provides an example of the cognitive skill of *translating words into action*. The teacher gives instruction in how to strike a match before opening the gas jet and then asks, "Do you understand what you have to do?" If the teacher lacks confidence in the students' skill of translating words of instruction into action, the task may be demonstrated as well as explained verbally.

Inferring cause-and-effect relationships is a critical cognitive skill in courses such as history. An example would be the reading of a text on the causes of the American Revolution which relates a number of incidents that could be placed in a pattern of cause-and-effect relations with varying long- and short-term effects. When the teacher asks, "Do you understand?" the meaning is, "Can you follow the pattern of cause-and-effect

BOX B　***The adolescent reasoning shift:
From description to explanation***

To study how adolescents develop their thinking skills over time, Edwin A. Peel had a group of school children between the ages of 9 and 15 read the following brief statement and answer the questions:

> Only brave pilots are allowed to fly over high mountains. This summer a fighter pilot flying over the Alps collided with an aerial cable railway and cut a main cable, causing some cars to fall to the glacier below. Several people were killed, and many others had to spend the night suspended above the glacier.
>
> 1. Was the pilot a careful airman?
> 2. Why do you think so?

The responses fell into four categories:

Category A. These were the least mature responses. The child responded yes or no, with irrelevant comment or denial of the premise, such as: "Yes, he was brave"; "Yes, the cable shouldn't be there"; "No, he was a show-off." Category A responses were infrequent; when they did occur they were given by the youngest children.

Category B. "No, because he hit the cable," and so on.

Category C. "No, because if he was careful he would not have cut the cable."

Responses of both the B and C types, which are limited to the circumstances of the problem, were given by children between the ages of 12 and 14.

Category D. Yes, no, or maybe, taking account of possible influences such as vision, weather, or state of the plane. These answers, which involve thinking that goes beyond the particulars of the information given, were given mainly by the 14- and 15-year-olds in the sample.

Thus Peel demonstrated that there is a developmental shift in children's reasoning from later childhood to adolescence, from descriptions of events to explanation.

Source: Edwin A. Peel, "A Study of Differences in the Judgments of Adolescent Pupils," *British Journal of Educational Psychology*, vol. 36 (1966), pp. 77–86.

relationships?" According to Peel, the main cognitive skills required to understand current affairs, history, and literature are a grasp of cause and effect, the ability to follow an argument, and the power to evaluate.

Seeing a problem in terms of higher-level concepts is another cognitive skill that is important in secondary schooling. In a high school physics course, for example, students can easily accomplish the wiring of a two-way electrical switch once they understand the principles of alternating current.

Using mathematical-logical abilities is required for deductive and inductive thinking. These formal reasoning skills, the same Piaget emphasizes, are important not only in math courses but in the evaluation of verbal problems as well. These skills are aspects of problem-solving ability that are important in all subject matter areas.

The application of formal thinking skills in making judgments is a demonstration of the problem-solving ability required in situations where no ready-made answers are available. These situations occur in the classroom whenever students are required to comprehend a problem or suggest a solution.

Students are frequently asked, for example, to translate information from one form to another, especially in math and grammar courses. The ability to expand a quadratic equation requires first translating the operations and symbols into the learner's natural language. The ability to pay attention and interpret messages also is required in most high school classes. Students have to be able to recognize part-whole and part-part relationships and to reorganize or rearrange them. They must be able to grasp the overall scheme or main idea as well as the supporting evidence. Also required are adeptness in the use or transfer of ideas, problem-solving and academic skills, and the ability to go beyond the information given and draw inferences.

The abilities of translation, interpretation, and drawing inferences are required to some degree in most high school classes. Typically they cannot be used in combination until adolescence, when the formal operational stage of thinking is usually reached.

THE SOCIAL-EMOTIONAL DOMAIN

Development and change in the social-emotional domain are insistent during the years of adolescence. If any single attribute may be said to characterize this period, it is the movement toward personal independence and the development of self-identity.

PERSONAL IDENTITY AND SELF-ESTEEM

Erik Erikson suggests that personality development during adolescence is concerned with the psychosocial crisis of personal identity versus role confusion (see Chapter 2). It would be helpful to assume that a sense of personal identity develops automatically, as an extension of the development of the self-concept in later childhood. This is not the case, however, because adolescents experience so many changes within themselves. There are too many present and future demands and too many decisions to be made. Personal identity results from commitments to occupational goals and a personal ideology. The first, including vocational choice and academic adjustment, provides direction in terms of educational needs and future priorities (such as getting married or going to college). The second entails the development of a consistent personal position on such matters as religion, politics, and ethics, as well as more immediate concerns such as drugs and sexual relations.

Unless these commitments are made with some degree of success, role confusion occurs. Role confusion might involve overidentification with popular cultural figures (rock groups, movie stars) or peer groups (cliques, gangs). Erikson also suggests that role confusion is reflected in passionate, though fleeting, plunges into ideological issues and commitments (unpopular wars, religious conversions, social struggles). Severe role confusion can result in social and emotional maladjustment.

Personal identity is the foundation for a sense of self-esteem, or feelings of worth or value in one's own eyes, which is developed through satisfactory interactions with other human beings. The adolescent regards the family, classmates, and teachers as important "others" with whom positive interaction is necessary. Self-esteem develops through accomplishments, success, and praise, and its lack can produce symptoms of emotional maladjustment. Thus interactions in the school setting can enhance or impede the development of self-esteem in adolescents.

Teenagers want to have relationships with adults, particularly those in positions of authority, that are quite different from the superordinate-subordinate relationships of childhood. In the instructional process the amount of interaction between a student and any given teacher diminishes significantly from what it was in elementary school. The youth's growth toward independence is partially responsible for the change, but so is the structure of most secondary school programs.

Students ordinarily spend only an hour a day or less in the presence of a particular teacher. In secondary school lecture or group discussion methods are more typical than individualized instruction. Most high school teachers have little time during the school day for contact with individual students, although some subjects, such as art, laboratory science, and perhaps mathematics offer somewhat more opportunity. This issue is explored in Chapter 13, which discusses the teacher's leadership role in the classroom.

College-bound students are more likely than others to initiate interactions with teachers. In general, warm relationships between students and adults in secondary school are most likely to involve faculty sponsors of activities such as the school newspaper or yearbook, coaches, or teachers in similar positions. The adult in such situations is frequently a high-status individual who controls access for the adolescent to favored activities and so has great ability to influence adolescent attitudes and behavior. Parents are often dismayed to find that what "coach says" carries more weight with their adolescent son or daughter than their own opinions.

The adolescent's main social energy, however, is devoted to building friendships and a social group. Membership in a larger social group

The secure, relaxed, and happy attitude of these teenagers is evidence that they have mastered the skills of peer relations, including those with members of the opposite sex.

provides a crucially important sense of security to adolescents. It is testimony that they are accepted members of teenage society. In addition, a circle of close friends (one or two, or perhaps more) not only gives a teenager someone to be with and to share activities with, it also constitutes a sounding board for his or her developing philosophy of life: "What is right?" "Who should you like or dislike?" "What are you going to do with your life?" The questions may never be formulated so pointedly, and the dialogues may continue throughout the years of secondary school, but the teenager uses close friends to build a sense of identity and try out different roles, positions, and attitudes. Adolescents who have no close relationships with peers not only are unhappy but lack a rudder to help them chart their course through these stormy years.

PEER GROUPS

During adolescence the developing learner's orientation shifts from the family to the peer group. The influence of peers in the schools is seen in data collected by Newman and Newman (1979), who found student-student interactions were almost six times as great as the student-teacher interactions which make up the instructional process.

Adolescents need the nurturance and security that other teenagers can provide, singly or in groups. Sometimes the high school student who is rebellious or withdrawn or who ignores academic responsibilities is sending a signal to the school asking for help with peer relationships. The need to belong to such groups, to conform to their norms and expectations, and to benefit from the learning possibilities that they afford is very powerful among adolescents. When teachers deal with stubborn students in high school, they do well to assist them into the mainstream of adolescent activities, rather than imposing sanctions upon them that emphasize their deviance from the group.

Types of Peer Groups

The social setting of the developing adolescent supports several peer groups, not just one. The nature and function of peer groups differ in early or late adolescence, and at any one time there may be more than one type of peer group to which an adolescent looks for support.

As we noted in Chapter 3, during the intermediate grades peer group affiliations tend to center around same-sex "gangs." Since physical mobility is limited for children of this age, the members usually are from the same neighborhood. With adolescence, however, the horizons widen. The child's range of acquaintances is extended beyond the immediate neighborhood, and peer group membership is no longer restricted to same-sex peers. As a result, adolescents have not only friends and best

friends, but casual acquaintances as well. In general, their peer relationships include three primary types: friendships, "the crowd," and
cliques.

The most personal type of peer group, *friendship*, is based on mutual
attraction. There is a tendency for friendships to be among members
of the same sex in early adolescence, but cross-sex friendships are more
common during the middle and late years of this period. Friendships
are typically more intimate, more open, and more intense than other
types of peer group relationships. Classroom friendship groups are described in Chapter 14.

Adolescents are struggling to adjust to a changing self, both psychologically and physically, and to meet the rapidly changing demands of
society. As a result they often experience doubts, anxieties, or resent-
ments which, in most situations, must be concealed. To admit them to
any but one's closest friends opens the door to possible misunderstanding, lack of acceptance, or, worst of all, amusement, scorn, or rejection.
When a meaningful friendship exists, such defensiveness is not required.
In such a relationship, "There is trust, there is no need to pretend, no
necessity for being on guard against betrayal of shared secrets. Adolescents who have a relationship of this kind can reprove each other without
condemning each other" (Conger, 1977).

The *crowd* is the least personal type of peer group. Its basic thread of
cohesiveness is shared activities. A crowd is made up of individuals who
share similar interests, likes, and social ideals rather than a mutual personal attraction, as is the case with friendships. This is the largest form
of peer group, and it centers more on organized social activities such as
parties that provide for interactions between the sexes.

The *clique* is smaller than the crowd and serves a different function,
centered around talking. Much of the conversation is an exchange of
information about the crowd and crowd activities. Essentially, a crowd
is made up of a number of cliques; clique membership appears to be a
prerequisite of crowd membership. Because they are smaller, cliques
permit a greater degree of intimacy and cohesion. At any one time an
adolescent may hold membership in a clique and a crowd, and be a "best
friend" as well.

OCCUPATIONAL GOALS

The choice of a vocation is one of the most important decisions adolescents must make, as well as a vital component of personal identity. Ideally
the choice is carefully thought out, but this is not always the case. Adolescents are always under pressure to choose a vocation. Their parents
have probably been asking for years, "What do you want to do when
you grow up?" Friends frequently inquire about plans after graduation,

The formulation of occupational goals is an important developmental task of adolescence. These youths will learn not only how to repair cars but also whether that is what they want to do for a living.

and counselors want to know whether college preparatory or vocational track courses are more appropriate.

Psychologists consider the formulation of vocational goals an important developmental task of adolescence, although the process starts earlier. During later childhood the sense of industry, which involves the ability to organize one's own time and energy in order to get chores and school work done, is developing, as we noted in Chapter 3. Learning to put work before play when it is appropriate is acquired during early adolescence. In the later teenage years, as a sense of identity as a worker emerges, preparations are made for an occupation through relevant work experience or education.

Vocational choice involves not only "How can I make a living?" but also "What am I going to do with my life?" An adolescent girl's choice of occupation, particularly, will influence the social roles she can later assume, as new career opportunities open up for women (see Box C).

Adolescents differ in the style with which they make occupational decisions (Newman & Newman, 1979). Some approach the choice of an occupation in a rational manner that calls for seeking out information

BOX C   *What little girls want to be when they grow up*

College women are considering traditionally male careers more than ever before, according to an annual survey of first-year students that was taken in the fall of 1980. This survey, which was conducted by UCLA and the American Council on Education, was based on questionnaires returned by 291,491 students entering 540 two- and four-year colleges and universities.

More than 1 woman in 4—27.2 percent—said she was planning a career in business, medicine, engineering, or law. This represents more than a 400 percent increase since 1966, when only 5.9 percent of women students indicated a preference for the four leading careers for men.

Changes were also noted in students' attitudes toward the role of women in society. The view that "women should receive the same salary and opportunities for advancement as men in comparable positions" was backed by 93.3 percent of the college men and women surveyed, up from 81.3 percent in 1970. The traditional idea that "the activities of married women are best confined to the home and family" received less support than in any previous year of the survey—26.6 percent, down from 47.8 percent in 1970.

and assuming personal responsibility for the choice. Others who base their decisions on fantasy or emotion may use intuition or "feeling," with little objective information. A few will let their career decisions be made for them. These adolescents take little responsibility for their decisions and see themselves as at the mercy of circumstance.

In formulating vocational choices adolescents have three primary sources: the family, peers, and the school. Sometimes the parental influence is direct; parents may insist an adolescent student goes to a certain school, selects a certain course sequence, or enters a profession the parent has chosen. Parental influence also may be exerted by making available a family business that the adolescent will some day inherit or by providing apprenticeship in a trade. About 90 percent of boys who chose farming as a career are sons of farmers, for example. Even if parents do not work directly with their teenagers they serve as occupational role models. Professionals particularly transmit vocational values; it is estimated that two thirds of all sons choose an occupation in either their father's status category or the next higher one.

Other occupational role models are peers and teachers. Peer influence tends to reinforce parental aspirations for children, in part due to the adolescent's tendency to pick friends whose goals are consistent with their parents'. Teachers particularly serve as points of reference for college-bound juniors and seniors, influencing their decisions about colleges and curriculums. There may be greater rapport between college-bound high schoolers and teachers than is true for the general school population. According to Rice (1978), college-bound juniors and seniors seek out and relate to teachers frequently and engage in discussions that are not restricted to subject matter.

ACADEMIC ADJUSTMENT

Regardless of students' desires or parents' aspirations, the practical basis for occupational choice is academic achievement. As with the career decision, the adolescent's academic adjustment is strongly influenced by peer group and parental attitudes and values, which overlap a great deal. Most adolescents select friends with educational goals that are similar to their own and their parents', as is the case with vocational choice.

In the middle and upper classes, parental influence with regard to life goals has been shown to be greater than that of peers (Newman & Newman, 1979). Adolescents may experience conflict and confusion when they encounter others who represent belief and value systems that are different from those they have been taught at home, however. When parents reject an adolescent's friends, it may be because of their concern that a different value orientation will weaken or replace that of the family. Thus a mother and father who share a strong belief in the value of higher education may try to dissuade their adolescent offspring from associating with friends who question whether going to college is worthwhile.

Self-esteem, as we noted at the beginning of this section, is built on a sense of personal identity, and its lack results from role confusion. The adolescent with low self-esteem may exhibit a form of social maladjustment called *social invisibility*. Socially invisible adolescents are not selected as leaders and do not participate actively in clique or crowd activities. As a result, these teenagers often experience loneliness and a sense of isolation.

The implications of self-esteem or its lack in adolescence are obvious. Self-esteem and academic achievement go hand-in-hand. Students who do not acquire positive self-esteem may well develop academic problems.

Anxiety and Alienation

The basis for many of the adjustment problems observed in the classroom is anxiety or alienation. Anxiety, worry, and fear are closely related emotions; all three are negative in the sense that they make a person feel uneasy and under stress. Some adolescent concerns have a basis in earlier stages of development, and others are characteristic of the teenage years. Most of them are derived from the normal course of development during adolescence.

Many adolescents worry about getting through school or about the grades they receive. This has been recognized as the primary cause of worry among junior and senior high school students. Other sources of anxiety are concerns about peer acceptance and personal characteristics, such as looks or personality, and an increase in sexuality which creates unfamiliar sensations and impulses. An important development hurdle during this period is acceptance of one's own body and its functions.

Every adolescent experiences some degree of anxiety and worry. While most can cope successfully, some cannot, and their social-emotional development suffers.

Young people who learn that the Amercian Dream of affluence and success is not for them, or who are unable to identify with the dominant cultural value of academic success in school, suffer blows to their self-esteem. They may become alienated from the school subculture; this is widespread among minorities and the poor, especially when adolescents fall into both categories. They have been poorly prepared socially or psychologically for academic success, and they may attend overcrowded and understaffed schools. Under such conditions, these adolescents are likely to experience a sense of powerlessness which leaves them feeling cut adrift from the mooring that provides security and a safe harbor for the individual personality.

Dropouts and Pushouts

Adolescents who feel powerless and who become alienated from the school subculture may voluntarily leave school before completing an academic program—they are dropouts. Others, particularly the poor, racial minorities, and the culturally different, may be forced out of school by expulsion, suspension, or arbitrarily administered discipline—they are pushouts.

Two 1975 Supreme Court decisions addressed the pushout issue. Onc prohibited school suspension without notice or a hearing (*Goss* v. *Lopez*), and the other determined that school board members could be held liable for violating a student's constitutional rights (*Wood* v. *Stickland*). Nevertheless, suspension and expulsion continue to be used by school policymakers as instruments for removing certain types of students from the schools. The school pushout problem has not been solved, any more than the long-standing dropout problem has been (Luty, 1982). They remain issues in the wider environment of the school which comprises the third dimension of the instructional process described in Chapter 1.

There are a number of reasons why students drop out if they are not pushed out: socioeconomic background, racial or ethnic prejudices, family position, personality problems, lack of interest, early marriage. No accurate data are available concerning specific or exact numbers involved, though U.S. Census Bureau data for 1976 indicated that 6 percent of teenagers between 14 and 17 were not enrolled in school. Up until age 14, attendance figures indicate very little difference in the percentages of white and nonwhite children who are not in school. After that age, a slightly higher percentage of nonwhites than whites leaves school. The socioeconomic background of the adolescent's family may be the most significant factor in determining whether schooling will be completed. In poorer circumstances, feelings of alienation, discrimination, boredom, or lack of motivation are more likely.

Dropouts usually are more emotionally immature and less well adjusted than high school graduates, though there are exceptions. Delinquent behavior often is exhibited by dropouts who are experiencing adjustment problems, and most delinquent dropouts come from broken or economically substandard homes (Rice, 1978).

For females, pregnancy or early marriage is a common reason for leaving school, but male adolescents seldom drop out to get married. In one survey (Gross & Osterman, 1971), over half of the female dropouts cited pregnancy or marriage as the reason. When teenagers drop out because of marriage, the likelihood of returning to finish school is very small. The lack of a high school diploma seriously limits any future social or economic potential, but without parental or outside help dropouts have little opportunity to return to school or continue to college. Early marriage, therefore, usually results in lower socioeconomic status. In a real sense, it can destroy an adolescent's freedom to grow, develop, and reach maximum potential.

The early identification of potential dropouts is a responsibility of the school. It need not wait until high school; in some cases, the roots of the problems go back to the preschool years. Two warning signals are a family background where a parent, brother, or sister has dropped out of school, and the learner's failure to master reading and comprehension skills by the fourth grade. By the time poor readers reach adolescence, they are working far below grade placement and are prime dropout candidates because of boredom, disinterest, or lack of ambition.

An adolescent who drops out is not necessarily intellectually retarded. As a group, when high school dropouts are compared with graduates, only a significant difference in average IQ is noted. In fact, the slight difference is typically not considered great enough to account for the differences in academic performance (Conger, 1977).

Instructional Answers to Academic Adjustment Problems

Academic adjustment problems can stem from a variety of sources in both the cognitive-intellectual and social-emotional domains. When the problems become unmanageable, dropping out may seem to be the course to take. The estimate that half of all high school females who drop out do so because they are pregnant or getting married suggests that information pertaining to sexual development and behavior could be used by educators to develop programs that would prevent this type of dropout problem.

Another factor that contributes significantly to the 6 percent dropout rate is the abuse of drugs by junior and senior high school students. It has been estimated that 5 percent of the school population uses drugs to an extent that interferes with the instructional process. These students are typically experiencing social or emotional adjustment problems such as low self-esteem, alienation, extreme anxiety, or worry. While treatment for drug use is usually outside the authority of the school, teachers must be aware of the problems and can devise ways to introduce them in the instructional process.

Both drug education and sex education can be integrated into the existing curriculum. The information on these topics presented in the following sections is designed to alert teachers to the issues and suggest ways they can be incorporated into school courses as a way of helping adolescents handle the problems.

ADOLESCENTS AND DRUG USE

Teenage drinking and drug abuse are serious problems in adolescence which have their roots in the social-emotional domain and can affect both the physical conditions and cognitive skills of students. The explanation may lie in rebellion against adult authority or imitation of adult ways (Akers, 1970). For schools, the challenge is to help students overcome both the cause and the effects of such practices. Teachers can provide learning programs that give accurate information on drug use and suggest realistic ways to prevent their abuse or to counter the consequences.

There is no definition of drugs that is agreed upon by all. From a psychological perspective, the definition we will use includes *those substances that influence behavior by altering feeling, mood, or other mental state.*

Alcoholic excesses therefore are considered in the same category as drug abuse. The classroom teacher should have knowledge of the symptoms of abuse of various kinds of substances and be sensitive to student behavior that abruptly changes from a normal pattern. An adolescent who withdraws from social interactions with classmates or suddenly starts to miss assignments and perform much below expectations should be carefully observed. School personnel are typically not trained to deal with an adolescent who comes to school drunk or stoned. At this point prevention is too late, and some form of intervention (or help) is required. Many communities have social service agencies that deal with this type of problem, and a good working relationship between the school and such agencies is a part of the third dimension of the instructional process. Most agencies equipped to deal with drug abuse also maintain supplies of educational materials which can be a valuable resource in a preventive drug education program.

In a national survey of drug use (DuPont, Goldstein, & O'Donnel, 1979), data were compiled on the frequency of use of various drugs by adolescents. Several conclusions can be drawn from the data on use of marijuana, alcohol, barbiturates, and amphetamines (see Table 4.1). Alcohol was by far the drug used most frequently by both the young adolescents and the high school seniors who were surveyed. Approximately one third of the younger respondents (between ages 12 and 17) said they had tried marijuana, a figure that rose to half by the senior year. The frequency of casual use (in the past month) dropped to less

Table 4.1

Reported frequency of drug use during early adolescence and at 12th grade

	Ages 12 to 17		High School Seniors	
Substance	**Ever Used**	**Used Past Month**	**Ever Used**	**Used Past Month**
Marijuana	28%	16%	56%	35%
Alcohol	53	31	92	71
Barbiturates	7	2	35	10
Amphetamines	5	1	23	9

Source: H. J. Parry, ''Sample Surveys on Drug Abuse,'' in R. L. Dupont, A. Goldstein, and J. O'Donnel (Eds.), *Handbook on Drug Abuse* (Washington, D.C.: U.S. Government Printing Office, 1979).

Table 4.2

Age of first drug use reported by high school seniors

Substance	Jr. High or Earlier	10th Grade	11th Grade	12th Grade
Marijuana	26%	12%	11%	6%
Alcohol	53	18	14	7
Barbiturates	8	7	6	3
Amphetamines	5	5	4	2

Source: H. J. Parry, "Sample Surveys on Drug Abuse," in R. L. Dupont, A. Goldstein, and J. O'Donnel (Eds.), *Handbook on Drug Abuse* (Washington, D.C.: U.S. Government Printing Office, 1979).

than one fifth for young adolescents and to approximately one third for high school seniors.

The survey also indicated that most high school seniors had had their first experience with alcohol or marijuana prior to or during junior high (see Table 4.2). In contrast, adolescents who used pills (barbiturates or amphetamines) were about as likely to experiment for the first time during the high school years as during junior high.

THE ADOLESCENT DRUG USER

Adolescent drug users can be placed in three rather broad categories: experimenters, intermittent users, and substance abusers. The vast majority of adolescents fall in the *experimenter* category; the substance (usually alcohol or marijuana) is tried out of curiosity or as a result of peer pressure. The *intermittent user* participates because it is the social thing to do in the clique or crowd. Use is likely to be confined to a setting like a party or concert, and the dosage is usually moderate and nontoxic. Probably less than 5 percent of the adolescent population that stays in school could be classified as *abusers*, or out of control. They may be experiencing adjustment problems in any or all of the three major areas of their lives: the home environment, peer relations, or the school.

One reason why adolescents take drugs is that they are available. Our society is bombarded with advertisements of the availability of chemical substances to help us stay awake, go to sleep, relieve pain, lessen stress, or improve our social status. Coupled with availability is the attitude of risk taking that characterizes adolescence, and the adolescent's abundant curiosity and sense of daring. Peer pressure from acquaintances who are using drugs also encourages experimentation and possible continued use.

Rebellion against parental authority is another reason frequently cited for taking drugs. Whether or not attempts to assert independence from parents will take this form is heavily influenced by the relationships between adolescents and parents. Those who have caring parents who try to keep the communication channels open are not so likely to turn to drug abuse. Adolescents whose parents are either extremely permissive or very autocratic are more likely to do so.

Escape from the pressures of life is another reason adolescents give for their use of drugs. The ability to cope with daily problems is an important developmental task during adolescence, and failure to accomplish it then can lead to greater problems in adulthood. Alienation and emotional disturbance can cause drug abuse which requires treatment.

The drugs adolescents use most frequently can be classified (as in Tables 4.1 and 4.2) as marijuana, alcohol, barbiturates, and amphetamines. Marijuana is an intoxicant which adolescents often use as a social drug, or icebreaker. Users contend that there are few harmful effects, but the THC (the mind-altering chemical) and other substances can remain in the body for a week or longer after marijuana has been smoked.

It has been estimated that by the end of adolescence somewhere between 75 to 90 percent of all teenagers have tried alcohol. Most of them engage in moderate use without symptoms of abuse, but problem drinking (defined as getting high or drunk once a week or more often) is engaged in by an estimated 5 percent of the teenagers in school.

Barbiturates comprise a class of drugs that are nonnarcotic depressants of the central nervous system, including sleeping pills and tranquilizers. Their use over a prolonged period in larger than prescribed dosages can lead to strong psychological dependency, followed by withdrawal symptoms when use is discontinued. An estimated three fourths of the drug-related deaths in the United States are due to barbiturates.

The two most frequently used stimulants in the United States are cocaine and amphetamines, which are more likely to be used by adolescents because they are cheaper and easier to obtain. Amphetamines have a marked effect on psychomotor activity and alertness, and there are many side effects: sleeplessness, lack of appetite, illusions, hallucinations, and a general state of hyperexcitability and irritability. Death from an overdose as the result of cardiovascular (heart) collapse is possible.

DRUG-RELATED INSTRUCTION

Opportunities for drug use exist for students in the early teenage years, among junior as well as senior high school students. To prevent the start of drug abuse, some information should be made available earlier; an instructional program in grade 5 or 6 could be beneficial as a preventive measure.

An even earlier start was suggested by the findings of a long-term study reported by Sheppard G. Kellam, director of the University of Chicago Social Psychiatry Research Center, in June 1982. This study found it was possible to predict which children will be drug and alcohol abusers (and cigarette smokers) as adolescents by observing their behavior in first grade. First-grade boys who were shy and aggressive had the highest risk; boys who were only aggressive had the next highest, and those who were only shy were next. Intelligence was a factor for both boys and girls; those who were bright tended to experiment with drugs earlier and more frequently. The researcher suggested the possibility of preventing drug and alcohol abuse problems among adolescents by developing programs to deal with the risk factors in the first grade. The success of preschool interventions such as Head Start was cited as a precedent for educational programs which improve first-graders' adjustment to school.

The principal aim of drug prevention programs in the school is to provide accurate information to potential users, not to preach against them. Preaching has not been proven to be a successful strategy. The approach usually takes a form such as:

> It is best not to indulge in drug use, since it can have potentially harmful physical and psychological effects. However, since the majority of adolescents experiment with drugs, out of curiosity or peer pressure, you should know something about what you are letting youself in for if you choose to follow this lead.

The subject matter of these instructional programs varies, but some general aspects of drug-related instruction are always included. Efforts are made to distinguish between drug use and abuse, for example. Abuse exists when use interferes with the student's social, psychological, physical, or academic well-being. It must be recognized that *all* drugs have abuse potential. Programs that do not include the entire spectrum of drugs (including tobacco and alcohol) may be considered hypocritical by many adolescents. In their opinion marijuana, for example, is not much different from tobacco, alcohol, or the medically prescribed mood elevators adults they know use to get through the day.

Techniques that are sure to destroy the effectiveness of drug education include exaggeration, distortion, sensationalism, and preaching (Boldt, Reilly, & Haberman, 1973). All-school programs, where everyone assembles in the auditorium or gym for a large-group presentation, also are not very successful, because a single lecture does not allow for sufficient time or attention. Moreover, large-group sessions are the least efficient medium for the instructional process, in terms of the instruction offered by the teacher or the attention paid by the students.

Two approaches are frequently used to incorporate drug-related information into the school curriculum (Boldt, Reilly, & Haberman, 1973).

One strategy is to develop a drug education curriculum that stands by itself and is a basic required course. The assumption for such an approach is that once students have pertinent information about the effects of drugs they will be prudent. Unfortunately, schools that have used this approach have generally found such courses are not very effective. Teachers may feel uncomfortable with the subject because students seem to know more about it than they do, although students' "street lore" includes much misinformation. Most teachers would have to undergo rather intensive preparation in order to handle such a course. Students and teachers also often have differing value systems. Regardless of the amount of information provided, unless the student is motivated to apply the facts to daily living, the program will not be a success.

The second approach is to fit drug-related information into the regular curriculum. With this approach, information is provided in the appropriately related courses. Chemical and pharmacological properties of drugs can be introduced in science courses, and psychological and social consequences of drug use and abuse would fit into the social sciences. The integration of drug-related information into the regular curriculum is not an easy task. Coordination is required in order to provide a sensible and meaningful instructional program.

SEXUAL BEHAVIOR
AND SEX EDUCATION

Sex education is one of the most controversial areas in the schools today. The issue is, first, whether schools should attempt such programs, and, if they do, what the content should be, at what level it should be introduced, and who should teach it in which courses. Acceptance of such programs reflects society's recognition of the school's role as a socializing agent. It also is an indication of the need for teachers to be aware of adolescents' concerns as an integral part of the instructional process at this level. Whether in a formal classroom presentation or an informal one-on-one discussion, the teacher must be able to provide accurate information about sexual behavior when a student requests it. It is important to keep the communication channels open and to help teenagers realize they have a personal choice about their own sexual behavior.

Adolescents spend a great deal of time during the school day either daydreaming or worrying about some aspect of sexual behavior. Research has found that males are more conscious of specific sexual impulses than females during adolescence, for reasons that have not been clearly defined. Sexual drive among females is likely to be diffuse and more integrated with love, reassurance, and affection. Exceptions exist, of course. Some females are as preoccupied with sex as males, although they would represent only a small proportion of the adolescent female population.

These differences in attitude are influenced by the sex-role stereotypes (or established notions) of contemporary American society. According to these standards, the girl should play a passive role in sexual relations, and the boy should take the initiative. If the boy threatens to go beyond the limits she sets, she is expected to serve as a calming influence. Although these sex-role stereotypes are gradually changing, in most communities social pressures still dictate appropriate sexual behaviors for both males and females.

SEX EDUCATION

For the most part, adolescents seek answers to their questions about sex from one another. Even with the trend to include some form of sex education in the schools, the majority of adolescents get their insight about sex from each other. Males seem to be more involved in the free discussion of sex than females are. Some information is given in families, but this varies considerably. In families where adolescents and parents discuss sexual behavior, attitudes, and so on, girls are more likely to participate than boys, perhaps because mothers are the primary source of information in these situations. In many families, parental attitudes are not conducive to such discussions. These parents seem to think that by ignoring this part of their child's development they need not be concerned with it. Others are simply too embarrassed or feel that the school should be providing such education.

When sex education is provided, in either the home or the school, it usually involves something being told rather than discussed. Sex education is "given," with no open exchange of information to encourage questions. Most sex education programs in the schools concentrate on the physiology of sex, providing instruction in such topics as the reproductive system or venereal disease. There is little information on the psychological aspects of sexuality or discussion of societal values. Consequently, information on sex is dispensed with scant attention to the fears, misconceptions, or perplexities of adolescents.

The adolescent is concerned with such practical questions as "Is it okay to have intercourse if you're in love?"; "Do you have to wait until marriage?"; and "Is oral sex normal?" (see Box D). Most parents and educators simply do not want to deal with these issues. When questions about sexual relations are introduced, they start to moralize, warn, or threaten. This is of no help to adolescents who are trying to analyze or evaluate the situations they find themselves in. The remedy might be to provide sex education for adults. Adults must overcome their inhibitions and neurotic attitudes about sexual behavior before they can provide insight as well as information for the developing adolescent.

BOX D *What bothers adolescents about sex*

In a survey of junior and senior high school students, a number of questions about sexual behavior were mentioned most frequently. As the list below indicates, the questions change from junior to senior high.

JUNIOR HIGH SCHOOL (Grades 7, 8, and 9):

How come when you think of girls, it turns you on?

How old do girls have to be to get pregnant?

It is harmful to your body to ejaculate?

To get pregnant, do you have to have your period?

How can you tell if you have VD?

How far do you have to go with a boy or girl before it is considered sex?

SENIOR HIGH STUDENTS (Grades 10, 11, and 12):

When you have a pregnancy test, do they go ahead and test you for VD?

Does being high help a woman have an orgasm during sex?

What side effects can you expect from taking the pill?

What contraceptives will stop you from getting VD?

Can you get an abortion without your parents knowing?

If a girl had sex with someone and you had oral sex with her, could you get VD?

SEXUAL DEVELOPMENT

The age at which young people reach puberty varies widely. At 14 some males have a beard and appear to be well on their way to adulthood, while others may still look and act like children. Such variability in the rate of maturation (or the onset of puberty) is normal and does not influence the final adult physical or sexual status. Adolescents, however, may not be able to take such a philosophical attitude toward their own development.

Generally speaking, early or late maturation appears to have a greater effect on males than on females. For the early maturing male, there are disadvantages as well as advantages. Adults and peers tend to expect much more of the 14-year-old boy who looks 17 than of the 14-year-old who looks his age. This expectation may create feelings of injustice in the teenager. An advantage for the early maturing male is that he is usually more self-confident in boy-girl relationships due to his earlier involvement in them. The advantage of physical maturity also can be put to good use in many activities, especially athletics. The early maturer may feel somewhat different but is not likely to feel insecure.

Early-maturing girls tend to be comparatively more self-confident, less anxious, more secure, and more relaxed. In a word, they are better adjusted than girls who mature later. A potential disadvantage of early maturity for girls is the mixed messages society sends about it. The adolescent female who is sexually attractive at an early age will be more likely to attract the attention of older males, and this is particularly undesirable if as a result the girl neglects relationships with others her own age or fails to develop as a mature person in her own right. A girl who becomes too concerned with her sexual attractiveness is vulnerable to the message that being pretty, arousing, and socially skilled are the attributes society expects of mature females.

Late maturers of both sexes are more likely to have poorer self-concepts and feelings of inadequacy or of being rejected. They may try to prolong the independence-dependence conflict with parents and other authority figures such as teachers. In order to minimize the psychological effects of late maturation, teachers should avoid treating such adolescents as younger than they really are. They should offer information that slow maturation is normal and counsel that the late bloomer will reach full physical and sexual maturity.

Human sexual development and behavior consist of three related components which result from either biological maturation or learning:

1. The biological-constitutional component—genetic, maturational, and present at birth.
2. The learned sex-role component—perception of the self as representing maleness or femaleness.
3. Genital-sex object preference—orientation to heterosexuality, homosexuality, or bisexuality.

The biological-constitutional component is concerned with the determinants of gender, which are hereditary; they are present at birth and develop as a result of maturation. The terms *male* and *female*, therefore, rightfully should be used to refer only to the biological aspects of sexuality. Biological development usually results in a predominance of anatomical and physiological structures that determine either maleness or femaleness.

The Influence of Learning on Sextyping and Sex-Role Identity

The determinants of sex-role identity, in contrast to the biological components, are environmental experiences, and the identity is learned throughout infancy, childhood, and adolescence. Social learning provides important information on society's definitions of feminine and masculine attitudes and behavior.

Whereas *male* and *female* are used to refer to biological characteristics, *masculinity* and *femininity* are properly used to describe the learned components of sex-role identity. *Femininity* refers to the behaviors, interests, and personality traits that are characterized by society as being more descriptive of females than males, and *masculinity* refers to those that are characterized as more descriptive of males. In the current view, an individual's personality traits, attitudes, and behaviors may be both masculine and feminine, and they may be influenced by the situation or setting.

An *androgynous* person is characterized by both masculine and feminine attitudes and behavior. Androgyny is not unusual in view of the way masculinity and femininity are usually assessed. The typical instruments used to determine sex-role identification (see Bem, 1974) require a person to indicate if an attitude or behavior is "true of me" or "not true of me." For example, "acts as a leader" is considered a masculine characteristic, and "affectionate" is considered feminine. Most people (regardless of femaleness or maleness) could probably indicate "true of me" in both cases. A well-adjusted person of either sex will use these behaviors when appropriate. The androgynous viewpoint regards women and men as equals and seeks to open up traditional male-female roles.

The learned sex-role component is complex. *Sex-role identity* refers to personality traits or attitudes that individuals believe they possess, and *sex-role preference* refers to traits or attitudes they prefer, which may not be consistent. *Sex-role adoption* refers to behaviors that are thought to be descriptive of either males or females. While sex-role adoption would be expected to be consistent with sex-role identity, in some cases it agrees more with sex-role preference. In the same way social or environmental situations influence sex-role identity, sex-role adoption is also affected by situational variables. Thus a woman may be assertive in a leadership role, or a man may be tender when expressing affection.

Achieving a sex-role identity or orientation is a major developmental task of adolescence. While identity has its roots in infancy and is fairly well formed by school age, sex-role behavior is an important aspect of social learning for the teenager. Developmental theorists suggest that adolescents become more androgynous as they attain higher levels of psychological maturity.

Sex Object Preference

Environmental conditioning and social learning are considered to be the determinants of genital-sex object preference. This involves what it is a person views as sexually arousing, to whom the arousal is directed, and with whom genital gratification or orgasm occurs. The standard outcome in this third component of human sexual development and behavior is considered to be monogamous heterosexuality. Homosexuality is a nonstandard developmental outcome for some 10 percent of the population.

For adolescents, a distinction should be made between a homosexual experience and a homosexual orientation. Societal attitudes about homosexuality may lead adolescents who have had a homosexual experience to become anxious or to experience guilt feelings. Early homosexual experiences typically take the form of sexual experimentation which may involve comparing sexual organs or masturbation. Relatively few adolescents establish enduring patterns that are primarily homosexual, however. At least half of all males and a third of all females have engaged in some form of sex play with members of the same sex, and most of them eventually have a heterosexual orientation (Conger, 1977).

SEXUAL ACTIVITY IN ADOLESCENCE

The communications media have been proclaiming a "new sexual morality" characterized by an open and honest approach to sexual behavior and an increase in sexual activity. The tendency is to view decisions about sexual involvement as a purely private matter, of concern only to the persons involved. There is evidence, however, that adolescents today are less preoccupied and concerned about sex than their parents were at that age (Conger, 1977). This is usually viewed as the result of a more honest and open attitude toward sexuality, instead of the atmosphere of secrecy, suppression, and guilt that confronted earlier generations.

The easing and tightening of restrictions on sexual activity, however, go in cycles which are related to numerous social forces, and sexual attitudes and behavior are no more relaxed today than they have been at other times in the past. This century has seen quite a variation in attitudes toward premarital sex, for example. Fifty years ago, adolescents were told that sexual activity outside of marriage was sinful and prevented the possibility of a happy marriage. Today most teenagers have read at least one article by a psychiatrist, sociologist, or other professional which suggests that no activity between consenting adults is necessarily harmful or really sinful.

A new element which was unavailable to preceding generations—the birth control pill—has had a profound impact on sexual attitudes and behavior. Adolescent girls used to be told that their only role was to bear and rear children. The pill and other contraceptives make a choice available and remove the fear of an unwanted pregnancy, so adolescents can easily be tempted to exchange their sexual fantasies for sexual activity.

The adolescent's decision to engage in premarital intercourse or to abstain is a personal one. While it may be true that almost half of all teenagers today have had intercourse by 18, the statistics also mean that not everybody is "doing it." Over half have not engaged in sexual intercourse by the time they graduate from high school (Conger, 1979).

How changing attitudes and values are reflected in behavior depends on the particular behavior and the age of the adolescent (Conger, 1977). For instance, the percentage of older (19-year-old) males who have engaged in masturbation appears to be no greater (90 percent) than during their fathers' generation, but reported instances have increased for younger adolescent males (13-year-olds) and adolescent females throughout the age range. Petting also seems to have increased in frequency, starting at a younger age. There also has been increased frankness about engaging in such behaviors.

Research has been directed mostly toward determining the incidence of sexual intercourse among adolescents. Although a bit dated, Sorensen's (1973) national sample of adolescents aged 13 to 19 is still one of the most representative data bases available (see Table 4.3). Sorensen found that 44 percent of males and 30 percent of females reported

Table 4.3

Sexual behavior by age and sex

Group	Males	Females	Average	Ages 13–15	Ages 16–19
Nonvirgins all adolescents who have had sexual intercourse at least once	59%	45%	52%	37%	64%
Currently active sexual intercourse during preceding month	30	33	31	15	45
Serial monogamists sexual relationship with one person	15	28	21	9	31
Sexual adventurers moving from one partner to another	24	6	15	10	18

Source: Adapted from R. C. Sorensen, *Adolescent Sexuality in Contemporary America: Personal Values and Sexual Behavior, Ages 13–19* (New York: Harry N. Abrams, 1973).

having had sexual intercourse prior to age 16, and the figures increased to 72 percent for males and 57 percent for females by age 19.

When Sorensen's data are compared with those compiled by A. C. Kinsey and associates in the late 1940s and early 1950s (Kinsey, Pomeroy, & Martin, 1948; Kinsey, et al., 1953), a general trend can be seen. There has been an increase in premarital sexual intercourse among adolescent females, most dramatically among younger girls (ages 13–16). Premarital intercourse has also increased among adolescent males, but it has not been as dramatic. Among males, the increase in sexual behaviors during early adolescence (ages 13–16) has been greater than for older adolescents (ages 16–19).

Pregnancy and Contraception

An unwanted consequence of the greater openness about sexual behavior and the corresponding increase in sexual intercourse is the growing number of pregnancies among teenagers. Even though about one third of all public schools have some type of sex education program, and parochial schools, especially, seem to be doing a good job of dealing with the issues, adolescents obviously have a lot to learn about sex. Sorensen (1973) found that nearly a third of all adolescents believed that if a girl truly did not want to have a baby, she would not get pregnant even though she had had sex without using any birth control procedure. Conger (1979) reported that less than a third of unmarried adolescent females having intercourse said they used the pill. A surprisingly larger number (55–75 percent) reported they had used no contraceptive device whatever in their first experience. Among those who had established a stable relationship, only 66 percent reported *always* using contraceptives. Reasons for not using them ranged from unavailability when needed to mistaken ideas that a girl could not get pregnant because of the time of the month, being too young, or infrequent intercourse. The Reagan administration announced its intention in April 1982 to require that parents be told when girls under 18 receive birth control prescriptions from federally funded clinics.

According to a widely quoted source (AGI, 1976), one million adolescent females between ages 15 and 19 (10 percent of the age group) can be expected to become pregnant *each* year, along with 30,000 teens under 15 years of age. Apart from the psychological and sociological difficulties of adolescent motherhood, pregnancies at this age are more likely to endanger the health of both mother and child.

Only a small difference in the use of contraceptive devices has been reported between poor and other adolescents or between various ethnic groups (Conger, 1977). There is a greater likelihood that white or non-poor teenagers will either get married or have abortions, however. Among the poor, especially, many pregnancies result in illegitimate children.

A recent study by Dr. Arthur B. Elster, director of adolescent services for the University of Utah Medical Center in Salt Lake City, revealed that a sizable proportion (36 percent) of illegitimate births among adolescents may be intentional. The teenage mothers surveyed gave such reasons as depression, rebellion, fear of abandonment, home environment, or loss of a loved one. Fear of abandonment led some girls to try to get pregnant in order to prevent a boyfriend from leaving. Occasionally, the boyfriend wanted a baby and the girl got pregnant to please him. The home environment cited involved an unspoken message that premarital pregnancy was acceptable. When a sample of primarily (91 percent) black teenagers were asked for their mothers' opinion of the pregnancy, only 3 percent said their mothers welcomed it.

CHAPTER 4 IN RETROSPECT

Most adolescents like school more for the social opportunities it provides than for its academic aspects. They like teachers who are cheerful, self-confident, and willing to demonstrate warmth and concern for others.

These likes are understandable aspects of the adolescent's development. In the physical-motor domain the most significant biological event is the onset of sexual maturity. Social-emotional development is influenced by factors in the cognitive-intellectual domain. The movement toward personal independence and the development of self-identity, for example, are complicated by the ability of adolescents to think hypothetically, or in formal operational terms, which increases the range of their choices. The ability to understand the ideas and feelings of others which develops at this stage contributes to the emergence of adolescent egocentrism.

The thrust of development in the social-emotional domain concerns the struggle to overcome role confusion and establish a personal identity. This is the foundation for a sense of self-esteem, which develops out of satisfying interactions with others—parents, teachers, and peers. These are also the principal influences on the adolescent's choice of a vocation, one of the most difficult decisions to be made in this period. The practical basis for the choice, however, often is academic achievement or a lack of it, which may produce such a sense of alienation that the student drops out of school.

Other reasons for dropping out—drug abuse and pregnancy or early marriage—are serious problems of adolescents which can adversely affect their adult lives. Both drug education and sex education can be integrated into the curriculum to provide the information adolescents need to deal with the growing need to make personal choices that they are encountering in contemporary American society.

1. What fundamental difference will it make to you as a teacher if your adolescent students are able to engage in formal operational thinking, in contrast to the concrete operational thinking that was characteristic of their earlier development?

2. Over the first several weeks of the fall, you have noticed a boy in one of your junior high school classes who is quiet, often unprepared for class, and who appears to have no friends in the class. What are several hypotheses you would formulate to explain his situation? What, if anything, would you try to do on behalf of this boy?

3. You are a teacher in a senior high school. A girl in one of your classes tells you that she is pregnant and she intends to remain in school throughout her pregnancy. On the assumption that the girl and most of her classmates are middle-class adolescents, what would you expect the dominant attitude toward this girl to be? What would your attitude be?

Adolescence

Conger, J. J. *Adolescence and Youth: Psychological Development in a Changing World.* New York: Harper & Row, 1977.

This is one of the best of a large number of introductory textbooks devoted exclusively to the topic of adolescence. It takes the typical survey approach and includes the standard chapters, well written. Its strength is its relevant, up-to-date coverage of such topics as adolescents and drugs and adolescent sexuality. The chapter entitled "Adolescents and the School" is recommended to teachers at the secondary level.

Teenage Sexual Activity

Alan Guttmacher Institute (AGI). *11 Million Teenagers: What Can Be Done about the Epidemic of Adolescent Pregnancies in the United States?* New York: Planned Parent Federation of America, 1976.

This is the most readily available of the informative sources concerning adolescent sexual behavior that have been compiled by Planned Parenthood Federation of America.

REFERENCES

Akers, Ronald L. Teenage drinking and drug use. In Ellis D. Evans (Ed.), *Adolescents.* Hinsdale, Ill.: Dryden Press, 1970.

Alan Guttmacher Institute (AGI). *11 Million Teenagers: What Can Be Done about the Epidemic of Adolescent Pregnancies in the United States?* New York: Planned Parenthood Federation of America, 1976.

Bem, S. L. The measurement of psychological androgyny. *Journal of Consulting and Clinical Psychology*, 1974, *42*, 155–162.

Boldt, R. F., Reilly, R. R., and Haberman, P. W. *A Survey and Assessment of the Current Status of Drug-Related Instructional Programs in Secondary and Elementary Educational Institutions.* Second Report of the National Commission on Marijuana and Drug Abuse. Washington, D.C.: U.S. Government Printing Office, 1973.

Conger, J. J. *Adolescence and Youth: Psychological Development in a Changing World.* 2nd ed. New York: Harper & Row, 1977.

Conger, J. J. *Adolescence: Generation under Pressure.* New York: Harper & Row, 1979.

Dupont, R. L., Goldstein, A., and O'Donnel, J. (Eds.). *Handbook on Drug Abuse.* Washington, D.C.: U.S. Government Printing Office, 1979.

Gross, R., and Osterman, P. *High School.* New York: Simon & Schuster, 1971.

Jacklin, C. N. Epilogue. In Michelle Wittig and Anne Petersen (Eds.), *Sex-Related Differences in Cognitive Functioning: Developmental Issues.* New York: Academic Press, 1979.

Jones, R. Human effects. In R. E. Petersen (Ed.), *Marihuana Research Findings: 1976.* NIDA Research Monograph 14. Washington, D.C.: U.S. Government Printing Office, 1977.

Kinsey, A. C., Pomeroy, W. B., and Martin, C. E. *Sexual Behavior in the Human Male.* Philadelphia: W. B. Saunders, 1948.

Kinsey, A. C., Pomeroy, W. B., Martin, C. E., and Gebhard, P. H. *Sexual Behavior in the Human Female.* Philadelphia: W. B. Saunders, 1953.

Luty, Carl. "Student Pushouts—Victims of Cultural Bias," *Today's Education,* April–May 1982, pp. 39–41.

Newman, Barbara, and Newman, Philip. *An Introduction to the Psychology of Adolescence.* Homewood, Ill.: Dorsey Press, 1979.

Peel, E. A. *The Nature of Adolescent Judgment.* New York: Wiley-Interscience, 1971.

Piaget, Jean. Intellectual evolution from adolescence. In Ann Floyd (Ed.), *Cognitive Development in the School Years.* New York: John Wiley & Sons, 1979.

Rice, F. P. *The Adolescent.* 2nd ed. Boston: Allyn & Bacon, 1978.

Sorensen, R. C. *Adolescence Sexuality in Contemporary America: Personal Values and Sexual Behavior, Ages 13–19.* New York: Harry N. Abrams, 1973.

The Exceptional Learner

The elementary and secondary schools in the United States have been constructed and staffed, for the most part, to offer a suitable education to the children of the citizenry. The history of public education in this country is a proud one. The schools responded courageously (and successfully) during the late 19th and early 20th centuries to the challenges posed by the large-scale emigrations to the United States from other countries, especially Europe. The public school systems of the nation, probably more than any other institution, made the "melting pot" image a reality. To do this, however, it was necessary for the schools to deal with very large numbers of children in uniform ways. Those who could not benefit from mass instruction, or who were unwilling to conform to the inflexible demands of the school, fell by the wayside.

Today we have strong social commitments that no child should be prematurely excluded from the educational system. Schools and instructional programs are much more flexible, and the existence of individual differences is widely recognized. Teachers have developed some productive ways of dealing with the differences among children, and materials and technology are available to cope, at least to some degree, with the difficulties of adapting the instructional process to children who are different from the majority.

A substantial minority of children across the nation are defined as "exceptional." In this chapter we consider the identification and description of those children and, to some degree, the educational approaches available for dealing with them (see Box A).

THE NATURE OF EXCEPTIONALITY

In terms of the developmental domains described in preceding chapters, children may be exceptional in their cognitive-intellectual, physical-motor, or social-emotional development. An understanding of the nature of exceptionality is basic to consideration of how schools can help exceptional learners attain a certain degree of educational development.

It has been estimated that as many as 20 percent of all children are exceptional in the broad sense that they deviate markedly from the average in one or more developmental capacities, such as intelligence, sensory or motor skills, or ability to relate to other people in the environment. Categories of exceptionality and estimates of their occurrence in the school-age population are listed in Table 5.1. Characteristics such as mental retardation, learning disabilities, and emotional problems are referred to as *handicapping conditions*. The intellectually superior, the

BOX A   *Widening the world of the teacher*

The efforts of educators to understand and teach all kinds of
children have constantly increased their areas of concern.
E. Paul Torrance recognized their efforts in these terms:

> Year by year educators in the United States have been coming
> closer to their dream of education for all children. The pursuit of
> this dream has taken educational psychologists into the worlds of
> the blind, the deaf, the emotionally disturbed, and the child who
> lives in poverty, as well as the worlds of the mentally retarded and
> the gifted. Educational psychologists have had to find out what
> effects blindness, deafness, an improverished environment, and
> emotional disturbance have on the functioning of the human mind
> and its development. They have had to search for educational
> procedures suited to the intellectual characteristics of these special
> groups.

Source: E. Paul Torrance and William F. White (Eds.), *Issues and Advances in
Educational Pscyhology*, 2nd ed. (Itasca, Ill.: F. E. Peacock Publishers, 1975).

academically talented, and the creative are also exceptional learners, but
they are at the upper extremes of learning ability and are often referred
to as gifted. In this chapter we will discuss exceptional learners at both
extremes.

MAINSTREAMING

The Education for All Handicapped Children Act (Public Law 94–142),
enacted in November 1975, set standards and regulations to be followed
by teachers and school systems. This federal legislation stipulated that
free, appropriate public education must be made available to all handicapped individuals between the ages of 3 and 18 (the upper age limit
was extended to 21 in 1980). There are exceptions for providing services
to preschoolers (ages 3 to 5) or young adults (ages 18 to 21) if inconsistencies exist between the federal mandate and individual state laws. An
implication of P.L. 94–142 is that local school systems cannot refuse to
enroll handicapped children.

Mainstreaming is the educational arrangement of placing handicapped learners in regular classes, to the extent that such placement is

appropriate. A basic premise underlying the practice is that handicapped students can benefit educationally and socially from interactions with nonhandicapped peers. A second premise is that separate educational experience, either in the same school building or elsewhere, results in "unequal education." It is also assumed that mainstreaming will work because handicapped students have more similarities to than differences from peers who are not handicapped.

The key to mainstreaming is the interpretation of the phrase "to the extent that such placement is appropriate." Mainstreaming does not mean the wholesale elimination of self-contained classrooms for handicapped learners only or the automatic placement of all handicapped students in regular classrooms for the entire school day. It also does not mean that nonhandicapped students' education can be jeopardized by the presence of handicapped students.

INDIVIDUALIZED EDUCATIONAL PROGRAMS

In cases where the placement of handicapped students in a regular classroom is appropriate, more than simple physical needs must be met. Each such student must be provided with an individualized educational program (IEP) geared to her or his own level of ability. Individual programs were not a new idea in 1975; the idea can be traced to the early 20th century (see Box B), but the emphasis then was quite different.

Table 5.1

Estimated prevalence of exceptional children of school age in U.S. population

	Percent of Population	Meets Federal Definition of Handicapping Condition?
Mildly mentally retarded	2.0%	Yes
Learning disabled	2.5	Yes
Borderline intelligence	6.7	No
Social-emotional problems	2.0	Yes
Speech disabilities	3.5	Yes
Orthopedic handicaps	0.5	Yes
Intellectually superior, academically talented, and creative	2.0	No

Source: Data from D. P. Hallahan and J. M. Kauffman, *Exceptional Children* (Englewood Cliffs, N.J.: Prentice-Hall, 1978) and G. P. Robb, L. C. Bernardoni, and R. W. Johnson, *Assessment of Individual Mental Ability* (New York: Harper & Row Publishers, 1972).

BOX B   *An early version of
the individual program*

The origins of policies and programs of education for special children such as the mentally retarded can be found in a little book by Arnold Gesell, director of the Psycho-Clinic at Yale University, published in 1925. In *The Retarded Child: How to Help Him,* Gesell noted that "deficient children" should not be neglected in the regular classroom if a special class or school could not be provided. Instead, he suggested, they should be taught with the Individual Program method. Demands on the teacher's time and creativity should not be excessive, he said, especially if some of the brighter pupils from the upper grades were used as monitors.

In Gesell's program, the retarded child was to participate in the regular classes of the day to the extent possible. Beyond that "busy work" (drawing, stringing beads, making paper chains, and similar activities) was to be available and, most important, there should be provisions for handicrafts and vocational work. Knitting, sewing, woodwork, and basketry were among the recommended activities, and there should be a table in the corner of the classroom for handwork and such accessories as a loom. Gesell strongly urged the use of older monitors to help the exceptional child and to control the teacher's work load. The monitors would receive "social education" from their role, he said.

The suggested daily schedule for a mentally retarded 12-year-old boy reprinted here could be adapted to any "deficient child," according to Gesell.

A special program for John Smith, age 12;
mental age 7; intelligence quotient 60.

9:00 to 9:15   *Opening Exercises.*

9:15 to 9:45   *Reading.* May read with class or with Monitor A (Fred Jones) who reads with him in the cloakroom or vestibule.

9:45 to 10:15   *Paper Work.* Monitor A (Fred Jones) sees to this; arranges for the material and gives help when necessary. This includes drawing, coloring pictures, making and filling in designs, paper cutting, cutting out pictures, etc.

10:15 to 10:30   *Recess.* Monitor B (Sam Robinson) is responsible for this period. He sees that John gets a chance to join some of the games; he may sometimes arrange special games for him; and he also sees to it that no one torments or imposes upon John on the playground or going to and from school. (It is important for the teacher not to neglect this.)

10:30 to 10:45   *Outdoor Chores or Errands.* Cleaning up yard, raking, spading flower beds or shrubs, sweeping, washing windows, errands, etc. (If there are not abundant opportunities, the teacher should make them.)

10:45 to 11:45   *Writing.* Copying words and figures, and writing exercises. Monitor C (Jane Brown).

11:45 to Dismissal   *Handwork.* Knitting, spool knitting, Dexter knitting (Bartholomew mat frame), braiding, etc.

1:30 to 1:45   *Reading.* (with regular group)

1:45 to 2:00   *Writing.* Monitor C.

2:00 to 2:30   *Seat Work.* Pasting: scrapbook of magazine pictures. Cutting out and pasting of geographical pictures for Geographical Scrap Book used by the regular classes in geography. (History, Nature Study, and other scrapbooks may be added to the series.) Monitor A and teacher supervise and direct.

2:30 to 2:45   *Recess.* (Monitor B)

2:45 to 3:30   *Industrial Work.* Weaving rag rug; brushmaking; making basket; woodwork at a bench in the basement or corner of the room (Monitor C or D). (The teacher may arrange with parents for early dismissal, so John can do definite chores at home. In many instances, it is desirable to have the deficient child attend school for only part of the day. Parents may readily cooperate on that basis.)

Source: Arnold Gesell, *The Retarded Child: How to Help Him* (Bloomington, Ill.:
Public School Publishing Co., 1925), pp. 83–84.

Teachers are primarily responsible for putting IEPs into practice, but the responsibility for developing them is shared. The law stipulates that this is a committee responsibility involving the teacher or teachers of the children, parents or guardians, and a representative of a local education agency or educational unit who is qualified to provide or supervise special education activities. When appropriate, the child is also present. In most cases, a local school administrator is also a member of the program committee.

The IEP must meet the educational needs of the handicapped student and include an assessment of the student's current level of educational achievement. At the beginning of the academic year annual educational goals must be formulated to specify the nature and level of skill attainment to be acquired by the student during the year. Since long-term or general educational goals require short-term or specific objectives, instructional objectives in the form of measurable behaviors must also be included, a process which will be described more fully in Chapter 15. The evaluation of short-term objectives and long-term educational goals must be undertaken on at least an annual basis, if not more frequently. The extent to which the handicapped child will participate in regular classroom programs must be stipulated, and where special services beyond those to be provided in the classroom are required they also must be specified.

While classroom teachers assume most of the responsibility for putting the IEPs of handicapped learners into operation, particularly as regards regular classroom activities, this does not mean that they are solely responsible for the education of these students. The other school personnel who help develop IEPs continue to participate in the instructional process of mainstreaming.

THE HANDICAPPED LEARNER
IN THE REGULAR CLASSROOM

The classroom teacher is likely to encounter certain types of handicapping conditions: mental retardation, learning disabilities, and emotional disturbances. Although other types may be observed, these account for the majority of cases. This does not mean, however, that the classroom teacher need anticipate that all mentally retarded students will be mainstreamed. Few, if any, severely or profoundly mentally retarded students are placed in a regular classroom.

Most handicapped learners who are mainstreamed are able to get along with regular classroom accommodations. At a lower level of functioning are those who regularly attend class but who require different instructional materials or services. Those with the lowest level of ability may spend part of the day in regular classes and part outside the classroom in special education classes. The greater the severity of the handicapping condition, the less the likelihood of mainstreaming.

Teachers who have been accustomed to the idea that such exceptional children belong in their own self-contained classrooms, where they are taught by special education teachers, may doubt their own abilities to include these children in the instructional process in their own classrooms. As with many new experiences, uncertainty creates a certain amount of fear. In large part, however, such doubts and fears have proved to be unfounded. Teachers have found that exceptional learners who are placed in regular classrooms are much better off socially and will learn from other students. A good resource teacher who provides appropriate learning materials or instructional help for exceptional children, so they always have something to work with, must be available, however.

An understanding of the developmental history of exceptional learners in all three domains—physical-motor, social-emotional, and cognitive-intellectual—is an essential consideration in the formulation of instructional plans that will meet these students' individual needs.

THE PHYSICAL-MOTOR DOMAIN

A number of handicapping conditions in the physical-motor domain can cause children to be placed in the exceptional category. Orthopedic handicaps such as cerebral palsy, epilepsy, and crippling accidents are obvious examples. Other handicapping conditions where organic or neurological involvement has been identified include aphasia, visual disabilities, and hearing loss. Here we will consider only two subtle forms of physically handicapping conditions: specific learning disabilities, such as dyslexia and minimal brain dysfunction, and speech disabilities. These account for approximately half of all the handicapping conditions seen in the schools. Students with these disabilities are likely candidates for mainstreaming, and classroom teachers should be familiar with the conditions. Specific remediation is carried out by a special education staff, but the classroom teacher must work closely with the specialists where unique materials or techniques are required for mainstreaming.

SPECIFIC LEARNING DISABILITIES

The central nervous system is a complex, intricate arrangement that includes the spinal cord and brain. Some children's systems simply function differently from those of the average child. The causes for this difference vary widely; in some cases, a specific cause is unknown. Many of the differences, therefore, are grouped as *specific learning disabilities.*

Specific learning disabilities have no single definition. For purposes of meeting the requirements of P.L. 94–142, however, the definition proposed by the National Advisory Committee on Handicapped Children can be adopted. According to this definition, a specific learning disability reflects:

> . . . a disorder in one or more of the basic psychological processes involved in understanding or in using language, spoken or written, which may manifest itself in an imperfect ability to listen, think, speak, read, write, spell, or to do mathematical calculations. The term includes such conditions as perceptual handicaps, brain injury, minimal brain dysfunction, dyslexia and developmental aphasia. The term does not include children who have learning problems which are primarily the result of visual, hearing, or motor handicaps, of mental retardation, of emotional disturbance, or of environmental, cultural, or economic disadvantage. (*Federal Register*, 1977, *42*, 250)

The principle of "discrepancy or disparity" is common to all definitions of learning disabilities. In cases so diagnosed, there is a glaring difference between the child's level of actual performance and his or her capacity to perform. Although this principle is widely accepted, there is no commonly accepted standard as to the magnitude of the discrepancy between achievement and potential, which typically increases the longer the child remains undiagnosed and in school. A discrepancy of one year between grade placement and actual level of achievement at second grade may indicate just as severe a problem as a three-year discrepancy at adolescence. There is no hard and fast rule as to "how discrepant" achievement and potential must be for a diagnosis of learning disabilities, but the rule of thumb in many instances is a rate of intellectual development that falls outside the range of mental retardation (IQ above 70), coupled with inability to profit from group instruction in the regular classroom. It is estimated that this condition accounts for up to 2.5 percent of the school population. It is more common than either mild mental retardation or emotional disturbances.

Dyslexia

The category of learning disabilities that has to do with reading difficulties is commonly called dyslexia, a disorder of the central nervous system which we first discussed in Chapter 2. In line with the environment-heredity controversy, attempts have been made to distinguish between reading disabilities that are of neurological origin and those that are learned or psychosocial in nature. Since the 1960s, however, the term usually has been applied to moderate to severe reading disabilities regardless of etiology (or cause). The psychosocial disadvantage of the learner's home environment is recognized as a possible cause of dyslexia as well as of mild mental retardation, as described in a later section of this chapter.

Table 5.2

Common types of errors made by dyslexic learners

Standard	Reading Error	Writing Error	Error Description
made		wade	Letter inversion
dog		god	Total reversal
dad		bad	Letter reversal
animal	aminal		Phoneme reversal
happen	happy		Structural confusion
album	alblum		Phoneme intrusion

While a specific cause for dyslexia has not been isolated, some interesting correlates have been found in research. Males are four times more likely than females to be affected. This factor, coupled with evidence that the disability can "run in families," suggests some as-yet unknown genetic influence. Dyslexic children may suffer from some central nervous system dysfunction.

Dyslexic learners typically have difficulty associating sound, meaning, and symbols. Words that look alike are frequently confused, or letters are reversed. Phonemes (or sound units) may be mispronounced, omitted, or inappropriately inserted. Oral reading is difficult and error filled for them, and silent reading may be accompanied by vocalizations or exaggerated lip movement. Reading comprehension is usually very poor.

Common examples of errors made by dyslexic readers are given in Table 5.2. The table also gives some examples of writing errors frequently made by dyslexic learners, who nearly always have difficulty with this skill. Deficiencies include letter reversals, poor structural formation of letters, inappropriate relationships between letters, and frequent misspellings. Many of these children also have difficulty with math.

With all these learning problems, remediation efforts usually are reasonably successful, and most dyslexic children can adapt to regular school activities. Other than these difficulties, many dyslexic children can perform at or above average in other academic areas. Dyslexia has no direct bearing upon children's social skills, so most dyslexic students can be integrated easily into the regular classroom.

Minimal Brain Dysfunction

Students suffering from minimal brain dysfunction frequently are characterized as inattentive, uncoordinated, or hyperactive. They have perceptual-cognitive difficulties and may exhibit a particular set of a number of other disabilities. The characteristics usually associated with this condition have been ordered in terms of the frequency with which they are cited by diagnostic personnel (Mordock, 1975). These characteristics are:

1. Hyperactivity—inability to restrict activity to a level appropriate to the situation.
2. Perceptual-motor impairments—inversion of letters, inability to print name, copy a triangle or square, or decode the alphabet.
3. Emotional lability—sudden, unexplained shifts from one emotion to another.
4. General coordination deficits—awkward gait, poor balance, problems with handedness; child appears clumsy.
5. Disorders of attention—short attention span, distractibility, repetition of errors even when corrective feedback has been provided for the learner.
6. Impulsivity—tendency to respond without thinking; usually characterized by high error rate.
7. Disorders of memory—poor memory for visually or auditorily presented material.
8. Specific learning disabilities—reading problems, math deficiencies, spelling difficulties.
9. Disorders of speech and hearing—stuttering, lisping, hesitations, hard of hearing; inability to discriminate accurately between sounds.

These characteristics are not observed only in children with minimal brain dysfunction, however. Several of them also apply to emotionally disturbed children. In some cases, the diagnosis of minimal brain dysfunction rather than emotional disturbance rests on an examination of family background. Children with attentional, perceptual, and reading difficulties who come from psychologically sound family backgrounds are more likely to receive a diagnosis of brain dysfunction. Behavioral performance associated with learning difficulties is varied, and causal factors are frequently ambiguous. The teacher cannot rely on a list of frequently observed characteristics to make such a diagnosis. Box C suggests how a picture of a child with minimal brain dysfunction can be created from diagnostic information.

Techniques for Remedying Specific Learning Disabilities

Children with specific learning disabilities can benefit from some group instruction, but when efforts to remedy these defects are incorporated into the instructional process the approach is usually individualized and highly specific in nature. The instructional techniques that have been developed for use with learning disabled students are applications of

BOX C *Diagnostic picture of a student with minimal brain dysfunction*

Larry M. Age: 9 years, 3 months
Full-scale IQ, 78; verbal IQ, 81; performance IQ, 79

Areas of minimal brain dysfunction:

1. Larry has not established a preferred hand. Sometimes he will switch from one hand to the other during the middle of a task. He is not proficient with either hand.

2. When asked to copy a triangle, Larry inverts the figure so that the base of the triangle is at the top (other reproductions are mirror images or reversals).

3. Drawing and writing are very poor. Letter reversals are common.

4. When presented with the outline of a picture, Larry cannot fill in the details. Often he even fails to recognize the picture on the basis of the outline.

5. Intersensory studies suggest a great deal of inadequacy. Specifically, Larry cannot feel an object (for example, a triangle) with his eyes blindfolded and then describe what he is feeling. He is unable to translate materials presented by touch into a concept.

the perceptual-motor, visual-perceptual, multisensory, or remedial reading approaches.

Perceptual-motor approaches to instruction reflect the early work of A. A. Strauss, who explored the possibilities of remediation through sensorimotor activities. Strauss recommended a nonstimulating classroom and specially designed instructional materials. The general educational plan was to reduce distracting stimuli, restrict working area (learning cubicles were suggested), provide a highly structured school program, and use learning materials that attract attention (Strauss & Lehtinen, 1974).

Newell Kephart, a well-known contributor to the field of learning disabilities, designed a different approach which emphasizes the need for the child to develop basic motor abilities and perceptual motor skills before academic tasks can be introduced (Kephart, 1960). Sensorimotor training in this approach involves the use of walking beams, trampolines, ocular-motor (or eye-hand) training, and rhythmic movement. There has been no extensive controlled research to determine the validity of this approach, but it has been widely accepted by special education personnel, and beneficial results have been attributed to the technique.

Marianne Frostig has been a leader in the *visual-perceptual approach* to the remediation of learning disabilities. She designed a program to develop skills in the perceptual areas of eye-hand coordination, figure-ground discrimination, shape constancy, position in space, and spatial relations (Frostig & Horne, 1964). While research data pertaining to the effectiveness of this remediation procedure are not clear-cut, Frostig's programs for remediation have been widely accepted and are frequently used in special education.

A *multisensory approach* to remediation developed by Samuel Kirk was based on the Illinois Test of Psycholinguistic Ability (ITPA), which Kirk developed with J. J. McCarthy in the 1960s. The ITPA evaluates various aspects of the communication process, including memory, cognition, and expressive and receptive abilities. Kirk advocates intensive training focused on improvement of the abilities identified by the ITPA as those in which a child is lagging in development (Kirk & Kirk, 1971). The abilities assessed include:

1. Ability to receive and understand what is heard or seen.
2. Ability to make associations and understand verbal authority relationships.
3. Verbal and motor performance.
4. Ability to bring closure to incomplete verbal and visual stimuli.
5. Visual-auditory sequential memory.

Although research pertaining to the reliability and validity of the ITPA has been questioned, the data are as good as those for any of the remediation programs.

The area in which teachers most frequently encounter the need for remediation efforts is reading. Eddie C. Kennedy (1977) has identified eight general principles of *remedial reading* instruction:

1. Begin reading instruction on a level at which the child can achieve success.
2. Build a background for understanding and enjoyment.
3. Teach new words thoroughly, and develop the meaning they will have in the selection.
4. Take plenty of time.
5. Help pupils gain confidence in themselves.
6. Be systematic in planning for instruction.
7. Provide for regular practice using the skills taught.
8. Provide for extensive reading from conventional materials.

The many different approaches that remediation efforts for learning disabilities have taken are in part due to the diverse nature of the handicapping conditions. While experimental attempts have been made to determine the effectiveness of various approaches, most of the data are of a clinical nature. Undoubtedly, each approach has been used successfully with some learning-disabled children. A teacher should not expect to use a particular remediation procedure with equal success for all children, however. The research data that are available do not indicate across-the-board success with all types of learning disabilities for any of the programs.

SPEECH DISABILITIES

Speech disorders afflict approximately 3.5 percent of the school-age population. Those that are frequently seen in classrooms can be placed in three major categories: articulation, timing, and voice disorders.

Articulation Disorders

Speaking errors in which the student omits or distorts word sounds, substitutes one word for another, or adds a word sound are articulation disorders. A familiar disorder in which one sound is substituted for another is *lisping,* as in substituting the *th* sound for the *s* sound, so that *said* is pronounced *thaid.* In another familiar articulation disorder, *lalling,* there is distortion of the *r* and *l* sounds. These disorders are frequently referred to as immature speech or "baby talk." As a group, articulation disorders are by far the most frequently observed speech disorders in the classroom.

Timing Disorders

Stuttering and cluttering are typical timing disabilities in speech. *Stuttering* involves the repetition of words or word elements, hesitations in speech, and the prolongation of speech sounds. Like articulation disorders, stuttering is a common occurrence when a child is developing as a speaker. The persistence of either of these disorders beyond appropriate ages is a source of concern, however. In the case of stuttering, many children stutter during early childhood but have outgrown the problem by the time they go to school. If the stuttering persists, special education services will be required. Some type of speech therapy is necessary because stuttering can become a source of social ridicule that can damage the learner's self-esteem. *Cluttering,* in which the speech is excessively rapid, erratic in rhythm, garbled, or unintelligible, is less frequently observed.

Voice Disorders

When the quality of speech is distorted to the point that it interferes with communication, voice disorders are said to exist. The cause of the disorder may be organic or transient. When the problem is organic, surgery may be required; transient disorders are typically outgrown. An adenoidal condition (growths of glandular tissue in the throat behind the nose) which interferes with voice quality may require surgery, whereas a teenage boy will outgrow the occasional jump of an octave or so in his speaking voice.

THE SOCIAL-EMOTIONAL DOMAIN

Children who suffer from severe emotional disturbances such as childhood schizophrenia or infantile autism require professional care. The social-emotional disturbances that do not preclude school attendance are less severe in nature. According to the estimates in Table 5.1 above, approximately 2 percent of all school-age children can be classified as emotionally disturbed.

Children's emotional disturbances may take the form of personality disorders (such as inhibition, anxiety, or neurotic reactions) or conduct deviance (such as delinquency, aggression, or character disorders). There is fairly close agreement on how emotional disturbances contribute to the development of inappropriate or self-defeating coping behaviors. Most definitions of these conditions take a developmental perspective and refer to impairment of social-emotional growth during some stage of development.

The learner's principal concerns in later childhood, as we noted in Chapter 3, are to conform to standards of behavior that have been set by the family, peers, and the school. These socialization agents also operate in adolescence, particularly as regards academic achievement

The good-natured combativeness of these boys is appropriate behavior for the playground, if not the classroom. Other children who are "behavior disordered" may have developed inappropriate or self-defeating ways of interacting with others.

and occupational choice and the sense of security that membership in a peer group can provide (see Chapter 4). When social-emotional development goes awry, we look to these same sources of influence for explanations. Interactions between the instructor and the learner in the instructional process, as well as parent-child interactions and peer-group affiliations, are all important influences in this developmental domain, but only the family is considered here.

FAMILY-CHILD INTERACTIONS

In a developmental perspective, child-rearing practices are viewed as important shaping influences on personality. Mordock (1975) has suggested that early parent-child interaction patterns can lead to the development of behaviors which may be labeled *mild emotional disturbances.* Every child experiences stress and conflict some of the time, and most children learn to deal with them most of the time. This means that they learn appropriate adjustment behaviors. For some, however, the learned behavior is inappropriate, and so when stress or anxiety is experienced their reactions also are inappropriate. The expression *self-defeating behavior* is used to describe such inappropriate reactions. People who react to stress with self-defeating behaviors may be described as being their worst enemies.

The emotional climate of the home is largely determined by the disciplinary pattern set by the parents. Most children can accommodate to either a directive, autocratic style of parental control or a permissive, democratic style. The most important factor in the emotional climate is the predictability of the discipline provided; the child must know what to expect. Parents who are ambivalent about being indulgent or punitive, or who vary in the warmth or nurturance they show their children, contribute to the development of feelings of confusion, insecurity, and anxiety (Williamson, 1972).

Two types of family environments which researchers have found often lead to behavioral disorders in children are autocratic family life and protective-interdependent family life.

The Autocratic Family Environment

Autocratic parents hold absolute views about behaviors and have very definite attitudes about the behaviors they expect of their children. Open resistance or deviation from acceptable criteria is punished. Parents of this type expect absolute obedience and unquestioned acceptance of their standards for behavior.

In families where autocratic control is consistently expected, the parents may vary in the degree of warmth they display toward their children. Autocratic nurturant (warm) parents control children through the use of reason, the deprivation of privileges, or the withdrawal of love, whereas autocratic nonnurturant (cold) parents rely almost exclusively on the control techniques of punishment and rejection. Cold parents are disapproving and inconsiderate and may disregard the need to communicate with their children.

Learners who have been exposed to either warm or cold authoritarian training may have high needs for achievement but tend to do poorly on unstructured tasks requiring abstract skills. They use a rigid approach to problem solving and are not likely to take conceptual risks.

One result of a consistently autocratic family environment may be obsessive-compulsive behavior. Compulsive behavior is a ritualistic form common in childhood which is considered a disturbance only when it consumes a disproportionate amount of time and energy. Normal compulsive behavior in children may run the gamut from eating only certain foods to not stepping on cracks in the sidewalk. In the classroom, compulsive behavior may be seen in children with an excessive concern for cleanliness (always washing their hands) or neatness (refusing to engage in activities because of concern for keeping clean). Obsessions are recurring ideas that consistently intrude on other thoughts. When a child develops compulsive acts to ward off guilt feelings initiated by the obsessive thoughts, the child is said to be exhibiting *obsessive-compulsive behavior.*

Depression is a learned feeling of helplessness that develops in children whose parents are autocratic and, at the same time, rejecting or nonnurturant. The rejection may be overt or may be due to the parents' own depression, but it leaves children feeling as if the events around them are beyond their control. In a school-age child, depression reactions may take the form of poor peer relations, loss of interest in activities, listlessness, or complaints of fatigue. If the symptoms persist, behavioral problems, poor school performance, or psychosomatic complaints may result.

The Protective-Interdependent
Family Environment

Parents in protective-interdependent families emphasize independent achievement but anticipate their children will fail, and they try to intervene before this happens. This form of overprotectiveness prevents children from developing a sense of individuality. Instead they develop a conditional dependence and may be quite mature before they recognize that they are not self-sufficient. Then they realize that any success has been due not to their own efforts but to their parents'.

This type of early family experience increases the likelihood that learners will rely too strongly on the support of others in unstructured situations. They may never learn to master a complex task alone because they always look to others for leadership. Children from these families exhibit high levels of anxiety whenever they are forced to take independent action. This can create problems at school where parents cannot always intervene, and such children are likely to depend too much on teacher support.

Children who are raised in protective-interdependent families are given the impression that they are secure only in their own homes. They function normally within the home but exhibit *marked inhibition* in other situations, attempting to handle anxiety by restricting their behaviors. Such children take little initiative, have few friends, seldom engage in activities of a voluntary nature, and may exhibit very patterned (i.e., safe) behavior.

In school, these children are described as extremely quiet and timid. Often they are overlooked in the classroom because they seem to blend into the crowd. Since they seldom take the initiative, their academic productivity is typically no more than what is required. Their lack of independence may cause them to look to peers for ideas, initiative, and leadership. In some extreme cases, they literally copy others whenever they can. Treatment for inhibition requires assertiveness training which involves the child in the school environment but includes the family. A favorable prognosis for the personality reorganization of children with these behavior disorders depends on the cooperation of the families involved.

THE SCHOOL'S ROLE WITH EMOTIONALLY DISTURBED LEARNERS

Opinions vary as to the role the school should play in helping students develop emotional well-being. At one extreme are educational theorists who see the school as responsible only for academic achievement. At the other are those who view schooling primarily as a socialization process and who regard the school's role as comparable, perhaps, to that of a mental health clinic. A more realistic perspective is that schools can do both—achieve cognitive educational goals and promote the mental health of students. A comprehensive mental health program for the schools like the one proposed by Clarizio (1979) utilizes three sequential types of prevention: primary, secondary, and tertiary.

In *primary prevention*, the target population is normal, healthy, school-age children, and the goal is to promote the continuation of good health practices. Curriculums designed to promote mental health in children include the causal approach, which Ojemann (1967) has been developing and evaluating with his associates for 40 years. The basis for this approach is that students will be able to cope and solve problems better if they understand the causes or motivations for their own behavior.

The causal approach can be introduced as early as kindergarten or the first grade, when realistic stories can be read by the teacher and then discussed and analyzed with the pupils. At the elementary and secondary levels, the causes or motives influencing people's behavior can be discussed within the context of social sciences and literature. Because the classroom teacher plays a very important role in this discussion, the teacher's own good mental health is essential in order to serve as an appropriate role model. Teachers who can model the causal approach in the classroom will help students develop good personal problem-solving skills.

In *secondary prevention* the target is high-risk children. Whereas primary prevention focuses on healthy children, secondary prevention focuses on the early identification of children with problems. These high-risk children are already experiencing visible problems that are presumed to be readily changeable. The goal is to identify them early, before the problems become firmly entrenched. The diagnosis of emotional disabilities during the preschool years, however, poses problems in accuracy of diagnosis and lack of concern by parents who consider a problem mild and "something to be outgrown." Clarizio (1979) says that the notion that early detection leads to efficent and effective treatment, though seemingly logical, remains an assumption rather than a fact.

A fundamental goal of *tertiary prevention* is the rehabilitation of socially or emotionally disturbed children so they can assume a productive role in school. Tertiary prevention requires the direct treatment of a child by a mental health specialist. Children with school phobias or disruptive obsessive-compulsive behaviors, for example, may be treated by a school psychologist. Therapeutic approaches commonly employed in schools include psychotherapy and various counseling techniques.

THE COGNITIVE-INTELLECTUAL DOMAIN

Exceptional intelligence refers to either very high or very low levels of intellectual ability, as measured by any of the various methods to be described in Chapter 6. Perhaps the top 2 to 3 percent of the population can be appropriately characterized as intellectually gifted. At the other extreme is an equal proportion of the population who are mentally retarded. The regular classroom teacher comes in contact with learners in both categories. This section describes what these opposite types of exceptional children are like and how they can be educated.

GIFTED LEARNERS

Interest in the gifted student is not a recent phenomenon. Lewis Terman was responsible for initiating the first longitudinal (or continuing) study of intellectual growth in 1921, and the series of reports entitled Genetic Studies of Genius has provided invaluable information about the development of human intellectual ability throughout the life span, as well as insights into the nature of giftedness (see Seagoe, 1975). Programs for the education of the gifted appeared in many cities in the 1920s in the wake of his first study, and there were brief flurries of interest in gifted children again in the 1950s and 1960s. A more recent resurgence of interest can be traced to the Study of Mathematically Precocious Youth initiated by Julian Stanley in the early 1970s, a project which regenerated interest in meeting the educational needs of gifted learners. This program is described in a later section.

Identifying the Gifted

Most educators and psychologists agree that the gifted category of exceptional learners includes more than just the intellectually superior. The definition of gifted could apply to high levels of ability in a number of areas, including intelligence, specific academic talent, creativity, leadership, ability in the arts, and psychomotor skills. Approximately 2 percent of the school population would meet one or more aspects of this definition.

A mark of truly gifted learners is the ability to *produce* educational output that is original, creative, and extremely advanced for their age. This product must be "useful," as contrasted with bizarre. Gifted learners share a number of common characteristics; as a group, the gifted are healthier, larger, and stronger than like-age peers. Their social-emotional adjustment is better than average for the group as a whole, and they are far ahead of their classmates in academic achievement. Even in elementary school, they may be three to eight years ahead.

Commonly used standards for identifying gifted students include performance on intelligence and creativity tests, teacher observations, and previous accomplishments. Since the administration of individual tests of intelligence is time-consuming and expensive, group tests are frquently used for screening. Students who score well on the group tests are given follow-up individual intelligence tests. When the individual tests are used to identify intellectually gifted children, a cutoff score of around 130 is conventionally assigned. Only about 2 percent of the population will earn scores that high or higher, depending upon the test used (see Chapter 17 for further information on standardized tests of intelligence). Creative potential is typically assessed by means of a creativity test, in which actual creative effort is appraised by analyzing a learner's previous

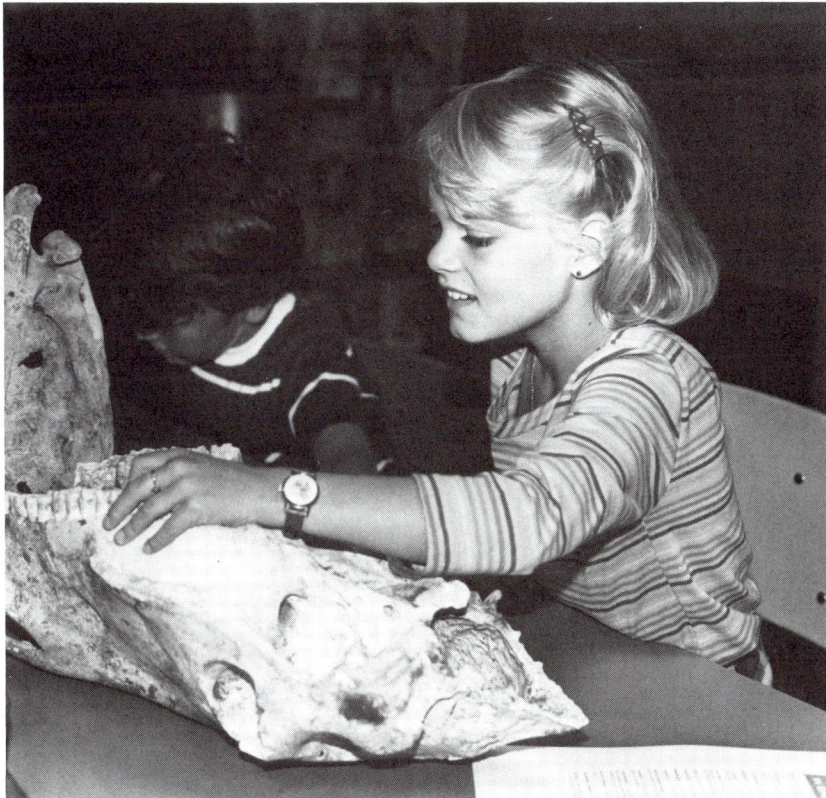

Gifted children can learn through independent study and inquiry. Programs for these learners encourage them to advance their knowledge in areas where they have special ability or interest.

accomplishments. Teachers also may be asked to nominate gifted students from their classes, though they have been found to be able to identify gifted children only about half the time. Frequently they include nongifted older children or hardworking "bright" students being pressured by parents. In order of accuracy, the identification procedures frequently used in selecting students for gifted programs are: previous accomplishments, intelligence test performance, teacher nomination, and performance on tests of creative potential.

Developmental Stages of Giftedness

The nature of the concept of giftedness is not only multifaceted, it also appears to mean different things at different stages of development. Programs for gifted and talented individuals must recognize that the characteristics of giftedness and talent are defined differently at different stages of learner development.

At the preschool level, *gifted* is most often defined in terms of accelerated intellectual potential. Such developmental characteristics as early language development or a high level of performance on an individual test of intelligence are observed. Since neither language nor intellectual ability have fully developed, the high potential is said to *predict* exceptional talent in creative thinking and problem-solving ability at maturity.

During the school years, giftedness is frequently related to academic achievement of an exceptional nature. A school-age child is rather complex in terms of developmental status, and talent can be exhibited in a number of ways. While intellectual potential is still considered important, the emphasis shifts to a focus on academic achievement.

Even in the early elementary education years, gifted children are identifiable in ways beyond their intelligence test scores. Exceptional talent in the fine or performing arts is beginning to develop, as is leadership ability. Achievement in all academic areas is characteristic of gifted children in these years. Even at this early age, giftedness means achievement as well as potential.

Gifted junior and senior high students readily use formal operational thought, and a designation of giftedness for them requires achievements that are exceptional in nature. Some of the most academically talented students have skipped grades in school and chosen early college admission. By adolescence, many gifted students have established a record of exceptional achievement, and the extent of giftedness is obvious. Their achievements can be defined in terms of usefulness and originality. This level of performance requires preparation, practice, and communication skills, complex skills which typically are not acquired prior to adolescence. High levels of achievement (talent) in leadership, the visual and performing arts, psychomotor ability, and academic areas are the focus of many talented and gifted programs at the secondary school level.

Gifted adults are typically identified after the fact. A gifted adult is a person who has made a significant contribution or produced a product that is extremely rare or original. Giftedness is usually attributed to those who invent, discover, or create. In all cases, there is a definable product that has been judged original and useful. Characteristics of gifted adults will be described in the section on creative thinking in Chapter 10.

Thus a transition has been made in identifying giftedness from conceptualizing it in terms of intellectual potential, to emphasizing academic achievement, to applying a standard of creative production. It is unfortunate that the apparent potential gifts of some children and youths fail to ripen into productive gifted adulthood.

Approaches to Educating the Gifted

Learning programs can be adapted for the gifted by changing the program content, the skills to be learned by the student, or the learning environment, or by accelerating the program. The approaches described here are general in nature, but they provide a frame of reference which can be used in encouraging intellectually superior or creative pupils.

Program Content   Much of the differential program content for the gifted stems from the secondary school curriculum reform movement of the sixties and seventies, which stressed high-level conceptualizations in math, science, and other content fields. Major evaluation studies have confirmed that the gifted respond to the special appeal of programs of this type.

An example of such program content is the Study of Mathematically Precocious Youth, established in 1971 at Johns Hopkins University by Julian Stanley. Young adolescents at the seventh- and eighth-grade levels who have demonstrated superior achievement in mathematics are identified by the progam and given accelerated instruction. In many cases, a child may travel daily to a nearby senior high school to attend mathematics classes, while remaining in the junior high school for all other subjects and activities. More rarely, general acceleration of one or more years of schooling is recommended. Stanley's (1977) position is that giftedness is not "general" but "specialized," so a potential mathematician need not be a political leader or have artistic talent. He does not subscribe to what has probably been the more popular view in recent years of providing "enrichment" activities for gifted children. In his view, an individual's special talents are best served by permitting and encouraging them to develop as fast and as fully as the educational system has the capacity to do so.

Program Skills: Problem Solving and Creativity   In adapting program skills to fit gifted learners, the objective usually is to develop capabilities in problem solving and creativity. These skills enable the gifted to engage in imaginative, productive thinking and encourage them to be less dependent on adult stimulation. They are discussed fully in Chapter 10.

Instruction in these program skills takes account of students who are gifted not only in general intelligence or content such as mathematics but who have specialized talents applicable in fields such as science or one of the fine arts. In recent years, some psychologists have recognized that most conceptions of human intelligence ignore or underemphasize creativity, and they have developed tests that purport to measure creative thinking ability. These can be used to identify children who have a potential to think in divergent and unusual ways. The principal one is the Torrance Tests of Creative Thinking, which will be described in Chapter 10.

Learning Environment   Changes in the learning environment to accommodate the gifted include a range of administrative devices: special schools, special classes, resource room programs and half-day programs, and individual tutorial work or mentor programs (Fox, 1979). All of these are designed to reduce the range of ability and performance within the instructional group and to get gifted children in touch with special teachers.

Though special facilities for the gifted and talented have taken several forms, in practice some of them, such as special schools for the gifted, are found only in metropolitan centers where there are sufficient population bases and adequate transportation systems. Learning centers have the same requirements, so a central school building or a portion of one can be designated a special center for the gifted on a community or districtwide basis.

Nonaccelerated enrichment classes have also been used to meet the needs of gifted learners. The concept of enrichment has not been well defined, however; if all it means is free time for busywork or games, it probably has little value for the gifted. Fox (1979) says that "Although many people advocate some free time or periods of incubation for the gifted, there is little evidence that gifted students can, without direction or training, profit from such experiences. Free time can, indeed, be lost time." Some types of enrichment have been found to be beneficial, however. Career education is not accelerative, nor is cultural enrichment, but both are of value not only to the gifted but also to the average student in the classroom.

Acceleration   Various attempts have been made to accelerate or speed up the programs for gifted students, in recognition of the 20 years or so that many of them must spend in the educational system before entering professional or scientific fields. Acceleration for high-achieving gifted students can occur at almost every level, from preschool to college. When reasonably planned, it has been found to result in no discernible physical or social damage.

The goal of educational acceleration is to provide gifted students with an opportunity to move quickly through basic subject material and advance to higher cognitive levels of abstraction and creative problem solving. Several approaches to educational acceleration have been practiced, most often in the past taking the form of grade acceleration, so a gifted student might complete high school at the age of 14 or 15. Early admission to college has also proven to be feasible for some 14- to 16-year-olds who are exceptionally talented in one field, usually mathematics. All such programs of acceleration, however, need to take the social-emotional development of individual children into account. Although acceleration may have educational benefits for gifted children, the age displacement can be harmful in particular cases.

Other educational acceleration techniques require neither early admission nor grade skipping. One way to accelerate the progress of gifted learners is through the use of *telescoped programs,* which present content that is normally covered in three or four years to a class of gifted learners in two or three years, usually in junior or senior high school. Subject matter acceleration is also useful for students who are exceptionally talented in one or more subject matter areas but who want to stay with their regular classes. A mathematically talented girl in the third grade, for example, may go to the fifth grade for math but return to her regular class for the rest of the day. The only objection to subject matter acceleration usually is the fear of administrators that a gifted child will exhaust the curriculum. This problem can be dealt with when there is cooperation between schools at different levels, such as the junior and senior high schools.

THE MENTALLY RETARDED

Directly opposite the gifted in terms of exceptional intelligence are the mentally retarded. A definition by Grossman (1977)—"Mental retardation refers to significant sub-average general intellectual functioning existing concurrently with deficits in adaptive behavior and manifested during the developmental period"—has been adopted by the American Association on Mental Deficiency (AAMD). For our purposes, these terms need to be clarified.

Mental retardation denotes a level of behavioral performance, with no reference to the cause of performance. *Intellectual functioning* is to be assessed by individual tests of intelligence. *Significantly subaverage* performance refers to a level of performance on a standardized individual test of intelligence of below 70 IQ (the finding of low IQ alone is not sufficient for making the diagnosis of mental retardation). In the *development period,* the upper age boundary for diagnosis is 18 years. *Adaptive behavior* refers to the way a particular child performs the tasks expected of someone of a comparable age from the same culture.

A great deal of attention is currently being paid to the adaptive behavior of children who are being evaluated. Adaptive behavior scales that can be used to assess a child's development are available. The skills considered in assessing adaptive behavior (see Box D) vary with age.

BOX D **Guidelines for assessing
a child's adaptive behavior**

INDEPENDENT FUNCTIONING
Evaluates the child's ability to function adequately outside the classroom. Self-help skills such as feeding self and basic hygiene are assessed. Adolescents may be asked to demonstrate their ability to prepare easy foods for themselves and others or to wash and iron their clothes.

PHYSICAL FUNCTIONING
Depending on age and severity of retardation, children may be asked to demonstrate such skills as climbing stairs, tossing a ball, riding a tricycle or bicycle, or jumping rope. Body control, with gross and fine motor coordination, is evaluated.

COMMUNICATION FUNCTIONING
Basic language skills and the ability to recognize single words (*stop, exit, men, women*) are evaluated. Skills include the ability to use the telephone and communicate by simple letter writing.

SOCIAL FUNCTIONING
The child's ability to participate in group activities and to interact cooperatively or competitively with others is assessed.

Mild Retardation

Concern with the mentally retarded in terms of school issues and learners of school age can largely be confined to the mildly retarded. This is the largest category of mental retardation, and mildly retarded children are most likely to be enrolled in regular school, comprising about 2 percent of the school population.

Many mildly retarded children are not identified before they enter school, because physically they are indistinguishable from others of the same age who are not retarded. During the preschool period they may be living in a family environment that is very supportive, and the parents may not sense "backwardness" in the child. At home the primary developmental tasks are language learning, motor learning, and socialization. At school the child is required to become more active in shaping the environment, and the nature of the learning tasks shifts. Motor and socialization skills are more or less assumed, and learning to read and write are the important tasks. These are the abilities that present the most difficulty for the mildly retarded, and they also are the foundation on which higher academic skills are built.

Though some mildly retarded children thus become visible in the primary grades, others are not identified this way until a second point in the learner's development, adolescence, is reached. This is the time when nonretarded peers are progressing to the formal operations stage of cognitive development, but mildly retarded learners are never likely to reach this level of cognitive maturity. The increasingly complex classroom demands at this time are usually beyond their level of comprehension. Subtle social changes also must be faced as adolescence unfolds. Society's norms for a higher level of social maturity present problems for the mildly retarded adolescent.

For educators or parents, the question is what can be expected as a result of the educational experience a mildly retarded child receives. The answer must be general in nature and may be inaccurate in some individual cases. Generally speaking, a mildly retarded person who remains in the educational setting until age 18 can be expected to develop academic skills that are common to fourth- or fifth-graders. This level of educational attainment is sufficient to permit mildly retarded young adults to become members of society. They may join the ranks of the dull-normal and become self-sufficient, able to live in marginal socioeconomic circumstances, and more or less "make it."

Psychosocial Disadvantage as a Cause   By far the majority of mildly mentally retarded learners encountered in the schools come from certain distinct backgrounds. In these cases, the intellectual retardation results from psychosocial disadvantage rather than cognitive development, another example of how the developmental domains overlap. Most of these children do not differ greatly from nonretarded age-mates.

Certain characteristics help identify mild mental retardation due to psychosocial disadvantage. The child must be measured as functioning at the retarded level on both an intelligence test and an adaptive behavior scale (see Box D). There must also be evidence of low intellectual functioning in the immediate family circle (aunts, uncles, cousins, etc.) as well. There must be *no* evidence that the lower functional level is due to a pathological brain condition. The home environment is usually impoverished, as defined in terms of poor housing, undernourishment, and inadequate medical care. A diagnosis of mild mental retardation due to psychosocial disadvantage, therefore, results from the absence of neurological involvement and the presence of a disadvantaged family background.

Learning Deficits   Mildly retarded learners, or slow learners, as they are often described, have varying strengths and weaknesses. Certain learning deficits, however, have been identified as characterizing the mildly retarded as a group. These are related to a lack of attentional, organizational, memory, or transfer skills, information on which is provided in Chapter 7.

Attentional deficits may be reflected in two ways: the learner may have a short span of attention or be easily distracted. In the latter case, the learner appears to be unable to focus on a task in an uninterrupted manner, and after several attempts all interest in the task may be abandoned.

Organizational deficits develop because the mildly retarded learner requires greater task structure than the average learner. While many children can learn on their own following the introduction of a problem, the retarded typically require more instruction, practice, and assistance. The steps in the learning task also must be smaller.

Memory deficits also characterize intellectually impaired children. The finding that they have poor short-term and long-term memory performance has been repeatedly confirmed. Rehearsal is necessary to retain information in short-term memory until it can be stored in long-term memory. The mildly retarded learner does not spontaneously rehearse, and so much information is lost because it does not get to long-term memory.

Transfer deficits mean the learner cannot successfully apply a previously learned skill or strategy to a learning problem at hand. The mildly retarded have a real problem with transfer; in a sense it appears they do not learn from previous experience. This produces the impression that they are always being confronted with totally new tasks for which they have no previous experience.

Labeling   Use of the term *mildly retarded* to denote a level of intellectual functioning that requires special educational provisions, as we have used it, has meaning to educators and psychologists. Such labeling can have serious consequences for the learner, however.

The labeling issue has at times been an intensely controversial issue. According to one line of thought, labeling can promote the development of a negative self-concept that can produce such effects as peer rejection, lowered aspirations, lower teachers' expectations, difficulties with adult adjustment, and dislike of bearing the label. Although all these effects are possible and no doubt occur in some cases, clear-cut evidence of them is lacking. Only "dislike of bearing the label" has consistently been found. No child or adolescent likes to be called retarded or to hear any of the more derogatory terms that sometimes are applied to them. Robinson and Robinson (1976) note, however, that

> It is not at all clear whether the label has changed their concept of themselves and/or their treatment at the hands of peers, teachers, and employers, or whether, in fact, they are fastening upon this label, their membership in a special class, or their admission to an institution, as a convenient target on which to blame their feelings of difference and incompetence.

Borderline Defectives

There is a fairly significant number of students who by current definitions are not handicapped. Their measured IQs fall between 70 and 79, and they are frequently placed in a regular classroom. While their rate of mental development is above the range of ability referred to as mental retardation, they perform much like mildly mentally retarded learners.

Borderline defectives share many of the characteristics of mildly retarded learners described above. In fact, from a teacher's viewpoint, they may function in much the same manner; after all, the difference in learning ability between students with IQs of 68 and 72, for example, is indistinguishable. These students should not be expected to be ready for reading, writing, spelling, or arithmetic when they enter school at age six. Most will not be ready for such skills until eight at the earliest. In some cases, they may be nine or ten before the beginning of such skills is evident.

The borderline defective's rate of educational development is slower, by about one half to three quarters, than that of the average child. The level of final educational attainment is also lower. It is probably unrealistic to expect these students to ever achieve much more than the average child has by the end of the sixth grade.

Educational goals for borderline defectives differ from those for nonhandicapped students. Programs for these learners usually stress the development of self-help skills, personal adjustment, and occupational competence. The instructional process includes such skills as personal hygiene, how to cope with daily living, and how to develop realistic aspirations. They also are given help in learning how to get along with their classmates, neighbors, and community members and how to develop occupational skills so they can become at least partially independent and able to engage in some productive activity.

CHAPTER 5 IN RETROSPECT

In recent years social commitments that no child should be prematurely excluded from the nation's educational system have involved the classroom teacher in efforts to adapt the instructional process to children who are different from the majority. These children may be exceptional in their cognitive-intellectual, physical-motor, or social-emotional development. It has been estimated that as many as 20 percent of all school-age children deviate from the average in developmental capacities such as intelligence, sensory or motor skills, and interpersonal relations.

Federal legislation enacted in 1975 provides for mainstreaming handicapped learners, or placing them in regular classrooms where this is appropriate. An individualized educational program must be developed by school personnel for each such learner, and the classroom teacher to whom the child is assigned is responsible for putting the program into practice.

In the physical-motor domain, some handicapping conditions can be classified as specific learning disabilities. These include dyslexia, or reading difficulties, and minimal brain dysfunction, which takes the form of such behaviors as lack of attention, uncoordination, or hyperactivity. The diverse nature of these handicapping conditions has resulted in many different approaches to efforts to remedy them. Another handicapping condition in this domain is speech disabilities, which can include articulation, timing, or voice disorders.

Children's social-emotional disturbances that do not preclude attendance in school may take the form of personality disorders such as inhibition or anxiety, or conduct deviance such as delinquency or aggression. The socialization agents which influence social-emotional development—the family, peers, and the school—also help explain the causes of such disturbances. Family-child interactions in autocratic or protective-interdependent families can produce behavioral disorders in the children. The school's role with emotionally disturbed learners is to promote mental health without sacrificing academic achievement.

In the cognitive-intellectual domain, exceptional intelligence refers to both the gifted and the mentally retarded. The gifted also may have above-average creative, leadership, artistic, and psychomotor skills. Learning programs can be adapted for them by altering the content, the skills to be learned, or the learning environment.

Mental retardation refers to substandard levels of performance and evidence of poor adaptive behaviors. Only the mildly retarded are likely to be enrolled in the schools, where their learning deficits may be related to attentional, organizational, memory, or transfer skills. Methods for testing the intellectual skills of learners at both extremes of exceptionality and the implications of group differences in intelligence will be described in Chapter 6.

1. Compare the various patterns of parent-child interactions discussed under the social-emotional domain heading. What behaviors are frequently observed in children from such families?
2. What level of academic development might be expected of a mildly mentally retarded learner? For which subjects would you expect such a student to be mainstreamed? What type of adult adjustment may be possible for some of these students?
3. Do intellectually superior children always grow up to make outstanding contributions as adults? Discuss reasons why various types of gifted learners may not develop into creative adults.
4. Creativity is valued in our society. What types of efforts or products would usually be deemed creative when produced by a first-grader, a high school sophomore, or an adult?

Exceptional Children

The writings of W. M. Cruickshank have been a major source of information about exceptional children since the 1960s.

Cruickshank, W. M. *Cerebral Palsy: Its Individual and Community Problems*. Syracuse, N.Y.: Syracuse University Press, 1966.

Cruickshank, W. M., Bentzen, F. A., Ratzeburg, R. H., and Tannhauser, M. T. *A Teaching Method for Brain-Injured and Hyperactive Children*. Syracuse, N.Y.: Syracuse University Press, 1961.

Cruickshank, W. M., and Johnson, G. O. (Eds.). *Education of Exceptional Children and Youth*. 2nd ed. Englewood Cliffs, N.J.: Prentice-Hall, 1967.

An excellent survey is provided by this book:

Mordock, John B. *The Other Children: An Introduction to Exceptional Children*. New York: Harper & Row, 1975.

Gifted Children

Historically, the volumes entitled *Genetic Studies of Genius* by Lewis Terman and others are considered classics. Currently, a series from Johns Hopkins University Press is highly recommended for those interested in the education of gifted children. It includes the following valuable resources:

> George, W. C., Cohn, S. J., and Stanley, J. C. (Eds.). *Educating the Gifted: Acceleration and Enrichment*. Baltimore, Md.: Johns Hopkins University Press, 1979.

> Keating, D. P. (Ed.). *Intellectual Talent: Research and Development*. Baltimore, Md.: Johns Hopkins University Press, 1976.

> Stanley, J. C., George, W. C., and Solano, C. H. (Eds.). *The Gifted and Creative: A Fifty-Year Perspective*. Baltimore, Md.: Johns Hopkins University Press, 1977.

> Stanley, J. C., Keating, D. P., and Fox, L. H. (Eds.). *Mathematical Talent: Discovery, Description, and Development*. Baltimore, Md.: Johns Hopkins University Press, 1974.

Mental Retardation

> Robinson, N. M., and Robinson, H. B. *The Mentally Retarded Child*. 2nd ed. New York: McGraw-Hill, 1976.

This standard reference deals with theory and etiology as well as cognitive, learning, and memory deficits. It gives diagnostic information, describes remediation of a psychological and educational nature, and covers problems that families of retarded individuals experience. A nice addition to standard coverage is a section on problems of adjustment in the community.

Learning Disabilities

> Bryan, T. H., and Bryan, J. H. *Understanding Learning Disabilities*. New York: Norton, 1966.

This is an excellent introduction to learning disabilities. A strength of the book is its characterization of the learning disabled.

REFERENCES   Clarizio, H. F. School psychologists and the mental health needs of students. In G. Phye and D. Reschly (Eds.), *School Psychology: Perspectives and Issues*. New York: Academic Press, 1979.

Fox, L. Programs for the gifted and talented. In A. H. Passow (Ed.), *The Gifted and Talented: Their Education and Development*. 78th Yearbook of the National Society for the Study of Education. Chicago: University of Chicago Press, 1979.

Frostig, M., and Horne, D. *The Frostig Program for the Development of Visual Perception: Teachers Guide.* Chicago: Follett, 1964.

Grossman, E. (Ed.). *Manual on Terminology and Classification in Mental Retardation.* Rev. ed. Washington, D.C.: American Association on Mental Retardation, 1977.

Kennedy, Eddie C. *Classroom Approaches to Remedial Reading.* 2nd ed. Itasca, Ill.: F. E. Peacock Publishers, 1977.

Kephart, Newell C. *The Slow Learner in the Classroom.* Columbus, Ohio: Charles E. Merrill Publishing Co., 1960.

Kirk, Samuel A. *Educating Exceptional Children.* 2nd ed. Boston: Houghton Mifflin Co., 1972.

Kirk, S. A., and Kirk, W. D. *Psycholinguistic Learning Disabilities: Diagnosis and Remediation.* Urbana, Ill.: University of Illinois Press, 1971.

Mordock, John B. *The Other Children: An Introduction to Exceptionality.* New York: Harper & Row, 1975.

Ojemann, R. Incorporating psychological concepts in the school curriculum. *Journal of School Psychology,* 1967, 5, 195–204.

Robinson, N. M., and Robinson, H. B. *The Mentally Retarded Child.* 2nd ed. New York: McGraw-Hill, 1976.

Seagoe, M. V. *Terman and the Gifted.* Los Altos, Calif.: William Kaufmann, Inc., 1975.

Stanley, J. C. Rationale of the Study of Mathematically Precocious Youth (SMPY) during its first five years of promoting educational acceleration. In J. C. Stanley, W. C. George, and C. H. Solano (Eds.), *The Gifted and the Creative: A Fifty-Year Perspective.* Baltimore: Johns Hopkins University Press, 1977.

Strauss, A. A., and Lehtinen, L. E. *Psychopathology and Education of the Brain Injured Child,* Vol. 1. New York: Grune & Stratton, 1974.

Williamson, R. C. *Marriage and Family Relations.* Rev. ed. New York: John Wiley & Sons, 1972.

Intelligence and Education

In the study of educational psychology, no concept is more important than intelligence in trying to reach an understanding of how children learn as they grow and develop. Its place in the cognitive-intellectual domain is obvious, but it also has a bearing on the physical-motor and social-emotional domains. This is especially true in the adolescent years, when the distinctions among the domains become less sharp, as we noted in Chapter 4.

The study of this concept is complex, and controversial issues have emerged in recent years. The need for teachers, parents, and others involved in the education of children to understand its nature is incontestable, however. The controversies surrounding the construct (or concept based on an intellectual understanding) of intelligence are in large part due to a lack of agreement about answers to a number of critical questions:

> What do we mean by intelligence?
>
> What are the effects of children's intelligence on their ability to learn and to succeed in school?
>
> Does attendance at school affect children's intelligence? If so, how, and to what extent?
>
> Does a person's intelligence change as he or she grows older, or is it a stable and essentially unvarying trait of the individual?
>
> How do schools determine how intelligent children are?
>
> Are the tests used to assess intelligence biased in favor of middle-class and against lower-class (especially minority) children?

In recent years more attention has been paid to such persistent issues, and research of the seventies and eighties has provided some answers and new ways of thinking about them. Still there are no conclusive answers to many questions about the nature and function of intelligence.

One teacher says to another, "Diane will be looking for things to do; she is a really bright child." A counselor tells a mother, "Robert will be spending an hour a day with a special teacher in our resource room. He just isn't able to keep up with the other students in his class in arithmetic." Or one child says to another, "You dummy! You don't even know how to play this game." Each of these people has made a judgment about someone's intelligence, but they would give various definitions of just what intelligence is.

Both children and adults attribute different characteristics to intelligent people of different ages. According to a first-grade boy, "being smart" means "They know a lot of stuff. 10 and 10 is 20. Some people are smart to do a lot of nice things for a lot of poor people—like give them money" (Yussen & Kane, 1980, p. 16). When a third-grade girl was asked what a six-month-old baby could do to show intelligence, she said, "Be able to sit up, not make a mess when he's eating; smile a lot," and a third-grade boy said an intelligent ten-year-old would "listen to the teacher, get things right on a test, read well." * Psychologists and educators, of course, have their own definitions of intelligence.

In this chapter we will describe the various ways intelligence is defined and the methods that have been devised to study and measure it. Information on the intelligence levels of students must be as valid and reliable as possible if the teacher's interactions with them in the instructional process are to be effective.

DEFINITIONS OF INTELLIGENCE

The ideas people have about what intelligence means, how it is demonstrated, and its sources (heredity, environment, or both) can be called *implicit theories of intelligence* (Sternberg et al., 1979). Implicit theories are important because they are used in everyday interactions with other people. The instructional process model introduced in Chapter 1 is based on the premise that teachers routinely make informal judgments of their students' capacities and at least partially use these judgments to decide on the level and amount of work to give to individual students. The match between the teachers' implicit theories and the behaviors exhibited by individual students undoubtedly also affects their expectations for the students' work.

The average person usually judges intelligent behavior on the basis of the age of the persons exhibiting it. A ten-year-old will be criticized for behaving like a two-year-old, for example. Table 6.1 lists the five characteristics cited most frequently by students in an undergraduate developmental psychology class who were asked to characterize intelligence in six-month-olds, two-year-olds, ten-year-olds, and adults. These students viewed problem solving and reasoning as being increasingly more important aspects of intelligence as people age and motor and perceptual skills as being increasingly less important. This judgment is supported by studies of human development, as shown in the preceding chapters in Part I. The set of traits for ten-year-olds and for adults given in the table exactly match, although the ranks vary. The initial appearance of each trait in a set is linked to characteristics that are rapidly changing at that age. For example, verbal ability appears for the first time for two-year-olds, who are rapidly expanding their vocabulary and general linguistic competence (Siegler & Richards, in press).

---

* Personal communication from Steven R. Yussen, November 1980.

Table 6.1

*Characteristics of intelligence at different ages
as perceived by undergraduate students*

Rank of the Characteristic*	Age at Which Intelligence Characteristic Is Evident			
	6 Months Old	**2 Years Old**	**10 Years Old**	**Adult**
1	Recognition of people and objects	Verbal ability	Verbal ability	Reasoning
2	Motor coordination	Learning ability	Learning ability; problem solving; reasoning (all tied)	Verbal ability
3	Alertness	Awareness of people and environment		Problem solving
4	Awareness of environment	Motor coordination		Learning ability
5	Verbalization	Curiosity	Creativity	Creativity

*Ranging from 1 for the most frequently mentioned characteristic
to 5 for the least frequently mentioned.

Source: Robert S. Siegler and D. Dean Richards, "The Development of
Intelligence," in Robert J. Sternberg (Ed.), *Handbook of Intelligence
Research* (Cambridge, England: Cambridge University Press, in press).

To determine children's ideas about what intelligence means, Yussen and Kane (1980) asked first-, third-, and sixth-graders a series of questions. Their responses involved concepts of knowledge, problem-solving ability, skills related to school or to interpersonal relationships, and arrogance. When asked about their own intelligence, the first-graders considered themselves more intelligent than the third- and sixth-graders did. Although large numbers of children at all three grade levels said that people's intelligence can change, younger children indicated that innate sources of intelligence are more important than experiences, while the older ones said that experiences are more important.

What do psychologists and educators mean when they refer to intelligence? There are many psychological definitions of the construct which relate to *explicit theories of intelligence*, those that are constructed by professionals based at least somewhat on research (Sternberg et al., 1979). In general, psychological definitions of adult intelligence include one or more of these characteristics: the aptitude for learning, the amount learned, adaptability, the ability to deal with abstractions, and problem-solving ability. These are quite similar to the characterizations of intelligent adults by undergraduate students listed in Table 6.1. Although learning, development, and intelligence are obviously related, the exact relationship is not known. However, the learning involved in intelligence is of all kinds, not just the type that is the object of the instructional process in the school.

PSYCHOLOGICAL APPROACHES TO THE STUDY OF INTELLIGENCE

There are three basic approaches to studying intelligence. The best known is the psychometric approach, which is concerned with the quantitative measurement of mental abilities and is known for the development of intelligence tests. The second approach is Piaget's conception of intellectual development, which was introduced in Chapter 2, and the third is information processing, which is based on the idea of the learner's interaction with information systems which was introduced in Chapter 3. Each of these approaches emphasizes different aspects of intelligence and has generated its own body of research, as well as its own measuring instruments.

The first two approaches utilize tests to measure people's intelligence. The scores resulting from these tests are not intelligence itself, however. A person's actual intelligence, like actual achievement, can never be known. People who receive the same scores on intelligence tests also exhibit many different behaviors in life. A person with an IQ of 130 as measured by a psychometric test or classed as a formal operational thinker by a test based on Piaget's theory may be a painter, an engineer, an assembly-line worker, a ski bum, or have no occupation at all. The most commonly used intelligence tests, those in the psychometric approach to intelligence, accurately predict school achievement for groups of students, especially in verbally oriented subjects. They are moderately accurate in their predictions for individuals.

All three approaches to the study of intelligence have grown out of perceptions of the construct that were based on people in the middle and upper classes in technologically advanced cultures with structured educational systems. Many other cultures would place higher or lower values on the knowledge, skills, and abilities included in these approaches, or would include others. If these cultures had developed the construct of intelligence as we use it, the content and measuring instruments probably would have been quite different.

THE PSYCHOMETRIC APPROACH TO INTELLIGENCE

The psychometric approach, best known for creating intelligence tests, views intelligence as a quantitative trait which is operationally defined as what intelligence tests measure. Intelligence, in this view, includes accuracy and power as well as speed. The more intelligent people are those who acquire more information and skills than their peers; they learn more, and they learn faster. They may seek out and use opportunities to learn, and they also learn incidentally. The emphasis in this approach is on behavior and learning.

Some people seem to have a great deal of knowledge about almost everything and can contribute to a conversation about almost any topic, from the latest count on the number of whooping cranes, to new economic theories and their relation to the national economy, to the common problems of the British car called the TR7. Some people absorb knowledge and skills after a single exposure to them, while others must spend hours going over and over the materials. Quick learners are universally regarded as highly intelligent and fit the psychometric view of intelligence very well.

Psychometric intelligence tests were developed during the late 19th and early 20th centuries, when compulsory educational systems were being initiated in the United States and many European countries. Prior to this time, only upper-class males had much access to the schools. In this country, Massachusetts was the first state to require school attendance by law, in 1852, and all the states had some form of compulsory school attendance by 1918. The initial goal of intelligence tests was to help deal with the wide range and diversity of skills and abilities represented in the population by making it possible to identify students at various ability levels. Then World War I made it necessary to test the intelligence of large groups of men drafted for military service. There was no time to analyze wrong answers, so the emphasis was on counting up the number of questions each man answered correctly and relating that number to an intelligence score. Tyler (1976) says the idea of intelligence as a quantity was thus firmly established.

Information on the format, scoring, and use of standardized psychometric intelligence tests in the classroom will be given in Chapter 17.

CLASSIFYING PSYCHOMETRIC THEORIES AND TESTS

One way to classify psychometric theories and their corresponding tests of intelligence is by the number of factors (or different but related aspects) each attributes to the overall construct of intelligence. This results in a threefold typology of unitary, or one-factor, theories and tests; two-factor theories and tests; and group-factor theories and tests. The theories and tests in these categories are those used most frequently in educational settings and research. Multifactor theories and tests comprise an additional grouping which is often included in this classification, but Guilford's theory and the tests derived from it, the major example in this grouping, are infrequently used in intellectual measurement in the schools.

Unitary Theories and Tests

A unitary theory of intelligence suggests that there is one general factor or aspect in intelligence, often referred to as *g*, for general intelligence. The tests associated with these theories give one main score, the IQ or intelligence quotient, which characterizes a person's intelligence based on the test's measurement. Neither Alfred Binet, creator of the original Binet Scale which is the forerunner of the Stanford-Binet Intelligence Scale, nor David Wechsler, creator of the three Wechsler intelligence tests, could draw on an explicit theory of intelligence while they were developing their tests. Nevertheless, their resultant measures characterize a person's intelligence through the use of a global (or overall, general) IQ score (Wechsler's tests also give a verbal and a performance IQ). This is the reason they often are considered unitary tests. They are the most frequently used individual tests of intelligence, and they also serve as the standards of comparison for newly constructed intelligence tests.

The Stanford-Binet Intelligence Scale   When Sir Francis Galton was expanding his work on human genetics in the 1880s he discovered that he needed a way of measuring people's characteristics so he could study genetic resemblance. As a result he established a laboratory where visitors could pay a small sum and have certain of their physical and sensorimotor characteristics measured. He believed that a person's intelligence could be measured through tests of sensory discrimination such as the highest pitch a person could hear, the exactness of an estimate of the length of a bar, or the ability to discriminate between different weights.

After contact with Galton, James McKeen Cattell established laboratories to continue work on intelligence testing in the United States. His tests included measures of strength, speed of hand movement, amount of pressure on the forehead needed to cause pain, reaction time, memory, and so on.

Binet, who is credited with developing the first intelligence test of the type currently in use, was hired by the French government to find a method of identifying students who would not benefit much from regular school attendance. He first examined tests like those of Galton and Cattell that tried to relate intelligence to physical and perceptual characteristics. Binet found that the results of these tests did not relate well to school performance or to teachers' judgments of students' brightness. So, first with Victor Henri and later with Theodore Simon, he worked on tests designed to measure "sound judgment," which was their definition of intelligence. The result was the first unitary test of intelligence, created in 1905. This was extensively revised; the first revision was introduced in 1908; and another, with only minor changes, appeared in 1911. These tests were not based on an explicit theory of intelligence at all but evolved through logic and trial and error. The 1911 revision worked quite well

---

BOX A *Binet's tests of "sound judgment"*

Items on the 1911 revision of the Binet intelligence tests were designed to measure the abilities of children at various ages. Developmental tasks at the ages of three, five, and seven are compared below.

At 3 years, the child can:	At 5 years, the child can:	At 7 years, the child can:
Point to the parts of the face as they are named	Choose which of two cubes is heavier	Identify missing parts of pictures
Repeat six-syllable sentences	Copy a square	Copy a diamond
Repeat two digits	Make a rectangle from two pieces of cardboard	Repeat five digits
Give own family name	Count four pennies	Count 13 pennies; name four common coins

Source: Adapted from Hans J. Eysenck and D. W. Fulker, *The Structure and Measurement of Intelligence* (Berlin: Springer-Verlag, 1979).

in identifying children who would not be successful in French schools (see Box A). This test was brought to the United States, where Lewis Terman of Stanford University translated it and revised it extensively. The result was the first edition of the Stanford Revision of the Binet Scale.

The most recent version of this test is the Form L-M Stanford-Binet Intelligence Scale (Terman & Merrill, 1960), which was renormed in 1972. It is administered by a trained psychometrician, counselor, or psychologist to individuals from the age of 2 through intellectually superior adults. The content is highly verbal in nature, consisting of many questions related to vocabulary, comprehension, and verbal reasoning. There are a few performance items, especially at the lower ages, in which the child is asked to actually do something, like build a tower from blocks. The results are given in one score, which is the unitary measure of intelligence. This test is moderately successful at predicting school achievement—as it should be, since it was explicitly developed to relate to school success.

Wechsler's Intelligence Tests   The Stanford-Binet was used as a criterion for assessing the Bellevue-Wechsler instrument, the original version of the newer Wechsler tests. Wechsler's intelligence tests also are designed to measure a single factor of intelligence, but in addition to the overall, global IQ score, they report two component scores, verbal IQ and performance IQ. Wechsler (1974) considered these to be the two main modes for intellectual expression. The tests include the Wechsler Adult Intelligence Scale—Revised, or WAIS–R, for people aged 16 and older; the Wechsler Intelligence Scale for Children—Revised, or WISC–R, for children from 6 years to 16 years, 11 months, and the Wechsler Preschool and Primary Scale of Intelligence, or WPPSI (pronounced *whip-see*) for children from 4 to 6½ years.

The WISC–R, for most students in elementary and secondary schools, consists of 10 subtests, 5 in the verbal area and 5 to measure performance, with one alternate subtest in each area. The verbal tests include information, similarities, arithmetic, vocabulary, and comprehension; the alternate is digit span. The performance subtests consist of picture completion, picture arrangement, block design, object assembly, and coding; mazes is the alternate. A brief description of the main subtests, as well as an example of an item similar to those in each one, is given in Box B. Like the Stanford-Binet, the Wechsler tests are moderately accurate in predicting an individual's academic performance.

Two-Factor Theories and Tests

Two-factor theories stress the bipolar nature of intelligence. These theories do not agree on the actual nature of the two factors, however.

Spearman's Theory   Like the unitary theorists, Charles Spearman believed that intelligence consists of a general factor, g. But he hypothesized that intelligence also consists of many specific factors, each known as s (for specific) and related only to a specific content area like mathematics or music. Thus, his two factors (g and s) are at different levels of generality, one general and the other specific to the area being measured.

According to Spearman, the relationships between tests purporting to measure intelligence are due to the presence of g. He felt, therefore, that intelligence tests should only measure g, since each s is unique to a content area and so is not useful for characterizing general intelligence (Anastasi, 1968).

No intelligence test has been developed specifically from Spearman's theory. Figure 6.1, however, illustrates his ideas about how intelligence might be measured with four tests. Tests 1 and 2 include tasks that contain large amounts of g and small amounts of s: They are strongly related to each other. Test 4 is moderately related to Tests 1 and 2 because success on Test 4 requires a moderate amount of g. Test 3 is not very related to the other tests because it includes very little g (Anastasi, 1968).

Figure 6.1

Model of Spearman's two-factor theory of intelligence (one general factor and many specific ones)

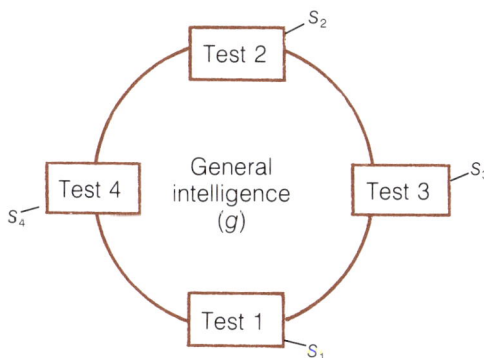

Source: Adapted from Anne Anastasi, *Psychological Testing*, 3rd ed. (New York: Macmillan Co., 1968), p. 327.

BOX B   *Measuring intelligence with the WISC-R*

The Wechsler Intelligence Scale for Children attempts to
measure the intelligence of students aged 6 to 16 with 10
subtests. In the following list, types of items similar to those
used in the test are given to the right of the test descriptions.

1. Verbal tests:	*Type of Item:*
A. **Information**—Amount of general information about life	How many nickels are there in a dime?
B. **Similarities**—Ability to analyze information	In what way are a dog and a bird alike?
C. **Arithmetic**—Ability to do simple arithmetic computations in a story problem within a time limit	Seven children picked 42 apples and divided them equally. How many apples did each child receive?
D. **Vocabulary**—Knowledge of word meanings	What does ridiculous mean?
E. **Comprehension**—Knowledge of and judgment about real-life situations	Why do we need firefighters?

2. Performance tests:	*Type of Item:*
A. **Picture completion**—Ability to find missing parts of pictures of common items within a time limit.	

B. **Ability and speed in arranging**
four or five pictures into an order
that tells a story

C. **Block design**—Ability and speed
in copying a design in a picture
using blocks

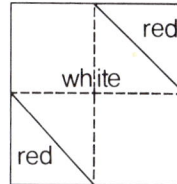

*Child is given four blocks, each with
some sides red, some white,
and some half red and half white.*

D. **Object assembly**—Ability and
speed in putting together a picture
puzzle of a common object (6 to 8
pieces)

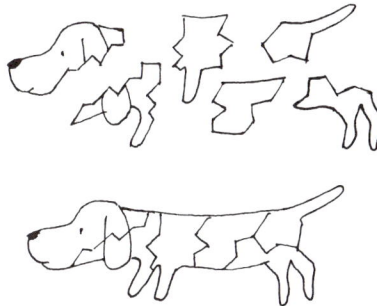

E. **Coding**—Ability and speed in
filling in marks in shapes to match
a key or filling in marks that are
associated with numbers

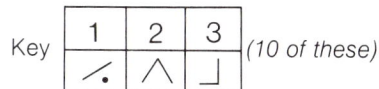

Key

(10 of these)

Exercise

(93 of these)

Source: David Wechsler, *Manual for the Wechsler Intelligence Scale for Children—
Revised* (New York: Psychological Corporation, 1974). Actual test items are not
used as examples.

Cattell and Horn's Theory   With Cattell, John Horn developed a theory of intelligence that includes two general factors (Horn, 1970). One of these, called *fluid intelligence* (symbolized g_f) relates to the actual structures of thinking, which are independent of the content of thought. Fluid intelligence includes neurological-physiological structures, basic unlearned organizational functions, and incidental learning, and it is related to such processes as memory, perception, and attention. It is considered culture-free because we are born with these structures; they reflect our genetic makeup. Their measurement also reflects environmental influences, however, because they can be affected at any time in the life span through damage to the physiological structures involved. The types of tests used to measure fluid intelligence include the Wechsler subtests of block design and digit span backwards, as well as many others.

The second factor in this theory is called *crystallized* intelligence (symbolized by g_c). It consists of the skills involved in learning cultural content, as well as the content itself. The types of tests used to measure crystallized intelligence include the Wechsler subtests of information and verbal comprehension, among others.

This theory is frequently used in research on the effects of aging on intellectual abilities. It did not spawn the development of specific tests but uses established intelligence tests for measurement. Some tests can be classified as measuring primarily fluid or crystallized intelligence, as in the examples given above. Other tests present tasks that can be solved using some abilities that are fluid and others that are crystallized. These include tests of general reasoning and semantic relations, such as verbal analogies and arithmetic reasoning.

Thurstone's Group-Factor Theory and Test

There is only one well-known example of a group factor theory of intelligence. This is L. L. Thurstone's (1938) primary mental abilities theory. At different times in his career, Thurstone theorized that intelligence consists of between 6 and 12 abilities that he called *primary mental abilities*, or PMA. The seven abilities he consistently found in research studies are: verbal comprehension, number ability, word fluency, spatial visualization, associative memory, reasoning, and perceptual speed. There is no general factor in this theory.

The PMA are measured by the Primary Mental Abilities Test. Thurstone's general ideas about the measurement of intelligence are shown in Figure 6.2, which includes three of the seven well-established PMA for purposes of illustration. In a test battery Tests 1 and 2 are strongly related because they both contain large amounts of the verbal comprehension group factor. Tests 3 and 4 are moderately related because of the number factor. Test 3 is also slightly related to Tests 1 and 2, due to sharing of the verbal comprehension factor. Tests 4 and 5 are mod-

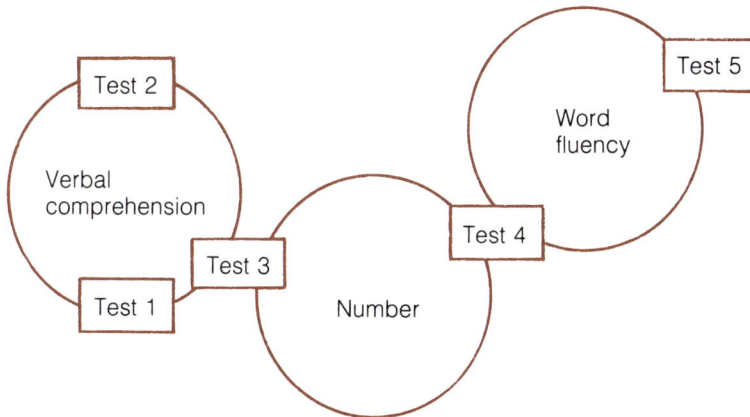

Figure 6.2

Model of Thurstone's group-factor primary mental abilities theory of intelligence (including 3 of the 7 most commonly found factors)

Test 2

Verbal comprehension

Test 1

Test 3

Number

Test 4

Word fluency

Test 5

Source: Adapted from Anne Anastasi, *Psychological Testing*, 3rd ed. (New York: Macmillan Co., 1968), p. 328.

erately interrelated through the word fluency factor and are unrelated to Tests 1 and 2 (Anastasi, 1968).

Comparing Factor Theories

The factor theories for measuring intelligence have some obvious differences, but some of the distinctions among unitary, two-factor, and group-factor theories are not at all clear.

Since Spearman emphasized *g* in measurement and in characterizing intelligence, his theory can be considered a single-factor theory like those of Binet and Wechsler. If the number of tests in a battery designed to measure intelligence is small, or if the tests are quite homogeneous in content, their relationships can be attributed to a single factor which can be called *g*, as Spearman's theory and Binet's and Wechsler's tests suggest. Yet, if these same tests are included in a larger, more variable battery of tests, *g* can become one of a series of group factors, as Thurstone's theory postulates. In fact, if the number and word fluency abilities, along with Tests 4 and 5, were omitted from the model of Thurstone's theory in Figure 6.2, the result would closely resemble the model of Spearman's theory in Figure 6.1. One test in a small battery may not be strongly related to the other tests in the battery, and so it can be considered as measuring a specific factor in Spearman's theory; yet, in a larger battery, that same test may be related to several others and so be considered a measure of a group factor (Anastasi, 1968).

Thurstone's PMA tests, representing a group-factor theory, are often split into two groups corresponding to Cattell's typology of fluid intelligence (such as the perceptual speed test) and crystallized intelligence (such as the verbal comprehension test). Yet Cattell's theory is a two-factor theory.

According to Yussen and Kane (1980), a clever test constructor can construct a test that supports any preferred psychometric theory, and a clever test user can select a battery of tests to support any theory. Scores from the accepted intelligence tests, however, are related, indicating that there is a general intelligence factor, g. These tests do vary in their relationships with each other, indicating that there is more to intelligence than just g. Intelligence tests that are highly related, and so mostly measure g, are those that involve complex mental tasks that require conscious mental manipulation to perform correctly (Jensen, 1980). It is probably most useful for educators to think of intelligence as consisting of both a general aspect, g, that is found in almost all academic tasks, as well as a series of group factors that are related to more specific, yet quite broad, aspects of tasks like number ability. In this vein, Wechsler's verbal IQ score relates to a child's g as well as a group factor associated with verbal ability.

PIAGET'S COGNITIVE-DEVELOPMENTAL APPROACH TO INTELLECTUAL DEVELOPMENT

When Piaget worked in Simon's Paris laboratory, his task was to create a French edition of some English reasoning tests. Thus the stage was set for Piaget to follow in Binet's and Simon's path, but he did not. In fact, he completely discarded the quantitative, factor view of intelligence. He was interested in how we think, not in what or how much we think, as in the psychometric theories.

Piaget theorized that people with the highest level of intellectual attainment have passed through four separate stages, each characterized by a *qualitatively* different kind of thought, as we noted in Chapter 2. Sensorimotor intelligence, generally found in infants, is intelligence characterized by action. Preoperational thought, usually found in preschool and early elementary school children, involves thinking based on direct perception, on what things are like. Concrete operational thought, normally found in elementary school children and perhaps half or more of the adolescent and adult populations, is related to concrete attributes of objects. Formal operational thought, which starts in adolescence for many people, involves considering the hypothetical. Evidence indicates that about half of the adults in this country have achieved the stage of formal operations (Siegler & Richards, in press). In some less technologically advanced cultures, no one may attain this stage.

Piaget's choice of intellectual tasks was primarily of philosophical interest, and his observations of how people of various ages perform on these tasks formed the basis of his theory. Intelligence tests based on Piaget's theory use these and similar tasks to try to identify the individual's current stage of intellectual functioning.

Archimedes's law of floating bodies, for example, is the basis for a task used to identify people who have attained the formal operational stage in their understanding of floating objects (Inhelder & Piaget, 1958). The task could easily serve as an item in a Piaget-type individual intelligence test. The student is given a large container of water, like a bucket; many different objects, each small enough to fit into the container of water; and a hollow cube to use in comparing the densities of the objects with the density of water. The task is to indicate which objects will float and which ones will not, and why. The student experiments with the materials and tries to formulate a general principle to explain why only some objects float. A student who is able to discover that objects whose densities are greater than that of water sink, while those that are less dense than water float, is classed as having attained formal operations in relation to this task.

Within each of Piaget's stages, different tasks are mastered at different times. In the concrete operational stage, for example, number conservation is mastered first, followed by solid quantity conservation, with weight conservation mastered last. (The principle of conservation was described in Chapter 3.) Any test developed from Piaget's theory, therefore, would need a series of items representing tasks within stages that are differentially achieved. The resulting stage classification is the person's intelligence score, based on *which* tasks the person solves rather than the *number* of tasks solved, as in the psychometric tests. Whereas credit is given for the correct answers in psychometric tests, in Piagetian tests credit is given for correct reasons for answers.

Although some Piaget-type tests are available, their development has been slow, and they are not widely used as tests of intelligence. At least part of the reason is that Piaget had no interest in developing intelligence tests based on his theory (Tyler, 1976).

THE INFORMATION-PROCESSING APPROACH TO INTELLIGENCE

When information processing, a concept which emerged about the time computers became available, is applied to the study of intelligence, the assumption is that people exhibit intelligent behavior by manipulating symbols. This approach aims at identifying and describing the symbols involved and the ways in which they are manipulated (Lachman, Lachman, & Butterfield, 1979). The symbols themselves may be words, images, or other representations yet unknown. The processes may be serial, or one symbol after another; parallel, or several symbols at the same time; or others that are yet to be identified.

No tests have been developed which use the information-processing approach to identify individual levels of intelligence. The emphasis instead has been on research designed to study either memory or problem solving.

Research on memory, which is very important to intelligent behavior, has identified four major memory-improvement strategies: rehearsal, or repeating the information to be remembered; organization, or putting the information into categories; elaboration, or linking the information together in meaningful ways; and allocation of more study time (Siegler & Richards, in press). More information on these strategies will be given in Chapter 7.

The contributions of information-processing research psychologists to an understanding of the processes of human problem solving also have been recognized (see Chapter 10). Information-processing research often examines problem solving through task analysis, by breaking a task down into small parts and determining how they can be combined into models that do or do not solve problems. In computer simulation, the computer is programmed to solve problems and study the various program models that are output. Information-processing research also may study problem-solving principles by using patterns derived from the errors and correct answers of people as they attempt to solve problems (Siegler & Richards, in press).

INTELLECTUAL DEVELOPMENT

Age is often used an an informal criterion for judging levels of intelligence, with results such as those shown in Table 6.1 at the beginning of the chapter. The characteristics undergraduates attributed to intelligent six-month-old infants were very different from those they attributed to 2-year-olds, 10-year-olds, and adults.

More scientific attempts to measure intelligence at various stages of the life cycle have produced data on how it develops in individuals and varies over time. The development of intelligence and its variable growth patterns from infancy through early and later childhood, adolescence, and adulthood have implications for the study of how people learn at home, in school, and in other social settings.

INFANCY

Infant intelligence tests like the Bayley Scale of Infant Intelligence measure sensorimotor skills, such as coordination, attention, knowledge of simple words, and visual tracking, in children from shortly after birth until about two and one-half years of age. There is little relationship between a particular child's scores on an infant test and on a later intelligence measure. This is due, at least in part, to the nature of intelligence; the behavior of infants, even very "smart" ones, bears little resemblance to what we think of as intellectual behavior in older children and adults. Moreover, infant intelligence tests measure very different skills and knowledge than the Stanford-Binet and Wechsler tests are designed to evaluate.

Infant tests are administered individually because of the age of the child and the nature of the tests. They can be useful in identifying gross developmental differences; for example, they will separate young children who are developing at a normal rate from those who are developing slowly. The tests also reveal specific problems, such as poor vision or hearing.

The finding that the growth of intelligence is most rapid during infancy and the preschool years led to the idea that intervention into intellectual development would be most beneficial at these times (Nichols, 1979). For intellectual development to proceed normally, infants first of all need adequate nutrition. Malnutrition experienced prenatally or during the first months or years of life results in mental retardation which may be permanent, depending on the timing and extent of the deprivation.

For a very young child who is sufficiently nourished, several other environmental variables may be important. Infants and toddlers need to be exposed to a great deal of verbal stimulation, including the labeling of objects and relationships, and to appropriate play materials. They need to be encouraged to achieve and to try to solve problems appropriate to their ages, both with help from adults and independently. Their cognitive interests, activities, and efforts must be positively reinforced. Activities such as these assist infants to develop the cognitive skills, as well as personality traits, that are associated with good intellectual performance. These personality traits include an internal locus of control, independence, trust in other people, and confidence in their own problem-solving abilities.

EARLY CHILDHOOD

During early childhood, from the age of about two until entrance into first grade, there are great changes in the child's intellectual functioning. Intelligence test results reflect these changes. Two of the most popular individual intelligence tests for this age group are the Stanford-Binet and the Wechsler Preschool and Primary Scale of Intelligence. These tests include questions designed to measure such factors as the child's knowledge of words (defining words), visual alertness and memory (finding what is missing from a picture of a common object), perceptual motor skills (copying a design with a pencil or with blocks), and logical thinking (telling how two objects are alike).

During this time intelligence is still quite unstable, and it is growing rapidly. Because of this, preschool intelligence is not related very strongly to later intelligence. Preschool intelligence test results should be used not to predict later school success but to identify extreme problems and individual differences in children's rates of development.

The same general types of experiences infants need for good intellectual development also are needed by preschoolers. They need to be actively involved with their environments and the people in them. Play with other children and alone is especially important during this time, both for cognitive and for social development. Preschool children develop cognitively through active interaction with concrete materials and playthings, such as sandboxes, tubs of water, dolls, and toy vehicles, as well as with other people. These materials allow them to explore the physical and logical relationships between objects. Interaction with adults, who model various cognitive activities, is also important. Children of this age respond positively to gentle prods toward achievement.

LATER CHILDHOOD AND ADOLESCENCE

The growth of intelligence continues to be very rapid until about age 10½, when it starts to slow down. From about six years of age, the stability of IQ scores from individually administered tests increases as children grow older. By preadolescence, the scores strongly resemble adult IQs; that is, most children with high IQ scores at 11 or 12 also tend to have high IQ scores at 20, 32, and 56, for example. IQs from group-administered tests do not begin to stabilize until between grades 4 and 7, and performance IQs from these tests are much less stable than verbal IQs (Hopkins & Bracht, 1975).

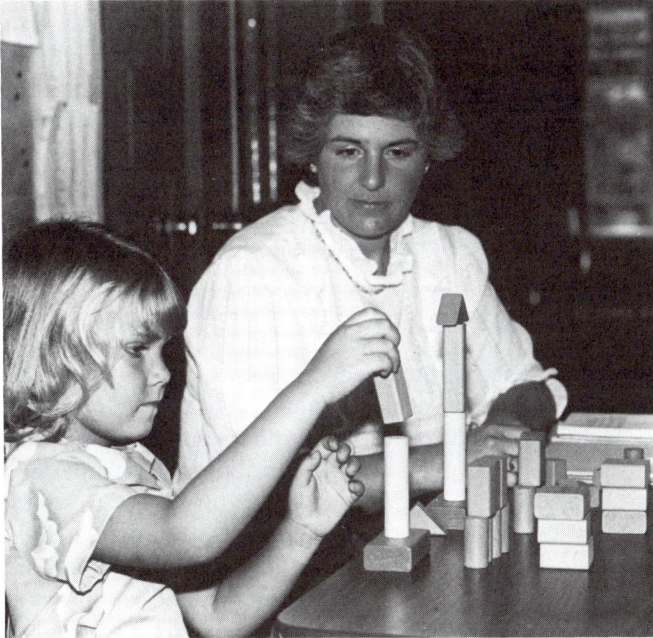

Individual assessments of intelligence, such as this block-building test, are advisable when exceptional ability has been demonstrated or a handicap as in hearing or speech is evident.

After the later childhood period, the IQ scores of most people vary with retesting within a small range, and the scores become increasingly more stable with increasing age. When most adolescents and adults are retested, their retest scores usually are within four or five points of their original scores. An occasional individual's score may change as much as 20 or 30 points from one testing occasion to another, however (Honzik, MacFarlane, & Allen, 1948; McCall, Applebaum, & Hogarty, 1973).

The Stanford-Binet and the Wechsler Intelligence Scale for Children—Revised (or the Wechsler Adult Intelligence Scale—Revised for adolescents 16 or older) are the most commonly administered individual intelligence tests for this age group. The questions are similar to those in the WISC-R (see Box B above). Students of these ages need to be exposed to material and skills of interest to them that are at levels slightly higher than their current levels of intellectual functioning. In elementary school, most students function at a concrete operational level and are interested in accumulating knowledge and experiences of various types. Middle-grade children often have hobbies that range from collecting matchbook covers to rock collections to memorizing the batting averages of favorite ball players. The attitudes and motives that inspire these hobbies often can be directed toward school-relevant material if it is made interesting to children of this age, applying the principles of intrinsic motivation described in Chapter 3.

In junior high and high school, many students think in concrete operational terms, but others are starting to think at formal operational levels in various subjects. The latter are eager to attempt experimentation and problem solving in areas important to them, such as unsolved scientific questions and social problems. Intrinsic motivation also can be used by teachers of these adolescents to present school material in ways that interest students and are relevant to their lives.

ADULTHOOD AND OLD AGE

Experts in the development of intelligence used to say that people's intelligence increases as they age, peaking somewhere between the late teens and 30 and declining slowly as they grow older until the late fifties or early sixties, after which it rapidly declines until death. This pattern of intellectual decline is obviously depressing to anyone over 30, which every person can expect to be at some point. The research that formed the basis for this conclusion was cross-sectional in nature and used unitary intelligence tests as the measuring instrument. The decline was attributed to many factors, but especially to age-related physiological changes in the central nervous system and sensory structures. Older people's senses were found to be less acute than those of younger adults, and their brains are smaller (Horn, 1970). Nevertheless, in many cultures older people are highly respected for their experience and knowledge. Unless people purposely shut themselves off, they are continually exposed to new knowledge and experiences, and some learning must take place. So how can older people be more knowledgeable and less intelligent at the same time?

Other researchers started studying this question using tests with more than one factor, such as Thurstone's Primary Mental Abilities Test. As Figure 6.3 shows, they found that the knowledge and skill aspects of intelligence, such as vocabulary, general information, similarities, judgment, and long-term memory, remain stable or continue to grow from the teens on through the fifties (Schaie & Willis, 1979). These areas correspond with Cattell and Horn's view of crystallized intelligence, or g_c, described above. Aspects of intelligence related to perception and speed, called fluid intelligence, or g_f, by Cattell and Horn, follow a different course, however. They do peak in the teens and decline from then through old age (Horn, 1970). Thus changes in intelligence and the corresponding changes in educability have been found to be due to performance changes, like speed, rather than to a decrease in learning ability (Schaie & Willis, 1979).

Figure 6.3

Approximate pattern of intellectual development over time

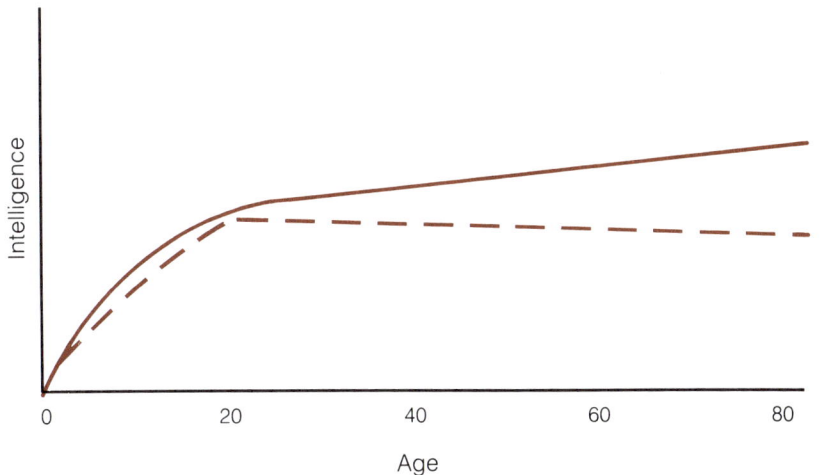

Source: Data from John L. Horn, "Organization of Data on Life-Span Development of Human Abilities," in L. R. Goulet and Paul B. Baltes (Eds.), *Life-Span Developmental Psychology: Research and Theory* (New York: Academic Press, 1970), and K. Werner Schaie and Sherry L. Willis, "Life Span-Development: Implications for Education," in Lee S. Shulman (Ed.), *Review of Research in Education 6* (Itasca, Ill.: F. E. Peacock Publishers, 1979).

Crystallized intelligence (g_c)

Fluid intelligence (g_f)

Teachers who work with adults, such as classroom teachers at PTA meetings, instructors in adult education classes, and many college professors, therefore need to use different teaching techniques and must be prepared for wider variations in ability, knowledge, skills, and interest levels. Speed of response should be minimized unless it is an integral part of the subject under study, and self-pacing by students and individualized teaching should be provided where possible. The subject matter must be of interest to adults, many of whom will not learn material that is meaningless to them. Adults also usually can leave school or drop a course at any time. The adult education teacher, rather than being primarily a director of learning, is a facilitator or resource person. The goal is to help adults maintain and transfer their knowledge and skills as much as it is to assist them in acquiring new capabilities (Schaie & Willis, 1979).

GROUP DIFFERENCES IN INTELLIGENCE

In the same way that individual differences in the three developmental domains are related to the heredity-environment controversy (see Chapter 2), so are mean differences in IQ among groups of people. In the case of group differences in measures of intelligence, however, a major point in the debate is how to determine a quantity called *heritability*.

Heritability (symbolized h^2) is the proportion of variability in intelligence in populations of people as they currently exist that is due solely to genetic contribution. Environmental effects and the interaction of genetics and environment are not included in this measure. While her-

Although tests reveal differences in the average measured intelligence of groups of people from different races, social classes, and occupations, students with the full range of cognitive abilities and skills have been found within each social class and racial grouping. It is not known whether racial differences are totally cultural or in part reflect biological differences.

itability is a description of the current state of affairs which does not include environmental effects, it does indicate how the distribution of intelligence within a group of people would change if either their environments or their heredities, or both, were changed within current existing ranges. It tells nothing about what would happen to intelligence if either the genetic or the environmental components, or both, changed *outside* their current ranges. Thus heritability is a characterization of a *group* under study, not of a trait. It does *not* mean genetically fixed (Lerner, 1976). We will consider the controversy over heritability in the next section, after examining the evidence that group differences do exist.

The most significant indication of group differences emerges when the *mean*, or average, intelligence test scores of large groups of people from different races, social classes, and occupations are compared. Differences in means are consistently found in research studies, even when different intelligence tests or achievement tests are used. Despite these mean differences, it is important to recognize that *people with the full range of cognitive abilities and skills have been found within each social class and racial grouping.*

MEAN DIFFERENCES IN IQ RELATED TO SOCIAL CLASS, OCCUPATION, AND RESIDENCY

There has been a great deal of research examining the mean differences in IQs for people in different social classes and occupations, as well as for people who live in rural, urban, and suburban areas. The results are interrelated, reflecting the close relations among social class, occupation, and residency. In fact, social class is usually defined in terms of occupation, area of residency, parents' educational level, or income.

Social Class Differences

According to Eysenck and Fulker (1979), the mean IQ for the middle class is about 107, while the mean for the lower class is about 92, a difference of about 1 *standard deviation*, the statistic used to indicate the difference between an observed score and the mean score (see Chapter 16).* This obviously simplified finding would vary depending on

---

* A standard deviation is a statistic that denotes the variability of scores in a distribution. For practical purposes, we can say that approximately two thirds of the scores in a normal distribution fall within 1 standard deviation of the mean, either above it or below it. If an intelligence test has a mean of 100 and a standard deviation of 15, then about 68 percent of the scores earned on it will fall between 85 and 115. Virtually all scores will fall within the range of plus or minus 3 standard deviations from the mean.

how the middle and lower classes are defined. Using the occupational frame of reference, Eysenck chose to define lower class as referring to those who have manual jobs and middle class as referring to those who have nonmanual jobs. These are mean IQs; people representing both extremes in intellectual ability will be found in each social class.

In this country, there has been a significant amount of upward and downward mobility between the lower and middle classes. In the 1950s, for example, it is estimated that between 30 and 35 percent of the men whose fathers held manual jobs moved to nonmanual ones, thus changing from the lower to the middle class. During this same period, however, between 25 and 24 percent of the men whose fathers held nonmanual jobs moved to manual ones and so changed from the middle to the lower class (Lipset & Bendix, 1959).

Occupational Differences

The relation of intelligence to occupational status is clear. When Harrell and Harrell (1945) analyzed massive data on Army General Classification Test scores for civilian occupations, they found that the average IQs of groups with professional and white-collar occupations, such as lawyers, teachers, and pharmacists, were 120 or greater. Groups with skilled manual labor occupations, such as mechanics and electricians, had mean IQs between 100 and 120, while those for groups with semiskilled manual labor jobs, like miners and truckdrivers, ranged between 85 and 100. These figures are only means, and much more variability in IQs can be found among semiskilled workers than among professional and white-collar workers. Therefore a truckdriver who is highly intelligent is more common than a lawyer who is dull.

One indication of the relation between intelligence and occupation is the eventual occupations of the persons studied in Terman's longitudinal study, which started in the early 1920s with a survey of over 1,500 children with IQs of 140 or more. The developmental histories of these persons over some 40 years were reported in a series called Genetic Studies of Genius, as we noted in Chapter 5. By the latest report (Oden, 1968), 86 percent of the 759 men who could be located in 1960 held professional or semiprofessional jobs, and some were nationally known scientists, writers, lawyers, diplomats, or executives. Other men reported different patterns: Some did not finish high school, and a few had been jailed. The patterns for women were quite different, probably due at least in part to the prevailing cultural standard of those times which dictated that careers were not important or even appropriate for women. Slightly less than half of these women were employed, but about 63 percent of those employed were in professional or semiprofessional jobs. Further, many of the unemployed women were civic leaders, engaged in prestigious, demanding volunteer work. So, in general, these high IQ people were involved in prestigious and often lucrative work.

The relation between IQ and job performance is not very strong, however (Jensen, 1980). There are several probable reasons for this, including the difficulty of measuring job performance and the fact that many occupations require special skills that are not measured by intelligence tests. So intelligence is important for some jobs, but many other characteristics enter into successful job performance. In Terman's study of the gifted, those who became successful had better physical and mental health, higher ambitions, and personalities that were attractive to other people (Oden, 1968).

Other studies have found that many people who were classified as mentally retarded in relation to IQ and low achievement in school can function adequately as adults in the world. In one such group, 62 percent of the men and 69 percent of the women were entirely self-supporting well into middle age, when the study ended, and 31 percent of the remaining men and 15 percent of the remaining women were partially self-supporting (Baller, Charles, & Miller, 1967).

Rural-Urban-Suburban Differences

Mean differences in IQ are also found when the urban or rural character of the place of residency is the variable of interest in the research study. Coleman (1966) found that children who lived in suburban areas had the highest mean IQ, while those living in rural areas had the lowest, and urban children were in the middle. Students in metropolitan areas of 50,000 people and above in grades 1, 3, 6, 9, and 12 had higher average ability and achievement scores than those who lived in rural areas. These results are comparable to those found for different occupations and social classes.

RACIAL DIFFERENCES IN IQ AND ACHIEVEMENT

Race differences have been studied most frequently with blacks because they are the largest racial minority in this country. Racial differences in IQ and achievement also are related to social class, occupation, and residency differences, with many minorities being clustered in urban or rural areas where they fill lower-class jobs. More whites than blacks achieve higher occupational status, at least partly because academic achievement is required for entrance into many careers (Scarr & Weinberg, 1976).

Although scores from infant intelligence tests are not stable, they do show consistent race differences between blacks and whites which favor blacks. Black infants have higher mean scores on the Bayley Scales of Infant Intelligence than white infants, for example (Bayley, 1965; Jensen, 1969). But, by school age, that difference has been reversed. The results of hundreds of studies indicate that the average IQ score for whites is about 1 standard deviation (15 points) above that for blacks. The Coleman Report (1966), which reported studies of about 60,000 students in 4,000 U.S. schools, found that whites and Orientals scored about 1 standard deviation above blacks on school achievement tests and on intelligence tests, whether verbal or nonverbal (see Chapter 14 for other results of this study). The mean IQs and achievement scores for the other disadvantaged racial minority groups, such as Hispanics and American Indians, generally fall between those for whites and blacks.

Figure 6.4, which compares distributions of IQ scores of two racially different groups, presents the distributions in graphic form. The distribution on the left is based on the scores of 1,800 black elementary school children (grades 1 through 6) selected at random for testing in 1960 from five southeastern states of the United States (Kennedy, Van de Riet, & White, 1963). The mean for that sample was 80.7, and the standard deviation for the distribution was 12.4. This particular mean is approximately five points lower than is usually reported for estimates of groups of black people when they take intelligence tests, perhaps due to a heavier density of rural than urban residencies in that region of the country. (Such regional differences are about the same for both blacks and whites.) The standard deviation of 12.4 is also somewhat lower than is usually found for black groups studied.

The distribution on the right is based on a large national sample of white school children. Their mean was 101.8, and the standard deviation was 16.4. These values conform to what is typically discovered when the intelligence of large samples of white students is estimated by existing measures of intelligence.

The difference in estimates of intelligence is usually slightly less than that reflected in Figure 6.4. Typically the difference lies between two thirds of a standard deviation and 1.33 standard deviations, with the mean falling at about 1 standard deviation. Since the standard deviations of most intelligence tests are 15 or 16 points, the common estimate of *obtained* differences in *measured* intelligence is about 15 points. Racial differences in academic achievement are congruent with these differences in measured intelligence (Jensen, 1980).

That these differences exist whenever large unselected samples of people are tested with existing measures of intelligence has been demonstrated many times (Jensen, 1980). Why the differences occur is not easy to explain. To say the least, the issue is a highly controversial one. Some public school systems in large cities have discontinued the use of standardized intelligence tests on the grounds that their scores are det-

Figure 6.4

*Approximate distribution of IQs for
black and white U.S. schoolchildren*

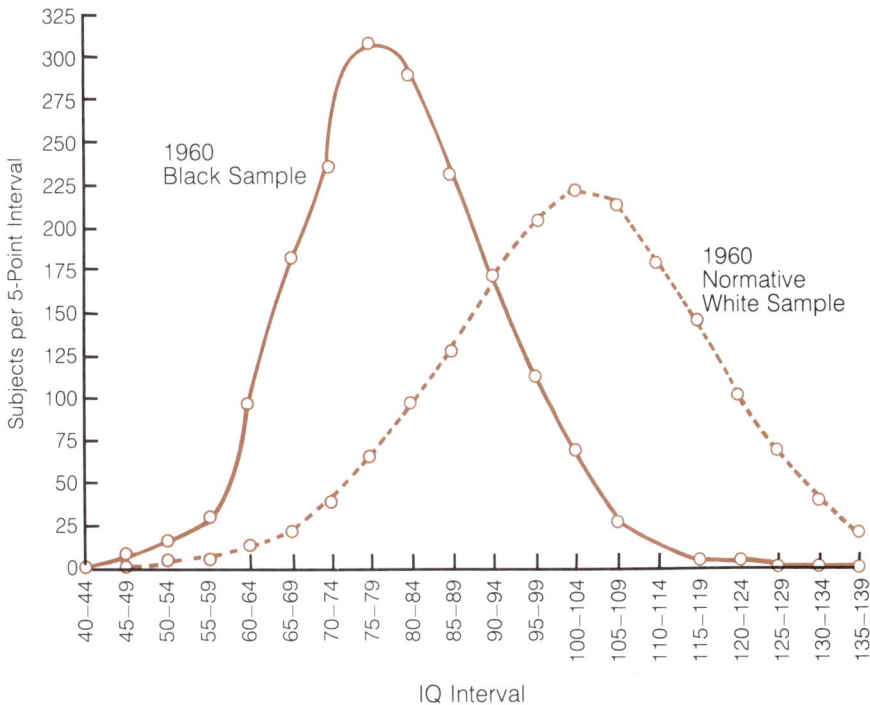

1960
Black Sample

1960
Normative
White Sample

Subjects per 5-Point Interval

IQ Interval

Source: W. A. Kennedy, V. Van de Riet, and J. C. White, Jr.,
"A Normative Sample of Intelligence and Achievement of Negro
Elementary School Children in the Southeastern United States,"
Monographs of the Society for Research in Child Development,
vol. 28 (1963), No. 6, Ser. No. 90. Adapted from Figure 2, page 68.

rimental to the welfare of minority children. Many people, including
professional educators and psychologists, are convinced that the tests discriminate against minority children because of the way they use language
and draw on cultural knowledge that is more accessible to children from
the white middle classes than it is to others. Efforts to devise culture-
fair standardized intelligence tests will be described in Chapter 17.

When U.S. IQ tests are translated into other languages, the results
are variable. Translating them into "Puerto Rican" Spanish did not improve the IQ means for Puerto Ricans and Mexican Americans; they

were lower, on the average, than the IQ means for whites on the English version of the test. When the performance subtests of the WISC were introduced into Japan, however, Japanese children between the ages of 5 and 15 had a mean performance IQ of 103, using the U.S. norms, compared to a mean score of 100 for white U.S. children of those ages. The WAIS and WPPSI performance subtests also have been used with the Japanese; when the results for all three IQ tests are combined, the mean performance IQ for Japanese is estimated to be about 107, compared to the U.S. norm of 100. Similar comparisons for the verbal scores are difficult to make because the questions had to be changed when translated into Japanese in order to make them relevant to the Japanese culture (Lynn, 1977).

All major bilingual groups in the United States have mean verbal IQs that are slightly, but significantly, lower than their nonverbal IQs, indicating the involvement of a language factor in the verbal scores. The language used on an intelligence test or used by the person giving the test has less and less effect on test scores as the time students spend in schools using the English language increases, however (Jensen, 1980).

INTELLIGENCE: GIVEN OR GOTTEN?

As the preceding section demonstrates, mean differences in IQs between groups do exist. But what they mean and what causes them are very difficult to determine. This has been the center of a great deal of controversy for years, especially in relation to the discrimination which has regularly closed off opportunities for members of minority groups in this country.

The issue provides evidence of the lack of objectivity of many research scientists who, like other people, operate from belief systems that affect the conclusions they draw. Their beliefs can determine the research questions they ask and the methods they use to study them, as well as their conclusions. Two small but extreme groups of scientists have reached opposite conclusions about whether intelligence is determined by the environment or heredity, an extension of the nature-nurture developmental controversy described in Chapter 2.

Some extremists say that the environment is primarily responsible for group differences in IQ. According to them, if environments and opportunities were equalized, racial, ethnic, and social class differences in intelligence would disappear because intelligence is "gotten" from the environment. At the other extreme are the strict hereditarians who say that no matter what is done with the environment, these differences will remain because intelligence is given to people through their genes, and different groups possess different gene pools. Most experts feel that the "truth" is somewhere in the middle, that both environment and genes significantly affect intelligence.

The controversy over the heritability of intelligence, or the proportion of variability in intelligence in existing populations that is due to genetics (as the term was defined in a preceding section) flared sharply in 1969 with the publication of an article by Arthur Jensen titled "How Much Can We Boost IQ and School Achievement?" The conflagration has had several outcomes. The best one is that a great deal of research on intelligence has been stimulated, and the quality of this research has improved more quickly than it would have without the debate (Nichols, 1979). Even so, there is no evidence that would allow the issue to be permanently settled, and there never will be. In order to settle the issue, there would have to be experimental research in which the genetics and the environments of people are controlled and manipulated by researchers, and in this case that obviously is not possible. People cannot be expected to mate just because their names are randomly drawn by a researcher or to allow their children to be taken from them and placed with different parents in a randomly selected environment. And, as of now, we cannot directly manipulate those genes that are responsible for a person's intelligence. So we use what evidence is available, primarily from nonexperimental sources. All of these sources include aspects of genes and environment that are not controlled and so cannot be used to settle the debate.

GENETIC AND ENVIRONMENTAL SIMILARITIES AND DIFFERENCES

One major line of research examines the IQs of people who share various degrees of genetic and environmental similarity. Identical twins have the same basic genetic makeup. Fraternal twins, siblings, or a pairing of a biological parent and child share half of their genes. Adopted children and their adoptive parents and siblings are genetically unrelated.

People living in the same home are assumed to have similar environments, while those in different homes are assumed to have different ones. In general, however, the environments of people in different homes may be quite similar or quite different. Children raised in the same home also may have somewhat different environments; the environment of the firstborn in a family is much different from that of the fifth child, for example. Moreover, as we noted in Chapter 3, girls often are raised differently than their brothers are because of the parents' expectations about appropriate sex-role behaviors.

If genetics makes all the difference in IQ, then being raised apart or together would not affect it at all. The groups most similar in IQ would be identical twins, since they are the most similar genetically. Groups with moderate similarity in IQ would be those sharing half of their genes, such as fraternal twins. Genetically unrelated people would not be similar in IQ at all.

If the environment makes all of the difference, then people in the same environments would have highly similar IQs, regardless of their genetic relationships. Similarities in IQs would decrease as the similarities in the environments decreased. So, for example, an adopted child's IQ would be quite similar to that of the adoptive parents and even more so to those of adoptive siblings, since they all would live together. Adopted children's IQs would be more dissimilar to their biological parents and siblings the more their adoptive environments differed from that of their biological families.

Research tends to support neither of these extreme positions but rather the influence of both genetics and the environment, with the major influence being genetics. Figure 6.5, based on correlations reported in Eysenck and Fulker (1979), shows the typical median value or range of values for the *correlation coefficients* between pairs of people in each of these groups.* Similar data were reported in other studies, such as Mehrens and Lehmann (1978) and Nichols (1979).

Each coefficient in the figure, signified by r, shows the similarity in the rank order of the IQ scores of the people in the two groups being compared. A coefficient of 0 means no similarity in rank order at all. A coefficient of 1 means perfect similarity, with the high IQs in one group being associated with the high IQs in the other. For a group of identical twins, for instance, a correlation coefficient of 1 ($r = 1$) would occur if the relative position of each twin from a pair was the same in each group. So if one twin had the highest IQ in one group, the other would have to have the highest IQ in the other group. Correspondingly, for the twin who had the lowest IQ in one group, that twin's sibling would have to have the lowest IQ in the other group too. In this case, the rank order of the twins' IQs in each group would match exactly. A correlation coefficient of about 0.5 indicates moderate similarity.

As Figure 6.5 shows, identical twins raised together are highly similar in IQs, while people who are unrelated to each other genetically and who do not live together have no similarity in measured intelligence. The groups follow the order of genetic similarity, with identical twins

---

*Variables are correlated when they vary together, but there is no implication that one varies because of changes in the other. The correlation coefficient indicates the magnitude of the relationship between the variables. Correlation coefficients can range from 0.00 to 1.00 and can be either positive or negative. The higher the coefficient, the better is the researcher's ability to predict where an individual's score on one variable will fall, given knowledge of his or her score on the other variable. Zero indicates no relationship, and perfect relationship is signified by 1.00. The sign of the coefficient indicates the direction of the relationship but has no effect on its strength. Thus, a correlation of -0.75 is equally as strong as one of $+0.75$.

Figure 6.5

Median correlations between IQ scores and genetic or
environmental similarity, as reported in major research studies

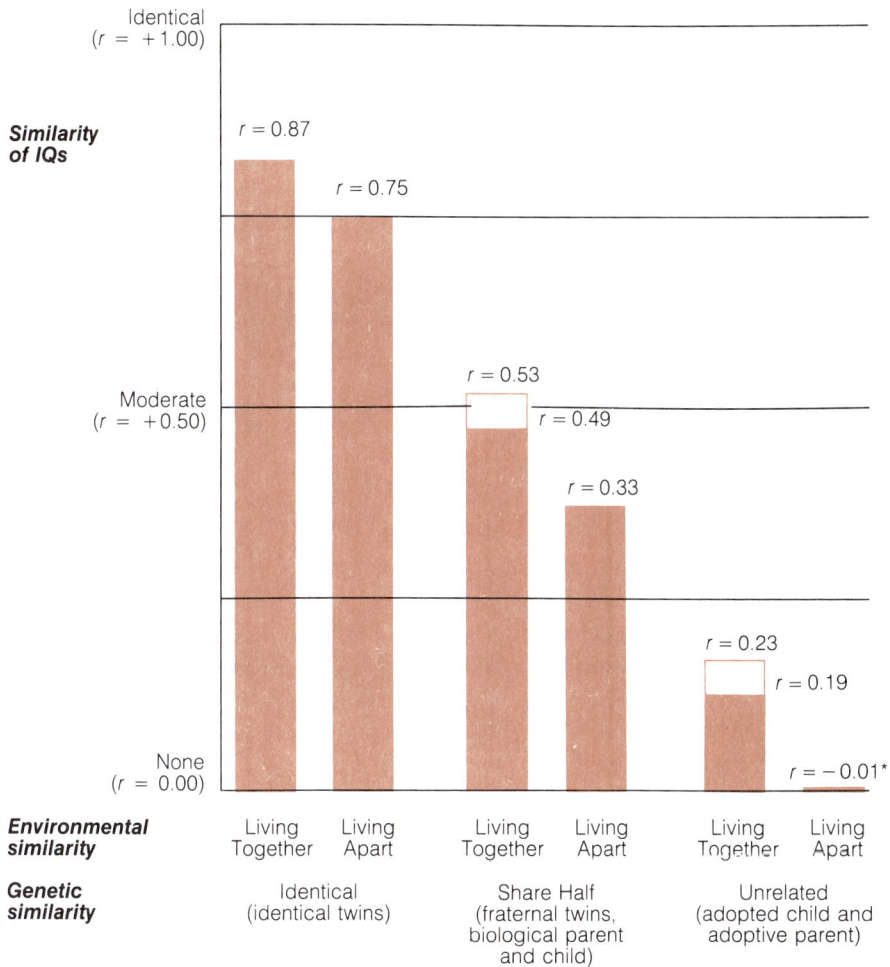

Identical
(*r* = +1.00)

**Similarity
of IQs**

r = 0.87

r = 0.75

Moderate
(*r* = +0.50)

r = 0.53

r = 0.49

r = 0.33

r = 0.23

r = 0.19

None
(*r* = 0.00)

r = −0.01*

Environmental similarity	Living Together	Living Apart	Living Together	Living Apart	Living Together	Living Apart
Genetic similarity	Identical (identical twins)		Share Half (fraternal twins, biological parent and child)		Unrelated (adopted child and adoptive parent)	

*This −0.01 is so close to 0.00 that it means no similarity in IQ scores.

Source: Correlations as reported in Hans J. Eysenck and D. W. Fulker,
The Structure and Measure of Intelligence (Berlin: Springer-Verlag,
1979) and other research. Ranges are shown where the majority
of research indicates such variability.

being most similar, groups sharing half of their genes at the midpoint in IQ similarity, and groups with no genetic similarity having the least similarity in measured IQ.

While genetics is obviously most important in these results, the environment still exerts a substantial influence. The IQs of genetically unrelated people in the same environment correlate between 0.19 and 0.23, which is significantly higher than the correlation of 0 for unrelated people living in different environments.

These research results clearly indicate that both genetics and environment affect intelligence. One useful way to think about this is that genetics sets the limits on the intellectual ability of an individual, while the environment places the intelligence of the individual within these limits.

Using the results of such similarity studies, Nichols (1979) found that between 75 and 80 percent of the variability in IQ scores for whites in the United States and in Northern Europe, within the current range of environments in these places, is due to genetics. Minority groups, including blacks, have not been adequately studied to allow heritability estimates to be made for them. Even if they had, heritability estimates apply only within racial groups, not between them.

PROSPECTS FOR RAISING INTELLIGENCE LEVELS

The research evidence on the environment-heredity controversy as it is related to group differences suggests bleak prospects for raising people's intelligence levels. It has shown that IQ is related to social class membership, occupation, and rural, urban, or suburban residence. Moreover, at least for whites, intelligence has been found to be highly heritable; that is, genetics plays a larger role in individual variations in intelligence than environment does.

According to Lerner (1976) and others, however, there is no evidence that the mean differences in intelligence and achievement between races that have been found are genetically determined. Within any group, in addition, there always are variations that are due to genetics; that is, all members of a group do not share the same heritability in regard to intelligence. Society therefore must work to reduce the differences between the groups, including differences by race, social class, sex, and so on. Two types of interventions related to environmental changes in the school and other life situations have been tried to accomplish this.

Effects of School Environment on IQ

It should be no surprise that school attendance has been found to result in increased academic achievement and probably in increased IQ. Jencks et al. (1972), for example, estimated that the IQ increases one point for every year a person stays in school past elementary school. This yields an increase of 4 to 6 points, almost one half standard deviation, for each person who completes high school. Husen (1951), who controlled for initial IQ in his research study, found that children who completed some secondary schooling had IQs between five and seven points higher than those who did not. Since people from the middle and high social classes are more likely to stay in secondary school than others, however, the effects of school are inextricably mixed with the effects of social class in both these results.

Compensatory educational programs based on the idea of raising the aptitudes and achievement levels of children from racial minorities or lower social class groups have been tried, but the results of such interventions are not clear-cut. As part of the War on Poverty, starting in 1964, the federal government funded Head Start for preschool-aged children, Follow Through for children from kindergarten through third grade, and other similar programs. The reasoning was that the home environments of children in certain groups do not prepare them for school, and so they enter at a disadvantage compared to children from the mainstream or majority culture. The compensatory educational programs were supposed to provide the knowledge and skills children need for successful performance in school and so correct the academic shortcomings which could limit the entire lives of disadvantaged children.

Initial evaluations of children who participated in Head Start often showed small gains in IQ and achievement, as well as in various personality characteristics needed for success in school, in comparison to children in a control group. Unfortunately, these gains did not persist after two or three years in elementary school (Weinberg, 1979). However, one conclusion agreed on by many is that an educational program should not necessarily result in an IQ gain anyway.

Evaluations of the Follow Through programs have produced contradictory results. Follow Through schools used one of several different instructional models which varied according to the roles of the teacher and the child as primary initiator or responder. At least initially, the evidence indicates, the direct instruction, language deficit model of Bereiter and Englemann (1966), in which the teacher was the primary initiator and the pupil the primary responder, resulted in the highest achievement in the basic skills, in comparison to the control programs and the other Follow Through programs. Nichols (1979) notes, however, that reexamination of the data showed that Follow Through children, as well as those in the other programs, did no better than children in the control groups.

Thus the effects of compensatory educational programs like Head Start and Follow Through are not clear. No educational intervention can possibly match adoption or intensive home intervention as a means of removing the learners' social class disadvantage, however.

Effects of Life Situations on IQ

Some very clear evidence that the environment does affect IQ scores comes from studies of adopted children. When children are placed in living environments that are significantly better than their biological home environments, their IQs increase dramatically. For example, Scarr and Weinberg (1976) studied about 130 black and interracial black-white children who were adopted into white families in which the parents were highly educated and above average in income and occupational status. Most of the children were one year old or less at the time of adoption. By the early to middle elementary school years these children had a mean IQ of 106, slightly above average, and also scored slightly above average on achievement tests. If they had remained in their biological homes, their mean IQ probably would have been about 90. Thus the change in environment was accompanied by an average increase of about 1 standard deviation in IQ, which is the difference between the mean IQs of blacks and whites in the general population. According to Scarr and Weinberg, if all black children were raised in homes similar to these good adoptive homes, their IQs should be 10 to 20 points higher. (This, of course, does not mean that the adoptive parents ought to be of a different race than the child. The critical variables are the intelligence and educational levels of the adoptive parents.)

Other studies of adoption have made similar findings. Skodak and Skeels (1949), for example, studied 180 children who had been adopted before six months of age. When 100 of these children were tested at about 14 years of age, their mean IQ was 107, with a range from 65 to 144. If they had not been adopted, Eysenck (1979) estimated, their mean IQ would have been 91; their biological mothers' mean IQ was 86.

Nevertheless, the same studies show a high degree of relationship between the adopted children's IQ and their biological parents' IQs. This is due to the nature of the correlation coefficient, which indicates how well the position of the child's IQ relative to the rest of the children's IQs (that is, the rank order) matches that of the rank order of the child's parents' IQ relative to those of the other parents. A change of environment does not change the child's relative position within the group of children; it raises all of the children's IQs, so the mean IQ of the adopted group increases. Thus, even if IQ were perfectly heritable for all people, large environmental changes would still change the IQ. Jensen (1969) indicated that the environment can shift IQ by 6 points for many people and can change it by 20 or 30 points for very deprived children.

It appears that intense, high-quality intervention in the original homes of very deprived children also increases IQ scores. In the Milwaukee Project, for example, mothers of children in poverty areas were given intensive training in child rearing, and the children eventually received educational interventions. Compared to a similar group, in elementary school the project children were significantly higher in IQ, with placement in the normal range while the control children were in the retarded range. It was difficult to obtain complete information on the ongoing project, however, which prevents accurate evaluation of its effects (Nichols, 1979). The estimated per-child cost for each year in the project was $10,000 (Eysenck, 1979).

While it has been established that large-scale environmental changes can affect IQs, the exact factors in the environment that cause the changes are unknown. The interventions that are really effective, like adoption, are so complex that it is imposible to identify the specific factors responsible for the changes. Research has identified environmental factors in middle-class homes that are associated with high and low IQs; for example, infants and young children who participate in language mastery experiences with adults have higher average cognitive achievement than other children (Carew, 1980). Parental expectations for achievement also are consistently related to higher cognitive performance in preschool and elementary school children. But these studies are not experimental in nature, so it cannot be concluded that these environmental factors actually cause higher performance.

INTELLIGENCE AND SCHOOL LEARNING

Classroom teachers cannot change a student's genetic input into intelligence. They can change the school environment, however. They can examine their rationale for ability grouping of students on the basis of social background characteristics, as well as past grades and recommendations and performance on standardized tests (see Chapter 14). They work with achievement in the here and now, not intellectual aptitude for the future. Although IQ is a moderately good predictor of achievement, so is past achievement. Other individual characteristics, such as motivation, and environmental characteristics like the amount of time students are given to learn also can affect school learning.

All these factors influence the nature of the teacher's interactions with learners in the instructional process. Because reading and problem solving are probably the most important life skills that anyone can acquire in school, these should be stressed for all students. For general testing purposes, many experts (e.g., Jensen, 1980) recommend that achievement tests, not intelligence tests, be used in schools. An IQ score alone is an insufficient basis for determining the readiness of any learner to benefit from classroom instruction.

Generally, the major differences between more and less intelligent children are related to speed and completeness in learning new material. Smarter children learn faster and more completely (Siegler & Richards, in press). Speed of learning, often called time to learn, or *TTL*, has been the basis for some interesting research. Gettinger and White (1979), for example, found that for fourth- and sixth-graders, TTL was more strongly related to school achievement as measured by standardized achievement tests than IQ was. This result held across four general content areas (vocabulary, spelling, mathematics, and reading). TTL varies depending on the achievement levels of the students, the difficulty of the tasks, and other instructor and student characteristics. This view of learning and intelligence fits well with the mastery learning idea (see Chapter 12), which suggests that time is the most important variable in learning and that, given enough time, almost everyone will master the necessary skills.

CHAPTER 6 IN RETROSPECT

There are three basic psychological approaches to the study of intelligence. The psychometric approach views intelligence as a quantifiable characteristic and uses traditional intelligence tests, such as the Wechsler and the Stanford-Binet, to measure it. Theories in this approach characterize intelligence as having one general aspect or factor, generally referred to as g, as in Binet's and Wechsler's theories; two factors, such as Spearman's theory of one g with many specific factors, each called s, and Cattell and Horn's theory of fluid and crystallized intelligence; or many group factors, such as Thurstone's Primary Mental Abilities view. The emphases in the psychometric approach are on measurement and individual differences. A second approach to intelligence is Piaget's theory, which views intelligence in a qualitative manner and maintains that highly intelligent people have passed through four successive stages of thought to reach their current level. Measures of current intellectual functioning are based on the tasks Piaget uses to characterize the stages, but tests of intelligence based on Piaget's theory are used primarily for research, not to indicate an individual's current intellectual functioning. The emphasis in this approach is on the structure of the intellect. The third approach is information processing, which tries to determine what symbols are involved and how they are manipulated to yield intelligent behavior. There are no intelligence tests based on this approach. The emphasis is on identifying commonalities in how knowledge is created and used.

Intelligence tests measure general learning, while achievement tests measure learning specific to school. Test results from both would tend to place a student at about the same cognitive level. IQ scores on standardized, individually administered, psychometric intelligence tests vary from about 40 to 160, with a mean of 100. They accurately predict school achievement for groups of students, especially in verbally oriented subjects, and are moderately accurate in their predictions for individuals.

Intelligence changes rapidly during infancy and the preschool period. It starts to stabilize at about five or six years of age and continues to grow and stabilize throughout the teens. Crystallized aspects generally maintain or continue to increase until old age, while fluid aspects decline from the teens on.

There are many interrelated mean group differences in IQ, including differences by social class, occupation, residency, and race. People in the upper and middle classes score higher on intelligence tests, on the average, than those in the lower class. People with professional and white-collar occupations have higher mean IQs than skilled manual laborers, and both groups have higher mean IQs than semiskilled manual laborers. Suburban people have higher mean IQs than urban people do, and both groups have higher mean IQs than rural people. From school age on in the United States, whites and Orientals score higher, on the average, on intelligence and achievement tests than Hispanics and American Indians, while all four groups score higher than blacks. Even with intelligence tests that are designed to be culture-fair, the majority groups, on the average, outscore the minority groups. Regardless of these mean differences, people at all levels of intellectual ability are found in each racial and social class group.

One reason for the differences in intelligence and achievement between groups is obviously discrimination. But a large body of research has examined data relating to the influence of heredity and environment on IQ and achievement. Heritability estimates indicate that between 75 and 80 percent of the variability in IQ for whites is due to genetics; accurate estimates have not been established for other racial groups. As genetic similarity between people increases, so does the similarity of their IQs.

Even so, the environment can exert a large influence on IQ. When children are adopted into homes that provide significantly better living conditions than their biological home environments, they often develop IQs between 10 and 20 points higher than they would have if they had stayed with their biological parents. In the Milwaukee Project, slum children who participated in the project had IQs in the average range, while the contols' IQs were in the retarded range. School intervention results are not as clear. Researchers cannot agree on whether Head Start and Follow Through have made any differences. In general, though, school attendance does increase IQ and achievement.

The classroom teacher should take learners as they come, make no assumptions about them based on race or social class membership, and assist each one to develop as much as possible. Each learner in school deserves the chance to be an individual rather than just a group member. Moreover, schooling is the basis for entry into many occupations, and occupational status and the income derived from working generally determine a person's standard of living and social class. These factors help set the general quality of the environment, which affects not only the adults involved but the children in the household too. And so the cycle begins again.

1. Which of the three approaches to intelligence described in this chapter (psychometric, Piagetian, information processing) most clearly fits your own conception of intelligence? Why? What does each approach have to offer teachers, and what educational implications can be drawn from each one?

2. Should a student's IQ scores be made available to the student, the student's parents, and/or the student's teachers? Why or why not? Do IQ tests have a place in education? If so, how should they be used? How shouldn't they be used?

3. How much can IQ scores change during (a) infancy, (b) childhood, (c) adolescence, (d) adulthood, and (e) old age? Discuss how the environment, disease, and personal characteristics contribute to IQ change at all age levels. Is nutrition important for infants' intellectual development?

4. IQ scores are related to social class, residency (rural, urban, suburban), occupation, and race. What environmental influences could contribute to these group differences? Should these four attributes be used to roughly estimate a person's IQ? Why or why not?

5. Suppose a white boy had the genetic potential to be classified as very superior in intelligence. His parents follow Mark Twain's suggestion and raise the boy in a barrel until he is 12, feeding him through the bunghole. Knowing that IQ is highly heritable for whites, do you think the boy at 12 years of age would be very superior in intelligence? At 30 years of age? Why or why not?

6. Should an educational program such as Head Start be expected to raise children's IQs? Why or why not?

Introductory Level

Evans, Ellis D., and McCandless, Boyd R. *Children and Youth: Psychosocial Development.* 2nd ed. New York: Holt, Rinehart & Winston, 1978.

This is a developmental text that has an especially good chapter on intelligence. The authors define the term, discuss its developmental aspects, describe the psychometric and cognitive-developmental approaches, and present the major influences on intellectual development (nutrition, family, interventions, and schooling).

Advanced Level

For many of the books and articles about intelligence at the advanced level, a basic understanding of the correlation coefficient is required. The three sources presented here emphasize different aspects of intelligence:

> Mehrens, William A., and Lehmann, Irvin J. *Measurement and Evaluation in Education and Psychology.* 2nd ed. New York: Holt, Rinehart & Winston, 1978.

Definitions and theories of intelligence, the heredity versus environment issue, the relationships of social class and race to intelligence, and the stability of intelligence are discussed. Also included are test descriptions (the Stanford-Binet and Wechsler tests, as well as infant and several group-administered tests, with example items).

> Siegler, Robert S., and Richards, D. Dean. The development of intelligence. In Robert Sternberg (Ed.), *Handbook of Intelligence Research.* Cambridge, England: Cambridge University Press, in press.

This chapter contains very complete discussions of implicit theories of intelligence, psychometric theories and tests, the Piagetian approach, and information processing, as well as discussing unresolved issues in intelligence.

> Jensen, Arthur R. *Bias in Mental Testing.* New York: Free Press, 1980.

Jensen's book, although controversial, contains some very interesting material. Chapter 2 (Tests on Trial) presents a summary of the major lawsuits concerning achievement and aptitude standardized tests. Chapter 3 (The Drive for Equality) discusses discrimination, bias, and fairness in testing; uses of tests (for assessment, diagnosis, placement, and selection); and affirmative action. Chapter 15 (Uses and Abuses of Tests) reiterates Jensen's position that standardized tests are not biased against blacks (they actually favor them in selection).

Anastasi, Anne. *Psychological Testing.* 3rd ed. New York: Macmillan Co., 1968.   **REFERENCES**

Baller, W. R., Charles, D. C., and Miller, E. L. Mid-life attainment of the mentally retarded: A longitudinal study. *Genetic Psychology Monographs,* 1967, *75*(2), 235–329.

Bayley, Nancy. Comparisons of mental and motor test scores for ages 1–15 months by sex, birth order, race, geographical location, and education of parents. *Child Development,* 1965, *36*(2), 379–411.

Bereiter, C., and Englemann, S. *Teaching Disadvantaged Children in the Preschool.* Englewood Cliffs, N.J.: Prentice-Hall, 1966.

Carew, Jean V. Experience and the development of intelligence in young children at home and in day care. *Monographs of the Society for Research in Child Development,* 1980, *45*(6–7).

Coleman, James S., Campbell, E. Q., Hobson, C. J., McPartland, J., Mood, A. M., Weinfeld, F. D., and York, R. L. *Equality of Educational Opportunity.* Washington, D.C.: Government Printing Office, 1966.

Eysenck, Hans J., and Fulker, D. W. *The Structure and Measurement of Intelligence.* Berlin: Springer-Verlag, 1979.

Gettinger, Maribeth, and White, Mary Alice. Which is the stronger correlate of school learning: Time to learn or measured intelligence? *Journal of Educational Psychology,* 1979, *71*(4), 405–412.

Harrell, T. W., and Harrell, M. S. Army General Classification Test scores for civilian occupations. *Educational and Psychological Measurement,* 1945, *5*(3), 229–239.

Honzik, M. P., MacFarlane, J. W., and Allen, L. The stability of mental test performance between two and eighteen years. *Journal of Experimental Education,* 1948, *17*(2), 309–324.

Hopkins, Kenneth D., and Bracht, Glenn H. Ten-year stability of verbal and nonverbal IQ scores. *American Education Research Journal,* 1975, *12*(4), 469–477.

Horn, John L. Organization of data on life-span development of human abilities. In L. R. Goulet and Paul B. Baltes (Eds.), *Life-Span Developmental Psychology: Research and Theory.* New York: Academic Press, 1970.

Husen, T. The influence of schooling on IQ. *Theoria,* 1951, *17*, 61–88.

Inhelder, Barbel, and Piaget, Jean. *Growth of Logical Thinking from Childhood to Adolescence.* New York: Basic Books, 1958.

Jencks, C., Smith, M., Acland, H., Bane, M. J., Cohen, D., Gintis, H., Heyns, B., and Michelson, S. *Inequality: A Reassessment of the Effect of Family and Schooling in America.* New York: Basic Books, 1972.

Jensen, Arthur R. How much can we boost IQ and scholastic achievement? *Harvard Educational Review,* 1969, *39*, 1–123.

Jensen, Arthur R. *Bias in Mental Testing.* New York: Free Press, 1980.

Kennedy, W. A., Van de Riet, V., and White, J. C., Jr. A normative sample of intelligence and achievement of Negro elementary school children in the southeastern United States. *Monographs of the Society for Research in Child Development,* 1963, *28*(6).

Lachman, R., Lachman, J. L., and Butterfield, E. C. *Cognitive Psychology and Information Processing: An Introduction.* Hillsdale, N.J.: Lawrence Erlbaum Associates, 1979.

Lerner, Richard M. *Concepts and Theories of Human Development.* Reading, Mass.: Addison-Wesley Publishing Co., 1976.

Lipset, S. M., and Bendix, R. *Social Mobility in Industrial Society.* Berkeley, Cal.: University of California Press, 1959.

Lynn, R. The intelligence of the Japanese. *Bulletin of the British Psychology Society,* 1977, *30,* 69–72.

McCall, R. B., Appelbaum, M. I., and Hogarty, P. S. Developmental changes in mental performance. *Monographs of the Society for Research in Child Development,* 1973, *38*(3), 150.

Mehrens, William A., and Lehmann, Irvin J. *Measurement and Evaluation in Education and Psychology,* 2nd ed. New York: Holt, Rinehart & Winston, 1978.

Nichols, Robert C. Policy implications of the IQ controversy. In Lee S. Shulman (Ed.), *Review of Research in Education 6.* Itasca, Ill.: F. E. Peacock Publishers, 1979.

Oden, M. H. The fulfillment of promise: 40-year follow-up of the Terman gifted groups. *Genetic Psychology Monographs,* 1968, *77*(1), 3–93.

Scarr, Sandra, and Weinberg, Richard A. IQ test performance of black children adopted by white families. *American Psychologist,* 1976, *31*(10), 726–739.

Schaie, K. Werner, and Willis, Sherry L. Life span development: Implications for education. In Lee S. Shulman (Ed.), *Review of Research in Education 6.* Itasca, Ill.: F. E. Peacock Publishers, 1979.

Siegler, Robert S., and Richards, D. Dean. The development of intelligence. In Robert J. Sternberg (Ed.), *Handbook of Intelligence Research.* Cambridge, England: Cambridge University Press, in press.

Skodak, M., and Skeels, M. M. A final follow-up study on one hundred adopted children. *Journal of Genetic Psychology,* 1949, *75,* 85–125.

Sternberg, Robert J., Conway, Barbara E., Ketron, Jerry L., and Bernstein, Morty. *People's Conceptions of Intelligence.* Paper presented at the annual meeting of the American Psychological Association, New York, 1979.

Terman, Lewis M., and Merrill, Maud A. *Stanford-Binet Intelligence Scale: Manual for the Third Revision, Form L-M.* Boston: Houghton Mifflin Co., 1960.

Thurstone, L. L. Primary mental abilities. *Psychometric Monograph,* 1938, No. 1.

Tyler, Leona E. The intelligence we test—an evolving concept. In Lauren B. Resnick (Ed.), *The Nature of Intelligence.* New York: John Wiley & Sons, 1976.

Wechsler, David. *Manual for the Wechsler Intelligence Scale for Children—Revised.* New York: Psychological Corporation, 1974.

Weinberg, R. A. Early childhood education and intervention: Establishing an American tradition. *American Psychologist,* 1979, *34*(10), 912–916.

Yussen, Steven R., and Kane, Patrick T. *Children's Conceptions of Intelligence.* Technical Report 546. Wisconsin Research and Development Center for Individualized Schooling, University of Wisconsin, July 1980.

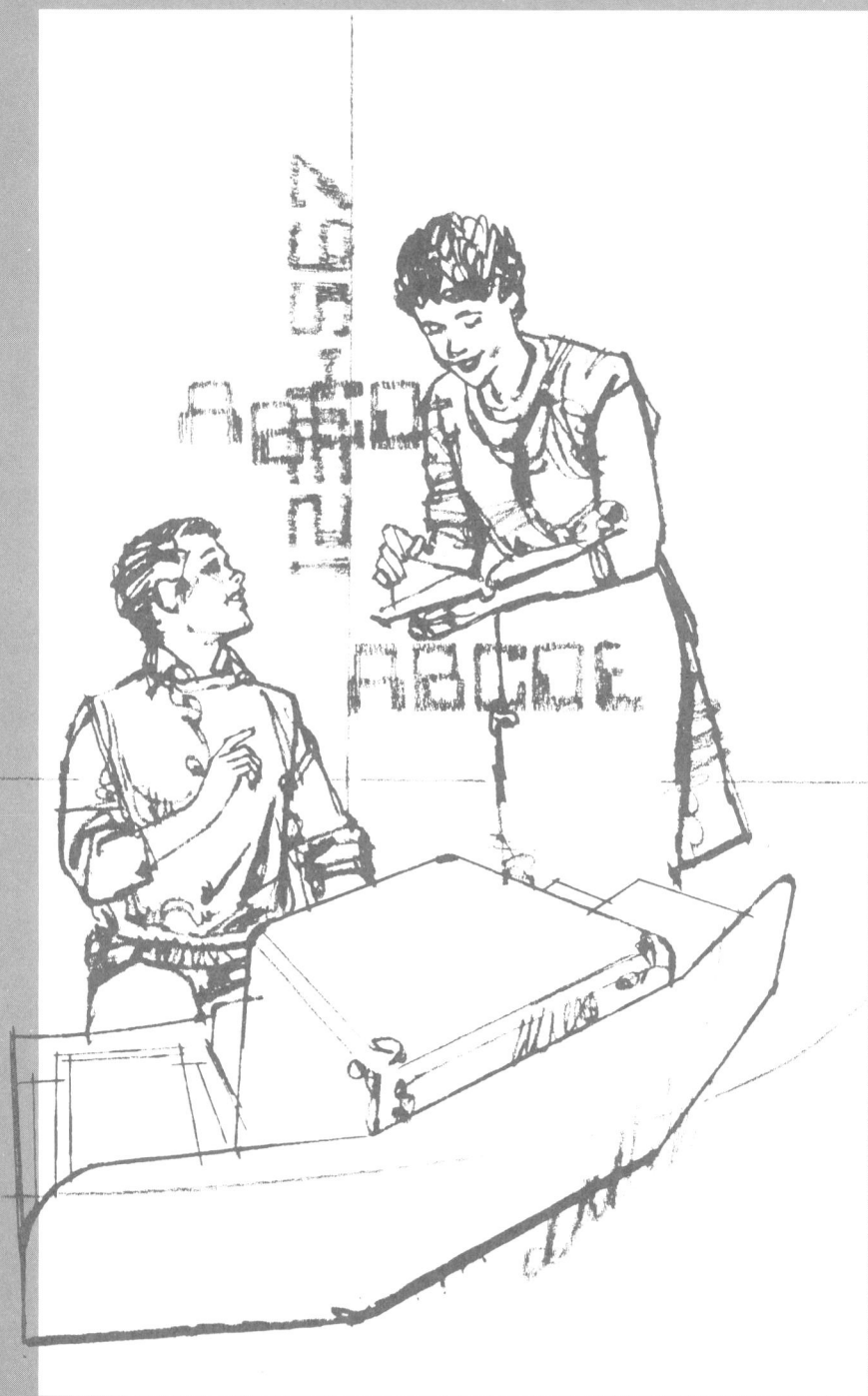

Learning, Thinking, and Motivation

Among all the reasons children and adolescents are required to attend school, "to learn" would be high on any list. Part II explores how children learn in school from many standpoints: how learning occurs; how beliefs, attitudes, and values are acquired or changed; how perplexing situations can be resolved by thinking; how students can be motivated to learn; and how learning and instruction are related.

Thinking, learning, and motivation are essential aspects of the instruction-learner interactions in the instructional process model introduced in Chapter 1. They apply to instruction provided to individual learners, or the first dimension of the model. But they are even more relevant to the second dimension, when the interactions are complicated by the need to present the instruction to classroom groups.

Chapter 7 examines how meaningful learning is added to the learner's cognitive structures, and Chapter 8 explains how behavior can be changed through reinforcement. Thinking is considered as an extension of learning in Chapter 10, which analyses reasoning in terms of critical and creative thinking, as well as problem solving. The relations between learning and the form of the instruction are examined in Chapter 12.

These chapters can provide an understanding of how learning takes place. But an understanding of why it occurs in some learners but not others depends on the individual learners' attitudes and values about the learning and their motivation to learn. These characteristics, which help determine the learners' readiness to learn, are examined in Chapters 9 and 11.

Learning as Cognitive Activity

 One of the first and most important jobs of the school is to teach children to read, write, and compute. These basic skills are indispensable in the learner's quest for knowledge about the world beyond his or her own immediate experience. Through such tasks as reading books, listening to lessons, and participating in discussions, students acquire bodies of knowledge which are refined, extended, and differentiated as the years pass and they undertake additional study. How the individual's organized bodies of knowledge, or *cognitive structure,* as we will describe them, are developed is a central concern of educational psychology. The teacher's interactions with students in the instructional process help them acquire accurate, comprehensive, and clearly defined structures that are appropriately interconnected with other such structures.

This chapter focuses on the learning of the information and concepts that are basic to large bodies of subject matter knowledge, such as literature, history, chemistry, and other fields of study. It examines how students learn subject matter as a cognitive activity, how they remember it, and how they apply, or transfer, what they have previously learned in learning new material. Because we believe that knowledge is learned more easily, and remembered and transferred better, if the learning process is *meaningful,* we will spell out what we mean by meaningful learning and meaningful material and contrast these concepts with rote (routine or repetitive) learning and material of limited meaningfulness.

THE NATURE OF SCHOOL LEARNING

Development and change in learners are the result of both maturation and learning, as we noted in Chapter 3. But all changes in behavior that are brought about by maturation are not classifiable as learning. Learning depends on the learner's *interaction* with the environment. A student may memorize a poem for English class or trace a frog's digestive system in the biology laboratory. In both cases, learning results from the student's active involvement with specific aspects of the environment: the poem or the frog.

Traditionally, learning has been defined as a change in behavior, more or less permanent in nature, which is the result of experience. We suggest altering this definition to include cognitive changes, or changes in how the learner views an aspect of the world, as well as behavioral changes. A high school boy studying biology who gains knowledge about the frog's digestive system by reading his textbook, examining the entrails of a frog he has dissected, and comparing his observations with the sketches in a laboratory manual may not undergo a directly observable or overt change in his behavior, but there will be a change in his understanding or comprehension of the topic.

This view of learning can be easily applied to the study of learning in schools. Many of the assignments that children and adolescents encounter during their elementary and secondary school years require the learning of new ideas and information. The changes students undergo as a result are sometimes, although not always, apparent as changes in behavior. Important changes also occur in the breadth and depth of their knowledge and understanding and in their ability to acquire additional ideas and information.

The tasks that teachers assign to implement the instructional process have several distinctive features. Perhaps the most important is their capacity to be learned in a *meaningful* way. When material is learned meaningfully it can be remembered for an indefinite length of time, and it can be related to other appropriate learning material. Meaningful learning, and the conditions that facilitate it, will be considered more thoroughly in a later section.

In addition to their meaningful nature, the learning tasks presented in school are often *conceptual* in nature. Over a span of years, the child is expected to learn broad, general concepts such as energy and force, or concepts of government, democracy, and justice. None of these concepts is learned once and for all, as it were. They all grow and undergo modification throughout the course of the learner's life cycle. There are many other less general concepts which children learn at different times in their school years and which may be more important to them at some times than at others. When concepts such as numerator and fraction in arithmetic, osmosis and mitosis in biology, or independence and revolution in social studies are learned in a meaningful way, not only are they more easily remembered, they also provide benchmarks, or points of reference, for organizing more specific information and details. Conceptual learning makes an important contribution to learners' ability to apply or transfer what they know to new situations.

Another characteristic of school learning is that it is often *cumulative*. Whether students remember or forget what they seemed to know at the close of a lesson is not a trivial matter. Tomorrow's reading lesson, for example, will incorporate the vocabulary learned today, and students who cannot remember those words will be unable to read the material. A girl studying American history must learn about the growth of individual liberty and freedom in England after the signing of Magna Carta. Otherwise she will not understand the formation of the Virginia House of Burgesses as an outcome to be expected from people who had lived in a monarchy whose rule depended on the allegiance of a parliament. The arithmetic pupil who is unclear about the concepts of division, fractions, numerators, and denominators will never master what percentage one number is of another.

Our concern in considering learning as cognitive activity is to determine how students *acquire* the cognitive tasks that are taught as part of the instructional process. Since learning ought to be permanent, we are also concerned with how they *retain* the material that is taught. And we want to determine the conditions under which what they learn can make it easier for them to master something else; that is, how *transfer* operates, and what the teacher can do to facilitate the process.

Some school learning tasks are not meaningful but depend on the acquisition of arbitrary, or fixed, associations. A student of French must memorize *fenêtre = window* or *neige = snow*. Labels or words that represent concepts may also have to be learned in this manner. Most psychology textbooks describe this as *associative* or *verbal learning* and explain the processes which govern it. The risk in school learning is that the material students learn as associations would make further learning easier or more effective if it were approached as potentially meaningful. This is why we have put so much emphasis on meaningful learning in this chapter.

BASIC PROCESSES IN SCHOOL LEARNING

School learning results from the interactions between environmental events and the learner's basic traits and disposition. In terms of the model of the instructional process described in Chapter 1, the relevant interactions are between the instruction (teacher, text, or program) and the learner, as determined by his or her cognitive development, prior learning, level of intelligence, and disposition to learn. The learner acquires learning through three basic processes: selective perception and attention; transformation and storage of selected information; and retrieval of the information. In the ongoing process, the learning acquired in turn affects the learner's selection of new environmental events, as Figure 7.1 shows.

Because the learner's intelligence, interest in the topic at hand, and attitude toward learning a task are not easily or quickly affected by environmental conditions, they are referred to as *basic traits*. A child with superior intellectual ability will learn most tasks more rapidly than one who has a low intelligence level. The brighter child will also remember the task better, if only because the learning has been more thorough, and will see more possibilities for its transfer, or implications for other learning, than a classmate who is intellectually less able. Even though intelligence may be somewhat altered with education, the changes do not come quickly, as Chapter 6 showed.

Several environmental events may occur simultaneously, even in the classroom, where the focus is supposed to be on the subject matter to

Figure 7.1

Basic processes in meaningful learning of school-type material

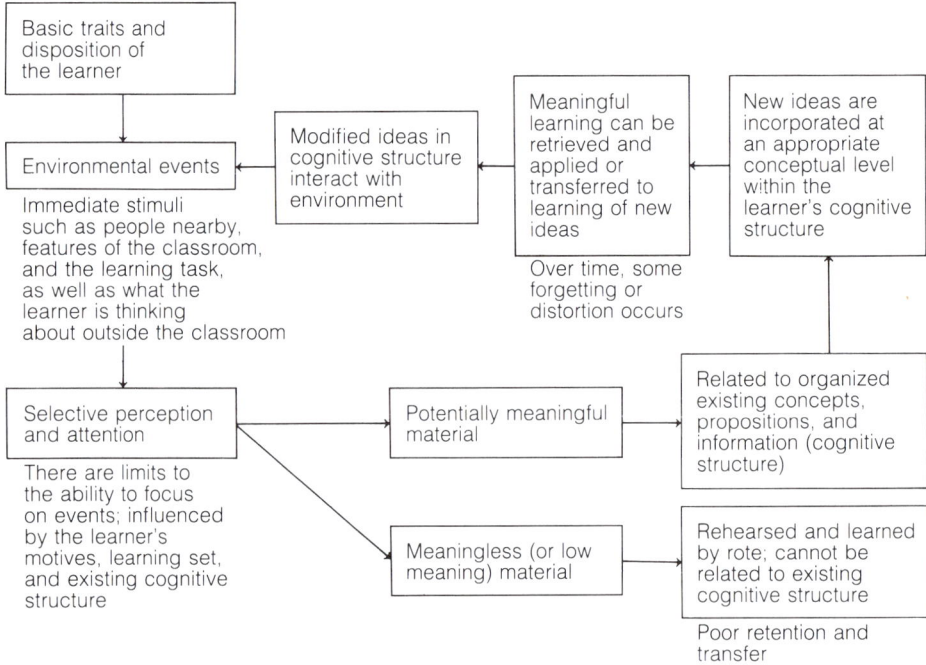

Basic traits and disposition of the learner

Environmental events

Immediate stimuli such as people nearby, features of the classroom, and the learning task, as well as what the learner is thinking about outside the classroom

Modified ideas in cognitive structure interact with environment

Meaningful learning can be retrieved and applied or transferred to learning of new ideas

Over time, some forgetting or distortion occurs

New ideas are incorporated at an appropriate conceptual level within the learner's cognitive structure

Selective perception and attention

There are limits to the ability to focus on events; influenced by the learner's motives, learning set, and existing cognitive structure

Potentially meaningful material

Related to organized existing concepts, propositions, and information (cognitive structure)

Meaningless (or low meaning) material

Rehearsed and learned by rote; cannot be related to existing cognitive structure

Poor retention and transfer

Source: Based in part on David P. Ausubel, Joseph Novak, and Helen Hanesian, *Educational Psychology: A Cognitive View*, 2nd ed. (New York: Holt, Rinehart & Winston, 1978), pp. 42 and 126.

be learned. Other students compete with the teacher for the learners' attention. Some learners may be preoccupied with events outside the immediate environment; they could be distracted by a coming ball game or their father's unemployment, for example. A teenaged girl may be waiting apprehensively for word that she has made the volleyball team, or a small boy may simply be tired, bored, or having an off day. For various reasons the stimuli the teacher wants students to attend to are not always the ones on which they are concentrating.

The learner, therefore, can seldom focus attention on all the stimuli in the environment. Attention is highly selective, and a person's attentional resources are limited. From the teacher's standpoint, it is important to draw students' attention to the materials that constitute the lesson of the moment. The teacher can influence the direction of attention to some extent by trying to establish an appropriate meaningful learning *set,* or state of psychological preparedness, in the classroom. Most pupils learn early in their years of schooling that teachers demand quiet in the classroom and always ask for the students' attention. Whatever other purposes such commands may achieve, they do help to limit the stimuli to which the learners are likely to pay attention. Paying attention, however, involves attending to the correct or appropriate aspects of the material under study. A geography teacher who vaguely waves at a wall map will fail to direct the class's attention precisely to the location that is critical for understanding a point, or the impact of a science demonstration may be lost if learners are looking at the wrong thing or expecting the wrong reaction.

Whether the material attended to will be stored in the learner's memory for future use is related to the meaningfulness of the material for the learner and how it is organized. To a large extent, whether or not the material is meaningful depends on the learner's existing cognitive structure of a topic; that is, what the learner already knows about it, and how *that* knowledge is organized. As new information is incorporated into the learner's cognitive structure, both the material and the cognitive structure are altered. Each learner's store of knowledge influences his or her ability to integrate and recall new information.

The learner's ability to retrieve information at a later time also depends on the form in which the material has been stored. If the acquisition and storage have been in a different form than the one in which it is later to be used, recall may be incomplete, or interference may occur. Another reason for advocating meaningful conceptual learning in schools is that such learning tends to have greater generality; that is, the greater the learner's understanding of the material, the greater his or her ability to transfer it, or apply it in a variety of settings.

A final point in the interactions which result in learning is reached when the learner's existing knowledge becomes an influence on how he or she selects or perceives new environmental events. A student who has never seen a Picasso may have little idea of what to look for in his paintings, for example, whereas the attention of a knowledgeable viewer will be focused at once on the painting's objects and their meaning.

THE FUNCTION OF ORGANIZATION IN LEARNING

One of the principal aids for learners in acquiring and retaining information is to organize it with various schemes. The process is easier if the task is organized for the learner or an effective procedure for organizing it is provided as part of the instruction. Suppose an American history teacher asks the class to name all the presidents of the United States. It would be surprising if a student responded, "Well, let's see . . . there was Millard Fillmore and James Garfield; Theodore Roosevelt, George Washington. . . ." A chronological order—Washington, Adams, Jefferson, and so on, down to the present chief of state—would be expected instead. Perhaps a better example of such organizational schemes would be a list of the Tudor English monarchs, in which the family name could serve as an organizer for the names of all the kings and queens of that line, from Henry VII in 1485 through Elizabeth I, who died in 1603. Teachers usually suggest appropriate organizing schemes to the class.

There is abundant evidence from laboratory investigations that people employ categories to organize and assist their recall of lists of words. In one of the first of these studies, Bousfield (1953) read 60 nouns aloud to college students and later asked them to recall as many of the words as they could. Although the words were read in random order, they could be categorized under four headings: names, animals, professions, and vegetables. When the students recalled the words, instead of following the random order they placed the words together in groups. The average number of words recalled was about 25.

Bousfield's study showed the tendency of adult learners to organize material for purposes of recall, but it told little about whether organization improves the amount of recall. In a similar study, different lists of names could be divided into two, three, or six categories (such as poets, artists, athletes, etc.). When Mathews (1954) made the categories explicit, students associated each name with its appropriate category as they read the list of names. Those who had learned lists divisible into six categories were able to recall more names from the total list than those whose lists could be placed into only two or three categories. Other students were given the same sets of lists but were not told the categories into which the names could be separated. They recalled about the same number of names as those who had been given the categories.

Several things happen when an individual is given material to learn and later is asked to recall or recognize it (Mandler, 1979). One is that the new information, after some preliminary coding, is incorporated into the learner's existing cognitive structures. Instructions for performance or output must also be translated into terms that relate to the organized structures into which the tasks fit.

DEVELOPMENTAL FACTORS IN ORGANIZING SKILLS

Young children do not usually cluster or organize tasks into categories, but older children do. Experimental data on children's use of organizing

As these students write down the main topics for a study of transportation, the teacher directs the class in organizing the material. School learning often involves classifying information and arranging it in hierarchical order.

strategies indicate that improvement in the skill occurs in all the years of elementary school, but not in a linear fashion (Ornstein & Corsale, 1979). For some tasks, only older children engage in organization, but there are other tasks that even young children will organize. A hypothesis that might account for the difference is that clustering varies with the strength of the individual's associations among items in a category. A young boy given a list of words to learn might place together the names of common tools, such as hammer, saw, and pliers, but might not organize labels for musical instruments with which he is less familiar.

One reason young children fail to organize new information is that they seem to lack a concept of what it means "to remember." Children do not always recall and use information that they are capable of organizing, but even third-graders can categorize if they are given explicit instructions in how to use an organizational strategy.

The growing body of knowledge about the development of the ability of children to organize information into meaningful categories, and to make use of strategies to plan such organization, suggests that teachers should present such planning strategies to young children as well as older ones. It seems that the failure to categorize, and thus to foster retention, is not entirely due to some lack in development. Rather it may be a simple lack of understanding by children that they can use what they already know to assist in the process of remembering.

The knowledge an individual has about a subject helps determine the strategy to be used in remembering new information about it. That is true for children as well as for adults. When Chi (1978) compared the memory for the location of chess pieces of a group of children who were proficient players with the memory of a group of adults who were novices at chess, the children's recall was superior to that of the adults. To determine whether these children possessed specialized knowledge about the chess pieces or would have superior memories for other information as well, Chi had both the children and the adults learn a digit-span task. Here, as expected, the adults were superior, and the interpretation was that the children used in the study had specialized knowledge which helped them remember the location of chess pieces. They would not, in any general sense, be superior in memory to a group of normal adults.

CONCEPT LEARNING

Concepts are general ideas which summarize a large number of examples or cases that have some essential qualities or elements in common but may differ from one another in particular ways. Educational psychology is concerned with how concepts are learned because they help organize knowledge and make it easier for people to remember things. The aid concepts give to the memory is enormous. Think of how difficult it would be to try to take account of all the details of every different specimen of dog or cat or person, to say nothing of more abstract ideas, if you did not have the capacity to generalize and abstract their common qualities or features.

Concepts also enhance the ability to learn subject matter content in a meaningful way. A learner who has a clearly delineated conceptual idea or outline of a topic has a much better opportunity to learn and remember particular information about it than one who must try to process and store incoming information without any conceptual hooks on which to hang all the details. Such a learner must try to memorize material by rote, perhaps with some help from mnemonic (or memory-assisting) devices. Ingenious as some of these devices are, they cannot match the assimilation that is possible when the learner has a meaningful, comprehensive cognitive structure into which new knowledge can be incorporated easily.

Some concepts are *concrete,* or represent real or actual things. Table and chair are typical of concrete concepts. It is seldom necessary to define such terms (although dictionaries do so), because even young children have clear concepts of them. Other concepts are *abstract;* we may have difficulty in communicating with one another about them because they do not mean precisely the same thing to everyone. Love, for example, is characterized by affection, commitment, and concern for a person or cause, but people have different overall conceptions of love, depending on their individual experiences.

The school years are filled with concept learning, which is assigned a central role in cognitive theories. Concepts are the building blocks of thought. They can incorporate many specific examples because they may be abstractions, and also because they are related to each other, ordinarily from the general to the particular. The concept of bird, for example, includes eagle and robin as well as penguin and ostrich.

THE DEVELOPMENT OF CONCEPTS

One of the most important tasks of the school is to assist the conceptual development of learners. Knowledge becomes usable if it is meaningful and so has generality or applicability. Students need clear, comprehensive concepts about the topics they are studying, and the relationships among these concepts should be clear and stable. These kinds of concepts make it easier for learners to acquire new information and to organize it within their broader concept structures.

One idea of how concepts are developed has been suggested by Herbert Klausmeier, who devoted several years to the study of children's learning of a series of concepts: noun, tree, equilateral triangle, and cutting tool. These concepts were chosen either for their subject matter connection, in the case of the first three, or because there was no direct teaching of the idea, in the case of the concept of cutting tool. Several hundred children in the 1st through 12th grades were tested in a complex study that ranged over three years and used a cross-section of students. Children were selected in the beginning from grades 1, 4, 7, and 10, and these groups were then tested on the concepts for three years in a row, thus supplying data about the development of the concepts in all 12 grades (Klausmeier & Allen, 1978; Klausmeier & associates, 1979).

Concepts develop, according to Klausmeier, through four levels: concrete, identity, classificatory, and formal (see Box A). It is important for children to develop concepts at the formal level because only then can the concepts be used for the mastery of principles or generalizations, which involve relationships among concepts, and for the solution of problems.

BOX A   *Getting to know the equilateral triangle*

According to Herbert Klausmeier, concept development takes place at four levels. The development of the *concrete and identity levels* of concepts occurs early, before the child enters school. Children who have concrete concepts of an object are able to discriminate it from other objects in the environment. If they have identity, they can recognize it as the same object even though it is seen in a different context. At this stage the child learns to discriminate between blocks of various shapes and other toys and to put a triangle-shaped block in the right space in a shape-sorter toy.

At the *classificatory level,* children are able to discriminate two or more examples of a concept from other objects in the environment and to treat them as equivalent. This is a crucial stage in concept development because it calls for the ability to generalize across examples of the concept, disregarding irrelevant differences. The concept at this level is stored in memory, available for later retrieval. Learners at the classificatory level are able to recognize instances of such concepts as the equilateral triangle and to discriminate them from negative examples. At this stage the child learns to sort out equilateral triangles from other triangular shapes, as in the following example:

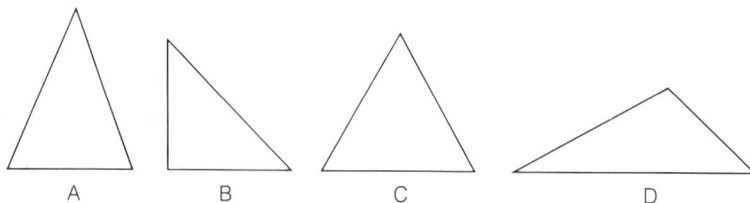

A   B   C   D

Draw an "X" through the triangle that has three equal sides.

At the *formal level,* the learner can define the concept and identify its attributes in a general way, not simply by classifying instances. A girl who has a formal concept of an equilateral triangle, for example, can define it as "a figure with three equal sides, three equal angles; a plane, closed, simple figure." Given one or more figures, she is able to evaluate the features of each one and determine whether the figure is a member of the class, and why.

The formal level of a concept is characterized by its meaning for the learner. The words in the definition and the relationships among them have meaning for the learner, rather than being simply memorized by rote. A child who has learned a concept at the formal level is able to use this knowledge of the concept to solve problems, such as the following:

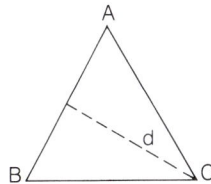

Given the triangle ABC with equal sides, and the fact that line *d* bisects angle *C*, how many degrees do angle *B* and angle *d* have combined?

A child with a formal understanding of the concept will recall that since an equilateral triangle has three equal angles, the sum of the two angles must be the 60 degrees of angle *B* and the 30 degrees of angle *d*. A child who has merely memorized the definition of the concept, without development of its meaning, would be unable to solve this simple problem.

Source: Herbert J. Klausmeier and Patricia S. Allen, *Cognitive Development of Children and Youth: A Longitudinal Study* (New York: Academic Press, 1978).

The significance for the teacher of how concepts are learned is not always recognized. Elementary and secondary school textbooks and courses are typically organized to stress the factual, informational, or narrative elements of the content. Concepts may be presented, usually through definitions accompanied by several examples, but often they are introduced at the same level of discourse as other content. Since the concepts of a course help to structure and to organize its content, they should be definitively presented. The learner's understanding and retention of material are improved when conceptual learning is clear and accurate.

Textbooks frequently use *definitions* as a way of teaching concepts to students. There are several kinds of definitions; in this chapter, for example, we used an *equivalence definition* to introduce the concept of cognitive structure. On the first page of the chapter you read that the term *cognitive structure* is equivalent to "the individual's organized bodies of knowledge." A bit later, in the discussion of concepts, we introduced concrete concepts both by using an equivalence definition (they are real things) and by the use of an *exemplary definition:* "Table and chair are typical of concrete concepts."

All the concept teaching in this chapter is not done by the presentation of definitions, however. Sometimes narrative accounts are used to exemplify and elaborate concepts. Box B, "How to Tell a Cat from a Dog," which will appear in the next few pages, is an example of such narrative teaching of the processes of generalization and discrimination that are the foundation of inductive concept learning.

THE INDUCTIVE PROCESS
OF CONCEPT LEARNING

Fundamentally, there are two ways a concept can be learned: through an inductive process or a deductive one. Young children's concept learning follows an inductive route, for the most part. An infant boy perceives an object such as his mother and, through repeated contacts with her, he learns to discriminate her from all other objects in the environment. The boy also learns to recognize her whenever she appears, whether in the nursery or the kitchen. Later he learns to signify her presence, or to demand it, by attaching a label to her—"Mama!"

Keep in mind, though, that maturation as well as learning is involved in this process, as we noted in the first part of this chapter. Since newborn infants lack a conception of permanence, objects they cannot perceive with their senses are gone forever, as far as they know. Most children are about one year old before they can apply a generic, or characteristic, label to the mother.

The labels children attach to the concepts they learn can be put in the form of a question: "How shall a thing be called?" (Brown, 1958). The principle of *frequency* is often the first determinant of the name to be used; children use the names they most often see or hear attached to certain objects. These labels also usually have *brevity*, but not always; a child learns that a particular object is a pineapple, for example, not a fruit. *Utility* seems to be the deciding factor. A father is more likely to ask a child to bring him "that apple" than "that piece of fruit."

Of course, children also attach to things the labels they are taught by their parents or others. This is important because communication depends on culturally shared meanings. Most people share a common core of meaning about a concept, but they may also have personal meanings for it that grow out of their individual experiences. The more special labels children learn for concepts, and especially the more they learn to label concepts differently than other people do, the greater their difficulty in communicating will be. Brown tells of one young boy who assigned the label "qua-qua" both to the concept of water and to the ducks that floated on it. Twins are notorious for developing their own language systems that are understood only by the two of them. Normally such deviations pass as soon as the children enter a broader society, and no great damage is done.

While the meaning of a concept is signified by attaching a label to it, the label is not the same thing as the concept. Concept meaning can be derived from meaningful learning of the dimensions and attributes that go together to form concepts and the limits that distinguish one concept from another. The labels of concepts, at least for the practical purposes of classroom learning, often must be learned as arbitrary associations, however. A class of eight-legged creatures is known as spider in English, for example, but as *arana* in Spanish. Even so, many labels, such as *triangle* and other compound words, are not strictly arbitrary but convey at least some of the meaning of what they represent.

How Concepts Are Learned by Induction

Experimental psychologists have studied concept formation or concept attainment through inductive means for many years, but the experimental tasks they have studied often do not represent real concepts. They have been of the order of "blue squares" or "red triangles," or *kun* means *love*. What has been learned from such studies is the problem-solving strategies that people employ to solve these gamelike puzzles, rather than knowledge about concept learning.

Not only does the child's earliest concept learning occur through induction, but to some degree, new concepts encountered in later life are also learned this way. Basically, the learning of concepts involves discriminating the differences among instances or examples of a class and generalizing about them. No one may point out the differences between cats and dogs to young children, for example, but they nevertheless

BOX B   *How to tell a cat from a dog*

Tommy was introduced to his first dog in the form of a family pet, Terry—a terrier, small, cuddly, and lovable, ideal for small children. Later he encountered Rex, the German shepherd belonging to a neighbor down the street. Rex is placid with children but a menace to those who trespass on his master's property, so Tommy's mother has firmly guided him away from the area Rex patrols.

The family pet and Rex are both dogs. Tommy hears them called by the same label, but they are dissimilar in so many ways. Their temperaments and purposes in life are different. So are their size, color, shape. Even such limited experience provides him with a primitive concept of dog because he abstracts from among all the differences those characteristics that the animals have in common.

Tommy discovers that his pet, Terry, and Rex each have four legs (he doesn't necessarily count the number of legs), no matter how different they look otherwise. Consequently when a new four-legged critter crosses his path, he identifies it as a dog. But the newcomer is the cat from across the street, and his mother's laughing contradiction of the term he uses must make Tommy wonder what kind of world he is living in. Tabby undeniably has four legs and is not appreciably different in size from Terry. Tommy must begin to discriminate how these two are *different,* for one belongs to one class, the other to another.

learn to distinguish between them (see Box B). They must use their own processes of inspection and cognition to memorize and abstract those differences, so that they begin to build related but different concepts about various four-legged creatures.

Limits to the Inductive Process

There are limits beyond which the inductive learning of concepts may not be productive or may interfere with the learning of other information. One limitation is that examples of a concept in the uncontrolled environment are likely to be encountered on a random and unpredictable basis. Thus, just at a time when children's conceptual learning would benefit from additional examples to verify or contradict their ideas about the nature of a concept, no more are forthcoming. Moreover, when the learner must interpret the examples that are encountered, there is a risk of forming a partial or distorted concept. Examples in the world at large may vary on numerous scores, but the small sample that happens to come the way of a particular learner never represents all the dimensions or attributes that define the category. Another limitation to learning solely by induction is that learners must depend on their own generalizations and efforts to define the concepts they encounter. For many concepts that is a difficult task, and most learners require some assistance in the form of definitions.

The most effective way to learn concepts may result from an artful blending of the processes of induction and deduction. Strictly inductive learning of real-life concepts involves a risk of partiality or distortion, but deductively learned concepts can rely too heavily on memorization and provide too little understanding of a concept.

THE DEDUCTIVE PROCESS OF CONCEPT LEARNING

Concepts to be learned at school are normally presented through deductive rather than inductive means (Carroll, 1964). School concepts, whether they are concrete or abstract in nature, are "real" concepts, not laboratory tasks. Learning such concepts often depends on the learner's prior conceptual knowledge. Because these concepts usually can be organized or classified, they also can be understood by nature of their relationships with other concepts.

Learning Concepts from Word Meanings

Any procedure that encourages the learner to process the meaning of a concept deeply will contribute to its meaningful learning. Research efforts to determine how concepts are learned by deduction have centered on the function of word meanings or definitions. One study found that 11- and 12-year-olds who were periodically asked to formulate the definition of an experimental concept later provided better definitions of it than those who had studied the same specific descriptions of the concept but had not been asked to define it as they learned it (Johnson & O'Reilly, 1964).

To test whether college students could learn concepts from definitions, Anderson and Kulhavy (1972) selected a series of extremely rare English words, such as *atavistic, cuprous,* and *besprent.* They provided college students with a single-sentence, dictionary-type definition of each word, such as: "Atavistic means reversion to a primitive type." Half of the students were told to compose a sentence of their own to illustrate the meaning of each new word, and the other half were instructed to repeat a given definition aloud three times. Anderson and Kulhavy reasoned that students who had to construct their own sentences would have to process the meaning of the words, whereas those who simply read the definitions aloud several times could do so without thinking very deeply about what the words meant. After these practice sessions, all the students took a multiple-choice test in which they had to choose the sentence that best exemplified the meaning of the test words. None of the sentences used the same language as the original definitions. The group who had composed their own sentences scored significantly better on the test, thus providing evidence in support of the investigators' belief about the role of semantic processing in learning concepts.

Other researchers adapted this procedure to see whether semantic processing would improve the word comprehension of remedial readers. Hudgins and Spies (1977) separated a group of sixth-, seventh-, and eighth-graders, all of whom were retarded by one year or more in reading, into three groups. One group was taught specific procedures for constructing meaningful sentences; another received practice in composing their own sentences for the new words, but with no direct instruction in the process; and a third group served as a control. Words were selected from the *Thorndike-Lorge Teachers Word Book*, and a single-sentence definition of each was provided. On the final test, which, as in the Anderson and Kulhavy study, required selecting the most appropriate example from a series of illustrative sentences, the highest average score was made by those students who had been given special instruction in making up meaningful sentences. The sentence-practice group was intermediate in score, and the control group lowest. This study suggests that increased semantic processing works with remedial reading students in much the same way as it does with competent college students. A simple, straightforward training program thus could be used to teach elementary school pupils a language arts skill that facilitates their ability to process word meanings.

Five methods teachers use to teach concepts were compared in a study by Johnson and Stratton (1966). Four groups of students were asked to study definitions of the words to be learned, or to complete sentences using the words, or to learn a classification method for them, or to study synonyms for the words. A fifth group was given a program with selected elements of all four of the other methods. There was also a sixth group which functioned as a control. Each of the 200 students in an introductory psychology class was given one of these six programs, distributed on a random basis. All were to learn the meanings of *alacrity, altercation, chide,* and *opulent* in 12 minutes. Nine days later a test which consisted of items of all the types studied by the different groups was administered to all the students. This made it possible to assess how much transfer had occurred from one method to another.

Johnson and Stratton attempted to construct each of the methods so it would operate at its most effective level. Students in the definitions group, for example, received material of this kind:

> When two or more people express different opinions, get excited, and contradict each other, the event is called an *altercation*. Thus an *altercation* is a social interaction characterized by heated exchange of opposing arguments. Now write a definition of *altercation* in your own words.

In the mixed program, the students had to abridge and reduce the examples and synonyms given. These students had only as much time for study as those in the other groups. Students using the mixed program studied more detailed material of this type:

> To *chide* someone is to talk to him to get him to correct his mistakes. *Chide* means to criticize or reproach. Thus a mother might *chide* her children for fighting with each other. An example might be a group of fellows poking fun at a boy with dirty clothes. Now write in your own words what *chide* means.

The results of the tests were clear-cut. Students who had been given the various single-method treatments scored better, on the average, than the group of control students who had received no instruction. But the group who had studied the mixed program scored significantly better than students in any of the four single methods. Johnson and Stratton found that transfer of learning from one task to another was complete. Even though they controlled the amount of study time for each group, students in the mixed program received a great deal more information about the words they were to learn.

These findings suggest that a learner who studies words as definitions, synonyms, and in other contexts has greater access to their meaning. These students had to remain active in generating their own definitions of the terms, once they had an opportunity to acquire additional pertinent information.

CONCEPT LEARNING AND THE INSTRUCTIONAL PROCESS

As we suggested in the preceding section, the learning of concepts in school might be improved by combining aspects of both inductive and deductive learning in the instructional process. Students can struggle a bit with formulating their definitions of concepts, as long as the teacher takes care to see that their final definitions contain all the significant elements. The active participation of the learner in devising definitions, as in other learning, is an important part of the process. Learners usually can acquire and demonstrate word meanings more effectively if they can produce a paraphrased form (expressed in their own language) of the definitions given by the instructor—the teacher, dictionary, or text-book. The possibility that students will be able to paraphrase meanings for a concept is one of the characteristics of potentially meaningful material which are described in a later section.

The availability of examples, both positive and negative, is also an aid in concept learning. If young children are learning the meaning of the concept of island, for example, pictures of many kinds of these land forms should be available to expand and supplement the meaning of the written definition, "a body of land surrounded by water on all sides." Negative examples, like pictures of continents and peninsulas, also can help sharpen the definition. A middle-grade teacher who wants to introduce the concept of a tarn, for example, might define it as a small mountain lake or pool. Children aged nine or ten should have good concepts of mountain, lake, and pool, but suitable photographs would help their comprehension (Carroll, 1964).

BOX C *Yes, but what does it* **mean?**

Can students entering college define words they do not know just from the way they are used in a sentence or paragraph? Freshmen today probably would fare no better than they did in a 1940 study by Helen Gibbons. She selected 24 words from a list of 50 that 85 percent or more of a group of 234 college freshmen could not define. Then she used each of these words in a sentence or paragraph of text and asked the students to determine its meaning. Overall, almost half of the students were not able to derive a meaning for an unfamiliar word when the only information they had about it was how it was used in context.

An example is the word *vicarious*, which was presented in the following way:

Part of our education is obtained directly through actual experiences; *vicarious* experiences which come through reading, pictures, lectures, art, and music are equally important, however, as a means of extending real experiences.

No answer or an incorrect answer was given to this item by 91 percent of the students. Students suggested the meaning of *vicarious* was "experiences obtained gradually," "indiscrete

Tarn is not a difficult concept for most children, especially if the contributing concepts are already well known, but it probably should be defined in order to avoid confusion with other concepts. There are many instances when new words are presented to the learner only through context, however. While it may be advisable to use context to provide the meaning of some concepts, others require fuller explanation or definition.

DERIVING MEANINGS FROM CONTEXT

Teaching from context is not the same as teaching a concept. The technique is most effective when a term to be learned labels a concept the learner already knows or one that needs only slight modification. Studies that have examined how such contextual learning occurs have found that more than one use of the term in context is necessary for students to be able to arrive at a dependable meaning (see Box C). Others have

experiences," or "the act of feeling, seeing, learning," and so forth.

Similarly, one third of the students could not adequately define the word *itinerant* after encountering it in the following sentence:

> In the beginning the teacher traveled from one locality to another to meet the students, thereby bringing into existence the *itinerant* schoolmaster.

Students described an itinerant teacher as "immoral," "a research schoolmaster," "intolerable," "humble," and so on.

Gibbons analyzed what students had to do with a sentence in order to construct an acceptable definition of a new word in it. She identified three skills the student must have:

1. The ability to see the relationship among elements in the sentence.
2. The ability to infer meanings from those given in the sentence.
3. The ability to paraphrase the meanings given.

Source: Helen Gibbons, "The Ability of College Freshmen to Construct the Meaning of a Strange Word from the Context in Which It Appears," *Journal of Experimental Education,* vol. 9 (1940), pp. 29–33.

found that the ability to infer meaning from context improves with age.

In one study of elementary school children, words to represent common objects were invented and embedded in groups of sentences which gave clues to their possible meaning (Werner & Kaplan, 1950). The word *corplum,* for example, was used this way:

> A *corplum* may be used for support.
> *Corplums* may be used to close off an open space.
> A wet *corplum* does not burn.

Eight-year-olds were unable to construct word meanings that were not tied to an idea in a given sentence. While the ability to infer more general meanings improved for older pupils, not until age 11 were most of them able to give meanings for the artificial words which were independent of specific sentences.

HOW SCHOOL LESSONS ARE LEARNED AND REMEMBERED

The instructional process presents students with large amounts of information to be learned during the school years. The material is far too much to be memorized and must be learned in a meaningful way if it is to be remembered for any length of time. The concept of meaningful learning and how it occurs is central to our consideration of learning as cognitive activity. It is derived in part from David P. Ausubel's assimilation theory of learning (Ausubel, 1969; Ausubel, Novak, & Hanesian, 1978). This section will describe assimilation as the end process whereby potentially meaningful information is remembered and incorporated into the individual's cognitive structure of an idea.

THE DISTINCTION BETWEEN ROTE AND MEANINGFUL LEARNING

An important part of Ausubel's theory of school learning concerns what he calls the "rote-meaningful" distinction. The term refers to two issues: the degree of meaningfulness of the task or the material to be learned, and the method or the process by which the learner approaches the task.

Learning tasks vary in how meaningful they are. Psychologists deliberately invented consonant-vowel-consonant (c-v-c) syllables as a way of controlling the meaningfulness of verbal learning tasks: *C-A-T* is highly meaningful; *L-U-X* is somewhat less so, and *Z-U-B* probably has little meaning, for example. A student who must learn materials of relatively little meaning is more or less forced to use techniques of rote learning, such as memorization through repetition and rehearsal. Efforts to build associations (*Z-U-B* is similar to *T-U-B*, and remembering the meaningless term may be easier if the similarity is recalled) may be helpful. Nevertheless, the ability to learn and, particularly, to remember such materials will not be very good. Large investments must be made in time and effort devoted to overlearning, and this may be impossible when extensive subject matter must be learned.

Meaningful material, in contrast, has relationships to other subject matter or bodies of knowledge that are not arbitrarily drawn. The high school student who begins study of the Russian Revolution of 1917 in a European history class already has a concept of revolution and some knowledge of the American War for Independence, the French Revolution, and possibly others. The Russian Revolution is also intellectually comprehensible in terms of historic events in Czarist Russia.

The materials students are asked to learn can vary appreciably in what Ausubel calls potential meaningfulness. He asserts that most school tasks have high meaning, but this is not always the case. Some materials must be learned as arbitrary associations, and, if they acquire meaning, it is only because they have been thoroughly learned.

Even though a lesson is potentially meaningful, it can be learned as though it were not. When material must be learned verbatim, as in memorizing a poem or learning foreign language vocabulary, some rote learning is inevitable. But when a lesson that need not be approached in this way is nevertheless learned in a rote fashion, some of the potential generality and versatility of the learning is sacrificed.

LEARNING AND REMEMBERING AS INFORMATION PROCESSING

To illustrate how information is acquired and remembered, we could follow Sue, a ninth-grade girl enrolled in a citizenship class, as she learns about the structure of our national government. The teacher presents the stimulus (an idea) by saying: "The federal government has several distinct branches. Who knows what they are called?" Sue perceives these words, together with other events in the immediate environment, in her sensory register or sensory memory (see Figure 7.2). The record she receives is a good and complete one, but it fades in a fraction of a second. Only those aspects of it that are carefully attended to are retained in short-term memory, where she may remember them for only about half a minute unless she rehearses (or studies) them or transfers them into her long-term memory store.

Sue retains the essence of the teacher's question while another student answers, "They're called the executive, the legislative, and the judiciary."

Figure 7.2

Information-processing diagram of the memory process

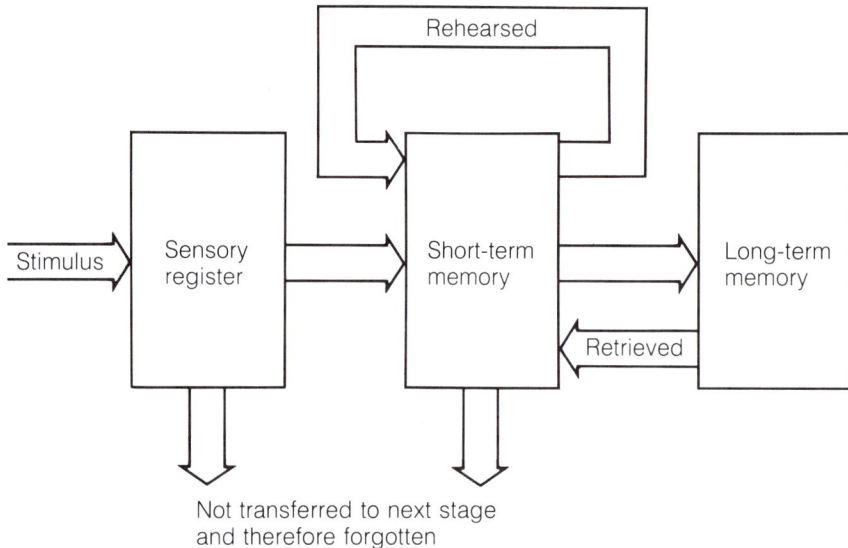

Source: Reprinted from *Memory* by Elizabeth Loftus, copyright © 1980,
p. 15, by permission of Addison-Wesley Publishing Co., Reading, Mass.

She wants to remember the terms, so she rehearses them silently. Her rehearsal in short-term memory may go something like this:

Branches of government: 1. Executive
                         2. Legislative
                         3. Judiciary

If Sue *overlearns* this information through repetitive study or rehearsal, she may succeed in storing it in long-term memory, where it could be retrieved later and returned to her short-term, or working, memory. The retrieval, though, would be limited, because all she has learned is the three names coded "branches of government."

Sue has another problem in that her attention span, or capacity of short-term memory, is limited, like everyone else's. Miller (1956) estimated it at seven items, plus or minus two. So all the while she is rehearsing the names of the branches of government and their associations, her ability to attend to what the teacher is saying is limited. She has to choose between abandoning her rehearsal and hoping she can remember the terms, or staying with it and thereby failing to take in and process subsequent information. It is easy to see that if incoming information lacks meaning, the rate at which it can be rehearsed with a hope of remembering it is low.

Thus the meaningfulness of the material to be learned plays a crucial role in learning. Sue doesn't just memorize the labels of the three branches of government. Knowing the functions performed by each one lends meaning to the outline she is learning: Congress makes the laws; the president sees that they are carried out; the courts rule on disputes about them. Though each branch performs many more functions than these, once she has a valid if simple picture of how the branches operate, she can assimilate new information about them with what she already knows.

Only a few items at a time can be kept in the short-term memory store, but if each item stores or encodes a much larger amount of information, the small number of words or terms rehearsed at any one time can represent a great deal of information. The availability in the individual's long-term memory (or cognitive structure, as Ausubel defines it) of generic terms such as generalizations and concepts makes it possible for new, incoming information that is more specific to be included under more general headings.

When learning is viewed as information processing, as in the systems-processing perspective of the learner taken in Chapter 3, the stimulus (an event in the environment that arouses activity) is introduced by the individual's sensory systems and recorded on the sensory register. Some part of the stimulus enters short-term memory, where it can be held by rehearsal, transferred into long-term memory, or forgotten. Material that is forgotten from short-term memory cannot be recalled, and retrieval from long-term memory can be slow and difficult if it is stored in a form that is different from the cues the learner uses to try to retrieve it. Meaningful learning is accessible because it is related to other material, and it can be recalled in alternate forms.

THE LEARNING OF MEANINGFUL MATERIAL

There is a decided difference for the learner between learning isolated information, such as the names of the branches of government, as in the example above, and learning the information in a meaningful way. The names can be memorized and used to answer the question, "What are the three branches of the federal government?" If they have not been connected to other defining information, however, that is about as much as can be expected. If meaningful learning has occurred, the learner can attach these labels to the cognitive structures, or organized and structured knowledge, he or she already has. The need for two

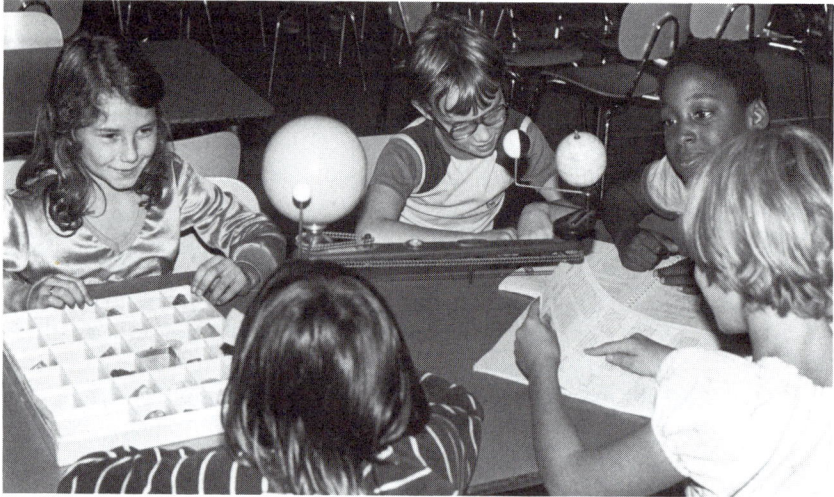

Understanding the relationships among the earth, the sun, and the moon is easier for students when they have concrete objects to examine. The textbook's explanations for why there are day and night and why the seasons change, for example, are more meaningful when children have opportunities for direct experiences with materials such as these.

houses in the Congress, one reflecting differences in population in the states and the other ensuring equal representation for each state, can be understood in terms of the compromise worked out among the writers of the Constitution to lessen the influence of the large states. Their composition, therefore, need not be memorized as an arbitrary bit of information.

It is up to teachers to make the meaningfulness of learning tasks apparent to students. For meaningful learning to occur, two conditions must be met: the learner must adopt a meaningful learning set, and the task to be learned must be potentially meaningful (Ausubel, Novak, & Hanesian, 1978).

Adopting a Meaningful Learning Set

In adopting a meaningful learning set, the student approaches the learning of new material with the assumption that the material possesses meaning. A student who treats a learning task as though it lacks meaning will learn the material by rote. A learner who assumes there is meaning in the material will study it and organize it in a way that tends to bring out its meaningfulness.

Expectancies, one of a series of control processes which, according to Robert Gagné (1977), govern all aspects of knowledge acquisition, learning, storage, and retrieval, is close to the idea of a learning set. According to Gagné, expectancies

> . . . represent the *specific* motivation of learners to reach the goal of learning which has been set for them, or which they have set for themselves. What learners intend to accomplish can influence what they attend to, how they encode the learned information, and how they organize their responses. An expectancy is a continuing set, oriented toward the goal accomplishment, which enables learners to select the outputs of each processing stage. (p. 16)

A learner who has an expectancy that content to be learned "makes sense" will approach it in her or his own terms, rather than learning it verbatim. The learner also will recognize the possibilities for relating the content to other knowledge and making comparisons and contrasts between the new and the old. Cognitive tasks such as classifying and categorizing information, organizing it from more to less specific, checking for connections between sets of data, and the like develop out of more general cognitive skills that play a useful part in meaningful learning. A learner with a meaningful learning set will engage in cognitive activity that is goal directed.

Identifying Potentially Meaningful Material

Material that is potentially meaningful can be *understood,* that is, it can be related in a meaningful way to other existing ideas, by at least some people. Novices in any field might find it difficult to follow the logic in an advanced thesis or to integrate its wealth of details into their limited cognitive structures, whereas advanced students could relate the ideas in the material in meaningful ways to ideas that already are present in their more extensive structures. Material without potential meaningfulness for a given learner must be learned with essentially rote techniques, as noted above.

Certain characteristics differentiate potentially meaningful material from tasks that have no possible meaning, such as lists of nonsense syllables. For one thing, it can usually be paraphrased, or expressed in language that is different from the language of the original message. Most teachers feel more confident that students comprehend material if they can express it in their own words (Anderson, 1972). There are exceptions, however (see Box D). Perhaps the most essential characteristic of potentially meaningful material is that it allows for connections to be made to other ideas or information.

BOX D *Say that again, please*

According to an education folk tale, a student taking a history test which called for essay-type answers included this statement in his reply: "The French Revolution wrote insulting letters to the American Revolution." When the teacher asked him to clarify his meaning, he insisted that was what she had said in class. After consulting her lecture notes she found that what she had probably said was: "The French Revolution corresponded in a rough way with the American Revolution."

Source: Arthur Gates et al., *Educational Psychology,*
3rd ed. (New York: Macmillan, 1948).

These characteristics help to make potentially meaningful material more resistant to interference than materials such as unrelated lists of words or nonsense syllables. Meaningful material is also more transferable than tasks that have been learned by rote, perhaps because a broader range of applications can be seen when the meaning, and not just the form of the task, is understood. (Interference and transfer are described in later sections of the chapter.)

WHAT STUDENTS REMEMBER ABOUT LESSONS

One way to examine how school lessons are learned is to investigate what is remembered about material after exposure to it. While students do recall particular words or phrases or special forms of expression, as might be expected, it has been found that they are much more likely to remember the idea or substance of a passage than the form in which the material was communicated (Bransfield & Franks, 1971). But, as Bourne, Dominowski, and Loftus (1979) observe, "what we do depends in large measure on what the demands of our task involve." If verbatim learning or recollection of a specific form or language is required, this will be accomplished. If there are no particular directions, learners are more likely to remember only the substance of meaningful passages.

The words and ideas that are recalled initially about a passage will probably be repeated later. Even errors in the initial recall of a passage may reappear, as Howe (1970) found in a study in which college students were presented with a brief excerpt from a Saul Bellow novel and then asked to recall whatever they could about it. Once a week for four weeks, they recalled the passage and then listened to it once more. The most striking finding of this study was that the second and subsequent recalls were heavily affected by the initial recall.

The ideas that are most likely to be recalled rank high in the context structure of the passage—that is, they have many other ideas or items of information subordinate to them (Meyer & McConkie, 1973). The evidence suggests that learners retain the more abstract and more important organizing ideas when they are required to read or hear a meaningful passage, but they may not remember less significant details.

People who are knowledgeable about a topic learn new information about it more quickly and easily than others. Learners must relate new information to what they already know, or their cognitive structures, and knowledgeable students can make connections between new knowledge and other ideas and information, which helps them to integrate it. This is much more difficult for students with limited knowledge. It has been suggested that the difficulties of mature learners with little knowledge are much like those of a young child struggling to learn something new, and age differences in learning may be reducible to knowledge differences.

COGNITIVE STRUCTURE

Cognitive theorists differ about how information is stored in long-term memory, but they do agree that retrieval of information depends on the learner's access to what is stored there. In Ausubel's theory of school learning the reference is not to long-term memory but to the learner's *cognitive structure,* or the organized representation of the individual's knowledge.* The richer and more fully delineated a learner's cognitive structure is, the more easily can new information be assimilated into the existing cognitive structure at an appropriate level of specificity or generality. Ausubel contends that the primary determinant of a student's learning is what he or she already knows. Voss's work described above

---

Cognitive structure is the term used by Ausubel and his colleagues to refer to individual learners' hierarchically structured bodies of organized knowledge (Ausubel, 1963, 1968; Ausubel, Novak, & Hanesian, 1978). Similar terms in current use include *knowledge structure* and *schema,* among others. These terms are not intended to be interchangeable, and there are differences among them. The field of knowledge about how learning takes place is expanding rapidly, but in this book we will use only *cognitive structure* to denote the learner's store of organized knowledge.

provides empirical support, and the logic is easy enough to understand once the organization of a cognitive structure has been explained.

A cognitive structure is an individual variable. That is, it is a property of the learner, not of the material to be learned. One way to think about classroom learning and teaching is that the task of the teacher and the learner interacting together in the instructional process is to modify and extend the learner's cognitive structure so it comes closer to either the teacher's structure or the structure of the content field.

Theoretically, the ideas in a person's cognitive structure are hierarchically ordered. At the top are the broadest and most general principles and propositions. Under these are categorized concepts and subconcepts, and at the bottom is the particular, detailed information about a topic. New information on a topic enters the cognitive structure, where it can be connected with or assimilated by an appropriate concept or proposition that is already organized there. At least initially, the meaningful relationship enables the learner to retain the new information as a distinctive fact, although with time it may become blurred and no longer retrievable as a separate item. One way to think about the dynamics of the system is in the same terms of storage and retrieval of information that apply to the memory process. If new and meaningful material is stored appropriately in a cognitive structure, it can be retrieved when necessary because the learner has access to it.

THE ASSIMILATION PROCESS

When new information about a topic enters the learner's cognitive structure, at first many of the particulars retain their distinctive characteristics, since they have recently been received on the sensory register and rehearsed by the learner (see Figure 7.2 above). With the passage of time, however, the basic new information becomes integrated with the ideas, concepts, and information already present in the learner's cognitive structure, and much or even all of the distinctive details are lost. That is, the learner can no longer recall them.

When a high school student of American history reads about secession from the union in 1861 and the formation of the Confederate States of America, for example, the details—which states participated, the ratification of the secession by state legislatures, the selection of Montgomery as the temporary capitol, and other particulars—are clear and become part of the learner's cognitive structure. Unless the learner rehearses or practices the details of the passage, however, many of them will fade. Finally nothing more may be retrievable than the recollection that in early 1861 several states in the southeastern part of the United States declared themselves independent of the union, an action which in turn led to the Civil War.

New potentially meaningful material is assimilated better when the learner has acquired a meaning for it that is clear and stable and has discriminated between the new material and other material with which it might be confused. The ideas already in the learner's cognitive structure also must have *clarity, stability, and discriminability*. One way in which this can be achieved is by overlearning the material, that is, by reading it and developing its meanings, not once but several times. Another is by comparing the similarities and differences between topics that are already known and a new but similar topic (the use of comparative advance organizers to do this is described later, in the section on transfer). If new material is not learned by one method or another, its chances of being incorporated into a learner's cognitive structure are lessened.

Ideas and information that already exist in the cognitive structure furnish anchoring points for incoming information. If the existing ideas are poorly understood or vaguely organized, they cannot function effectively in this capacity. Thus a student who fails to acquire clear concepts of the history, precepts, and religious teachings of Buddhism will lack the knowledge needed for subsequent study of Zen Buddhism. The study may even be harmed in the sense that there will be interference between what was studied earlier and the knowledge the learner is attempting to acquire.

INTERFERENCE AS A SOURCE OF FORGETTING

The learning and remembering of school lessons was likened to information processing in the preceding section (see Figure 7.2 above). All lessons do not follow the procedure of being held in long-term memory—or the cognitive structure—and returned to short-term memory when the learner calls them up, however. Some part of the learning is forgotten, as Figure 7.2 shows.

One reason material is forgotten is that it is not potentially meaningful, and so connections cannot be made to the learner's cognitive structure. Another reason is *interference*, which occurs when students learn something that is rather like something they have learned before, and the new learning makes it difficult for them to recall what they already know. Hunter (1964) regards interference as the major cause of forgetting.

There is a long-standing scholarly dispute about whether interference only occurs when the learning tasks are such things as nonsense syllables or lists of words, or whether it also applies to meaningful materials, such as textbook passages or other content to be studied in school. The results of recent research (some of which is described below) have suggested that interference also occurs in the learning of meaningful material.

STUDIES OF INTERFERENCE

One aspect of interference that has been investigated in psychology laboratories is the effects of *interpolation,* or the insertion of different material in a task, on people's ability to recall something they have previously learned. Usually in these studies students are required to learn one or more lists of nonsense syllables or words, and then they are given an interpolated activity to perform which may not bear any relationship to the first task or may be quite similar. The students then attempt to recall the first task. The amount of interference (or the opposite, facilitation of memory) that a particular type of interpolated activity accounts for can be inferred by comparing the recall scores of students with equal ability who learned the same initial task but were given different interpolated tasks.

An example is a study reported by Hunter (1964) which showed that the closer the interpolated activity comes to the original one, short of identity with it, the greater is the amount of interference. A group of students learned lists of adjectives, and then some of them read jokes and others learned nonsense syllables or synonyms for the adjectives before being asked to recall the original list. Those who had read the jokes in the interval were still able to recall 45 percent of the adjectives, much more than the others. The poorest rate of recall (only 12 percent) was for students who learned synonyms for the original adjectives.

In the study of how interference operates, an interference theory has developed which specifies the relationships between interpolated learning and ability to remember the previous task. According to Hunter (1964), these relationships include:

1. The greater the similarity between the original and the interpolated activities, the greater the interference.
2. Interference is related to the extent of the interpolated learning. A student who is actively involved in learning for an extended period will experience more interference than if the original learning can be followed by rest, a tennis game, or dinner, for example.
3. Interference is lessened if the original task is thoroughly learned.

Another factor which can cause interference in learning is competition among responses. This happens, for example, when a student is asked to learn a new association for an already familiar stimulus or a new answer for a familiar question. Response competition was observed in a study by Myrow and Anderson (1972) which tested whether interference operates in the learning of school-type materials. This study used original passages describing two mythical primitive tribes which had complex clan systems, one based on occupations and the other on the stars. When students were asked questions about the clan system of one tribe, and the possible answers included the directly competing response about the other tribe, interference occurred. In this classroom example, the results were consistent with the effects of directly competing responses found in the learning laboratory.

Interference also occurs in daily life, however. Hunter suggested, for example, that the more active the individual, the greater the likelihood of interference. To look at this issue, one third of the passages in the Myrow and Anderson study were unrelated to one another. For example, one tribe was said to live as foresters and the other as hunters. When students were asked questions about the occupations of the first tribe after having read about both of them, there was some decrease in their recall, but it was not significant. Thus, when the questions were designed to follow the demands of interference theory (identical stimuli, competing responses), interference occurred. But when more real-life situations were tested (as with questions on foresters and hunters), the effects of interference were not significant. As Myrow and Anderson noted, "We seldom teach students different answers to the same question. If retroactive interference is generated in prose only when the materials are so closely similar, we must question the efficacy of the interference model as an inclusive explanation of forgetting in the classroom" (p. 308).

In an early experiment on interference and facilitation in school learning, Ausubel, Robbins, and Blake (1957) concluded that interference is "an important determining factor in forgetting only in artificial laboratory situations employing nonsense learning tasks, and is at most a relatively minor variable in the retention of most newly learned school materials" (p. 341). This conclusion was supported in a study a decade later by Ausubel, Stager, and Gaite (1968) which examined the effects of both interpolated learning and overlearning on interference with school-type learning materials. In this experiment high school students read a passage on Zen Buddhism. Two days later half the students read the same passage again, and two days after that some of the students studied material on Buddhism in a passage which was different from but related to the original one, while others read an unrelated passage about drug use. At the end of the week all the students took a multiple-choice test based on the Zen Buddhism passage.

The students who had read the Zen Buddhism passage twice had the highest scores, thus demonstrating the positive effect of overlearning. Moreover, students who had read the related Buddhism passage as an interpolated activity scored better than those who had studied the unrelated passage about drugs. Thus reading an interpolated passage with content similar to but conflicting with the original learning material did not produce interference, as the theory would predict. On the contrary, these students experienced *facilitation* in their learning, perhaps because, as Ausubel suggests, they could use the Buddhism passage to review and clarify the concepts presented in the Zen passage. Both were ideational, of the type that students encounter daily in the classroom.

The issue of whether school learning is subject to interference when sequences of related information are presented to learners has not been resolved. Ausubel's contention that facilitation rather than interference is to be expected appeals to teachers, and it certainly conforms to their daily experience in the classroom. Students know more in June than they did in September. Their scores on standardized achievement tests reflect this, and teachers can see the progress from their own records. If the increments of improvement are not obvious from day to day, they are surely evident between September and January, from then until spring recess, and so forth. Teachers feel comfortable with the idea that memory and school learning are helped rather than hindered by the instructional process.

TRANSFER OF LEARNING

The topics of interference and transfer are closely related in the consideration of learning as a cognitive activity. Transfer occurs when something students *already know* influences their ability to learn something new, in either a positive or a negative direction. An American driver in England, where cars are driven on the left, for example, would find that earlier training and attitudes interfere with the task of learning to follow British rules of the road.

Transfer of learning is a major topic in educational psychology. Our emphasis here is upon the transfer of *knowledge*, both in terms of how new information is acquired and assimilated into an existing cognitive structure, and in the sense of how the existing cognitive structure (that is, what the learner already knows) can facilitate the learning of new knowledge.

The history of the study of transfer of learning (or transfer of training, as it is sometimes called) is long and varied, however. Scholars used to believe that transfer is automatic, brought about by the training of mental *faculties*, an obsolete term for very general mental attributes that can be strengthened through appropriate practice. The faculty of memory, for example, was said to be improved by continuous practice at memorizing, and it was thought that students who had extensive practice in memorizing could apply that faculty to the memorization of new material of all kinds. Classical languages were considered particularly good for that purpose, and the study of mathematics was thought to improve the faculty of reasoning. It was believed that the accomplished mathematician not only could reason well in a mathematical way (which would be accepted by psychologists today as well as a century ago), but also had an improved general ability or faculty for reasoning that would make it possible to reason effectively about any kind of issue or problem.

Transfer of training is a very broad topic. It applies not only to the transfer of knowledge but also to the transfer of bodily skills, attitudes, general principles for action, and other areas. Edward L. Thorndike, who introduced a theory of transfer by identical elements, acknowledged the broad scope of transfer. Some people even argue that education, beyond the point of initial learning of the basic skills, is a continuing process of transfer.*

Ausubel's assimilation theory of school learning is concerned with the transfer not of habits or skills but of ideas in the learner's cognitive structure. When Ausubel says that the best predictor of new learning is old learning, he suggests that the ideas which are already stored in a learner's cognitive structure influence the course of new learning, as we have already seen. Thus the existing cognitive structure is the central variable that affects the transfer or application of learning in learning new material. Furthermore, since school learning tasks are ordinarily sequential and cumulative, the weight of what students already know about a topic exerts a strong positive influence on their ability to learn the next idea or body of factual information that fits into their cognitive structures. Ausubel's insistence that learners must make their ideas clear, stable, and discriminable in their cognitive structures and Hunter's principle that the best proof against interference and forgetting is mastery of the original learning have a clear bearing on the concept of transfer.

When students must study new information that is not closely related to their current knowledge, they are likely to treat it as though it lacked meaning even though it is potentially meaningful. If no clear, appropriate concepts for organizing the information are present in their cognitive structures, the options available for incorporating the new material are limited. The learner may have to approach the learning task through rote memory, which, as we have noted, sacrifices some of the potential generality and versatility of the learning.

ADVANCE ORGANIZERS

An advance organizer in learning materials is a device, usually an introductory passage, which is designed to facilitate learning when there is no appropriate frame of reference for new material in the learner's

---

*For further information about transfer beyond the scope of this chapter, an excellent older book by Ellis (1965) or Gagné (1977) can be consulted.

cognitive structure. This type of learning aid is designed to supply elements of a missing or inadequate cognitive structure so the learner can assimilate potentially meaningful material that is unfamiliar.

Rarely, however, is a learner's cognitive structure totally lacking in previous knowledge or concepts that can be related to new content. Organizers not only provide "ideational scaffolding," as Ausubel puts it, they also help students call to mind information they already have that is relevant to the new learning task. For mature students, who are likely to have more general information at their disposal, the advance organizers may be comparative in nature. *Comparative organizers* not only supply some of the conceptual structure into which new ideas to be learned can be integrated, they also compare related topics the learner is presumed to know about with the material to be introduced.

An advance organizer is usually a relatively brief passage of text which precedes the new material to be learned. It provides a conceptual organization into which the learner can integrate the more detailed and lengthier new material. Ausubel recommends the use of advance organizers with new material that is likely to be studied by learners who have no relevant concepts in their cognitive structures to which they can relate it. An advance organizer is designed not to give the learner a preview or an overview of a new learning task but to establish some abstract, limited ideas that can function in the same way as a more advanced learner's cognitive structure would.

According to Ausubel, advance organizers should be written in more general, abstract, and comprehensive terms than the learning material that follows. The logic is clear enough, since new ideas tend to be classified with a larger category or under more general principles when they are assimilated in a person's cognitive structure. From a theoretical position Ausubel's argument is consistent and compelling. If an advance organizer is presented at the same level of discourse as the more detailed learning task it precedes, it cannot serve the necessary organizing and assimilating functions. At a more practical level, however, an advance organizer must be written so that it can be comprehended by the learner, or it cannot serve the purpose of providing cognitive structure and marshaling the relevant information already in the learner's possession.

Experimental Tests of the Idea

In Ausubel's (1960) initial experimental attempt to test the effectiveness of advance organizers, college students were randomly assigned to experimental or control groups. The students were to study a lengthy passage on the metallurgical properties of plain carbon steel, written at a level ordinarily found in a first-year college chemistry textbook. This specialized topic would not usually be learned in such a course, and advanced chemistry students were eliminated from the study.

Two introductory passages for the topic, each about 500 words long, were constructed. One was a historical review and the other, the advance organizer, was more abstract and general; it did not contain any specific information that would directly help readers to score better. Students in the control group read the historical passage, and those in the experimental group read the organizer. This reading was repeated two days later, followed by reading of the entire learning passage. After another three days a multiple-choice test was administered to all the students, and those who had read the advance organizer scored significantly higher. Ausubel concluded that an advance organizer can be an effective means for assisting students' learning and retention of potentially meaningful, but new and unfamiliar learning material.

The effectiveness of comparative organizers was tested in much the same way (Ausubel, 1961). College students in the experimental group studied a lengthy passage on the doctrines and sacred teachings of Buddhism, using an advance organizer that systematically compared the major points of Christianity and Buddhism. The comparison was intended to remind these students of concepts about Christianity that most of them would have encountered, and which they could use to make comparisons and contrasts with unknown concepts about Buddhism. Retention was checked 3 days after the study of the advance organizer and again after 10 days. Not only did the readers of the comparative organizer have better retention, compared to control subjects, but so did another group of students who had read an advance organizer about Buddhism that did not attempt to draw the comparisons with Christianity.

Students who had a clear and well-defined cognitive structure about Christianity were not helped much by advance organizers of either kind, however. That is as expected, since the purpose of the organizer is to provide minimal cognitive structure where none exists. It has also been found that students lacking verbal skills are helped most by advance organizers. Because they are less able to organize, categorize, and place new material into meaningful superordinate and subordinate positions, they need the organizers to help them comprehend and retain the information.

There is a solid background of theory for evaluating the concept of the advance organizer. As we noted in the preceding section, cognitive structure is the major influence on the student's retention and transfer of meaningful material, and an advance organizer is a way of providing such structure for a student who has none. Research studies have also supported the idea, but the effects of advance organizers have not been uniformly positive. The concept of the advance organizer is a controversial one which has been the object of several major research literature reviews in recent years (Barnes & Clawson, 1975; Hartley & Davies, 1976;

Lawton & Wanska, 1977). In some cases failure to find the predicted effects of advance organizers is clearly the result of poor research or poorly constructed advance organizers. Other investigations that are well designed and conceptualized, however, also have failed to find these effects.

The facts that the concept of the advance organizer continues to arouse controversy and to generate research speak well for its significance. Even its critics recognize the connection of organizers to the assimilation theory of school learning. If the logic of Ausubel's contention that cognitive structure is hierarchically organized, and less general concepts and information are subsumed by and assimilated with broader propositions, is accepted, the use of advance organizers can be seen as a powerful aid to meaningful learning and remembering.

CONCRETE VERSUS ABSTRACT ORGANIZERS

Another view of the advance organizer is that, rather than being abstract and general, as Ausubel maintains, it should provide concrete reference points for the learner or analogies to familiar ideas the learner already has. James Royer (1979; Royer & Cable, 1975, 1976) has demonstrated that college students transfer the ideas they learn in one passage to a second abstract passage that is based on similar concepts or processes. In this regard his ideas are close to Ausubel's contention that accumulated knowledge in the learner's cognitive structure does not interfere with new learning and may in fact facilitate it.

In one experimental study of the issue, Royer and Cable (1975) asked college students to read two passages, one on electrical conductance and the other on heat transfer. The specifics of the topics are different, but both share such concepts as temperature, pressure, and impurities. Two versions of each learning passage were prepared, one in concrete form and the other an abstract version. The concrete passage used simple, familiar illustrations; for instance, in describing impedance, impurities in a metal were said to have the effect of an object such as a cigarette package inserted in the midst of a string of falling dominoes. A student might receive a learning passage on either of the two topics first, and it might be either concrete or abstract. The results showed that the best recall of ideas in the second passage was made by the students who had received the concrete version of the passage they read first. Moreover, those who received passages on the second topic which were abstract after they had read concrete versions of the first topic achieved the best overall recall scores. The magnitude of the recall differences was impressive—at least 40 percent higher than for any other combination of passages and concrete-abstract order.

Royer's procedures may not be as contradictory of Ausubel's conception of advance organizers as this finding suggests, however. The concrete referents of the initial passage call to mind ideas, events, or processes of a general nature which are broadly applicable; that is, which not only fit the specific case of the initial passage when it is read but are also transferable to a different phenomenon, such as the second passage. That is precisely the purpose of an advance organizer: to help learners mobilize and bring into their consciousness appropriate concepts and information which they have previously acquired and which will transfer to new situations. Ausubel cautions that the generality of an organizer is limited because it must be comprehensible to the person who is to study and use it. Royer points out that organizers may have to include concrete referents or images, analogies, and the like to make immediate contacts for learners between the ideas of the material being studied and the more general ones that exist in their study of knowledge.

MEANINGFUL LEARNING IN THE INSTRUCTIONAL PROCESS

Meaningful material, as the concept has been described in this chapter, is essential for successful interaction between learners and instructors in the instructional process. The learner will have difficulty assimilating and transferring material that does not fit into her or his cognitive structure about a topic. Care must therefore be taken to assure that the instruction is potentially meaningful for the learner.

While the instruction may be a text or programmed learning unit as well as a teacher, as we noted in Chapter 1, the classroom teacher has the principal role in assuring that students will learn in a meaningful way. This section suggests techniques teachers can use to guide meaningful classroom learning. They are cast in the form of a series of directives: insist, demand, stress, and so on. The language should not imply that the teacher is the sole judge of what the student learns or the sequence or method by which the material is to be assimilated, however. The instructional process is an interaction in which students may select their own learning tasks or pursue objectives that are of interest to them. The teacher's role is not to curtail the students' part in the process but to offer guidance to enable them to acquire, retain, and transfer what they do learn in as meaningful a way as possible.

1. *Take account of differences among individual learners.* Some of the differences in learners' basic traits and dispositions are stable and pervasive, such as intelligence and temperament. Others are more easily

influenced or more transient. Attitudes, for example, are not easy to change, but they can be influenced more easily than intellectual ability. Factors such as fatigue may be subject to change on a day-to-day basis.

Communication in the instructional process depends on the individual learner's cognitive development, prior knowledge, intelligence level, and disposition to learn. Lessons geared to the class as a whole may be satisfactory for the majority of pupils, but they will inevitably fail to provide meaningful learning for some of the more advanced or slower-learning class members. Almost any school or teacher should be able to meet the needs of individual learners without extraordinary strains on budget or personnel. Individual assistance from the teacher or the use of peer tutors in the classroom do not require special materials or equipment or additional expenditures. Individualization also can be enhanced with programmed instruction, computer-assisted learning, multiple sets of textbooks, or audiovisual aids such as single-concept filmstrips. No system has yet been found that perfectly meets all the individual differences of learners, but a teacher concerned with the meaningfulness of learning can make reasonable progress toward providing it.

2. *Channel and control the events to which the learner pays attention.* Little cognitive learning is achieved incidently, that is, without the learner's attention. Teachers sometimes confuse "paying attention" with "maintaining order." Attention fluctuates, even when the learner is reasonably involved in the learning task, and so some redundancy, or perhaps needless repetition, should be built into the instruction. This may consist only of repeating from time to time the label of a concept or the name of a person whose achievements are being discussed. The student's attention must be activated, but it must also be organized and directed toward the meaningful aspects of what is to be learned.

3. *Keep the learner actively and appropriately engaged in the learning process.* In the interactions of the instructional process the student's learning depends more directly on what the learner does and less directly on the teacher's behavior. In subject matter learning, especially, the teacher should counsel students in the techniques of learning: "Don't just memorize this, try to understand it," "What connection do you see between this and the experiment we did yesterday?" "Why do you think that happened?" Active involvement of the learner means intellectual involvement. The deeper and more thorough the semantic processing the learner engages in is, the more meaningful will be the learning.

The teacher's questions are a good way to engage students actively in the instructional process. All but the most routine questions have some arousal value for students (Bull, 1973), but only a small percentage of the questions asked in classrooms require any intellectual effort. Many teachers also fail to allow enough time for students to provide thoughtful replies to questions that require organization of data or the application of facts to a new situation. A student who fails to answer at once is likely to be passed over (Hudgins, 1971, Chapter 8).

4. *Stress the meaningfulness of the learning.* Teachers ought to have a more comprehensive view of the subject matter than students do. Tasks within a course or unit of instruction that are an integral part of the study may appear to learners as just so much busywork, unconnected to anything else they are doing. The teacher's continual attention should be directed to helping students see the relationship of current learning tasks to what has gone before and what is to follow. Learners have a right to know what it is they are expected to do and to learn. They can organize their efforts to learn better if they know and understand the objectives of the tasks they are being asked to undertake (Gagné, 1977).

The better the learner's comprehension, the more likely it is to depart from the verbatim language or examples of either the teacher or the textbook. A teacher who stresses meaningful learning has to be prepared to evaluate student responses in terms that may go beyond answer books or laboratory manuals. If credit in tests or recitations is given only for answers phrased in the same terms as those used by the teacher or textbook, the learner is likely to resort to rote memorization of content and answers to questions. The effort to learn in a meaningful way is likely to be abandoned (Ausubel, Novak, & Hanesian, 1978).

5. *Insist that one task be mastered and comprehended before the learner undertakes the next.* A primary cause of confusion or interference in learning is the learner's effort to acquire new learning before a previous related task has been well learned. Ausubel has repeatedly stressed the necessity for stability, clarity, and discriminability of ideas in the learner's cognitive structure. An idea should be clear to the learner, learned thoroughly enough to be retained for a period of time and understood well enough that it can be differentiated both from other ideas already in the cognitive structure and from new but similar ideas still to be learned. Then it can provide a basis for learning which enables the learner to acquire, subsume, and retain new ideas in her or his cognitive structure.

The clarity, stability, and discriminability of previous learning is also a valuable gauge of how fast the pace of classroom instruction should be. If the learning has been thorough, the time required to learn new ideas will be reduced because a foundation is already available to the learner. Some teachers believe that how well they do their job is related to how fast they introduce new material. It is true that more content can be "covered" in that way, but effective learning will probably suffer for all but the fastest learners in the class. Other students will be reduced to meaningless forms of learning, or they will suffer unnecessary interference if the pace exceeds their ability to integrate previous ideas into their cognitive structures.

6. *Emphasize the possibility of transfer of what is already known to the acquisition of new learning.* The course of acquisition and retention of new material can be shortened and strengthened when learning is meaningful. The teacher should suggest that students try to make connections and applications of what they have already learned to what remains to be learned. By definition, meaningful tasks are related to one another. For a learner who knows the fundamental ideas and principles of a field, the integration of more detailed information can follow naturally, but only if the learner takes advantage of the prior knowledge. The learner who does not try to transfer prior knowledge to new learning tasks may retreat, at least in part, to learning by rote and thus be denied the opportunity to develop the fullest meaning of the learning tasks.

CHAPTER 7 IN RETROSPECT

The role of teachers in the instructional process includes assuring that their students will remember what they learn at school and be able to apply or transfer it to new learning. This is an ambitious objective because students are exposed to many new stimuli each day, and they neither learn nor retain much about many of them. The teacher's task is made easier, however, by the fact that most of the learning is potentially meaningful; that is, the material can be learned in a meaningful way, so it can be connected to or related with other pertinent ideas and bodies of knowledge.

Teachers and students alike facilitate the instructional process when they recognize the meaningful nature of what is to be learned and acknowledge the importance of learning it in a meaningful way. Meaningful learning is integrated into the learner's cognitive structure of a topic, where it is connected with other substantive material to which it is related. The learning therefore is stored more easily for future retrieval and is also available for application to appropriate new situations. In contrast, most material that is learned by rote memory cannot be easily connected or integrated, and so it tends to be lost unless it is thoroughly overlearned or is reviewed and rehearsed periodically.

Concepts, or abstract representations of a large number of particular instances of an object or event, are an important part of meaningful school learning. Through their definitions or verbal labels, concepts make it possible for learners to summarize a great deal of information with very little direct cognitive activity. Because concepts are stored at an appropriate level of cognitive structure, they are also available for retrieval and application to related concepts or additional bodies of knowledge.

One major contemporary idea of how learning and remembering occur relates the processes to information-processing systems. In this view, learning begins when learners *pay attention* to stimuli in the environment. If they do not pay attention, little or no learning will take place. If they do give sufficient attention, new information enters short-term memory, from which it can ultimately be transferred to long-term memory (or cognitive structure, to use Ausubel's term). Once in the long-term store, memories are relatively permanent. Even so, to recall information for current use or application, it must be retrieved once more into the short-term or working memory. How information is stored in long-term memory affects its accessibility. Material that has been learned in a meaningful way is stored in the cognitive structure so the learner has easy access to it.

The advance organizer is an important aid to the acquisition of new potentially meaningful material which also provides a basis for transfer to new learning. This brief, general statement gives the learner an "ideational scaffolding" to which new information or ideas can be attached as they become available. Although the research evidence for advance organizers is partly positive and partly negative, the idea holds much promise as a way of advancing meaningful school learning.

QUESTIONS
FOR
DISCUSSION

1. Take some time to think about a topic you know well—something in your major subject, or the subject you teach, or a hobby. Write (at least in outline form if not in full detail) what you would say to a child to whom you wished to explain that subject. Then examine what you have written. Did you include a detailed, technical account of the subject, or a more general one that hits some of the conceptual highlights of your field? Compare what you wrote with Ausubel's ideas about cognitive structure and how new ideas are incorporated.

2. What is a concept? What is the difference between a concept and a definition? The chapter argues that concepts should be taught through a blend of inductive and deductive experiences. Give an example of how that might be done, using a concept with which you are familiar.

3. Following Ausubel's assimilation theory, the chapter stresses the importance of *meaningful* learning. Students sometimes construe learning material that has personal importance to them or that they judge to be "relevant" as being meaningful. Is that the sense in which the chapter uses the term? Can subject matter content such as appears in a textbook lack personal importance for a learner but still be meaningful? Why or why not?

4. One of the conditions for meaningful learning to occur, according to Ausubel, is for the learner to adopt a meaningful learning set. What does that mean? What other type(s) of learning set(s) might a student take?

5. Why is meaningful material retained in cognitive structure longer than material that lacks meaning?

READINGS
FOR
REFLECTION

Cognitive Views of Learning

Cognitive views of learning and memory have become increasingly available in book form in recent years. We have listed only a few of those that might be cited.

Introductory-Level General Texts

Ausubel, David P., Novak, Joseph, and Hanesian, Helen. *Educational Psychology: A Cognitive View.* 2nd ed. New York: Holt, Rinehart & Winston, 1978.

Farnham-Diggory, Sylvia. *Cognitive Processes in Education.* New York: Harper & Row, 1972.

Gagné, Robert M. *The Conditions of Learning.* 3rd ed. New York: Holt, Rinehart & Winston, 1977.

Introductory Level (special reference to memory)

Bartlett, Frederick. *Remembering.* Cambridge, England: Cambridge University Press, 1932.

This book is a classic. Written over half a century ago, it continues to stimulate investigations of human memory. The style is fresh, readable, and interesting. This book is well worth reading by any student.

Loftus, Elizabeth. *Eyewitness Testimony.* Cambridge, Mass.: Harvard University Press, 1979.

The author has adapted her technical knowledge of human memory to the special case of eyewitnesses. Although the book is written principally for attorneys and students of the law, it is also an interesting application of the psychology of memory to a set of important human problems.

Advanced Level

Bourne, Lyle E., Dominowski, Roger L., and Loftus, Elizabeth F. *Cognitive Processes.* Englewood Cliffs, N.J.: Prentice-Hall, 1979.

Other Theories of Learning

Theories of learning are both more numerous and more diverse than the ones that have been selected for discussion in this book. Students who want to explore that diversity more fully might consult the two books listed below.

Introductory Level

Hill, Winfred F. *Learning: A Survey of Psychological Interpretations.* 3rd ed. New York: Thomas Y. Crowell & Co., 1977.

Advanced Level

Bower, Gordon H., and Hilgard, Ernest R. *Theories of Learning.* 5th ed. Englewood Cliffs, N.J.: Prentice-Hall, 1981.

This book, first written by Ernest Hilgard in 1948, places psychological learning theory in a historical and philosophical framework. There are chapters devoted to early theorists, such as Thorndike and Pavlov, as well as to contemporary theories. Some effort is made to consider the implications of theory and research in learning to educational issues, but the emphasis is on examination and analysis of theories of learning for the serious student of psychology. This is an excellent reference for the student of educational psychology who wants to acquire broader knowledge of learning theory.

REFERENCES

Anderson, Richard C., and Kulhavy, Raymond W. Learning concepts from definitions. *American Educational Research Journal,* 1972, *9,* 385–390.

Ausubel, David P. The use of advance organizers in the learning and retention of meaningful material. *Journal of Educational Psychology,* 1960, *51,* 267–272.

Ausubel, David P. The role of discriminability in meaningful verbal learning and retention. *Journal of Educational Psychology,* 1961, *52,* 266–274.

Ausubel, David P. *The Psychology of Meaningful Verbal Learning.* New York: Grune and Stratton, 1963.

Ausubel, David P. *Educational Psychology: A Cognitive View.* New York: Holt, Rinehart & Winston, 1968.

Ausubel, David P. *Readings in School Learning.* New York: Holt, Rinehart & Winston, 1969.

Ausubel, David P., Novak, Joseph, and Hanesian, Helen. *Educational Psychology: A Cognitive View.* 2nd ed. New York: Holt, Rinehart & Winston, 1978.

Ausubel, David P., Robbins, Lillian C., and Blake, E., Jr. Retroactive inhibition and facilitation in the learning of school materials. *Journal of Educational Psychology*, 1957, *48*, 334–343.

Ausubel, David P., Stager, Mary E., and Gaite, A. J. H. Retroactive facilitation in meaningful learning. *Journal of Educational Psychology*, 1968, *59*, 250–255.

Barnes, Buckley R., and Clawson, Elmer U. Do advance organizers facilitate learning? *Review of Educational Research*, 1975, *45*, 637–659.

Bourne, Lyle E., Dominowski, Roger L., and Loftus, Elizabeth F. *Cognitive Processes*. Englewood Cliffs, N.J.: Prentice-Hall, 1979.

Bousfield, W. A. The occurrence of clustering in the recall of randomly arranged associates. *Journal of General Psychology*, 1953, *49*, 229–240.

Bransfield, John D., and Franks, Jeffrey J. The abstraction of linguistic ideas. *Cognitive Psychology*, 1971, *2*, 331–350.

Brown, Roger. How shall a thing be called? *Psychological Review*, 1958, *65*, 14–21.

Bull, Sheelagh. The role of questions in maintaining attention to text. *Review of Educational Research*, 1973, *43*, 83–87.

Carroll, John B. Words, meanings, and concepts. *Harvard Educational Review*, 1964, *34*, 178–202.

Chi, M. T. H. Knowledge structures and memory development. In R. Siegler (Ed.), *Children's Thinking: What Develops?* Hillsdale, N.J.: Lawrence Erlbaum Assoc., 1978.

Ellis, Henry C. *The Transfer of Learning*. New York: Macmillan Co., 1965.

Gagné, Robert M. *The Conditions of Learning*. 3rd ed. New York: Holt, Rinehart & Winston, 1977.

Hartley, James, and Davies, Ivor K. Preinstructional strategies: The role of pretests, behavioral objectives, overviews, and advance organizers. *Review of Educational Research*, 1976, *46*, 239–265.

Howe, Michael J. A. Repeated presentation and recall of meaningful prose. *Journal of Educational Psychology*, 1970, *61*, 214–219.

Hudgins, Bryce B. *The Instructional Process*. Chicago: Rand McNally, 1971.

Hudgins, Bryce B., and Spies, James J. Improving word comprehension of remedial readers. *Journal of Educational Research*, 1977, *70*, 299–303.

Hunter, Ian M. L. *Memory*. Rev. ed. Baltimore: Penguin Books, 1964.

Johnson, Donald M., and O'Reilly, C. A. Concept attainment in children: Classifying and defining. *Journal of Educational Psychology*, 1964, *55*, 71–74.

Johnson, Donald M., and Stratton, R. P. Evaluation of five methods of teaching concepts. *Journal of Educational Psychology*, 1966, *57*, 48–53.

Klausmeier, Herbert J., and Allen, Patricia S. *Cognitive Development of Children and Youth: A Longitudinal Study*. New York: Academic Press, 1978.

Klausmeier, Herbert J., and associates. *Cognitive Learning and Development: Information-Processing and Piagetian Perspectives.* Cambridge, Mass.: Balinger Publishing Co., 1979.

Lawton, Joseph T., and Wanska, Susan K. Advance organizers as a teaching strategy: A reply to Barnes and Clawson. *Review of Educational Research,* 1977, *47,* 233–244.

Mandler, George. Organization, memory, and mental structures. In Richard C. Puff (Ed.), *Memory Organization and Structure.* New York: Academic Press, 1979.

Mathews, Ravenna. Recall as a function of number of classificatory categories. *Journal of Experimental Psychology,* 1954, *47,* 241–247.

Mayer, Richard E. Information processing variables in learning to solve problems. *Review of Educational Research,* 1975, *45,* 525–541.

Meyer, Bonnie J. F., and McConkie, George W. What is recalled after hearing a passage? *Journal of Educational Psychology,* 1973, *65,* 109–117.

Miller, George A. The magical number seven, plus or minus two: Some limits on our capacity for processing information. *Psychological Review,* 1956, *63,* 81–96.

Myrow, David L., and Anderson, Richard G. Retroactive inhibition of prose as a function of the type of test. *Journal of Educational Psychology,* 1972, *63,* 303–308.

Ornstein, Peter A., and Corsale, Kathleen. Organizational factors in children's memory. In Richard C. Puff (Ed.), *Memory Organization and Structure.* New York: Academic Press, 1979.

Royer, James M. Theories of the transfer of learning. *Educational Psychologist,* 1979, *14,* 53–69.

Royer, James M., and Cable, G. W. Facilitated learning in connected discourse. *Journal of Educational Psychology,* 1975, *67,* 116–123.

Royer, James M., and Cable, G. W. Illustrations, analogies, and facilitated transfer in prose learning. *Journal of Educational Psychology,* 1976, *68,* 205–209.

Werner, Heinz, and Kaplan, Edith. The acquisition of word meanings: A developmental study. *Monograph of the Society for Research in Child Development,* 1950, *15*(51).

A Reinforcement Interpretation of Learning

When learning is considered as a cognitive activity, as in the preceding chapter, the emphasis is on its meaningful nature, taking account of the internal processes the student uses to relate incoming information to existing knowledge or to retrieve or recall what has already been learned. Cognitive theorists are concerned with the changes in students' understanding and comprehension that result from learning. Another group of learning theorists, who interpret learning in terms of environmental reinforcement and conditioning, are more concerned with the changes in students' *behavior* that result from learning. This reinforcement interpretation of learning is the topic of this chapter.

According to reinforcement theory, a response is strengthened when it is followed by a reinforcing stimulus. A simple classroom example concerns a fourth-grade teacher who wants her pupils to raise their hands to be recognized. She asks a question that generates much excitement among the children, and several of them begin to speak at once. But one boy sits quietly with his hand raised, and in a moment the teacher calls on him to give the answer. That stimulus of recognition by the teacher reinforces the boy's hand-raising response, and it becomes more likely that the next time he wants to participate in a class recitation he will sit quietly and raise his hand.

EVALUATION OF COGNITIVE AND REINFORCEMENT LEARNING THEORIES

Whereas the cognitive psychologist explains learning through such concepts as meaning, understanding, and knowledge in the cognitive structure, the explanation of the reinforcement or behavioral psychologist is based on stimuli and responses and the relationships between them. A behavioral psychologist would consider the terms used by cognitive interpreters of learning to be subjective and unnecessary. In explaining why he is not a cognitive psychologist, B. F. Skinner (who developed the concept of operant behavior, which will be discussed later) referred to Ivan Pavlov's classical conditioning experiment:

> In Pavlov's experiment a hungry dog hears a bell and is then fed. If this happens many times, the dog begins to salivate when it hears the bell. The standard mentalistic explanation is that the dog "associates" the bell with the food. But it was Pavlov who associated them! Associate means to join or unite. The dog merely begins to salivate upon hearing the bell. (Skinner, 1978, p. 97)

Skinner concludes that there is no evidence that the dog salivates because it associates the stimulus and response cognitively.

The behavioral psychologist's view of learning is that a response occurs, which is then reinforced or strengthened by a subsequent stimulus. A girl reaches into the cookie jar at home and is rewarded (reinforced) by getting a cookie. The next time the pangs of hunger strike an hour before dinner time, she may reach once more for the cookie jar. If she reaches into an empty jar and comes away without a treat, her behavior may be altered. That is, she is less likely than before to approach the jar, at least until someone has had time to restock it. From the behavioral standpoint, it is unnecessary and unwise to suggest mental concepts or events as a form of explanation.

The behavioral psychologist's insistence on the power of environmental events to shape behavior and disregard for the roles of internal representation and cognitive processes in human learning have been rejected by many students of learning theory. The behaviorists' view of human nature is considered by critics to be simplistic, impoverished, and lacking in the richness and texture needed to explain a phenomenon as complicated as the behavior of human beings. The behaviorist sees human behavior in external and mechanistic terms: A person responds to something in the environment, this response is reinforced, and then it becomes stronger. This view does not seem to take into account the independence of human beings and the individual's ability to think, reason, plan, hope, try, or despair. In view of the complicated, sometimes contradictory, but always interesting human scene, it is difficult to accept the principle that behavior is shaped, maintained, and extinguished solely through external means. The implied denial of humanity keeps many students, teachers, and others from taking it seriously.

There is some validity to the concept of reinforcement in cases such as evaluation of students' behavior with test scores or grades. It is not difficult to understand, for example, that adults work hard day after day in order to support their families; work is rewarded with money which helps to meet basic needs. Yet it is hard to believe that all the activities of either students or workers are conditioned by the relationships between their behavior and reinforcements whose existence or occurrence may not even be evident.

Work, for example, has several functions. Fathers (and, increasingly, mothers) have learned since childhood that as adults it will be their responsibility to support their families. Most adults have so internalized that value that they feel it as a positive desire, not solely as an obligation. Furthermore, their work is not simply a means to such an end but, to varying degrees, it is also the result of a career decision which may have been preceded by years of education and experience. Personal decisions about a mate, a family, a home, and a creed to live by also influence work life. It is likely that all these decisions are made through the individual's power of reasoning, coupled with a personal sense of values formulated while growing up. Attempts to reduce all these decisions and values to contingencies (or dependent interactions) between behavior and reinforcement provide an unsatisfactory explanation of how the work ethic operates in individuals.

In educational psychology concerns are often expressed about behaviorism and its applications in the classroom in the form of operant conditioning techniques. These techniques are based on the simplistic idea that behaviors can be shaped and maintained through contingencies of reinforcement, and the conditions under which academic behaviors are learned are by no means simple. Skinner's analysis of human behavior is more comprehensive and humane than most classroom applications of reinforcement theory would suggest, however. Teachers or consultants who use such techniques regard the ability to alter or to shape human behavior as a straightforward matter of "rewarding" children with candy or tokens or free time, and there are pitfalls in such token economies in the classroom. Careful planning must precede applications of reinforcement theory designed to shape academic behavior.

In the final analysis, whether school learning is approached from a cognitive or a reinforcement position, the application of a theory of learning to the teaching of subject matter content depends on the teacher's thorough understanding of the fundamental concepts and propositions of the field to be taught, including the sequences or structures that enable the learner to acquire mastery of the field. An obvious first principle of the instructional process for the teacher is to be an expert in what is to be taught; in this sense, "content" must predominate over "method." In reinforcement terms, the content of a subject provides the key to the sequencing of the operants to be conditioned, the building up of successive approximations to the final performance that is desired. Whether or not the learner's interactions in the process earn a response of "good" is trivial, compared with the reinforcement the learner receives from the "click" of understanding the subject matter or the satisfaction of acquiring the ability to apply it to new situations.

BASIC CONCEPTS OF REINFORCEMENT AND LEARNING

Skinner differentiates between two basic kinds of conditioning: respondent (or classical) and operant (or instrumental). The principles of respondent conditioning were discovered in Pavlov's experiments with hungry dogs which were briefly described in the quotation above, and operant conditioning, proposed by Skinner, is the basis for classroom applications of reinforcement theory.

RESPONDENT OR CLASSICAL CONDITIONING

Pavlov established the existence of respondent (or classical) conditioning in his experiments with the salivary responses of dogs to unconditioned (meat) and conditioned (bell) stimuli (see Figure 8.1). Two well-known American behaviorists, John B. Watson and Rosalie Raynor (1920), provided a different example. They suggested that fear (as of loud noises or loss of support) is an innate response of human infants, and other emotional responses could be conditioned by pairing a new stimulus with one that elicits the innate fear reaction. To test their belief, they placed an 11-month-old boy, Albert, on a large table and introduced a white laboratory rat into the area. The baby showed some interest and curiosity in the rat, but no fear. But then they made noise directly behind Albert

Figure 8.1

The process of respondent conditioning

Before conditioning:

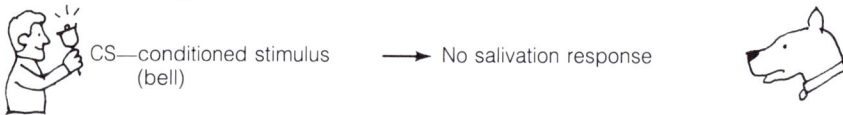

CS—conditioned stimulus (bell) ⟶ No salivation response

UCS—unconditioned stimulus (meat) ⟶ UCR—unconditioned response (salivation)

During conditioning:

CS (bell) + UCS (meat) ⟶ UCR (salivation)

After conditioning:

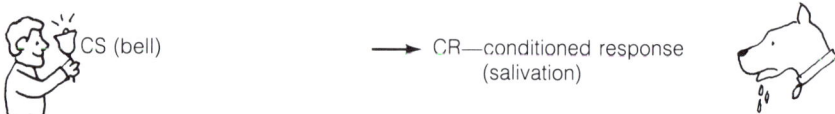

CS (bell) ⟶ CR—conditioned response (salivation)

Source: Adapted from Dan G. Perkins, "Classical Conditioning: Pavlov," in George M. Gazda and Raymond J. Corsini (Eds.), *Theories of Learning* (Itasca, Ill.: F. E. Peacock Publishers, 1980), p. 36.

by striking an iron bar with a heavy mallet, and the child reacted with fear to the noise. The bar was struck each time the rat was presented to the baby. Finally, when the rat was shown to Albert without being preceded by the noise, he responded emotionally to the rat.

Thus the loud noise (an unconditioned stimulus) was presented, and it elicited an unconditioned response (fear). Through pairing the noise with the rat, the rat eventually became a conditioned stimulus. It was then no longer necessary to bang on the iron bar to elicit the fear response from the frightened infant. Albert was afraid of the rat.

The principle of conditioning in this example is exactly the same as that in conditioning a dog to salivate to a bell. Pavlov and Watson both believed that classical conditioning accounts for all learning, but today most stimulus-response psychologists make the same kind of distinction between classical and instrumental, or respondent and operant, conditioning that Skinner does.

OPERANT CONDITIONING

Skinner coined the term *operant* to signify a class of responses or behaviors that operate on the environment.* Responses such as walking, reaching, grasping, and speaking all fall within the broad class of operant responses, which are under the individual's voluntary control. For example, you may agree to extend your arm on a signal from the instructor, such as a tap on the desk with a pencil. But you can control how far or how high you extend your arm, and you can even decide not to respond at all to the signal. If a doctor strikes your patellar tendon with a rubber mallet, though, your knee will jerk, whether you want it to or not. That response is reflexive, involuntary.

When an operant response occurs and is followed by reinforcement (such as food or praise), that response becomes more likely to be repeated in the future under similar circumstances. For a girl who has been reinforced for writing her name in cursive letters rather than printing it, for example, the probability increases that she will use cursive letters again when she must write her name. As that response is reinforced on repeat occasions, cursive writing will finally supplant her earlier printing response.

The Operant Level

The conditioning of a response depends in the first place on its occurrence, or in the language of the behaviorist, its *emission*. If the girl in the example above did not know cursive writing she could not use it, and

---

*For practical purposes, the terms *operant* and *instrumental* are interchangeable. Throughout this book we have referred to such responses as operants.

there could be no reinforcement of the response. Most of the operants in which the school has any interest are complex, and students exhibit them at different levels of performance. The skills do not occur fully developed; if they did, there would be no need to teach them. The key to a teacher's success in using reinforcement principles in the classroom is the ability to diagnose the child's current behavior and to plot a course of increasingly complex responses that will move the child steadily in the direction of the ultimately desired behavior.

This idea of the operant level is an important one. A response cannot be reinforced and made stronger unless it occurs. The teacher therefore cannot shape new, more elaborate responses that depend on another behavior unless the first behavior has been emitted by the learner and conditioned. Suppose a new teacher has just been brought in to take charge of an unruly fifth-grade class. He knows something about operant conditioning and behavior modification, and he wants to apply his knowledge to the new class. He knows, for example, that the way to condition the class's behavior is to wait for the response that he wants to occur and then reinforce it. But as the morning wears on, he finds the behavior of the group growing worse and worse. The operant level, that is, the *frequency* of occurrence of the response that he wishes to reinforce, appears to be close to zero. He cannot reinforce the class because they never behave in a way that he wishes to encourage.

TYPES OF REINFORCEMENT

Reinforcers can be classified in several ways. One major distinction is between primary and secondary reinforcers. Food, for example, which is often used in animal investigations and sometimes in studies of human beings, provides primary reinforcement. The term *primary reinforcer* applies to any stimulus that helps satisfy a primary or basic drive, such as food, water, or sex. But behavior can be reinforced by other stimuli as well. For most human beings, a stimulus such as the approval of friends or receiving money is reinforcing. A *secondary reinforcer* does not itself satisfy primary drives, but it has been conditioned to a primary reinforcer. Money, for example, cannot be eaten or drunk, but it can easily be converted into a chosen primary reinforcer. In fact, because of the range of choices that secondary reinforcers make possible, Skinner calls them *generalized reinforcers*. The availability of reinforcers can be very great because they do not always need to fill primary needs; smiles, words of praise, the "feel" of a clean golf shot, and many other stimuli also acquire reinforcing properties. Classroom teachers have a variety of reinforcers at their disposal. A smiling "good" from one teacher may not have the hoped-for reinforcing qualities another teacher or a student's friends can obtain, however.

*This student, working independently with automated
instructional devices, receives precise reinforcement as she
moves through the sequences of the learning material.
Provision for such activities releases the teacher from the
constant need to serve as reinforcer for the class.*

Reinforcers can also be classified as positive or negative. A *positive reinforcer* is simply the presentation of a reinforcing stimulus. A student receives positive reinforcement when a test paper is returned with a grade of A or a note that says "Excellent! Keep up the good work!" An exhausted teacher is positively reinforced by the receipt of her paycheck. The presentation of the stimulus is reinforcing.

Sometimes, though, the operant behavior is reinforced by a *negative reinforcer,* or the removal or withdrawal of a stimulus. Suppose you have a throbbing abscessed tooth and you rush to the dentist, who removes the nerve so the pain ends. The trip to the dentist is reinforced because his action removed the painful stimulation you had been suffering. Or the mother of an unhappy baby who cries all night finally plugs her ears, and the sound level is sharply reduced. Next time the baby cries, Mother hunts for her ear plugs. The fifth-grade teacher finally can stand the noise and disorganization no more and shouts "Be quiet!" at the class. Surprised, they are quiet, and the blissful silence reinforces his shouting.

Students often think that negative reinforcement and punishment are the same thing, but they are not. Negative reinforcement, like any other reinforcement, strengthens the behavior that it follows. It is called negative because it involves the removal of harmful or unpleasant stimuli. Punishment, on the contrary, calls for the presentation of unpleasant or harmful stimuli or the withdrawal of a reinforcer. A simple example is the case of a small child who misbehaves by knocking down his baby sister, a severe violation of family rules. Father raps junior's bottom smartly two or three times to discourage him from repeating the behavior—that is, he presents negative stimuli. Psychologists since E. L. Thorndike at the turn of the century have had great trouble in deciding what effects punishment has on behavior. Mild punishment administered today may suppress junior's naughty behavior. Tomorrow, however, if he is thwarted by his baby sister again, his behavior may again be marked by aggression.

EXTINCTION

Just as the reinforcement of a response tends to strengthen it or make its occurrence more probable, the *absence* of reinforcement tends to weaken the response. The extinction of a response is said to be due to a lack of reinforcement. The strengthening of a response through reinforcement and its extinction for lack of reinforcement can easily be seen where there is little or no previous history of reinforcement. An example is the behavior of a little girl riding on the subway with her mother. They are seated opposite a grandfatherly gentleman who laughs when the child hides her eyes with her hands and plays peekaboo. The laughter reinforces and excites the child, who again and again clasps her hands over her closed eyes. Several more times the gentleman laughs, but after a while he has had enough of little girls and returns his attention to his newspaper. The child continues the game for a while longer and may become unhappy at the withdrawal of her playmate's attention. Sooner or later, however, something else will distract her, and there will be no more peekaboo attempts.

Extinction rarely occurs in such a straightforward manner, however. Responses can become so strong that they continue to be repeated, more or less unchanged, even though they are rarely or never reinforced. Schedules of reinforcement, which have been studied to determine the effects of intermittent reinforcements on the maintenance of behavior in strength, are described in a later section.

STIMULI

There is a close relationship between stimulus and response in classical conditioning. In Pavlov's experiments with dogs, a salivary response was elicited by the presentation of food. After conditioning, the sound of a bell or a whistle, or whatever was used as a conditioned stimulus, elicited a similar response. The individual cannot consciously suppress such a response. It is, as we have already said, involuntary.

On the other hand, the stimulus cannot call forth a wide range of responses. If conditioning has been to salivation, salivation is elicited when the stimulus is presented, not smiling, or standing on one leg, or reciting poetry. The stimulus need not be precisely the one used in conditioning for the response to be elicited. A sound of different pitch or volume from the one used in conditioning trials will still elicit the conditioned response, although the strength of the response will diminish, depending on how different the new stimulus is from the old one. This phenomenon of *stimulus generalization* is well known in everyday life. A girl meets another girl for the first time, but she feels as though she knows and likes her. The stranger reminds her of Beth Brown, who was her best friend when she was 10 years old. She tends to respond to the girl in the same way as she did to Beth.

In operant conditioning, the role of stimuli is less definite but more flexible. Operants are emitted rather than elicited, and often an operant cannot be connected to a specifiable stimulus. As everyone knows, infants cry a good deal. Sometimes there may be a specific reason for this, such as hunger, gas, or a wet diaper, but often crying, which is operant behavior, has no discernible stimulus. A great deal of operant behavior eventually comes under the control of stimuli. Much of the socialization process, including formal education, can be thought of in these terms. Behavior is reinforced under some conditions but not others.

Stimuli can come to have a discriminative capacity, that is, they can signal when a response may be reinforced and when it will not be. You know that you can drive a car safely through an intersection when the traffic light is green. The green light is a *discriminative stimulus;* it tells you that moving through the intersection is an appropriate thing to do. At an elementary school, a bell rings five minutes before classes begin in the morning. The children playing in the schoolyard line up, ready to enter the building. The bell is a discriminative stimulus for forming lines and abandoning play. Or, before the professor enters the lecture room, college students sit reading or talking. When she enters, the students' reading and conversations gradually cease. The professor's appearance is a discriminative stimulus for paying attention to her.

THE SHAPING OF BEHAVIOR: ACQUIRING NEW OPERANTS

The instructional process is designed to bring about change or modification of knowledge or behavior, as we noted in Chapters 1 and 2. An essential principle in the reinforcement interpretation of learning is the variability of human behavior which makes change possible. The reinforcement of behavioral responses could have no effect if behavior were fixed or unchangeable, and learning would not be possible.

The young teacher with the unruly fifth-grade class who was introduced earlier did not think he could use reinforcement with his students because they never behaved as he wanted them to. Ultimately, his own behavior—shouting at them—was reinforced when he obtained quiet with this means. Had this teacher applied reinforcement principles to achieve the behavior change he wanted (quiet!), he could have used a strategy of the following order. Whenever a lull occurred in the noise level of the class, even though the behavior only roughly approximated the teacher's goal, he could have reinforced it. Since the effect of reinforcement is to strengthen behavior, the lull probably would have gradually occurred more frequently, and the undisciplined behavior would have diminished or disappeared. Because behavior is variable, as the average classroom behavior more closely approached what the teacher was after, he could have reinforced those behaviors that best approximated his goal.

Skinner (1978) describes a simple classroom demonstration he has used to show college students of psychology how a response is shaped. A pigeon is placed in a cage on a table in the lecture room. A line is drawn on the far wall of the cage at the highest level the pigeon's head normally reaches. Sighting through a peephole, Skinner watches for an occasion when the bird's head rises above the line and then gives reinforcement. If this is repeated whenever the bird's head exceeds the height of the line, the pigeon soon struts about the cage with its neck stretched to its utmost. While shaping of this sort is much easier to achieve than shaping the behavior of a class of rowdy children, to say nothing of shaping their academic behavior, still the pigeon demonstration includes the fundamental elements used to shape behavior of any sort. The variability of behavior must be recognized, whether a pigeon's responses are being shaped or a complex concept is being taught to students. The individual's *capability* for the desired response is what makes the shaping of behavior possible. If behavior were inflexible, shaping would be impossible.

Behavior can be shaped through a series of *successive approximations,* or a sequence of responses that increasingly approximate the desired one. In the pigeon demonstration, the first stretch by the pigeon that Skinner reinforced did not exemplify the final response he wanted. It was an approximation, just as the lull in the fifth-grade noise level would be an approximation to what the teacher wanted. If approximations are reinforced in the beginning, more and more of the behavior of the organism (the pigeon or the child, in these examples) comes to resemble the desired performance. Because there is always response variability, some of the later responses will be more like what is wanted than the responses that were initially reinforced. The experimenter, or the teacher, discontinues reinforcement of responses like the early ones, thus allowing them to undergo extinction.

Reinforcement therefore is administered on a *differential* basis, so that only desired responses are reinforced. A few minutes after the first neck-stretching response was reinforced, the pigeon made many even higher stretches. A response that was considered worthy of reinforcement at the outset would not be rewarded at this later time. As the shaping process continues, the standard for reinforcement may be altered several times.

Thus, through a combination of successive approximations and the differential reinforcement of responses, new behavior is shaped. The procedure can be applied by teachers who want to shape new academic responses by their students. Its effectiveness rests on the teacher's ability to specify the student behaviors that are necessary and to recognize them unequivocally when they occur, so the teacher knows when to provide reinforcement.

SHAPING SCHOOL LEARNING
WITH PROGRAMMED INSTRUCTION

One reason the reinforcement interpretation of learning appeals to educators is that Skinner and others have amply demonstrated the applicability of operant conditioning procedures to the instructional process. Most notable in this regard, perhaps, was the impetus Skinner gave to the use of programmed instruction and teaching machines in the 1950s and early 1960s.

Skinner observed that most recommendations for the improvement of education had neglected the study and analysis of teaching, focusing instead on raising standards, improving textbooks, or altering the curriculum. In his view, "Whether by intention or necessity, teachers have been given less to teaching than to holding students responsible for learning" (Skinner, 1961, p. 378). He suggested that efforts to teach by means of programs and machines would encourage careful analysis of how information, concepts, and skills are learned by children and how content must be organized and presented so it can be taught effectively. There is a world of difference between "teaching" and "holding students responsible for learning," of course. The former casts the instructor as a knowledgeable guide through the pitfalls of learning, while the latter assigns only the role of judge and evaluator to the teacher. Many teachers still construe their role in the instructional process as one of selecting and assigning tasks for students, and then evaluating the degree to which the tasks have been achieved.

Skinner's first foray into education (Skinner, 1954) suggested that the knowledge acquired about learning and the shaping of behavior in the psychology laboratory, and the technology to study it there, had important applications to what he viewed as the more important, more complex world of the classroom. A skill subject such as elementary arithmetic might have, he judged, as many as 25,000 contingencies of reinforcement, and each combination might have to be reinforced several times for a child before it is well learned. A single teacher could not provide so many reinforcements for each child and time them with the child's responses to the numerous number combinations. This could be done much more effectively by programs and machines, and the simple technology required to make such reinforced practice possible was available. Skinner insisted that teachers ought not to be expected to serve as a reinforcing mechanism of that sort, because they have more important things to accomplish in the classroom. Teaching machines were seen as one way to free the teacher's time and intellect to pursue the more elevated aspects of the instructional process without sacrificing the practice needed by students.

Teaching Machines

Teaching machines and the instructional programs fed through them were designed to apply operant conditioning principles to teaching. The machines used instructional programs divided into a very large number of segments or *frames*, each of which presented a small amount of new learning. Usually this was just one concept or a variation of a concept. The frame had one or two blanks in it representing key words to be selected or provided by the learner.

An early teaching machine consisted of a manually operated device in which the frame of learning material appeared in a small aperture at the left. The student would read it and then provide the answer on a line of paper exposed at the right. The paper and the program were on rollers, and both advanced when the student pushed a button at the bottom of the machine. The student's attention was closely channeled and focused, since one frame, or small item of information, appeared at a time and had to be responded to before the next frame would appear.

Characteristics of Programmed Instruction

The reinforcement principles applied in the programs used by the early teaching machines have survived in the form of other types of programmed learning machines. An example of how a child's response is shaped through programmed instruction is given in Box A, which reproduces the six frames used in an exercise at the third- or fourth-grade level to teach children to spell the word *manufacture*. The student is kept responding in an active way throughout the exercise. He or she is not expected to know how to spell *manufacture* at first but is asked to copy it from a model. Then parts of the word (various Latin roots) are blanked out, and the student must produce them independently. After the practice afforded by the first five frames, the student must spell the word independently in frame 6.

The intention in programmed instruction is that students will learn by making responses (as opposed to choosing from multiple responses) that are immediately reinforced. Conditioned reinforcers are commonly used; for example, the next frame (bit of instructional material to be learned) is withheld until the student's response to the present frame is correct. What the learner "thinks" or "understands" is not important. What he or she *does* is! If, after completing the sequence in Box A, students can correctly spell *manufacture* in the spaces allocated in frame 6, independently of any cues, hints, or prompts, the successive approximations provided by the five previous frames have shaped their behavior correctly for the purpose.

Several assumptions about the learning of school-type material were incorporated into the early instructional programs. Some of these assumptions have not withstood research testing and school experience, and some have been revised.

A necessary assumption of programmed instruction is that the subject matter has an appropriate sequence, in which each step must be mastered before advancing to the next. This assumption is built into what are called *linear programs,* which compel students to respond to each frame of a program, even though they may have already mastered it. Later, *branching programs,* which begin with a problem or exercise and offer several alternative answers, were developed. Each answer moves students to a different portion of the program which fits their prior knowledge.

Another assumption is that the learner should respond actively to each learning frame and receive reinforcement for a correct response. In the spelling frames in Box A, for example, the reinforcement is the appearance of the next frame or step in the learning process.

In programmed learning it is also assumed that the learners should attend to a small amount of material at any one time and should make an active response to it. Therefore the subject matter is divided into a very large number of very small steps. And, since it is assumed that

BOX A   *Learning to spell with a programmed sequence*

In a programmed learning sequence, the student sees only one frame (numbered item) at a time. The second is not revealed until the first has been completed correctly, and so forth. The student cannot return to already completed frames, and the total exercise is never shown together at one time, as it appears below.

1. **Manufacture** means to make or build. *Chair factories manufacture chairs.* Copy the word here:

   □ □ □ □ □ □ □ □ □ □ □

2. Part of the word is like part of the word **factory.** Both parts come from an old word meaning *make* or *build*.

   m   a   n   u   □ □ □ □   u   r   e

3. Part of the word is like part of the word **manual.** Both parts come from an old word for *hand*. Many things used to be made by hand.

   □ □ □ □   f   a   c   t   u   r   e

4. The same letter goes in both spaces:

   m   □   n   u   f   □   c   t   u   r   e

5. The same letter goes in both spaces:

   m   a   n   □   f   a   c   t   □   r   e

6. Chair factories

   □ □ □ □ □ □ □ □ □ □ □
   chairs.

Source: B. F. Skinner, "Teaching Machines," *Science*, vol. 128 (October 24, 1958), pp. 969–977, Figures 1 and 2.

learners tend to learn the responses they make, the success rate should be very high.With the material presented in small steps, the demand level of the content could be kept so low that few students would make more than an occasional error in their study of a program.

Prospects for Programmed Instruction

Studies of the effectiveness of programmed instruction in the late 1960s and 1970s failed to find significant advantages for the procedure. A survey of four case studies in Chicago; Manhasset, N.Y.; Provo, Utah; and Denver by the Fund for the Advancement of Education (1964) found that programmed instruction was useful in enriching or improving instruction on specific topics, but the goal of large-scale individualized instruction was seldom achieved.

Programmed instruction now provides help with only a small part of the instructional process, and teaching machines have virtually disappeared. Advances in the use of programmed instruction are being offered, however, by developments in computer-assisted instruction, which is discussed in Chapter 12.

THE MAINTENANCE OF BEHAVIOR: SCHEDULES OF REINFORCEMENT

When a response is being learned, frequent reinforcement is important. As the young child struggles to "print" his *a*s and *o*s, the teacher wants to be nearby to provide information and encouragement: "That's good, Jean. Don't go below the line. Here, let me show you. See? The top of the letter touches the sky, and the bottom is on the ground. Now try it again. Oh, that's wonderful! Do it again." Continuous reinforcement like this, the reinforcement of a response each time it occurs, is difficult to provide, however, particularly when it must be done by a classroom teacher who has many pupils to supervise. Often responses are reinforced only occasionally.

If a response is strong, it is not easily extinguished because of infrequent reinforcement. In fact, a response that has been reinforced continuously will disappear faster when reinforcement stops than one which has only been intermittently reinforced. Our everyday observations confirm this. Suppose you have been trying to telephone a friend but you cannot reach him; maybe he is out of town or working late. So you will try again tomorrow or the next day, and since he is away from home a good part of the time, you will keep it up until you contact him.

Intermittent reinforcement helps to maintain behavior in strength. Once a response has been well learned, it is usually extinguished only through repeated lack of reinforcement. The natural contingencies of reinforcement that occur in people's daily lives supply reinforcement on

An obviously warm relationship assures that this teacher's praise will be reinforcing for this particular pupil.

an intermittent and usually random basis. Many habits have been strengthened by the occasional reinforcement they receive. Individuals may be oblivious to the fact that such random reinforcement governs their behavior, but the examples are legion. One is the beggar, shambling along the city streets, who one day picked up a five-dollar bill lying in the gutter and who forever after kept his eyes on the gutter, although he never again found even a nickel there.

Different types of reinforcement schedules determine the pace at which intermittent reinforcement is administered, which in turn affects the individual's rate of responding. Only behavior that has been well learned will be maintained in strength, however. If a student is just beginning to acquire a skill or an interest, intermittent reinforcement will not have the desired effects. Suppose a teenager, after much urging from his parents, has started to play tennis. After two consecutive days of playing, he is beginning to enjoy it. When he arrives for the third day, the courts are closed for repairs, and they will not reopen for two weeks. It is probable that by then the adolescent's interest will have shifted elsewhere. A veteran player might be highly annoyed by the interruption, but two weeks later he would appear at the court, racquet in hand.

TYPES OF REINFORCEMENT SCHEDULES

In detailed investigations of the effects on responding of various reinforcement schedules, Ferster and Skinner (1957) identified four principal types. Two are *interval* schedules, in which the first response, after a specified period of time, is reinforced. The other two are *ratio* schedules, which make reinforcement of a given response contingent on the production of some previously determined number of responses. The basic difference between the two sets of schedules is that the interval schedules depend on the *passage of time* before a response can be reinforced, whereas the ratio schedules involve a certain *number of responses* being performed.

The person whose behavior is being reinforced may not be able to establish either the interval or the ratio. It usually is easier to control reinforcement under a ratio schedule, however, because the rate at which the required responses are produced can be adjusted. Ratio schedules generate higher rates of responding than interval schedules do. Imagine how different children's behavior would be at an Easter egg hunt if they were told that the first child to find an egg at the end of ten minutes would win a prize, or if they were told the prize would be given to the first child to find ten eggs hidden around the lawn.

The number of responses necessary for reinforcement, or the length of time between reinforcements, may be either *fixed* or *variable*. On a fixed schedule, a specific period of time or number of responses is required before the next response is reinforced. With a variable schedule, reinforcement occurs on the average once for every predetermined period of time or number of responses, but any given response may be reinforced. These schedules are thus much less predictable than fixed schedules.

Combinations of the fixed or variable and ratio or interval characteristics result in the four major schedules of reinforcement shown in Box B. Other instances of how the different reinforcement schedules might be expected to function in a classroom or everyday life are described below.

The different schedules of reinforcement generate widely different rates of responding and differences in resistance to extinction. The

BOX B *Examples of the four schedules of reinforcement*

	Fixed	*Variable*
Interval	The teacher tells the class to read silently for five minutes, after which she asks a question about what has been read. For several minutes children sit quietly and read, but as the five-minute mark approaches more and more hands are raised.	Joe tries to catch his barber, Bill, just as Bill returns from lunch. Ordinarily Bill enters the shop about 12:30 p.m., but he may return as early as 12:15 or as late as 1:00 p.m.
Ratio	The chemistry teacher awards "extra credit" for every fifth experiment students write up.	A weekend tennis player hits about one-quarter of his shots well. Some days his play is exceptionally good. Other times he misses many shots during games or hits the ball poorly.

graphs shown in Box C were drawn from data on the pecking responses of pigeons in experimental cages when they were presented with food as a stimulus, not the responses of human beings in everyday situations. Nevertheless they illustrate how rates of responding and resistance to extinction are affected by different schedules of reinforcement and how resistant to extinction behavior can become. It is no wonder, then, that a teacher's gentle admonition, "Please don't do that anymore," often has little or no effect on the behavior of a child.

Fixed-Interval Schedules

In an elementary classrom where spelling tests "for the record" always are given at nine o'clock on Friday mornings, reinforcement in the form of a weekly grade places the pupils' spelling activity on a fixed-interval schedule. The pupils are free, and even encouraged, to practice and rehearse their spelling words any time during the week, but the only time the response is reinforced is at the nine o'clock Friday test.

As illustration 1 in Box C shows, fixed-interval schedules produce fairly low rates of responding, depending on the length of the interval. The appropriate behavior tends to occur only toward the close of the interval, since it is the very next response that is reinforced. For example, campers line up outside the mess hall three times each day, with some of them arriving a little while before meals are served in order to be at the head of the line. If you are asked at ten o'clock in the morning why no one is standing at the door of the mess hall, you would think your questioner rather stupid: "Why, because lunch isn't served until 12 noon. It would be pointless to stand in the hot sun for two hours." Or you might say that meals are served at fixed intervals. Behaviors associated with eating (such as milling around the mess hall) will remain unreinforced until the proper time has arrived.

Variable-Interval Schedules

If a spelling test is given once a week, *on average,* but the test may come unannounced at any time, the teacher is using a variable-interval schedule. A teacher who substituted this technique for regular weekly tests might find that students were studying their daily work more diligently, the average test scores were higher, and most of the children seemed to prefer this method of testing.

Illustration 2 in Box C shows a characteristic rate of responding for variable-interval reinforcement. Even though the number of reinforcements per unit of time is the same under this schedule as with a fixed-interval schedule, the pigeons used in this experiment responded at a more rapid and steadier rate. In both of the classrooms described above, spelling tests were given on the average of one a week. But in the first class the time is specified; in the second, where the quizzes occur on average at the rate of one a week, the student's studying will remain more continuous because of the greater difficulty of predicting when they will be asked to spell "for the record."

Fixed-Ratio Schedules

An example of a fixed-ratio schedule is a program adopted to teach mathematics to high school students who had not succeeded in the normal courses. Most students in the remedial course are young men 17 or 18 years old who have outside jobs and are more interested in earning

BOX C *Pigeons or pupils:*
How reinforcement affects
responding and resistance

Does how often a pigeon pecks a key in a laboratory have anything to do with how a student's attitudes or behavior about learning can be changed? The graphs shown here are based on data supplied by laboratory observation of pigeons who had been placed in standard experimental (or "Skinner") boxes and deprived of food for a certain period. They record responses which consisted of a pigeon's pecks at a key in the box; these responses were reinforced with food on different schedules, as indicated by the short dashes at various points along the curves. When the findings of how the birds' responses varied with the type of reinforcement they received are applied to humans, they suggest why it is so hard to extinguish a student's learning behavior and allow for new learning.

The graphs clearly show how the relationship between the administration of reinforcement and the birds' responding changes as the type of schedule of reinforcement changes. For example, in the first graph (fixed-interval responding), the first response to occur at the end of a predetermined time interval is reinforced. When that happens, the rate of responding diminishes toward zero until well into the next interval. The rate of responding in a high fixed-ratio schedule, however, appears to be independent of the administration of reinforcement. Part B of the third graph shows that the bird continuously pecks the key as rapidly as it can, despite the lack of reinforcement.

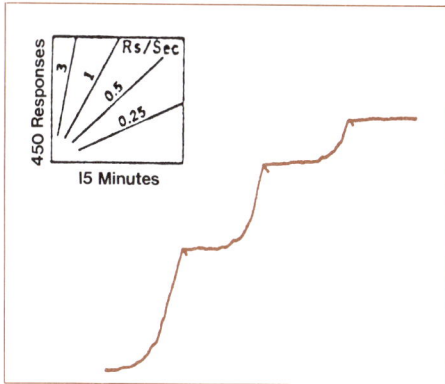

1. The "scallop" effect characteristic of fixed-interval responding. The number of responses increases towards the end of the interval, then subsides after reinforcement.

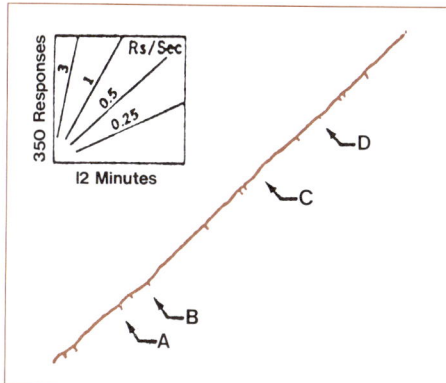

2. A portion of a reinforcement curve for a bird on a variable-interval schedule. The average interval between reinforcements is three minutes, but the reinforcement interval may vary from a few seconds to six minutes. Time is counted from the previous reinforcement. This schedule generates a much higher and steadier rate of responding than the fixed-interval schedule.

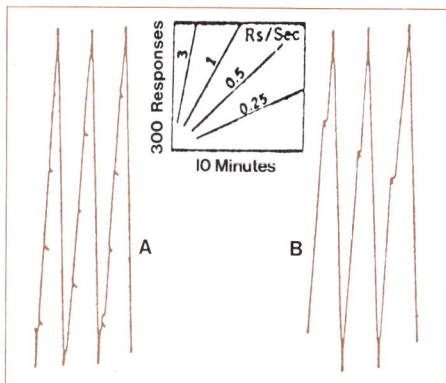

3. Portions of two fixed-ratio schedules. In record A reinforcement occurs for the 210th response, and in record B the 900th response is reinforced. To obtain such high ratios, of course, the experimenter must begin with much lower ones and gradually increase the ratio. Otherwise the response would undergo extinction. After a response had been maintained on a fixed ratio of 900 and reinforcement was then stopped, the pigeon emitted 73,000 responses during the first four and one-half hours of extinction.

Source: From The Analysis of Behavior by James G. Holland and B. F. Skinner, p. 124. Copyright © 1961 by McGraw-Hill Book Company. Used with the permission of McGraw-Hill Book Company.

money than going to school. The high school's grip on them is tenuous at best. They remain in school because they wish to have a high school diploma, but any of them would rather drop out than put up with people or things they find demeaning. The students must learn enough mathematics to warrant a year's credit in the subject, which is required for graduation, but the learning must occur under conditions that do not threaten the learners' concept of themselves as independent young adults.

The teacher secures multiple copies of numerous mathematics textbooks and workbooks, everything from general mathematics to trigonometry; so they can be used on an individual basis. The students work on topics of interest to them and in which they are not already proficient, at their own speed. The teacher remains at her desk most of the period so they have access to her if they want help.

Each topic has a set number of exercises to be worked. The teacher will give instruction and feedback, but the students must work the exercises themselves. The exercises are not graded but must be completed before the unit test is taken. A student receives credit for the unit by scoring at least 80 percent on the unit test. Successful completion of at least 10 unit tests is required for credit for a semester's work, but students must learn some mathematics to pass the tests; just completing the exercises is not reinforced. The exercises must be done carefully before the unit test is administered. Reinforcement in the form of a successful unit is contingent not on the passage of time, as in waiting for a quiz at the end of the week, but on a specific number of responses, completing the exercises before taking the test.

Variable-Ratio Schedules

The reinforcement schedule that most closely resembles everyday experience is the variable-ratio schedule. In the laboratory a particular ratio of reinforcement is selected; for example, every 5th or 80th or 900th response, on the average, will be reinforced. Because any response may theoretically be reinforced, however, the schedule generates very high resistance to extinction. If you have ever stood in one of the large Las Vegas casinos and watched the fervor with which people play the slot machines, you can understand something of the power of this reinforcement schedule. Although the machines are not programmed in accordance wth scientific data about variable-ratio schedules, the results are similar. A player inserts a coin and loses; another and loses; another and wins five in return. When the player will be rewarded is uncertain to the player, who wins often enough to maintain the "lever depressing" response. Few players win sufficiently often to break even at the end of an evening's play, however.

But playing the slot machines is a relatively rare event, and a variable-ratio schedule applies to everyday life in many ways. You may not receive good news in the mail, such as a letter from an old friend, very often, but you continue to anticipate the mail's arrival each day. You may read daily newspapers, although you find good news or articles of great interest or merit only once in a while. You go on rooting for the home baseball team although, statistically at least, it will win the World Series only once every 26 years. Some teams are even less fortunate, yet they may have the most diehard fans! The examples are innumerable.

STUDIES OF SCHEDULES
OF REINFORCEMENT
IN THE CLASSROOM

Adults often strengthen the learned behaviors of children or students without intending to do so. This is apt to happen when the children's demands or misbehaviors persist and their intensity increases. The adults grow weary of the struggle, and the children have their way. An unwanted response, in a form and at a level that may be especially undesirable, is strengthened. Elementary teachers often have an intuitive understanding of this principle, even if they are not familiar with schedules of reinforcement in a technical sense. Before dismissing their classes for lunch, or to go home, they insist that the furniture is placed in its proper position, books and papers are put away, and the children line up quietly. Teachers know that if disorganized behavior is even occasionally permitted, it will become increasingly difficult to control the behavior of the class.

Research data on schedules of reinforcement have come principally from laboratory experiments on the behavior of animals, and their effects on classroom academic performance have not been conclusively proven. Nevertheless, the results of educational studies that have varied the intervals between tests for college students and between report cards for third-grade children suggest that the laboratory conclusions about reinforcement schedules can be generalized to the more complex human conditions of classrooms.

To determine how varying the interval between tests on course material would affect the studying behavior of students of educational psychology, Mawhinney et al. (1971) controlled their access to the course materials. In order to use them, the students had to enter an observation room equipped with one-way mirrors. The experimenters noted how often each student appeared and the time each one spent reading the assigned materials. In one experiment, a total of 12 students took a brief test every day during the first two weeks of the experiment, followed by a longer test administered three weeks later. Then the entire cycle was repeated; two weeks of daily testing, followed by another longer test three weeks after that.

The daily testing schedule produced the steady studying (responding) that is associated with low-value fixed intervals. In the first cycle, the average daily study period was 64 minutes long; in the second it increased to 73. When the students were tested once every three weeks, the scallop effect characteristic of longer fixed-interval schedules appeared (see Box C above). Students tended to be absent more often and to study for briefer periods early in the cycle, and their study periods lengthened as the time for the test approached. The average study times for the 12 students are shown for each session in Figure 8.2. During the first three-week cycle the average was almost identical with the figure for the daily tests (just about 64 minutes). But the mean for the second three-week cycle climbed to 84 minutes, even though the values for the early days

Figure 8.2

Patterns of study for alternating daily and three-week tests by educational psychology students

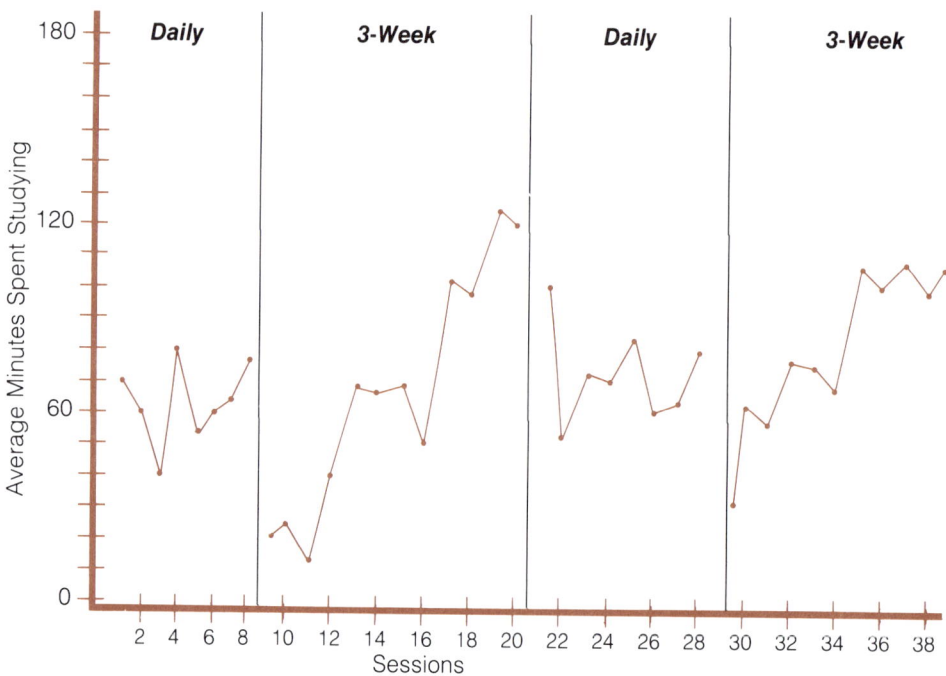

Source: V. T. Mawhinney, D. E. Bostow, D. R. Laws, G. J. Blumenfeld, and B. L. Hopkins, "A Comparison of Students' Studying Behavior Produced by Daily, Weekly, and Three-Week Testing Schedules," Journal of Applied Behavior Analysis, vol. 4 (1971), p. 262.

were quite low. It seems that the repeated shifting from a lower to a higher interval has the same effect on college students' study behavior as it has on pigeons' disc pecking.

The effects of fixed-interval and random-interval reinforcement schedules on third-grade children's academic work, in both quantity and quality, were examined by Saudargas et al. (1977). These children attended a school in which instruction was highly individualized. On Monday each child received an assignment sheet for the week with a minimum of 15 reading assignments, 5 arithmetic assignments, and not more than 5 other assignments in other subject areas such as social studies and science. The children normally were given report cards to take home at the close of school each Friday afternoon, showing their parents how much of the week's work they had completed. Assignments were marked "complete" only if the scores were at least 85 percent correct. Thus there was some check on how well the children did their work, not just the amount of information they processed.

For experimental purposes, a record was kept of the percentage of the assigned work completed. At the end of the first week, when reports went home, the average was 83 percent of all assignments completed. Then during a two-week period reports were sent home at the rate of between seven and nine a day, on a random basis. The only stipulation was that each child must receive at least one report each week. The first week under the variable schedule the completed assignments averaged 93 percent, and the second week just under 111 percent were completed (this was possible when the children also did extra assignments). When the fixed schedule was restored for a week, completion dropped to 74 percent, but when the variable time schedule was reinstated the following week, the rate soared to 154 percent.

The teacher of this class had been trained in individualized instruction, and repeated observations throughout the course of the school year revealed that her pupils were academically engaged about 75 percent of the time, and they completed weekly assignments at about an 85 percent rate. Yet when the home report reinforcement schedule was shifted from a fixed to a random interval, the productivity of the pupils went up dramatically. Both the teacher and the pupils expressed their preference for the random-interval schedule. It is not known whether the accelerated academic production would be sustained if the variable schedule were used on a continuing basis. As an important control in this study, the teacher approved an assignment as completed only if it were essentially done correctly. This provides some assurance that the heightened rate of production did not occur at the cost of accuracy or quality of the children's schoolwork.

These brief classroom studies are not completely analogous to laboratory investigations of schedules of reinforcement. In the latter, a particular response is reinforced, either after a time interval has elapsed or when a specified number of responses has been emitted. In the educational studies, tests or home reports were administered at appointed times, and independently of response contingencies. Saudargas and his colleagues make the explicit point that assignment completion rates for individual children were unpredictable and not comparable to those produced by laboratory organisms.

Nonetheless it seems clear that variations in classroom events that resemble the conditions of interval or random schedules of reinforcement will produce changes in amounts or rates of studying behavior. These are reminiscent of the experience with laboratory schedules, although not identical with them. Teachers who want to intensify students' responses, such as studying or practicing already learned responses, should find it worthwhile to try new schedules of reinforcement in the classroom and then observe their effects over time.

THE TEACHER'S ROLE IN REINFORCEMENT

The reinforcers that teachers can use in the classroom are largely related to the verbal nature of the instructional process. The teacher's language is a vehicle for showing approval or disapproval and supplying information about how well the pupil is doing. Classrooms are highly verbal in nature, and most reinforcement comes in the form of feedback from the teacher on students' performance or behavior. We have shown how tests and reports can be used to vary schedules of reinforcement, for example.

Regular or special classroom activities also can be reinforcing. Many children love to read or do arithmetic problems, science experiments, or other types of academic tasks, and opportunities for such activities can be used as reinforcement. Teachers sometimes use the promise of a preferred activity as an inducement to students to do something else ("I'll read the next chapter of Tom Sawyer to you if we have a good geography period"). They may also provide free time in which children can select their preferred activities (Premack, 1965).

REINFORCEMENT OF STUDENTS THROUGH VERBAL FEEDBACK

For the most part the instructional process is conducted by verbal means. Assignments are made, textbooks are read, exercises are completed, new subject matter is presented, and discussions are held between the teacher and students. Recitations, or exchanges consisting of questions from the

The teacher helps reinforce students' learning experiences by providing ongoing information and encouragement. Because her attention must be divided among all the members of the class, she can offer reinforcement to individual students only occasionally.

teachers and answers from the pupils, are the principal type of classroom interaction. Teachers use all their verbal exchanges with students as vehicles for reinforcing those academic behaviors they wish to strengthen and punishing or discouraging the ones they would like students to abandon.

It is important, therefore, to know how language is used in the classroom to provide reinforcement and what its consequences are. According to Bellack et al. (1966), the language teachers and students use in the classroom takes definite forms. The most frequent type of interaction is a simple "teacher-question, pupil-answer, teacher-feedback" model. Classroom verbal exchanges take many other forms, also, but most of them are variants on this model, which is the principal means teachers use to convey feedback to students.

To find out what kind of feedback teachers provide and its effects on students, Zahorik (1968) observed lessons in several third- and sixth-grade classrooms. Although the teachers he observed used some 175 different patterns of feedback to expand or comment on their students' answers in recitations, just 16 patterns accounted for 70 percent of all the feedback. Moreover, a fourth of the feedback was delivered in only three patterns:

1. The teacher repeats a pupil's answer, approves it, and goes on to the next topic in the lesson.
2. The teacher asks a child to develop his or her answer more fully.
3. The teacher praises a child's answer, confirming its correctness, and then goes on to the next topic.

It might be helpful for teachers to cultivate alternative feedback patterns, especially of the type that would supply more information and explanation about the adequacy of student responses.

How the teacher's feedback affects pupils' subsequent behavior (that is, its effectiveness as a reinforcer) has also been studied. Travers and others (1964) found that students' retention of information is heavily dependent on their direct interaction with the teacher. In the artificial and contrived experimental situation they used, however, some children were not allowed direct participation in the lessons.

Praise as a Reinforcer

Teachers may use praise as a reinforcer in the classroom, but it does not always function that way (Brophy, 1981). For a child who dislikes the teacher or school, the praise might not be reinforcing. And, as children grow older, approval by a peer group may be more effective in shaping their behavior than what the teacher says. This is particularly true for adolescents, as we noted in Chapter 4.

Teachers are more apt to express disapproval than approval, according to observations of the behaviors of over 100 teachers in every grade between 1 and 12 reported by White (1975). At most grade levels (and in all of them above the primary grades), the feedback of disapproval from teachers is greater than approval. It makes a difference, though, whether the feedback is being offered for substantive (subject matter) or managerial (disciplinary) behaviors. Teachers are more likely to offer praise for children's substantive work, especially in the primary grades, but more likely to disapprove of their managerial activities. In fact, teachers rarely reinforce appropriate pupil behavior of a managerial sort. Comments such as, "I'm glad you are on time," or "You've behaved very well today," are infrequent. And approval rates go down as grade level goes up. It is more likely that students will be reinforced by the substance of their work at more advanced grade levels, or by test grades or other types of feedback. The teacher can appropriately praise a young child in terms that would be embarrassing to both of them if the child were a preadolescent or older.

REINFORCEMENT FOR THE TEACHER

One reason teachers express disapproval more often than approval is that immediate disapproval of a pupil's misbehavior is reinforcing to the teacher—it tends to stop the misbehavior. Such temporary resolutions usually do not provide long-term solutions of the underlying problems responsible for the misbehavior in the first place, however.

Recitations, which we have described as the principal form of classroom verbal interactions, are also reinforcing for the teacher (White, 1974). They have been criticized for dullness and triviality, but they are still widely used. When students answer a teacher's questions, it is a sign that they are paying attention and they are learning. The teacher's use of questions is therefore reinforced. If the teacher's questions are too complex or abstract, however, pupils will not respond to them, an embarrassing outcome for everyone. When the questions are easier, more children participate in the recitation, and more of the questions can be answered correctly more often. Care with construction of the questions for a recitation thus determines how reinforcing their use will be for the teacher.

If teachers were evaluated and reinforced on the basis of their teaching, rather than their ability to maintain quiet and orderly classrooms, White suggests, recitations might be replaced more widely with methods that offer intellectual stimulation and imaginative learning experiences for students. Her idea that it is always wise to look for the sources of reinforcement behind persistent behavior (such as recitation) is an interesting way to think about what teachers as well as students do in classrooms. It echoes Skinner's observation that more attention should be paid to the way teachers teach than to the way they evaluate student progress.

PLANNED VERSUS NATURAL CONTINGENCIES OF REINFORCEMENT IN THE CLASSROOM

Because the contingencies of reinforcement that occur naturally in the classroom can be reinforcing to teachers, they may encourage the preservation of methods (such as recitations) that are not as powerful in their influence on student learning as they ought to be. Planned reinforcement contingencies can have a much greater effect. The impact on students' studying behavior caused by intermittent schedules of reinforcement applied to the timing of tests and home reports has been demonstrated. The strength of programmed instruction also lies in the carefully arranged contingencies between the stimuli of the instructional program, the students' response, and the reinforcement provided by the teaching machine or programmed textbook.

The typical classroom teacher may not be able to make direct applications of operant procedures to everyday classroom teaching or to maintain the applications over an extended period. Even if the applications can be made indefinitely, their early consequences for shaping classroom behavior and pupil learning may not continue but may fade when the novelty of the procedures wears thin. These issues are considered in Chapter 12, as part of the discussion of learning and instruction.

CHAPTER 8 IN RETROSPECT

The emphasis of this chapter is on the *behavior* of learners in contrast to their cognitions, as was true of Chapter 7. Behavior is shaped through the presentation, or sometimes the withholding, of stimuli that are called reinforcers. Behavior is strengthened when it is followed by a reinforcing stimulus.

The academic behavior of learners can be shaped by appropriate sequences of reinforcing contingencies. They should be designed so that the learner is reinforced for making responses that approximate the desired academic or intellectual performance, and not reinforced for responses that are not relevant to, or that would interfere with, the desired response. For many sophisticated behaviors, the correct or complete response cannot be performed initially. Then a process of successive approximations, in which early responses of the learner that are close to the desired ones are reinforced, can be used. As a result of differential reinforcement applied as learning continues, responses that were reinforced early in the learning process no longer receive reinforcement but are extinguished as the learner becomes increasingly capable of making the appropriate or correct responses.

Concepts about reinforcement are useful not only in shaping behavior but also in maintaining behavior in strength. Such schedules of reinforcement show in general that once responses are acquired, they are made resistant to extinction if they are reinforced only some of the times they occur, rather than every time. A response that is always or continuously reinforced is highly susceptible to extinction. Once it fails to be reinforced, it may fade rapidly. Well-learned responses that are gradually shifted from high to low rates of reinforcement may continue in great strength.

There are several ways in which the concepts of operant conditioning have been applied to practical problems of education. One of these is programmed instruction. Another is the use of schedules of reinforcement to maintain or to increase students' studying behavior. A third application is contingency management, in which teachers follow a careful plan for the reinforcement of student behaviors in the classroom (see Chapter 12). If contingency management is to be effective teachers must have clear-cut rules for the administration of positive reinforcers.

1. How are respondent and operant conditioning different from each other? Give an example of each that is applicable to the school or to the classroom, other than those cited in the chapter. **QUESTIONS FOR DISCUSSION**
2. Select a reasonably straightforward academic task you might wish to teach to a student. Show how the final performance could be shaped through a series of successive approximations. Pay special attention to identifying the assumptions you make, for example, about the knowledge or skills your pupil begins with, and the series of steps or chains you expect him or her to go through in acquiring the final behavior.
3. List reinforcers the teacher has available to help shape or maintain students' behavior. How different are the reinforcers the first-grade teacher can use from those accessible to the senior high school teacher?
4. Write an additional set of examples for the four types of schedules of reinforcement in Box B. Use teachers and students as the subjects of your illustrations.
5. In what sense and to what extent is the parent's or the teacher's role to control the behavior of the learner? What does control mean in the context of education and child-rearing? What obligation does it impose upon the person doing the controlling?

The references cited at the end of Chapter 7 are also applicable to the discussion of reinforcement in this chapter. **READINGS FOR REFLECTION**

Reinforcement Theory and Operant Conditioning

The writings of B. F. Skinner are the major source of scientific and intellectual information about operant conditioning. Much of his work is technical or of primary interest to other scholars and social scientists.

The books listed below provide a representative sampling of Skinner's ideas which should be of general interest to college students.

Holland, James G., and Skinner, B. F. *The Analysis of Behavior.* New York: McGraw-Hill, 1961.

This book presents the basic concepts of Skinner's system in a programmed text format. It is interesting not only for the ideas it contains but also because it illustrates Skinner's belief that those ideas can be applied to practical considerations of education, such as college students learning about operant conditioning.

Skinner, B. F. *Walden Two.* New York: Macmillan Co., 1948.

This book is Skinner's statement of a utopian society. It is cast in the form of a novel, but it is more interesting if approached as social philosophy than as fiction.

Skinner, B. F. *Science and Human Behavior.* New York: Macmillan Co., 1953.

This is Skinner's basic statement about the scientific study and analysis of human behavior. If you are going to read only one of Skinner's books, this probably should be the first choice.

Skinner, B. F. *Cumulative Record.* 3rd ed. New York: Appleton-Century-Crofts, 1972.

This is a carefully selected and edited collection of Skinner's major research reports and shorter papers. Judicious sampling of its contents can provide a good concept of the wide-ranging interests Skinner has entertained throughout his career.

Bandura, Albert. *Principles of Behavior Modification.* New York: Holt, Rinehart & Winston, 1969.

One of the major applications of operant conditioning is behavior modification. This is a comprehensive statement of its principles.

REFERENCES Bellack, Arno A., Kliebard, Herbert M., Hyman, Ronald T., and Smith, Frank L., Jr. *The Language of the Classroom.* New York: Teachers College Press, Columbia University, 1966.

Brophy, Jere. Teachers praise: A functional analysis. *Review of Educational Research*, 1981, *51*, 5–32.

Ferster, Charles B., and Skinner, B. F. *Schedules of Reinforcement.* New York: Appleton-Century-Crofts, 1957.

Fund for the Advancement of Education. *Four Case Studies of Programmed Instruction.* New York: 1964.

Holland, James G., and Skinner, B. F. *The Analysis of Behavior.* New York: McGraw-Hill, 1961.

Mawhinney, V. T., Bostow, D. E., Laws, D. R., Blumenfeld, G. J., and Hopkins, B. L. A comparison of students' studying behavior produced by daily, weekly, and three-week testing schedules. *Journal of Applied Behavior Analysis,* 1971, *4,* 257–264.

Premack, David. Reinforcement theory. In David Levine (Ed.), *Nebraska Symposium on Motivation,* vol. 13. Lincoln: University of Nebraska Press, 1965.

Saudargas, Richard W., Madsen, Charles H., Jr., and Scott, John W. Differential effects of fixed and variable-time feedback on production rates of elementary school children. *Journal of Applied Behavior Analysis,* 1977, *10,* 672–678.

Skinner, B. F. The science of learning and the art of teaching. *Harvard Educational Review,* 1954, *24,* 86–97.

Skinner, B. F. Why we need teaching machines. *Harvard Educational Review,* 1961, *31,* 377–398.

Skinner, B. F. *Reflections on Behaviorism and Society.* Englewood Cliffs, N.J.: Prentice-Hall, 1978.

Travers, Robert M. W., Van Wagenen, Keith, Haygood, Danielle H., and McCormick, Gary. Learning as a consequence of the learner's task involvement under different conditions of feedback. *Journal of Educational Psychology,* 1964, *55,* 167–173.

Watson, John B., and Raynor, Rosalie. Conditioned emotional reactions. *Journal of Experimental Psychology,* 1920, *3,* 1–4.

White, Mary Alice. Is recitation reinforcing? *Teachers College Record,* 1974, *76,* 135–142.

White, Mary Alice. Natural rates of teacher approval and disapproval in the classroom. *Journal of Applied Behavior Analysis,* 1975, *8,* 367–372.

Zahorik, John A. Classroom feedback behavior of teachers. *Journal of Educational Research,* 1968, *62,* 147–150.

The Learning of Attitudes and Values

Many kinds of learning at school involve feelings as well as thoughts. It is necessary for someone to teach a young child to learn to read, for example, but it also is desirable to help the child learn to love to read—quite a different thing, but with just about as important an outcome. Children in school should learn to like themselves, their peers, school, and a variety of school subjects, and they should also come to like learning for its own sake.

As children mature into adolescents and adults, one goal of their education in a democratic society is the acquisition of such values as freedom of choice, equality, cooperation, and self-reliance. Students should not only learn how government works, for example, but should also acquire values that express the importance of voting in an informed way. As they learn the subject matter of music, biology, social studies, and mathematics, they may also learn to appreciate good music, to respect nature, to regard as equals people from different cultures, and to enjoy using mathematics.

The instructional process can be structured to help students learn or acquire beliefs, attitudes, and values about themselves, others, objects, and events, and to allow teachers to facilitate this learning. This is the principal topic of this chapter, and the conclusion is that teachers should not attempt to indoctrinate students with certain values but instead should help them learn a process for resolving value dilemmas for themselves. The instructional process is concerned with students' attitudes and values because adults care about what children feel and how they act, as well as what they know or think. In order to make beliefs, attitudes, and values a part of the process, teachers must have an understanding of them and how they can be learned or changed.

THE RELATION OF BELIEFS, ATTITUDES, AND VALUES

Beliefs, attitudes, and values affect each other, and together they affect the actions of individuals. A person rarely has an attitude toward something without also having a belief about it. A teacher may have a favorable *attitude* about drinking coffee and enjoy her morning cup, for example, but she also *believes* that the caffeine makes her more alert, and being alert helps her work harder, and hard work is an important *value* of hers. Attitudes about things or persons usually have a basis in personal beliefs and entail corresponding values. As indicated in Figure 9.1, a person's beliefs and attitudes are generally integrated within a broader value framework.

Figure 9.1

Relationships among values, beliefs, and attitudes

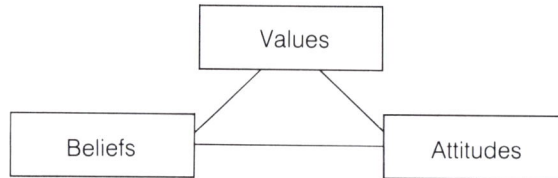

Values

Beliefs

Attitudes

Attitudes can involve feelings about objects (spinach), persons (teachers), and events (tests). A student may dislike spinach, like the challenge of a tough test, and regard Mrs. Hastings as a favorite teacher. Beliefs differ from attitudes in that they involve the information a person has about an object, such as the belief that you are 20 pounds overweight, that Alan has an IQ of 90, or that Sara never raises her hand before answering a question. Beliefs involve cognitions, or thoughts, whereas attitudes involve affect, or feelings. Values include both beliefs and attitudes (thoughts and feelings) and are standards and principles for judging worth. Honesty, equality, freedom, and justice are examples of values. Values are more general than attitudes and beliefs. A person may have only a relatively few (20–30) values but hundreds of attitudes and beliefs about objects, from specific and insignificant items such as chicken noodle soup to more general, more important issues such as nuclear disarmament.

THE LEARNING OF ATTITUDES

An attitude is a learned predisposition to respond in a consistently favorable or unfavorable manner with respect to a given object (Fishbein & Ajzen, 1975; Gagné, 1977). These are all attitude statements: "When I look at myself in the mirror, I like what I see," "I like to read books," "Math is yucky," and "I don't like Andrew." In each of these statements there is an object (self, books, math, Andrew) which is evaluated positively or negatively. Attitudes are not inherited; they are learned through some sort of experience. For example, your mother may have told you that you are nice looking; you may have heard other students say they dislike Andrew; or you may get poor grades in mathematics. Certain experiences leave you with positive feelings, while others leave you with negative feelings.

ATTITUDES AND BEHAVIOR

Most people believe that it is desirable to be physically fit, though obviously not everyone is. In fact, many people who say they agree with the goal of physical fitness overeat, smoke cigarettes, and rarely exercise. This probably does not mean they have negative attitudes toward physical fitness, however. How then are attitudes related to behavior?

Attitudes are linked to behavior through a complex set of beliefs, values, and expectancies. Consider the example of two students, both of whom value friendships over physical development. Molly joins her friends after school to talk, eat, and listen to records and never participates in any sports activities, while Cathy finds she can make friends by playing on the soccer team after school. For Molly, participating in after-school sports is inconsistent with being with her friends. While she may have positive attitudes toward both being with friends and physical fitness, the after-school situation favors one behavior over another. Molly's decision to reject sports participation is an easy one if she thinks she might not be accepted by her teammates. Whatever the reason, Molly presents quite an interesting challenge to the physical education instructor who must try to mesh such attitudes and sports participation.

Attitudes have an intuitive appeal as explanations for behavior. When students drop out of school, it is easy to write them off as having negative attitudes toward school and society. Or when students get low grades, they may say the teacher doesn't like them. Such explanations are often convenient excuses; while they may help explain events, they do not accurately represent the complex attitude-behavior relationship.

Specific behaviors are not easily predicted from attitudes, as Fishbein and Ajzen (1975, p. 15) have noted: "An attitude is a 'general' predisposition that does not predispose the person to perform any 'specific' behavior." For example, if Mark believes that history books are boring, full of details and big words, and that history tests mean memorizing a lot of facts, he may have an unfavorable attitude toward the study of history. As a consequence, he would avoid courses in history as electives and would not read nonrequired history books, but still he might study quite diligently for the history tests he has to take. Here, the student's attitude is predictive of his general orientation toward history as an area of study, but it does not affect all his specific behaviors. In trying to predict specific behaviors, such as why Mark studies for his history tests, it is necessary to look at the consequences of this behavior and how he values these consequences. He may believe that studying for history tests leads to good grades, and good grades are very important to him. Another example is given in Box A, which explores the values and beliefs high school students have about the consequences of taking French courses and how this affects their course-selection behavior.

BOX A   *The French connection:*
Attitudes and behavior about
learning a foreign language

The head of a high school French department was concerned about a drop in enrollments in the introductory French course which had occurred when learning a foreign language was eliminated as a requirement for graduation. This was a highly competitive, upper-middle-class high school in which 90 percent of the students went on to college. Most of the students believed that foreign language courses were difficult, and many believed they did not have a high aptitude for learning a foreign language. In a recent survey the department head had discovered that most students had positive attitudes toward learning about other cultures and learning foreign languages, but they had negative attitudes about taking foreign language courses themselves.

Problem

How can the department head increase enrollments in French courses?

Problem analysis

The department head knows that students have a negative attitude toward foreign language courses which seems to stem from their belief that taking such courses will result in low grades. Thus, if she wants students to take French courses, she

A MODEL OF ATTITUDE LEARNING
AND CHANGE

Children in the first stages of social-emotional and cognitive-intellectual development (see Part I) learn attitudes through experiences with the consequences of their actions and behaviors (Fishbein & Ajzen, 1975). If the consequence of reading a book is pleasure, for example, they may learn to like books. The pleasure a child associates with books may be generalized to all situations of reading, or it may be limited to bedtime stories read by a parent. A child who has had pleasant experiences with reading may come to anticipate in thought the positive consequences of reading. As an adult he or she may daydream about getting home from

must change their attitudes toward foreign language courses
and change their expectation that taking French will result in
failure or low grades.

Solution

The department head decided that she must entice students
into a direct and positive experience with French, making use of
their positive attitudes toward studying other cultures. She
offered a mini six-week course in French culture which was
made highly attractive to students because it involved numerous
field trips to museums, French plays, and movies. She also
redesigned the entire introductory French language curriculum,
using a mastery approach.* The key features of the program
were advertised to students in the following way:

> Sign up for a new experience in learning the French language.
> Learn at your own pace with individualized feedback in the
> language laboratory. You can only receive an A or B or no credit.
> Complete one unit at a time and set your own goal for an A or B.
> When you meet the objectives of a unit, you will earn an A or B.
> You may drop the unit and start over again at any time.

---

*Mastery learning is described in Chapter 12.

work, settling down in an easy chair, and becoming engrossed in an
Agatha Christie murder mystery.

Initially, most attitudes are probably learned through such direct experience with events that arouse positive and negative feelings. As children develop the capacity to think about their feelings, they come to
anticipate these positive or negative experiences and then act in ways to
approach or avoid them. Because these thoughts and feelings often can
be generalized to similar or related situations, children also can learn
attitudes indirectly (vicariously) by observing the positive or negative
experiences of others. More mature and more sophisticated thinkers
may learn about the positive or negative consequences of actions through
logic and reasoning, without having either direct or vicarious experience

with the attitude object. These three approaches to the learning of attitudes—direct experience, observation, and logical reasoning—will be described in the sections to follow.

An attitude is the affective or emotional evaluation a person makes about objects or persons. A specific attitude is found by evaluating the attributes of the object on a dimension of like-dislike. As an attitude object, school, for example, may involve such attributes as a brick building, teachers, rules, classmates, books, or tests. A student's attitude toward school is a function of how he or she evaluates these different attributes. If more of them are evaluated positively than negatively, a positive attitude results. Those attributes that are most closely associated with school in the student's thoughts are the ones that will be most dominant in shaping these attitudes. A boy's attitude toward school might be somewhat negative if the first thought he has when he thinks of it is, "I have to take tests which I could fail." If he thinks first of classmates and social events, he would have a more positive attitude.

The cognitive and reinforcement principles of learning presented in Chapters 7 and 8 also apply to the study of how people learn what attributes are associated with attitude objects and how they acquire the positive or negative evaluations they place on these attributes. One key difference, however, is that the learning of attitudes is a function of each person's unique personal history. Thus, various persons' attitudes toward the same object (such as school) are quite different. Attitudes are formed through learning processes involving direct experience, vicarious experience, or logical reasoning, by means of which people learn to associate the attributes of an attitude object with positive or negative outcomes: "I do well (positive outcome) on tests (attitude object)," "I do poorly (negative outcome) on tests." People learn to represent these experiences in their thoughts as expectancies about whether a positive or negative consequence results. Thus, *the evaluation of an attitude object is determined by whether its important attributes are associated with positive or negative consequences.*

People do not always approach situations with either positive or negative attitudes, however. Students, for example, can have a relatively neutral attitude toward a teacher or course when they have had little direct experience with a new teacher or subject matter and have not heard any rumors or other evaluative accounts about it from their peers. In these cases, the teacher can start from a neutral point to try to develop positive attitudes in the students. The students do not know whether to expect positive or negative consequences from interaction with a new teacher, unlike a teacher who has been in the school for a time and has developed a reputation among students ("Miss Phillips is nice but she makes you work hard"). Similarly, students starting a new subject like algebra or a course on the American novel may approach it with neutral attitudes. Teachers also can make a course *appear* new and different, as the head of the French department did in creating a "new experience in learning the French language" (see Box A above). Advertisers attempt to do this when they announce a "new and improved" brand X. You may not have liked the *old* brand X, but the advertiser is hoping you will hold a more neutral attitude toward the "improved" product until you try it.

Thus learners may have neutral, negative, or positive attitudes toward their participation in the instructional process. When the students' attitudes toward learning are neutral or positive, the instruction can be designed to achieve attitude learning and development. When their attitudes are negative toward learning or undesirably positive (as with disciplinary problems), the instruction should be geared to attitude change.

Suppose the boy described above who associates school with the attributes of tests and classmates has a teacher who wants to help him develop a more positive attitude toward school. According to Fishbein and Ajzen (1975), attitudes can be changed in one of three ways:

1. By altering the strength of the association of the attributes with the attitude object.
2. By changing the consequences associated with the various attributes.
3. By changing the evaluations of those consequences.

The teacher might decide to focus the change efforts on the association of the attribute, test, with the attitude object, school. She could try to *change the student's close association* of test and school by simply reducing the number of tests and replacing them with assignments. Or she could *create new beliefs* about the consequences of taking tests. To do this the teacher could use the mastery approach (see Chapter 12), in which the consequences of the test constitute a chance for improvement, or provide an opportunity for those who pass a test to go to a music or art learning center, or just allow them to begin another unit. In this example, trying to *change the negative evaluation* associated with failing a test would be rather difficult, since failure arouses strong feelings of displeasure.

In the example in Box A, before the head of the department redesigned the French course, students associated taking any foreign language course with the attribute, difficult, and the negative consequence, failure. The students placed a negative evaluation on this attribute because they believed that taking a difficult course would be likely to result in failure. Failure was particularly distasteful in this case because they perceived that it would prevent them from achieving the important goal of getting admitted to college. Since changing such a strong negative evaluation is not easy, instead the attributes and consequences that are associated with taking a French language course had to be changed.

Culture was a *positively evaluated attribute,* so the department head attempted to *strengthen its association* by inviting students to learn about French culture without the burden of learning a new language. Then she attempted to *create new beliefs about the consequences* of taking a foreign language course by guaranteeing that students could not fail the course in French; that is, they assuredly would earn either an A or B or no credit.

Whatever the goal of the instructional process in regard to student attitudes, the methods for achieving attitude learning and change fit the same model. Some combination of direct experience, vicarious experience or observation, and logic or reasoning is needed to develop or modify attitudes in the desired direction.

ATTITUDE LEARNING THROUGH DIRECT EXPERIENCE: RESPONDENT AND OPERANT CONDITIONING

The respondent (or classical) and operant (or instrumental) conditioning procedures introduced in Chapter 8 can be applied to attitude learning and change. In these cases the conditioning process involves the learner's direct experience with the consequences associated with attributes of the attitude object.

RESPONDENT CONDITIONING

In respondent conditioning, as we noted in Chapter 8, learning is regarded as an association between a stimulus and a response. In the same way Pavlov associated a bell with meat for dogs, an unconditioned stimulus (food) which elicits an unconditioned response (hunger) is paired with a neutral stimulus (dining hall). Through repeated pairings of this type, the neutral stimulus becomes a conditioned stimulus which begins to elicit a conditioned response that is the same as the unconditioned response, despite the absence of the unconditioned stimulus (the sight of the dining hall elicits feelings of hunger, although no food is present). In attitude learning, when the conditioned response replaces the former unconditioned response, it becomes the consequence of the attitude object. Unconditioned responses related to attitudes have a strong emotional component such as fear, anxiety, relaxation, pleasure, or elevated body temperature or blood pressure. Students who learn attitudes through respondent conditioning therefore can develop rather strong emotional reactions to previously neutral stimuli. The announcement of a midterm exam, for example, often elicits anxiety.

The famous study of 11-month-old Albert's reaction to a white rat by Watson and Raynor (1920) which was described in Chapter 8 showed how easy it is to condition a negative attitude. Whenever a loud noise was paired with the appearance of the rat, Albert cried. The loud noise was an unconditioned stimulus which produced the unconditioned response of fear in Albert. After a while this fear response was triggered by just the sight of the rat. In fact, Albert quickly generalized the fear response to other white, furry objects, including a white rabbit and even a Santa Claus mask.

Respondent conditioning is the earliest form of learning most children experience in their lives. They learn to respond to their parents with positive, warm feelings because the parents hold them during breast or bottle feeding. Later, in the absence of feeding, the parents produce this same warm emotional response. In conditioning terms they take on the status of a conditioned stimulus and serve as the cue for later conditioning. For example, a parent may hold a small child while reading a book aloud. The physical touch and presence of the parent produces a positive emotional response in the child, and through repeated experiences involving the parent, child, and book, the child develops a positive response to books.

Voices also can create very strong responses in infants. A soft, soothing voice can elicit a relaxation response, whereas a loud, harsh voice can elicit a startle response. Responses to these voice tones may be partly responsible for negative emotional reactions to failure and new experiences. Failure is part of the developmental process. A toddler who is learning to walk, for example, is not bothered if she loses her balance; she just gets up and tries again. If the little girl is reprimanded in a harsh voice for exploring or doing things a parent does not want her to do, however, she may develop a negative emotional reaction to any situation where she is uncertain how she is supposed to behave. Eventually she may develop a fear of failing, and when she gets to school and discovers that school presents many opportunities for failure she is likely to devise strategies to avoid it, such as procrastinating or psychosomatic symptoms of headaches or stomachaches.

To change a negative attitude, counterconditioning procedures can be used. In *counterconditioning*, the negatively conditioned stimulus (e.g., schoolwork) is paired with some positive stimulus—such as fun activities, peer interaction, food, or a soothing tone of voice—which elicits a positive, desired response. A teacher could involve students in many activities that are not evaluated, praise them for trying things that are new or difficult, and consistently use a soft, soothing voice in the classroom.

An example of how counterconditioning can be used to develop positive attitudes in students toward an isolated child in the classroom was reported in a study by Early (1968). The teacher made numerous com-

Figure 9.2

Respondent conditioning model of attitude learning

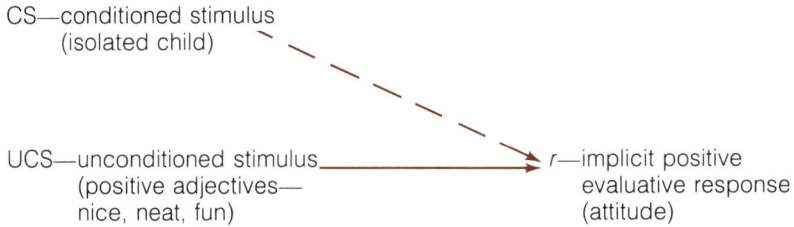

CS—conditioned stimulus
    (isolated child)

UCS—unconditioned stimulus   *r*—implicit positive
    (positive adjectives—   evaluative response
    nice, neat, fun)   (attitude)

ments about the isolated child and used the child's name in conjunction with words such as nice, fun, and neat. Through this counterconditioning, the students began to accept the isolated child and ask the child to join their activities. A respondent conditioning model based on Early's study is shown in Figure 9.2.

OPERANT CONDITIONING

In operant conditioning, the student engages in some behavior which is followed by some type of reinforcement. The reward or reinforcing stimulus is made contingent on the occurrence of a specific behavior. The mastery learning approach used in the French language course described in Box A relies heavily on the principles of operant conditioning. The subject matter is broken down into small, sequential steps to give students a high probability of succeeding on each part. A positive attitude is developed because the students experience positive consequences for studying each unit of the course.

Favorable attitudes arise from the experience of success (Gagné, 1977). A beginning piano student may have a negative attitude toward practice because he makes so many mistakes, but as he becomes more proficient his attitude toward practice should become more positive. Or a girl who gradually becomes more capable at swimming begins to like to swim more and more. In the same way, positive attitudes toward mathematics, reading, or history tend to follow experiences of success in these activities, while attitudes of dislike probably result from repeated instances of failure. High grades have been shown to result in more positive attitudes toward a subject than low grades (Bostrom, Vlandis, & Rosenbaum, 1961). As Chapter 11, on motivation, will show, students who experience repeated success develop positive attitudes toward their own competence, while those who experience failure develop more negative attitudes about their abilities (Mager, 1968).

Providing rewards or incentives to students can be effective in helping them develop certain skills or positive attitudes toward learning. There are difficulties with the use of simplistic classroom applications of reinforcement theory, however, as was pointed out in Chapter 8. The shaping of academic behavior is a complex matter which requires careful analysis and planning. There is even some evidence to suggest that incentives can have detrimental effects on student behaviors and attitudes, especially when they already have positive attitudes toward a subject or activity. Incentives also can produce negative reactions when they are used in a coercive manner. If students feel they must engage in activities for which they have low regard in order to receive such rewards as grades or recognition, they are likely to respond negatively to them and to feel manipulated. Reinforcements or incentives can be useful in getting students to engage in certain activities and put effort into them, and they can serve as the basis for the development of positive attitudes toward these activities. Incentives alone, however, cannot make students value learning.

CONDITIONING FAVORABLE CLASSROOM ATTITUDES

While individual students differ in what is reinforcing for them, there are procedures teachers can adopt to increase the likelihood that each one will find learning an enjoyable activity and the classroom a pleasant place. Generalizations based on the principles of conditioning suggest ways teachers can help students establish favorable attitudes toward school and learning.

The teacher's personal style should reflect caring and concern for students, as well as excitement and enthusiasm. The more teachers enjoy the classroom and their role in the instructional process, and the better they communicate this feeling to the students, the more likely are the students to also consider learning enjoyable.

When new topics or activities are introduced, connections should be built to other positive experiences the students have had. Things about which they are likely to have negative attitudes—"different" children, tests, homework, etc.—should be identified, so the instruction can be designed to produce positive consequences. Tests and homework, for example, can be presented as steps toward improvement rather than evaluations of ability, which can be negative.

The classroom should be a place where students can work and achieve success. For students who are having difficulty succeeding, the instruction can be broken down into smaller, easier units. For students who are

Children from a minority culture can help build positive attitudes toward it in both themselves and others. As they share their pride in their heritage, their classmates may come to see them as knowledgeable about its history and symbolism and to associate them with the beauty of the art.

finding the lessons too easy, the challenge can be increased by making additional or larger assignments. Teachers should determine individual students' likes and dislikes and use the information to individualize the reinforcements offered. When the instruction reflects students' likes, the learning behavior is more intrinsically motivated, and fewer or simpler rewards are needed (see Chapter 11).

Many commonly used discipline procedures, including various kinds of punishments, have the undesirable effects of creating in students negative attitudes toward many aspects of school. Teachers must continually weigh the negative attitudinal consequences of discipline procedures against what is to be gained by using them. (Chapters 11 and 13 give some positive approaches to classroom control.)

The teacher is the leader of the classroom, as Chapter 13 will show, and therefore the teacher is an attitude object about which students quickly form positive or negative evaluations. The teacher's position is difficult: being overly punitive can create too many negative associations, but not setting and enforcing any standards could cause the students to lose respect. The teacher traits or characteristics students value vary at each of the developmental stages described in Part I. Young children need and probably appreciate nurturance more, whereas older learners may appreciate a "caring" teacher but place a higher value on intelligence and logic. Different sexes, social classes, socioeconomic structures, and cultures also identify desirable characteristics of teachers differently. No one can tell teachers what these characteristics are, since the standards are subject to change to fit the circumstances and the times. Teachers therefore must develop skills for learning what teacher characteristics their students evaluate positively and negatively and then adapt their teaching style accordingly.

ATTITUDE LEARNING THROUGH VICARIOUS EXPERIENCE: OBSERVATIONAL LEARNING

With instrumental and classical conditioning, students develop attitudes through direct experience with the consequences associated with the attitude object. A second approach to learning or changing attitudes is by observing others; in this process, attitudes are learned indirectly and vicariously. Albert Bandura (1977) maintains that attitudes are learned by observing the attitudes that are verbally expressed or acted out by others. This observed information is internally represented in some manner (visual images, verbal codes) and can be expressed at a later time. Children are known to learn a great deal simply by observing the behavior of adults.

In a now-classic study based on the principles of observational learning, or modeling, Bandura (1965) had four-year-old children observe a film in which an adult behaved aggressively toward an inflated plastic Bobo doll. One group of children observed the adult being rewarded with treats for behaving aggressively (aggression associated with positive consequences), a second group observed the adult getting punished (aggression associated with negative consequences), and a third group observed the adult receiving neither rewards nor punishments for aggressive behavior. When the children were then placed in a room with the Bobo doll and other toys, those children who had seen the aggressive behavior rewarded behaved more aggressively toward the doll than children in either of the other two groups. Those who had seen the adult punished exhibited the fewest aggressive behaviors, but when the children were offered incentives to reproduce as many responses as they could remember, even they modeled the aggressive behavior of the adult.

Thus observing the adult being punished only temporarily suppressed their own aggressiveness; it did not interfere with the learning and recall of the aggressive behavior.

Many feelings toward objects (fear of snakes), people (liking for a teacher), and events (intrigue with travel to faraway places) are learned by observing others respond in a similar manner. A teacher may acquire a negative attitude toward a student from hearing other teachers complain about the child's behavior. Similarly, students behave quite differently for teacher A and teacher B because they observe how others are rewarded or punished in these teachers' classrooms. The degree to which individuals learn certain attitudes or behaviors through observation, according to Bandura (1977), can be influenced by a number of factors, including: (1) characteristics of the model, (2) consequences associated with the model's behavior, and (3) characteristics of the observer.

It is easy to see how characteristics of a model encourage imitation of a behavior from the testimonials of celebrities in advertising. Athletes and TV stars endorse products ranging from breakfast cereals to facial creams to garbage bags, although their influence may have little to do with their area of expertise. Individuals who attract attention are more likely to be modeled. Observational learning can also be enhanced when a behavior has been shown to result in positive reinforcement or punitive consequences. In the same way that observing a model being rewarded for aggression encourages observers to adopt the behavior, seeing students receive praise from the teacher for their hard work may entice other students to work harder for these rewards. And students who repeatedly see others come out of the principal's office looking troubled may react negatively to even passing by the office, though they never have been called in. One characteristic of the observer which has been found to encourage modeling is past experience with being reinforced for imitating others.

INSTRUCTIONAL USE
OF MODELING PRINCIPLES

For many students school fails to offer many positive role models. There are too few adult males at the elementary school level, too few females in the sciences at the secondary level, and little ethnic representation in faculties at all levels. In urban areas, particularly, many students may exhibit antisocial behaviors. Television, movies, and books present cultural stereotypes of desirable and undesirable behaviors, particularly with respect to sex-appropriate behaviors, and children's attitudes toward themselves and others are often based on how closely they match these projected characteristics. The absence of positive role models or the presence of negative models can have significant effects on children's expectations and goals and the standards they adopt for their conduct.

Observational learning is ongoing and continuous. Children pick up new behavior, consciously and unconsciously, almost every day by watching parents, teachers, peers, and others. They may adopt both the desirable and undesirable habits of others they regard as models. Almost every action of a teacher or parent in the presence of children, therefore, has the potential of being modeled. Teachers can capitalize on this continuous modeling process by making every effort to be desirable models. They can channel the powerful influence of peers by having students volunteer to demonstrate various desirable behaviors. The support of others in the school community, including parents, other teachers, and administrators, should also be enlisted in the modeling process.

In this context, however, the modeling process is incidental and unsystematic. The teacher can make more structured applications of the principles of modeling to the instructional process. Modeling is most useful in getting students to develop positive attitudes toward engaging in certain types of behaviors, such as those that are considered appropriate in the classroom.

Steps in Modeling Behaviors and Attitudes

A series of instructional steps to enhance learning in general—and attitude learning in particular—through observation and modeling was developed by Bandura (1977). It includes:

1. A conceptual presentation which informs students about the appropriate behaviors and the desirable characteristics of the model and links the model to desired activities and positive consequences. The purpose of such a presentation is to describe the behaviors in which students are expected to engage and to focus on the desirable aspects of imitating a person like the model.
2. A demonstration of the model engaging in the behavior and receiving positive consequences. Such a demonstration could be in the form of a film, filmstrip, slide show, videotape presentation, or live acting and role playing.
3. A chance for students to try out or rehearse the behaviors modeled and experience the associated positive consequences.
4. A discussion with students to help them make a commitment to using the behavior.
5. Follow-up discussion to help students monitor their new behavior and associated attitudes.

A teacher might implement these steps to help students develop a positive attitude toward the scientific method, for example. The processes of slow, careful planning and checking and rechecking of procedures and results can become tedious and boring for students. To develop a unit to improve this attitude, the teacher could follow the steps outlined above, as described in the following paragraphs.

1. Conceptual Presentation   The teacher presents the steps of the scientific method, emphasizing the need for careful planning, monitoring, and checking of results. Students are asked to identify scientists they respect and admire, as well as others who could use the scientific method, such as executives, administrators, and medical technicians. One or two local citizens could be invited to come to the class to talk about the value of the scientific method in their work, stressing the *positive consequences* of using the method. Magazine articles or biographies describing others' use of the scientific method and demonstrating how it resulted in positive consequences could also be studied.

2. Demonstration of the Model   In this step someone must visually demonstrate the steps of the scientific method, with an emphasis on careful planning, monitoring, and checking. The teacher could give a slide demonstration showing a student working through the steps at a lab desk in biology or chemistry, or show a film of a scientist or expert going through the process. If such audiovisual materials are unavailable, the teacher could do a demonstration of the method or have a former student do one. The processes and positive consequences of planning, monitoring, and checking should be clearly shown.

3. Rehearsal and Feedback   Each student should then be given a chance to rehearse the procedure. This could best be done in groups of two or three with one student practicing the procedures and the others observing how well careful planning, monitoring, and checking procedures are followed. The observers would then give feedback to the student presenters. This process would continue until all students had had a chance to *rehearse and succeed*.

4. Commitment   This step could be accomplished by having students discuss the merits of the procedure, problems of implementation, and methods of overcoming the problems.

5. Follow-up   Some class time should be set aside on a regular, frequent basis (every week or every other week) to discuss student use of scientific procedures and the associated positive consequences.

ATTITUDE LEARNING THROUGH REASONING AND PROBLEM SOLVING

The third approach to attitude learning and change involves logic and reasoning. In this approach, students who have at least achieved the concrete operational thought stage are required to think critically about their past, present, or future behaviors and consider the consequences in a logical manner. The approach uses the basic problem-solving process, which will be examined in Chapter 10 as one of the three principal processes of thinking. In any application, the problem-solving process consists of several steps which combine the following components in some way:

1. Statement and analysis of the problem.
2. Consideration of alternative courses of action.
3. Examination of the probable consequences of each alternative.
4. Choice of the best alternative and preparation of a plan for carrying it out.

ATTITUDE CLARIFICATION CONFERENCES

One way to use problem solving in connection with student attitudes is to examine in student-teacher conferences questions such as "What does fighting in the playground accomplish?" or "Does cutting class matter?" Procedures for such attitude clarification conferences have been developed by William Glasser (1969) and Herbert Klausmeier (1973). The conferences may involve interactions between the teacher and the entire class, a small group of students, or a single student. During the discussions students examine the motives for and consequences of their behavior and become more aware of the reasons for it. As they become skilled at reasoning about their behavior, these skills can be generalized to other situations.

In order to conduct attitude conferences, the teacher must be skillful in the use of interpersonal relations and discussion techniques. If there is good rapport with students and an atmosphere of involvement, Glasser and Klausmeier recommend a meeting agenda like the one below:

1. Exposing the problem for discussion—students describe the situation and the objects, behaviors, and consequences that are involved.
2. Making a judgment about the behavior—students examine the consequences of their actions and state whether these consequences are desirable or undesirable.
3. Identifying alternative consequences or various possible actions—students "brainstorm" different ways of behaving which might have more positive consequences.
4. Making a commitment to a selected course of action—students make a contract in which they develop an action plan with specific behavioral goals.
5. Behavioral follow-up—students set a time to report on the success of their action plan.

A report of such a conference is given in Box B.

BOX B   *Learning to like Laura:*
A student-teacher attitude conference

Teacher
exposes
problem for
discussion

Teacher: It's time for our weekly conference. Remember, I want you to learn to think about problems and to find ways of acting that will solve them, without my having to tell you what to do or how to do it. One problem that we are going to face very soon is that a new student will be joining our class next week. School has been in session for eight weeks, and we have established some regular routines and habits. I am particularly concerned with how we can accept Laura—that is her name—into our classroom because she is handicapped and has never attended a regular school.

Jack: What kind of handicap does she have?

Teacher: She has a severe speech and hearing impediment. Laura has received special training for the first five grades, but now she feels ready to come to regular classes. What kinds of problems do you think she might have when she comes into our classroom?

Nancy: She might have trouble hearing. (Ha Ha! Students laugh at such an obvious statement.)

Teacher: That's right, she will, but she will sit here at the front of the room.

Joe: That'll mean that one of us in the front row will have to move!

Teacher
asks for
a judgment
about
desirable
behavior

Teacher: Well, we certainly aren't going to force anyone to move. But how is such an attitude helping us solve the problem?

Mary: It's not. I think we all have to be willing to make some sacrifices. (Other students nod in agreement.)

Teacher
summarizes,
refocuses
problem,
asks for
alternatives

Teacher: Can we agree that Laura must sit somewhere, and it would be best if she sat at the front of the room? (Students nod.) The problem, then, is—What seat will she sit in, and who will have to move? What suggestions do you have?

Ben: We could decide by drawing straws, but how do we decide where the person moves to?

Kara: Yeah! I don't mind moving, but I don't want to end up at the back of the room.

Fred: We have two extra chairs at the back of the room. That's where you will go unless we move more than one person.

Jack: Why can't we take one of those chairs and move it up next to the teacher's desk? That way no one has to move.

Chorus of class members: Yes, good idea!

Teacher asks students to examine the consequences of an action

Teacher: It seems to me that we want to make Laura feel like one of the rest of us. How do you think she will feel if she sits up here, by herself, next to my desk?

Susan: She wouldn't like it. She'd feel left out.

Jeff: Yeah, she'll stick out like a sore thumb.

Robert: Certainly, all eyes would be on Laura. (Students laugh at the image.)

Tom: I have an idea. Since no one person wants to move, why don't we all move?

Dennis: You mean everyone would get a new desk?

Tom: Yes!

Teacher asks students to consider consequences of various alternatives

Teacher: We now have three or four good suggestions. Let's list them on the board. (Teacher lists suggestions.) Do we have any more to add to this list? (No response from students.) OK, let's evaluate some of these possible alternatives. We've already decided that sitting up here would be very uncomfortable for Laura. What about these other suggestions?

Neil: I like Tom's idea. That way everyone makes an equal sacrifice. (Other students nod in agreement.)

Continued on next page

Box B continued

Teacher: OK, but how will we make specific assignments for this new seating arrangement?

Tom: How did you assign us at the beginning of the year?

Teacher: Before I answer that, I want to say that I think it is important for everyone to feel comfortable with the new seating arrangement. I don't think it would be good if someone resented Laura because she made them move. I think this should be our standard for accepting a solution. (Students make a number of suggestions and discuss their merits. Finally they decide to go with putting 25 numbers into a hat and drawing them out.)

Teacher asks for commitment

Teacher: Now that we have made this decision I want us to try it out so we are sure we will be happy with it. We will make the new seating arrangements tomorrow. After two days, I will ask each of you to sign a petition stating that you are happy with your new seat.

Mary: Maybe it's not good to be attached to a seat. I think we should vote now to change seats every six weeks.

Joe: Good idea. Then we can include Laura in our next discussion of seating arrangements.

Commitment and follow-up

Teacher: If you'll agree we will make this part of your commitment to see this through and to continually reevaluate our decision. (Students agree.)

Teacher asks for reflection about possible positive consequences of an event

Teacher: I think we have accomplished enough for one day. But this topic is an important one, so for our next meeting we can talk about what positive or good things are likely to happen because Laura is coming to our classroom.

LEARNING ATTITUDES ABOUT ONESELF: THE SELF-CONCEPT

The self-concept represents the sum total of an individual's experience, not only as viewed by others but also as perceived by the self. As we noted in Part I, it is present in infancy and early childhood in primitive forms of self-control and self-esteem and begins to be structured in later childhood, when it emerges as an expression of the individual's sense of self as an object and as a doer. In adolescence the self-concept is strengthened by development of a sense of personal identity and higher self-esteem.

Failure to develop a positive self-concept can trouble an individual throughout the life cycle. John Quincy Adams's life, for example, was one of extraordinary achievements, but he harbored feelings of self-doubt, inadequacy, and failure. He distinguished himself as a foreign minister, congressman, secretary of state, and president, and yet at the age of 70 he wrote "my life has been a succession of disappointments. I can scarcely recollect a single instance of success in anything that I ever undertook" (Kennedy, 1956, p. 30).

The self-concept can be defined as a set of perceptions, beliefs, and attitudes that a person has about himself or herself. A teacher might describe herself in the following way: teacher, tall, ambitious, artistic, sports fan, mother. These perceptions not only describe how she views herself, they can also be ranked in order of personal importance, and they are invested with an evaluative component. Certain attributes may evoke positive evaluations, while others involve negative connotations. Being a teacher might be evaluated positively by someone who feels competent about teaching, who expects positive evaluations from students, and who teaches at a good school. But teacher attributes might be evaluated negatively by a teacher who feels overworked with too many students, who must handle many behavior problems in class, and who thinks parents do not respect her position.

This evaluative component of the self-concept is generally labeled *self-esteem*. It is learned by comparing ourselves to others, from feedback we receive about ourselves, by observing the consequences of our behavior, and from our perceptions of cultural values. For example, if Sara finds herself consistently outperforming classmates, she might judge herself to be capable and smart. Children who are physically handicapped or unattractive may see themselves as undesirable by society's values.

HIGH VERSUS LOW SELF-ESTEEM

The self-concept integrates the individual's experiences and gives them personal meaning. One process that has been found to distinguish persons with high versus low self-esteem is how they explain success or failure. Children with high self-esteem generally attribute success to their capabilities (I succeeded because I am smart and capable) and perceive failure as atypical of themselves (I failed because I wasn't feeling well; I didn't study the right material). For these children, success experiences are motivating; they maintain high expectations for their performance, anticipate future success, and through a self-fulfilling prophecy, are likely to experience continued success. There is, in fact, substantial evidence linking high self-esteem to high achievement in school (Brookover, Patterson, & Thomas, 1964). Self-esteem and achievement seem to be related in a reciprocal process; high esteem produces high expectations and resulting high achievement, and the successful performance reinforces a positive self-evaluation.

Children who have low self-esteem reject success and believe that failure is typical of them. Failure seems to confirm their already low self-evaluation and to operate like a negative self-fulfilling prophecy (Ames & Felker, 1979; Maracek & Mettee, 1972). These children typically have a history of rejection and failure and are locked in a cycle of defeatism, and (unlike high self-esteem children) they are not easily uplifted by positive feedback or successful experiences. Donald Felker (1974) paints a rather bleak picture for the child with low self-esteem, pointing out that there is no action a teacher can take that a child with a negative self-concept will not interpret in a negative way, no matter how positively others might interpret the action or how positively the teacher might mean it.

There is evidence to suggest that children who have positive and negative views of their social competence interpret social outcomes differently. Children who view themselves as socially competent take personal credit for positive social encounters and reject negative encounters. In contrast, children who regard their social competence negatively do not take credit for positive social encounters and blame themselves for negative ones. Thus there is a tendency to behave in a manner that is consistent with one's self-view. Felker (1974) suggests this is why a positive self-concept is so important:

> The self-concept is like an inner filter—every perception that enters the individual must go through the filter. As each perception passes through the filter, it is given meaning, and the meaning given is determined largely by the view the individual has of himself. If it is a negative view, every experience is stamped with a frown. If it is a positive view, every experience is stamped with a smile. (p. 9)

The sources of feedback and evaluation from others that children receive for their developing self-concepts are the same as the principal agents of socialization in child development described in Part I: the parents and the home environment, peers and peer groups, and the school. In the first few years of childhood parents provide the pri-

*Experiences in which children are active doers and
achievers contribute to their positive concept of themselves.
Teachers can provide opportunities for such activities both
in the classroom and outside it.*

mary source of feedback and evaluation. They also serve as models of behaviors which children can observe to learn how to treat themselves and others. When children enter school a wider range of social experiences becomes available, including interactions with peers. The number of people who can serve as models and evaluators increases dramatically. On an average day students may encounter not only fellow students but the bus driver, teachers, the librarian or resource person, the lunchroom supervisor, the principal, teacher's aides, and so on. With school, certain areas of the self-concept become extremely important, particularly in the academic and social areas. The school situation presents children with the first real opportunity to test their abilities. Those who experience early success are likely to develop a firm foundation for building a positive self-concept. Early failures can cause children to lose confidence rather quickly, and as a result they may develop negative attitudes toward learning.

THE SCHOOL'S ROLE IN DEVELOPING POSITIVE SELF-CONCEPTS

The schools provide the most readily available vehicle for encouraging the development of positive self-concepts in children. They also can be a means for intervening early to help children with low self-esteem correct it before they come to accept failure as typical of themselves. Educational efforts to promote positive self-concepts have taken three main approaches: training children in specific academic and social skills, modifying the classroom environment, or teaching a system of positive self-evaluation.

Training in Academic and Social Skills

The first approach to encouraging positive self-concepts focuses on skill training in the cognitive-intellectual and social-emotional domains. Behaviors in these areas correlate strongly with the self-concept. Many children with low self-esteem, for example, experience a great deal of academic failure and social rejection in a school setting. If a child can acquire specific skills that are necessary for achievement (such as vocabulary words for reading), improved performance will be a source of personal satisfaction and heightened self-esteem (Calsyn & Kenny, 1977). Similarly, social skills training (Cartledge & Milburn, 1980) can enhance children's social acceptance among their peers (Oden & Asher, 1977). Other methods which have not demonstrated the same ability to produce long-term changes in social acceptance include grouping practices and the assignment of special tasks or leadership roles. Once the necessary skills are mastered, the child's accomplishments lend a sense of personal responsibility and encourage favorable attitudes toward both the activities and the self.

Modifying the Classroom Environment

The second approach to self-concept development involves modifying the classroom environment. Within the traditional competitive structure of most classrooms, many students engage in self-defeating behaviors—dropping out, cheating, not trying—that are likely to lead to future failure or punishment. Replacing the competitive structure with cooperative-based learning has been associated with enhanced self-esteem (Blaney et al., 1977; Covington & Beery, 1976). Proponents of cooperative learning contend that students are more likely to feel that their contributions are important, more likely to receive feedback from their peers, and less likely to feel anxious about their performance, all of which contribute to positive self-esteem. A cooperative learning environment has been found to foster positive attitudes toward others and toward the school, as well as toward oneself (Johnson & Ahlgren, 1976; Johnson et al., 1976; Johnson & Johnson, 1978; Slavin, 1977). Effects of cooperative, competitive, and individualistic classroom climates on students' feelings of capability and self-confidence are examined in Chapter 11.

Teaching a Self-Evaluation System

The third approach to improving students' self-concepts views self-concepts as comprising a functional (or dysfunctional) self-evaluative system. How children evaluate themselves depends on the standards they set for their behavior. When the standards are too severe, their behavior is a constant basis for self-criticism, but standards that are too low do not create a feeling of involvement or motivation. Children with low self-concepts often make excessive demands on themselves and evaluate themselves harshly when they do not meet their own expectations.

Teachers can help children develop their own internalized systems of positive self-reinforcement through modeling, instruction, and reinforcement. If the standards children set for their behavior and how they evaluate themselves in relation to those standards are realistic, the children are likely to feel challenged to meet them. And, when the goals are achieved, they are likely to feel a sense of personal responsibility and accomplishment. Felker (1974) has suggested five keys teachers can use to help students develop positive self-evaluation systems:

1. Adults, praise yourselves. Teachers can model the process of self-praise by praising themselves in front of the class and congratulating themselves for small and large accomplishments.
2. Help children evaluate themselves realistically. Teachers should guide students to understand that they do not have to be perfect but should show improvement.
3. Teach children to set realistic goals. In individual or small-group conferences, teachers should discuss students' goals and specify the standards to be used in evaluating their work.

4. Teach children to praise themselves. Skillful questioning strategies should be used to encourage students to acknowledge their accomplishments.
5. Teach children to praise others. Teachers can model this behavior by praising achievements and encouraging students to praise each others' schoolwork and behaviors.

Since the self-concept is a filter through which all new experiences pass and are interpreted, it is relatively stable and difficult to change. This is why it is necessary to intervene early and promote positive self-concepts in individual students, before they can be trapped in a cycle of failure. Changes in the classroom's competitive spirit and emphasis on formal evaluation also must be considered if students' self-concepts are to be improved.

Table 9.1

Composite rankings of terminal values for American men and women

Terminal Value	Male (N = 665)	Female (N = 744)
A comfortable life	4	13
An exciting life	18	18
A sense of accomplishment	7	10
A world at peace	1	1
A world of beauty	15	15
Equality	9	8
Family security	2	2
Freedom	3	3
Happiness	5	5
Inner harmony	13	12
Mature love	14	14
National security	10	11
Pleasure	17	16
Salvation	12	4
Self-respect	6	6
Social recognition	16	17
True friendship	11	9
Wisdom	8	7

Source: Data from Milton Rokeach, *The Nature of Human Values* (New York: Free Press, 1973), p. 57.

THE LEARNING OF VALUES

Values are concerned with personal standards and principles for judging worth. They establish the criteria by which we judge people, their actions, and various other objects in our environment as being good and worthwhile or undesirable and worthless. An individual's values are organized into a value system which provides a comprehensive set of standards to guide actions, justifications, judgments, and comparisons of self and others.

Researchers maintain that the average person has somewhere between 20 and 40 values which actively serve as guiding principles. Milton Rokeach (1973) differentiates between two categories of values—terminal and instrumental, as listed in Tables 9.1 and 9.2. To determine a person's value hierarchy, the individual is asked to rank order the 18 values in

Table 9.2

*Composite rankings of instrumental values
for American men and women*

Instrumental Value	Male (N = 665)	Female (N = 744)
Ambitious	2	4
Broadminded	4	5
Capable	8	12
Cheerful	12	10
Clean	9	8
Courageous	5	6
Forgiving	6	2
Helpful	7	7
Honest	1	1
Imaginative	18	18
Independent	11	14
Intellectual	15	16
Logical	16	17
Loving	14	9
Obedient	17	15
Polite	13	13
Responsible	3	3
Self-controlled	10	11

Source: Data from Milton Rokeach, *The Nature of Human Values* (New York: Free Press, 1973), p. 58.

each list from 1 to 18, for most to least important. The results of one such large-scale values survey among men and women are presented in these tables. For the terminal values, both men and women ranked "a world at peace," "family security," and "freedom" as the top three values. For the instrumental values, "honest" and "responsible" ranked first and third for both men and women, but men ranked "ambitious" second while women gave "forgiving" this rank.

These lists are averages, and there is a wide range of individual differences. A woman who, contrary to the average, ranks "ambitious" at the top of her list of instrumental values probably would be career oriented and would set high, but attainable, goals for herself. She could find herself in conflict over various choices, such as having a career or having children. She might value success in working in a competitive environment more than maintaining a home and nurturing children, or she might try to accomplish both.

VALUE DEVELOPMENT AND CHANGE

Because of the central position of values in the relations among values, beliefs, and attitudes (see Figure 9.1 above), a change in values is likely to have a more dramatic impact on thoughts, feelings, and behavior than a change in a single belief or attitude. Rokeach adapted John Dewey's conception of a "felt difficulty" as the beginning of all education to explain how values are learned and changed:

> This "felt difficulty" is a more or less consciously experienced affective state of self-dissatisfaction, a dissatisfaction arising from some cognitive discrepancy between self-conceptions and performance in a given situation or class of situations. Does my total performance in this situation—what I said, what I did, and most important, what it signifies about myself—measure up to whatever conception I have of myself as a competent person? as a moral person? Most, if not all, activities a person engages in end, at least implicitly, with some evaluation of his performance. To the extent that a person perceives a discrepancy between self-conceptions and performance, he experiences it emotionally as a "felt difficulty" or state of self-dissatisfaction. (Rokeach, 1973, p. 226)

Thus the fundamental prerequisite for values learning, development, or change is seen as a perceived self-dissatisfaction. Rokeach suggests three basic ways a teacher can induce a "felt dissatisfaction":

1. Expose students to information about the ideas and behaviors of others, pointing out how they differ from the students' own beliefs and behaviors.
2. Induce students to adopt behaviors which differ from their own beliefs and prior behaviors.

The school is an imparter of values, sometimes subtly, often consciously and deliberately, as in these children's morning salute to the flag. Group values are also expressed in the list of helpers to keep the classroom orderly.

3. Give students information about their own belief systems in order to make them consciously aware of contradictions that may exist below their level of awareness.

Rokeach asserts that information about the contradictions within a person's belief system should motivate the individual to make cognitive or behavioral changes to remove or reduce the inconsistencies.

VALUES EDUCATION

Teaching about values and the use of value activities in schools have been controversial because many parents are concerned that teachers will impose their own values on students. As we will point out in Chapter

13, teachers are charged with defining the values and needs of the social system and teaching them to students. For society, the problem is *whose* values, preferences, and needs will be taught. For the teacher, the problem is how to preserve social order and transmit the values of society while fostering a feeling of independence and individualism in students (see Part III).

If the explicit discussion of value questions is excluded from the curriculum, another value is implied—that value considerations are not important in the schools (Postman & Weingartner, 1969). The goal of science, for example, generally is to discover knowledge and truth. Knowledge and truth are certainly worthy values, but at what human expense? Is it right or wrong to test mind-altering drugs on people without their consent? To experimentally spray dangerous chemicals in a populated area? To sterilize institutionalized, mentally retarded individuals? If such value questions are not discussed as part of science, then students may be left with the impression that value considerations are unimportant, perhaps even with the idea that science and technological advancement can proceed without weighing their human impact.

Thus, we cannot wish value considerations away. They arise because education is expected to affect how students make decisions, and decision making involves value considerations. The focus of the values teaching activities and problem-solving strategies presented in this chapter is on the *process* of weighing alternatives in a decision, not on the specific beliefs or values that students should acquire.

GIVING STUDENTS A CHOICE OF WHAT TO VALUE

The proper focus of values education, we believe, is to help students practice strategies for assessing values and making choices, rather than deciding what students should value and attempting to indoctrinate them. In our view, teachers should avoid telling students what they should value. This type of teaching, also called *moralizing,* uses such techniques as instilling fear about the consequences of certain acts, appealing to conscience, or citing good behavior examples from history or literature. According to Fraenkel (1977), these techniques do not seem to work. In a classic study by Festinger (1964), for example, high school students were given strong, moderate, and minimal fear-arousing appeals regarding oral hygiene. Students who were exposed to the strongest fear-arousing appeals were the least likely to change their behaviors and showed little conformity to the recommended oral hygiene methods.

Instead of moralizing about the desirability of accepting authorized values, the teacher's proper role is to help students seek out the reasons behind the recommendations of authority figures. In this way the students can learn to think critically and to avoid blind acceptance of others' values. They can learn to make intelligent decisions when the opinions or values of authorities conflict or an established authority is questioned. Problem-solving strategies also can help them make personal decisions to resolve the felt dissatisfactions they encounter in their own value systems.

PROBLEM-SOLVING STRATEGIES FOR VALUES EDUCATION

A number of educational researchers have developed programs of values education which are designed to help students become consciously aware of how values guide their behavior and show them how to deal rationally with seeming contradictions in values they encounter. Values education offers help to students in coping with the kinds of conflicts and decisions that emerge in their everyday interactions with others. It helps them develop a rational decision-making approach toward values-related questions such as:

> What occupation should I choose so that I don't spend my life, like so many other people, in boring, unfulfilling jobs?
>
> Should I smoke marijuana with my friends?
>
> Should I cheat to help a friend get a passing grade?
>
> Should citizens participate in elections even if they do not like any of the candidates?

Programs in values education usually have as a general objective the development of more rational individuals who will take account of their value priorities and consider the consequences of their actions when they make decisions. In essence, these programs seek to educate students in *strategies* for thinking or solving problems about themselves and their own behavior. It is difficult to specify the exact learning conditions for the development of problem-solving strategies, but the instructional process can be structured to provide conditions that are favorable to such activities. After presenting value-related problem-solving strategies, teachers should provide repeated opportunities for students to apply them to their own value dilemmas.

Most strategies of values education use some form of the problem-solving process with the basic components described above. First, students define the problem and evaluate the relative importance of their own and others' values and goals. Then they consider alternative courses of action and logically examine the positive and negative consequences of each one. Finally they select the one that is most supportive of their value priorities and prepare a plan for carrying out the selected course of action. In the values education programs described in the following paragraphs, students practice one or more problem-solving strategies.

The strategies and programs reviewed in this section are for the most part directed to students of high school or college age. This is understandable because adolescence is a particularly crucial period in the life cycle during which young people can reevaluate and consolidate their value systems. However, they do not arrive at adolescence without basic values already integrated into their personality structure. Although specific classroom programs for sorting out values with younger children are not presented here, the kind of discussion described in Box B (Learning to Like Laura), for example, is replete with values considerations. Teachers must make appropriate changes in the problems and topics for studying values with younger children, but the basic principles remain the same. The goal is to demonstrate to the children that values are an integral and indispensable part of the curriculum (What is the responsibility of the government to the poor? Is it fair for the lives and talents of young men but not young women to be taken for service to the nation?), without trying to prescribe what their values should be.

Setting Value and Goal Priorities

Rokeach's instrumental and terminal value scales (see Tables 9.1 and 9.2 above) can be especially useful in helping adolescents plan career goals and consider other major decisions. Students are asked to rank the values from 1 to 18 "in order of their importance to *you,* as guiding principles in *your* life." After the students have selected their values priorities they are asked to list their major goals in areas such as career satisfaction, status and respect, personal relationships, leisure satisfactions, learning and education, and spiritual growth. The students then consider their goals in terms of relative importance, ease or difficulty of attainment, and degree of conflict. Finally the students compare their value rankings and goal lists in response to the following questions:

Do the values support the major goals, or do they conflict?

Are some personal values in conflict with career goals?

How does my present schoolwork compare with my values and goals?

Does this explain any satisfaction or dissatisfaction with my present situation?

What implications does this examination have for my future plans?

As part of this exercise, students may also be asked to discuss their value and goal rankings with each other in small groups. Variations of these activities are easily used with junior high, high school, college age, and adult students.

Considering Alternatives and Evaluating Consequences

Activities that have been developed to help students consider alternatives and evaluate their consequences focus on discrepancies between their own and others' beliefs and behaviors. This approach, sometimes called *values clarification*, shows students how to use problem-solving techniques to think critically about their values and how they may differ from others'. One problem confronting adolescents, in particular, is conformity: "My friends have different goals and values than I do." Values education stresses the norm that it is acceptable to hold different values and beliefs. The initial step is making students aware of what others think and feel.

Values voting provides a simple, quick method for getting students to show what they believe. Students find out how many of their beliefs are shared by others, and the idea that others often see issues quite differently is established. The procedure for values voting begins with the teacher reading aloud a series of questions students can respond to with a show of hands. Simon, Howe, and Kirschenbaum (1972) suggest the following examples:

> How many of you . . .
>> Think teenagers should be allowed to choose their own clothes?
>> Will raise your children more strictly than you were raised?
>> Watch TV more than three hours per day?
>> Think the most qualified person usually wins in school elections?
>> Think there are times when cheating is justified?
>> Could tell someone they have bad breath?
>> Think going steady is important in order to achieve social success?
>> Regularly attend religious services and enjoy them?

Following each question the students express their positions on it. (They might raise their hands if they agree with the statement and point thumbs down if they disagree. Those who are undecided could fold their arms.) When the list of questions has been completed, students discuss the positions they have taken and the teacher stresses acceptance and understanding of the different points of view.

Another activity involves an *alternative action search* in which students are presented with short episodes which call for some proposed action. The teacher presents the vignette to the students, orally or in writing, and asks them what they would do in such a situation. Individual students write down what they would do, and together they discuss their different views in small groups or with the entire class. Two sample vignettes from Simon, Howe, & Kirschenbaum (1972) which require students to evaluate the consequences of possible actions are:

> You are walking behind someone. You see him take out a cigarette pack, withdraw the last cigarette, put the cigarette in his mouth, crumple the package and nonchalantly toss it over his shoulder onto the sidewalk. You are twenty-five feet behind him. Ideally, what would you do?

> You see a kid three or four years younger than you shoplifting at the local discount store. You're concerned that he'll get into serious trouble if the store detective catches him. What would you do?

In another activity which also provides students with practice in searching for alternatives, the teacher presents a values issue or problem with topics such as ways to save time, to help out on community projects, or to improve race relations in school. Each student is then given three to five minutes to brainstorm his or her ideas on the problem, after which they all meet in small groups to generate more alternatives and consider the consequences of their ideas. The students are then asked to present the three or four alternatives they like best. As a follow-up to this activity, the teacher may ask them to examine and reconsider their alternatives in relation to their own individual value priorities.

Acting on Values

When students explore values issues, they may be ready to do something about them—that is, to act on their values. Among the many ways students can act on their values is through more in-depth study of various subject matter areas. The emphasis is on identifying discrepancies between beliefs and behavior. For example:

> Health sciences—students could research the facts on the effects of smoking and circulate them, or start a smokers' anonymous club.

> Science—students could study values questions about chemicals in the environment by surveying the presence of chemicals in their city, study the effects of different chemicals on animals and people, write their congressional representatives, or plan a poster campaign or a demonstration project in a shopping center.

> Social studies and history—students could study the changes in family life from early settlement days or make a movie of family life in suburbia or the city today.

> Arithmetic—students could survey the cost of products in a number of stores over a period of time. They can petition store owners, make suggestions, circulate their information, or write articles for the newspaper.

VALUES ACTIVITIES IN THE INSTRUCTIONAL PROCESS

The use of values activities in academically oriented high schools might be considered "soft," but schools also have been criticized for teaching knowledge and facts but not decision making. Wales (1976) and others (Fraenkel, 1977; Simon, Howe, & Kirschenbaum, 1972) have argued that good decision making involves not only a sound knowledge base but also an understanding of the value dilemmas involved. Business and law schools have been criticized for graduating students who are technically competent but who lack any sense of social justice. Wales contends that if students never practice making value choices in school, they will be ill prepared for effective decision making in the real world.

Values education can emerge as an extension of the academic curriculum, as suggested above, or it can be made a part of the course of study. In this case the problem-solving strategy of values education described in the preceding section is placed in the format of discussion of an academic subject. The six steps in the high school lesson plan in *Death of a Salesman* given in Box C illustrate this process. The teacher has students discuss the value dilemmas of the major characters in the play, and then they relate these value dilemmas to choices and decisions they are making or will have to make in their own lives.

HIGHER-LEVEL MORAL REASONING IN THE SCHOOL

Moral values are reflected in judgments of what behaviors are right versus wrong, fair versus unfair, just versus unjust. Some of the more difficult judgments people must make involve a conflict between two or more values. Imagine yourself faced with the following moral dilemma: In a large metropolitan area, a Nazi organization wants to stage a march through a predominantly Jewish suburb, many of whose residents were survivors of the Nazi concentration camps. You must choose between the civil rights of the Nazi group to march and demonstrate on the one hand and the potentiality of violence and the sentiments of the residents of this suburb on the other. What are the values involved in this conflict? Should the Nazi group be permitted to march? Why or why not?

On the basis of evidence of how people respond to moral dilemmas such as this one, Lawrence Kohlberg (1966, 1969) developed a six-stage theory of moral development classified into three levels: preconventional, conventional, and postconventional. The levels and the six stages are listed in Figure 9.3. To assess a person's level of moral development, Kohlberg typically presents a dilemma in story form which involves a conflict between two or more values. The individual is first asked what should be done and is then asked several questions which relate to the

BOX C *A plan for studying the values
in* Death of a Salesman

This lesson plan for analysis of the value dilemmas, alternative actions, and consequences of action in Arthur Miller's play *Death of a Salesman* includes six steps.

STEP 1

Set value priorities

After reading the play, students consider the major characters: Willy Loman (the salesman), Linda (Willy's wife), Bif and Happy (his sons), and Ben Loman (his brother). For each character, they rank order the following values according to what they think that character considered most important versus least important:

> A sense of accomplishment.
> Family security.
> Pleasure.
> An exciting life.
> Self-respect.
> Mature love.

After students rank order the values for each character, they rank order them for themselves. They answer: What is important to you? Least important? Then they form into groups of four or five to discuss, compare, and contrast their lists of values for each character.

STEP 2

State alternative courses of action and evaluate consequences

Students meet in groups to discuss one or more of the following focus questions:

Focus question 1. When he graduated from high school Bif accompanied his father on a business trip. Describe what happened in Willy's hotel room when Bif came in unexpectedly and discovered his father with a woman in the bedroom. What did Bif do? On what values was he operating? What other possible actions could he have taken? What are the consequences of each alternative action? What action would you have taken? How are these actions consistent or inconsistent with your value priorities?

Focus question 2. When Willy goes to the headquarters of his company to seek a desk job, he is told that the company is progressing in many new areas, and, they must make room for younger employees. Even though Willy has worked for the company most of his life, he is told that it has no obligation to him. What values are operating in this interaction? Do you agree or disagree with the action the company took? Why? Why not? What responsibility does a company have to an older employee? With what value priorities is your opinion consistent? Inconsistent?

STEP 3

Relate actions, consequences and values to students' own life experiences

Focus question 1. During one scene of the play, Linda communicates to Bif: "Pick up this stuff; I'm not your maid anymore." While Bif wants to please his mother, he wants to be his own man. What should Bif do? (Students, working in groups, list at least three possible courses of action.) What are the possible consequences of each action?

Focus question 2. Have you ever experienced a similar interaction with one of your parents? (Students write short scenarios of such an interaction, based on personal experience if possible. They share scenarios in small groups and discuss.) On what values did you operate? What did you do? What else could you have done? What were the consequences of your action? Would any other action have had more favorable consequences in terms of your value priorities?

STEP 4

Implement actions consistent with value priorities

Students role-play scenes demonstrating effective parent-child interactions, that is, those consistent with stated value priorities.

STEP 5

Act consistently over time

Students make a plan of action for dealing with situations involving a value dilemma of conforming to authority versus expressing independence. They identify key situations where this dilemma is likely to arise at school, home, and so on; identify possible courses of action and consequences; and select a reasonable action sequence. Students report back periodically on their progress in implementing their plan.

reasoning behind the person's choice of action. One of Kohlberg's best known stories is as follows:

> In Europe, a woman was near death from cancer. One drug might save her, a form of radium that a druggist in the same town had recently discovered. The druggist was charging $2,000, ten times what the drug cost him to make. The sick woman's husband, Heinz, went to everyone he knew to borrow the money, but he could only get together about half of what it cost. He told the druggist that his wife was dying and asked him to sell the drug cheaper or let him pay later. But the druggist said no. The husband got desperate and broke into the man's store to steal the drug for his wife. (Kohlberg, 1969, p. 379)

Follow-up questions for this situation might include:

> Should Heinz steal from anyone, even if his wife is dying?
>
> Do you think laws always should be obeyed?
>
> Do you think Heinz has an obligation to steal the drug?

Kohlberg sees moral development as sequential, with each stage representing a higher level of reasoning that is qualitatively different from the stage preceding it. Individuals do not skip stages, although their progression through them may be fairly rapid or slow. People who are exposed to arguments one stage above their own tend to prefer the higher level of reasoning, but they are unable to comprehend reasoning that is more than one stage beyond their own. According to Kohlberg (1969), concrete operational thought is necessary for conventional moral reasoning, and formal operational thought is necessary for postconventional reasoning. Generally, moral reasoning advances from the preconventional level to the conventional level between the ages of 10 to 13. Conventional moral reasoning continues to dominate the reasoning of most American adults, and only a small proportion use postconventional reasoning.

Kohlberg suggests that teachers can facilitate higher-level moral reasoning by presenting moral dilemmas for students to discuss. The problems may be hypothetical, as in the story about Heinz, or derived directly from the curriculum. A science class, for example, might consider whether scientists should engage in genetic research. Moral issues also may deal with real problems, such as whether a student should report another who is involved in selling drugs. News articles abound with moral issues. The discussion of moral problems is important in applications of Kohlberg's theory because these values are most susceptible to change when students are exposed to moral reasoning that is higher than their own. The discussion should guide students to become unsure of their own thinking (a "felt dissatisfaction") and move to reconsider and restructure it to accommodate the higher-level position.

Figure 9.3

Kohlberg's stages of moral development

Level I: Preconventional
Individuals are responsive to cultural labels of good and bad but focus on the rewarding or punishing consequences of their actions and the power of those who enforce the rules.

> **Stage 1:** Obedience and punishment orientation—deference to superior power and avoidance of punishment.
> **Stage 2:** Self-satisfying orientation—concern with satisfying one's own (and, occasionally, others') needs.

Level II: Conventional
Individuals conform and are loyal to the social order and seek to maintain it and to meet the expectations of others.

> **Stage 3:** Good-girl, good-boy orientation—interest is in pleasing others within the conventions of society and with regard for stereotypes of natural behavior.
> **Stage 4:** Law and order orientation—desire to maintain the social order for its own sake and to show respect for authority.

Level III: Postconventional
Individuals make a clear effort to define their own values and principles, apart from the authority of others.

> **Stage 5:** Contractual-legalistic orientation—critical examination of rules; consideration for the rights of others and majority welfare.
> **Stage 6:** Conscience and principles orientation—right is defined by one's own conscience and by universal principles which are abstract and ethical like the Golden Rule, rather than concrete and moral like the Ten Commandments.

Source: Lawrence Kohlberg, "Stage and Sequence: The Cognitive Developmental Approach to Socialization," in David Goslin (Ed.), *Handbook of Socialization Theory and Research* (Chicago: Rand McNally & Co., 1969), p. 376.

Teachers' uses of questions are critical in eliciting conflict in students' thinking. They may ask why, present complications (Suppose the student selling drugs is your cousin?), probe the student's reasoning (What obligations do you owe to a friend?), or ask for clarification of terms (What kinds of drugs are you referring to?) (Fraenkel, 1977; Hersh, Miller & Fielding, 1979). The classroom climate should be a cooperative and open one in which students, individually and in groups, can explore a variety of moral issues that are relevant to them. The primary role of the teacher is facilitation and confrontation, that is, facilitating the group discussion and confronting students with conflicting points of view to incite cognitive conflict which can lead to change.

A CRITIQUE OF VALUES EDUCATION ACTIVITIES

The development and use of values education activities such as those described in this section have received much attention from educators in the past few years. The drive to develop curriculum activities based on the ideas of Kohlberg, Rokeach, and others doing basic research and theory has been so intense, in fact, that it has outstripped the accumulation of solid validating evidence for the use of these activities in examining goals and priorities, choosing alternatives, examining consequences, and taking action. The activities described here are intuitively reasonable and have been reported extensively (Fraenkel, 1977). A solid research base, however, has not been established to validate their effectiveness, and criticisms of each approach have been advanced.

For example, while it seems useful to follow Kohlberg's suggestion to present students with moral dilemmas to discuss, his theory relies heavily on the concept of stages. Kohlberg states that students cannot understand each other if they are more than one developmental stage apart, so what is the teacher to do if the pupils in a classroom are in more than one stage? Are the stages distinct and separate? How can teachers diagnose the developmental level of each student? Answers to such questions have not been forthcoming. Moreover, at any developmental level, moral judgment probably varies as a function of the particular issue.

It is widely acknowledged that developmental trends do exist in moral judgments, but social learning theory (Bandura, 1977) takes account of the many social factors that influence moral reasoning. From the social learning perspective, standards for rightness and wrongness are a function of the person's own direct experiences, the experiences of others, and the unique characteristics of the specific situation. In this view, it is through experience, not stages, that particular dimensions evolve as relevant and important.

Another potential difficulty is that the values clarification activities, including values voting and discussions of consequences, require students to publicly admit to their attitudes. When students have opinions that deviate significantly from the perceived norm, it may be difficult, particularly for adolescents, to take public stands (Stewart, 1975). Perhaps the most serious weakness of values clarification is an overemphasis on the process of valuing, while ignoring the facts or information required to deal intelligently with values issues (Fraenkel, 1977, pp. 46–48). As we will note in Chapter 11, effective decision making requires both accurate knowledge and awareness of the values involved.

Rokeach's approach also has focused on becoming more aware of one's personal values and various inconsistencies among them. While most of his work has a solid research base, it has not received the widespread attention of curriculum theorists that the other approaches discussed here have. It is a good technique for helping students become aware of their own value priorities, and such information could be very useful for career and college counseling. More work is needed, however, before his approach can be easily integrated into the instructional process.

TEACHERS' ATTITUDES AND VALUES AND THE INSTRUCTIONAL PROCESS

As we have suggested, attitude and value learning is an ongoing process which occurs regardless of whether the teacher specifically plans for it. Teachers convey the school's values by the extent to which they offer students choices, by their selection of curriculum materials, and by their efforts to treat all students equally. Successful implementation of attitude and value learning thus depends on the teacher, a decision maker who has a great deal to say about what should be taught and how it should be taught. The teacher is also an ongoing model of attitudes and values associated with instructing, exercising control over, and caring for individuals. Perhaps the most difficult part of the teacher's task is to work with a variety of students who have different attributes, traits, and readiness characteristics in a way that is free of bias and that encourages all students to achieve maximum academic and social progress. (This is the teacher's paradox to be described in Part III.)

The interactions of teachers and students in the instructional process thus are strongly affected by the teacher's attitudes and values. Brophy and Good (1973, p. 17) describe the importance of teachers' attitudes in this manner:

> Since no two teachers or students have the same personality, a given student will provoke somewhat different reactions in each of the

different teachers he meets. We can also predict certain generalities, however: certain kinds of students will be liked by most teachers, and others will be disliked by most teachers. To the extent that a teacher experiences a strong emotional response to a student and forms clear-cut attitudes toward him, teacher-student interaction will be affected for better or worse.

HOW TEACHERS' EXPECTANCIES AFFECT STUDENTS

Certain student characteristics are more likely to be viewed by teachers as desirable or valuable. A study by Feshbach (1969) found that most teachers preferred to have rigid, conforming, and orderly students who are dependent, acquiescent, and passive. They least preferred students who are independent, active, and assertive. Teachers can form rather spontaneous judgments about students based on information from other teachers or administrators and direct encounters with students. While some teachers may be accurate in their perceptions of the abilities, motivations, and personalities of their students, others have distorted perceptions of them. Brophy and Good (1973, pp. 25–26) give the following examples of a first-grade teacher's reports about three of her students:

> *Robert*
> Robert is very slow, tries to certain extent. I'm afraid he's going to have to work real hard to get out of the first grade—as it appears now. He's overgrown for one thing. He's not a repeater.

> *Louise*
> Louise is going to be, I believe, one of the best students in the room. She's interested, does her work and gets through and very quiet. What I mean, she doesn't talk or cause much disturbance or anything.

> *William*
> Can't think of anything on him.

The information teachers receive about a student's ability, motivation, personal habits and traits, or background is translated into a set of expectancies about whether the student has the potential to succeed. *Based on these expectancies, the teacher begins to anticipate positive or negative consequences that may result from interacting with the student.*

Generally, teachers anticipate positive interactions with students who succeed academically and who behave in appropriate and helpful ways in the classroom. Negative interactions are usually anticipated with students who fail or create behavior problems. Over time these positive and negative interactions affect the teacher's positive or negative attitudes toward particular students and become translated into expectancies for them. Moreover, these expectancies can be generalized beyond the specific situation in which the behavior occurs to a wide variety of the students' behaviors. When the teacher overgeneralizes these expectancies or bases them on insufficient data, differential treatment of students can result.

Research has shown that teachers' expectancies can affect student performance in both positive and negative directions. If the expectancies are based on false information, particularly information that contributed to negative expectancies, the consequences could be quite undesirable. The same is true if teachers have accurate information and expectancies but are unwilling to change their beliefs when confronted with new performance data. In many ways, expectancies are normal, and when they are based on accurate data and are flexible, they may constitute a functional set of attitudes and beliefs for teachers. They have the potential of being quite harmful in the instructional process if they are based on small amounts of information, on stereotypes, or on hearsay and other types of unreliable data (Brophy & Good, 1973, chap. 11).

Most educators agree that teachers' expectations are of greatest concern when particular students are regarded as not very capable or chronic behavior problems. The teachers then inadvertently behave in ways which limit these students' potential achievement. Teachers tend to create a warmer socioemotional climate for students they believe are brighter; they nod, smile, make eye contact, and are generally more supportive and friendlier with these students. By contrast, students who are judged lower in ability are given fewer opportunities and less difficult material to learn, and their academically related interactions with the teacher are less frequent. The differential treatment of high- and low-ability students appears to be most profound in a large group setting, where the teacher fears losing control of the group as a result of boredom or a generally unpredictable environment (see Chapter 13). From the teacher's perspective, low-expectancy students are most likely to bore other students, cause disturbances, be inattentive, and generally make classroom life unpredictable. When teachers work with very small groups or on a one-to-one basis, the expectancy effects and resulting preferential treatment of certain students seem to disappear (Cooper, 1979).

What can teachers do to avoid the negative consequences of their expectancies? Should they avoid forming any opinions about student capabilities, or is this even possible? Should they hold equally high expectations for all students? Assessing students' capabilities at any point can be very useful when the teacher is planning instructional units, but holding the same expectations for all students does not make sense from a motivational point of view. Students who cannot meet the expectations are likely to give up, while others may find them unchallenging. Thus teachers must make individual estimates of students' potential if they are to maintain a reasonable pace of learning and motivation for the students as a whole. The effects of personal and situational factors on student motivation will be described in Chapter 11.

Teachers can avoid some of the problems associated with expectancies by focusing on concrete, first-hand information about students. Expectations are more likely to be accurate if they are based on actual performance data. Recent performance records may be useful if they refer to specific subject-matter areas or skills, but global predictors of ability and perceptions and evaluative comments from other teachers are likely to result in inaccurate assessments. Teachers also can make an active effort to focus on positive characteristics by making a list of each student's positive behavioral characteristics and reviewing and adding to it from time to time. They should try to communicate their positive expectations to the students. While all students may not be able to achieve at the same high level, they all can make progress and improve on their past performance. Instructional formats that move away from large-group instruction, such as individualized and mastery programs, can help teachers establish individually appropriate goals, but student progress should be reassessed frequently. Teaching in a large-group setting requires considerable practice in encouraging inquiry and creative exploration of ideas by all students.

THE EFFECTS OF TEACHERS' ATTITUDES ON INSTRUCTIONAL DECISIONS

Teachers' ability to adapt instructional plans to deal with the effects of expectancies depends in part on how they understand their own values and attitudes. As transmitters of learning about values and attitudes, teachers must be explicitly aware not only of the values orientation of the school but of how these values and attitudes affect all their instructional decisions and moment-to-moment teaching behaviors. According to Cooper (1979), expectancy effects are most likely to have an undesirable impact on teacher behavior when teachers perceive the situation as "out of control"; that is, they have few, if any, ideas about how to produce a positive outcome with a particular student. Feeling "in control" is of course related to the expertise, skill, background, and training of the teacher, but it is also related to the teacher's value orientation. It is much easier for teachers to feel in control when classes are small or when students are passive and acquiescent, rather than active, independent, and assertive.

According to Brophy and Rohrkemper (1981), when a student's behavior interferes with the teacher's instructional goals, the teacher is more likely to form a negative attitude toward the student; the teacher blames the student and is more likely to treat her or him punitively.

When the student has a behavior problem which does not interfere with any of the teacher's important goals, the teacher takes a more open and helpful stance toward the student. Brophy and Rohrkemper call these "teacher owned" and "student owned" problems, respectively:

Teacher-owned problem
> Defiant students: Children who resist authority and carry on a power struggle with the teacher. They want to have their own way and not be told what to do. They might resist verbally by saying, "You can't make me," or by making derogatory statements about the teacher to others. They might resist nonverbally by making grimaces or by deliberately doing what the teacher says not to do.

Student-owned problem
> Students rejected by peers: Children who seek peer interaction but are rejected, ignored, or excluded. These children may be forced to work and play alone, lack social skills, or often are picked on or teased.

With teacher-owned problems, teachers are more likely to use strategies characterized by frequent punishment and short-term control. With student-owned problems, they are likely to encourage and support students and pursue long-term mental health goals designed to help them develop coping techniques and self-approval (Brophy & Rohrkemper, 1981).

Teacher-owned problems are affected most by the teacher's own values. A teacher who believes obedience is important will have more teacher-owned problems with an active, assertive child than one who places a high value on independence, for example. Consider how a teacher who has completed the Rokeach values survey (see Tables 9.1 and 9.2 at the beginning of the preceding section) and has ranked "helpful," "loving," and "responsible" near the top of the list would react to the following case of Jeff in the Brophy and Rohrkemper (1981) study:

> Jeff tries hard but is the lowest achiever in the class. This week you taught an important sequence of lessons. You spent a lot of extra time with Jeff and thought he understood the material. Today you are reviewing. All the other students answer your questions with ease, but when you call on Jeff he is obviously lost. (Brophy & Rohrkemper, 1981, p. 298)

We might speculate that this teacher would believe there is still hope for Jeff, and further work with him might pay off. Helping others benefits this teacher's own sense of self-esteem, and the teacher might conclude that it is possible to spend extra time with Jeff without sacrificing the needs of other students. It may be, however, that the most rational course of action would be to refer Jeff for special tutoring and to pay more attention to the more capable students in the class. Determining which approach—helping Jeff or referring him for remedial help—is correct would require a careful examination of all the factors in the situation.

In any case, teachers should continually examine their own values and attitudes and assess the impact of these values on their instructional decisions. This cannot be a single static act; value systems change over time as people encounter new experiences and challenges to previously held assumptions. The more teachers are aware of how values and attitudes are learned, the more able they will be to make rational decisions about students and instruction.

CHAPTER 9 IN RETROSPECT

The instructional process is concerned not only with how students acquire cognitive knowledge but with how they acquire beliefs, attitudes, and values. The proper role of the teacher in this process, we believe, is to give students a choice of what to believe, like, and value, not to indoctrinate them with the value systems of others.

Attitudes may seem to provide simple explanations for behavior, but the relationship is complex. Specific behaviors are not necessarily predictable from attitudes, which are learned predispositions to respond favorably or unfavorably toward an attitude object—a person, thing, or event. A person's evaluation of an attitude object is determined by whether the person associates the attributes of the object with positive or negative consequences. A person also can have a relatively neutral attitude toward an object. Efforts to change any type of attitude may try to change the strength of the association between the attributes and the object, the consequences of the attributes, or the evaluations of the consequences.

Attitudes are learned or changed through some combination of three processes—direct experience, vicarious experience or observation, and logical reasoning. In the direct experience approach, respondent and operant conditioning principles are related to the learner's experience with the consequences associated with the attributes of the attitude object. Teachers can use this approach to condition favorable classroom attitudes. The vicarious experience approach is tied to observational learning, or the modeling of behaviors and their consequences for learners. In the reasoning and problem-solving approach, students are required to think critically about their behaviors and consider the consequences in a logical manner.

Attitudes about oneself are reflected in the self-concept, or the set of perceptions, beliefs, and attitudes that individuals develop as a result of how they and others view their experiences. A positive self-concept and high self-esteem enhance learners' expectations for themselves, which in turn improves their behaviors and academic performance. Schools can help students develop positive self-concepts by teaching the necessary academic and social skills, modifying the classroom environment, or presenting a system of positive self-evaluation.

Values establish the standards for judging things, people, and events and evaluating them favorably or unfavorably. A change in values is likely to have a greater impact on behavior than a change in either beliefs or attitudes. Values learning, development, and change emerge from a person's perceived self-dissatisfaction, and values education should acquaint students with strategies for resolving the values dilemmas that result. These strategies employ problem-solving techniques and are designed to help students choose what to value. Rokeach's instrumental and terminal value scales and Kohlberg's six stages of moral development provide useful categories as a basis for such discussion and decision making.

Successful implementation of attitude and values learning depends on the teacher, whose own attitudes and values directly affect the instructional process. Teachers' expectancies about the positive or negative consequences of interactions with particular students can affect student performance and behaviors both positively and negatively. As a result, teachers should base their expectancies of students on complete first-hand information, try to form positive attitudes and communicate them to students, and tailor the instruction to individual students.

---

1. Select a short lesson in music, art, history, grammar, or mathematics. Imagine that the students have never been exposed to this content before, and you want them to develop a positive attitude towards it. Prepare a list of procedures and activities you would use in the lesson to develop positive attitudes. Include activities that reflect respondent, operant, and observational approaches to attitude learning.
2. Prepare one or two learning activities related to each of Felker's five keys for helping students develop positive self-concepts. Develop these activities for an elementary or secondary school class.
3. Suppose you want to integrate some values education activities within the standard curriculum. For a curriculum subject with which you are familiar, identify areas of the content that might involve values considerations, and describe some specific values learning activities

**QUESTIONS
FOR
DISCUSSION**

that would relate to those areas. These activities should help students practice one or more of the problem-solving strategies for making value-related decisions described in this chapter.

4. Take the Rokeach Survey of Values yourself; that is, rank order the 18 terminal and 18 instrumental values listed in Tables 9.1 and 9.2. What values do you think will be most important to you in your role as an educator? Based on these values, what emphasis will you place on social, academic, personal growth, and development outcomes of education?

5. How would a child at Kohlberg's preconventional level of moral development and a child at the conventional level differ in their views of authority? How does each type of child relate to authority?

**READINGS
FOR
REFLECTION**

Felker, Donald W. *Building Positive Self-Concepts.* Minneapolis: Burgess Publishing Co., 1974.

This readable text has value as both a broad-based theoretical summary and a source of practical suggestions for improving the self-concept of children. It sketches theoretical background and research on self-concept and then introduces "five keys" for improving it. The book makes a case for how children can be taught to think positively about themselves and their performance through systematic instruction in strategies of self-reinforcement.

Fraenkel, Jack R. *How to Teach about Values: An Analytical Approach.* Englewood Cliffs, N.J.: Prentice-Hall, 1977.

An excellent analysis of the process of valuing and its relevance to schooling is provided in this book, which has a solid theoretical and research base. It draws on the work of Rokeach, the values clarification of Simon, Howe, and Kirschenbaum, and the moral reasoning approach of Kohlberg. The need for students to be able to identify, analyze, and assess alternative policies and procedures, along with their consequences, in an intelligent and rational manner is stressed.

Simon, Sidney B., Howe, Leland W., and Kirschenbaum, Howard. *Values Clarification: A Handbook of Practical Strategies for Teachers and Students.* New York: Hart Publishing Co., 1972.

This book is extremely useful for values clarification activities in the classroom. It explains values clarification strategies that are adaptable for both elementary and secondary school-age students.

Advanced Level

Fishbein, Martin, and Ajzen, Icek. *Belief, Attitude, Intention, and Behavior: An Introduction to Theory and Research.* Reading, Mass.: Addison-Wesley, 1975.

This book for advanced students explores current research and theory on attitudes. It reviews major theoretical approaches to the learning of attitudes and describes the authors' own research, which relates behavior to attitudes through specific intentions and beliefs.

Rokeach, Milton. *The Nature of Human Values.* New York: Free Press, 1973.

This advanced text on the social psychology of values discusses the development of questionnaires for assessing terminal and instrumental values and presents the theory that values are the most important part of our self-belief systems. Research on procedures for bringing about values change in individuals is also described.

REFERENCES

Ames, Carole, and Felker, Donald. Effects of self-concept on children's attributions and self-reinforcement. *Journal of Educational Psychology,* 1979, *71,* 613–619.

Bandura, Albert. Influence of models' reinforcement contingencies on the acquisition of imitative responses. *Journal of Personality and Social Psychology,* 1965, *1,* 589–595.

Bandura, Albert. *Social Learning Theory.* Englewood Cliffs, N.J.: Prentice-Hall, 1977.

Blaney, Nancy, Stephan, Cookie, Rosenfield, David, Aronson, Elliot, and Sikes, Jev. Interdependence in the classroom: A field study. *Journal of Educational Psychology,* 1977, *69,* 121–128.

Bostrom, Robert, Vlandis, John, and Rosenbaum, Milton. Grades as reinforcing contingencies and attitude change. *Journal of Educational Psychology,* 1961, *52,* 112–115.

Brookover, Wilbur, Patterson, A., and Thomas, S. Self-concept of ability and school achievement. *Sociology of Education,* 1904, *37,* 271–278.

Brophy, Jere E., and Good, Thomas L. *Teacher-Student Relationships: Causes and Consequences.* New York: Holt, Rinehart & Winston, 1973.

Brophy, Jere E., and Rohrkemper, Mary M. The influence of problem ownership on teachers' perceptions of and strategies for coping with problem students. *Journal of Educational Psychology,* 1981, *78,* 295–311.

Calsyn, Robert J., and Kenny, David A. Self-concept of ability and perceived evaluation of others: Cause or effect of academic achievement? *Journal of Educational Psychology*, 1977, *69*, 136–145.

Cartledge, Gwendolyn, and Milburn, JoAnne F. *Teaching Social Skills to Children*. New York: Pergamon Press, 1980.

Cooper, Harris M. Pygmalion grows up: A model for teacher expectation communication and performance influence. *Review of Educational Research*, Summer, 1979, *49*(3), 389–410.

Covington, Martin V., and Berry, R. G. *Self-Worth and School Learning*. New York: Holt, Rinehart & Winston, 1976.

Early, C. Joan. Attitude learning in children. *Journal of Educational Psychology*, 1968, *59*, 176–180.

Felker, Donald W. *Building Positive Self-Concepts*. Minneapolis: Burgess, 1974.

Feshback, Norma D. Student-teacher preferences for elementary school pupils varying in personality characteristics. *Journal of Educational Psychology*, 1969, *60*, 126–132.

Festinger, Leon. Behavioral support for opinion change. *Public Opinion Quarterly*, 1964, *28*, 404–417.

Fishbein, Martin, and Ajzen, Icek. *Belief, Attitude, Intention, and Behavior: An Introduction to Theory and Research*. Reading, Mass.: Addison-Wesley, 1975.

Fraenkel, Jack R. *How to Teach about Values: An Analytical Approach*. Englewood Cliffs, N.J.: Prentice-Hall, 1977.

Gagné, Robert M. *The Conditions of Learning*. New York: Holt, Rinehart & Winston, 1977.

Glasser, William L. *Schools without Failure*. New York: Harper & Row, 1969.

Hersh, Richard H., Miller, J., and Fielding, G. *Models of Moral Education*. New York: Longman, 1979.

Johnson, David W., and Ahlgren, Andrew. Relationship between student attitudes about cooperation and competition and attitudes toward schooling. *Journal of Educational Psychology*, 1976, *68*, 92–102.

Johnson, David W., Johnson, Roger T., Johnson, Jeanette, and Anderson, Douglas. The effects of cooperative vs. individualized instruction on prosocial behavior, attitudes toward learning, and achievement. *Journal of Educational Psychology*, 1976, *68*, 446–452.

Johnson, David W., and Johnson, Roger T. Cooperative, competitive, and individualistic learning. *Journal of Research and Development in Education*, 1978, *12*, 3–15.

Kennedy, John F. *Profiles in Courage*. New York: Harper, 1956.

Klausmeier, Herbert. Learning and human abilities. In *Educational Psychology*. New York: Harper & Row, 1973.

Kohlberg, Lawrence. Moral education in the schools: A developmental view. *School Review*, 1966, *74*, 1–30.

Kohlberg, Lawrence. Stage and sequence: The cognitive developmental approach to socialization. In David Goslin (Ed.), *Handbook of Socialization Theory and Research*. Chicago: Rand McNally, 1969.

Mager, Robert F. *Developing Attitude toward Learning*. Belmont, Cal.: Fearon Publishers, 1968.

Marecek, Jeanne, and Mettee, David R. Avoidance of continued success as a function of self-esteem, level of esteem, certainty, and responsibility for success. *Journal of Personality and Social Psychology*, 1972, *22*, 98–107.

Oden, Sherri, and Asher, Stephen. Coaching children in social skills in friendship making. *Child Development*, 1977, *48*, 495–506.

Postman, Neil, and Weingartner, Charles. *Teaching as a Subversive Activity*. New York: Delacorte Press, 1969.

Rokeach, Milton. *The Nature of Human Values*. New York: Free Press, 1973.

Simon, Sidney B., Howe, Leland, W., and Kirschenbaum, Howard. *Values Clarification: A Handbook of Practical Strategies for Teachers and Students*. New York: Hart Publishing Co., 1972.

Slavin, Robert E. Classroom reward structure: An analytical and practical review. *Review of Educational Research*, 1977, *47*, 633–650.

Stewart, J. S. Clarifying values clarification: A critique. *Phi Delta Kappan*, 1975, 648–689.

Wales, Charles E. *The guided design systems approach*. Report prepared for Exxon Education Foundation Impact Program. Morgantown, W.Va.: Freshman Engineering, Department of Engineering, 1976.

Watson, John B., and Raynor, Rosalie. Conditioned emotional reactions. *Journal of Experimental Psychology*, 1920, *3*, 1–4.

Thinking

Learning and thinking are closely related processes which often merge. Indeed, meaningful learning, whose importance in cognitive activity was explored in Chapter 7, closely approaches and may involve thinking. The student who understands the Pythagorean theorem, for example, can apply it to the solution of appropriate measurement problems. For meaningful learning to take place, learners must classify new data, compare and contrast new ideas with those already in their store of knowledge, and search for connections or relationships between information presented to them and information they already have. All of these are indications that the learner is thinking.

We will use the term *thinking* in a general sense, to signify the individual's reflective and productive preoccupation with some type of theoretical or practical material. The idea being thought about may be as concrete as how to keep rabbits out of the garden or as abstract as the expression of a complicated concept within the disciplined form of a sonnet. It may be as complex and urgent as creating a desegregation plan for an urban school district, or as simple and pleasant as planning a barbecue for one's friends.

Thinking is a natural part of the child's development, in both the cognitive-intellectual and social-emotion domains as defined in Part I. It is the means by which children's cognitive structures are maintained and expanded and the boundaries of their world are constantly widened (see Box A).

ESSENTIAL CHARACTERISTICS OF THINKING

Most human predicaments demand some type of thought. Specialized knowledge, techniques, or procedures may be required, as is the case in engineering, medicine, or the law. But there are some essential characteristics of thinking that are always present, regardless of content or circumstances.

When people are thinking, their behavior departs from routine patterns. A teacher questioning her class who hears an answer from a student that doesn't make sense will probably pause and try to decipher the child's response. If she cannot do so, she may ask another question to help her understand where the learner's reasoning went astray. Or a physician taking a routine health history from a patient may become alert at the mention of a significant symptom or condition and seek additional information to assist his diagnosis.

The first common characteristic of thinking, then, is that it demands *attention*. When we encounter a perplexing situation, our senses seem to

BOX A · *The wide line between thinking and being told*

For children, thinking is a more active way of learning than instruction they only receive passively. The following example by Helen Marksberry illustrates how the process of thinking helps children learn for themselves:

> Five year old Wendy was taking a ride with her father. They passed a cement truck, and Wendy said, "That's a cement mixer. It has sand and water and cement in the round part, and that part goes around so the sand and water and cement will get mixed up and stay mixed up." She went on to tell where the cement mixer might be going and what would happen when it got there. After giving all this information, she looked at her father and said, "Do you know how I know this? I thought it." Then she said thoughtfully, "You don't have to think in school. The teacher tells you."

Source: Mary Lee Marksberry, "Sizing up Assertions," *Elementary School Journal*, vol. 76 (1976), p. 289.

quicken. We look or listen, or we pause and search our memory as we try to classify the unusual circumstances in terms that make it understandable. When behavior has been pushed or pulled out of its accustomed ruts, restlessness or discomfort is experienced, and it will not pass until the situation can be understood or altered or resolved.

Second, thinking demands *flexibility,* or openness to possible alternatives that may resolve the perplexity. Sarnoff Mednick's Remote Associates Test (1968), for example, presents trios of seemingly unrelated words and asks learners to come up with a fourth word that connects all three. An example might be:

birthday   line   political

To find a word that ties these three words together, a person might begin by thinking of birthday *gifts,* which might be associated with political but hardly with line. Political *meeting* fits one word and not the other two, but *party* meets the requirement of fitting all three. The elapsed time necessary to find the correct association is usually only a fraction of the time required to read this paragraph, but the process underlying the solution utilizes the same kind of review or assessment of alternatives.

It should not be surprising that the best thinkers are often people with the largest stores of both general and specialized information. An individual who knows a lot of things has a better chance of uncovering suitable alternatives during a review of possibilities. But knowledge in itself is no guarantee of good thinking. The individual must be able to retrieve suitable alternatives from memory and to see appropriate fits or relationships among ideas.

A third characteristic of thinking is that it requires *time for reflection* and for the construction and consideration of alternative possible solutions. The British psychologist Edward DeBono (1969) distinguishes between vertical and lateral thinking. Most people do vertical thinking most of the time; they dig ever deeper intellectual holes for themselves. Lateral thinking is analagous to drilling many shallow holes, all in different places, to find new kinds of approaches to thought.

A first trial solution to a problem, or the first idea for a story or speech or other intellectual activity, will probably not be as high in quality as the idea or solution that occurs as a result of persistent efforts to generate additional possibilities. Maltzman (1960) found this result in a variation on the standard word association task ("When I say a word, you answer with whatever word comes into your mind"), in which participants were given the same words repeatedly and asked to provide a different response each time. As the number of trials increased it became more difficult for participants to supply associations, but those they did give were increasingly rare. And when Parnes (1959) asked adult and college students to suggest numerous uses for broom handles, coat hangers, or other everyday objects, they found that the answers rated as best in quality by independent judges always came in the second half of the time period.

With routine tasks there is a great deal to be said for the tendency of common responses to occur early in a person's thinking. If you ask the produce clerk at the supermarket how much tomatoes are a pound, you expect a quick and accurate reply. And if you ask this question just after I do, you should receive the same answer I did. The reason for thought is that an idea is perplexing because it is incomplete or unsatisfactory. If a quickly available answer would fix the difficulty, there would be no need to think.

Fourth, thinking requires some direction or *plan*. It has a purpose. Most children have no set plan for working a puzzle that requires separating two interlocked pieces of metal, for example; they simply manipulate the pieces this way and that, until finally they stumble on the correct positions and the pieces come apart. Such trial and error behavior may lead to the solution of simple problems, but this is not what we mean by thinking.

To improve students' thinking, a variety of work-study skills is taught as part of the instructional process. In middle or junior high school, for example, teachers of English and social studies first require students to write a term paper or long report. The children learn the processes of identifying topics, writing note cards, making detailed outlines, drafting first versions, and then editing and revising them. As these stages are checked by the teacher, feedback to the learner suggests whether the work needs to be more complete or better organized. In the framework of a lifetime of thinking, such efforts to teach children to be planful and systematic in selecting and organizing information are invaluable. The same may be said for the specialized, disciplined thinking required in laboratory science, mathematics, or the other major branches of study.

Fifth, thinking demands an involvement or *commitment* from the thinker. A person must be motivated to think, rather than accepting predetermined answers or settling for the commonest ways to resolve perplexities. As Chapter 11 will show, motivation involves the organization of the individual's energies, an extremely important point in the consideration of thinking. Thinking requires energy, focus, and a determination to persevere until the best or the correct or the most suitable formulation has been found. Since this does not usually happen quickly or easily, or without concentrated and perhaps extended thought and effort, it is imperative that the learner be motivated to make the effort.

Thinking, then, refers to an individual's deliberate, directed effort to generate a suitable (and perhaps original) idea for resolving a perplexing situation or an observed or felt dissatisfaction (see Chapter 9). The idea, which may take many forms, is the result of the individual's application (or redefinition or reconstruction) of his or her own knowledge or experience in a form that fits the situation. Thinking is further characterized by the individual's focused energy, persistence, and willingness to arrive at a solution or understanding.

In this chapter we will classify the processes and outcomes of thinking into three categories: problem solving, critical thinking, and creative thinking. These skills were introduced in Part I as various aspects of development of the learner in the cognitive-intellectual domain.

PROBLEM SOLVING

It is a common experience for students to encounter mathematics problems of the following kind: "The sum of Mary's age and Ann's age is 30. In three years Ann will be twice as old as Mary. How old is Mary now? For younger children, a more manageable problem might be: "A garden plot is 45 feet long and 20 feet wide. How many square feet does it contain?" Both of these are problems in the sense that the answer to

Thinking requires time to reflect and to consider alternative approaches and the consequences of decisions, whether the problem is a move in a game of chess or the intricate design of a scientific experiment.

them is not immediately available; no solution has been memorized. But there are set procedures which are communicated in the instructional process to make it possible to solve such problems. Middle-grade children, for example, learn that the area of a rectangle is found by multiplying its length by its width. If questions about the area of garden plots and other like quantities are asked at the same time the child is learning how to find the area of rectangles, the "problems" represent little more than varied practice on an arithmetic process. Little thinking is required.

A problem occurs when the individual is confronted with a situation for which he or she does not have a solution, and for which no set pattern or procedure to provide one exists. Thus problem solving involves the characteristics of thinking enumerated in the preceding section. The application of past experience to the problem is very much a part of problem solving, but the applications are rarely direct or auto-

BOX B   *Problem solving for short people*

Pete, a tenth-grader, had been unhappy ever since classes started at the senior high school. He was too short for his age, but in the elementary and junior high schools his lack of height had not presented great difficulties. Now he was surrounded by older adolescents, and his 5'2" frame, strong torso, and thick neck had become the butt of incessant jokes. One day, in the cafeteria, Pete overheard one too many derogatory remarks aimed at him, and he swung at another boy.

Pete's counselor, Mr. Mathews, tried to get Pete to talk about the problem. As far as Pete was concerned, the problem was with the other students who called him names. "That may be true, Pete," Mr. Mathews tried to reason, "but do you think there's any way the school can stop them from doing it?" Pete reluctantly agreed that another approach would have to be tried. Mr. Mathews pointed out that as long as Pete defined the problem as "something the kids shouldn't do to me," and the solution as, "I'm going to hit them!" he would be in constant trouble, not only with his peers, but with the authority of the school as well. They talked about several other ways of defining the problem, but none of them suited Pete. He could ignore the remarks, or laugh at the offenders, or kid them back: "How's the oxygen supply up there?" Pete only scowled. These were not solutions, as far as he was concerned. Several weeks later he hit another name-caller, and this time he was suspended from school for three days.

Later in the semester, when Mr. Mathews encountered Pete in the hall and asked how things were going, Pete replied "Pretty good. I joined the wrestling team, and I'm doing real good." By spring, when the wrestling season ended, Pete had won most of his matches, and he was regarded as an up-and-coming wrestler in the district. He had enhanced his status and his self-esteem by making use of his size, weight, strength, and aggressiveness. No doubt his anger toward the taunts of his peers was redirected at his wrestling opponents. If classmates continued to joke about his height, Pete no longer heard them or cared what they said. He had proved to himself that he could succeed in an area that was important to him.

matic. In order to solve a problem, one must first understand what the problem is. That may call for reconstructing or redefining the problem as it first appears, and adapting one's prior knowledge or experience in some way that fits the demands of the current problem (see Box B).

REFLECTIVE THINKING

The idea that thinking only occurs when the thinker is faced with a "felt difficulty" or problem was first expressed by John Dewey, as we noted in Chapter 9. A disturbance occurs, and the individual must search for a way out of it. Some tentative plan or solution is required, and it must be tested for adequacy. The role of prior learning and experience is important in this process, but so are the ability and willingness of the individual to think reflectively about the problem. Dewey stressed that effective problem solving depends on the learner's disposition to suspend judgment while the process of inquiry goes forward.

For many people, the uncertainty and ambiguity of an unresolved problem arouses tension. They feel uncomfortable, and if they have a choice between reaching an immediate decision or postponing it for a time to consider alternatives and gather additional data, they are likely to choose the easier, faster decision.

SEEING RELATIONSHIPS

In Pete's problem described in Box B, his decision to join the wrestling team was not directly related to the difficulties he was having with his peers. After reflective thinking, he understood that if he took action which made him feel more secure within himself as a competent individual, the insults directed at him would lose their effectiveness.

In one view of problem solving, finding solutions depends on the ability to see relationships between or among key elements of problems. A classic example was reported in Wolfgang Kohler's studies of the mentality of apes. One of the animals had previously learned to use a pole to rake in food from a place outside its cage. Kohler complicated the situation by moving the food to a more distant point and placing in the cage two poles that would have to be connected to provide a rake long enough to reach the food. At first the ape persisted in reaching for the food with a single pole, though it was much too short. As long as the two poles lay apart from each other in the cage, the animal failed to see a relationship between them, but when they were placed next to each other it seemed to "see" that together they would make a pole long enough to reach the food. The problem was solved at that point, even though, in fact, the ape had considerable difficulty in joining the two pieces together.

BOX C *The beautiful transformation*

Max Wertheimer studied problem solving by observing how children learned to compute the area of a parallelogram. His report noted that:

> Some children reached the solution with little or no help in a genuine, sensible, direct way. Sometimes, after strained concentration, a face brightened at the critical moment. It is wonderful to observe the beautiful transformation from blindness to seeing the point!

Wertheimer gave no help at all to a five-and-a-half-year-old girl when he asked her to compute the area of a parallelogram:

> Given the parallelogram problem, after she had been shown briefly how to get at the area of the rectangle, she said, "I certainly don't know how to do *that*." Then after a moment of silence: "This is *no good here*," pointing to the region at the left end, and *no good here*," pointing to the region at the right.

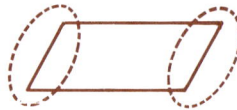

> "It's troublesome, here and there." Hesitatingly she said, "I could make it right here . . . but . . . ." Suddenly she cried out, "May I have a pair of scissors? What is bad there is just what is needed here. It fits." She took the scissors, cut the figure vertically, and placed the left end at the right.

Source: Max Wertheimer, *Productive Thinking* (New York: Harper & Bros., 1959), pp. 47–48.

Max Wertheimer (1959) made a similar point in his studies of children's mathematical problem-solving ability. He observed that even quite young children can understand the logic of how to determine the area of such forms as a parallelogram (see Box C).

THE NEED FOR FLEXIBILITY

Most people persist in behaving in their accustomed ways unless there is some force in the environment that induces change or variability in their behavior. Learning results when there is enough flexibility in the situation to permit new solutions to be considered and alternatives to be tested.

One of the biggest casualties in the 1980s recession was the automobile industry, which had introduced the ideas of mass production and the assembly line and helped change the daily lives of people around the world. The success of the manufacturing and marketing strategies of the industry may have carried the seeds of its disaster. Despite reports of petroleum shortages and sharp increases in the price of gasoline, U.S. auto manufacturers were inflexible about their production format, and Detroit continued to turn out large, gas-hungry cars long after the demand for small, fuel-efficient models took hold. The availability of high miles-per-gallon, relatively inexpensive foreign imports, coupled with the inflexibility of the domestic industry, seriously weakened the major producers. By the time American automakers responded to changes in the marketplace and began to turn out smaller, lighter models, buyer confidence was lacking, interest rates were too high for purchasers, and unemployment and inflation had seriously weakened buying power.

Flexibility is required in problem solving because, by definition, the problem's existence is due to a lack of appropriate available solutions or fixed patterns of response. The classic example of how a mental set, or fixed way of thinking, interferes with the ability to see that other or simpler solutions are possible was provided by the "water jar" problems devised by Luchins (1942). This is a good way to establish quickly a set pattern or routine way of solving problems that is relatively difficult to overcome. The problems work in this fashion:

> Given three jars, jar A holds 21 quarts of water, jar B 127 quarts, and jar C 3 quarts. Obtain 100 quarts of water. The experimenter helps the solver see that 100 quarts can be obtained by filling jar B with 127 quarts, and then pouring 21 quarts into jar A, and filling jar C twice (for 6 quarts). This leaves the desired 100 quarts. The formula B − A − 2C is established. It works on an ensuing series of similar problems, and may continue to be used on later problems that can be solved more directly, for example, by the formula A plus C or A minus C.

Luchins points out that even highly intelligent and well-educated adults are susceptible to rigidity in problem solving. He also observes that when teachers insist on blind obedience to routine ways of doing things in the classroom, the mental set is more likely to constrain students' learning. Students who are allowed to participate in deciding how a classroom will operate and who can see that flexibility is valued are more likely to be flexible in their own problem-solving efforts. Chapter 12 will contrast the effects of open classroom situations with those in which the teacher directs the instruction.

Lack of flexibility in problem solving is also revealed in "functional fixedness," a term first used by Duncker (1945) to describe the idea that an object used for one purpose is not readily perceived as fulfilling a different function. To study this effect Adamson (1952) asked participants to mount three candles vertically on a board, using available materials such as small cardboard boxes and thumbtacks. The appropriate solution is to light a candle, melt some wax on top of the box, mount the candle on the box, and then tack the box to the board. In one experimental condition the materials were packed in the boxes, which were thus seen as containers rather than possible candleholders. Twice as many people solved the problem correctly when the boxes were displayed empty, as part of the equipment to be considered for use.

PROBLEM-SOLVING INSTRUCTIONAL PROGRAMS

Problem solving can be presented to students in the instructional process as a technique for thinking about subject matter or as a series of skills to be mastered in their own right. In both cases the skills must be presented in some sort of content framework, however. As DeBono (1976) points out, a difficulty in programs to teach thinking to schoolchildren is the necessity to use some type of content as a vehicle for discussion. DeBono contends that the content may so dominate the lesson that the class literally "glides past" the occasion for developing thinking skills, even though they are the central purpose of the lesson.

The Productive Thinking Program

One program to teach the skills of problem solving which avoids traditional subject-matter content is the Productive Thinking Program (Covington et al., 1972). This curriculum for middle-grade students consists of a series of 16 lesson booklets plus an excellent student activity book. The lessons and activities are organized around a number of "thinking guides," such as "Take time to find out what the problem is you are trying to solve," and "Don't jump to conclusions." The thinking guides are not taught as precepts; instead the lessons engage students in interesting puzzles or mysteries, from which the thinking guides emerge.

One lesson presents the riddle of two valuable coins that are missing from a dealer's collection. The reader is given a number of items of information that rule out chance disappearance; for instance, the windows were screened, and no one had tampered with them. A suspicious character was waiting in an outer office to view the collection at the time the disappearance was discovered, so apparently he did not take them. The point of the lesson is that sometimes it is necessary to assume the impossible (the suspicious character *is* the culprit) and then figure out how it could have occurred.

The goal of the Productive Thinking Program is to teach general problem-solving skills which are applicable to various situations that can occur in children's lives but which are not neatly tied to a subject area like science or arithmetic. As the program was under development, careful field tests of its effectiveness confirmed that children who study the program and have appropriate practice will improve their general problem-solving skills. In one study Olton and Crutchfield (1969) sought to achieve maximum learning and transfer of the skills among fifth- and sixth-graders. Supplementary exercises in the activity book were added to the basic 16 lessons to extend transfer to school-related problems. Teachers who used the program were encouraged to participate actively by guiding and stimulating discussion.

The participants in this study were 50 fifth-graders drawn from two classes. Half the children in each class received instruction, and the other half were controls. The two groups were closely matched for IQ and achievement scores. All of the children took problem-solving tests just before the instructional period. For the next eight weeks the experimental group studied the materials for about one hour a day, and the control pupils were given a program consisting of general educational activities such as movies, stories, and other interesting projects, none of which utilized productive thinking. A posttest was given at the end of the eight-week period. Distributions of the 23-item composite productive thinking scores for the instruction and control groups are shown in Figure 10.1. A significantly higher proportion of the instruction group scored above the median of the combined groups, compared to the control group.

Superior performance was maintained by the instruction group over the controls in the follow-up test given six months after the completion of the unit, supporting the contention that the skills of thinking were well retained. A good amount of transfer was also evident for the instructed pupils, as seen by their performance on some of the follow-up test items. For example, the "nameless tomb" problem challenges the

Figure 10.1

Composite productive thinking scores of fifth-grade pupils

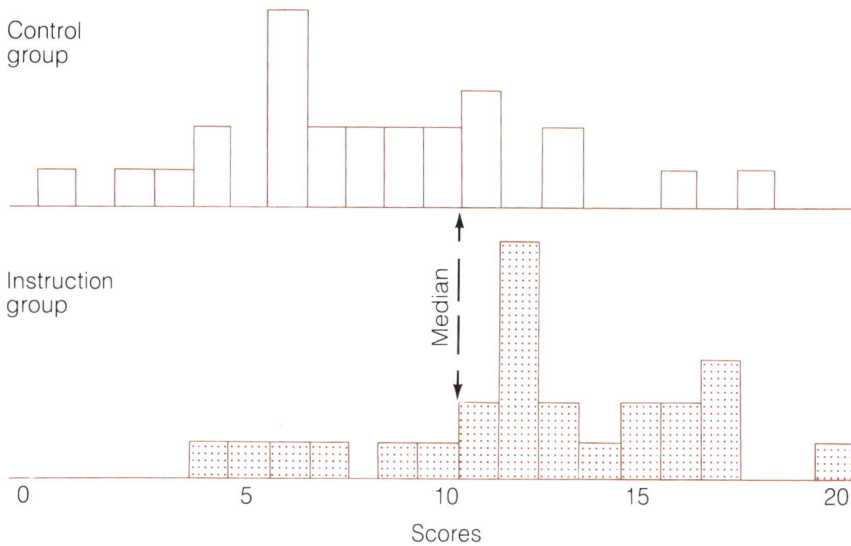

Source: Adapted from Robert M. Olton and Richard S. Crutchfield,
"Developing the Skills of Productive Thinking," in P. Mussen,
J. Langer, and M. V. Covington (Eds.), *Trends and Issues in Developmental
Psychology* (New York: Holt, Rinehart & Winston, 1969), p. 81.

child to determine which of 10 people is buried there. Simple facts in
the problem statement can eliminate 7 of the 10, and a single clue makes
one person the obvious choice, but a learner who is not flexible enough
to break a mental set is unlikely to respond to the clue. Of the control
students, 37 percent eliminated the seven possible occupants, and 58
percent went on to solve the problem correctly. Corresponding scores
for the instructed group were 69 and 91 percent.

A more impressive indication of the transfer power of the program
is the result of the pupils' work on the problem which called for writing
an essay on poverty. They were free to write whatever they felt about
the topic, and the essays were scored on three points: (1) the number
of descriptions of poverty given, (2) the number of cases of poverty
mentioned, and (3) the number of suggestions about how poverty might
be ended. The instruction and control groups did not differ in the
number of descriptions of poverty given; their basic fund of knowledge

about the problem was about the same. But the instruction group listed on the average five causes of poverty, almost three times as many as were named by the control pupils. Since the learners were not asked to cite causes, this suggests more active thinking by the instruction group. Only 5 children in the total group of 50 proffered suggestions for ending poverty, but 4 of the 5 came from the instruction group. The evidence speaks well for the positive impact of the Productive Thinking Program on the development and use of active thinking skills by children.

Studies of Other Problem-Solving Programs

Using the Productive Thinking Program as a model, Greer and Blank (1977) designed a series of programmed booklets to test whether certain types of responses typically given by impulsive, nonanalytic children could be modified. The program used six booklets, each aimed at a particular skill or principle: delaying immediate responses; identifying relevant and irrelevant clues to problems; using information-seeking questions to elicit clues; listing all the facts in a problem and combining them to produce possible solutions; evaluating possible solutions in light of the facts given in a problem; and practicing these skills independently. Students were asked to evaluate their own solutions according to the information or clues they discovered.

To test this program, Greer and Blank trained a group of fifth-grade children in 14 30-minute sessions, and then each child was given four "mystery" problems to solve. The responses were scored for the amount of time the children committed to studying and evaluating the problem, and the total number as well as the types of questions they asked while considering it. The major finding of this study was that this type of programmed instruction increases the length of time children pursue solutions to problems and the quantity and quality of their questions about the process. The effect of checking the impulsiveness of the least restrained and most nonanalytical children was negligible, however.

Children's social problem-solving skills have also been studied. Social problems depend on the same intellectual and cognitive processes as other kinds of problems do, but they involve other people, and their solutions must be worked out by interaction among the participants.

McClure, Chinsky, and Larcen (1978) studied the social problem solving of elementary school pupils with a program using six problem-solving components. It was designed to assure children that problems are to be expected as a natural part of life, that they should be able to solve many of their own problems, and that it is important to learn to stop and think instead of impulsively rushing ahead with a solution. The components stressed identifying a problem correctly, collecting and organizing pertinent data, setting both long- and short-term goals, generating multiple solutions to problems, and taking account of the potential consequences of solutions. The final component called for placing all these skills and procedures into a unified strategy that could be used to solve a given problem.

Instruction in this program was by means of videotapes featuring child actors about the same age as the third- and fourth-graders who participated in the study. The students were assigned to one of four conditions, a control group and three others which were shown the appropriate videotape one day a week. On the following day, children in one group participated with an adult leader in a *discussion* of the strategy demonstrated on the videotape. A *role-playing* group acted out the consequences of alternative strategies of solution. The *television* group saw each videotape but had no special activity other than their regular social studies class the following day.

At the end of the six-week training program, the role-playing treatment was found to have the strongest effect on the children's problem-solving behavior, although the ability to think about problem solving was also enhanced by other videotape showings. The best opportunity for transfer from the training to real-life situations seemed to be provided by the role-playing technique. That is an understandable outcome, because as part of their training the children had to do the thinking and engage in the acting that are part of social problem solving.

TEACHING STUDENTS TO SOLVE PROBLEMS

Rather than using programs like those described above to teach problem-solving skills to students, teachers can incorporate the skills into their treatment of subject matter content. They also can provide opportunities to students for practice with the basic components of problem solving and allow them time to search for the best possible alternative solution.

Problem-Solving Subject Matter

A direct application of problem solving to content is the use of story or word problems in arithmetic or mathematics lessons (problem test items are described in Chapter 16). Here the learner's ability to make meaningful translations of the language of the problem into mathematical operations is critical. Teachers are often concerned with the inability of students to follow the logic of such word problems, and researchers have found support for this concern.

Anthony and Hudgins (1978), for example, found that fifth-graders have difficulty with two-step problems because they overlook one of the steps. A problem may state:

> Four girls and three boys in our class have rock collections. If each of them brings five rocks to school, how many rocks will there be altogether?

A poor problem solver may answer either 20 or 15, depending on which part of the problem he or she pays attention to. Similar failures occur with other problems, all of which fall under the heading of not paying attention to all the information provided by the problem, or misunderstanding what the problem calls for or what outcome the learner is to achieve.

Another reason students have difficulty with word problems is that they are unfamiliar with the language used, especially key words that give cues about which arithmetic operation to employ. There is evidence that special instruction in the vocabulary of word problems can improve achievement (Johnson, 1944). Success has also been found with a procedure that teaches high school mathematics students to translate the everyday language of problems into a series of mathematical statements (Dahmus, 1970). An example of this technique is:

The sum of 6 and a number is the same as the difference between 32 and the number.

      6 plus n =   32 minus n

Find the number.

                        n = ?

Perhaps the most important thing about children's problem-solving performance is that it improves with practice. To test this, Pace (1961) stressed understanding of the demands of the problem with an experimental class of fourth-graders; a control class received no special instruction but worked the same sets of problems. Right after the instruction, the performance of the experimental class was superior, but eight weeks later, the control class was also solving more problems than before. This was clearly a function of the additional practice these class members had received, even in the absence of any direct instruction about "how to do it." Pace's finding is especially relevant because many teachers shy away from the problem-solving pages or units of arithmetic programs. The students do poorly and have negative attitudes about the activity (and indirectly, at least, about the teacher who makes them participate in it). Teachers also may experience failure as they try to teach arithmetic problem solving. So both parties tacitly agree to avoid it, though, as Pace suggests, continued practice and a little tenacity could improve students' problem-solving performance.

Practicing the Problem-Solving Process

Another way teachers can improve students' problem-solving abilities is by providing opportunities for practice with the various components of the problem-solving process which were described in Chapter 9 in relation to the learning of attitudes and values. The principal components are defining the problem accurately, considering alternative solutions to it, evaluating the solutions, and acting on the chosen one.

Defining the Problem   Before a problem can be solved, it must be identified correctly. This is easier to do in some cases than in others. A boy who longs for an expensive pair of Western boots may view denial of his request as parental rejection, when it is nothing of the sort. The real problem may be a restricted budget that imposes hard decisions upon his parents. If the child's definition of the problem were accurate, his attitude toward his parents and their relationship with him might also be altered.

Sometimes the nature of a problem is not immediately apparent. If your car refuses to start on a damp winter morning, you may need time (and perhaps help) to diagnose the difficulty. If you jump to an erroneous conclusion about the problem, you could waste time, effort, and money and still fail to start your car.

Proposing Alternative Solutions to the Problem   Most problems can be solved in more than one way, and this includes the major problems that confront our nation and our time in history. There is no single textbook answer to any of them—recession, inflation, peace, food, industrial production, and countless others. The arguments of economists with different theoretical orientations or of political opponents are ample evidence that alternatives are available. Nevertheless, educators often act as though for every problem there is a single solution.

Because the first idea that occurs in response to a question is likely to be the least original and imaginative, the time and effort invested in generating additional ideas pays off. In the same way, when problems are open to alternative solutions, the more thought given to how the problem may be resolved, the higher is the quality of the solution that is likely to be proposed. Sometimes the first idea loses out as additional data are acquired. This is the reason that agencies such as the Federal Drug Administration suspend judgment, sometimes for years, before they give approval to the marketing of a new medical product. "Marry in haste, repent at leisure" thus reflects the wisdom of the ages.

Evaluating Solutions before Acting on Them   In L. L. Thurstone's tests of deductive reasoning, the problem solver is told that a certain Captain Watts and his son James have been found shot to death on a rifle range. Was it murder, suicide, or accident, and how did it happen? Several facts are provided: both died instantly; a gun was found under the body of the father but not the son; powder burns were found on the coats of both men; the captain was devoted to his son, but there was suspicion that the son was eager to inherit the father's estate (Burack, 1950). Problems of this kind, especially if they are constructed with the subject matter students are studying, provide excellent practice opportunities for learners to examine how well alternative solutions account for the facts of a case.

Taking Time for Problem Solving

Most models of problem solving that schoolchildren encounter in everyday life emphasize fast, easy, and happy solutions. In a one-hour television show minus commercials, for example, the viewer is treated to the prompt solution of crucial problems such as love, marriage, and murder. When miraculous medical cures seem to take place in minutes, it is not surprising that children become discouraged if their problems do not yield easily or quickly to painless solutions.

The time constraints of school also affect students' problem-solving efforts. A chemistry student, for example, has to wrap up her experiment at 9:59 because at 10:04 she must be in a mathematics class in order to devote 55 minutes to working on geometry problems. Virtually all the problems students must work in school are assigned, rather than growing out of their own intellectual interests and pursuits. Furthermore, they have a single correct answer: "X equals 3," and nothing else. Too often an incorrect answer is simply counted wrong, rather than being used as an occasion for the class and the teacher to examine the learner's reasoning processes.

Teachers as well as students are constrained by the compartmentalized, time-oriented nature of the school and the classroom. Problem solving is discouraged in school systems that divide days into brief but equal periods of time or that value textbook teaching, with its externally imposed problems and single right answers. Nevertheless, teachers can find occasions to encourage learners to undertake problems for days or even weeks instead of a single class period. Some responsibility must be accepted by the learner for selecting problems, defining them, searching for alternatives, and examining the possibilities in light of the facts discovered.

Problem solving can be a difficult part of the instructional process for the teacher because the interests and specialized knowledge of students become diversified. Most textbooks and teachers' manuals are geared to "whole class" lessons. And, instead of filling the authoritative and managerial roles with which teachers are most comfortable, problem solving requires them to serve as advisers and consultants. There also is the possibility, particularly in basic courses, that the fundamental knowledge and principles students need may be lost in the search for more interesting challenges.

PROBLEM SOLVING AS INFORMATION PROCESSING

Major progress in understanding the processes of human problem solving has been made recently by information-processing psychologists, who view thinking, as well as learning and remembering, in information systems terms (see Chapter 7). Groundbreaking work in the area was extensively reported by Allen Newell and Herbert A. Simon in *Human Problem Solving* (1972). Since information-processing theories of thinking stress the systematic storage and retrieval of large bodies of information, computer simulations of human thinking have often been used as the research method in these types of investigations.

The strategies used by thinkers are of special interest to information-processing behavioral scientists, who often select problems for study which reflect complicated sequences of decisions and moves rather than lifelike qualities. Bourne, Dominowski, and Loftus (1979), for example, devised a series of problems such as "orcs and hobbits" (formerly "cannibals and missionaries"). Three orcs and three hobbits are on one side of the river, and all need to be transported to the far shore. There is a single boat that will hold only two passengers at a time. If orcs ever outnumber hobbits, the orcs will eat the hobbits. How should they get across?

Other information-processing analyses use problems closer to those of the elementary or secondary school, and the outcomes are of much more appeal to the student of educational psychology. A study of problem solving by Greeno (1978) dealt with the strategies used by high school students when they are given problems in geometry to solve (see Box D). Another study used the Wertheimer parallelogram problem described above in Box C. Resnick and Ford (1981) gave 10- and 11-year-old children training in two tasks. One was to construct a rectangle and place blocks on it which each covered an area of one square inch. By filling the rectangle with such cubes and counting the number, the children could determine the area of the rectangle. The second task was to *transform* nonrectangular objects into rectangular shapes by cutting off protruding ends with scissors and placing them where they would convert the shape to a rectangle. The children did not practice this task with parallelograms.

In the problem-solving phase of this study, the children were given two shapes, one a rectangle and one a parallelogram, and some cubes and were asked to find the area of the parallelogram. About half the children independently transformed the parallelogram into a rectangle and applied the cubes. The other half had to be given a hint to use the scissors before they made the transformation. Many of the children attempted to place cubes on the parallelogram. When told by the experimenter, "That's wrong," some removed all of the cubes and started

BOX D *A computer program for solving geometry problems*

To study how high school students solve problems, James Greeno asked students to talk aloud about their thinking processes as they worked on geometry problems. Then he developed a computer program, called PERDIX, which substitutes information-processing techniques for the strategies used by human problem solvers. By copying the steps of the students, the computer program provides a detailed picture of their problem-solving strategies.

One problem Greeno used was of the following type:

Lines *a* and *b* are parallel, and lines *m* and *n* are parallel. Angle *p* = 40°. What is the measure of angle *q*?

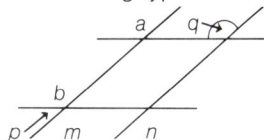

PERDIX first inquires whether any information is available in the problem that would permit the value of angle *q* to be read off directly. Since there is not, the program sets up a subgoal to find a quantitative relationship between the measure of the unknown angle and the 40° of angle *p*. There is no direct relationship between them, and so PERDIX sets up another subgoal. After several subgoals have been identified, it draws an inference that some angles are related to each other, such as supplementary angles. Finally the program establishes that pairs of angles within the field are congruent with each other, and so it provides the value of the unknown angle.

PERDIX is more systematic and more comprehensive than the typical high school student of plane geometry would be expected to be. The two do appear to share some strategic moves, however. PERDIX, like the human problem solver, begins the process of problem solution by stating a goal to be achieved that is proximate to the question of the problem: "Can I read the value of the angle directly from the figure?" When that is not possible, the program establishes a subgoal one step removed from the solution and continues that process until a subgoal is reached that can be achieved.

Source: James G. Greeno, "A Study of Problem Solving," in Robert Glaser (Ed.), *Advances in Instructional Psychology* (Hillsdale, N.J.: Lawrence Erlbaum Associates, 1978).

over from scratch. Others removed some of the cubes or tried a new rearrangement of them on the parallelogram. To Resnick and Ford, this meant that the children behaved differently because they had different goals in mind. Until their goal included transforming the original figure into a rectangle, they could not comply with the request to find its area.

PROBLEM SOLVING AS RULE-GOVERNED BEHAVIOR

Cognitive psychologists view problem solving as behavior that is governed by rules. Robert Siegler, for example, demonstrated that children's scientific problem solving is characterized quite early by rules which become more elaborated, qualified, and comprehensive from early and middle childhood through midadolescence. In terms of Piaget's developmental stages (see Part I), the rule that governs preoperational thought is partial and simplistic and frequently leads to incorrect solutions. The rules employed in formal logical reasoning are closer to the rules of science.

Siegler's work on this topic is interesting because of the technique he developed for inferring the rules a child uses to solve a problem. He also demonstrated that at intermediate stages children may solve problems incorrectly that they could previously solve, and later they will again be able to solve these problems correctly. This can happen when a child formulates a rule which is more elaborate than an earlier one but which is still incomplete, thus leading to some incorrect solutions.

Figure 10.2

Balance scale apparatus used to infer students' problem-solving rules

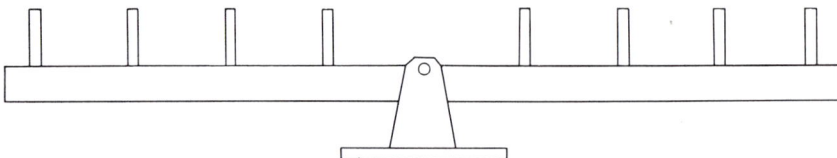

Source: Adapted from Robert S. Siegler, "The Origins of Scientific Reasoning," in R. S. Siegler (Ed.), *Children's Thinking: What Develops?* (Hillsdale, N.J.: Lawrence Erlbaum Associates, 1978), p. 112.

One sort of problem Siegler (1978) used with children and adolescents at several age levels will clarify the significance of this effect. Figure 10.2 shows a balance scale apparatus with weights that could be placed on any of the four pegs on each side of the fulcrum. Problems consisted of showing children the scale with one or more weights applied at various points and asking them whether the scale would balance or to which side it would tilt. Models of four rules, in order of increasing accuracy and completeness, that might govern children's reasoning about the balance scale problems were devised, and the percentage of correct answers for children using the different rules for each problem was predicted. Figure 10.3 shows the various positions in which the scale was

---

Figure 10.3

Predictions for percentage of correct answers and error patterns when different problem-solving rules are used

Problem Type	Rule			
	I	*II*	*III*	*IV*
Balance 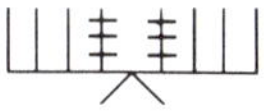	100	100	100	100
Weight 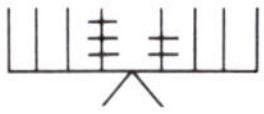	100	100	100	100
Distance 	0 (Should say "Balance")	100	100	100
Conflict-Weight 	100	100	33 (Chance Responding)	100
Conflict-Distance 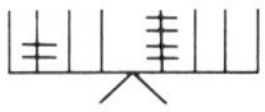	0 (Should say "Right down")	0 (Should say "Right down")	33 (Chance Responding)	100
Conflict-Balance 	0 (Should say "Right down")	0 (Should say "Right down")	33 (Chance Responding)	100

Source: Adapted from Robert S. Siegler, "The Origins of Scientific Reasoning," in R. S. Siegler (Ed.), *Children's Thinking: What Develops?* (Hillsdale, N.J.: Lawrence Erlbaum Associates, 1978), p. 115.

presented to the children and the predictions offered by each rule. In the conflict-weight problem, for example, the prediction was that children who operate with Rule III will be correct only one third of the time, whereas all others, even those who operate with lower level rules, will consistently get the problem right.

Siegler presented this problem to a sample of 120 students at four age levels—5, 9, 13, and 17—in a girls' upper-middle-class private school. The rule models correctly characterized the predictions of almost 90 percent of the total sample. Accuracy was poorest (80 percent) for the five-year-olds but increased to 100 percent for the oldest group of girls. This bears out Siegler's contention that "what develops" in scientific reasoning is children's ability, with advancing age, to encode more and more relevant aspects of the problem situation.

CRITICAL THINKING

Critical thinking does not always require a productive response from the thinker the way problem solving does. Instead it may result in an evaluation or a judgment to accept or to reject an idea or argument. Ennis (1962) defined critical thinking as the ability to make reasonable assessments of statements, to which we would add that critical thinking is best thought of as an attitude or a persistent disposition to make such assessments. An individual who is thinking critically will try to understand the basic elements of the argument under study, array the evidence, both pro and con, on the topic, and then decide whether the weight of the evidence does or does not support the argument. By examining the interpretations of others, students learn to evaluate their own thinking. The value of debate, controversy, and passionate dialogue in stimulating critical thinking and generating ideas will be pointed out in Chapter 14.

In the modern technological world, our critical thinking skills are overtaxed on many issues. Entire populations may benefit from or be harmed by decisions concerning the construction and use of nuclear power plants, for example, but few citizens have the necessary technical education and experience to evaluate objectively the arguments on either side of this issue. Students who have been educated in critical thinking should have the skills needed to help them learn how to assess judgments that their own knowledge cannot provide. These skills include inferential reasoning, the detection of assumptions, and the recognition of possible sources of bias. Since the ability to use them depends on the thinker's background of knowledge and experience, developmental considerations are involved in teachers' efforts to encourage the acquisition and application of critical thinking skills by students.

DEVELOPMENTAL CONSIDERATIONS
IN CRITICAL THINKING

Critical thinking depends more than anything else on the learner's ability to reason logically. Evidence about the development of children's logical reasoning, such as the conclusions about the cognitive-intellectual domain reported in Part I, suggest that in very young children the ability to reason one's way through logical tasks is limited. Such limitations can be expected to affect the level and quality of critical thinking in which children of various ages can engage.

A series of logical thinking tests administered to pupils at the fourth-, sixth-, eighth-, and tenth-grade levels by Roberge (1970) provided evidence of this developmental trend: As children grow older their ability to solve a variety of logical tasks improves. Younger children in his study had difficulty with all the logical forms, and even the adolescents rarely reasoned correctly about principles which lead to invalid conclusions such as affirming the consequent, as in: All As are Bs; x is a B; therefore x is an A.

It has been argued that critical thinking is dependent on the thinker's ability to reason in a formal way. Piaget's position, for example, was that children younger than 11 or 12 cannot handle propositional logic. Younger children are not altogether unable to reason logically, however. Ennis (1975) pointed out that children as young as six or seven can perform certain classes of conditional reasoning, and Roberge suggested starting instruction in school at about the fourth-grade level with some of the easier to master logical forms, such as: All As are Bs; x is an A; therefore x is a B. The presumption is that systematic training would hasten children's logical development, especially their ability to think about logical matters in the school curriculum.

The judgments of adolescents were studied by E. A. Peel at the University of Birmingham in England to find out how their reasoning about ideas changes from one age level to the next. He found that at midadolescence (about age 14), marked changes in critical thinking begin to differentiate the explanatory thinking of older adolescents from the more restricted or descriptive accounts of younger children. (This is the adolescent reasoning shift which was described in Box B in Chapter 4.) The dramatic increase in frequency of well-reasoned arguments and the shift from description to explanation may occur anywhere between the ages of 14 and 16 or 17, depending on the difficulty and conceptual sophistication of the material under study (Peel, 1966).

Peel (1973) also demonstrated that the progression of reasoning from restricted and descriptive through a series of steps to explanatory also unfolds when the topic is drawing inferences from literature. Secondary school students who had read Somerset Maugham's *Of Human Bondage* were asked a series of questions that demanded predictions about a character's reactions to a particular issue in the novel. Mature judgments ("explicit discussion of the dynamics of the crisis situation and possible consequences") first appeared to a marked extent in students over the age of 14. With more difficult scientific material, the same sort of progression from descriptive to explanatory accounts was found, but the age at which explanation emerges was greater. With technical scientific data, Peel found students' mental age (around 18) a better predictor of explanation than chronological age.

TECHNIQUES FOR ENCOURAGING
CRITICAL THINKING
IN YOUNGER CHILDREN

While younger children may lack all the skills of formal operational thought (see Part I), they can learn to test the validity and the truth of their own or other people's assertions at home, in preschool, or in the lower grades of the elementary school. Situations where early critical thinking can occur, like four-year-old Scotty's love of playing "true or false" with his mother, Pamela, were studied by Marksberry (1976):

Pamela: Cows can fly.
Scotty: False. Cows can't fly. They don't have wings. Now it's my turn. Babies can crawl.
Pamela: True. Mommie can crawl.
Scotty: False.
Pamela: I caught you. Look. (And she got down on the floor and crawled.)
Scotty: O.K. Snakes can climb trees.
Pamela: Hm-m-m. I don't believe I've ever seen one climb a tree.
Scotty: It's true! Don't you remember the snake that crawled up the tree at the zoo? I caught you.
Pamela: You're right. You know because you actually saw it. Now it's my turn again. (And the game continued.) (p. 293)

This game helped Scotty learn that true assertions can be agreed on by following common rules of evidence. In another example, Marksberry pointed out how a kindergarten teacher who had the child's development of thinking skills in mind helped one small boy detect his overgeneralization and its effect on his ability to draw conclusions.

It was clean-up time in the kindergarten. Timmy, a new child, had been chosen to put the large blocks in the cupboard. For a few minutes he was very busy carrying them to the shelves. Then he came running to the teacher with the complaint, "Susan did all of my work."

"Would you tell me just what Susan did?" the teacher asked. "She did my work." "Yes, you told me that, but I want to know exactly what she did." "She put the large blocks away." "How many did she put away?"

"The one she was using for a doll bed." "Just that one?" "Yes." "Then did she put all the large blocks away?" "No," Timmy said. "Is she doing all of your work?" "No," Timmy smilingly said. "That's right," the teacher said as she put her arm around him and gave him a little hug before he ran back to his work. (p. 293)

One of the best and most ambitious of the systematic efforts that have been made to facilitate critical thinking by elementary school pupils was a project conducted in the middle 1960s by Hilda Taba. Her work was especially notable because she deliberately set out to develop a social studies curriculum which integrates skills of thinking with the learning of socially useful information. Although Taba (1966) believed that the intellectual skills children would learn from her curriculum would transfer to thinking in other situations, they were not taught as separate general skills but as an integrated part of the learning of social studies.

Two of the thinking skills Taba's curriculum was designed to teach were called inferring and generalizing and application of principles. Her description of these skills (see Table 10.1) specifies the cognitive activity in which the children are to be engaged, the underlying mental operations, and the kinds of questions teachers might ask to draw out (or elicit) these activities. There is at least a rough hierarchy in each of the cognitive activities. The children must first learn to identify points in a discussion and to distinguish between relevant and irrelevant information before they can relate the points to each other and establish cause-and-effect relationships, for example.

The Taba curriculum was based on a thoughtfully developed rationale about the growth of children's thinking. Its effectiveness, however, was not easy to demonstrate. Taba and her colleagues conducted extensive field tests, but the clear significance of children trained in her curriculum, compared to classes of control children, did not emerge as was hoped. Hudgins (1977) gives a more detailed analysis of this field experiment and why it failed.

Some points about teaching critical thinking to children in elementary school have been made in other studies. One is that children's thinking can be assisted by teaching them to use or create concrete materials, sketches, or diagrams to visualize a problem. Morgan and Carrington (1944) used three-step series problems which have simple relationships but which are difficult for young children to understand. The children were given a task such as: "John has fewer marbles than Bill. Tom has fewer marbles than John. Who has the fewest marbles?" They were then shown how to sketch piles of marbles for each boy, showing his share in relation to the others':

John   Bill   Tom

Table 10.1

*Details of two basic thinking tasks
in the Taba social studies curriculum*

Cognitive Task 2: Inferring and Generalizing

Cognitive Activity	*Underlying Mental Operations*	*Eliciting Questions*
1. Identifying points	1. Differentiating, distinguishing relevant information from irrelevant	1. What did you note? see? find?
2. Explaining identified items of information	2. Relating points to each other; establishing cause-and-effect relationships	2. Why did so-and-so happen? Why is so-and-so true?
3. Making inferences or generalizations	3. Going beyond what is given; finding implications, extrapolating	3. What does this mean? What would you conclude? What generalizations can you make?

Cognitive Task 3: Application of Principles

Cognitive Activity	*Underlying Mental Operations*	*Eliciting Questions*
1. Predicting consequences, explaining unfamiliar phenomena, hypothesizing	1. Analyzing the nature and the dimensions of the problem or condition	1. What would happen if . . . ?
2. Explaining and supporting the predictions and hypotheses	2. Determining the causal links leading to a prediction or hypothesis	2. Why do you think this would happen?
3. Verifying the predictions and hypotheses	3. Using logical reasoning to determine the necessary conditions and the degree of universality of the prediction or hypothesis	3. What would it take for so-and-so to be true? Would it be true in all cases? At what times?

Source: Hilda Taba, *Teaching Strategies and Cognitive Functioning in Elementary School Children,* Cooperative Research Project No. 2004 (San Francisco: San Francisco State College, 1966), pp. 40, 42.

The impact of this training was most marked for the third- and fourth-graders, who were at an age where they were not quite able to work out relationships without concrete props. The fifth-graders were also helped to a degree, but control fifth-graders did about as well.

At least by the middle grades, children can learn to make use of numerous skills and abilities that contribute to critical thinking. For an experiment in developing thinking in children, Hyram (1957) taught seventh- and eighth-graders a seven-unit program in logical thinking which covered these topics: (1) the nature of thinking in general, (2) tools of thinking, (3) the nature of definition, (4) the nature of inductive inference, (5) the nature of deductive inference, (6) the nature of experimentation, and (7) common errors in thinking. According to his evaluation at the end of the semester, students who were given the program knew more about the types of logical thinking than a control class of seventh- and eighth-graders who did not receive it.

CRITICAL THINKING IN SECONDARY SCHOOLS

Most efforts to teach critical thinking to students of secondary school age employ subject matter such as geometry or social studies. With the increasing differentiation of studies for older students, specific approaches to critical thinking skills are unlikely to have much practical value, although they may be useful as an outline or a guide to planning instruction. A high school senior who is asked to judge the inferences in an argument about the future level of the gross national product, for example, cannot do so effectively without reference to the basic concepts and analytical tools of the economist. At the same time, however, instruction in a subject, be it economics, English, geometry, or any other, will not necessarily improve the student's ability to reason about it.

The available evidence suggests that students' reasoning skills can be improved if the instructional process is aimed at critical thinking about a particular branch of knowledge. Numerous studies have demonstrated the possibility of improved thinking in subject matter studies when the objectives of critical thinking are made an integral part of the instructional process.

Studies of Instructional Methods

There have been some classic studies of critical thinking instruction in high schools, such as Fawcett's *The Nature of Proof* (see Box E). Although by the standards of educational psychology his book is an old one, several of his principles are as valid today as they were in 1938. He said, for example, that students need to understand the objectives of their in-

BOX E   *How to generate light without all that heat*

A gifted teacher, H. P. Fawcett, used his high school geometry class in the 1930s as a vehicle for teaching students how to do critical thinking, which he called *the nature of proof.* Fawcett believed that students *could* learn to think as a result of studying geometry, but whether or not they *would* learn to think depended heavily upon how the course was taught.

Fawcett wanted his students to learn to define important words in arguments and to insist that others do so too. He challenged them to call for evidence about arguments they were asked to accept, to identify the assumptions upon which arguments are based, and to evaluate conclusions before they accepted them. One year the high school students were having heated arguments about whether awards should be given to students for "outstanding achievement." He deliberately allowed members of the geometry class to debate the issue. After long disagreements and unproductive discussions, he helped the students to see that they were having trouble in communicating with one another and reaching agreement because everyone was too excited—too emotionally involved in the topic.

The teacher suggested that reasoned thinking is easier to do when the content to be thought about is neutral, or at least less emotion arousing. "A theory of space," he told them, provides such content, and the students happily accepted his direction. They thus used their unemotional study of geometry as a way of working toward the teacher's objectives about thinking.

As time passed and the students developed some competence in critical thinking, Fawcett had them apply this new skill to nonmathematical arguments and evaluations, some of which were emotional subjects. For example, students evaluated newspaper editorials and editorial cartoons, political opponents' arguments, and so on. Thus his students were learning to do critical thinking and to apply or transfer those thinking skills to everyday problems.

Although considerable class time was devoted to activities which were not mathematical in nature, end-of-course examinations show that Fawcett's students had learned as much geometry as students in control classes.

Source: H. P. Fawcett, *The Nature of Proof.* 13th Yearbook, National Council of Teachers of Mathematics, 1938.

struction; if they are to learn the skills of critical thinking, the skills must be clarified and taught in explicit, unmistakable terms. Similarly, Fawcett's understanding that material with emotional or affective influence on students should be introduced gradually helped them learn to transfer the basic skills and attitudes of critical thinking to commonly encountered problems of daily life that call for reasonable assessment.

Contemporary studies of thinking in high school classes may lack the scope and eloquence of Fawcett's early work, but their general conclusions have been consistent with the approach he suggested. Tomera (1974), for example, demonstrated that secondary school students who were taught skills of observation and comparison in a science class were able to retain those skills over an extended period (five months) and could transfer them without loss to other material. Seventh-grade pupils were taught how to observe either twigs or algae in several lessons during which they observed and characterized numerous individual examples of one or the other. Then they practiced making comparisons among similar examples, and a measure was taken of how well they performed the observations and comparisons. Five months later the students were given examples of algae to observe and compare if they had earlier been trained to study twigs, and vice versa. Their skills transferred easily from one type of object to the other.

Tomera followed a carefully designed method of teaching children to make observations and comparisons. It specifies precisely what the learner is to observe and how comparisons among examples should be made. Practice is built in, and allowance is made for learning from classmates' comments in group discussion. The method, which stresses the operations involved in observation and comparison, follows these steps:

1. Study of specimens with clear, distinct identifying characteristics.
2. Making observations, followed by class discussion.
3. Preparation of laboratory drawings.
4. Study of a second specimen or example in the same way.
5. Comparison of both specimens in class discussion.
6. Repetition of the entire procedure, with additional examples.

Whether Tomera's procedure for teaching skills such as observing and drawing comparisons transfers to issues outside the science classroom has not been tested directly. Teachers could emphasize the generality of these skills and encourage students to apply them more broadly. The introduction of examples from other fields in the training procedures (as Fawcett would suggest) should also result in improved transfer.

In most critical thinking programs, students learn to make decisions for themselves and to arrive at and stand by their conclusions independently. This is in contrast to more conventional educational approaches which call for the presentation of information and established conclusions to students (see Box A above). There is considerable evidence that critical thinking can be enhanced when teachers encourage students to rely on their own reasoning and reach independent conclusions.

Class discussions are often designed to increase students' mastery of subject matter, Gall and Gall (1976) concluded in a summary of the massive literature on the discussion method. Discussions tend to ebb and flow, however, and the rate of introduction of new material may be low. Therefore the gains may not be so much in the acquisition of information as they are in the level of thinking students engage in. Apparently as students participate in discussions (covertly, as well as overtly), they process the materials being discussed differently than if simple comprehension and storing of new information were called for.

A social studies educator (Weeden, 1977) suggests that teachers can use consideration of social problems as a basis for increasing high school students' independence and decision-making ability. The details of recurrent social issues may be different from generation to generation or century to century, but the general form of the problems is the same. He uses as an example the trial of Galileo by the church in 1633. Galileo was defending the right to pursue truth wherever it might lead; the pope and the church feared that new ways of learning and thinking would undermine the status quo. The fundamental issue posed by Galileo's trial arises whenever new modes of thinking, inquiring, or living emerge in society. Weeden suggests that schools can teach children to ask questions about these persistent issues and to make independent decisions about them in contemporary life, rather than simply learning the lessons and the conclusions of the past. To do this requires restructuring the classroom roles of both teachers and students.

An example of the outcomes of such transformations was given in Egleston's (1973) report comparing inductive versus traditional methods of teaching high school biology with laboratory experiments. For a unit on cell physiology and nutrition, Egleston arranged the inductive laboratory group so they independently explored each concept of the unit in the laboratory, followed by class discussion of the concept. This was the reverse of the more traditional procedure which was followed with another class, which first received instruction about the concepts and then entered the laboratory to observe and confirm the correctness of the instruction and the preceding discussion.

There were 10 laboratory exercises in the unit, each accompanied by a quiz. For the first several exercises the inductive class did less well, but as the weeks passed and the students became familiar with the arrangement, their achievement matched (and by the end of the unit, surpassed) that of the traditional class. Egleston also maintained records on the teacher-pupil interaction which showed that students in the inductive class behaved in more independent ways; they were more likely to look up information for themselves rather than receiving or seeking assistance, and they were more inclined to initiate questions about activities instead of simply responding to the teacher's questions. The teacher's behavior was also altered; she was placed more in the capacity of a consultant and adviser than an imparter of information. Egleston makes the point that the transition of these roles involved some adjustment by both the teacher and the students, since the achievement of the inductive group was initially poorer but later became superior to that of the traditional group. Thus teachers may have to change in order to promote student independence and critical thinking, and such changes are not without a certain amount of difficulty and initial lack of success.

Many studies of the teaching of critical thinking have used the Watson-Glaser Critical Thinking Appraisal to assess critical thinking skills. This test measures students' thinking in five areas: (1) inference, (2) detecting assumptions, (3) deductive reasoning, (4) interpretation, and (5) evaluating arguments. Smith (1977) used this instrument to compare gains in critical thinking of college students enrolled in 12 courses in several disciplines. He found gains in critical thinking when student participation was high, the faculty member encouraged students' ideas, and there was considerable peer-to-peer interaction in the classroom. No cause-and-effect relationships were established in this study, however. Perhaps students who are good critical thinkers tend to participate more and to interact more vigorously with other class members as well as the instructor, and they may have good ideas that instructors wish to encourage.

CREATIVE THINKING

The appropriateness of teaching creative thinking may be more open to question than the teaching of problem solving or critical thinking skills. Some people see it as having a place in a limited area of the curriculum, such as art or music, while others regard it as properly restricted to a relatively few students such as those with artistic talent or the gifted described in Chapter 5. We believe the instructional process offers broad opportunities to involve all children and adolescents in creativity. In the same way every student is expected to work on problem solving and learn how to assess arguments, though they all will not become scientists, mathematicians, or scholars, education in creative thinking and the chance to learn how to think in divergent terms should be part of the education of every child, though all will not become actual creators.

This position is not shared by all educators and theorists. Ausubel, Novak, and Hanesian (1978) for example, regard the creative person as *qualitatively different* from other people. Correlates of creative production such as word fluency or adaptive flexibility, or other psychological variables that are measured on tests of creative thinking, are considered to be normally distributed in the population. The creative individual is not merely at the high end of this distribution but is distinctly different from others. And creative talent is not general and content-free, as it is conceived in measures of creative ability, but highly specific to music, literature, physics, or some other subject area in which contributions demand creative talent.

We do not suppose that an instructional process that challenges children to think creatively in mathematics and science and social studies, as well as in art, dramatics, or creative writing, can transform a child of average intellectual and creative potential into a Mozart, a Monet, or a Molière. Nevertheless, every child can benefit from experience with the discipline of creative thinking, by becoming sensitive to gaps and errors in existing situations and searching for new, not immediately apparent ways of answering questions or solving problems. Children who are asked to think about long-standing problems in their own terms may come to understand that knowledge is manmade and imperfect, and truth is not written once and for all but is subject to reevaluation and reconstruction as the human mind suggests new, more adequate ways of conceptualizing it.

CONCEPTS OF CREATIVE THINKING

Creative thinking is a productive process in the sense that it results in a new idea or product. The outcome may be artistic, scientific, or of a more practical nature. Originality lies at the heart of the creative process, but it is not the sole criterion of creativity. Whatever the idea or solution, it must be appropriate to the situation where it is to be used.

Guilford's Structure of Intellect Model

Joy P. Guilford's (1966) structure of intellect model has been a major source of ideas about creativity (see Figure 10.4). He drew attention to the fact that human intelligence consists of numerous factors, including what he labels *divergent production* (or divergent thinking) operations, in which the major factors are fluency, flexibility, and elaboration. These factors, together with some examples of tests for each, are described in Table 10.2. Guilford's overall idea of creativity is the ability to generate many different kinds of images, words, or phrases in response to a particular stimulus.

Figure 10.4

Guilford's structure of intellect model

Operations

Cognition
Memory
Divergent production
Convergent production
Evaluation

Products

Units
Classes
Relations
Systems
Transformations
Implications

Contents

Figural
Symbolic
Semantic
Behavioral

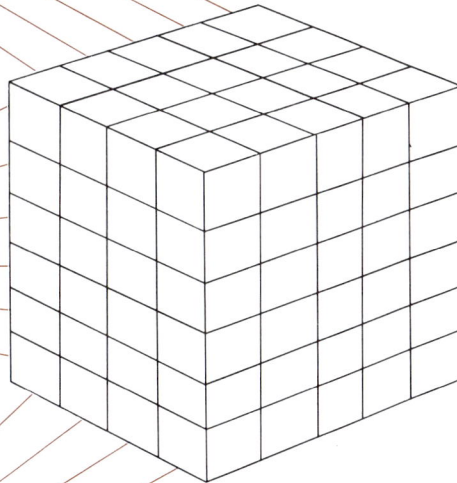

Source: Adapted from J. P. Guilford, "Intelligence: 1965 Model,"
American Psychologist, vol. 21 (1966), p. 21. Copyright 1966 by the American
Psychological Association. Adapted by permission of the author.

Table 10.2

Divergent-thinking factors according to Guilford

Factors	Sample Tests
Fluency factors Ideational fluency— the rate of generation of a quantity of ideas	List objects that are round and edible. List all things you can think of that are solid, flexible, and colored.
Associational fluency— the completion of relationships; may also apply to the construction of analogies	List words that mean about the same as "good." List words that mean about the opposite of "hard."
Expressional fluency— the ability to construct sentences	Write as many four-word sentences as possible using the same initial letters, without repeating any words. Use these letters: W __ c __ e __ n __ .
Flexibility factors Spontaneous flexibility— the ability to shift classes of responses without being directed to do so.	List all the uses you can think of for a common brick. (Score is only for the number of classes; e.g., *build* something, *drive* a nail, *grind* up for red powder.)
Adaptive flexibility— originality; production of original responses (with verbal material)	Plot titles. Listen to a very short story and then make up as many titles for it as you can. (Commonplace titles contribute to score for ideational fluency. Responses rated as "clever" are scored for originality.)
Elaboration— production of a variety of implications	Given the bare outline of a plan, produce the detailed steps required to make it work.

Source: Joy P. Guilford, "Factors That Aid and Hinder Creativity," *Teacher's College Record*, vol. 63 (1962), pp. 380–392.

The Torrance Tests of Creative Thinking

E. Paul Torrance, a long-time student of the role of creative thinking in education, defines creativity as:

> . . . a process of becoming sensitive to problems, deficiencies, gaps in knowledge, missing elements, disharmonies, and so on; identifying the difficulty; searching for solutions, making guesses, or formulating hypotheses about the deficiencies; testing and retesting these hypotheses and possibly modifying and retesting them; and finally communicating the results. (Torrance, 1966, p. 6)

To Guilford's factors of fluency, flexibility, and elaboration, Torrance added originality as a fundamental concept. (Originality is included in fluency in Guilford's list of divergent-thinking factors in Table 10.2.) Torrance defines fluency as the ability to produce numerous items that fulfill essentially the same purpose. A good writer, for example, avoids repetition by substituting synonyms instead of using the same tired words time after time. Flexibility is similar to fluency, but it involves the ability to alter the level or class of thinking. A child asked to list the uses of a nail, for example, probably would respond with, "hammer boards together," or "tack soles on shoes." A more flexible thinker might categorize these suggestions as "building purposes" and also see nails as useful weapons, dividers for a filing system, and so on.

For Torrance, as for most people, the originality of thinking lies at the heart of the creative process. He sees originality as a matter of the statistical infrequency of an idea; that is, the rarer the idea, the more original it is. But originality cannot be inferred from infrequency alone. The idea must have "creative strength"; that is, it must reflect energy and thought, and it must fill the required gap, or solve the creative problem. An idea which is unusual but which does not meet the other criteria of creativity is not an original contribution.

The Torrance Tests of Creative Thinking, published in 1966, are one of the few major published efforts at measuring creative ability. The tests have two parts, one measuring verbal ability and the other figural ability. In the figural test, for example, the person taking the test is presented with a series of random lines or shapes which are to be completed in a limited time as an original and meaningful entity, complete with a label or title. The other parts of the test use different stimulus materials which require the production of a large number of different responses, thus stressing divergent production abilities. The Torrance tests have rather limited predictive validity (see Chapter 15), with the highest validity found for the originality factor. But because of the abstract nature of the construct of creativity, it may be difficult to produce a test that would yield much higher validity (Torrance, 1972).

Another commercial effort to measure creative thinking is the Remote Associates Test of Mednick (1968). The theory on which Mednick's test is based is *association;* essentially, he argues that the more creative individuals are, the more able they are to see relationships between objects or words that are normally regarded as far apart in meaning. A disadvantage of the Mednick test is that it is very difficult even for students in senior high school, being normed for college students, graduate students, and professional groups. The Torrance tests, on the other hand, can be used with very young children as well as with adults.

The usual alternatives of tests of creative thinking for the identification of potentially creative students have been teacher or peer nominations.

These seldom correlate with subsequent evidence of creative productivity, however, as we noted in Chapter 5.

THE CREATIVE INDIVIDUAL

Some of the most interesting and important findings about creative people have been reported at the Institute for Personality Assessment and Research at the University of California at Berkeley. Research on creative people conducted there under the direction of MacKinnon (1966) and Barron (1966) assessed personality characteristics of highly creative members of well-defined groups such as architects and writers. People of demonstrated outstanding creative talent are chiefly characterized by their independence and autonomy and their commitment to discovering and expressing the truth. They also usually have a disregard for the pursuit of money where their creative talent is concerned, although many of the creative people studied at Berkeley became affluent as a result of the commercial success of their work.

According to MacKinnon (1966), what most generally characterizes the creative individual in the Berkeley studies is:

> . . . his high level of effective intelligence, his openness to experience, his freedom from crippling restraints and impoverishing inhibitions, his esthetic sensitivity, his cognitive flexibility, his independence in thought and action, his high level of creative energy, his unquestioning commitments to creative endeavor, and his unceasing striving for solutions to the ever more difficult problems that he constantly sets for himself.

Characteristics of Creative or Intelligent Students

The similarities and differences between adolescents they identified as either creative *or* highly intelligent were studied by Getzels and Jackson (1962). The mean IQ of the intelligent group was 150, which is extraordinarily high, whereas for the creative group it was 127, which is at least as high as the mean at most of the good secondary schools in the nation. Thus, although the members of the creative group scored lower in IQ than those in the highly intelligent group, they were nonetheless very bright young people, as well as more creative than those in the other group.

The groups did not differ from each other in academic achievement or motivation. Getzels and Jackson suggest that intellectual creativity accounts for the superior achievement of the creative group, but these students were intelligent enough to achieve well in any academic environment. Teachers generally preferred highly intelligent students over average students, but they did not significantly prefer those in the creative group, nor did they prefer the high IQ students over the creative group.

Some differences appeared between students in the two categories when they were asked to rank order a set of qualities (1) as they preferred them for themselves, (2) as they make for adult success, and (3) as they are valued by teachers. The bright students' rankings were very similar for all three categories; what they valued in personal qualities was highly congruent with the characteristics they believed teachers like in students and also with what they thought would contribute to adult success. The creative students' list of personal preferences was independent of what they perceived as likely to make them successful in the future, and it was negatively related to how they believed teachers would rank the qualities. Table 10.3 lists the qualities and the personal preferences assigned to them by each of the two groups.

The creative group was more likely to consider a wide range of potential occupations, especially unconventional ones, and to make an early commitment to an occupation. When both groups were asked to write stories in a very short time (three to four minutes) in response to picture stimuli, the creative students made much greater use of stimulus-free themes, unexpected endings, humor, incongruities, and playfulness. The adolescents who were identified as creative seem to have much in common with the proven creative adults of the Berkeley studies. Long-range,

Table 10.3

Preference rankings of eight qualities by two groups of gifted adolescents

Qualities Ranked	Rankings by	
	High IQ Group	Creative Group
Character	1	3
Emotional stability	2	1
Goal directedness	3	4.5
Creativity	4	6
Wide range of interests	5	4.5
High marks	6	7
IQ	7	8
Sense of humor	8	2

Source: Data from Jacob W. Getzels and Philip W. Jackson, *Creativity and Intelligence: Explorations with Gifted Students* (New York: John Wiley & Sons, 1962), p. 167.

longitudinal studies of the development of creative people are not available, but this cross section provides a glimpse of such individuals at ages 15 to 18.

Other studies have been conducted with adolescents identified as creative by teachers, using completed creative products such as original scientific work, paintings, or short stories. In these studies by Anastasi and Schaefer (Schaefer & Anastasi, 1968; Anastasi & Schaefer, 1969) the creative adolescents, in contrast with control groups who were similar in academic achievement but not noted for creative productivity, shared a continuing and persistent commitment to their special field of interest. Most of these students were only 17 or 18 and had taken up their creative endeavors at a very early age.

Anastasi and Schaefer found intriguing differences between young people whose creative fields are in the arts, such as painting or writing, and those whose specialty is in the natural sciences. Science students tended to identify closely with their fathers, who were likely to be following conventional career paths, whereas the artistic teenagers reported more identification and support from their opposite-sex parents. Home environments were characterized as cultural and intellectual, with music, good books, and interest and instruction in the arts. Among males, artistic adolescents did not have much interest in sports, either as spectators or participants, but science students were likely to have participated in one or more sports.

One other difference between the arts and science students in these studies is of interest in educational psychology. The data came from biographical inventories which the students filled out in their later high school years, giving no reasons for their opinions. The creative writers frequently attributed their interest in writing to teachers and experiences they had encountered in their elementary school years, but the science students did not make such attributions. The reason may be that elementary schools provide much richer language and creative arts curriculums than science courses, or that science courses and experiences are not offered in most schools below the junior and senior high school level.

Highly creative students were also compared with highly intelligent students by Torrance (1972), with two important differences. His studies were done with elementary school children, and they included a group who were *both* creative and had high IQs. It is from such a population that truly creative people would be expected to emerge.

For Torrance's test at the University of Minnesota Laboratory School, samples of children were identified as creative or intelligent. The two groups were not significantly different in academic achievement, as measured by two well-known sets of standardized achievement tests. The high IQ children were found to be better known to their teachers than the creative children, and the teachers considered them to be more desirable students. The preference extended to both high IQ–low creativity pupils compared to those who were high on both variables. Teachers saw children who were both bright and creative as more unruly and dominant, more independent and ambitious, but also as friendlier and more studious and hard-working than either of the other two groups—creative or intelligent only.

The highly creative and intelligent children were also perceived by their teachers as the most talkative and having unusual but good ideas. They could quickly generate new ideas if original plans went awry. Furthermore, their peers paid attention to them and considered them as being talkative and having good ideas, but often wild or silly ones. The bright but not so creative children had the most friends, the creative but less bright ones the fewest.

To try to confirm the contentions of Torrance and others that creative children are more nonconforming, Wodtke and Wallen (1965) observed boys at the fourth- and fifth-grade levels, only some of whom were identified as creative. They had a good deal of difficulty in observing behaviors reliably, but their findings showed that the behaviors of creative children do not fit neatly into conceptual packages. For example, they did not find creative pupils to be any more nonconforming than their less creative classmates, but they did rate creative pupils as being more alert and as initiating less talk in the classroom.

ENCOURAGING CLASSROOM CREATIVITY

An interesting parallel to how creativity is regarded in the classroom can be found in Kaplan's (1963) observations of creativity in industrial laboratories. If a director is responsible for testing 500 substances for antibiotic effect, for example, the scientists working for him must concentrate on those tests. Creative scientists might abandon the routine work and pursue their own original projects. The director cannot tolerate this because his success depends on the required productivity. Creative scientists are not highly prized, because the director's goals and achievements are jeopardized by their autonomy.

Pressures toward conformity of the same sort can be seen in classrooms where teachers stress the completion of sets of mathematics problems or chemistry experiments on a set schedule, and according to the formulas set up by textbooks and laboratory manuals. While individualistic approaches to problems might lead to genuine insight for a student, they are apt to be discouraged because they interfere with the classroom equivalent of productivity. The instructional process should allow for occasions when students are permitted and even encouraged to strike out on their own and look for new solutions and approaches that are

*These young artists are practicing the art of self-criticism.
A classroom climate that encourages creativity gives learners
freedom to explore their talents, while stressing their
responsibility to discipline their efforts.*

not prescribed by the teacher or the textbook. Failure to allow opportunities for students to explore, manipulate, wonder, invent, or propose can stifle students' imaginations.

The thinking done in school is analogous to DeBono's (1969) concept of lateral thinking, which was described in the first section of this chapter. Lateral thinking seeks to generate as many alternative ideas as possible, not to pursue the first promising one. DeBono sees the fear of being wrong as the greatest deterrent to the ability to come up with new ideas. Children learn, from their earliest years, that being mistaken is shameful. Teachers intensify these feelings when they insist on the needs to maintain classroom productivity and to be correct. The classroom should provide at least an occasional chance to try out ideas in a psychologically safe setting.

Torrance (1965, p. 43) identified five principles teachers can apply in rewarding creative thinking in the classroom:

1. Be respectful of unusual questions.
2. Be respectful of imaginative, unusual ideas.
3. Show your pupils that their ideas have value.
4. Occasionally have pupils do something "for practice," without the threat of evaluation.
5. Tie in evaluation with causes and consequences.

When Torrance undertook a series of small-scale studies to see how teachers use these principles, he found they were widely accepted, but perhaps more at the level of lip service than of action. He concluded that teachers rarely apply the principles at all in their daily work with young people.

To encourage the emergence of students' natural creativity, the instructional process should provide for the establishment of a classroom climate which encourages creative performance and emphasizes divergent thinking—the ability to propose alternatives, to see multiple solutions, and to find new ways to behave. If creativity is to have any value for the learner, however, it must be disciplined. The child poet must learn some of the critical standards for poetry while pursuing self-expression, and the school must provide the tools needed to communicate inner feelings, even if the communication is only to the child across the aisle or the teacher or the poet's mother. Creativity demands continuing emphasis on divergent thinking, coupled with discipline. The teacher can foster the learner's creative development by encouraging alternative ways of learning, providing the necessary skills, and holding the expectation that the learner's talent will emerge.

CHAPTER 10 IN RETROSPECT

Thinking and learning are related, similar processes. Meaningful learning requires the learner's attention and active involvement in trying to organize new material and integrate it with existing knowledge. In the same way, the thinker must be sensitive to problems, alert to the possibilities of using previous knowledge or skills in a new fashion, and flexible in approaching problems, difficulties, and solutions. Thinking and meaningful learning both involve active participation and intellectual processing by the learner.

While some solutions to problems may be formulated quickly, most thinking requires time and sustained effort for reflection to occur. Thinking can be categorized as problem solving, critical thinking, and creative thinking. Research investigations in all three areas reflect some progress in teaching individuals to think better, but they also signify the difficulty of doing so. Current knowledge of how thinking can be improved through experience or instruction is limited.

A problem exists when a thinker encounters an obstacle there is no obvious way to surmount; that is, when habitual or routine ways of responding are to no avail. A particularly interesting study aimed at improving learners' problem solving is the Productive Thinking Program, which has demonstrated an ability to improve several general (that is, widely applicable) intellectual skills which are useful in problem solving. Teachers also can teach students to solve problems by stressing the problem-solving aspects of content or subject matter, providing opportunities for practice with the components of problem solving, and allowing time to search for the best alternatives. Different views of problem solving are taken by information-processing psychologists, who regard it as an information-processing operation, and cognitive psychologists, to whom it is rule-governed behavior.

Critical thinking, or the reasonable assessment of statements, is characterized by the thinker's ability to suspend judgment until evidence about an issue can be collected and evaluated. An attitude that critical thinking is important in school and everyday life is helpful. Numerous small-scale investigations have demonstrated the possibility of teaching children individual intellectual skills that may contribute to critical thinking, but it has been much more difficult to show that long-term curricular efforts can improve children's critical thinking. Taba's effort with elementary school children was well designed, combining a social studies curriculum and methods of teaching geared toward critical thinking, but the results did not support her hypotheses that children's thinking would be improved.

Creative thinking is a productive process which results in an original idea or product. In Guilford's structure of intellect model, it is represented by divergent production or thinking, which calls for the generation of many different responses to a stimulus.

The role of creative thinking in the schools has not been well defined or established. Critics contend that true creativity is extremely rare and is qualitatively different from normal intellectual abilities, so the idea of "teaching creativity" is erroneous. Nevertheless, psychologists such as Torrance and Mednick have developed tests of what might be called general creative thinking. Research at the University of California also has provided information on the abilities, attitudes, and personality structures of creative people, identified at the top of their fields as adults. Creative individuals tend to be not only highly intelligent and original, but also independent and autonomous.

Whether "true creativity" can be taught or not, the instructional process can be designed to assist normal children to express unusual and innovative ideas by looking for nonroutine responses or solutions. A climate for creativity in the classroom stresses disciplined behavior and a learning environment that provides opportunities for unevaluated efforts and is generally supportive of creative endeavors.

1. At the beginning of the chapter, six essential characteristics of thinking were defined. Recall an episode in which you had to do some thinking, either in or out of school. How well do these six elements conform to your experience? Would you suggest the addition of other characteristics?

2. The emphasis of psychologists such as Kohler and Wertheimer in problem solving is on seeing relationships among parts of a problem. How does the role of *understanding* those relationships contribute to problem solving?

3. Does the *ability* of a child to think in a critical way change as he or she grows older? Obviously older children can process more information, and they have greater knowledge. Is that the only difference, or is there a basic alteration in the process or skills of thinking between, say, a lower-grade elementary school child and a student in senior high?

4. What would you do in a general way to foster students' critical thinking? Are some studies such as geometry superior vehicles for such a purpose? Or can any subject matter be offered in a way to assist critical thinking? Give one or two specific reasons for your answer. Provide at least one example.

5. What difference, if any, do you see between *originality* and *creativity?* You might want to review the discussion of the Torrance Tests of Creative Thinking and Mednick's Remote Associates Test before you answer.

6. Covington and his co-authors subtitled their Productive Thinking Program "A Course in Learning to Think." The emphasis is on general skills and attitudes about thinking, rather than content in science, history, or other subject areas. What are the merits of such an approach?

7. In your opinion, can schools teach students how to think? Your answer might be that it is possible to teach separate skills of thinking, which might or might not lead to general improvement in students' thinking. You should consider these factors:

   a. What do you mean by thinking?

   b. What is the nature of human ability needed for thinking, and how easily can it be modified?

   c. What strategies are available to the school to provide instruction in thinking, broadly conceived?

Problem Solving

Introductory Level

Davis, Gary A. *Psychology of Problem Solving: Theory and Practice.*
New York: Basic Books, 1973.

Davis brings together reviews of two different bodies of research literature—psychological theory and research on problem solving, and research and training programs from education and industry.

DeBono, Edward. *The Five-Day Course in Thinking.* New York:
Basic Books, 1967.

The title is a bit misleading in that the book contains not *one* five-day course in thinking, but three, dealing with insight and sequential and strategic thinking. This is a do-it-yourself book; each problem requires a few simple props and a considerable amount of thinking. The activities are absorbing and worthwhile. DeBono's orientation encourages what he calls lateral rather than vertical thinking.

Advanced Level

Kohler, Wolfgang. *The Mentality of Apes.* New York: Humanities
Press, 1925.

This is the classic book on animal problem solving, written about Kohler's extensive experiments with chimpanzees while he was interned on Tenerife during World War I. The struggles of the chimpanzees to solve problems leading to food are probably the most often cited studies on problem solving in the history of psychology.

Wason, Peter C., and Johnson-Laird, Philip N. *Psychology of
Reasoning: Structure and Content.* London: P. T. Batsford, Ltd.,
1972.

In this report of numerous investigations of human thinking conducted by the authors, the studies are tied closely to standard topics of logic, such as deduction, induction, and syllogistic reasoning. The experiments described are interesting, and many of them are related to daily problems of reasoning, as in the chapter on understanding regulations. The writing is good, but the book, on the whole, is technical and fairly difficult.

Bartlett, Frederic. *Thinking: An Experimental and Social Study.* New
York: Basic Books, 1958.

One of England's most eminent psychologists explores the characteristics and relationships of scientific, artistic, and everyday thinking.

Wertheimer, Max. *Productive Thinking.* Enlarged ed. New York: Harper & Row, 1959.

This collection of papers, written by the founder of the school of Gestalt psychology, is rewarding reading for the serious student of educational psychology. Wertheimer was interested in the differences between what he called productive thinking and reproductive thinking, the "blind" application of previous learning. Teachers who want their students to learn in a meaningful way have much to profit from by reading this classic.

Critical Thinking
Introductory Level

Thouless, Robert H. *How to Think Straight.* New York: Hart Publishing Co. (no date).

This book was first published in 1932 under the title *Straight and Crooked Thinking* and revised and published under its present title in 1939. (The edition cited here is a paperback and is fairly recent.) The author, a British philosopher-psychologist, provides a most interesting introduction to how people apply and misapply logic to the problems and arguments of daily life. The book was written for the public at large, not for teachers, but it is a good source for the teacher who is more interested in the applications of logic than in logic as a formal study.

Two books about critical thinking that were written for teachers are:

Aylesworth, Thomas G., and Reagan, Gerald M. *Teaching for Thinking.* Garden City, N.Y.: Doubleday & Co., 1969.

Burton, William H., Kinball, Roland B., and Wing, Richard L. *Education for Effective Thinking.* New York: Appleton-Century-Crofts, 1960.

Advanced Level

Dewey, John. *How We Think.* Gateway edition. Chicago: Henry Regnery Co., 1971.

Dewey's famous book for teachers was published originally in 1910. A revised and extended version which appeared in 1933 was reprinted in 1971 in paperback form, making this fine volume readily accessible to teachers. The three parts are devoted to the nature of reflective thinking, logical considerations in thinking, and the training of thought.

Other recommended advance-level texts are:

Black, Max. *Critical Thinking.* 2nd ed. Englewood Cliffs, N.J.: Prentice-Hall, 1952.

Ennis, Robert H. *Logic in Teaching.* Englewood Cliffs, N.J.: Prentice-Hall, 1969.

Creative Thinking
Introductory Level

Barron, Frank. The psychology of the creative writer. *Theory into Practice,* 1966, *5,* 157–159.

MacKinnon, Donald W. What makes a person creative? *Theory into Practice,* 1966, *5,* 152–156.

These articles (referred to in the chapter) in the same issue of *Theory into Practice* give brief and nontechnical but definitive statements about creative people.

Davis, Gary A., and Scott, Joseph A. *Training Creative Thinking.* New York: Holt, Rinehart & Winston, 1971.

This book of readings is particularly useful because it includes papers that were written for use in industrial, engineering, and corporate settings as well as educational ones. For teachers, a glimpse into some of these other organizations and their procedures for coping with creativity can be enlightening.

Osborn, Alex F. *Applied Imagination.* 3rd rev. ed. New York: Charles Scribner's Sons, 1963.

This widely publicized book popularized the idea of brainstorming.

Advanced Level

Rugg, Harold. *Imagination.* New York: Harper & Row, 1963.

Harold Rugg had a long and sometimes controversial career as a professor at Teachers College, Columbia University. After retirement he reflected about the process of creativity and produced this book, incomplete at the time of his death, which is a provocative synthesis and interpretation of a wealth of knowledge about the topic.

Koestler, Arthur. *The Act of Creativity.* New York: Macmillan Co., 1964.

This book by a renowned writer and scholar is a fascinating series of essays which explore the area deeply from various scientific and scholarly points of view. It is an outstandingly readable volume and well worth the time to read all of it, but sections can also be read independently.

Adamson, R. E. Functional fixedness are related to problem solving. *Journal of Experimental Psychology*, 1952, *44*, 288–291.

Anastasi, Anne, and Schaefer, Charles E. Biographical correlates of artistic and literary creativity in adolescent girls. *Journal of Applied Psychology*, 1969, *53*, 267–273.

Anthony, Barbara, and Hudgins, Bryce B. Problem solving processes of fifth-grade arithmetic pupils. *Journal of Educational Research*, 1978, *72*, 63–67.

Ausubel, David P., Novak, Joseph, and Hanesian, Helen. *Educational Psychology: A Cognitive View*. 2nd ed. New York: Holt, Rinehart & Winston, 1978.

Barron, Frank. The psychology of the creative writer. *Theory into Practice*, 1966, *5*, 157–159.

Bourne, Lyle G., Dominowski, Roger, and Loftus, Elizabeth. *Cognitive Processes*. Englewood Cliffs, N.J.: Prentice-Hall, 1979.

Burack, Benjamin. The nature and efficacy of methods of attack on reasoning problems. *Psychological Monographs*, 1950, *64* (Whole No. 313).

Covington, Martin V., Crutchfield, Richard S., Davies, Lilian, and Olton, Robert M. *The Productive Thinking Program: A Course in Learning to Think*. Columbus, Ohio: Charles E. Merrill Publishing Co., 1972.

Dahmus, Maurice E. How to teach verbal problems. *School Science and Mathematics*, 1970, *70*, 121–138.

DeBono, Edward. Information processing and new ideas—lateral and vertical thinking. *Journal of Creative Behavior*, 1969, *3*, 159–171.

DeBono, Edward. *Teaching Thinking*. London: Temple Smith, 1976.

Duncker, Karl. On problem solving. *Psychological Monographs*, 1945 (Whole No. 270).

Egleston, Judy. Inductive versus traditional methods of teaching high school biology laboratory experiments. *Science Education*, 1973, *57*, 467–477.

Ennis, Robert H. A concept of critical thinking. *Harvard Educational Review*, 1962, *32*, 81–111.

Ennis, Robert H. Children's ability to handle Piaget's propositional logic: A conceptual critique. *Review of Educational Research*, 1975, *45*, 1–41.

Gall, Meredith, and Gall, Joyce. The discussion method. In N. L. Gage (Ed.), *The Psychology of Teaching Methods*. 75th yearbook, National Society for the Study of Education, 1976.

Getzels, Jacob W., and Jackson, Philip W. *Creativity and Intelligence: Explorations with Gifted Students*. New York: John Wiley & Sons, 1962.

Greeno, James G. A study of problem solving. In Robert Glaser (Ed.), *Advances in Instructional Psychology*. Hillsdale, N.J.: Lawrence Erlbaum Associates, 1978.

Greer, R. Nancy, and Blank, Stanley S. Cognitive style, conceptual tempo and problem solving: Modification through programmed instruction. *American Educational Research Journal*, 1977, *14*, 295–315.

Guilford, Joy P. Intelligence: 1965 model. *American Psychologist,* 1966, *21,* 20–26.

Hudgins, Bryce B. *Learning and Thinking.* Itasca, Ill.: F. E. Peacock Publishers, 1977.

Hyram, George H. An experiment in developing thinking in children. *Journal of Experimental Education,* 1957, *26,* 125–132.

Johnson, Harry C. The effect of instruction in mathematical vocabulary upon problem solving in arithmetic. *Journal of Educational Research,* 1944, *38,* 97–110.

Kaplan, Norman. The relation of creativity to sociological variables in research organizations. In Calvin W. Taylor and Frank Barron (Eds.), *Scientific Creativity: Its Recognition and Development.* New York: John Wiley & Sons, 1963.

Luchins, Abraham S. Mechanization in problem solving—the effects of Einstellung. *Psychological Monographs,* 1942, *54* (Whole No. 248).

MacKinnon, Donald W. What makes a person creative? *Theory into Practice,* 1966, *5,* 152–156.

Maltzman, Irving. On the training of originality. *Psychological Review,* 1960, *67,* 229–242.

Marksberry, Mary Lee. Sizing up assertions. *Elementary School Journal,* 1976, *76,* 289–295.

McClure, Lawrence F., Chinsky, Jack M., and Larcen, Stephen W. Enhancing social problem-solving performance in an elementary school setting. *Journal of Educational Psychology,* 1978, *70,* 504–513.

Mednick, Sarnoff A. The remote associates test. *Journal of Creative Behavior,* 1968, *2,* 213–214.

Morgan, John J. B., and Carrington, Dorothy H. Graphical instruction in relational reasoning. *Journal of Educational Psychology,* 1944, *35,* 536–544.

Newell, Allen, and Simon, Herbert A. *Human Problem Solving.* Englewood Cliffs, N.J.: Prentice-Hall, 1972.

Olton, Robert M., and Crutchfield, Richard S. Developing the skills of productive thinking. In P. Mussen, J. Langer, and M. V. Covington, *Trends and Issues in Developmental Psychology.* New York: Holt, Rinehart & Winston, 1969.

Pace, Angela. Understanding and the ability to solve problems. *Arithmetic Teacher,* 1961, *8,* 226–233.

Parnes, Sidney J. Effects of extended effort in creative problem solving. *Journal of Educational Psychology,* 1961, *52,* 117–122.

Peel, Edwin A. A study of differences in the judgments of adolescent pupils. *British Journal of Educational Psychology,* 1966, *36,* 77–86.

Peel, Edwin A. *The Nature of Adolescent Judgment.* New York: Wiley-Interscience, 1973.

Resnick, Lauren B., and Ford, Wendy W. *The Psychology of Mathematics for Instruction.* Hillsdale, N.J.: Lawrence Erlbaum Associates, 1981.

Roberge, James J. A study of children's ability to reason with basic principles of deductive reasoning. *American Educational Research Journal,* 1970, *7,* 538–596.

Schaefer, Charles E., and Anastasi, Anne. A biographical inventory for identifying creativity in adolescent boys. *Journal of Applied Psychology,* 1968, *52,* 42–48.

Siegler, Robert S. The origins of scientific reasoning. In R. S. Siegler (Ed.), *Children's Thinking: What Develops?* Hillsdale, N.J.: Lawrence Erlbaum Associates, 1978.

Smith, Daryl G. College classroom interactions and critical thinking. *Journal of Educational Psychology,* 1977, *69,* 180–190.

Taba, Hilda. *Teaching Strategies and Cognitive Functioning in Elementary School Children.* Cooperative Research Project No. 2004. San Francisco: San Francisco State College, 1966.

Tomera, Audrey N. Transfer and retention of transfer of the science process of observation and comparison in junior high school students. *Science Education,* 1974, *58,* 195–203.

Torrance, E. Paul. *Rewarding Creative Behavior: Experiments in Classroom Creativity.* Englewood Cliffs, N.J.: Prentice-Hall, 1965.

Torrance, E. Paul. Predictive validity of the Torrance Tests of Creative Thinking. *Journal of Creative Behavior,* 1972, *6,* 236–262.

Torrance Tests of Creative Thinking. Princeton, N.J.: Personnel Press, 1966.

Weeden, Kenneth. Teaching decision making in secondary social studies. In Dana G. Kurfman (Ed.), *Developing Decision-Making Skills.* 47th yearbook, National Council for the Social Studies, 1977.

Wertheimer, Max. *Productive Thinking.* Enlarged ed. New York: Harper & Bros., 1959.

Wodtke, Kenneth W., and Wallen, Norman E. Teacher classroom control, pupil creativity, and pupil classroom behavior. *Journal of Experimental Education,* 1965, *34*(1), 59–65.

Motivation

Motivation is a scientific concept, but it is also part of the human experience. Children learn motives from their own experience, as de Charms (1968) notes: "The child knows that he wants things and learns that he can do something to get them, that his wanting is the motive for his behavior." In early childhood, particularly, thinking is centered on the child's own perspective, as we noted in Chapter 2. Judgments are made from an egocentric position, based on a history of personal experiences that tell children what they can and cannot do, what they do and do not want to do, and, in later childhood, their concept of the self-as-doer, which helps them understand that they themselves do things (see Chapter 3).

When adults attempt to explain a child's behavior, they often use words and phrases like these:

David works hard in science because he:
 . . . wants a good grade.
 . . . wants to please his parents.
 . . . feels he has to live up to his sister's reputation.
 . . . thinks it's fun.

In each of these examples, David's behavior is described as purposive, or goal directed. He is involved in science to achieve good grades, recognition from others, or for the pure enjoyment of the task. In fact, he probably is pursuing a number of these goals at the same time.

Motivation concerns the "why" of behavior. It cannot be directly observed; it must be inferred by observing the direction, intensity, and consistency of behavior over time. To judge whether David is motivated, for example, we may observe that he checks science books out of the library, enters a project in the science fair competition, and gets so involved in his science experiments that he may not hear the class bell. From a teacher's perspective, motivated students initiate activities on their own, complete assigned work on time, and persist when they experience difficulty. If two students are approximately equal in overall ability, the one who spends more time working on a task is likely to be judged as trying harder and being better motivated. Motivation concepts help explain what initiates or energizes behavior, what directs it toward certain ends, and what maintains it over time.

PERSONAL AND SITUATIONAL FACTORS IN MOTIVATION

Expressed in statistical terms, behavior (B) is generally viewed as a function of characteristics of the person (P) and the environment (E):

$$B = f(P \times E)$$

The person characteristics are typically described as needs, such as the need to achieve or to influence others. They are an explanation of behavioral differences among people in similar situations. Students with a high need to influence others may get actively involved in the student council and other school organizations, while those with a low need may participate only minimally. People who behave consistently in various situations also may be described in terms of personal dispositions: "He's lazy; he never completes his work on time," or "She's really smart; she always gets As." The environmental characteristics are external to the person and refer to features of the situation: in the school these may be teacher demands, grading practices, seating arrangements, or curriculum materials. Variations in the environment also can explain inconsistencies or differences in a single person's behaviors; a student may work very hard in teacher A's class but not at all in teacher B's class, for example.

The relationship between the personal and environmental or situational factors can be seen in the following example: A young girl is about to enter a tennis match. Predicting the outcome of the match depends on certain characteristics of the girl as a tennis player (ability, amount of time she has practiced, physical condition) and of the situation (how good the opponent is). If the opponent is not very good the girl can probably win, even though she may not have practiced very much. But if the opponent is skilled, the girl's characteristics as a player become very important. If she doesn't apply all her personal resources to the task, she is not likely to win. Whether she decides to exert maximum effort to win depends on how skillful she perceives herself to be, relative to her opponent. The right mix of personal and situational factors yields maximally motivated behavior. It is not always possible to achieve this mix, but it is possible, as we shall see, to modify the situation and to change how the individual perceives self and situation so as to increase motivation.

When little consideration is given to the relationship between the classroom situation and student characteristics in the instructional process, student achievement will primarily be determined by ability or aptitude, according to Bloom (1976). Those students who are better prepared and have a disposition to learn will achieve more. When the situation is carefully matched to student characteristics, however, student motivation is increased, so more students can learn more. Bloom suggests that motivational factors alone probably account for about 25 percent of the variation in achievement among students. Therefore, despite differences in individual students' ability or aptitude, when the classroom climate allows attention to motivational factors it can influence what the students accomplish.

THE MOTIVATED STUDENT

Why do some students do so well in school and others do so poorly, even though they could do much better? A cognitive approach to student motivation is concerned with how students interpret certain types of feedback and how it affects their feelings about themselves and the situation, as well as their subsequent behaviors. One student may react to a low test score by studying harder, while another may withdraw and give up. These different behaviors evolve from the different thoughts and feelings the students have about the test score information. In the classroom these thoughts involve beliefs about their own ability, beliefs about the causes of success and failure, and beliefs about specific actions that will lead to a goal.

When students who are motivated to achieve fail, they react quite differently than failing students who are less well motivated. Motivated students are more likely to say "What did I do wrong, and how can I correct it so I can do better next time?" rather than "I must be dumb." They believe that the amount of effort they expend determines how well they succeed, and they focus on their effort and specific skills—factors that can be controlled and improved with practice. Unmotivated students, in contrast, are likely to rely on external reasons to explain their failures, such as, "The teacher used tricky questions," "The book was boring," or "The reading was too hard." These external factors are not easily controlled, so these students learn to doubt their ability to accomplish their goals, and they develop strong negative feelings about their self-worth. In order to avoid a negative sense of self-esteem, they often stop trying or deny the importance of the assignment, test, or subject matter. When given a choice of activities, unmotivated students will avoid choosing those that are associated with such goals, and when forced into a situation (tests, homework) where they must deal with them, they may get anxious, engage in distracting activities, or withdraw. All of these reactions are likely to lead to more failure.

Motivated and unmotivated students not only think differently about failure, they also think differently about success. Motivated students have a high hope of success and a positive attitude toward goal attainment, and they do not think too much about the possibility of failure, unlike unmotivated students who spend a great deal of time wondering whether they will fail and worrying about the consequences. Instead of worrying about failure, motivated students think about specific actions they can take to accomplish the goal: "I will quickly read the chapter as an overview, then I will write out the major points, and finally, I will read the chapter thoroughly, taking detailed notes on the specific points." As a consequence, they spend more effective time on the task, and, since

---

BOX A *Motivations in a ring toss game*

Allan and Beth and Christina and David and Erin are playing a ring toss game. The object of the game is to get as many rings as possible over a peg. The distance from the peg is marked off in 2-foot intervals, and points are given for each ringer according to the distance from which the ring was thrown. For example, a ringer from 2 feet earns a player two points, a ringer from 4 feet earns a player four points, and so on.

The scoreboard shows the distances the five players threw from and the number of ringers they got out of four tosses in each round (number in parentheses).

	Allan	Beth	Christina	David	Erin
Round 1	2′ (4)	4′ (3)	6′ (1)	8′ (0)	16′ (0)
Round 2	2′ (4)	2′ (4)	4′ (3)	6′ (1)	16′ (0)
Round 3	2′ (4)	4′ (4)	6′ (2)	16′ (0)	16′ (0)

After the game, the players are questioned about their strategies in choosing the different distances.

Allan says that he is not very good at games like this, so he wanted to make sure that he could make a ringer: "I didn't care about the number of points, I just didn't want to try from far back because I was afraid I'd miss."

---

on-task behavior is correlated with achievement, they are more likely to be among the successful ones.

When motivated students achieve a goal, they usually feel very good, congratulate themselves, and take pride in the accomplishment. Unmotivated students, however, view success as a lucky break or as something easy enough for anyone to accomplish. Thus they take less pride in their performance. The fantasies of these types of students also differ. Motivated students often imagine themselves in achievement settings engaged in challenging activities and accomplishing desired goals. The fantasy results in very positive feelings about themselves and about achievement. For negatively motivated students, thinking about achievement generates anxious and tense feelings which may further inhibit their ability to act effectively.

Beth moved closer to the peg on the second trial and then moved farther back for the last trial. She also says she was afraid or nervous but felt a little more confident after the second trial, so she moved farther back.

Christina stood a moderate distance from the peg the first time. She says she didn't want to stand too close or too far away: "If I stood too close, it wouldn't be a challenge, but if I stood far away, it would have been just a matter of luck. I really felt I could make it from 6 feet, but then when I missed I decided to move a little closer. Then when I made the ringers, I decided to move back again. I felt really good when I made them."

David indicates that he stood at 8 feet on the first trial because he thought he was good at things like this: "It was much harder than I thought, so I decided to move a lot closer. But for the last trial, I thought I might be lucky enough to get one ringer, so why not take a chance."

Erin says she felt it was just a game: "I thought I'd just have some fun. It didn't matter if I got any ringers—maybe I'd be lucky."

Source: Dennis Shea and Karl Jackson, "Motivation Development Training with Teachers," in Richard de Charms (Ed.), *Enhancing Motivation: Change in the Classroom* (New York: Irvington Publishers, 1976).

Some differences in the motivational approaches of a group of students playing a game are described in Box A. All used motivational concepts in describing their behaviors. Some talked about the *challenge* of the game, while others said they were *lucky* in throwing from a distance. For some of the players, receiving points was an *incentive* for taking a larger *risk*. One student was *afraid of failing* and played in such a way that assured success for himself. Another student felt very *satisfied* when she was successful in her attempt.

Individuals who are motivated to achieve think differently about a game than those who are less well motivated. They respond to challenge; they take a risk but do not want their success to be a matter of luck. They are confident and have positive expectancies about achieving their goals. They feel good when they take a moderate risk and are successful.

As in classroom learning, in setting any goal people evaluate the task in relation to their abilities, the incentives for performing, and the probabilities of success. The consequences of behavior either affirm their perceptions of their ability or discomfirm it and suggest a need for reevaluating their perceptions of both the task and their ability.

Being motivated to succeed in academic areas is only one possible goal for which students may be motivated. They also have thoughts about their ability or competence to relate to others and to make friends. These beliefs determine whether or not they will initiate social contacts, include others in their activities, or be socially active. Students motivated to achieve social or affiliative goals believe in their social competence; like students seeking achievement goals, they focus on greater effort or the development of new social skills when they meet with social rejection. Students lacking confidence in their social abilities are less likely to initiate social contacts, except in "safe" situations. They are not likely to know how to develop the very social skills they need. Motivational principles thus may also be focused on socially oriented goals such as a sense of belonging, interpersonal effectiveness, and social success.

NEEDS THEORY

The concept of need is used by theorists to explain behavior that is directed toward goals to satisfy individual needs. When motivation is defined in terms of a concept of human needs, two broad classes can be identified:

1. Needs that are related to the survival, existence, and protection of the individual—food, water, security.
2. Needs for psychological well-being—belonging, freedom, self-esteem, competence, mastery.

MASLOW'S HIERARCHY OF NEEDS

Abraham Maslow's need theory is probably the one that has been best developed. Maslow (1968, 1970) theorized that unsatisfied human needs create tension, which serves as a force to direct behavior toward goals that will restore the individual to a balanced psychological position. A state of tension generates behaviors to reduce the tension, which eventually results in a rewarding and satisfying state. In this sense, student behavior (e.g., making friends, mastering reading skills) can be viewed as fulfilling certain needs. The unfulfilled need is the motivator for the behavior designed to fill that need.

A fundamental part of Maslow's theory is a hierarchy of needs in which lower-order or more basic needs must be satisfied before the next higher-order need can be effective as a motivator. Maslow's hierarchy of needs, from lowest to highest, is:

1. Physiological needs.
2. Safety needs.
3. Belongingness and affiliative needs.
4. Esteem needs.
5. Self-actualization needs.

The basic physiological needs comprise the lowest order of need and the strongest. These needs must be satisfied before goals evolving from higher-order needs can be pursued. Maslow describes physiological needs as "prepotent," meaning that they have the greatest strength until they are reasonably well gratified. Thus, according to Maslow, people have multiple needs or motives, and certain needs take precedence over others. Children understandably find it difficult to concentrate on school work if the classroom environment is punitive, if they are not accepted by their peers, or if they are hungry or sick.

Maslow's highest need state, self-actualization, differs from the other needs in the hierarchy in one important respect. Physiological, safety, belongingness, and esteem needs are caused by deficiencies. When there is a deficiency or a state of deprivation, the individual is driven toward a goal to eliminate that deficiency. A hungry person seeks food, a child who is not socially secure seeks friendship. Self-actualization, in contrast, can be satisfied by growth, not tension reduction. Self-actualization is a continuous process of growth; the motivation "to become everything that one is capable of becoming" (Maslow, 1970, p. 46) is never fulfilled for most people.

Physiological and Safety Needs

The two lowest orders of needs can be satisfied by goals that sustain life, such as shelter and water, and provide protection from physical or psychological threat. Until these needs have been met, people cannot be motivated toward higher-level goals. Victims of starvation spend most of their time thinking and fantasizing about food, and a child who comes to school tired or hungry finds it hard to interact in learning. Federal subsidies for breakfast and lunch programs were designed to satisfy this need. A motivationally sound instructional process would have children work on tasks that are more difficult and require more concentration in the early morning, when they are most physiologically alert and best able to concentrate (Rosenshine, 1976).

Children also have a basic need to feel secure, both physically and psychologically. Teachers and parents who are inconsistent in their demands stifle children's initiative, and the lack of structure in a permissive environment may be just as overwhelming as an overly structured and inflexible one. According to Glasser (1969), in a good school children know the rules and help make and agree with them; the rules are changeable and are consistently enforced.

Belongingness and Affiliative Needs

Everyone has a need for love and affection. Infants have been found to develop into more psychologically healthy children if they have had close personal contact with a caregiver. This is one reason the American Pediatric Association recommends breast feeding and holding the baby closely in bottle feeding.

In school settings, attempts to satisfy affiliative needs are translated into goals to make friends, to be included in group activities, and to be accepted by others. When children's needs for love and affection are frustrated, and they fail to develop friendships or become isolated from classmates, they may become hostile or aggressive toward others and the system, or they may withdraw. Eventually they may drop out of school or develop mental health problems. Gronlund (1959), using sociometric data from one school system, reported that as many as 20 percent of the children in the middle school grades could be classified as socially unaccepted by others.

Because social isolation may be due to a lack of social skills, attempts have been made to train children in various friendship behaviors in order to improve their classroom status. Oden and Asher (1977) identified a group of third- and fourth-graders who were not well accepted by their peers and instructed them over a four-week period in four friendship-making behaviors:

1. Participation—getting started, paying attention.
2. Cooperation—taking turns, sharing.
3. Communication—talking and listening.
4. Validation and support—offering help and encouragement.

In the coaching sessions the children were verbally instructed in the social skills and given an opportunity to try them out in a practice session. Not only did these children make substantial gains in social acceptance among their peers, but these gains were still evident one year after the training. Teachers can also provide opportunities for children to relate to others by using small-group instructional methods (such as Jigsaw and TGT, described later) and peer tutoring. Research has shown that when learning involves a cooperative effort, students develop more positive feelings toward each other and the class as a whole. In this manner, students can achieve affiliation goals while working toward learning goals.

Esteem Needs

Esteem needs are directly related to a person's sense of self-worth, which Covington and Beery (1976) define as the individual's evaluative appraisal of himself or herself, particularly his or her ability to achieve. Positive self-evaluations are reflected in statements like: "I am a good person; I am good in math; I have good ideas," and negative self-evaluations by statements such as: "I do not like myself; I am dumb; I can't do anything right." Students who view themselves positively and have confidence in their ability generally work harder on classroom tasks and strive to succeed. If the sense of self-esteem becomes threatened, however, they may act to protect themselves in ways that are counterproductive. A girl who does not study for a test, for example, avoids any evaluation of her ability. Even though she will probably fail, the failure cannot imply that she lacks ability, because she did not try. Covington and Beery describe this behavior as "failure with honor." Students may try to protect their self-esteem by dropping out, trying just hard enough to get by, cheating to get ahead, or putting down other students for studying or getting good grades.

Students' feelings of self-worth are threatened most when the instructional process produces a classroom climate which is diffuse and ambiguous (Johnson, 1981). In such a classroom the goals are often unclear, and one student's accomplishments are measured against another's. A competitive climate is probably the one classroom factor that provides the greatest threat to student motivation and self-esteem. Even students who are high in self-esteem are not impervious to the negative effects of competition. Ames (1978) found that, contrary to what might be expected, high-self-esteem children engaged in more self-derogatory behavior following a competitive loss than low-self-esteem children did. One of the conclusions from this study is that over time, failing in a competitive setting is likely to affect negatively even the high-self-esteem child's feelings of competence and self-worth.

Classroom competition can be explicit, as in grading on a curve, or it can be implicit, as in certain grouping practices, teacher communications, and the ways students use to gain the teacher's attention (see Chapter 13). The competitive, individualistic orientation of most American schools often blocks opportunities for students (both high- and low-achieving) to improve performance and develop self-esteem (Johnson, 1981). The section on improving student motivations later in this chapter describes cooperative, competitive, and individualized classroom climates and how they affect students' abilities to feel worthwhile and self-confident.

Self-Actualization Needs

Maslow defined self-actualization as a need for growth and development that builds on needs for achievement, competence, and independence.

Self-actualization also includes concepts of mastery and creativity. This higher-level need emphasizes the seeking, learning, and striving aspects of behavior.

A number of other psychologists have focused on a similar motive in human behavior which involves attempts to interact effectively with the environment. Robert White (1959) described this need as a desire to experience *competence,* which is unique to humans because they have a great capacity to learn. According to White, the competence motive is activated by a desire to deal effectively, or competently, with the environment. Similarly, for Richard de Charms (1968), human behavior reflects a "motivational propensity to be effective in producing changes in the environment." This propensity is described as a striving for *personal causation*—a desire to be the "origin" of one's behavior. Individuals who are "origins" believe that their behavior is self-determined, that they have freedom of choice, and that they are doing what they have personally chosen to do. An origin is motivated to engage in creative, productive behavior that is personally satisfying. The opposite of the origin is a "pawn," or a person who is controlled by external forces. A perception of oneself as a pawn reduces the motivation to act on the environment. De Charm's personal causation training programs are described later in the section on instructional methods.

The ideas that tie these different views of self-actualization together are an individual motivation to be autonomous and to master and adapt to the environment, as well as a belief in personal responsibility.

NEEDS THEORY AND THE INSTRUCTIONAL PROCESS

When needs theory is taken into account in the instructional process, the objective is to improve students' ability to recognize and satisfy their needs and eventually to achieve a degree of self-actualization. Charles Wales, for example, views the general objective of education as to help students achieve self-actualization goals, so they acquire a sense of competence and independence. He has defined three specific educational goals of self-actualization: knowledge, values, and decision making (Wales & Stager, 1977). Self-actualization is based on the ability to make decisions, which is supported by both knowledge and values, as shown in Figure 11.1. A decision based on knowledge or values alone is likely to be unbalanced, as with the scientist who ignores values in making decisions, the idealist who fails to consider what is feasible, or the politician who ignores both knowledge and values.

Wales has developed a system of instruction, called *guided decision making,* to accomplish the educational goals related to self-actualization. Initially this was designed for introductory courses for engineering stu-

Figure 11.1

Relationship of knowledge, values, and decision making to self-actualization

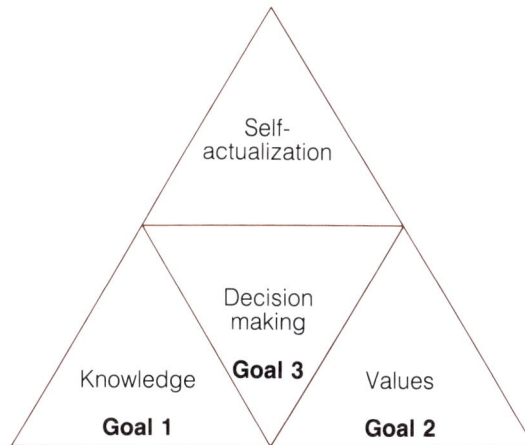

Self-actualization

Decision making

Knowledge **Goal 3** Values

Goal 1 **Goal 2**

Source: Adapted from C. E. Wales and R. A. Stager, *Guided Design* (Morgantown: West Virginia University, Freshman Engineering Department, 1977).

dents at West Virginia University, but it has been extended to almost all subject matter areas and grade levels. In this approach, students are presented with an open-ended problem which establishes a need for decision making. For example, students in a high school health or home economics course might be given the following vignette:

> The students at Crestville High have made numerous complaints about the quality and quantity of food served in the school cafeteria. As a group, you have been appointed to investigate the nutritional value, preparation, and the attractiveness of the food. Your committee is to complete its investigation within six weeks and provide a report which lists the major problems and makes specific recommendations for improvement.

These problems first establish a need for knowledge (goal 1). The above problem creates a "need" for knowledge about nutrition and the preparation of food. Knowledge-level goals are accomplished first through outside activities in which self-study materials may be coordinated to the textbook or library and research materials. Students are tested on their ability to recall and interpret the material, and they discuss the open-

The school should create a need for knowledge, not just supply it. The boys examining this bone may have their curiosity stirred, one of the principal ways to create a thirst for knowledge.

ended problems in small groups. In the process, they can become independent thinkers and develop their values and skills in communicating, presenting, defending, and criticizing ideas (goals 2 and 3). The students gain respect from others by making contributions to the discussion, and the group provides an environment where students' needs for belonging can be satisfied. The result of the group work is a written paper or project which is submitted to the teacher for final evaluation.

The challenge of solving open-ended problems may threaten the safety-security needs of beginning students. These students are first taken step-by-step through the decision-making or problem-solving process—defining the problem, considering alternative solutions, evaluating the solutions, and synthesizing the "best" possible solution into a detailed plan of action (see Chapter 10). Once students have mastered these steps in a group setting, the guidance is removed and they work independently on similar types of problems. This allows them to satisfy their needs for individual achievement and self-actualization.

ACHIEVEMENT THEORY

The theory of achievement motivation, which has become exceptionally influential, was originally formulated by David C. McClelland et al. in *The Achievement Motive* (1953). The achievement motive has been used to predict such diverse events as a student's academic performance and a country's economic growth, and it has been applied to such controversial areas as sex and racial differences in motivation.

There are two basic motives at the heart of achievement theory: *a motive or need for success* (symbolized M_s) and *a motive or desire to avoid failure* (symbolized M_{af}). These are competing motives in that one pushes the individual to undertake an achievement task ("I want to try out for the school play"), and the other pulls the person in the opposite direction ("I'm afraid to try out because I might not get the part I want"). If the motive to achieve success is greater than the motive to avoid failure, this person will probably try out; but if the motives are equal in strength or if the motive to avoid failure is stronger, the person is not as likely to do so. The strength of these motives is considered relatively stable over time, but most people would experience both motives to some extent.

The theory of achievement motivation had its origins in needs theories, which did not specify how to measure the existence and strength of a person's needs. Henry Murray (1943), a prominent needs theorist, hypothesized that people's thoughts and fantasies reflect their need states. To assess the magnitude of a need, he developed the Thematic Apperception Test (TAT), in which people are asked to write stories to interpret ambiguous pictures. The theme is provided by the viewer's personality, that is, people project their own needs into the story. An early study by Atkinson and McClelland (1948) used the TAT to assess the hunger need in three groups of men who had not eaten for 1, 4, or 16 hours. In the stories they wrote, the number of references to food and means for getting food increased with the number of hours of food deprivation.

A MEASURE OF THE MOTIVE TO SUCCEED

While early research made it clear that the magnitude of physiological needs could be assessed, Atkinson and McClelland were more interested in developing a measure of the need for achievement. Using the ambiguous stimuli in the TAT, they asked students to write stories in response to several questions. The stories were then scored to determine the strength of the projected achievement motive.

As the example in Box B shows, the TAT story is first scored according to whether or not there is any expressed concern for achievement. For example, does the story reveal a concern for competing with some external standard of excellence ("I want to break the record on my next attempt") or with an internal standard ("I want to do better next time")? Is there a concern with doing something unique ("I will invent the first electric bicycle") or with being involved in a long-term effort ("I know I will have to work a long time to achieve what I want")? If the story has one of these achievement themes, it is given a score of 1 and then scored for 10 specific achievement-related thoughts, with one point for each thought. (Some examples of these achievement thoughts are given in Box B.) A story can receive a total score of 0 (no achievement theme present) to 11 (1 point for a general theme plus 10 points for specific thought components). Summed over a series of stories, this unique scoring system of the TAT measures the relative strength of the motive to achieve success.

A MEASURE OF THE MOTIVE
TO AVOID FAILURE

Just as people look at a situation and think about succeeding, they may also think about failing. Anticipating an upcoming final exam, you may think about improving your performance from the midterm exam, and you may imagine how great you would feel if you got an A in the course, but you may also have twinges of anxiety about taking the exam and not doing as well as you hoped. The amount of *anxiety* people feel in an achievement or testing situation is indicative of their motive to avoid failure. To some degree, everyone is caught somewhere between a need to achieve success and a desire to avoid failure.

The device most commonly used to measure this motive is an anxiety questionnaire such as the Test Anxiety Questionnaire by Mandler and Sarason (1952). A person high in anxiety might indicate agreement with statements such as:

> I get so nervous while taking an exam, I never do my best.
> I block on many questions even when I know the answers.
> Time pressures make me do worse than what I can really do.

THE RESULT: ACHIEVEMENT MOTIVATION

To some extent, everyone has both the motive to approach success and the motive to avoid failure. Every achievement situation elicits some tendency to seek success and some tendency to avoid failure. The real question is, which is the stronger motive: Is $M_s > M_{af}$, or is $M_{af} > M_s$? The right answer can provide important information to schools and teachers about a student's likelihood of undertaking a task and putting forth the effort to complete it. This information could be used to predict

BOX B   *Measuring the will to succeed with the TAT*

A student taking a Thematic Apperception Test is shown a picture depicting two women in a laboratory, both dressed in white lab coats. One is standing in front of some chemistry equipment holding what looks like a test tube, and the other is next to her.

The following questions are provided as guides:

1. What is happening? Who are the people?
2. What has led up to this situation? What has happened in the past?
3. What is being thought? What is wanted? By whom?
4. What will happen? What will be done? By whom?

This is the story the student writes:

> A well-known female scientist is demonstrating her latest discovery to another female colleague. The scientist has spent years working on a new process for converting wood chips into a gasoline substitute cheaply. The scientist is looking for advice on how to have her process adopted by the large energy firms without being pigeonholed or totally killed. She will go to the government for help and will ultimately get a small plant running.

To measure the extent of this student's achievement motive, a scoring system is applied to the story. It is first given a point for being about achievement. Note the statement about long-term involvement ("has spent years working on a new process"). Since the story is about achievement it can be scored for the more specific categories. One point is given for the instrumental activity with an outcome ("She will go to the government for help and will ultimately get a small plant running"), environmental obstacle ("how to have her process adopted by the large energy firms without being pigeonholed or killed"), and nurturant press ("looking for advice; . . . will go to the government for help"). Since the main theme of the story is achievement, a fifth point is given. Overall, the story is scored +5.

Source: John W. Atkinson, *Motives in Fantasy, Action, and Society* (New York: D. Van Nostrand Co., 1958).

whether or not certain types of behaviors might occur, such as the following:

Sarah decides to drop a chemistry course.

Michael believes he can get a B if he studies more.

Sherry goes out for the softball team.

Allan watches TV instead of studying for his exam the next day.

In these examples, Michael and Sherry are approaching achievement situations, but Sarah and Allan appear to be avoiding them.

Individuals high in achievement needs ($M_s > M_{af}$) are known to prefer tasks of moderate difficulty. Their thinking might go something like this: "An easy task is not challenging, and even if I succeed I don't feel I've really accomplished something. But a task that is too hard is too risky to be worth the effort. A task that is neither too hard nor too easy offers the best challenge, with a reasonable chance of success if I work for it." It is precisely this combination, a challenge and a chance of success, that most attracts a person who is high in need for achievement. In fact, when the task is moderately difficult, individuals who are high in achievement needs are most likely to persist, even when they encounter difficulty.

In the same sense that individuals with high achievement needs have a desire to succeed, those with low achievement needs ($M_{af} > M_s$) have a strong desire to avoid achievement situations. In test situations, they are likely to rush through the questions, not recheck their answers, and daydream, all of which help them avoid the feeling of being in an achievement situation. Research shows that these students work harder and show more persistence when a task is perceived as being either very easy or very difficult. Tasks of moderate difficulty produce negative or failure-avoiding motivational patterns, such as not trying or procrastinating. A low need for achievement produces some tendency to avoid any achievement situation, but situations that are in the intermediate range of difficulty are most anxiety producing.

Individuals high and low in achievement needs not only are likely to choose different types of tasks to work on, they also are likely to use different strategies in their attempts to solve problems and to experience different levels of success. Students who want to succeed choose tasks of moderate difficulty; they are persistent in their efforts to complete a task successfully, and they tend to use more strategies that are directed toward task mastery. Students who are more concerned with avoiding failure than with being successful may select tasks that are extremely easy or too difficult, thereby avoiding any challenge or threat to their ability. They are more likely to give up when difficulty is experienced and less likely to use appropriate problem-solving strategies. Thus it is easy to see that the individual with a high achievement need is, indeed, more likely to be successful.

The case examples below suggest the contrasting ways high- and low-motive students might prepare for an exam:

> Cara, who is preparing for a final exam in social studies, has a need for achievement that is greater than her need to avoid failure. As she reviews her past performance, she notes that she received 2 Bs and 3 Cs for the five previous marking periods. Therefore she wants to get a B on the final so her average for the year will be a B. Cara estimates that getting an A on the final would probably be too hard, and she could get a C with only a short review session. She decides that obtaining a B is a moderately difficult task, and she is motivated to study hard for the test. She starts studying three weeks ahead of time, organizing her notes and chapter outlines and writing out a careful study schedule. She follows this plan carefully and looks forward to the challenge of the test.

> Mike, a classmate, has a similar record for the previous period and is also preparing for the exam. He usually is quite anxious about doing poorly on tests, which prevents him from realistically confronting the need to prepare for them. Therefore Mike does not think much about his social studies final until the night before the exam. Now the task of getting a B is extremely difficult. Mike settles down, studies very hard, and stays up until 3 A.M. reviewing the text and his notes. He hopes the test will be easy.

Two factors that can increase the achievement motive in students who otherwise have a strong inclination to avoid failure have been identified by Raynor (1970). One factor involves some form of external incentive. A boy may not be very interested in trying out for the baseball team, for example, but if his closest friends are going to try out and his father wants him to, he might decide to do so because of the extrinsic value of being with his friends and pleasing his father. A teacher has to be very judicious in using external motivators, however, because the incentives must be valued by the student. A second factor that may enhance the achievement striving of a student involves how the student perceives the behavior. In the student's view, an activity should be linked to valued goals; the activity level increases when a goal is being pursued. The key factor in determining whether a person will approach or avoid a situation is the difference between M_s and M_{af}, but when there is some extrinsic reward or the activity is seen as instrumental to some valued goal, the motivation to approach the situation is increased.

ATTRIBUTION THEORY

Attribution theory, like achievement theory, begins with the assumption that people differ in how they think about success and failure. But attribution theory is more concerned with identifying and classifying specific thoughts related to the approach and avoidance of achievement situations. These thoughts are *causal explanations* given in answer to such questions as, "Why did I succeed?" or "Why did I fail?" or, more specifically, "Why did I flunk biology?" or "Why did Greg get a better part in the school play than I did?"

The major recent contributor to the development and elaboration of an attribution theory of achievement has been Bernard Weiner (1979; Weiner et al., 1971; Weiner & Kukla, 1970). He suggests that when people ask "why" questions about their performance, they answer them with explanations using one or more causal categories, such as *ability, effort, task difficulty,* or *luck.* These causes can be assigned three primary dimensions: internal versus external, stable versus unstable, and controllable versus uncontrollable (see Table 11.1). Ability and effort are seen as factors that are internal to individuals, while task difficulty and luck are external factors. Effort is the one factor that is under the person's own control. You can control how much you study for an exam, how hard you work at an exercise program, or how much time you devote to one course over another. You cannot immediately control how much activity you have, how hard the task is, or the amount of luck you have.

According to attribution theory, how a person thinks about success or failure affects her or his motivation to achieve. The following case study

---

Table 11.1

Dimensions of causes of success and failure

| Controllability | Internal | | External | |
	Stable	Unstable	Stable	Unstable
Uncontrollable	*Ability:* I am good at sports.	*Mood:* I was upset about an argument with my parents, and I couldn't concentrate on the test.	*Task difficulty:* The map assignments are very difficult.	*Luck:* I had two final exams scheduled on the same day.
Controllable	*Typical effort:* I like history, so I always work hard.	*Immediate effort:* I concentrated on each word as the teacher read the spelling list.	*Teacher bias:* Because I am nice to the teacher, she likes me.	*Unusual help from others:* My mother helped me with my algebra homework.

Source: Categories from Bernard Weiner, "A Theory of Motivation for Some Classroom Experiences," *Journal of Educational Psychology,* vol. 71 (1979), pp. 3–25.

demonstrates how different thought patterns can lead to very different types of achievement strategies.

> Donna and Stephen both receive a D on the first exam in introductory psychology. Donna explains her poor performance in the following way: "I feel bad that I didn't do better. The exam was fair, but I just didn't study enough. I know I can do better in this course." In contrast, Stephen says, "I'm unhappy with my grade. The exam questions were tricky, and you had to be lucky to get a decent test score." Donna attributes her low performance to a lack of effort, but Stephen makes excuses for his performance by attributing his performance to bad luck. Because Donna believes she didn't study hard enough, she decides to implement a new study schedule and to follow it diligently. Donna also decides to attend optional review sessions prior to the second exam. Stephen does not change his behavior, and he does not attend any review sessions. He tells his friends that the tests are tricky and claims all he wants to do is pass the course.

The thought-feeling-action sequences for the two students are quite different. While both are unhappy with their grades, Donna attributes her performance to a controllable factor, while Stephen attributes his to a more uncontrollable factor. Donna's attributions lead her to try new achievement-oriented strategies, and she expects that her future performance will improve, while Stephen remains "stuck" in a pattern of ineffectiveness, expecting a barely passing grade.

TEACHERS' ATTRIBUTIONS

Attribution theory can also help teachers understand how to evaluate and help students. Suppose a grade school teacher has given an exam and must convey some feedback to the pupils. Three students did very well on the test, but each demonstrated a different level of ability and motivation in his or her performance:

> Theron doesn't have much ability, but he tried very hard.
> Roberto has a great deal of ability, but he didn't try very hard.
> Candy has high ability and tried very hard.

If the teacher can give each student from one to five gold stars, who would get the most and the least?

Three other students did very poorly on the test. These students also demonstrated different levels of ability and motivation:

> Teddy tried hard, but he doesn't have much ability.
> Kendall did not try very hard, even though she has a lot of ability.
> Morgan did not try hard, and she doesn't have much ability.

The teacher can give from one to five red stars to each of these students, all of whom failed the test. The student she evaluates most negatively would get the most red stars.

Students who role-played teachers in a study by Weiner and Kukla (1970) would give the most gold stars to Theron, who tried hard but has little ability, and the least gold stars to Roberto, who has high ability but did not try very hard. They would give the most red stars to Kendall, who has a great deal of ability but did not try, and be most protective of Teddy, who tried very hard but didn't have much ability. The results of this study are shown in Figure 11.2; students were rewarded for trying hard and punished most for lack of effort.

Figure 11.2

Evaluation (reward and punishment) as a function of ability and motivation

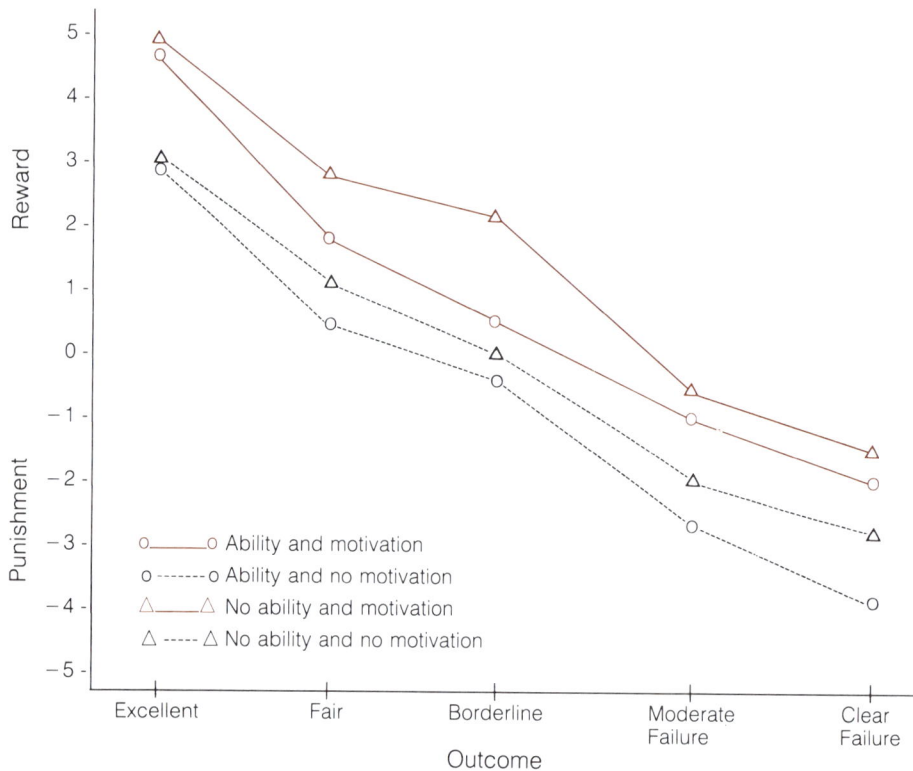

o———o Ability and motivation
o - - - - -o Ability and no motivation
△———△ No ability and motivation
△ - - - -△ No ability and no motivation

Source: Adapted from Bernard Weiner and Andy Kukla, ''An Attributional Analysis of Achievement Motivation,'' *Journal of Personality and Social Psychology*, vol. 15 (1970), pp. 1–20. Copyright 1970 by the American Psychological Association. Adapted by permission of the author.

Table 11.2

Causal explanations for success and failure

Achievement Motive	Success	Failure
High motive	Ability/Effort	Lack of effort
Low motive	Task/Luck	Lack of ability

ATTRIBUTION THEORY AND ACHIEVEMENT MOTIVATION

Attribution theory assumes that individuals high in need for achievement explain their successes and failures differently than individuals low in this need do (see Table 11.2). The research of Weiner and his colleagues shows that there are very distinct differences in the way these two types of individuals think about achievement situations. Persons high in achievement motivation believe they are successful because they have the ability or because they work hard, and they reward themselves by saying, "I'm proud and confident of the future." Persons low in achievement motivation do not believe that effort leads to success; instead, they think their success is due to external factors like luck or an easy task, and so they take little pride in their accomplishments.

High- and low-achievement-motivated individuals also differ in how they explain or attribute failure. Those with high achievement motivation attribute failure to a lack of effort. They are angry with themselves because they believe they should have done better. These students do not question their ability; they believe they can succeed in the future if they try harder, change their strategy, or in some way modify their approach. In contrast, low-achievement-motivated students attribute failure to a lack of ability, which is a stable and uncontrollable factor; therefore they experience lowered esteem and feelings of helplessness.

The causal explanation of these high- and low-motive groups can be linked directly to specific behavioral differences (see Figure 11.3). As we noted in the preceding section, students with high achievement needs or motives are more likely to initiate achievement activities, to work with greater intensity, to persist longer in the face of failure, and to choose tasks of moderate difficulty. By attributing success to their ability and effort, high-motive students feel a sense of pride in successful accomplishment, and this heightened sense of reward increases their desire to *initiate* future achievement actions. People tend to like and want to continue what is rewarding. Since the low-motive group makes external rather than internal ascriptions for success, their self-esteem is not enhanced, and they are not as likely to continue or to initiate achievement efforts.

Figure 11.3

*Thought-action sequences based on attributional
analysis of achievement motivation*

Individuals' Achievement Motive	Achievement Event	Attribution	Emotion	Future Behavior
High	Molly wins a blue ribbon in skating.	I won because I practiced four hours a day for the last six months (sustained effort).	I feel proud.	I want to keep skating and to do well; I know I will have to keep up a diligent practice schedule.
Low	Jack is elected to the student council.	I was elected because I was the only senior running (easy task).	I'm happy.	I don't know how I would do in a real contest; thus, I do not know if I will run for office again.
Low	Jacob is turned down by the college he selects as his first choice.	I must not be smart enough (low ability).	I feel very bad and depressed.	It doesn't really make any difference now which college I go to; I probably won't do very well anyway.
High	Jana loses her position as starting guard for the basketball team.	I must have let down in my concentration (inadequate effort).	I'm mad at myself for letting this happen.	I'm going to practice on my own an extra hour each day.

Causal attributions are also related to *persistence* behavior. Because
individuals with high achievement motives ascribe success or failure to
effort, which they can increase or decrease at will, they can anticipate
the possibility of succeeding in the future by planning to work harder.
Low-motive students attribute success to luck and failure to ability, so
they can only anticipate more failure; achievement striving therefore is
likely to subside. Thus high-motive persons are more likely to perceive
the value of expending energy and effort in the pursuit of their goals.

Causal explanations also explain why high-motive persons prefer tasks
of moderate difficulty, whereas low-motive persons select those that are

very easy or very hard. Success at an easy task is almost assured, and failure at a hard task can be attributed to the task itself; but failure at a moderately difficult task focuses low-motive persons on their ability—the attribution that makes them feel most anxious. Because high-motive students focus more on their effort when they succeed or fail, they continue to feel competent about accomplishing any task. They select moderately difficult tasks because they can reasonably expect to succeed.

INTRINSIC MOTIVATION: THE MOTIVATIONAL GOAL OF EDUCATION

An intrinsically motivated student undertakes a task like mathematics, reading, or music because he or she enjoys the task for itself, as we noted in Chapter 3. A girl who is intrinsically motivated to read will read not for the approval of her parents or to get good grades, but because she likes to read the stories. For a student with such intrinsic motivation, failure is not a negative reflection on ability, but rather a minor setback or problem to be overcome by trying a new approach. In a sense, failure is not even perceived as failure, but rather as information indicating the need for a different strategy. Such an attitude toward learning obviously contributes to a lifelong desire for the subject. In John Dewey's words, "The most important attitude that can be formed is that of desire to go on learning."

It is clear from attribution theory, however, that a lifelong desire for learning is dependent on a belief that effort is the basis for learning goals. It is also clear that not everyone believes in this effort-outcome relationship. According to Covington and Beery (1976), students who believe that goals are accomplished through effort are success oriented. These students steadily gain confidence in their abilities and come to see themselves, while in school and later in their working life, as equal to most tasks. When success-oriented students encounter failure, they are most likely to blame it on insufficient effort, as we have seen. Therefore failure is viewed as a natural part of the learning process, not as a characteristic of the learner (e.g., "I must be an ignorant person"). Success-oriented students want to base their decisions on available knowledge and present values, and they are willing to run the reasonable risks of failure which are necessary in order to achieve. They focus on the challenge of the learning task and are not distracted by worry and self-doubt. In contrast, failure-avoiding students feel continually threatened and harbor secret doubts about their ability. These students fear that they lack ability and despair of succeeding well enough in the future. Since to them failure means a lack of ability rather than a lack of effort, it threatens to deny them their respect and esteem. Thus their primary motivation is avoiding failure, even if it means hindering their chances for success.

At the core of intrinsic motivation is the thought pattern of the student. A teacher can get a failure-oriented student to perform by offering some reward or threat of punishment (see Chapter 8), but such extrinsic reinforcement techniques will not result in a lifelong desire for learning. Extrinsic motivators only result in temporary states of motivation, and the motivation is lost as soon as the reward is removed.

INCREASING STUDENT MOTIVATION

As we noted at the beginning of this chapter, academic achievement, like all behavior, is affected by both situational and personal factors. Student motivation, therefore, should be related to both the situational factors of the instructional process and the classroom environment and to the personal factors of the student's ideas about what goals are important and how to attain them, beliefs about the causes of successes and failures, and needs for affiliation, esteem, and competence.

COOPERATION, COMPETITION, OR INDIVIDUALIZATION

The classroom climate and the nature of the instructional process are important determinants of student motivation. They affect how students relate to each other and to the task, how they attribute their successes and failures, and what they believe about their social and academic competence. The process may be designed so that students work independently or interdependently, and the type of interdependence may be positive, as in cooperation, or negative, as in competition. Students can cooperate in groups toward a common goal, or they can compete against each other to see who can do the best job, accomplish the task first, or get the most personal recognition or attention. They also can work independently and individually on tasks toward their goals. The relation of these various goal structures and group processes will be examined in Chapter 14.

The issue of whether cooperative or competitive learning environments contribute most to student achievement has endured in psychological and educational research since the beginning of the century. Many unanswered questions remain, but there is a substantial amount of evidence linking competition to less desirable outcomes such as aggressiveness, cheating, lowered motivation, and failure-avoiding behaviors, while cooperation is linked to more desirable outcomes such as

Competition with other people can bring out the best in a student. A better incentive, though, may be to compete against a standard of excellence or against one's own best earlier efforts.

positive peer relationships, higher achievement, positive self-esteem, and interracial acceptance (see Johnson & Johnson, 1975; 1979). There is also consistent evidence that students prefer cooperative learning situations to those that are competitively structured (Johnson & Johnson, 1975).

Nevertheless, each type of goal structure can have positive and negative consequences, and, under certain circumstances each may be desirable, depending on the outcomes that the instructional process seeks to achieve, avoid, or accept. A competitive game format may provide a fun and exciting way of practicing a new skill, but repetitive use of the traditional spelling bee, for example, can be demoralizing to a poor speller. Using cooperative groups to accomplish a goal encourages peer tutoring, and successful accomplishment of the goal may enhance the self-esteem of low-achieving students. But, as a study by Ames (1981) has shown, when a group turns in a poor performance, hostility and blame may be directed at low-achieving students or those who contribute little to the group product. Individualistic structures may help students develop a sense of independence and enable the teacher to match individually prescribed goals to students' performance, but if they are overused students may also develop a sense of isolation.

It is our position, therefore, that students can learn to develop internal standards of excellence best if they are exposed to a variety of learning environments. An individualized environment can help students learn to focus on their past performance as a source of information for setting future goals and standards. A cooperative learning environment can help students attain higher levels of achievement and develop a sense of responsibility to others. And a competitive environment can help students identify standards of excellence where they are otherwise ambiguous. Determining the most yards rushed in a single football game is a matter of knowing what someone else has accomplished, for example, but solving a certain number of math problems is a matter of knowing what students themselves have done in the past, and making an important scientific breakthrough is usually a matter of careful scholarship and joint inquiry. None of these has much to do with the social comparison processes of competition, which can lead to the setting of false or unrealistic standards rather than internally referenced criteria for performance.

According to Matthews et al. (1980), the most successful people have a strong desire to work but focus on internal standards of excellence rather than comparing themselves to how well others are doing. "Making it on your own" thus means being able to look within oneself for goals, criteria of excellence, and resources to meet personal standards. It is not necessary to look to the accomplishments of others as motivation.

INSTRUCTIONAL PROGRAMS AIMED AT MOTIVATIONAL DEVELOPMENT

Many students in elementary and secondary schools fail or cease trying because they doubt their ability, see no purpose in school, or feel they have no control over their learning. The thoughts and feelings these students have about themselves, others, and the school interfere with their performance, and teachers can do much to prevent and remedy these motivational problems.

During the past ten years, educational researchers have devised and tested programs aimed at the motivational development of students. Field tests have often been conducted in the urban and low-income areas where motivational problems abound. The programs are broadly based on the three theoretical perspectives presented in this chapter: need, achievement, and attribution. Some of them focus on restructuring the learning environment; that is, they reduce competition, replacing it with cooperative and individualized approaches. This modification of the learning environment typically results in a focus on student effort rather than ability. It enables students to satisfy their affiliation needs and allows them to work on goals appropriate to their ability levels. Other programs focus on helping students learn to set goals of moderate difficulty and to think differently about success and failure; that is, students are taught how to think like achievement-motivated persons. Basically, these programs aim to prevent or reverse a negative motivational cycle by changing students' thought patterns or by changing the conditions that contribute to them.

Cooperative Learning

Many cognitive and affective educational objectives can be achieved best through cooperative models of classroom learning, according to David W. and Roger T. Johnson (1974, 1975, 1979). They reviewed a substantial amount of research comparing cooperative to competitive and individualistic structures and concluded that cooperatively structured learning environments promote intrinsic motivation, enhance students' beliefs about their social competence, and improve their attitudes toward classwork and school. In general, they found that cooperation increases achievement, particularly the achievement of low-ability students when they work in heterogeneous groups. The finding that cooperation fosters positive interpersonal relationships is not surprising, since it provides opportunities for students to work interdependently and help each other. The finding that it also improves achievement, however, establishes a strong case for increasing the frequency of cooperative-based learning in the classroom.

In their work with teachers, Johnson and Johnson found that many of them think they are implementing cooperative learning when they have students sit together at a table, discuss an assignment, tutor or help one another, or share learning materials. While these experiences may contribute to or be necessary for cooperative learning, it is also necessary to assign a group goal or objective and evaluate the group as a unit according to the quality of the group product. Cooperation means working toward a common goal, such as writing a report or producing a set of answers to mathematics problems, whether the goal is assigned by the teacher or set by the group members. The classroom must be arranged so that students are clustered together and have free access to resource materials. Thus the classroom environment must be open, not restrictive, and the teacher's attitude must be supportive, not prohibitive. In cooperative learning, the teacher's role is to observe and consult with the groups. The teacher might make suggestions to improve their progress, encourage students to seek new resource materials, ask questions to stimulate thinking, recommend dividing the task into separate parts, and provide support for their efforts.

Anyone who has ever worked as part of a group is well aware of one of the most persistent problems—how to get everyone to do his or her share of the group work. In cooperatively structured learning both the students' lack of experience in developing cooperative skills and school or classroom pressures to maintain the instructional pace contribute to these problems. To alleviate them, Johnson and Johnson suggest that the teacher observe and monitor the groups to make certain everyone is participating. Occasionally asking students to explain their own parts of the work emphasizes that all group members are responsible for it. Students also need time to reflect on the group's accomplishments and discuss how well the group has worked together. The final step in cooperative learning is evaluation of the group product. Johnson and Johnson recommend a criterion-referenced system of evaluation in which all group members receive the same grade.

A major consideration in using cooperative learning is to provide groups with achievable goals. Whether or not a group is successful in accomplishing its goal may be more important than whether the groups' members contribute equally to the group product. When a group is unsuccessful, the group members not only judge themselves rather harshly, they also attempt to impart blame to one or more of the group members (Ames, 1981).

Teams-Games-Tournaments (TGT)

A modified cooperative program for learning is Teams-Games-Tournaments, developed by DeVries and Edwards (1973). It involves both cooperative groups and intergroup competition. TGT is particularly attractive because it utilizes the diversity of student abilities in the classroom and makes the learning of basic skills more interesting. The effectiveness of TGT has been demonstrated in a wide variety of field settings, across different age levels and subject matter areas (Slavin, 1978). Compared to control classrooms, in classrooms using TGT the amount of time students spent on their work and academic achievement were both increased, and interracial relations were improved.

When students are assigned to cooperative teams for TGT, all ability levels are represented on each team, and the teams are fairly comparable in overall ability. Team members first practice and tutor each other on the skills or material to be learned (e.g., spelling lists, mathematics problems, historical events). Then, using a game format, teams compete against each other in a tournament in which students at the same ability levels on each team answer questions and earn points for their teams according to their performance. A unique aspect of this approach is that low-ability students can contribute as many points to their team totals as high-ability students, because the students compete only against others at their own ability levels. Thus each individual has a chance to contribute to the goals of the group, and the strong incentive value of competition can be utilized.

To simplify the TGT program and make it more compatible to actual classroom practices, Slavin (1978) eliminated the use of games. In his Student Teams Achievement Divisions (STAD) program, students are assigned to cooperative teams with mixed ability levels, as well as to divisions according to their achievement levels. Each division represents one achievement level in the class, and all the divisions are represented on each team. Students work in their teams to learn the assigned material and then compete with their divisions on quizzes. The actual composition of the divisions is known only to the teacher and is changed when necessary after each quiz.

Jigsaw

The jigsaw method combines group cooperation with peer tutoring. Jigsaw is a highly structured approach in which each student learns a skill or part of a lesson and teaches it to others. Students are first divided into groups, and each group member is given part of an assignment. In one lesson (Aronson, 1978), the students were to learn the life story of Joseph Pulitzer. A biography was divided into six equal parts, with each member of a group receiving one part. Each student had to master his or her own part before teaching it to the other members of the group. To facilitate this process, students from all groups who received the same part of the biography met to discuss it, ask each other questions, and rehearse to make certain that each student knew the information. The students then returned to their original groups and taught each other their parts of the lesson. Each student was then tested on the entire life of Pulitzer.

Aronson compares the jigsaw method to a puzzle in that the students must work together to complete the picture. The students become valuable and necessary resources to each other. The jigsaw model differs from Johnson and Johnson's cooperative learning in that the students perform and are evaluated on an individual basis, not as a group. Research has shown that putting students in the role of teachers and in the cooperative group situation improves their beliefs about their ability. Students with a history of low achievement have been found to change their attributions about their performance; they begin to attribute success, but not failure, to their own ability. Not only do these students begin to view themselves as more capable and competent, but they are viewed similarly by others. This new pattern of attribution seems to result in more task involvement and better achievement.

Individually Guided Motivation (IGM)

The model for individually guided motivation, developed by Klausmeier et al. (1973), is a totally individualized approach to increasing student motivation. The model centers on regularly scheduled teacher-student conferences. The purpose of the conferences is to help students set realistic learning goals and become self-directed in their behavior.

In IGM programs, students not only learn how to set goals, but because the goals are based on their prior levels of achievement, they also learn

---

BOX C *Reading for fun and profit*

An individually guided motivation program relies on a series of student-teacher conferences to encourage students to set and achieve their own goals in a particular subject area. A reading program, for example, might be designed to build positive attitudes toward reading and to advance a student's reading level.

This is a conference with 10-year-old Lynn, whose reading score on the Iowa Test of Basic Skills in September was 4.8, almost one grade equivalent higher than the national average. Before the program, she had read only two easy books in an eight-week period. During the eight weeks of the conference period, in contrast, she read 36 books, some of which were much more difficult than any she had tried before. Her reading score at the end of the school year was 6.7.

Teacher. Hello, Lynn! Will you sit down right here next to me? What books did you read this week? Do you have them written down on your record sheet? [Focuses student attention.]

Lynn. I read a lot of books this week. I read *Lucky and the Giant, Encyclopedia Brown, Tony's Treasure Hunt,* and *Henry and the Club House.*

Teacher. My, you *have* been reading a lot. Very good! So much more than you used to. [Provides feedback and reinforces desired behavior.] Why don't you tell me about Henry and his club house. I see you brought it along. Did he really build a club house?

Lynn. Yes, Henry and his two friends built it in Henry's backyard. They got some old wood from a man in the neighborhood who had to tear down his garage. And the club house had windows and a floor and everything. They wouldn't let any girls in their club house. They made a sign saying, "No girls allowed. This means you.". . .

that effort is the key to success. The goal is challenging but based on their present skill levels. The procedures the teacher uses are intended to reinforce students' efforts and get them interested in and committed to working toward the next goal. During the conferences the teacher uses a variety of behaviors—modeling desired behaviors and attitudes, giving feedback regarding students' progress, correcting problems, reinforcing students' efforts and progress, and helping students set goals for the next conference (see Box C).

Teacher. I see a picture here of a man spraying water on two dogs that are fighting. What happened? [Asks questions to check on retention and comprehension of book.]

Lynn. Oh, that's when Henry was trying to sell a subscription to the new neighbors. Henry's dog, Ribsey, and the neighbor's dog got into a fight and they had to spray water on them to stop it.

Teacher. Did you enjoy the book about Henry?

Lynn. I really did! Because it had a lot of funny things that happened in it.

Teacher. That's fine. [Reinforces positive comment about reading.] Did you have any trouble with any of the words in the story? [Checks whether book was of appropriate difficulty.]

Lynn. Oh, no. It was easy.

Teacher. What would you like to read next week?

Lynn. I think I want this one, *The Peculiar Miss Pickett.* [Student sets goal.]

Teacher. Is that the only one? O.K. But before you decide for sure, why don't you read the first page aloud to me? [Assesses difficulty level of reading material. In this case, the teacher knew that Lynn tended to choose books that were too easy for her. Lynn reads. It seems to be on the right level.] That sounds like it's going to be a good book! Do you think you can finish it by next week? I'd enjoy hearing about it.

Lynn. I will. You know, Mrs. _____, I'm going to try to read all the books on this shelf!

Teacher. That's very good, Lynn. [Utilizes the individual's need to achieve; reinforces expression of positive attitude.] But remember that there are a lot of good books in the library too. Good-bye. Don't forget your conference next week.

Source: Herbert J. Klausmeier and William Goodwin, *Learning and Human Abilities,* 4th ed. (New York: Harper & Row, 1975), pp. 239–241.

BOX D *Realistic goal setting with the origin spelling game*

For the students in de Charms's personal causation training program, the spelling game was the most popular unit, and many of the teachers considered it the most successful one: "It taught them how to set a moderate goal. They learned immediately the dangers of setting one that's too high and also they learned that there is no satisfaction in setting one that's too low. . . . Also this was something easy to transfer to areas other than just the spelling game."

The spelling game was built around the sixth-grade spelling books that presented 20 new words each week. De Charms describes it as follows:

> On Monday the children took a pretest on the words for that week. Tuesday and Wednesday were devoted to practice in any way that the teacher or workbook suggested. Thursday was the day for the game. By Thursday the teacher had checked the Monday papers and had marked correct and incorrect words and kept the list herself. The children began by choosing two teams as in a traditional spelling bee. When they were ready, the teacher called the first member of team A.
>
> "John, what would you like to try, an easy word, a moderately hard word, or a hard word? If you spell the easy word correctly your team will receive 1 point. Correct spelling of the moderately

Personal Causation Training

De Charms describes personal causation as being the "origin" of one's behavior, as was noted previously in this chapter. An integral part of the origin concept is realistic goal setting. "Origins" are positively motivated persons who have feelings of confidence ("I can do it"), set their goals within their skill levels, feel a commitment to and strive for these goals, and take responsibility for their behavior. "Pawns" are negatively motivated persons; a pawn feels powerless and tries to protect his or her ability by setting unrealistically high or low goals. Personal causation training involves creating those conditions that will help students feel and behave like origins.

An origin classroom, according to de Charms (1976), is likely to be characterized by:

> . . . the teacher's warm acceptance of the children along with her firm, consistent rules and high expectations for their behavior. Controls from

hard word gives 2 points. Hard words result in 3 points. Incorrect spelling of any word results in no points and I will spell it for you."

John was faced with setting a goal, and unbeknownst to him the difficulty of the words was scaled according to his own ability. The teacher had in front of her his spelling paper from Monday. An easy word was one he spelled correctly on Monday; a moderately hard word, one he spelled incorrectly on Monday but had a chance to study; and, a hard word was from a future list tailored to his ability. John's teammates were allowed to consult with him on setting his goal, thus giving group support.

We decided not to tell the children the method of selection of words to see if they did, in fact, have more success with moderately difficult words and tend to choose them more often as time passed. The teachers were initially concerned that the children would think it unfair to change standards for each child, but their fears were quieted, as the children heartily approved. As the children said, even the worst speller could get two points for his team if he studied the words he missed. The teachers also wondered if the children would start looking at future spelling lists and apparently some did. In the context of the game this might be considered cheating, but hardly something to be discouraged.

Source: Richard de Charms, *Enhancing Motivation: Change in the Classroom* (New York: Irvington Publishers, 1976), pp. 72–73.

within the children are enhanced whenever possible, but external controls may be used when clearly designed to promote the good of the children. The goal is to convert external control to control from within. (p. 175)

To show how this classroom climate might be achieved, de Charms developed an extensive training program elementary school teachers can use to improve students' motivation. One of the most successful aspects of the program was a spelling game with the underlying purpose of helping students set realistic goals in their academic work (see Box D). Another part of the program which emphasized realistic goal setting involved training students in origin behaviors, specifically helping them to determine their own personal goals and to plan activities for achieving them. Over a five-week period, the students completed various exercises to help them think like origins. In one they were asked to set one goal for that day and to consider the activities necessary for reaching the goal, the help that might be needed, and the importance of taking responsibility for their own behavior. Other exercises asked them to consider the importance of their goals to themselves and to examine the goals in relation to their present levels of ability.

Based on their observations over an eight-week period, the students identified a set of eight characteristics that typify origin-like behavior. These included commitment to a task, work-oriented behavior, concentration and attentiveness, assumption of personal responsibility, creativity in artistic arrangements and illustrations, avoidance of overt anxiety and pretentious behavior, interaction with students and the teacher, and a capability to master problems and to cope with situations (de Charms, 1976, p. 118).

IMPROVING TEST CONDITIONS

A recurring aspect of classroom life is test taking, both teacher-made quizzes and standardized aptitude and achievement tests. For many children, a testing situation arouses extreme anxiety; they begin to doubt their ability, anticipate doing poorly, and engage in a variety of self-defeating thoughts prior to and during the test. For these children, such motivational problems are likely to interfere with test performance, so that, in all probability, the test will underestimate their true achievement. Some students try to get out of the testing situation as soon as possible by rushing through the questions. Others doubt their own knowledge and turn to guessing. Still others move so slowly and cautiously through the test in their efforts to avoid failure that they do not finish.

When poor test performance reflects motivational problems rather than learning deficits, the motivational conditions surrounding the test procedure must be reevaluated. Extensive research by Hill (1980) and associates has shown that changing or optimizing the testing conditions to reduce anxiety and pressure improves the performance of anxious children, particularly those from minority and low-income groups. Hill suggests three ways to improve the testing situation: (1) reduce the time pressures, (2) change the way a child reacts to difficult experiences during a test, and (3) familiarize the child with the mechanics of the test.

Stringent time pressures seem to be the principal reason for poor performance by anxious students. When time requirements are relaxed, performance improves substantially, and when time pressures are completely removed, anxious children work much faster and more accurately and cheat less. They have been found to solve more arithmetic problems more quickly than when they must work under time limits, for example. Time limits cannot always be avoided, however, particularly with standardized tests. To change the way failure is experienced while taking a test, students can be informed, in advance, of the difficulty of the test and told how to cope when they have trouble. They can be taught new cognitive strategies that emphasize effort and some type of self-instruction. Test performance also can be substantially improved by providing practice with the mechanics of the test in a relaxed setting, well in advance of the testing situation.

Hill's research has shown that anxious children often have the ability to do the work but perform poorly because of motivational difficulties. If the testing conditions are less than optimal, poor performance that results from learning problems cannot be separated from those that are due to motivational problems. Other suggestions for providing optimal testing conditions will be given in Chapter 16, for teacher-made tests, and Chapter 17, for standardized tests.

ATTRIBUTION TRAINING

Attribution training is most concerned with how students respond to failure. Some children react with increased persistence and actually improve their performance after they fail, while others give up and their achievement continues downward. Research by Dweck (1975, 1977) shows that it is not achievement or ability level that differentiates these two groups, but to what they attribute their failures. As we noted above in the section on attribution theory, children who persist after failure have high achievement motives and attribute their performance to a lack of effort. They believe they can change their performance: "If I try harder, I can do better." Children with low achievement motives continue to fail and blame this on their lack of ability. To them failure seems to be insurmountable; no matter how hard they try, they believe they cannot succeed: "I can't do it, and there is nothing I can do about it." Children who believe they lack the ability to succeed and cannot change the situation demonstrate a "helplessness" syndrome.

Attribution training or retraining is designed to help children who display helpless behaviors following failure. The purpose of these programs is to teach them to attribute their feelings to effort rather than ability. As a consequence of this training, they should respond to failure with increased effort and greater persistence—achievement behaviors that increase the likelihood of success.

In one study Dweck (1975) conducted 25 daily attribution retraining sessions with children who had been identified as "helpless." The children were allowed to experience both success and failure at working mathematics problems, and when they failed they were told that it was due to insufficient effort. At the conclusion of the training these children no longer gave up when they encountered failure; most actually improved their performance following failure. Based on attribution theory, the change in performance following failure occurred as a consequence of the change in attribution.

Other research on attribution training has shown that attributions can be modified through reinforcement procedures. Andrews and Debus (1978) verbally reinforced children for making effort attributions and cued them to the attribution when necessary, following success with "You really tried hard" and failure with "Sometimes we haven't worked hard enough." They also found that training increased the frequency with which these children attributed success or failure to their own efforts and increased their persistence when they encountered failure.

MOTIVATION IN THE INSTRUCTIONAL PROCESS

Motivation holds an equal position with learning and thinking as the major variables in the interactions between teacher and learner in the instructional process. Because the learner is not a passive recipient of learning but will act on it or react to it in many ways, as we noted in Chapter 1, the motivation of the learner is an essential part of the process. It is represented by the learner's disposition to learn, one of the student readiness characteristics which determines the possibility of effective teacher-student communication.

The instructional programs described in the preceding section suggest ways in which teachers can direct the motivation of students to accomplish their goals in the instructional process. They are based on the motivation principles described below, which can be viewed as strategies for enhancing students' motivation in the classroom. While these principles are stated in the form of imperatives or directions, they provide general guidelines for teachers rather than prescribing procedures to be followed rigidly.

1. *Reduce competition in the classroom.* Social comparison can be eliminated by having students work toward individually prescribed or group goals. Competition should be geared to the ability levels of the students so that all have a chance to succeed, and they should focus on their own past performance as they set new goals for themselves, rather than on what others are doing or have done. The goals should be concrete and measurable, and the grading system should be made contingent on meeting these goals. If performance expectations are communicated clearly, everyone knows the criteria for success. Grading on the curve should be avoided, to reduce competition; individual contracts and criterion-referenced tests can be used instead.

2. *Promote students' beliefs in their competence; encourage realistic goal setting.* Students are more success oriented if school tasks and assignments are matched to their abilities. Task analyses in which students' entry characteristics are assessed before they begin a task are one way to do this. The tasks should be neither too easy nor too hard, so they require some effort but are not frustrating. Success is made available to more students if they are allowed to learn at their own rates.

Students might write individual development plans or contracts to accomplish specific goals which are realistic in relation to their past performance. The teacher can help students gain a realistic view of their strengths and weaknesses, make sure the plans are complete, and anticipate most obstacles. The teacher also should offer praise for specific accomplishments and evaluate the plans as they are implemented, to provide evidence of success.

3. *Encourage students' effort attributions.* Students should be given individual feedback when they fail and shown concrete steps they can take to improve. Teachers can model how success is attributed to effort by describing personal experiences in which they accomplished tasks by trying hard to succeed. Students might read stories and biographies describing individuals who have accomplished goals through effort and discuss individually or in groups the reasons why people succeed or fail. The discussion should focus on how attitudes, interests, and efforts are related to succeeding. To emphasize the importance of effort in academic tasks, students should work on instructional units with short-range goals and receive points for doing more difficult work than they previously attempted.

4. *Provide for peer support for academic effort.* Students can help one another when they are divided into small groups for short topical discussions, to work on projects, or to assist each other with lessons. Various projects that will be evaluated, as well as nonevaluated activities such as planning a picnic, creating a poster, or participating in cooperative team games, should be provided.

5. *Increase students' involvement in learning.* Students should be given opportunities to select activities, assignments, due dates, and those with whom they want to work, as well as their own methods and pace of learning. They can be involved in relating the curriculum material to their own experiences and problems. Flexible time scheduling allows students to put as much effort into a learning experience as they wish. It is important that each student be allowed to contribute something to a group discussion or assignment. Individuals can be made responsible for different parts of a task, assigned to take various perspectives or positions in a discussion, or given different resource materials to use.

6. *Reduce anxiety in achievement situations.* Students must have sufficient time to complete assignments, tests, and other work so they do not worry

about them. They should have opportunities to practice taking tests and learn strategies for effective study and test taking. Performance expectations should be stated in concrete, measurable terms, and a variety of grading practices, including narrow categories (A, B, C or 70–80, 80–90) as well as broad categories (pass-fail), and some activities that are not evaluated or graded, should be used. Classroom rules that are kept short and simple and that communicate expected behaviors also help reduce anxiety. A relaxed classroom atmosphere can be developed by using good communication techniques and actively listening to student concerns.

7. *Provide for students' affiliation needs.* Varied procedures should be used for grouping students: according to shared interests, similar ability levels, friendship patterns, and at random, for example. They should have time to talk to each other about personal affairs as well as academic tasks. Games or activities that require team effort also help students satisfy their needs for affiliation and belonging.

CHAPTER 11 IN RETROSPECT

Motivation represents the "why" of behavior. It cannot be observed but must be inferred by observing the direction, intensity, and consistency of behavior over time. Both personal and situational factors affect behavior and help explain how it differs in and among people. Student motivation is related to the feedback they receive on performance and how it affects their feelings about themselves and the situation.

Needs theory is concerned with behavior that is directed toward goals to satisfy individual needs. In Maslow's theory, both physiological and psychological needs are arranged in a hierarchy in which lower-order needs must be satisfied before the highest-order need, self-actualization, can be attempted. This is a need to be autonomous and independent and to be able to master or adapt to the environment, as well as a belief in personal responsibility.

At the heart of achievement theory are two competing motives—the need for success and the desire to avoid failure. Measures of the magnitude of these needs or motives, devised by Atkinson and McClelland, made it possible to determine which is the stronger motive of the two for an individual. People with high achievement needs have a desire to achieve, and those with low achievement needs try to avoid achievement situations.

Attribution theory is concerned with the causal explanations people give to account for their success or failure. When persons high in achievement motivation succeed, they attribute it to their own ability or effort. If they fail, they believe the failure is due to a lack of effort. Those who are low in achievement motivation attribute success to external factors like luck or an easy task and failure to a lack of ability. Intrinsically motivated students undertake a learning task because they enjoy it, not for rewards such as grades or approval. To them a failure is just a minor setback to be overcome with a new approach.

Students' needs for affiliation, competence, and esteem can be frustrated or enhanced by the classroom climate and by teachers' expectations and evaluations of them, which are affected by the teachers' attributions or explanations for how students perform. A number of educational strategies aimed at preventing or alleviating motivational problems have been developed. Some involve modifications in the classroom environment, such as cooperative learning and Teams-Games-Tournaments; others, such as personal causation or attribution training, are more directly focused on changing students' thoughts and beliefs about success and failure.

QUESTIONS
FOR
DISCUSSION

1. What behaviors would lead a teacher, parent, counselor, etc., to suspect a child of having a high motivation to avoid failure? What kind of action plan might make the child more success motivated?
2. Recall recent situations in which you were (a) studying for a test, (b) involved in a game or contest, and (c) working on a project of your own choosing. What were your thoughts in each situation? How confident were you about succeeding? How important was it for you to do well? Were you worried about your performance? How did you plan the strategies you would use? How did you feel? Why do you think your thoughts and feelings were different or similar in these situations?
3. Maslow defines a hierarchy of five needs or motives. How can schools help students satisfy these needs? How do schools frustrate students' need satisfaction?
4. Imagine yourself in an achievement situation. What are you doing, thinking, and feeling in your fantasy?
5. Consider the following situation. Jackson and Allan are both having some difficulty in mathematics. But while Jackson believes he isn't doing well because he isn't trying hard enough, Allan believes he isn't doing well because he isn't very smart. How is the behavior of these two students likely to differ? Suppose their math teacher also believes that Allan isn't very capable and that Jackson isn't putting enough effort into his work. How do you think the teacher will behave toward each student?

**READINGS
FOR
REFLECTION**

Arkes, H., and Gaske, J. *Psychological Theories of Motivation.*
Belmont, Cal.: Wadsworth Publishing Co., 1977.

This excellent source book on the psychological theories of motivation describes eight basic motivational paradigms, from more classical biological and psychoanalytical approaches to cognitive consistency and causal attribution. It is useful as a starting point for any serious student of motivation.

Covington, Martin V., and Beery, R. G. *Self-Worth and School Learning.* New York: Holt, Rinehart & Winston, 1976.

This readable, short paperback on the self-worth theory of motivation postulates that students are motivated to enhance and protect a belief in their ability to succeed. The model draws heavily from attribution theory and presents theory, research, and many concrete suggestions for structural change in the classroom.

De Charms, Richard. *Enhancing Motivation: Change in the Classroom.* New York: Irvington Publishers, 1976.

A complete look at a motivation change project, from its inception to documentation of the results, is presented in this book, which gives theoretical background and suggests a wide variety of activities for classroom application. Of specific interest are the descriptions of the motivation training done with teachers and in classrooms.

Johnson, David W., and Johnson, Roger T. *Learning Together and Alone: Cooperation, Competition, and Individualization.* Englewood Cliffs, N.J.: Prentice-Hall, 1975.

These authors provide extensive information about the three types of goal structures—competitive, cooperative, and individualistic—and how to use them and evaluate the outcomes. Research on the outcomes of each type of goal structure is reviewed. This book provides the know-how for studying classroom learning environments and using cooperative learning in the classroom.

Maslow, Abraham. *Motivation and Personality.* 2nd ed. New York: Harper & Row, 1970.

Chapters 3 through 7 of this book offer a theory of motivation that is based on holistic and humanistic principles. This somewhat advanced reading provides a basic statement of self-actualization theory.

Weiner, Bernard. A theory of motivation for some classroom experiences. *Journal of Educational Psychology,* 1979, *71,* 3–26.

This important journal article presents a cognitive theory of motivation which explains how causal explanations for success and failure are related to students' attempts to maintain their self-esteem and achievement behaviors. Weiner is the foremost authority in the study of attribution theory in educational settings. Such topics as hopelessness, helping behaviors, liking, hyperactivity, mastery, and evaluation are included.

New Releases

Ames, Russell, and Ames, Carole (Eds.). *Research on Motivation in Education: Student Motivation.* New York: Academic Press, in press.

Nicholls, J. G. (Ed.). *The Development of Achievement Motivation.* Greenwich, Conn.: JAI Press, in press.

Stewart, A. J. (Ed.). *Motivation and Society.* San Francisco: Jossey-Bass, 1982.

REFERENCES

Ames, Carole. Children's achievement attributions and self-reinforcement: Effects of self-concept and competitive reward structures. *Journal of Educational Psychology,* 1978, *70,* 345–355.

Ames, Carole. Competitive versus cooperative reward structures: The influence of individual and group performance factors on achievement attribution and affect. *American Educational Research Journal,* 1981, *18,* 273–287.

Andrews, George, and Debus, Ray L. Persistence and causal perception of failure: Modifying cognitive attributions. *Journal of Educational Psychology,* 1978, *70,* 154–166.

Aronson, Elliot. *The Jigsaw Classroom.* Beverly Hills, Cal.: Sage Publications, 1978.

Atkinson, John W., and McClelland, David C. The projective expression of needs: II. The effect of different intensities of the hunger drive on thematic apperception. *Journal of Experimental Psychology,* 1948, *38,* 643–658.

Bloom, Benjamin S. *Human Characteristics and School Learning.* New York: McGraw-Hill, 1976.

Covington, Martin V., and Beery, R. G. *Self-Worth and School Learning.* New York: Holt, Rinehart & Winston, 1976.

De Charms, Richard. *Personal Causation: The Internal Affective Determinants of Behavior.* New York: Academic Press, 1968.

De Charms, Richard. *Enhancing Motivation: Change in the Classroom.* New York: Irvington Publishers, 1976.

DeVries, David L., and Edwards, Keith J. Learning games and student teams: Their effects on classroom process. *American Educational Research Journal,* 1973, *10,* 307–318.

Dweck, Carol S. The role of expectations and attributions in the alleviation of learned helplessness. *Journal of Personality and Social Psychology,* 1975, *31,* 674–685.

Dweck, Carol S. Learned helplessness and negative evaluation. *UCLA Educator,* 1977, *19,* 44–49.

Glasser, William L. *Schools without Failure.* New York: Harper & Row, 1969.

Gronlund, Norman E. *Sociometry in the Classroom.* New York: Harper & Row, 1959.

Hill, Kennedy T. Motivation, evaluation, and educational testing policy. In Leslie J. Fyans (Ed.), *Achievement Motivation.* New York: Plenum Press, 1980.

Johnson, David W. Student-student interaction: The neglected variable in education. *Educational Researcher,* 1981, *10,* 5–10.

Johnson, David W., and Johnson, Roger T. Instructional goal structure: Cooperative, competitive, and individualistic. *Review of Educational Research,* 1974, *44,* 213–240.

Johnson, David W., and Johnson, Roger T. Cooperative, competitive and individualistic learning. *Journal of Research and Development in Education,* 1978, *12,* 3–15.

Johnson, David W., and Johnson, Roger T. Cooperative learning: The power of positive goal interdependence. In R. Chasnoff (Ed.), *Structuring Cooperating Learning: The 1979 Handbook.* Minneapolis: Cooperation Network, 1979.

Klausmeier, Herbert J., Jeter, J. T., Quilling, M. R., and Frayer, D. A. *Individually Guided Motivation.* Madison: Wisconsin Research and Development Center for Cognitive Learning, 1973.

Mandler, George, and Sarason, Seymour B. A study of anxiety and learning. *Journal of Abnormal and Social Psychology,* 1952, *47,* 166–173.

Maslow, Abraham H. *Toward a Psychology of Being.* 2nd ed. New York: Van Nostrand Reinhold, 1968.

Maslow, Abraham H. *Motivation and Personality.* 2nd ed. New York: Harper & Row, 1970.

Matthews, K., Helmreich, R., Beane, W., and Lucker, G. W. Pattern A, achievement striving, and scientific merit: Does pattern A help or hinder? *Journal of Personality and Social Psychology,* 1980, *39,* 962–967.

McClelland, David C., Atkinson, John W., Clark, Russell A., and Lowell, Edgar L. *The Achievement Motive.* New York: Appleton-Century-Crofts, 1953.

Murray, Henry A. *Thematic Apperception Test Manual.* Cambridge: Harvard University Press, 1943.

Oden, Sherri, and Asher, Stephen R. Coaching children in social skills for friendship making. *Child Development,* 1977, *48,* 495–506.

Raynor, Joel O. Relationship between achievement-related motives, future orientation, and academic performance. *Journal of Personality and Social Psychology,* 1970, *15,* 28–33.

Rosenshine, B. Classroom instruction. In N. L. Gage (Ed.), *The Psychology of Teaching Methods.* 75th Yearbook of the National Society for the Study of Education, 1976.

Slavin, Robert E. Student teams and achievement divisions. *Journal of Research and Development in Education,* 1978, *12,* 39–49.

Wales, Charles E., and Stager, R. A. *Guided Design.* Morgantown: West Virginia University, Freshman Engineering Department, 1977.

Weiner, Bernard. A theory of motivation for some classroom experiences. *Journal of Educational Psychology,* 1979, *71,* 3–26.

Weiner, Bernard. *Theories of Motivation: From Mechanism to Cognition.* Chicago: Rand McNally, 1972.

Weiner, Bernard., Frieze, I., Kukla, A., Reed, L., Rest, S., and Rosenbaum, R. *Perceiving the Causes of Success and Failure.* Morristown, N.J.: General Learning Press, 1971.

Weiner, Bernard, and Kukla, Andy. An attributional analysis of achievement motivation. *Journal of Personality and Social Psychology,* 1970, *15,* 1–20.

White, Robert W. Motivation reconsidered: The concept of competence. *Psychological Review,* 1959, *66,* 297–333.

Learning-Instruction
Relationships

Our society sets two distinct productivity goals for the schools: to produce evidence of academic achievement by children and adolescents, and to produce self-directed learners who know how to plan and are responsible for their actions. In the 1980s the concern with conceptual development and learning seems to be the stronger of the two. Because it is not necessarily true that an instructional process that results in academic achievement also cultivates independence and self-directed learning, we will keep both of these types of goals in mind as we examine the relationships between the instruction and the learner in the process.

A decade or so ago, the emphasis in educational psychology was on meeting the needs of individual learners—not just their needs for academic achievement but their requirements for ego strength, a sense of identity, satisfying relations with others, and ability "to become." In the 1980s, in contrast, the principal concern is with how educational outcomes that can be directly and immediately measured are related to the ways classroom time is utilized. A likely research conclusion is that children learn more when they devote more time to academic pursuits and less time to the arts and other activities that cannot be measured on standardized achievement tests.

Planning activities with others in a group, deciding what learning tasks ought to be undertaken, and taking some responsibility for achieving those tasks do not help children learn arithmetic tasks, for example. When teachers are well organized and task oriented and lead the class as a group, increases in academic achievement that can be measured in relatively straightforward ways ought to be the outcome of the instructional process (see Chapters 16 and 17). But changes in children's abilities to make decisions for themselves or to profit from mistakes in planning tasks badly or failing to plan them at all are difficult if not impossible to measure quantitatively. Working on such skills and abilities in the classroom may appear untidy, compared with the orderly, organized environment of teacher-led classrooms (see Box A).

The central focus of this chapter is on the analysis of forms of instruction that produce academic learning outcomes. Generally these are the kinds which are called cognitive and which can be measured by standardized or teacher-made tests of academic achievement. School achievement of other types such as the learning of attitudes and values and of motives (considered in Chapters 9 and 11) are also significant factors in the instructional process, however.

The contemporary approaches to instruction that will be discussed in this chapter can be at least roughly classified according to how they attempt to deal with the range of individual differences in academic achievement. Some approaches, such as computer-assisted instruction,

BOX A   *What did you learn today in school, Tammy?*

Tammy is a student in a second-grade classroom. During the reading period children who are not in the group that the teacher is working with directly are to study by themselves. They can read, do arithmetic, or visit one of the several interest centers—the library, the science corner, and so on—in their interesting, pleasant classroom.

When Tammy works independently, she does not seem to be very efficient, however. She taps her pencil on her desk a lot and wanders around the classroom, and she doesn't always seem to know what to do.

Undoubtedly, if the teacher exercised more direct supervision, Tammy and her classmates would use their study time more productively. In D. C. Berliner's terms, *academic learning time* would be increased.[*] If the small increments of additional study time that would be realized each day were accumulated over a large number of such days, they would, presumably at least, result in increased achievement.

But probably the opportunities Tammy has as a second-grader to experience being an independent learner will contribute to her sense of autonomy and ability to assume responsibility. Studies of young children have shown that mothers' willingness to allow preschoolers independence, consistent with their age and stage of development, makes them more independent later.[†] It may be that this is a more enduring educational outcome for Tammy than the extra achievement that would result from additional direct instruction. This essentially is the issue addressed in this chapter.

---

[*]David C. Berliner, "Using Research on Teaching for the Improvement of Classroom Practice," *Theory into Practice*, vol. 19 (1980), pp. 302–308.

[†]Robert R. Sears, Eleanor E. Maccoby, and H. Lewin, *Patterns of Child Rearing* (Evanston, Ill.: Row, Peterson & Co., 1957).

aptitude-treatment interactions, and learning for mastery, try to individualize instruction to some degree. Others treat a classroom, particular subject matter, or same-grade-level students as essentially homogeneous groups in which achievement can be advanced by teaching aimed at the large middle (or average) segment. Examples are direct instruction and contingency management.

DIFFERENCES IN ACADEMIC ACHIEVEMENT

In the course of development in the various domains, human beings come to differ from one another in many ways, as we showed in Part I. Some of the most relevant differences for those interested in the education of children concern academic achievement. Even when particular segments of a school population are selected for special attention, as in the programs for academically talented and gifted children discussed in Chapter 5, the results are never homogeneous, as might be expected.

For example, Suppes (1964) found in an early study on computer-assisted instruction in arithmetic that the fastest student in a group of gifted learners completed the entire first-grade arithmetic curriculum in about four weeks, whereas the slowest one required about six weeks to reach the same point (see Figure 12.1). By the end of the seventh week, these two first-graders, both of whom were considered bright, were apart by almost a third of the second-grade curriculum, and Suppes was reluctant to forecast what the maximum separation between them would be after this class had continued for another couple of years. The rate at which these children were working problems and proceeding through the curriculum exceeded expectations, despite the teachers' efforts to discourage intensive competition. He concluded that "These comparisons are, I think, a fair representation of the very large differences to be expected among even very bright children when the rate of progress of the individual child is not tied to that of the group" (p. 81).

To determine the nature and extent of the range of differences in academic achievement, we will examine differences between or among groups and differences within members of a group. The first analysis compares ranges of differences in achievement among students in different countries, different parts of this country, or different schools and colleges. The concept of high school graduate, for example, can have a quite different meaning with regard to the amount of academic achievement it represents, depending upon which high school is being considered. Similarly, there are wide variations in achievement within a classroom or at the same academic level within a school.

Figure 12.1

*Progress of fastest and slowest
of 40 gifted mathematics students*

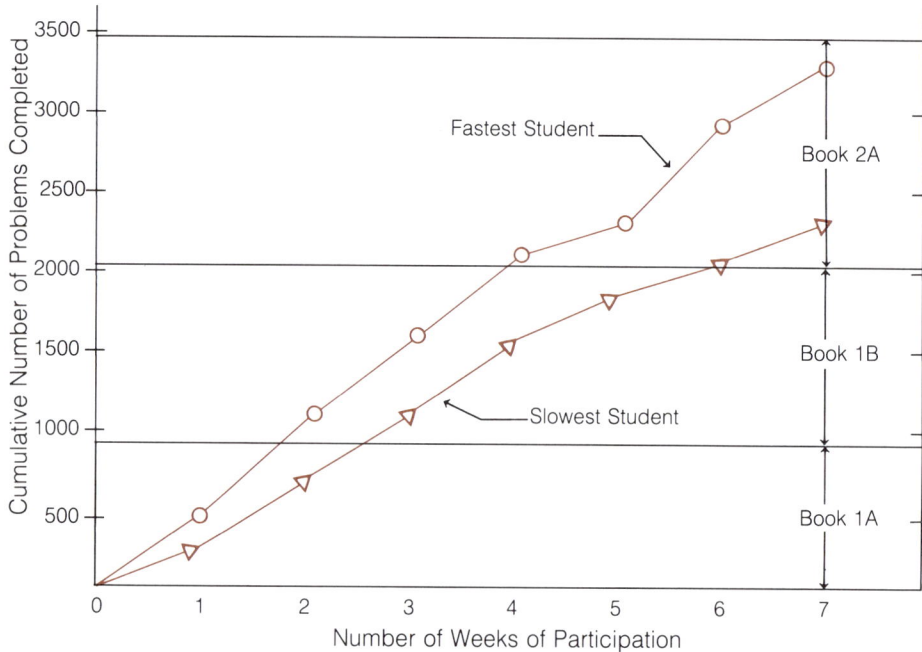

Source: Patrick Suppes, "Modern Learning Theory and the Elementary School
Curriculum," *American Educational Research Journal*, vol. 1, no. 2 (1964), p. 81.
Copyright 1964, American Educational Research Association, Washington, D.C.

DIFFERENCES IN ACADEMIC
ACHIEVEMENT AMONG GROUPS

One of the best known reports on education in the United States was
based on a study by Learned and Wood (1938; summarized in Willerman, 1979), who tested thousands of high school and college students
in Pennsylvania. One of their broadly based tests of academic achievement, consisting of more than 1,200 multiple-choice items, revealed conclusively that the number of years students had attended high school
and college was an imperfect predictor of their level of general culture.
When they considered achievement at the 80th percentile for college

seniors as the criterion for college graduation and disregarded the actual year in college, they found this "graduating class" would consist of 28 percent of the seniors in their sample, 21 percent of the juniors, 19 percent of the sophomores, and 15 percent of the freshmen (size differences among the classes account for a total below 100 percent). Moreover, the top 10 percent of the high school seniors scored better than 75 percent of the college sophomores, and higher than 50 percent of the college seniors on this test.

Learned and Wood also examined educational achievement of college students by major and found that engineering students scored highest. Students preparing to teach high school were found to be poorly prepared. According to Willerman (1979), "Learned and Wood point out that a large proportion of these prospective high school teachers knew less than many of the high school students that they would soon be teaching. They doubted that these teachers were of the intellectual caliber to be successful high school teachers" (p. 173).

More recent investigations have made different comparisons, but they also verify the wide variation in educational attainment. Bloom (1974) summarized a host of studies of education in rural and urban and national and international settings and reported some striking similarities. In studies of educational achievement in the United States that had been published in the mid-1950s, for example, the mean educational achievement of students in the state with the highest attainment was 1 standard deviation higher than the mean achievement in the poorest-scoring state. Another way to express the relationship is that students in the state with the lowest achievement records reached only an eighth-grade education level for 12 years invested in schooling, compared to students in the state with the highest achievement records. More or less the same 8:12 ratio was found in comparisons of achievement between the most and least favored schools and communities in the United States.

According to Bloom's interpretation of the International Study of Educational Achievement, in which researchers from 12 countries participated (Harnqvist, 1975), the same result—eighth-grade achievement for 12 years of schooling—also describes the achievement relationships between the highest and lowest scoring developed nations. If developing nations are included in the data, the level diminishes to sixth-grade achievement for the lowest scoring nations.

DIFFERENCES IN ACADEMIC ACHIEVEMENT WITHIN GROUPS

Differences within groups include the range of differences among students at a certain grade level in a school, or the range a teacher might encounter in a particular group or class of students. According to Bloom

(1974), if elapsed time is used as the measure of learning rate, the slowest learning pupil will require roughly five times as long to learn a task as the fastest learner.

Most classroom teachers at either the elementary or the secondary level can expect pupils' achievement levels to vary by at least three or four years, and they may vary by six or eight years. Special grouping arrangements may reduce the variation, but they cannot eliminate it. Individual differences in educational achievement and rate of learning for new content are a fact of school life, and programs of instruction must take them into account. Thomas and Thomas (1965) analyzed the achievement test scores of a fifth-grade class in a working-class school, for example, and found that only a few achievement scores were at the fifth-grade level. Some fell a year below, and about an equal number were a year or two above grade level. A small number of these fifth-graders were achieving at the ninth-grade level or beyond in reading, mathematics, social studies, and science.

RELEVANT VARIABLES IN INSTRUCTIONAL METHODS

Two types of variables affect instructional methods most directly. One is the nature of the learning task, and the other is related to how much time is allotted to study and learning, as well as how the time is used.

TASK ANALYSIS

Analysis of the nature of a learning task reveals the sequential or hierarchical characteristics of what is to be learned, which helps determine the order of the instruction. Suppose the task is long division, that is, division in which the divisor has at least two digits. The student must be taught how to set up the division example, find a trial quotient, place the product beneath the appropriate two or more first digits of the divisor, find the remainder, and so forth. The obvious starting point is estimating a trial quotient.

Tasks that are sequential may also involve hierarchies. In teaching the sequence of long division, it is assumed that the student already has mastery of the various intellectual skills and number facts required to complete the exercise. A simple step like estimating a trial quotient can only be accomplished if the student already has the skills of division, multiplication, and subtraction, as well as a concept of place value. The process of long division therefore is hierarchical in the sense that some intellectual skills are necessary before others can be learned. In the same way, children's difficulties with long division involving decimals have less to do with the added requirement of working with decimals than with the fact that they have failed to master the process of long division of whole numbers.

TIME AS A CENTRAL VARIABLE IN SCHOOL LEARNING

Some college students use their time efficiently; they listen carefully to lectures, take good notes, study with concentration, and can work for long stretches without apparent effort or fatigue. To others, study must be punctuated by long walks, coffee breaks, or socializing with friends. Other things being equal, in elementary and secondary school as in college, the person who studies attentively and at length obviously learns more than the student who studies less.

A model of school learning in which time is a central variable was proposed by Carroll (1963), who reasoned that how much of a task students learn depends on how much time they actually spend on it in relation to how much time they would need to master it. The amount of time a learner requires to learn is determined by:

1. The learner's aptitude for the task—a student with a high aptitude for learning French vocabulary requires relatively less time than one with a low aptitude, for example.
2. The learner's ability to understand instruction, which consists of general intelligence and verbal skills—the higher these are, the less is the time needed to learn.
3. The quality of instruction.

Theoretically, the time required to learn will be the least for any student when the quality of instruction is the highest. But this variable interacts with the aptitude and ability variables, so that the quality of instruction has unequal effects on students of different abilities. The higher the student's ability, the less is the impact of low-quality instruction.

Two other variables which are measurable in time and which also affect the degree of learning are opportunity to learn, defined as the amount of time the school provides for the learner to study a given task, and perseverance, the amount of time the student actually spends in studying. Suppose Jon is assigned the task of learning the meaning of 20 French words. He could master them in an hour of fairly concentrated study, but the teacher provides only the final 15 minutes of the day's French period for individual study. If Jon is to master the task, he must persevere; that is, he must devote another hour to his preparation for tomorrow's class. Opportunity to learn and perseverance are basic to the mastery learning model, to be described in a later section.

INDIVIDUALIZED METHODS OF INSTRUCTION

Individualized instructional programs are designed to take account of the knowledge base and intellectual strengths and limitations of individual learners. In terms of the first dimension of the instructional process described in Chapter 1, they focus on the individual learner's stage of cognitive development, prior knowledge, and level of intelligence, as well as the learner's disposition to learn. Contemporary programs that utilize individualized methods include computer-assisted instruction, aptitude-treatment interactions, and mastery learning.

COMPUTER-ASSISTED INSTRUCTION

Computer-based learning programs developed out of the earlier programmed instruction which was based on the application of operant conditioning principles to teaching procedures (see Chapter 8). Because modern computers have extensive memory capability and easy access for purposes of retrieval, it is not necessary for a computer-based instructional program to offer the same sets of stimuli and responses to each learner who uses it. Use of the computer frees individual learners from being held in check by slower-learning classmates or being forced ahead before they have mastered necessary background concepts or skills. The learning curves of the fastest and slowest gifted learners who used a computed-based program for a fifth-grade mathematics curriculum, as shown in Figure 12.1 above, are evidence of this effect. Thus, although computers have been mostly used to provide drill and practice, they can offer much greater flexibility in instructional methods.

The rush to develop and disseminate computers and computer-assisted instruction (CAI) programs for educational purposes began in the 1960s. Much of this investment in time and resources was based on expectations for rapid diffusion and adoption of computer-assisted instruction, which did not occur at that time. The problems of producing suitable, affordable computers (hardware) and appropriate, effective learning programs (software, or courseware, the term used in education) were too complex, even when they were adequately financed. The early promise of CAI as a major influence in the classroom began to fade, though some programs, such as Suppes's (1964) computer-assisted instructional program in mathematics and a computer program in beginning reading developed by Atkinson (1972), were quite successful.

Continued work on CAI hardware and software was stimulated in 1971, when the National Science Foundation undertook the support of two major computer-assisted instructional projects. One of these was Programmed Logic for Automated Teaching Operations (PLATO), de-

*As computers become more available and easier to use, the
school's long-standing objective of meeting individual
differences may be easier to accomplish.*

veloped at the University of Illinois. Plans were to make PLATO accessible to a million or more users and to utilize communication by satellite (Bunderson & Faust, 1976).

With improvements in technology, the price of computers has been greatly reduced. At least three major difficulties still stand in the way of widespread acceptance of computer-assisted instruction, however. One is the unavailability of a variety of proven educational programs as computer courseware. Teachers must be prepared to evaluate the numerous programs that are being produced in response to this need, particularly in regard to how a program reflects theories on learning, cognitive development, and other aspects of educational psychology (Dean, 1982).

A related problem is the lack of a computer language that developers and authors of instructional materials can use without having to become proficient in computer programming. Teachers also should be able to create or adapt materials for computer use in their own classrooms. BASIC is the most common programming language in education; it is compact, easy to use, and suitable for solving computational problems, but it is clumsy in applications to words and language. Furthermore, it comes in various versions which are not interchangeable. Some proficiency in this language is necessary for those who use computers in the classroom, however (Dean, 1982). Other languages, such as PILOT, PASCAL, and LOGO, hold promise for some educational purposes.

The third obstacle to computer use in the classroom may be more obstinate, since it will not yield to improvements in technology. This difficulty is teachers' objections to the use of computers in education. Many teachers do not understand computers, and they are apprehensive that the devices will usurp the teacher's historic role in the instructional process. Skinner (1954) anticipated, correctly, the same objection from teachers when he introduced the concept of programmed instruction and teaching machines (see Chapter 8). In Skinner's view, the purpose of the teaching machine was to free the teacher to perform those educational acts that require the touch of a human being, though he did not suggest what those acts are.

Perhaps even more threatening is Christopher Evans's (1979) suggestion that the value of computers is not so much what they can teach as the way they can teach it. He proposes that the new generation of teaching computers will be "genuinely smart"—that is, able to adjust their responses constantly. By structuring their communication to fit the situation, they will give students the impression that they are "interested" in teaching. Such interaction is much closer in spirit to the way instructors and learners exchange information than the teaching machine was. Evans notes that a technology capable of providing interactive personal teaching is available; the need is to determine the best methods for doing so and the effectiveness of these methods when they are put into practice.

In any case, as Bunderson and Faust (1976) observe, "the teacher's role is radically changed—though not necessarily for the worse—when computers are introduced in a substantial manner into the instructional process. They become managers, helpers, provokers to creativity, instructional developers, and serve less as a kind of delivery system" (p. 89). In effect, the teacher's role is oriented more to consultation than to the traditional leadership function to be described in Chapter 13.

APTITUDE-TREATMENT INTERACTIONS

Another aspect of individualized instruction that has been examined is aptitude-treatment interactions, based on the idea that an instructional program may yield different achievement results for students with a particular ability or aptitude than it yields for students as a whole. Students who are more independent, for example, may achieve comparatively more in a social studies inquiry program, because the inquiry method provides opportunities for students to set their own goals, discover relevant information, interpret it, and so on (Peterson, 1979). This does not mean that an inquiry approach to the teaching of social studies is superior for all students, merely that independent students perform better in this program than students do on the average.

The idea of aptitude-treatment interaction (ATI) is not new. Such educational platitudes as "There is no single best method" and "It depends upon the nature of the learner" have been around for years. Cronbach and Snow's (1977) extensive review acknowledges the existence of ATIs but cautions that knowledge and understanding of these interactions is limited, and no such interactions have been "so well confirmed that they can be used directly as guides to instruction."

As we noted in Chapter 6, some theories about the nature of human intelligence and how it is measured consider it to be a single unitary ability, and others regard it as composed of a group of primary mental abilities or a large number of separate intellectual factors. Cronbach and Snow found that in interactions between intelligence and instructional treatments, general ability was a better predictor of achievement outcome than specialized abilities. They concluded that "tests of general ability relate to subsequent performance in just about the way achievement tests at the start of the course do" (p. 497). Therefore little if any better prediction of achievement should result from replacing tests of general intelligence with tests of more specialized ability and using the results as a basis for adapting instruction to the learner. This is particularly true for low-achieving students.

Another fundamental question about aptitude-treatment interactions is whether individual differences in achievement can be reduced or eliminated by fitting instruction to the learner more closely. Cronbach and Snow argue that they cannot, because of the pervasive correlation of general ability with learning outcomes.

Aptitude-treatment interactions can occur for personality traits as well as for intellectual abilities. Research has found correlations between teacher and student beliefs and achievement in college psychology courses, for example. At the elementary school level, it has been found that anxious students achieve better under the supervision of self-controlled teachers, compared to teachers whose styles are more spontaneous or who are themselves obviously anxious.

Although the findings of aptitude-treatment interaction research fall short of providing dependable generalizations on which instructional principles can be based, two points are clear. One is that such interactions exist, and some of the areas in which they occur are known. The other is that as understanding of how to conduct fruitful research in this area grows, the validity of the findings will improve. Today's student of educational psychology may not derive much direct benefit from the current level of knowledge, but ATI is an important area to monitor for the future.

MASTERY LEARNING

It is Benjamin Bloom's (1974, 1976) contention that, for basic learning skills, virtually all pupils—perhaps as many as 95 percent—can master what is ordinarily achieved by only the top 20 or 30 percent of learners. As a rationale he cites Carroll's formulation of the relationships between time and learning which was described in the preceding section. The learner's general intellectual ability, especially in the early stages of learning, is a major determinant of how fast learning occurs. It has been estimated that the fastest 5 percent of learners master new material about five times as rapidly as the slowest 5 percent do. But the assumption exists that, given sufficient time, most other learners could learn as well what the fastest 5 percent learns. One major reason many learners fail, according to this conception, is that they are not allowed adequate time to master the first lesson before they must learn a second, and a third, and so on. To the degree that learning is sequential, that is, later learning depends on earlier learning, failure to master the early lessons will have harmful effects on learning later in the series. In theory, at least, this effect can be alleviated by ensuring that the learner who does not initially master a task is given the time and help needed to do so before undertaking learning on a subsequent task.

Classroom procedures for mastery learning consist of the following steps:

1. A pretest over the course or unit is administered to the entire class.
2. The teacher uses ordinary means of instruction to teach the first section or unit of the course.
3. A test over the first section or unit is administered to the class.
4. Students who do not achieve mastery on the test receive instruction by means of alternative materials on just those portions of the unit with which they had difficulty.
5. An alternate form of the test is administered.
6. Steps 4 and 5 are repeated as necessary.

The example of mastery learning given in Box B illustrates how the model operates and suggests some of the practical issues for the instructor when it is used in the instructional process.

Some Practical Questions about the
Mastery Learning Model

Few educators would quarrel with the goal of mastery learning. They have been searching for years for ways to increase the proportion of students who benefit from instruction. The promise of the mastery learning model is great, but there has not been sufficient experience, especially with intact classes over extended periods such as an entire school year, on which to base firm conclusions.

Some of the questions about mastery learning are persistent problems in the conduct of classroom teaching for which no satisfactory solutions have been designed. The fact that the mastery learning model also encounters some of these problems does not mean that it is unworkable. Teachers also may resist implementing mastery learning techniques if they perceive the model as disturbing their daily routine or imposing additional burdens of materials preparation and record keeping.

One of the most difficult managerial problems this model poses for the teacher is the need to have available several alternative forms of instructional material and tests. It is not likely that a student who did not learn from the initial materials will learn much better by repeating them. Repeating the same test, given the rather brief time intervals between tests, maximizes the effects of memory and practice on test scores and overestimates the students' mastery of the content on the second administration. To expect teachers to prepare alternative materials and tests of their own may be unrealistic, however.

Another problem is what to do with the early masters while the non-masters are receiving additional instruction. If the teacher halts instruction on the topic until the slower learners have caught up, this seems to impose an arbitrary limit on the rate at which the faster children can advance. And what are the faster learners to do during the interval? It is one thing if legitimate enrichment or extended activities are available to challenge these learners, and quite another if they are simply asked to mark time and wait for their slower peers to catch up.

If the teacher permits the original masters to continue with the course, however, the learners in the classroom will soon be spread out over a number of units. In short order, it may be necessary to teach a class in which each pupil is operating at his or her own rate of speed and the instruction is highly individualized. From the standpoint of learning that may be a very effective solution, but most classrooms are not organized to allow such extensive individualization.

Whichever of these alternatives (or others) a teacher selects, certain conditions are necessary if the long-range outcomes of mastery learning are to be positive. The necessary organizational structures must be in place, and the instructional and testing materials must be provided in

BOX B *Mastering matrix arithmetic*

The power of the mastery learning model in presenting instruction in matrix arithmetic was demonstrated in a brief, small-scale investigation by Lorin W. Anderson. For this study 90 eighth-grade students were randomly assigned to three classroom groups of 30 each. One class was treated as a mastery class, and the other two were taught in traditional, or nonmastery, fashion. Three arithmetic lessons were taught on consecutive days; the first dealt with the terminology of matrix arithmetic, the second with special issues, and the third with operations (addition and subtraction). After each lesson, the children took a test on its content, and 80 percent correct (16 of 20 test items) was set as the mastery level.

In the two nonmastery classes, a record was kept of how many students failed to achieve mastery after each lesson, but no further instruction was given. In the mastery class, however, the teacher used the following procedure. Students who had not achieved mastery after a lesson were given *alternative instructional materials* to study that were keyed to the parts of the test they failed. As each child finished studying, he or she took an *alternative form of the test* which consisted only of items keyed to the content that had not been mastered in the first place.

An example might be a girl who passed on 14 items and failed on 6 items in the test given after the first lesson. She

sufficient quantities and in a form that can be used easily and routinely by classroom teachers.

Another major consideration is not only of practical significance, but the workability of the model hinges on it. A principal assumption on which mastery learning is based is that learners who do not at first master new content can do so if they are given additional time in which to study and are provided with alternative forms of instruction. This assumption is based on Carroll's concept of opportunity to learn described above; that is, the school may not give everyone sufficient time to master content, so more time must be provided. His concept of perseverance also enters in, for unless the learner uses the additional opportunity, no learning will result. Perseverance is a motivational concept; students who fail to learn something the first time are normally those who are most reluctant to invest additional time in learning. The A student who can would receive instructional material geared to the content covered in the six items she missed. After she studied that material, she would take six new test items based on the content. Her score on this second test would be added to the first. If the sum equaled 80 percent or more, she would have mastered the lesson. If she still did not reach mastery, a second alternative test and a second alternative instructional procedure, peer tutoring by a student who had mastered the content, would be made available.

Several results of this study help explain the mastery learning model. One is that an estimate of arithmetic achievement that correlated highly with students' achievement on the first lesson did not correlate well with results for mastery learning by the end of the third lesson. By the third lesson, also, students in the mastery class who had not initially met the criterion required no more time to study the lesson than students in any of the groups who had attained mastery from the original instruction. Theoretically, therefore, if additional time and help are made available *early* in the course of instruction to learners who need them, their learning of later parts of the overall task (which may be a course or extended unit) should proceed much like that of the other students.

Source: Lorin W. Anderson, "An Empirical Investigation of Individual Differences in Time to Learn," *Journal of Educational Psychology,* vol. 68 (1976), pp. 226–233.

solve all the geometry problems wants more of them to work on, while the pupil who fails a geometry test is not likely to respond positively to the offer to spend more time trying to learn the material.

There is another practical problem that educators have grappled with for generations. One reason students fail is that they do not come to school regularly, and when they are in school they have added difficulty in learning what they encounter because they have missed so much. That encourages them to stay away from school more. Some students create vicious circles of this sort for themselves. But mastery learning may help solve this problem. Bloom has made it clear that it can help slower students catch up within a matter of additional hours of instruction, so their academic deficits need not be strung out over years. The best time to implement a mastery learning model is at the beginning of a course of instruction, and it should be continued only so long as it is useful.

That added opportunity to learn and extra help will pay dividends if they are provided at the beginning of instruction has been found in small-scale studies such as the one by Anderson (1976) described in Box B. Larger-scale classroom studies that involve students with long-standing histories of failure are needed before conclusions can be reached about the motivational effects of the mastery learning model. Mastery learning should prove to be more successful with young children than with adolescents, because older students may have greater academic deficits and a history of failure that make it more difficult for them to respond to additional opportunities to learn and assistance with the learning. If the additional help of mastery learning could only be given to very young children who are just beginning to experience difficulty or to older ones, the odds would greatly favor helping the young child.

GROUP INSTRUCTION METHODS

The most typical classroom instruction method probably consists of a teacher working face to face with a group of about 25 to 30 students. The goals toward which the teacher and students are working could vary, but they undoubtedly involve some kind of academic achievement. While the style or form of instruction is not fixed, there is sure to be discussion or recitation led by the teacher, with roughly equal proportions of individual study or seatwork (Good & Beckerman, 1978). The teacher's instructional roles thus include leading discussions, imparting information, tutoring, and supervising students' study.

Hundreds of thousands of classrooms are functioning at any one time, and there is really no way to know how instruction is being presented in all of them or which method is dominant. There is no central classroom monitoring service to provide such data. When we piece together reports of how instruction is conducted that have appeared in the professional and research literature, however, the picture is similar to the one described above. Over the years, there has been a striking consistency to the reports. When Stevens (1912) studied high school classrooms in New York City, the teachers were asking questions so rapidly she wondered when the students found time to think. More than half a century later, Bellack and others (1966) concluded that the teacher's major task in the classroom was "soliciting" (asking questions) and the student's job was to "respond" (answer them). Summary studies of classroom recitation, such as Dale and Raths (1945) and Hoetker and Ahlbrand (1969), found these patterns to be both persistent and pervasive. The dominant method when a teacher interacts with a classroom group of students, as specified in the second dimension of the instructional process, is direct instruction in which the teacher presents the instruction and the students collectively receive it.

DIRECT INSTRUCTION

Definitions of direct instruction vary; for Good (1979), for example, the image is active teaching:

> A teacher sets and articulates the learning goals, actively assesses student progress, and frequently makes class presentations illustrating how to do assigned work. Direct instruction does not occur when teachers do not actively present the process or concept under study, when they fail to supervise student seatwork actively, or if they do not hold students accountable for their work. (p. 55)

Although direct instruction does not prescribe how teachers should teach, it does have certain common characteristics. The emphasis is on defined educational goals, those that can be tested by standardized achievement tests and batteries (see Chapter 17). The instruction is focused, and in line with Ausubel's theory of meaningful school learning (see Chapter 7), the students' roles are to listen, observe, read, study, and incorporate into their existing cognitive structures the meanings in the material to be learned.

As a general approach to the instructional process, direct instruction increases the time students devote to learning tasks. Because the teacher is usually directing the entire group, in either an instructional or supervisory capacity, the students have few opportunities to socialize or waste time. There is abundant evidence to support the commonsense notion that learners achieve more when they devote more time to their studies (Good, 1979; Gage, 1978; McDonald, 1976; Stallings, 1977). The measurable effects of direct instruction seem to demonstrate superior academic achievement, compared to less formal, more open educational arrangements. But objectives that can be measured by standardized achievement tests do not represent the full array of educational goals in which the society takes an interest, as Part III will demonstrate.

The Persistence of Direct Instruction

Direct instruction continues to dominate in the nation's classrooms, despite instructional innovations such as programmed instruction, team teaching, open classrooms, differentiated staffing, and many others. Good (1979) suggests that a major reason for the survival of direct instruction is that it works. That is true, but an understanding of why it works is fundamental to our perception of the instructional process.

Teachers are influenced by the way in which they were themselves taught as children, as we noted in Chapter 1, and most teachers today

grew up with the expectation that instruction occurs in self-contained classrooms. The teacher is in charge of the classroom, which means that he or she is responsible (or *accountable*, as the term will be used in Chapter 18) for what takes place there. Most instructional innovations would alter the situation in which the teacher has to work, without providing a new role for the teacher or altering the teacher's responsibilities as they are perceived by the teacher, the school system, and society as a whole.

If an innovation like computer-assisted instruction, for example, were thoroughly implemented in a classroom, all the pupils would soon be working on completely different tasks in each subject area. This adaptation to accommodate individual differences among children would mean a fundamental change in the way the students and the teacher work together. Even if there are provisions for a management system to keep the teacher informed of the goals and progress of each child, the traditional instructional role of the teacher would be greatly changed. Individualized methods would predominate over large-group or small-

No single instructional style or method achieves all educational objectives equally well. Children may gradually learn to plan and to make decisions more effectively if they are given some freedom of choice. Direct instruction seems to favor acquisition of those cognitive goals that are ordinarily measured by standardized tests of achievement.

group instruction, and the classroom setting would be greatly altered to allow children to work at terminals and carrels. The management capacity of the teacher also would be changed, as we noted above. Instead of managing a large group or at most several small groups of students, the teacher would direct most interactions to individual children.

From the point of view of learning, the effects of such changes in the instructional process may well be positive, and they probably would improve the academic achievement of students. Unless the total context of schooling is also changed, however, the diffusion of educational innovations will be resisted. To promote their acceptance, or at least their consideration, teacher education programs ought to be developed that thoroughly examine variations in the way instruction is delivered and provide training in their use and effects. Teachers need to know how evaluations of instruction can be achieved with these new methods, how instruction proceeds with them, and what the expectations are for the behavior of the teacher. When these teacher education programs are transferred to school settings, teacher behavior is more likely to be guided by the specialized knowledge and skills they have learned, and their resistance to change will be lessened. Until expectations about teacher behavior undergo this transformation, the method of direct instruction can be expected to continue to be the dominant one in U.S. classrooms.

CONTINGENCY MANAGEMENT

Contingency management describes a type of group instruction which is based on attempts of classroom teachers to bring about changes in the behaviors of pupils through the application of operant conditioning principles. As Skinner (1972) observed, operant conditioning can be applied not only to academic learning but to the teacher's other major obligation of classroom management or control. Reinforcement is administered for desirable behaviors, and when students are in their seats, attending to academic work and not interrupting classmates, their academic achievement will improve, even though teachers do not use operant conditioning procedures directly on the children's study habits, methods of acquiring and processing information, and so on. In this sense, contingency management facilitates academic achievement.

Contingency Management in Inner-City Schools

The Atlanta (Georgia) public schools provided an effective demonstration of the ability of classroom teachers to bring about changes in the behaviors of pupils by applying operant conditioning principles over the course of an entire school year (Rollins et al., 1974). Results of the program, called Project Success Environment, provide evidence that student behavior can be shaped and maintained for a protracted time, not just in brief demonstration periods, and that with minimum training competent teachers can successfully use educational innovations.

The project was conducted in four public schools on the fringe of inner-city Atlanta—a middle school and its three feeder elementary schools. Over 700 children were involved. The population of the schools was black; educational achievement was low, and many of the children came from poor homes. The families of over half of the pupils enrolled in one of the elementary schools had annual incomes below $2,000.

The 16 experimental teachers, who volunteered to participate in the project, were given three weeks of training in behavior modification and individual instruction. An early task was to specify simple rules for appropriate classroom behavior. Elementary teachers agreed on:

1. Stay in your seat.
2. Work hard.
3. Pay attention.
4. Raise your hand to speak.

Each teacher was free to interpret the rules to suit a particular class.

Teachers were asked to use the policy of "ignore and praise." Children's behaviors that were appropriate to the well-defined classroom rules were to be reinforced, and inappropriate acts were *not* to be punished, but ignored. In situations that might require the teacher's intervention, "time out" could be called, and children could be separated from the group for a time.

At the outset several types of reinforcers, including M and M candies, were given to the children on a continuous and somewhat predictable schedule. After several days, reinforcements were given much more intermittently and unpredictably. Rewards could be "bought" with cards, marked by the teacher, which at first were filled by 25 checks but eventually required 150. During the third and fourth months of the project, the rewards were gradually shifted from tangible items to activities. Children could turn in their check cards for school time in an activity room, where there were games, toys, records, and so on matched to their developmental interests. There was little effect on the children's behavior when the tangible reinforcements were discontinued, perhaps because the shift was made very slowly and the children were informed that a change was coming some weeks in advance. A principal difficulty with the use of token economies in school (see Chapter 8) has been the failure of the conditioned behavior to hold up when the tokens are no longer forthcoming.

Classrooms were arranged as a mastery center and five special-interest centers or stations, and pupils in a class were divided into three groups by ability. While one group received instruction and a second worked at completing its assignments, the third was able to move among the interest centers. These included library corners, a place for science materials, one with art supplies, a communications center, and one with games and puzzles. This not only provided variety in learning activities but permitted the teacher to interact with the students on an individual or small-group basis.

Effects of the Program Behavioral observations conducted in project and control classes often during the experimental years of Project Success Environment revealed that project teachers administered significantly more positive reinforcement to their pupils and significantly fewer punishments, compared to teachers in control classrooms. The frequency of disruptions by children diminished sharply in the experimental classrooms, and disturbances remained relatively low throughout the school year (see Figure 12.2). Observation of pupil attention supported the assumption that the greater the involvement of students in academic tasks, the better their learning will be. Children in the project

Figure 12.2

Mean number of disruptions per 15 minutes by grade-level groups in Project Success Environment

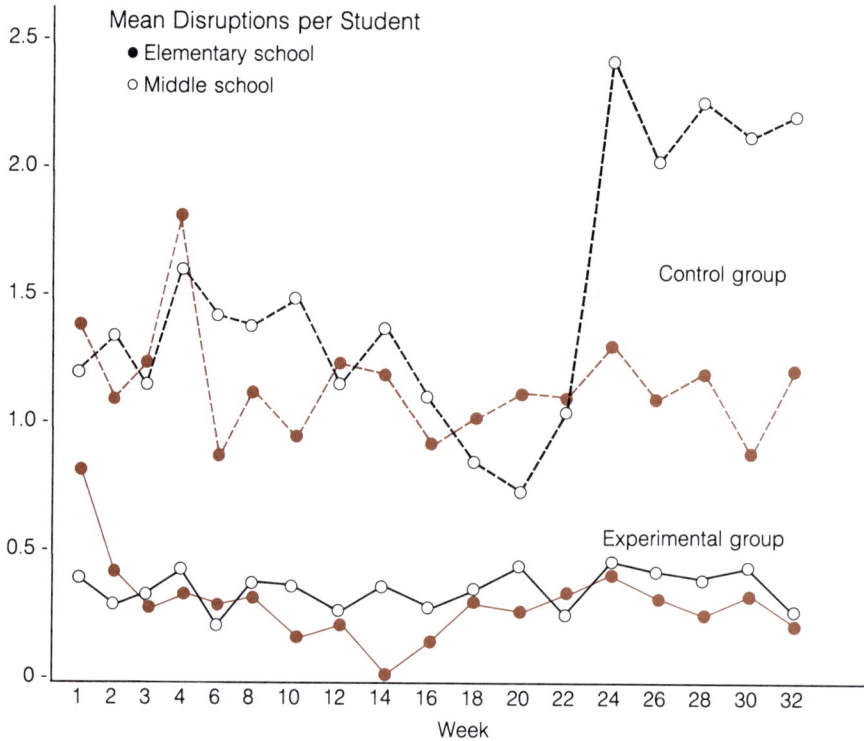

Source: Adapted from H. A. Rollins, B. R. McCandless, Marion Thompson, and W. R. Brassell, "Project Success Environment: An Extended Application of Contingency Management in Inner-City Schools," *Journal of Educational Psychology*, vol. 66 (1974), p. 174. Copyright 1974 by the American Psychological Association. Adapted by permission of the authors.

classes increased their involvement from about 75 to more than 90 percent; no appreciable change in attention was observed in the control classes.

Academic achievement in reading and arithmetic was measured at the start and the end of the school year in both project and control classes. For all grade levels, the mean gain for both subjects in project classes was 0.69 year, just double the 0.34 year's gain made by the control children. While the project children were well below the average gain in one school year of 1.00 year in academic growth for the population as a whole, they were still appreciably ahead of the controls. Repeated scores on the California Test of Mental Maturity were higher for project than for control children, except at the first-grade level.

Thompson et al. (1974) points out that of the 16 experimental teachers, all but one, in their view, were able to make contingency management work in the classroom. Thus the principles of operant conditioning apparently can be mastered and applied consistently and continuously by most ordinary teachers. A subsequent study with elementary teachers essentially repeated the findings; student disruptions were decreased and student involvement or attention increased by about 50 percent, compared with control classes. Most of the teachers were able to implement the contingency management procedures, though the in-service training was minimal.

BEYOND ACADEMIC ACHIEVEMENT

In some ways contingency management as an instructional method is very close to direct instruction, which has been found to improve academic achievement. When Peterson (1979) reviewed studies of both traditional or direct instruction and education in open classrooms (see Chapter 13), students taught by direct instruction were found to do somewhat better on tests of academic achievement, but those in more open classrooms do a little better on tests of creativity, problem solving, and abstract thinking. Students who regard themselves as the center of control of their own behavior do less well under direct instruction than students who attribute their success or failure to external sources of control (see Chapter 11). And students of low ability are likely to achieve better under direct instruction than in classroom settings that provide freedom to choose activities and participate in planning. The differences are small, however, and the weight of the evidence in this and other studies is not conclusive.

Peterson also observed that whether or not direct instruction is used in a classroom depends on the objectives toward which the teacher is working. For improvement in basic skills with low-ability students, direct instruction may be the best choice. But the lives of low-ability and disadvantaged children may allow little diversity outside of school, so the teacher also has an opportunity to provide an environment that allows for choice and encourages students to solve problems and to think in creative ways. These are valid considerations in the use of contingency management in the classroom. The designers of the Atlanta studies may have been acknowledging them with their use of interest centers in the classrooms, which gave teachers and children opportunities to interact on an individual or small-group basis. This facilitates pupil planning of activities, divergent thinking, and educational objectives which go beyond academic achievement. Teacher-student interactions in classroom groups will be examined in Part III.

CHAPTER 12 IN RETROSPECT

Students in classrooms differ widely among themselves in academic and other educational achievement. This is a persistent characteristic of schools and schooling. Educators and psychologists continue to search for the "one best method" of providing instruction, but none seems to fill the bill particularly well. Whether instructional methods can be developed that drastically reduce differences in educational achievement is a controversial issue.

Instructional methods are of two basic types: methods that stress individualization and methods that emphasize the use of group instruction. Among the former are aptitude-treatment interaction, computer-assisted instruction, and the mastery learning model. Among the latter are direct instruction and contingency management instruction.

Aptitude-treatment interactions do exist, and their importance for instruction is acknowledged. Despite years of intensive investigation, however, such interactions have not led to the discovery of major innovations in instruction. Some interactions are with general intellectual ability, and others have been found with personality characteristics, notably the motivational effects of anxiety and conformity.

The introduction of computer-assisted instruction has not resulted in universal acceptance in the nation's schools, as was anticipated at one time. As computers become less expensive, and as appropriate hardware that can be easily installed and software or courseware that can be used without programming expertise become available, their acceptance is growing. A principal advantage is that they can quickly provide systematic feedback to teachers about their students' progress and difficulties. The movement will be inhibited, however, unless teachers learn to assume quite different roles for their interactions in the classroom.

The mastery learning model focuses on the relationship between time and learning. If students whose initial learning is poor are provided with additional time and instruction to master beginning lessons, ultimately their learning will require proportionally less time. Another way to express this idea is that initially high correlations between general intelligence or aptitude and specific learning tasks diminish during the course of mastery learning.

Average classroom achievement has been found to be higher where direct teaching is the instructional method, compared to more open or individually organized classrooms. This is true when achievement is measured by standardized achievement or other academic knowledge tests. In direct teaching the teacher controls the attention and activities of the group. In less-controlled classrooms, students may devote considerably less time to the ordinary learning tasks which are reflected in test scores. But they may also have more opportunity to increase their independence and autonomy, and to learn other social and intellectual skills that develop over time. Tests are not available to measure this type of equally important educational achievement.

QUESTIONS FOR DISCUSSION

1. This chapter asserts that productivity goals for American schools are concerned with academic achievement or the development of self-directed learners. What do these terms signify? Which, if either of them, is more important? Why do you think so?
2. In many school districts there is a surplus of teachers, and the number of teaching positions available continues to decline. What effect would you expect this situation to have on the quality of students who are now preparing to teach? Why?
3. The text expresses skepticism about the ability of technology (such as programmed instruction or computer-assisted instruction) to become a major force in classroom instruction unless the part the teacher plays is redefined to accommodate the change. What changes in the teacher's traditional role would have to be made to reach such an accommodation?
4. What are the major strengths of the mastery learning model? the major weaknesses?
5. What are the characteristics of direct instruction that account for its long-standing acceptance as a mode of classroom instruction?
6. Would contingency management be successful in classrooms at different social and economic levels than those studied in Project Success Environment? Why or why not?

READINGS FOR REFLECTION

There are several excellent contemporary books that review and summarize the literature and the controversial issues discussed in this chapter. All of the references cited in this section are technical and are intended for advanced students or scholars in the field. Educational psychology students who develop an interest in a particular aspect of an instructional issue can benefit from an appropriate chapter or paper, however.

Relevant readings can be found in:

Cronbach, Lee J., and Snow, Richard E. *Aptitudes and Instructional Methods.* New York: Irvington Publishers, 1981.

Peterson, Penelope L., and Wahlberg, Herbert J. *Research on Teaching: Concepts, Findings, and Implications.* Berkeley, Cal.: McCutchan Publishing Corp., 1979.

Willerman, Lee. *The Psychology of Individual and Group Differences.* San Francisco: W. H. Freeman, 1979.

Willerman, Lee, and Turner, Robert G. (Eds.) *Readings about Individual and Group Differences.* San Francisco: W. H. Freeman, 1979.

REFERENCES

Anderson, Lorin W. An empirical investigation of individual differences in time to learn. *Journal of Educational Psychology,* 1976, *68*(2), 226–233.

Atkinson, Richard C. Ingredients for a theory of instruction. *American Psychologist,* 1972, *27*(10), 921–931.

Bellack, Arno A., Kliebard, Herbert M., Hyman, Ronald T., and Smith, Frank L., Jr. *The Language of the Classroom.* New York: Teachers College Press, 1966.

Bloom, Benjamin S. Time and learning. *American Psychologist,* 1974, *29*(9), 682–688.

Bloom, Benjamin S. *Human Characteristics and School Learning.* New York: McGraw-Hill, 1976.

Bunderson, C. Victor, and Faust, Gerald W. Programmed and computer-assisted instruction. In N. L. Gage (Ed.), *The Psychology of Teaching Methods,* 75th Yearbook of the National Society for the Study of Education, Part I. Chicago: University of Chicago Press, 1976.

Carroll, John B. A model of school learning. *Teachers College Record,* 1963, *64*(8), 723–733.

Cronbach, Lee J., and Snow, Richard E. *Aptitudes and Instructional Methods: A Handbook for Research on Interactions.* New York: Irvington Publishers; Halsted Press, 1977.

Dale, Edgar, and Raths, Lewis E. Discussion in the secondary school. *Education Research Bulletin,* 1945, *24,* 1–6.

Dean, Jay W. What's holding up the show? *Today's Education,* April–May 1982, pp. 21–23.

Evans, Christopher. *The Mirco Millennium.* New York: Viking Press, 1979.

Gage, N. L. *The Scientific Basis of the Art of Teaching.* New York: Teachers College Press, Columbia University, 1978.

Good, Thomas L. Teacher effectiveness in the elementary school. *Journal of Teacher Education,* 1979, *30*(2), 52–64.

Good, Thomas L., and Beckerman, Terrill M. Time on task: A naturalistic study in sixth-grade classrooms. *Elementary School Journal,* 1978, *78*(3), 192–201.

Harnqvist, Kjell. The international study on educational achievement. In Fred N. Kerlinger (Ed.), *Review of Research in Education 3.* Itasca, Ill.: F. E. Peacock Publishers, 1975.

Hoetker, James, and Ahlbrand, William P., Jr. The persistence of the recitation. *American Educational Research Journal,* 1969, *6*(2), 145–167.

Learned, William S., and Wood, Ben D. *Student and His Knowledge: A Report to the Carnegie Foundation on the Results of the High School and College Examinations of 1928, 1930, and 1932.* Bulletin No. 29, Carnegie Foundation, 1938.

McDonald, Frederick J. Report on Phase II of the Examining Teacher Evaluation Study. *Journal of Teacher Education,* 1976, *27*(1), 39–42.

Peterson, Penelope L. Aptitude by treatment interaction effects of teacher structuring and student participation in college instruction. *Journal of Educational Psychology,* 1979, *71*(4), 521–533.

Peterson, Penelope L. Direct instruction: Effective for what and for whom? *Educational Leadership,* 1979, *37*, 46–48.

Rollins, H. A., McCandless, B. R., Thompson, M., and Brassell, W. R. Project Success Environment: An extended application of contingency management in inner-city schools. *Journal of Educational Psychology,* 1974, *66*, 167–178.

Skinner, B. F. Contingency management in the classroom. *Cumulative Record: A Selection of Papers.* 3rd ed. New York: Appleton-Century-Crofts, 1972.

Skinner, B. F. The science of learning and the art of teaching. *Harvard Educational Review,* 1954, *24*(2), 86–97.

Stallings, Jane. How instructional processes relate to child outcomes in a national study of follow through. *Journal of Teacher Education,* 1977, *27*(1), 43–47.

Stevens, Romiett. *The Question as a Measure of Efficiency in Instruction: A Critical Study of Classroom Practice.* Contributions to Education, No. 48. New York: Teachers College Press, Columbia University, 1912.

Suppes, Patrick. Modern learning theory and the elementary school curriculum. *American Educational Research Journal,* 1964, *1*(2), 79–93.

Thomas, R. M., and Thomas, S. M. *Individual Differences in the Classroom.* New York: McKay, 1965.

Thompson, Marion, Brassell, William R., Persons, Scott, Tucker, Richard, and Rollins, Howard. Contingency management in the schools: How often and how well does it work? *American Educational Research Journal,* 1974, *11*, 10–28.

Willerman, Lee. *The Psychology of Individual and Group Differences.* San Francisco: W. H. Freeman & Co., 1979.

The Social
Psychology of
the Classroom

Part III represents the converging interests of psychology and
sociology in the instructional process and the institution of
education. Psychology is concerned with motives, attitudes, and
behaviors, and sociology with the structure and operation of groups
in society. The social psychology of the classroom is concerned with
the operation of school groups, reflecting the focus of social
psychology on the reciprocal ways individuals and small groups
influence and are influenced by one another.

   The two chapters in this part provide extensive information on the
second dimension of the instructional process—instruction provided
to learners in groups. This is the most common setting for school
instruction, which is affected in significant ways by group dynamics
and processes. The teacher's leadership roles in different classroom
settings are described in Chapter 13, and the effects of groups on
students' status, self-esteem, and academic achievement are
examined in Chapter 14.

   These chapters also are concerned with the third dimension of the
process, the external environment. The public's view of teaching as a
profession influences their expectancies about individual teachers'
behaviors, and the ways teachers interpret their responsibilities to
society affect their relationships with others in the classroom and
the school. An example of an educational problem which has
implications as a social issue is ability grouping, which can limit
the capacity of students from disadvantaged homes to better their
social and economic positions.

Classroom Leadership

In studying the science and art of teaching it is necessary to specify its various forms and styles and how they are related to the context in which the instruction is presented. Teachers take on different roles and perform various functions in their interactions with students as members of a classroom group. These social forces, together with the formal organization of the school, the teacher's personal characteristics, and the public's view of teaching, all influence a teacher's leadership style, and this in turn affects the classroom climate and the academic achievement of the students.

Classroom leadership is perhaps the most challenging and exciting task the teacher undertakes. Many skills, varying according to the social and institutional setting, are required. Teachers are subject to a crush of organizational, community, student, and personal pressures as they direct the instructional process, as Figure 13.1 shows.

Community pressures are derived from the public's view of the teaching profession and can take the form of public input into small and large

Figure 13.1

Influences affecting the teacher as leader

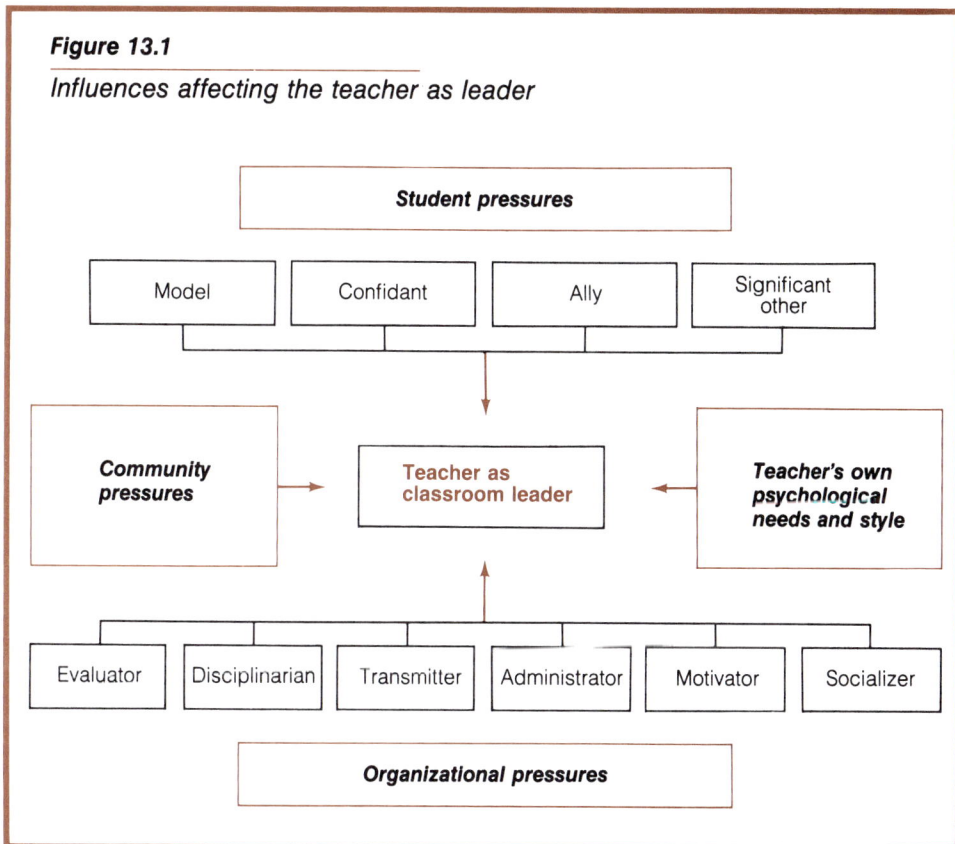

educational decisions which directly affect the teacher's position as classroom leader. Teachers' personal characteristics, dispositions, and needs directly affect the leadership style each one adopts. Their perceived roles as model, confidant, ally, or significant other to the students also bears on their behavior as the classroom leader, and organizational pressures are exerted by the requirements of their various roles as evaluator, disciplinarian, transmitter, administrator, motivator, or socializer.

HOW SOCIETY'S VIEW AFFECTS THE TEACHER'S STYLE

Education is the largest "industry" in the United States. Over 50 million students are enrolled at the elementary and secondary levels nationwide (Grant & Lind, 1978). And teaching is the single largest occupation in the country; to instruct these young people and to coordinate and guide their training, over three million teachers are employed by public and private school systems.

The size of the educational institution is matched only by the demands and responsibilities of teaching positions. Teachers are expected by parents, administrators, and members of the community to teach pupils not only facts and figures but socially prescribed ways of behaving, the ability to interpret and appraise the motives and actions of others, and how to behave both independently and in harmony with the rest of society. This is no small order! To accomplish such a multiplicity of tasks and expected outcomes requires thoughtful, deliberate leadership and organization. Some instructors are able to handle the rigors of the job much better than others; the best teachers seem to motivate and direct the learning of students almost effortlessly, though much time and thought may be invested in the development of their unique teaching styles.

The large membership of the teaching profession and its nearly universal contact with every citizen has made it a very public property. Controversies over teacher salaries, curriculum and textbook selections, and school closings or reductions in force due to declining enrollments in many areas are given prominent news coverage. As teachers organize to protect their interests, they may be pictured outside the classroom as being militant, self-righteous, and self-centered.

The teacher's ability to lead in the classroom is inevitably affected by the public's view of the teaching profession. Misconceptions and stereotypes, reinforced by the entertainment and news media, affect the public's attitudes toward teachers, which take such forms as:

Teachers are overpaid—they only work nine months of the year.
Anybody could babysit for 20 kids like they do!
Students today don't learn one-half as much as I did when I was in
school. What do teachers do all day long?

Although there are indications that the prestige associated with teaching has remained fairly constant, if not slightly increased, in the past 40 years relative to other occupations (Hodge, Siegel, & Rossi, 1966), the public image of teachers as a group is not a constructive one. Generally it impedes a teacher's efforts to establish an appropriate classroom climate and to provide effective leadership.

Adults' impressions of what teachers do in school are based on their own prolonged exposure to schooling, so they tend to consider their notions of what constitutes good and bad teaching as being fairly accurate. While they may have clear impressions about how good or bad the teachers were that they encountered in their own student days, they would find it difficult to state precisely what made these individuals either effective or uninspired instructors. The public's criteria for evaluating teachers' styles seldom have an informed basis.

DEVELOPING A TEACHING STYLE

Teachers develop their own classroom styles as a result of how they were taught themselves, as well as their temperament and disposition, knowledge of the subject matter, and professional acquaintance with education and teaching, as we noted in Chapter 1. Because they usually do not teach in the presence of their peers or other adults, they must form opinions of their own effectiveness. The teacher is almost solely responsible for establishing classroom management procedures, leadership styles, and the details of the instructional process. Reinforcement for the teacher's methods and strategies comes from interpreting the feedback from students in response to the instruction, as was shown in the model of the instructional process in Chapter 1.

The isolation of teachers in their classrooms is due to both the social structure of the teachers' position and the organizational structure of the school. Lortie (1975) found that almost half of the teachers he interviewed said they had "no contact" at all with their peers during the course of their work, and "The major psychic rewards of teaching are earned in isolation from peers, and they can hamper one another by intruding on classroom boundaries" (p. 193). In an illuminating study of a small-town school in New England, McPherson (1972) found that classrooms were off limits not only to observers from the community at large but also to other teachers in the school. She observed the teachers' apparent belief that

> . . . it was not one teacher's job to tell another teacher how to teach. It was quite proper for one teacher to be a model of discipline and order for another to follow, or for one teacher to inform another about the school rules and her responsibilities on the playground or in the

lunchroom, but no teacher should invade another's classroom when teaching was going on; no teacher should belittle or question another teacher in front of pupils or parents; each teacher should support and back up the actions of a colleague in public. (p. 64)

The principle of noninterference means that teachers keep their teaching to themselves in their own classrooms. Severe discipline problems may be passed on to the principal, and students with profound learning difficulties may be referred to an education specialist. But most learning and behavior problems must be dealt with quickly and without the help of others, in the confines of the classroom.

While the school principal, as the administrative head, is responsible for the establishment of the general teaching and learning environment, the segmented nature of the instruction and the structural and physical arrangement of the classrooms allow teachers a great deal of autonomy in the organization and management of their classrooms.

THE TEACHER AS A LEADER OF THE CLASSROOM SOCIETY

The classroom is a relatively self-contained mini society comprised of diverse group members, as we noted in Chapter 1. The combinations of students and instructors contribute to a unique climate for each classroom. There is little carryover from one classroom setting to the next, and group membership and leadership are defined anew each time classrooms are restructured.

Complicating the tasks of molding group identity and establishing the teacher's authority is the fact that the students may not want to be in the classroom in the first place! Students come to the school setting from a variety of backgrounds and bring with them a highly mixed set of motivations, aspirations, and abilities. Students are in a sense "conscripted"—that is, they have no choice as to whether or not they will attend school. They also have little voice in the selection of their teachers, and their input into how the class is run may be severely limited. The teacher, therefore, is confronted with the task of molding a diverse set of wills, talents, and personalities into a group that can interact in the common tasks of the instructional process.

However competent teachers might be in their subject areas, before they can present the instruction they must first fit the collective body of students to a uniform set of learning tasks and expectations. This is complicated because the basis for student assignment to a particular group is usually simply membership in a certain age category or educational level, not particular interests or friendships. Tenth-graders may be fairly uniform in age and perhaps even in height and weight, but certainly all are not equally disposed (or able) to read *Julius Caesar* or *Macbeth*. Perhaps even fewer care whether butterflies belong to the genus lepidoptera or arachnid. Yet a teacher must mold 20 or more wills to read and comprehend such material.

Although many schools attempt to group students within ages according to ability, the groupings may not coincide with the students' own preferences. For example, Brenda might resent being placed in an "advanced" math class because her best friend Janine, whom she would like to be with, was assigned to an "intermediate"-level class. Thus the teacher's first task in bringing structure to the classroom is to persuade students that they *want* to be in a particular class when in fact they all know they *must* be there. The involuntary nature of school attendance also means that some students who may not want to be in school at all or who are limited in their ability to profit from the experience are enforced recruits to the system. Yet the school system as a whole, and individual teachers in particular, are charged with the responsibility of producing graduates with at least minimal competence in a variety of subject areas.

In addition to transmitting cognitive information such as facts and figures and methods of processing the information, schools are also responsible for the socialization of young people so that they can function in an adult world, as we noted in Chapter 1. The expectations, attitudes, and behaviors associated with adulthood may not be of much importance to an adolescent, however. Therefore the teacher must not only serve as a model of prescribed forms of adult behavior but must also convince students that certain ways of acting are important to their future social and economic well-being. Because adulthood is a distant state for most young people, the payoffs for "proper behavior" are sometimes difficult to comprehend. In general, the younger children are, the more tangible they like their rewards to be. The promise of a "smiley face" on second-graders' papers may be sufficient reward to carry them through an assignment. It is doubtful whether promise of a better-paying job some day would have the same effect, however.

Some high school students have similar difficulty in seeing the link between a good grade in civics, for example, and their occupational aspirations. (Indeed, some readers of this text may be wondering what the study of educational psychology has to do with becoming a good teacher. Have faith!) The example of Larry, a student with above-average ability attending a rural high school in Iowa, is not unusual:

> Larry attends school daily, is usually punctual, and is polite to his teachers, but he rarely shows interest in his school work. He occasionally completes his homework assignments and does not seem to be bothered by mediocre grades. Before and after school Larry works hard on his

father's farm, which he expects to take over some day. Repeated attempts to discuss his below-par performance with his parents have failed. Larry's teachers and counselors have given up trying to persuade his parents to take time off from the family farming chores to discuss his school work.

Larry is puzzled by the need to take plane geometry, in which he must memorize seemingly useless theorems and postulates. Likewise, he is bored by the study of lines of succession among European monarchs and wonders how analyzing the blood imagery in Macbeth will help him produce a better crop of soybeans some day. Now, in his senior year, Larry is cutting classes with increasing frequency. If he continues skipping he may find himself unable to receive his diploma because of failure to meet state attendance requirements for graduation.

There are many Larrys in our education system. Although their stories vary, the problem is similar: How does the teacher make learning *interesting and rewarding* for them?

Teachers have few resources available to promote desirable individual and group behavior. The most commonly used are rewards and punishment in the context of operant conditioning, as described in Chapter 8. First they must establish the importance of these resources in the students' eyes, however. The job of the teacher is considerably more complex than simply lecturing, grading, and assigning tasks; it involves motivating, persuading, organizing, initiating, and guiding. In short, the classroom teacher must be a *leader*.

THE NATURE OF LEADERSHIP

Our examination of the concept of leadership can start with the definition given by Hollander and Julian (1968): "Leadership in the broadest sense implies the presence of a particular influence relationship between two or more persons" (p. 890). Since leadership is a multifaceted process, it is difficult to define it simply and completely, however. We can think of it as the behavior of a person which initiates, necessitates, or results in new interactions or processes in a social group or social system. But even this expanded definition ignores the central characteristic of leadership: There is no leadership unless there also is a "followership" (Getzels, 1973). Leadership does not exist in social isolation. In order to lead one must have followers—individuals who consent to be led by mutual agreement and not as a result of bribes, coercion, threats, or force.

In this sense leadership is *entrusted* authority which is *voluntarily* given by a group or society to an individual. *Authority* is power which is regarded as legitimate and is attached to a specific role or position. The right to authority and leadership is generally not associated with a specific individual but rather with the office that a person holds. Many Americans did not like Richard Nixon as a man and did not agree with the decisions he made and the manner in which he led the country, for example. But until he violated the responsibilities of his office, his *right* to exercise power and control was not in question. He was the president, and by nature of the socially defined responsibilities and powers of his office he legitimately wielded power and authority. Similarly, in the classroom, teachers have power and authority precisely because they are teachers; they occupy positions which, because of school rules and social convention, are imbued with power.

Classroom leadership, as distinct from command, is a function of teachers' personal relationships with members of the groups under their charge. Students must view teachers' roles and responsibilities as legitimate. Thus, whereas the *right to command* may be inherited with a social position, *formal leadership* is a *privilege* which can be ascribed voluntarily only by the group submitting itself to the direction of an individual. Power therefore resides in the group membership and is granted to the leader on the basis of a particular quality or set of competencies. *Informal leadership* exists when an individual, regardless of position or rank, is able to influence the actions of others. While teachers are the formal leaders in the classroom, in most classrooms there are several student informal leaders as well. These students are able to mold the wills of their subgroup constituencies and use their influence to reinforce or countermand teachers' directives.

A leader, then, may be defined as a person voluntarily vested with authority within a group who initiates, guides, and directs the realization of the group's objectives. Leadership is frequently conferred on a single group member who is designated as the person in charge of an activity, but direction and influence may be provided by any group member, depending on the situational characteristics and the organizational character of the group. Although teachers may have a controlling interest in leading in the classroom, therefore, they share authority and influence with others.

THE LEADERSHIP TASK OF THE TEACHER

Effective leaders manage to harness the individual strengths and dispositions of a group's members to accomplish a common task. For the teacher, this often means introducing routine and regimentation into the daily lives of students who are used to behaving in settings such as the home where activities are minimally structured. At home play is begun and ended when the child is intrigued by or loses interest in a certain activity. Movement about the house is relatively unrestricted. In school, children may find the rigidity of time schedules, the fixed sequential nature of activities, and the necessity to seek permission to

BOX A   *A morning in the life of Sarah and Joshua*

There are many differences between the home environment and that of the classroom. The following excerpts from observational diaries of the activities of a four-year-old sister and six-year-old brother on a typical schoolday morning illustrate how the two settings vary in the freedom and spontaneity they provide.

Sarah, age 4:

8:30 A.M. Sarah wakes up, gets out of bed, and looks at the storybook her mother read to her last night. Then she goes to the kitchen to eat breakfast.

9:15 A.M. Breakfast finished except for her Poptart, she turns on television and watches Sesame Street. She then plays with the family cat and a new box of checkers while Big Bird and company entertain in the background.

10:00 A.M. She returns to the breakfast table to finish her Poptart. Mother dresses her, and she runs next door to play with Heather on her swing set. Activities shift between playing house, reenacting scenes from *The Empire Strikes Back*, and begging Heather's mom for juice and cookies.

11:15 A.M. Her mother takes her to the store and they stop at the library, where Sarah entertains herself watching the gerbils and playing with the puzzles in the children's room.

12:00 Noon Sarah dozes on the way home in the car. She decides she wants a peanut butter and jelly sandwich for lunch. Then she goes to her room, reads another story, and lies down for her nap.

Joshua, age 6:

8:30 A.M. Joshua leaves for school with the warning, "Hurry or you'll be late!"

8:45 A.M. The first bell rings. Joshua and his classmates hush as Mrs. Lollar, their teacher, walks into the room.

8:50 A.M.	The students are told to take out their readers and open them to page 63. They take turns reading aloud for 20 minutes.
9:10 A.M.	The students are told to begin reading to themselves a new story which starts on page 70. There is silent reading for 10 minutes.
9:20 A.M.	Mrs. Lollar tells the class to take out their math books (groans from some of the students). Groups of students are assigned to put homework problems on the board. Joshua requests and is refused permission to go to the bathroom—Mrs. Lollar tells him to wait 30 more minutes until recess begins.
9:50 A.M.	Recess begins, and the children are told to stand in line and march single file to the bathroom and then form another line in front of the drinking fountain.
10:00 A.M.	Art class begins. The children are directed to paint a picture of a farm scene. Joshua is reminded 20 minutes later to remain in his seat and to work by himself without talking. After another 20 minutes, the entire class is warned to stay in their seats and stop talking.
10:45 A.M.	The students are told to clean up their desks and pin their pictures on the bulletin board.
11:00 A.M.	Mrs. Lollar leads the class in a story about American Indians, involving the children in song and dance. Joshua is scolded for dancing out of turn. The percussion section of the student rhythm band is warned not to bang too loudly on their drums.
11:35 A.M.	The class is told to put away their instruments and sit quietly until lunch period begins. Joshua wonders why Mrs. Lollar says "I don't want to hear one more word out of you for the next five minutes."
11:45 A.M.	Lunch period begins. Joshua goes to the school cafeteria for one half hour of uninterrupted freedom.

engage in even the most personal tasks, such as going to the bathroom, to be bewildering and objectionable. To the teacher, however, structure and predictability are essential in order to maintain order and accomplish instructional objectives.

The difference only two years and the fact of school attendance can make in the daily routines of a brother and sister are detailed in Box A. Students like Joshua must be persuaded that restrictions placed on them that appear to be individually limiting are prescribed for the benefit of the group. Most importantly, the teacher must be careful to ensure that rules and exceptions to them are applied fairly and impartially to all members of the group. For most children like four-year-old Sarah, life at home is unplanned and relatively structure free. Attention is immediate and highly personal, hence gratification is seldom delayed and is usually positive.

In general, parent-child relationships are characterized by intense personal ties of affection and may be described as *particularistic,* or devoted to a particular subject. Teacher-student relationships may be personal and particularistic at the early stages of schooling, but as students get older and classroom groups are more transient and diversified, the instructional process becomes less particularistic and more *universalistic,* or equally applicable to all (Getzels, Lipham, & Campbell, 1968). First- and second-grade teachers are in many ways surrogate parents who must help ease youngsters into the real world of objective rewards and punishments. This function of the teacher gradually diminishes as students mature and learn to accept the more impersonal basis for valuing pupils that grows out of the school's need to set and follow standardized rules and regulations. Schools operate on the principle that procedures and rewards are to be administered in a universalistic fashion, so teachers relate to all students, regardless of who they are, what they look like, or what their gender is, on the basis of the same explicit criteria (Dreeben, 1970).

The distinction between particularistic and universalistic has profound implications for teachers in their leadership capacity, as Getzels (1973) notes:

> An interpersonal relationship is particularistic when the nature of the interaction is determined by what the individuals mean to each other personally; emotional rather than functional ties define the mutual rights and obligations. In the universalistic relationship matters are reversed; emotional considerations become secondary to functional considerations, and the rights and obligations are determined on impersonal rather than personal grounds. Leader-follower relations in primary groups are usually particularistic, leader-follower relations in bureaucratic organizations are predominantly universalistic. (p. 18)

This first-grade teacher has mastered the art of giving individual attention while keeping the other students at work on the class project. The teacher's leadership task is to harness the individual strengths and dispositions of class members to accomplish a common educational goal.

The Teacher's Paradox

Because of their leadership task, teachers are confronted with a dilemma. Effective leadership of the instructional process requires routine procedures, such as standardizing homework formats, beginning lessons promptly, and limiting recess to established time periods. But all students do not function at their best in such a structured environment, and some cannot cope with the rigidity of schooling. Attention spans and interest levels vary from student to student and from subject to subject. When adults find it frustrating to be interrupted in the middle of a conversation or an interesting book, we can hardly expect a student engrossed in a reader to welcome the announcement, "All right class!

It is time to put away your readers and take out your math books—quickly, please."

To the extent that good teaching is measured by the amount of material covered in a class and how well students learn it, teachers must be concerned with efficiency and equity. They can realize these outcomes by making automatic responses to everyday situations and creating emotional distance and depersonalization in teacher-pupil relationships. Students are concerned with their self-concepts and have a claim on the personalization of relationships, however. Like everyone else they have good and bad days, and their enthusiasm, patience, and diligence are anything but constant. They have emotional and intellectual highs and lows and are grateful when special allowances are made for them. Nevertheless the teacher must treat all the students as objectively and equally as possible by avoiding personal, emotional attachments and basing evaluations of students on either a group standard or a set of absolute criteria.

There are many students who flounder socially and academically because a teacher did not give them that extra spark of personal attention which might have kindled the flame of enthusiasm and enhanced their self-confidence. The following example concerns a misunderstood American Indian girl:

> Sheila is a bright, soft-spoken Navajo student who is enrolled in the 11th grade of Suagarro City High School. Although she does fairly well in school, her teachers cannot understand why she rarely speaks in class, and when she does why it is in such a perfunctory way.
>
> Her parents usually drop Sheila off at school, as often as not 10 to 15 minutes after the first class has begun. When called on in class she rarely looks at the teacher and never glances at her classmates while she is reciting. Her English teacher has noticed that ever since her classmates laughed at a pronunciation mistake she made several weeks ago, she has not volunteered to answer any questions, nor has she replied when directly called on in class. She seems neither pleased nor displeased with the grades she gets on her assignments and exams, despite the constant encouragement that her teachers give her.
>
> Even though Sheila's grades are excellent, her perplexing and sometimes seemingly rude behavior in class has caused at least two teachers to write mediocre recommendations for her for college scholarships. Without financial assistance it is highly unlikely that she will be able to attend the university.

Teachers are bound by organizational demands to be impartial, and at the same time they are charged with maximizing each student's potential. This is *the teacher's paradox*. It challenges the best of instructors, and its resolution demands the best of the teacher's leadership qualities.

PERSONALITY ATTRIBUTES
OF CLASSROOM LEADERSHIP

The teacher's leadership style determines his or her success in resolving the teacher's paradox and providing all students with impartial but individualized guidance in the instructional process. There has been considerable research on the personal attributes that contribute to an effective leadership style, but it has not been definitive because two factors hamper the research process: Stable personality traits are difficult to measure reliably, and they are affected by situational factors. Personalities are influenced by mood and circumstance; people may display one dimension of their personality when taking one role and quite another in a different one. In the same way, one type of leadership behavior may not be as effective in one group as it is in another, due to variations in group structure and different combinations of behaviors and expectations among the group members.

Except in experimental situations examining leader effectiveness, it is difficult to determine whether changes in leadership style affect group behavior or shifts in group structure accommodate new leadership styles. In regard to teacher leadership, the question is whether teachers modify their instructional and leadership styles to fit the characteristics of their classes, or class members accommodate themselves to the demands of individual instructors. More than likely, both are relevant, which complicates the task of sorting out causal relationships between personal teacher characteristics and the realization of classroom goals.

Perhaps even more difficult is the problem of identifying group leadership as such. Steiner (1964) considers leadership to be "one of the most elusive terms in the language of group dynamics," and the search for a definitive study of personality characteristics as correlates of leadership is intriguing. If it is assumed that personal qualities are both learnable and changeable, and if it can be demonstrated that certain characteristics are related to a person's capacity to influence or dominate social groups or situations, it follows that personality modification could substantially affect leadership ability. Even if changing personality traits were relatively simple, however, there is a substantial school of thought which maintains that leadership is an innate quality which cannot be developed easily, if at all. An example is Aristotle's fatalistic observation that "From the hour of their birth some men are marked out for subjection, and others for command." Observers today simply recognize that people vary in their ability or willingness to take charge of a group or a situation.

Studies of teacher leadership have not identified a single dominant personality characteristic as a determinant of leadership, but a number

---

Table 13.1

Personality correlates of leadership

Personality Traits	Nature of Relationship
Flexibility	Dogmatism and rigidity about suggestions of group members discourage the group receptivity of leadership efforts. Consideration from the leader facilitates group drive and freedom of action. An authoritarian personality is detrimental to leadership.
Assertiveness	Individuals who are vocal and have high levels of self-confidence and ascendant power orientations have much group influence. Structuring the expectations of the group produces group cohesiveness and loyalty.
Sensitivity	Ability to judge the opinions and feelings of others is likely to be found in leaders. Leaders are able to predict group opinion or shape consensus in line with predicted group attitudes and can accurately assess key individual opinions as well as the group position. Leaders' consideration of the welfare of members and receptivity to their contributions allow expression of the group drive.
Persuasiveness	Structuring expectations reinforces group norms, roles, and goals of the group, which in turn enhances the strength of the group and identification with the organization. The productivity of task-oriented and interaction-oriented members is higher under persuasive than coercive leaders.
Intelligence	Although this is technically not a personality trait, it interacts with the four traits in establishing influence and primacy in groups.

---

of variables have repeatedly been at least moderately correlated with it. The most prevalent characteristics and their relation to leadership, as listed in Table 13.1, are flexibility, assertiveness, sensitivity, persuasiveness, and intelligence. Classroom teachers may not possess all of these traits, but the higher their composite ratings on these items, the higher is the probability that they will be recognized as strong leaders. In an educational setting, the consideration for students that teachers demonstrate and their ability to initiate structure (or direct the work explicitly) while reinforcing group goals and objectives appear to be the two most important determinants of leadership (Halpin, 1957).

The criteria for identifying leaders should not be confused with the criteria for evaluating them. You may admire a teacher for having the ability to mold student wills, maintain discipline, and accomplish objectives, but you still may disagree with that teacher's procedures and goals. In short, you may be impressed by a teacher's leadership *capacity* but find the teacher's *style* of leadership distasteful. Most adults can remember a former teacher with a classroom style which was unpleasant but which nevertheless was effective in making them learn. In the same way, few people would deny that Woody Hayes was extremely successful at leading his football teams to their goals, but his style of coaching and his treatment of team members and opposition players were severely criticized.

DETERMINANTS OF CLASSROOM LEADERSHIP

The web of instructional leadership is spun from thin filaments of group membership, trust, cooperation, and universalism. It forms a fragile network connecting teachers with students in the human need for personal, affective relationships. It is threatened by the compulsory nature of teacher-student relations and by the vested rights and authority of teachers, but the members of a group have considerable power in evaluating leadership behavior and initiating consequences for it. When the group membership rejects or seriously questions not only the leadership style but the values and organizational structure upon which the leader's legitimacy is based, the leader-follower relationship is in jeopardy. To understand why this is so we must consider what determines classroom leadership and accounts for its legitimacy.

Classroom leaders can be placed in the threefold typology of leaders developed by Eric Berne, a physician who popularized the study of groups. Berne's (1963) three kinds of leaders are:

1. The responsible leader—the person who fills the role of leader in the organizational structure is responsible to others higher up.
2. The effective leader—the person who makes the actual decisions in a group (and who may not have a role in the organizational structure) is the most *important* member of the group.
3. The psychological leader—the person who is able to mold group solidarity through personal influence and persuasion is the most *influential* member of the group.

It is possible for a single individual to have all three types of leadership, but usually they are shared by a number of group members. In a classroom context, the responsible leader is always the teacher or a designated substitute. Classroom teachers must pass students' academic and behavioral successes and deficiencies up to the school organization and pass institutional directives down to the classroom group.

Effective and psychological leadership may be vested solely in the teacher or be shared with the members of the class. In an autocratic classroom environment, teachers have the first and only say in decision making. But in democratic and open classes instructors share their leadership functions with class members (see Box C below). Psychological and effective types of leadership in schools vary with the personalities of the teachers and the extent to which they entrust responsibility to their students, which determines the leadership styles and classroom environments described in a later section.

When teachers are only marginally entrusted with "followership" by the class, one or more of the class members who enjoys the respect of other students may be instrumental in influencing the direction of activities instigated by the responsible leader. For example, although the biology teacher wants to assign a lengthy homework exercise due on Monday, he modifies the assignment at the request of Mary, one of the better students in the class, who politely informs him that the students already face two exams in other classes that same day. The strength of effective leaders like Mary is to a large part determined by the distribution of authority and type of leadership style adopted by the teacher, who is the responsible leader.

Psychological leaders in the classroom are usually popular and respected individuals who can garner support for a leader's initiative but who are not instrumental in formulating such an initiative. In *sociometric* studies of classrooms (Moreno, 1960), the psychological leaders are usually identified as the classmates most students would like to be with. In Figure 13.2, an example of a classroom sociometric design, each numbered circle represents a student in a small class of 12 members. The lines represent the answers each pupil gave to the question, "Who are your best friends around here?" A line with an arrow on both ends, such as that connecting students 2 and 12 in the figure, indicates that the students named each other in their responses. A line with a single arrow like that between students 5 and 2 indicates that the friendship relation is one sided; that is, pupil 5 mentioned pupil 2, but not vice versa.

Sociometric diagrams of this sort allow a researcher to put together a picture of classroom relationships and lines of influence among group members. They provide graphic representations of how the class members group themselves into friendship alliances (see Chapter 14). Similar diagrams could be constructed from responses to the questions, "Whose opinion do you value most in this class?" or "Which members of the class do you think care most about you as a person?"

Figure 13.2

Classroom sociometric design

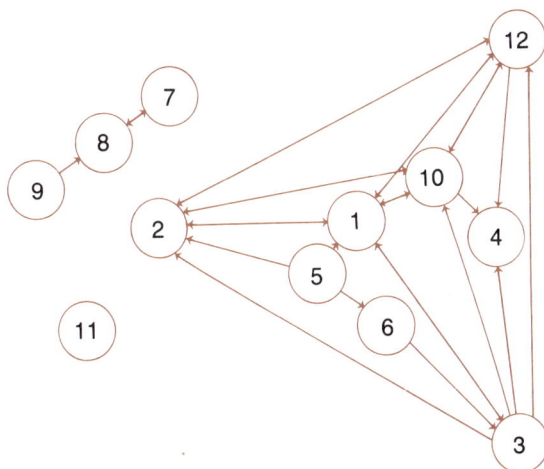

Source: J. L. Moreno, Helen H. Jennings, and others (Eds.), *The Sociometric Reader* (Glencoe, Ill.: Free Press, 1960), p. 513.

In the greatest number of choices (5) in Figure 13.2, students 2 and 1 were identified as being among others' best friends. Student 5 mentioned peers 2 and 1, but they did not reciprocate the feeling. Teachers should be aware of such patterns of friendship and deference in their classrooms, because student leaders in such friendship alliances can help cajole, persuade, and encourage other students. Enlisting the cooperation and support of student 1 in the figure, for example, would probably have a persuasive influence on the other students who are bound to him or her by their interpersonal relationships. Student 11, however, would have little influence on group activities and decision making. This pupil is a social isolate, a best friend to no one in the group. Punishing or rewarding isolated students will have little direct bearing on the rest of the group. But punishing a pupil central to the membership of a group brings guilt and a shared embarrassment to the others.

In reinforcement terms, the reasonable and just imposition of sanctions (rewards and punishments) serves to unify the group and strengthen their relationship with the classroom instructor. Flagrant abuses by teachers of their leadership role also promote solidarity in the class—but directed against the teacher. When a teacher's behavior is inconsistent or appears to be illogical to the students, his or her status as an effective and psychological leader diminishes and the responsibility is gradually, but not always explicitly, assumed by the class members. A teacher who operates solely on the basis of institutional power and authority quickly loses effectiveness. Teachers who are not aware of the class needs and the sociometric structure of the classroom group handicap themselves in the performance of two of the important components of their leadership functions.

In most classrooms, however, the responsible leadership and the effective leadership roles are at least shared by the teacher with pupils. Two important variables which are external to the classroom group help to determine the type and quality of teacher leadership: institutional characteristics and personality attributes.

INSTITUTIONAL CHARACTERISTICS

Formal educational instructions have most of the characteristics of the organizational form called a *bureaucracy*. As Bidwell (1965) has noted, school systems display, at least in a rudimentary form, the following hallmarks of a bureaucracy:

1. A functional division of labor—instruction allocated to teachers, coordination to administrators, and learning to students.
2. Definition of staff roles as offices—with recruitment and promotion of teachers and administrators based on merit and competence, specified performance expectations, and universalistic interactions between students and teachers.
3. A hierarchy of offices—with descending levels of authority and formal channels of communications, in which principals have power over teachers, who have authority over students.
4. Operation according to strict procedures—with limits placed on individualistic, discretionary actions and aims and objectives being institutionally defined.

Roles and Norms

In the division of labor and offices in any organization, associated with each position are one or more roles which the officeholder is expected to fill. School administrators, for example, are not expected to personally supervise the daily instruction in classrooms, but they are expected to resolve conflict between teachers and students quickly and efficiently. Student roles include demonstrating attention and interest in what the teacher has to say (even though it may not be very interesting), handing papers in on time, and showing deference to the teacher and respect for others.

Roles are expected patterns of behavior anticipated of someone who holds a particular status, office, or position in a society or group. The prescribed behavior is determined by the social norms of the group.' *Norms* are principles or standards designated to regulate and guide behavior that is deemed proper and appropriate by the group. They are the standards which are relative to a particular group, and they are binding on all members of the group.

Although most people subscribe to one set of general social norms, they occupy a number of different roles during the course of the average day. As a college student you may also be a parent—but at the same time a child of your own parents. Depending on which role you are filling at a given time, your behavior will change. Problems develop when it is necessary to fill two overlapping or conflicting roles at the same time. For example, a bride who wants to be respectful to her mother-in-law might find it frustratingly difficult to engage in her new role of independent householder and spouse when she is still viewed as the young, inexperienced partner of the mother's equally young and inexperienced son.

Role expectations are related to previous experiences with individuals occupying similar positions, and models of role performance are used in determining what constitutes appropriate and desirable behavior. For example, the manner in which we raise our children is strongly influenced by how we ourselves were raised. Some of our actions as parents emulate role relationships our parents embodied; others repudiate early experiences.

INSTITUTIONAL ROLES OF THE TEACHER

Teachers' roles within the institution of the school are determined by the nature of their expectations and assumptions about what constitutes appropriate behavior in the classroom. The way they conceptualize their roles is affected by their perception of how the public and other teachers, administrators, and students view them.

One of the principal influences on teacher behavior (as identified in Chapter 1) is how the teacher was taught. Wright (1959) suggests that teachers are strongly influenced in carrying out their roles by the type of teacher from their own school days with whom they identify most, and they are psychologically socialized into adopting one of three distinct teacher models as the basis for their own teaching behavior. These role types, which Wright credits Fritz Redl with identifying, are the patriarchal sovereign, the leader, and the tyrant (see Table 13.2).

Patriarchal sovereigns are demanding, exacting instructors. Students are in awe of them yet respect them for their knowledge and high

Table 13.2

Three teacher role types

Role Types	Role Characteristics	Character of Teacher-Student Relations
Patriarchal sovereign	Stands for order, discipline, and tradition Values ingrained and subconscious; deep morality Explicit, high-quality work standards	Unquestioned acceptance of values by students Student respect mixed with anxiety Emphasis on gratification from verbal rewards
Leader	Expects work and discipline in class Looks and behaves like a young person Strong sympathy with children's emotional and physical needs Altruistic and independent Prone to ideological rebellion	Adoration by students and acceptance of values Danger of particularistic attachments by students and emotional disequilibrium Openness and honest expression
Tyrant	Intolerant of irregularities Disciplines continuously and capriciously Invokes tricks, rules, and revenge	Punitive treatment toward students Teacher stresses weakness in students to hide own shortcomings Strict obedience demanded and little sympathy toward students Exploitation of students

Source: Benjamin Wright, "Identification and Becoming a Teacher," *Elementary School Journal*, April 1959.

standards. These teachers epitomize the aloof, scholarly, compassionate, intellectual pedagogue. They are self-assured, but justifiably so. Such teachers command respect and reverence by their knowledge and bearing, and their social distance from students is compensated for by their fairness and impartiality.

Whereas the sovereign type of leader sees the class as a unit rather than a collection of individuals, the leader type pays attention to individuals in the class and identifies with their problems and concerns. Leaders are friends as well as superiors who gain student trust and cooperation by building interpersonal relations. The friendship and empathy they offer encourage and motivate students to make academic gains. Leaders usually are popular with students but may be charged with betrayal or favoritism.

The tyrant, like the patriarchal sovereign, is concerned with order and regularity, but for different reasons. The patriarch manages the class to promote maximum learning and discussion, but the tyrant regulates it to establish a seat of power and control. Tyrants consider results to be more important than consistency in controlling behavior. They perceive violations of authority as a personal threat rather than a challenge to the position of leadership. The tyrant's authority exists because of fear and control of sanctions, not knowledge and empathy, and students respond to their directives in order to avoid reprisals. Most students encounter a tyrant at least once during their schooling (see Box B).

The theoretical work of George Herbert Mead (1934), Charles Horton Cooley (1909), and Peter Berger and Thomas Luckmann (1967), among others, has indicated that people not only shape their behavior as a result of observing role models, they also act in ways that are congruent with the expectations they think *others* have of the person occupying a role. Teachers, for example, behave not only on the basis of what they feel they should be doing but also in *anticipation* of how they feel others will respond to their behavior. Deliberately giving lower than average grades on essays may make students try to improve their marks on the next one, for example. Some college professors have a reputation for giving difficult midterm exams and grading them strictly, to strike fear into the hearts of their students and perhaps motivate them to work even harder during the second part of the semester. (Of course, some students may get so discouraged that they drop the course.) Elementary teachers try to find out what types of lessons please their principals so they can maximize their chances of a good rating on their in-class critiques.

Thus teacher behavior, leadership style included, represents a complicated response to past personal experiences, collegial patterns of behavior, and administrative, peer, and student expectations of performance in the teaching role.

ROLE CONFLICT

While bureaucracies such as a school organizational unit are theoretically characterized by strict delineation of roles, in practice the boundaries separating role expectations can be quite easily penetrated. The effective or psychological leaders in a classroom may be students, as we noted at the beginning of this section. Furthermore, the roles students and teachers occupy in the external environment may impinge on their group membership roles. For example, an adolescent deeply involved in a lover's quarrel may find it difficult to concentrate on the role of student. More directly, teachers who are anti-Semitic in their personal lives may find it difficult to apply the principles of fairness and equity to the Jewish students in their class.

BOX B   *The Teacher as Tyrant*

The following version of the tyrant teacher type, which was presented in an early book which examined the sociological aspects of teaching, is primarily of historical interest. Willard Waller described the tyrant as follows in 1932:

> Inadvertently we sat a little straighter in our chairs when we heard our teacher's step in the hall. He was a rough man, and bad-tempered, and we never knew where his temper was going to break out next. This morning he paused in the doorway and looked us all over before entering. There was on his face not the shadow of a smile, and the expression which left no doubt in any of our minds that he was not happy over the thought of having to spend the hour with us. We had the impression that he did not like us and would not regret an opportunity to punish us. The suspense was heightened as he looked over the class. He walked into the room; slowly, deliberately, and with a slight swagger he made his way toward his desk. He looked at a little boy in the back row. "Johnson," he said in that deadly way he had, "I told you to write yesterday's lesson four times. Where is it?"
>
> "It's on your desk, sir," says the small boy in a very small voice.
>
> "Well, it had better be. Where did we stop yesterday? You tell us, Jones, that's all you can do. We've got to make use of you."
>
> "Page 96, line 7," said Jones, apparently not offended.
>
> "Sir," said the teacher.
>
> "Yes, sir," answered Jones, mechanically.

Role conflict confounds many teacher-student relationships. To assist students with learning difficulties, for example, teachers particularize their instruction and personalize their techniques. In doing so, however, they are confronted with the teacher's paradox described above: the need to negotiate the fine line between impartial, unconcerned aloofness and outright favoritism. Can the disciplinarian and evaluator also be a guide and confidant, especially when all of these roles take place in the highly public environment of the classroom? In the example below, the trauma felt by Kristin in her relations with peers, parents, and teachers illustrates how difficult it is for the individual to compartmentalize various roles, and how easy it is for roles to interfere with one another.

We returned to the lesson. "All right, Jones, try to translate the first sentence."

Jones began, "When the lights were turned on . . ."

"Oh, Lord, no, no, nonono! Sit down. Shut up. That will do from you. *Prima luce* does not mean when the lights were on. Why did I ever call on such a dumbbell as you. I'll never be able to teach you anything. You're too smug and too conceited. Why don't you ever get next to yourself? Palmer! All right, Palmer!"

"I'm afraid I can't today, sir."

"Why not?"

"I don't understand that sentence," said Palmer, in desperation.

"Ha, ha. I know that trick. Translate the next sentence."

"I can't sir."

"Well, then, translate any sentence in the assignment. You can't?" His voice raised, and we knew that the storm was going to break. His voice filled the room. "Now, listen here, Palmer. I'm damned good and tired of the way you act anyhow. All you do in this class is take up a chair." He walked up to Palmer's chair and began to shake his fist in his face. "I want you to know that I'm tired of your damned nonsense." Exhausted, he sank back into his chair.

Source: Willard Waller, *The Sociology of Teaching* (New York: John Wiley & Sons, 1932), pp. 270–271.

Kristin's troubles had begun the night before, when she arrived home an hour and a half late from an outing with a girlfriend. Kristin's explanation that being late was due to her friend's decision to stop and visit her boyfriend did not dissuade Kristin's parents from grounding her for the next two weekends.

In the morning, while Kristin is eating breakfast and hastily reviewing some notes in preparation for a quiz in civics, she discovers that her two-year-old brother has torn out two key pages from her text. In anger and frustration she hastily storms off to school, not realizing until the beginning of second period P.E. class that she has left her gym clothes at home. She learns she will have to spend an hour after school in the coaches' room as a result.

Coming out of the cafeteria at lunchtime, she notices that the boy who she hoped would ask her to the spring dance is holding hands with a cheerleader. During her first afternoon class Mr. Olson, the biology teacher (who also has had an upsetting day), lectures her in public about how today's students disrespect their teachers. He says Kristin is obviously daydreaming and not paying attention to a thing he is saying. Mr. Olson is at a loss to explain how this mild criticism makes Kristin break down in tears and run from the room.

THE LEGITIMACY OF CLASSROOM ROLES

Another of the characteristics of roles in a bureaucratic setting is that although the individual occupying a specific position may be replaced, the role and its essential duties remain the same. Though individual teacher personalities and teacher-pupil relationships have much to do with classroom leadership, there is an institutional component which resides in the leadership role per se and is determined by the relative position of the role or position in the organizational hierarchy.

Leadership entails directing group efforts to the accomplishment of designated goals. In order for leadership to be effective it must be regarded as legitimate by those at whom it is directed. This means that both the *process* of direction and the *objectives* themselves help determine whether effort will be expended to complete an assigned task. Students decide how much effort to put into a learning task both by the way they feel about how the teacher structures the *learning activities* and by how interested they are in *what is to be learned*. Ideally, teachers arouse interest through their teaching techniques and convey a sense of purpose for mastering the material.

Institutional Role Components

Student support for the accomplishment of assigned goals usually can be secured because they regard the teacher's leadership as legitimate. Certain aspects of the teacher's role position contribute to this legitimacy.

First, teachers are older than their students. Especially with younger children, age unquestionably represents wisdom and good judgment. In general, the sizable age difference between teachers and students enhances their influence and persuasiveness.

Second, the objectives of instruction are often institutionally defined. For example, all third-graders in most schools use the same books and must accomplish similar tasks and objectives. Support for the teacher's leadership role is buttressed by nonpersonal, institutional demands and expectations. The school system is considered responsible for the routinization and standardization needed to ensure a uniform product of a certain quality.

Third, the definition of teachers' status and roles in the school helps ensure their position as leaders. Authority is invested *directly* in teachers by others' expectations of the role and the power accorded their position in the hierarchy of relationships within the school. Regardless of their personal characteristics, by definition of their role teachers have authority over students in a school, as the following example shows:

> As soon as the between-class bell rings, Scott and Bill hurry out of their classroom, duck down the science corridor, and go just outside the rear delivery door. Bill offers a cigarette to Scott, and both boys puff hurriedly to finish before the next class bell rings. Miss Clifford, the psychology teacher, rounds the corner and catches the boys taking their last prohibited puffs.
>
> Miss Clifford admonishes the pair and asks for their names. Scott replies that it is none of her business, since she isn't one of their teachers. Because the boys refuse to give her any information, she orders them to report to the principal's office immediately. Bill knows that his size would prevent the timid Miss Clifford from physically taking him to the office, so he replies, "Who's going to make me?" Miss Clifford says that she herself would not, but since the boys had violated the rules of the school and since she was charged, as were all other teachers, with enforcing those rules, she will report the incident to the principal. He would probably begin an investigation that would not end until the boys were identified and punished. "Now," she says, "you can either follow me down to the principal's office or take your chances on the principal not finding out who you are." Scott and Bill silently follow Miss Clifford as she strides to the main office.

In this confrontation, Scott and Bill recognize that in the organizational hierarchy of the school they have considerably less power than Miss Clifford. Although they might have little respect for her personality, they knew that she has superior resources at her disposal by nature of her organizational role. This gives legitimacy to her right to administer sanctions as well as to direct the accomplishment of goals.

Teacher-Student Relations Components

Authority for the exercise of leadership also comes from the teacher's personal characteristics and the modes of rewards and punishment used in the classroom. The final say in the operation of a classroom is the teacher's, but students can wield considerable power and influence in instructional groups by withholding their cooperation. Their interpersonal influences can be used in support of or opposition to the leadership of the teacher.

Some teachers may try to rely on the statement, "Just do it as I told you, because that's the way it's done" as a motivating technique. But the appeal to habit, tradition, or even the teacher's role power will not be effective as an inducement if the need for the activity and the potential rewards are not clear. And a personal, emotional appeal by teachers will work only as long as they are in the good graces of their students (Dreeben, 1971).

Teachers cannot rely on the emotional ties of the family in their attempts to lead students. Family members enjoy close, intense, and enduring emotional attachments. Children seek approval and love from their kin and are motivated to behave as they think their family members would like them to. By setting examples and through direct instruction, the family models attitudes and behavior for the willing child. Reprimands and punishment are received quite differently in the context of a sustained, close, emotional relationship than they are in the brief encounters structured by organizational constraints that usually take place between students and teachers.

Teachers find it easier to maintain control and leadership if they have used personal resources such as trust, understanding, and empathy in their interactions with students to build a reservoir of goodwill the students can draw on. Every social system or group has some rules which are only as effective as the willingness to enforce them, but because they can be invoked at any time they remain a threat. Being called to account for violations is at the discretion of the authority controlling them. You may exceed the 55 mph highway speed limit and be relieved when you flash past a hidden patrol car and the officer lets you go. Similarly, teachers ignore occasional violations of classroom norms, such as talking to classmates, checking answers, or failing to turn in homework. Both the teacher and the student know that a rule has been violated, but by not making an issue of it each time the teacher establishes goodwill.

Teachers also need to call on the full cooperation of their students from time to time. Students can sense when a teacher is not feeling well or is emotionally upset or wants them to be on their best behavior in front of others. When they go beyond classroom norms to assist their teachers, the credit is recorded on a mythical classroom accounting ledger. As long as the account between teachers and students remains relatively balanced, harmony prevails. If either side bankrupts the system, cooperation becomes extremely difficult to achieve. Repeated attempts by teachers to overdraw from their source of credit will exhaust the supply. When this happens, their leadership must rely on institutionally ascribed authority, and leadership based solely on power is never effective or long-lived.

Authority of the type found in schools relies almost entirely on sanctions (rewards and punishments) to ensure compliance. But sanctions are prone to devaluation; the more common they are and the more frequently they are used, the less value is placed on them by recipients.

For example, the value of a B report card grade or a gold star diminishes as students come to expect these rewards for minimal effort. Likewise, as scoldings and disciplinary attention become more frequent or severe, they can be tolerated by students more easily.

ROLES OF THE TEACHER AS CLASSROOM LEADER

Within the general framework of classroom leadership, teachers provide group guidance in a number of specific ways. The principal leadership duties of teachers are:

1. To transmit and impart factual information to students.
2. To supervise the development of moral values and norms in students.
3. To initiate and administer long-range and short-run activities and goals of class membership.
4. To evaluate students' academic performance.
5. To motivate students to realize their achievement potential.
6. To discipline and apply sanctions to class members' behavior.

These functions are described in terms of teachers' roles in the sections below.

THE TRANSMITTER

In the instructional process, the instructor presents information to students, who are expected to add meaningful material to their cognitive structures by applying the skills of reasoning and problem solving and critical and creative thinking. The instructor's approval is more than an endorsement of their academic competence. It symbolizes to the group what the norms of acceptable behavior or standards are and reinforces actions and activities which support those norms.

As the classroom leader the teacher must address individual needs as well as group needs. He or she facilitates individual learning by engaging the group in collective discussions of issues, asking leading questions, and getting students to share difficulties with the group. Through collective approaches to problem solving, the teacher also helps fill students' needs for affiliation with other group members. The teacher marshalls the individuals and the group to the common task of information gathering and processing, setting criteria for status and prestige by offering rewards and encouragement.

THE SOCIALIZER

As representatives of the community, teachers are charged with defining for students the values, preferences, and needs of the social system of which the school is a part. The problem is *whose* values, preferences, and needs will be taught, as we noted in Chapter 9. Èmile Durkheim, in a landmark book, *Moral Education* (1961), said that as the interpreter and enforcer of behavior in the classroom, the teacher has the duty of creating a consensus among students concerning legitimate and acceptable conduct. He argued that the best way to treat a student's failure to conform to expected patterns of behavior is to muster group displeasure against the offender. According to Durkheim, one of the chief responsibilities of the teacher as a group leader is to "Make students *want* to do what they *must* do."

Durkheim's position has often been criticized as an argument for the preservation of the status quo. Proponents are ultimately concerned with the problem of how the teacher preserves social order and transmits the values of society while at the same time fostering independence and individualism for the individual members of the group.

Most societies are heterogeneous and are characterized by a pluralism of social norms and values. After the family, schools are the principal guardian of social norms; formal schooling is perhaps the only common experience for citizens of the United States. Issues such as the right to say prayers in the classroom, the adoption of certain textbooks, and the provision of bicultural programs for ethnic minorities are part of this controversy. Although school boards interpret community values to the school, the teacher must translate them in the classroom.

We suggested in Chapter 9 that students should have the freedom to choose values. Teachers can present a particular value structure through three principal avenues of moral training or socialization. First, students are influenced by the actions and beliefs of *significant others*. These are individuals who share close personal relationships and whose behavior and sentiments are important to one another. Attractive and respected peers, parents, and siblings provide the most likely significant relationships. Teachers themselves often occupy the role of significant other to students in their classes, though they are limited by norms against particularistic displays of attachment. Effective classroom leadership involves identification of the student's classroom significant others and drawing on their influence to motivate and reinforce classroom activities.

Second, students are influenced by activities which have high degrees of *instrumental reward;* that is, they can be used to complete assignments or are recognizably important in students' relationships with others. Teachers can develop in pupils a positive feeling for such activities or values (Holsinger & Theisen, 1977). If, for example, cooperation among

As a lunchroom supervisor, the coach maintains order by insisting on acceptable norms of behavior. The group reaction to the disciplinary effort reflects others' regard for both the pupil and the teacher.

students on a class project is rewarded by a grade which is higher than the teacher would give for individual effort, cooperation will be valued as a mode of group behavior. Independence, achievement orientation, and participation are only a few examples of value orientations that can be learned indirectly when teachers demonstrate the utility of practicing them.

A third way teachers transmit values is through *exemplification*. This is the process of incorporating impersonal rules or general practices which are characteristic of the social organization of a group or an institution. Exposure to the teacher's leadership style and patterns of reward and punishment eventually create pressures to which students respond by forming value impressions. For example, if a teacher always promptly returns assignments, is ready to begin the class when the bell rings, and is consistent in the daily routine, the pupils in the class gradually learn punctuality and regularity. Teachers' repetitions of certain behaviors serve as a model of conduct for their students, despite individual personality differences among students which can lessen the effects of classroom procedures and the teacher's leadership style (Holsinger, 1976).

THE INITIATOR AND ADMINISTRATOR OF GOALS

Because daily school activities are segmented, with abrupt beginnings and endings, it is difficult for students to see the outcomes of the instructional process. Even when teachers make daily objectives clear to a class, students often have only a vague comprehension of how these goals fit into the overall educational plan. The classroom leader must persuade the students to internalize the class's behavioral and attitudinal objectives as their own. Unless this is accomplished, the leadership will be based on authority and coercion instead of compliance. Reliance on authority alone erodes the legitimacy of the leader's position and may even affect the way students value goals identified by the teacher.

The realization of short-term, day-to-day goals is often shrouded in uncertainty for both the teacher and students, since the measure of their accomplishment is how well they agree with the long-range objectives assigned to the group. Knowledge acquisition is incremental (or realized bit by bit), and progress is drawn out over lengthy periods (a month to an entire school year), so the pleasure of mastering the material is often deferred and only partially realized. Motivational techniques therefore focus on immediate goals. As Lortie (1975) notes, "It may well be that the emphasis in pedagogy on breaking teaching up into short units (e.g., lesson plans, study units) stems from this lack of knowledge about long-range instruction. Teachers are more likely to experience reward if they can punctuate their work, concentrating on short-range outcomes as a source of gratification" (p. 212).

To measure the accomplishment of goals, criteria of performance must be established that are relevant to both the teacher and the student. The teacher must conceptualize the goals for the class and put them into operation, usually alone and without the aid of systematic, clearly defined guidelines. He or she must determine whether student potential should be a consideration or there should be a single standard that applies to all students in the class. Furthermore, when the class objectives conflict with the psychological needs of the students, the teacher must seek a balance between the academic goals and the students' expressive or emotional needs. Otherwise, Lortie (1975) says, "excessive demands for effort will produce alienation, but excessive consideration will lead students to 'take advantage' of the situation" (p. 155).

The teacher must therefore address not only institutional and group needs but manage concern and attention for the goals of individuals within the group as well. Within the class, smaller groups of students band together in relationships which may be relatively stable or only temporary. Cells of students may develop through their recognition of "consciousness of kind"—the awareness of belonging to a certain category on the basis of similar interests, attitudes, or objectives. Effective classroom leaders must recognize these groups and their objectives.

THE EVALUATOR AND MOTIVATOR

Evaluation is perhaps at the heart of teaching behavior. It not only helps to monitor the progress of students but also provides one of the few tangible means of rewards for the teacher and student. Evaluation reinforces learning behavior and motivates students to different levels of achievement. As group leader and evaluator, the teacher is in a position to provide feedback on student performance which affects both the cognitive-intellectual and social-psychological development of the pupils.

The teacher's role in objective testing and measurement of knowledge is described in Part IV. The psychological impact of evaluation is even more complicated. By the time students reach high school they are well acquainted with various types of grading procedures and have been socialized to accept the meaning and importance attached to rewards for achievement. At the elementary level, however, they must learn the value of a gold star or a "smiley face" on their work. They must be persuaded by repeated patterns of reward that these symbols are proxies for achievement according to class standards. Thus pupils learn that achievement is rewarding and hence desirable.

Rewards in the form of grades and praise, especially when they are distributed in front of peers in the classroom, are instrumental in the formation of a student's self-concept. *Self-concept*, as we defined the term in Part I, refers to the objective and subjective information and evaluations that comprise our thoughts and feelings about ourselves. Most evaluative feelings are derived from *comparison*—with *others*, with our *"ideal" selves*, and with our *perception of the expectations of others* relative to social or group norms. As we have noted, for some pupils a teacher may be a significant other whose opinions are valued because of personal attachment or the power and authority they represent.

The noted social psychologist Charles Horton Cooley (1909) suggested the importance of the *looking-glass self* in shaping the self-concept. He theorized that we are constantly subjected to interpersonal situations in which we receive "reflected appraisals" of ourselves from others around us. As we process those impressions, we develop expectations and attitudes of ourselves which are in line with how we perceive others we see. For example, in the classroom, students receive appraisals and feedback constantly, not just through the verbal and written evaluations of the teacher but through interactions with peers. Over time, the appraisal of others becomes rather clear, and students place themselves into a perceived classroom hierarchy of ability, personal appearance, popularity, and so on. Thus their self-concepts are either reinforced or brought into line with what they feel is the groups' evaluation. Since teachers at least partially control the frequency and style of group communication, they have indirect control over exchanges which affect the development of students' self-concepts. The impressions they convey to students about their ability rest heavily on the comparisons made with others.

Effective classroom leaders are aware of the multifaceted nature of the self-concept. During the course of classroom interactions, behavior patterns appropriate to a particular aspect of the self-concept are activated. The teacher's ability to locate which aspects of the self should be appealed to is the key to solving motivational problems for students.

THE DISCIPLINARIAN

Some of the benefits and limitations of sanctions (rewards and punishments) as a leadership tool have been discussed earlier. While it is not to the advantage of either the teacher or the students for negative sanctions to be involved frequently, if at all, the teacher must establish authority and maintain order in student groups. As we have noted, without control, leadership and with it the instructional process will collapse.

CLASSROOM LEADERSHIP STYLES

The organizational structure of the school specifies the mandatory roles all teachers must adopt, but each teacher has discretionary power to select the roles he or she will emphasize in the classroom. Because of this variability and the differences in the other influences on the teacher's leadership style—public opinion, personal attributes, and student relationships—teachers differ widely in how they approach the implementation of the instructional process and control of student behaviors. The three basic types of leadership styles are autocratic, democratic, and laissez-faire (see Box C). Each has different implications for the exercise of authority and the methods to be used in influencing and motivating the membership of the group.

BOX C *Three models of classroom leadership*

The teacher's leadership style represents a personal approach
to the various roles that must be assumed in the classroom. The
teacher's position in relation to the students is essentially
different in each one.

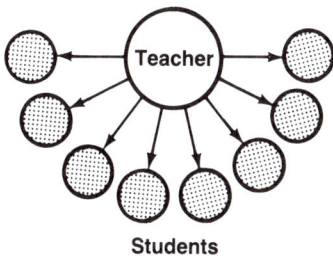

Students

1
Autocratically structured
classroom model—the teacher
is aloof; communication goes only
one way, from teacher to students.

2
Democratically structured
classroom model—the teacher
is approachable;
communication goes two ways
between teacher and students.

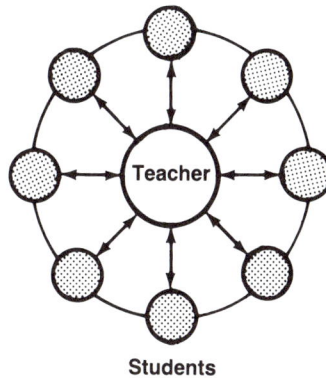

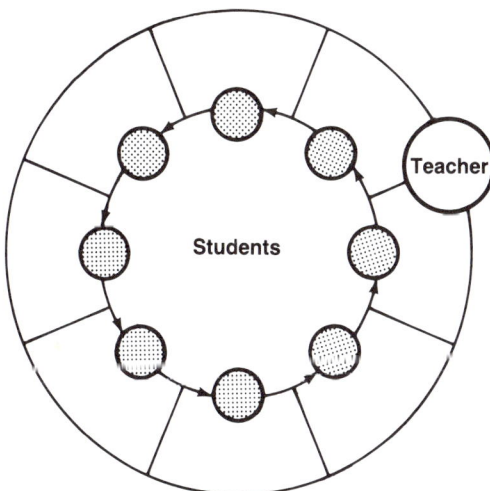

Students

Students

3
Laissez-faire structured
classroom model—the
teacher rarely interferes;
communication goes one way,
among students.

In educational settings, the teacher may not consciously choose a particular leadership style. Rather the leadership represents an amalgamation of approaches which fit the daily demands of the classroom environment. Although it is tempting to give one leadership style more credence than others, each must be analyzed in the context in which it is implemented.

THE AUTOCRATIC OR AUTHORITARIAN STYLE

In the autocratic or authoritarian style the leader remains aloof from the group, and all policies, processes, and objectives are transmitted from teacher to student. Classroom policies are determined solely by the teacher. Work tasks are dictated to students, and even the choice of companions is at the discretion of the teacher. The activities and tasks the student must perform are usually revealed in segments, so that future events are only vaguely defined. The teacher-student relationship is based on automatic and unquestioned response to directions and characterized by uncertainty and role ambiguity.

Autocratic leaders usually offer praise and criticism in a personal, individualistic fashion. They rarely engage in group activities or active involvement with students, except to demonstrate or elaborate on points made during presentations to the group. Communication between teacher and student usually is at a superficial level, and warmth and emotional attachment rarely enter into the relationship. The teacher's conception of the leadership role best fits the model of the tyrant described above.

THE DEMOCRATIC STYLE

Democratic principles of leadership allow class members to generate group activities and shared work responsibilities. Communication between students and teachers is characterized by bilateral decision making and student participation in discussions and in the setting of objectives. In most democratic classroom environments, the teacher initiates and directs the instruction, but many of the classroom activities and decisions are determined in consultation with or on the approval of the group. The teachers and students establish a two-way channel of communication, in which students interact with one another and with the instructor.

Research has shown that both autocratic and democratic leadership styles have a substantial impact on the classroom learning environment. Autocratic leaders are likely to remain distant from students and to be concerned with classroom management and procedures rather than learning outcomes. Democratic leaders, in contrast, promote a free exchange of attitudes and ideas and do not allow their own positions to govern the actions of the group. Investigations of leadership styles have confirmed that participatory classrooms produce higher group satisfaction and more receptivity to new ideas and change. Ryans (1952, 1960) found that teachers who were regarded as understanding, attentive to pupil needs, and consistent were more likely to have students who demonstrated interest, participation, enthusiasm, and desirable behaviors than autocratic instructors were.

In its purest form, a democratically structured classroom group would formulate all policy and make all decisions in group discussions, with direction and assistance from the teacher. Activities are generally sketched out in advance for students, but the teacher's input to group decision making is limited to suggestions, curricular or technical advice, and the procedural implications of various activities. The teacher provides a general framework of conduct and instruction, while the division of tasks, designation of short-run objectives, and assignment to subgroups are left up to class members.

The Hierarchical-Cooperative Model

Both the autocratic and democratic models of classroom organization are ideal types. Few teachers strictly fit either the purely autocratic or democratic molds; most are at one time or another likely to engage in one or more types of leadership behavior. Although teachers may have a dominant mode of operation, they adjust their leadership styles to meet the situation, as dictated by the mood of the class, the type of instructional technique being employed, and the teacher's disposition. When students do not respond to prods by a democratic teacher, for example, the procedure may be modified by delegating authority to several key members of the class and making them responsible for the coordination of activities.

This hierarchical subtype of cooperative classroom preserves the egalitarian relationship between teacher and students of the democratic style but allows the teacher to influence the group. The influence comes indirectly through contact with the membership as a whole and directly through contact with key members of the group. In practice most classrooms are organized in at least partly hierarchical or autocratic fashion; no matter how the teacher implements egalitarian procedures, the institutional power invested in the teacher inherently unbalances the teacher-student power relationship. For this reason, complete trust by students and their full cooperation are difficult to achieve.

THE LAISSEZ-FAIRE STYLE

A third major leadership style which found its way into educational circles when nonstructured, open classrooms were introduced in the late

1960s is the *laissez-faire* approach. This approach to management and leadership, which is not widely practiced today, minimizes the teacher's participation in structuring activities. Punishment is rarely necessary because activities and objectives are determined by the students. Studies have shown that student anxiety may be higher in this context than in either autocratic or democratic settings, but there is also evidence that certain types of emotional gains are realized.

In the open classrooms found in schools today, the teacher has a consultative or cooperative position as pupils plan their own goals and undertake their learning. The truly laissez-faire approach to leadership is generally not well regarded, particularly in schools with conventional educational programs. This style is not suited to organizational environments which emphasize task completion and the mastery of goals. To many teachers, as well as parents and administrators, the freedom accorded to individuals and the secondary role of the teacher in this model suggest an abdication of management and leadership responsibilities rather than a reformulation of them. The infrequent, spontaneous teacher comments and the unregulated, uncharted course of events which characterize laissez-faire leadership do not fit the teacher's role expectations. The term *more open classrooms* is used in this text (and elsewhere in education) to refer to models that are comparatively more democratic than autocratic in style or that allow for more participation by students as compared to traditional teacher-directed instruction, as described in Chapter 12.

CREATING A CLASSROOM CLIMATE

Whichever leadership style teachers adopt, they are concerned most with the task of maintaining control. Teachers must create order and discipline before they can teach. Lortie (1975) reports that, on average, teachers spend approximately 40 percent of effective class time on monitoring and disciplinary activities, much to their displeasure.

The ways teachers administer a class and students respond to their direction combine to form a *classroom climate*, or psychological environment, in which learning takes place. The climate not only affects the learning which takes place in the group but also governs the affective or emotional results of classroom interactions.

Classrooms which are relatively open or participatory are likely to have certain characteristics, according to Epstein and McPortland (1979):

1. Movable furniture and varied instructional spaces.
2. Several activities going on simultaneously.
3. Students freely moving among activities.
4. Several teachers supervising activities.

Table 13.3

Effects of more open and traditional classrooms
on cognitive and affective change

	Results *(percent of studies)*			
Variable *(number of studies)*	Open Better	Traditional Better	Mixed Results	No Significant Differences
Academic achievement (102)	14	12	28	46
Self-concept (61)	25	3	25	47
Attitude toward school (57)	40	4	25	32
Creativity (33)	36	0	30	33
Independence and conformity (23)	78	4	9	9
Curiosity (14)	43	0	36	21
Anxiety and adjustment (39)	26	13	31	31
Locus of control (24)	25	4	17	54
Cooperation (9)	67	0	11	22
Overall average	39	4	24	33

Source: Adapted from Robert Horowitz, "Effects of the Open Classroom," in Herbert Walberg (Ed.), *Educational Environments and Effects* (Berkeley, Cal.: McCutchan Publishing Co., 1979), p. 286.

5. Informal student-teacher relations.
6. Emphasis on individualized instruction.
7. Infrequent direct supervision of student tasks and assignments.

Whether participatory classrooms and democratic teaching styles promote learning better than more traditional models was investigated by Horowitz (1979). As Table 13.3 shows, of the 102 studies of academic achievement he reviewed, nearly half (46 percent) found no significant difference in the cognitive achievement of students in open as opposed to traditional classrooms; 14 percent found open classrooms better and 12 percent found traditional classrooms better. When the size of the effects of classroom style was examined, traditional teaching styles produced slightly higher achievement scores than open styles. These slight gains were offset, however, by the superior performance in the open classrooms on the social-psychological variables. Although approximately one third of the studies indicated no differences on these dimensions, nontraditional approaches to classroom instruction did favor the development of such characteristics as creativity, independence, and cooperation.

One of the chief criticisms leveled against participatory classrooms and laissez-faire leadership styles is that these arrangements may breed uncontrollable discipline problems. Disciplinary efforts detract from the time the teacher can devote to teaching and evaluation. Moreover, teachers' expectations about academic achievement are affected by their appraisals of troublesome students, as we noted in Chapter 9. Thus a teacher's evaluation of a student's academic ability may be influenced by the pupil's history of behavior.

Introducing new styles of leadership and trying to redefine traditional roles in the classroom are difficult undertakings. Educational institutions and, for the most part, the people working in them have been trained to handle recurring problems in traditional ways, as Novotney and Tye (1973) have observed: "First, education is fraught with traditions and bureaucratic structures. Second, those who are promoted and put into positions of responsibility are people who have learned to adhere closely to those traditions and structures." As a result, conformity to traditional methods of classroom conduct are perceived to have tangible payoffs for the teacher. In the short run, customary approaches to instruction and classroom management result in favorable ratings by supervisors who expect traditional forms of behavior from their teachers.

Schools are not only bureaucratic organizations themselves, they are also units within even more highly structured school districts. The emphasis in the system is on efficiency and the perpetuation of offices and functions from one year to the next. In such a system the rewards go to those who are stable and consistent and who have the personality traits that have been recognized as traits typical of higher level administrators.

In teaching, as in most other occupations, extended exposure to the organizational environment causes individuals to internalize the values and standards of performance held by their superiors. In this sense classroom leaders come to embody the organization's values. For *dynamic* leadership to exist, however, the leader must also work to change existing values and procedures and initiate new ones which may be more productive. A dynamic leader sets the pace for change within the organization or group and marks a trail for others to follow. The bureaucratic characteristics of formal educational institutions, however, make it difficult for leaders to propose or try out innovative forms of instructional techniques or teacher-student relationships.

CHAPTER 13 IN RETROSPECT

Leadership is authority which is voluntarily entrusted to an individual by a group. In the classroom group the formal leader is the teacher. Authority is attached to the teacher's role or position and regarded as a legitimate means of power. The classroom group may also have informal leaders or students who are able to influence the actions of the other members. Both types of leaders are vested by the group with power or influence to initiate, guide, and direct the realization of the group's objectives.

Group leaders can be classified as responsible (the leader in the organizational structure), effective (the most important member in making decisions), or psychological (the most influential member). In the classroom group the responsible leader is always the teacher or a designated substitute. Effective and psychological leadership may be vested solely in the teacher or be shared with class members. The type and quality of teacher leadership are determined by institutional characteristics and personality attributes. The teacher may follow the style of a patriarchal sovereign, leader, or tyrant, but these roles and others adopted by the teacher or group members may come into conflict in the teacher-student interactions of the instructional process.

Through their leadership styles, teachers help create a classroom climate. These environments are of three general types: democratic, autocratic, and laissez-faire. In general, more open classrooms foster the growth of social-psychological characteristics such as independence, curiosity, and cooperation. More traditionally structured environments seem to have a slight advantage in increasing achievement scores, however.

The leadership task of the teacher is complicated by the need to reconcile considerations for the class as a collective group with the intellectual and psychological needs of individual pupils. The teacher's paradox describes the dilemma of the teacher who is bound by the notion of equal treatment of all students on the one hand and the need to dispense special help and consideration to some students on the other. Classroom leadership requires a skillful mix of teaching behaviors— applying rules and procedures impartially, predictably, and consistently, and giving attention to the uniqueness of each student's problems and competencies. The teacher's personal traits and teaching behaviors are scrutinized by class members for evidence of approval and encouragement, as well as to uncover signs of favoritism or rejection. Satisfying the student's self-concept needs may be the most difficult part of the leadership task for the teacher to perform.

As leaders, teachers are expected to encourage students, especially when they must learn difficult concepts or their performance is below par. Relieving student anxiety, bolstering egos, and offering reassurance may be just as important to the development of a child in the social-emotional domain as the dissemination of factual information in a classroom is in the cognitive-intellectual domain. The perceived relevance and fairness of punishments and rewards administered in the classroom have a bearing on this aspect of classroom leadership. The objectivity of the teacher in assessing students' daily work and making periodic reports of progress (or lack of progress) is another factor, as Part IV will show.

1. In the discussion of teachers' institutional roles we referred to Wright's classification of them as tyrants, patriarchal sovereigns, and leaders. Think back to your elementary or secondary school days. Did any of your former instructors fit these prototypes? Can you think of any teachers who don't fit into these categories? What are their characteristics, and how would you label them?

2. If you are thinking about becoming a teacher, is there any single instructor you have encountered who has been instrumental in convincing you about your career choice? Is this person a teaching model for you? What characteristics of this instructor would you like to have in your own teaching?

3. When you think of an elementary school teacher, what image do you see? On a sheet of paper, quickly list the first ten descriptive words or phrases which come to your mind. Compare and discuss your descriptors with those of other students. Do you have a different set of images for secondary teachers?

4. In this chapter we distinguished among psychological, responsible, and effective classroom leadership. Have you been in a classroom where the teacher did not perform all those roles? Who did perform them? How did this arrangement affect the conduct of the class?

5. Have you ever been in an open classroom? How did it differ from other class arrangements you have experienced or observed? Did you like this experience? Why or why not?

Introductory Level

Jackson, Philip. *Life in Classrooms.* New York: Holt, Rinehart & Winston, 1968.

There are few more readable, cogent observations of what goes on from day to day in classrooms. Jackson artfully captures the demands placed on students and teachers by the structure and organization of the school.

Illich, Ivan. *Deschooling Society.* New York: Harper & Row, 1970.

This book is highly critical of formal education and hence quite controversial. It suggests that schooling demands that teachers *indoctrinate, not lead.* His work explains how teachers can be leaders only if education is taken out of schools and placed back in the community where it belongs, according to Illich.

McPherson, Gertrude. *Small Town Teacher*. Cambridge, Mass.: Harvard University Press, 1972.

This is an engaging social-psychological-anthropological account of life as a teacher in a small New England school. The author analyzes the complex leadership roles of the teacher and links them to the multitude of pressures exerted by peers, students, administrators, and the public.

Coleman, James. *The Adolescent Society*. New York: Free Press, 1961.

Although this book is over 20 years old, few other works capture so well pupil and teacher relationships in a school. The sections on formation of peer groups and classroom subgroups are essential reading for anyone concerned with classroom leadership and group management.

Dreeben, Robert. *The Nature of Teaching*. Glenview, Ill.: Scott, Foresman & Co., 1970.

Although the entire book is recommended for prospective teachers as an excellent overview of teaching as an occupation, Chapter 3 is especially relevant to the material contained in this chapter of this book. Dreeben assesses the organizational constraints placed on teachers which limit their leadership independence.

Advanced Level

Berger, Peter, and Luckmann, Thomas. *The Social Construction of Reality*. New York: Doubleday & Co., 1967.

This book is a major theoretical treatise on how and why we perceive ourselves and others the way we do. Students interested in how roles are determined and self-concepts are formed will find this book challenging but invaluable.

Bruce, Joyce, and Weil, Marsha. *Models of Teaching*. Englewood Cliffs, N.J.: Prentice-Hall, 1972.

This book offers a detailed description and critique of a host of classroom instructional models. Students who want to explore the linkages between the structuring of social relationships in classrooms and social and cognitive change will find this a rich resource of material.

Dunkin, Michael, and Biddle, Bruce. *The Study of Teaching*. New York: Holt, Rinehart & Winston, 1974.

The authors of this book have pulled together an immense amount of research on various aspects of teaching and concisely summarized it.

Chapter 5 dealing with classroom climate, Chapter 6 on management and control, and Chapter 7 on the classroom as a social system provide numerous reports on leadership influences and teaching styles.

> Bennett, Neville. *Teaching Styles and Pupil Progress.* Cambridge, Mass.: Harvard University Press, 1976.

An in-depth study of elementary classrooms which illustrate a variety of teaching styles. Bennett focuses on the costs and benefits associated with instruction in an open setting.

> Walberg, Herbert (Ed.). *Educational Environments and Effects.* Berkeley, Cal.: McCutchan Publishing Co., 1979.

This is an excellent collection of articles covering virtually all aspects of the importance of teachers and their roles in creating educational climates. The effects of various learning settings on cognitive and affective change are explained both theoretically and empirically.

REFERENCES

Berger, Peter, and Luckmann, Thomas. *The Social Construction of Reality.* New York: Doubleday & Co., 1967.

Berne, Eric. *The Structure and Dynamics of Organizations and Groups.* New York: Grove Press, 1963.

Bidwell, Charles. The school as a formal organization. In James G. March (Ed.), *Handbook of Organizations.* Chicago: Rand McNally & Co., 1965.

Cooley, Charles Horton. *Social Organization.* New York: Scribner's, 1909.

Dreeben, Robert. *On What Is Learned in School.* Reading, Mass.: Addison-Wesley Publishing Co., 1970.

Dreeben, Robert. American schooling: Patterns and processes of stability and change. In B. Barber and A. Inkeles (Eds.), *Stability and Social Change.* Boston: Little, Brown & Co., 1971.

Durkheim, Émile. *Moral Education.* New York: Free Press, 1961.

Epstein, Joyce, and McPortland, James. Authority structures. In Herbert Walberg (Ed.), *Educational Environments and Effects.* Berkeley, Cal.: McCutchan Publishing Co., 1979.

Getzels, Jacob W. Theory and research on leadership: Some comments and some alternatives. In Luvern Cunningham and William Gephart (Eds.), *Leadership: The Science and the Art Today.* Itasca, Ill.: F. E. Peacock Publishers, 1973.

Getzels, Jacob W., Lipham, J. M., and Campbell, R. F. *Educational Administration as a Social Process.* New York: Harper & Row, 1968.

Grant, Vance, and Lind, C. George. *Digest of Educational Statistics 1977–78,* Table 3, p. 7. Washington, D.C.: U.S. Government Printing Office, 1978.

Halpin, A. W. *The Leadership Behavior of School Superintendents*. Chicago: Midwest Administration Center, University of Chicago, 1957.

Hodge, Robert, Siegel, Paul, and Rossi, Peter. Occupational prestige in the United States: 1925–1963. In Reinhard Bendix and S. M. Lipset (Eds.), *Class, Status and Power*. New York: Free Press, 1966.

Hollander, Edwin, and Julian, James. Leadership. In Edgar F. Borgatta and William Lambert (Eds.), *Handbook of Personality Theory and Research*. Chicago: Rand McNally & Co., 1968.

Holsinger, Donald. The schooling environment as a context for individual modernization. Unpublished manuscript, 1976.

Holsinger, Donald, and Theisen, Gary. Education, individual modernity and national development: A critical appraisal. *Journal of Developing Areas*, 1977, *11*(3), 323.

Horowitz, Robert. Effects of the open classroom. In Herbert Walberg (Ed.), *Educational Environments and Effects*. Berkeley, Cal.: McCutchan Publishing Co., 1979.

Lortie, Dan. *Schoolteacher*. Chicago: University of Chicago Press, 1975.

McPherson, Gertrude. *Small Town Teacher*. Cambridge, Mass.: Harvard University Press, 1972.

Mead, George Herbert. *Mind, Self and Society*. Chicago: University of Chicago Press, 1934.

Moreno, J. L., Jennings, Helen H., and others (Eds.). *The Sociometric Reader*. Glencoe, Ill.: Free Press, 1960.

Novotney, Jerrold, and Tye, Kenneth A. *Dynamics of Educational Leadership*. Los Angeles: Educational Resource Association, Inc., 1973.

Ryans, D. G. A study of criterion data. *Educational and Psychological Measurement*, 1952, *12*, 333–344.

Ryans, David G. *Characteristics of Teachers*. Washington, D.C.: American Council on Education, 1960.

Sharp, Rachael, and Green, Anthony. *Education and Social Control: A Study in Progressive Primary Education*. London: Routledge & Kegan Paul, 1975.

Steiner, Ivan D. Group dynamics. In Paul R. Farnsworth, Olga McNemar, and Quinn McNemar (Eds.), *Annual Review of Psychology*, (Vol. 15). Palo Alto, Cal.: Annual Reviews, 1964.

Wright, Benjamin. Identification and becoming a teacher. *Elementary School Journal*, April 1959.

Classroom Groups

There are all kinds of classrooms and school groups—quiet or noisy, busy or lazy, chaotic or well organized. In some classes students can relax and be at ease with classmates and the teacher, and in others the pressure to perform and the resulting tension and anxiety are so great as to be almost visible. The same course can be taught to two different classes in the same way and yet have very different outcomes, as James McMillan (1980) notes:

> One class seems to respond better, to ask more stimulating questions, and to be more alert than the other class. At the end of a semester I think of one class very fondly as a group of people who became a cohesive, happy unit and shared my positive feeling about the course. I remember the other class more as work with few satisfactions or rewards for me or the students. (p. 1)

What accounts for the differences in these learning situations? Is one classroom climate more conducive to the mastery of material than the other? Can learning be facilitated or hindered by the selection and grouping of the students in the class or the relationships between the teacher and the students? Do subgroups of students based on socioeconomic status, race, or sex affect their members' achievement and aspirations?

We will examine these questions in explaining the nature of groups in the school and how they affect the social and organizational environments for the instructional process. Although learning takes place at the individual level, the ratio of as many as 30 students to one teacher in the classroom requires the formation of student subgroups for both administrative and instructional purposes. These groups may be created by the teachers or the school administration or they may be organized by students, either according to explicit criteria, as in the case of clubs like the Thespians or the National Honor Society, or implicitly, on the basis of friendships, ability, or social class.

Teachers facilitate the formation of groups in the classroom by the way in which they structure activities and organize the learning environment. Some instructors emphasize group work and class discussion, while others favor direct instruction—the lecture and recitation style of teaching (see Chapter 12). Each grouping and each style of classroom organization utilizes a unique set of rules, both official and unofficial, which govern the expectations and behaviors of the members of the group. Thus each configuration of students and teachers represents a different environment and set of norms which determine how classroom situations are perceived and evaluated. Because of the variety of student personalities and backgrounds in various classrooms, there are different group responses to the learning environment and teaching style. In secondary school, these interactions are renegotiated each time the school bell rings and a new class is called to order. At the elementary level, groupings are more stable because a fixed body of students constitutes a class which meets with a single teacher for the entire day, and usually for an entire school year.

An effective teacher draws on the strengths, allegiances, and self-concepts shared by members of classroom groups to promote a desire to learn and achieve, just as a basketball coach tries to inspire motivation, enthusiasm, and team spirit among the players. To understand the dynamics of group formation and group processes, we must first examine some of the identifying characteristics of formal and informal affiliations.

THE NATURE OF GROUP IDENTIFICATION

Everyone is a member of certain groups, and some people belong to many of them. Memberships are determined by design as well as by accident or circumstance. Groups may be formed because of the voluntary desires or involuntary assignment of the members, or their basis may be the members' innate, unchangeable characteristics.

Voluntary groups are made up of individuals who have chosen to affiliate themselves for a specific reason or because of their identification with a common set of goals, interests, or characteristics. The Shriners, Greek fraternities and sororities, local booster clubs, and Rotary clubs are all examples of collections of people who have willingly bonded together to pursue common activities and shared goals.

Involuntary groups are comprised of people who have been assigned a common status or have organized together to engage in similar tasks. The individuals may be uninterested in or even opposed to membership in the organization, but nevertheless they may be drafted or coerced into participation. Prisoners are most certainly involuntary members of groups in penal institutions. As we noted in Chapter 13, in U.S. schools the student body is an involuntary group; though most students may attend willingly, some do so not because they *want* to but because they *have* to! One of the dilemmas for the classroom teacher is how to stimulate those students who enjoy school and at the same time interest those who view it with little enthusiasm.

Practically speaking, an involuntary group is not really a group but rather a collective. A *collective* is a gathering of people who do not meet in face-to-face involvement but who are engaged in a common activity or who have a common characteristic which helps form their identity (Mills, 1967). Groups are characterized not only by the voluntary or involuntary nature of their membership but also by face-to-face interactions and communications, a common goal or goals, and an awareness of and identification with a set of common beliefs and attitudes. As leaders, teachers can utilize these characteristics in developing their institutional and personal authority in the classroom (see Chapter 13).

Most people are members of both voluntary and involuntary groups, even though they may consciously identify themselves only with memberships that are voluntary. Everyone also has *ascriptive memberships,* or associations with which they are born or inherit, such as race, sex, and social class. These involuntary associations may affect a person's ability to choose voluntary membership in other groups. In the U.S. population, for example, 51 percent is female, which can automatically mean discrimination in job hiring, pay, and promotion. Another 16 percent of U.S. citizens is black, and certain clubs and private organizations systematically exclude them from membership on the basis of their color or ancestry. These involuntary identifications may also lead people into particular voluntary associations. Although black students' associations are technically open to all interested parties, for example, membership is usually reserved for those who are identified as blacks.

AFFILIATION, GROUP BOUNDARIES, AND GROUP STATUS

The need to belong or to affiliate with others was identified in Chapter 11 as one of the five basic needs of humans. The desire to be with others may be based on a need for information that only others can provide or on a search for rewards through the recognition of others. Most reasons for becoming a part of a group can be classified as either extrinsic (external) or intrinsic (internal) in nature.

The distinction between extrinsic and intrinsic motivation also was made in Chapter 11. *Extrinsic* motives are linked to tangible payoffs of a social or economic nature. A student's desire to become a member of the French club, for example, might be due to a desire for help with learning the language. Club membership could provide another student with a chance to exercise leadership in a smaller, more congenial group setting than the classroom. Joining a group might even provide an opportunity to meet a "special someone" of the opposite sex. *Intrinsic* motives are those that provide psychological satisfaction to the individual. A student might join a coin club for the primary reason of sharing a keen interest in numismatics with others or for the extrinsic motive of improving a collection by trading with others who have similar interests.

Students are affiliated with all kinds of large formal and informal groups, but on a day-to-day basis they usually define themselves and their activities in terms of rather focused criteria of group membership. Bill and May may think of themselves first as members of the advanced college preparatory stream of students. Most of their friends are fellow students who are also members of the academic elite. John and Sally, however, identify themselves as athletes more than scholars. The main focus of their school life is on sports, and the majority of their friendships and conversations are sports related. The less general the criteria for group membership are, the more likely they are to cross the boundaries of ascriptive membership.

The process of defining our identity can be viewed as analogous to peeling away the layers of an onion. As we gradually expose the layers of our self we reach the levels of our identity which are most central to us. Other individuals who share the characteristics defined by these layers will probably be members of our most highly valued group affiliations. In response to the question, "Who am I?" many people will identify themselves first by a surname: "I am Marie Jones." This suggests that the members of Marie's family are of central importance to her. If she then defines herself as a singer, it is likely that she associates with individuals who share this interest. Friendships are not made solely on the basis of common, mutual interests, however. Personality, race, social class, and other factors also affect social interaction.

In most classrooms the pupils differ in such variables as social class, ability, ethnicity, race, and religion (the effects of similar factors on group differences in intelligence were discussed in Chapter 6). These identifying classifications are not mutually exclusive, however. The formation of group affiliations in school rarely occurs solely on the basis of a single characteristic. Voluntary group membership is determined by a complex interplay of ascriptive and performance-based characteristics. Students have many identities, each of which is valued in different ways by different sets of peers.

A person's place in any system of social ranking, whether it be a classroom, a club, or an athletic team, is defined by the sum of membership affiliations and the combined status those memberships confer. Memberships in groups are varied and numerous, and status relative to others may be defined by the importance of a particular group membership among the individuals with whom the person interacts. In most high school yearbooks a list of activities and school organizations accompanies the picture of each graduate, and it would probably not be too far off the mark to identify the individuals with the highest status in the class solely by the length of their lists of membership affiliations. But belonging to many groups does not in itself confer status, unless the clubs and activities are recognized as prestigious in their own right. A seat on the student council is generally more likely to be regarded as awarding status than would be, say, the presidency of the Hot Rod Club, though students with an interest in cars and mechanics might disagree. Most people have a multitude of interests and therefore place varying values on their activities and those of others. This complicates the task of defining group boundaries and allocating status and respect within them.

Satisfaction with group membership is likely to be based on the rewards the individual derives from the affiliation. But payoffs to membership are always viewed relative to those accruing to other individuals in the group. A member who discovers that she does not completely share the norms, values, or goals of a particular group begins to examine critically the costs and benefits of membership. If she perceives that the respect and deference accorded to her by other members of the group are inconsistent with what is demanded of her, the bonds of membership will begin to unravel. The gap between the emotional investment required of membership and the returns flowing from it is referred to as *status inconsistency*. In groups where the characteristics and interests of the majority of members are substantially different from those of a single member, the lone individual begins to feel isolated and detached from the group. As the boundaries of the membership appear to circumscribe the individual motives for attachment to the group less certainly, the person who is different begins to look to other groups with which to share more common interests.

PRIMARY GROUP MEMBERSHIP

The varied, often conflicting memberships that students bring to the classroom may contribute to or detract from their cognitive-intellectual and social-emotional development and learning. The most intimate personal relationships take place in what Charles Horton Cooley labeled *primary groups*. Members of these groups are mutually committed to the welfare of the group, and they participate without question in all matters related to it. Membership in primary groups changes little over time and is seldom affected by external social pressures to change. Almost every individual is a member of at least one primary group.

The family provides the most important primary group attachment. It is the principal group during the first few years of life, when children are most susceptible to the influence and guidance of others, and the most lasting one. Status and responsibility in the family are determined primarily by relative chronological age. Age is used by parents and others as a general benchmark against which standards of proficiency and the appropriateness of tasks are measured. A three-year-old is told that she is not yet old enough to help wash the dinner dishes, which is the job of her eight-year-old brother. A six-year-old sister is chastised for spilling food on the table; when she complains that the three-year-old does the same thing and asks why her parents don't scold her, too, she is likely to be told that the three-year-old is younger and doesn't know any better.

The brother can stay up one-half hour later than his six-year-old sister because he is two years older. In these ways responsibilities and evaluations in the home are made relative to age and are not measured against an absolute standard.

Moreover, parents and other family members are *subjective* judges and evaluators of their kin. The family unit is tied together by emotional bonds of love and intimacy, which conveys unquestioned status and privilege to each of its members. Consequently, most children have little *objective* sense of their abilities relative to same-age peers. Parents may make comparisons to children outside the family, but the evaluation and its conveyance to the child are heavily tainted by love, loyalty, and familial closeness.

As children grow their circle of friends and acquaintances broadens beyond the immediate family. Play groups comprise an expanded circle of friends, and each group may have its own norms of behavior and unwritten rules governing membership. The four-year-old boy who "doesn't know how to share," for example, may be shunted to younger play groups by his same-age peers until he can comply with the group's rules of conduct. As new roles and new friendships are created; the importance of old groupings either fades away or persists. The child's exposure to others increases, but the number of his or her primary group affiliations stays relatively constant even though the groups may change. The number of *secondary groups*, or less personal, more institutional groups, that the individual belongs to increases dramatically, however.

SCHOOL GROUP ATTACHMENTS

Since the school is the center of activity for much of a young person's day, the majority of group attachments for children of school age are schooling related. A child entering school encounters for the first time a situation in which companions have been selected solely on the basis of age. But, while the age is the same, the classroom often includes children of a wide variety of family backgrounds and ability levels. Perhaps never before has the child been so aware that other young people of the same age are different in many ways: They may be more attractive, brighter, or more industrious, or uglier, duller, or lazier. For some youngsters the realization that they differ from their peers in ways that the teacher and other school officials consider significant may be intimidating. Despite the similarity of ages in most American classrooms—80 percent of classmates are within about seven months of each other in age—students are quick to discover that their classmates vary markedly in levels of educational preparation and ability, as well as personal and physical characteristics.

Elementary school children generally form primary groups from within the ranks of their own classmates (friendship alliances in a classroom are described in the section below on individuals and groups). This is less likely to be the case at the secondary level, when the importance of age differences among students diminishes and the mix of students and classes increases. Over time students develop expectations of each other based on the roles each has occupied in their past relationships. Some students may emerge as troublemakers, others will be looked to for leadership, and still others will develop reputations as class clowns or those who always know the answers.

Because students are generally drawn from the community at large, particularly in the public schools, classrooms can be thought of as mini societies which are affected by forces operating in society as a whole, as we noted in Chapter 13. Consequently, the issues which concern individuals and groups outside the school are likely to be brought to bear on the coordination and control of what goes on in the classroom. The relation of the instructional process to the external environment is the third dimension of the instructional process model which was introduced in Chapter 1. An example of an area in which public input affects educational decisions is the ability grouping of students and the related topic of educational equality.

ABILITY GROUPING

In facilitating the instructional process, the teacher must deal with a mixed group of students. For each grade level a set of general objectives is specified which is supposed to be accomplished each school year (see Chapter 15). The substantial differences in students' readiness characteristics—cognitive development, prior knowledge, level of intelligence, and disposition to learn, as specified in the instructional process model—make it likely that some pupils will accomplish much more than the defined tasks for the year, while others will accomplish less. It is the teacher's task to organize the class in such a way that all students perform to the best of their ability and their potential is realized.

Some educators maintain that in certain subjects students' talents will be used more fully if they are placed in a classroom which includes both high- and low-ability students. Such a mixed grouping theoretically enhances the slower learners' achievement because they can profit from the cognitive example of their more capable peers. The motivation of low achievers also is spurred by the competition and student models they encounter. Critics of mixed ability grouping maintain that most students learn more quickly when the classroom group includes only students of similar ability. The process of stratifying or constructing classroom groups according to ability is commonly known as *tracking* or *streaming*.

THE TRACKING CONTROVERSY

The principal criticism in the continuing controversy surrounding ability grouping, or streaming or tracking, is that it indirectly contributes to the perpetuation of social class inequities in society. Critics argue that students of lower socioeconomic backgrounds enter school less well prepared, socially and/or academically, than other children. Because the orientation and value system of the school reflect the dominant middle-class culture, students from poor backgrounds have a more difficult time adjusting to school and do not progress as rapidly as their peers. Consequently, they are tracked into lower ability groups where less is expected of them. Assignment to a specific ability group may in fact be a better indication of social class differences than of academic potential.

Thus, according to critics, the process of schooling perpetuates rather than reduces the differences between students of different social origins. Inferior position becomes a self-fulfilling prophecy: The act of grouping within the classroom tends to reinforce and legitimize lower-class students' insecurities by assigning them to positions in second- and third-rank ability groups. Their inferior position in the academic ranking system within the classroom mirrors their secondary social position in society, and they internalize and accept their subservient position in the school and extrapolate it to the larger social system. These students bring their educational and occupational aspirations and expectations into line with their position in the tracking system. Consequently, the critics argue, stratifying classrooms by ability inhibits rather than motivates lower-class student achievement and restricts rather than enhances their life chances.

Assignment to a low-ability group can have a very depressing effect on a child's enthusiasm for schooling and a profound impact on the child's self-esteem (see Box A). Rewards in the classroom are based on performance, and students in the lower tracks receive less valuable forms of approval than those in the upper tracks. Classroom status, therefore, is highly associated with the ability group or academic strata in which a student is placed.

The process of differentiating among students and labeling them mirrors the social stratification of society. In effect, the tracking system of the schools prepares students for allocation to a hierarchy of later social and occupational positions. Grouping by ability in the classroom corresponds to assigning status in the adult population on the basis of occupational prestige and the related factors of income and educational attainment, the principal criteria of social class. Even the terms used to

BOX A   *I'm starting to think they're right*

Assignment to ability groups in school can reflect and perpetuate social class differences. An example of how children perceive their assignment to a low-ability group is given in the following portion of an interview with an 11-year-old black student:

"The only thing that matters in my life is school and there they think I'm dumb and always will be. I'm starting to think they're right. Hell, I know they put all the Black kids together in one group if they can, but that doesn't make any difference either. I'm still dumb. Even if I look around and know that I'm the smartest in my group, all that means is that I'm the smartest of the dumbest, so I haven't gotten anywhere at all, have I? I'm right where I always was. Every word those teachers tell me, even the ones I like most, I can hear in their voice that what they're really saying is, 'All right you dumb kids. I'll make it as easy as I can, and if you don't get it then, then you'll never get it. Ever.' That's what I hear every day, man. From every one of them. Even the other kids talk that way to me too."

"You mean the kids in the upper track?" I asked, barely able to hold back my feelings of outrage.

"Upper tracks? Man, when do you think I see those kids? I never see them. Why should I? Some of them don't even go to class in the same building with me. If I ever walked into one of their rooms they'd throw me out before the teacher even came in. They'd say I'd only be holding them back from their learning. I wouldn't go near them," he grumbled. "And they wouldn't come around us neither, I'm sure."

Source: Thomas J. Cottle, "What Tracking Did to Ollie Taylor," *Social Policy,* vol. 5 (July–August 1974), p. 24.

describe ability groupings within the classroom frequently reflect the relative social status of members of those groups. Rist's (1973) study of the urban school, for example, reported that in one elementary classroom student groups were named "lions," "tigers," and "clowns," according to their ability level. It is easy to guess which of these groups was at the low end of the tracking scheme! But it is not always the low-ability students who suffer from mixed ability grouping. In his study of schoolteachers, Lortie (1976) quoted one elementary instructor who lamented, "I know my greatest fault is that I neglect the brightest children. I work with the slow group first. Then I feel guilty about the brighter ones, that I haven't given the time I should but there are just so many minutes in the day" (p. 147).

Despite examples of this sort, in general the effect of ability grouping on attitudes toward school and the development of self-esteem is not clear. Studies have indicated that tracking has a positive effect on some students and a negative one on others. In at least four studies low-ability students have been shown to develop positive self-images in mixed classes, while the self-concept of high-ability students has declined (Drews, 1962). Other research hints that both groups may gain or lose.

Generalizing about the effects of tracking is difficult because the results of the practice are related to the psychological and emotional maturity of the individual students as well as to the manner in which teachers treat differences and similarities in the classroom. For example, a two-year age difference among early elementary school children is marked by pronounced physical differences. An eight-year-old has advantages of size and experience over a six-year-old which may inhibit equal classroom participation, even though the younger child may be the intellectual equal of the older one. Play groups and semiorganized playground games like keep-away or tag rarely crosscut classroom (and age) boundaries, even though some of the younger students may be able to compete very favorably with older ones.

As students get older, age and relative size are less important as distinguishing characteristics. At the senior high school level, 10th-, 11th-, or 12th-grade students vie for the same positions on academic teams and for the same sets of grades in classes such as woodshop and home economics. For college students ascriptive characteristics such as age and size have almost no bearing on class assignments or academic competition. The implications of age or ability tracking, therefore, must be considered in relation to the stage of schooling.

Grouping by ability is a prevalent practice in the United States, where it is estimated that streaming is practiced in over 75 percent of the elementary and secondary schools (Findley & Bryan, 1971). School policies usually determine how students are to be assigned to ability groups.

Ability grouping has been found to have a positive effect on some students and a negative effect on others. How the practice affects students' self-concepts and academic achievement has not been clearly demonstrated.

They may suggest the use of several objective or subjective measures by the teacher, including:

1. Past grades and recommendations from teachers.
2. Performance on standardized achievement measures such as the Iowa Test of Basic Skills (see Chapter 17).
3. Background characteristics of the student, such as race, social class, and ethnicity.

No matter how irrelevant socioeconomic status, race, ethnicity, and even physical appearance may be to academic performance, these are all factors which consciously or unconsciously impinge on the teacher's construction of groups. This is true whether the groups actually exist or are merely groupings in the teacher's mind. When blind experiments were conducted in which essays to be graded had student pictures attached to them but no names, teachers consistently assigned the highest grades to compositions accompanied by pictures of the most attractive children. Other investigations have revealed that the more a student resembled an "ideal-typical" middle-class child, the higher were the appraisers' performance expectations. Everyone carries a lifetime of psychological baggage containing an array of socialized anticipations and responses to various stimuli. Teachers are no exceptions, and their perceptions may have tremendous consequences for the future well-being of their pupils, as we will note in the section on mixed ability grouping.

Consequences of Tracking

The most convincing argument yet put forward for ability grouping, or tracking, is that it helps teachers concentrate group resources on those pupils who need them. When the range of ability levels within a classroom group is narrow, few pupils will be significantly above or below the level of the lesson being taught by the instructor. Over all, less time and fewer resources are wasted for the minimum number of pupils in a tracked situation, and performance can be enhanced by a closer match of teaching methodologies to pupil needs.

Opponents of tracking argue that reducing differences among students in classroom groups restricts the types of social experiences they are exposed to. When students are presented with an artificial conception of social reality, their short-run experiences in the school can be adversely affected. In the long run, too, their adjustment to the larger social system may be impaired.

Persell (1977) concluded, after reviewing 271 reports of research on tracking, that although some assignments were made on the basis of social class and other ascriptive characteristics, even when ability levels were similar, the placement of students had little effect on their academic performance. She notes that

> . . . separation into ability groups has no clear-cut positive or negative effect on the average scholastic achievement of the students involved. There is a slight trend toward improving the achievement of "high ability" groups, but that is offset by substantial losses by the average and low groups. A number of studies, however, indicate that gains for the "high ability" group appear only when the content, materials and teaching methods are enriched for them and when they are "pushed." (pp. 92–93)

Persell suggests that the improved performance of high-ability groups, therefore, is due to the differentiated instructional process used for them, rather than ability grouping as such.

These comments reveal the most disturbing finding about ability groupings: The best students have preferential access to the highest quality schooling resources. Studies have demonstrated, for example, that in some schools the lower streams of students have been assigned the poorest teachers (Hargreaves, 1967). High-track students may also have better access to counselors, laboratory equipment, and educational opportunities outside the school, such as field trips (Hegns, 1974).

It appears, then, that the most serious concern about ability tracking is not that the process hinders or enhances learning. Rather it is that it saddles students with labels which are not easily shaken off and which may be applied on the basis of their ascriptive characteristics rather than their aptitude.

EDUCATIONAL EQUALITY: THE COLEMAN REPORT

To investigate the reasons for differences in educational achievement among students, the largest survey ever conducted of the American educational system compiled data on 45 school characteristics related to students, teachers, and instructional programs and facilities. The results, published in 1966 under the title *Equality of Educational Opportunity*, came to be known as the Coleman Report after James Coleman, the principal investigator.

This research was conducted during the height of the civil rights movement in the United States. Most educators and politicians expected the findings to demonstrate that differences in educational performance between whites and blacks and among students in different areas were due primarily to variations in the funds available to individual schools and the quality of physical resources available to students. If these hypotheses were borne out, it was thought, policymakers should then be able to develop intervention strategies and programs to bring about an equalization of the resources available to educational institutions. Ultimately, the thinking went, these actions would equalize achievement levels among the schools.

The appeal of this interpretation was that when educational inequality was defined as differences in achievement levels, it could be traced to inequities in the *process of education* rather than the social system as a whole. Therefore inequality could be reduced by changing patterns of expenditures and equalizing resources among the schools. From a policy standpoint, these are tasks which could be rather easily implemented. Producing educational equality would then be the responsibility of the schools and not the communities or the society in which the educational institutions are embedded.

The Coleman Report, however, generated evidence that differences in resources have very little effect, if any at all, in explaining differences in achievement. The educational and occupational background of the students' parents was the single most important predictor of achievement. One of the most significant conclusions of the report was that students from low socioeconomic status (SES) backgrounds do not perform as well as their peers from higher status schools because they are not exposed to models of students with high achievement and attainment aspirations. Because of this, the report speculated, it was likely that the only way differences in achievement could be improved was through a reallocation of *students*, not resources. One way of accomplishing this, it was suggested, was to expose pupils from low socioeconomic backgrounds to the motivational norms and aspirational models of students from upper- and middle-class backgrounds. The idea was that characteristics important to cognitive learning would be transmitted through the normal socialization process of schools in middle- and upper-status communities.

The Coleman Report was only the first of a number of achievement studies which developed similar interpretations of performance data. The recognition of the importance of social grouping they inspired helped promote the practice of busing students across school district lines in the quest for educational equality.

CLASSROOM IMPLICATIONS OF MIXED ABILITY GROUPING

Although the effects of the Coleman Report have been felt mainly at the administrative level of the school, the idea of shuffling students on the basis of race and socioeconomic characteristics has profound implications for the classroom instructor. Should teachers continue to group students by ability, putting the most able students in the same class and the least able in another, regardless of the resulting racial composition of the classrooms? Would separating the best students from the poorest maximize the learning potential of each group, assuming that this permits the teacher's efforts to be better directed to the specific problems of each group? Or, in light of the Coleman Report, would mixed ability grouping enhance learning for both sets of students? Can lower-SES, less well-prepared students benefit from the role models provided by upper-SES students, who may have higher expectations and ambitions?

It is generally recognized that the influence of students' social class origins and ethnic and racial background on ability grouping noted above can result in classroom groups which deprive certain children of the opportunity to reach their academic potential. Research on the social psychology of organizational behavior indicates that the actions of groups are affected by the structure of the organization and the background characteristics of the members of the group. In most schools, for example, classrooms are divided fairly evenly between females and males. In the philosophy of many single-sex boarding schools, however, identical socialization experiences for girls and boys are not regarded as desirable, and so they are educated separately. The federal mandate for coeducational physical education classes has prompted outcries from those who foresee socially as well as physically injurious results of the practice.

Parents have similar fears about the effects of racial and social class mixing in the classroom. They are afraid their children will learn bad habits from others who do not understand the "proper way" to behave, or their progress will be held up by less intelligent students who ask "stupid questions." Opinions like these are, to be sure, stereotyped overgeneralizations, and often they reflect the exceptions to the rule rather than the rule itself. But they do express concerns about the effects of peers as role models on children's learning.

Support for the role model explanation of achievement was found in a review of the research on the effects of racial composition on achievement and aspiration by Boocock (1980). She concluded that the smaller the percentage of minority students in a school, the higher will be their relative academic achievement, especially at the lower grade levels. But this relationship is true *only* when white and nonwhite students are placed in the same classes. When minority students are grouped together in classes, their achievement is poorer than if they were in nonintegrated schools. Boocock also found that the aspirations of black students in all-black schools are higher than those of blacks in predominantly white schools. This result has been attributed to the students' misperceptions of their own ability which result from their achievement in a largely noncompetitive academic environment. That is, high academic achievement which is measured relative to one's immediate peers can result in an unrealistic perspective of true ability, unless a more objective comparison is made to students in more competitive schools.

Perhaps unintentionally, teachers do categorize their pupils and set expectations for them based upon the students' physical appearance and social class, as we noted above. Most people are more favorably disposed to individuals who seem to share their beliefs, attitudes, and values. Since most teachers are middle class in origin, or at least have had extensive socialization in middle-class norms and values, they are more apt to identify with, and so regard more positively, students who come from similar middle-class backgrounds. As a result, many teachers regard the chances of success, both academically and socially, for middle-class children more favorably. Thus academic grouping may be not only an index of demonstrated ability and performance, but also a projection of expected achievement levels that are associated with general group characteristics rather than an individual's abilities and potentials.

But surely when teachers become aware that students' performances are incongruent with their expected achievement, the students will be transferred into an appropriate ability group—or will they? Unfortunately, most of the time they are not (Jackson, 1964). The likelihood of a student being transferred out of a group into one of higher or lower status is relatively low. Jackson found that although 40 percent of all students in his study should have been transferred from one ability group to another on the basis of their performance, only 5 percent of them actually were.

The early classification of students on the basis of criteria unrelated to performance, such as sex, appearance, race, and SES, thus is not easily overcome during the schooling process. Furthermore, the longer students remain in their groupings, the more likely they are to adopt the group's average achievement level or expectations. Their performance is then brought into line with their expectations. In the presence of others for any length of time, students generate self-expectations which are congruent with their perceptions of the expectations others have of them. If both the self and "other" opinion is low, self-concept may decline, and eventually performance will diminish.

EFFECTS OF SELF-ESTEEM AND PEER EVALUATIONS

Earlier in this chapter we compared the way individuals identify dimensions of their self-consciousness to peeling away the layers of an onion. In each of these perceived layers there is also a qualitative assessment of how well the person fits the defined roles. You may identify yourself as a student or an athlete, for example, but how good are you as a pupil or team member?

The term *self-concept* refers to the way individuals characterize and evaluate themselves in the many roles they take in their daily lives. The self-concept is not formed on the basis of any single function the individual performs, however; rather it is a developmental personality factor which emerges in later childhood as a sense of self-as-object and self-as-doer (see Chapter 3). An adolescent girl may think of herself as an excellent student but a terrible athlete; fluent in French but an abominable artist; a compassionate friend but a jealous competitor. Cumulatively these self-appraisals let her take stock of herself relative to her expectations for herself and those others seem to have for her. Some self-judgments are made in comparison to an abstract idea: "I want to be able to play the piano flawlessly." Few of us, however, ever realize perfection, and our successes and failures are sometimes measured in relation to the achievements of others and sometimes in relation to a standard of excellence. What matters is not whether we play a piece well enough to please ourselves but where we stand in relation to how well the piece can be played.

Through a process of repeated comparisons we develop a conceptualization of what our relative capabilities and limitations are in each of the roles we occupy. We also develop an awareness of what others' expectations are of us. Young boys, for example, learn of others' opinions of their baseball ability by the order in which they are selected by team captains at the start of sandlot games. A high-ability student's status might be indicated by peers who ask, "You got an A again, didn't you?" when papers are handed back, or a teacher may say, "I wonder who got the 23% on this test?" knowing that the class will name the low achiever.

Favorable evaluations from peers contribute to a positive self-image; negative appraisals inhibit the development of a strong self-image. In Figure 14.1, the solid directional lines represent paths of influence from peer evaluation to self-esteem. The higher students' self-concepts are,

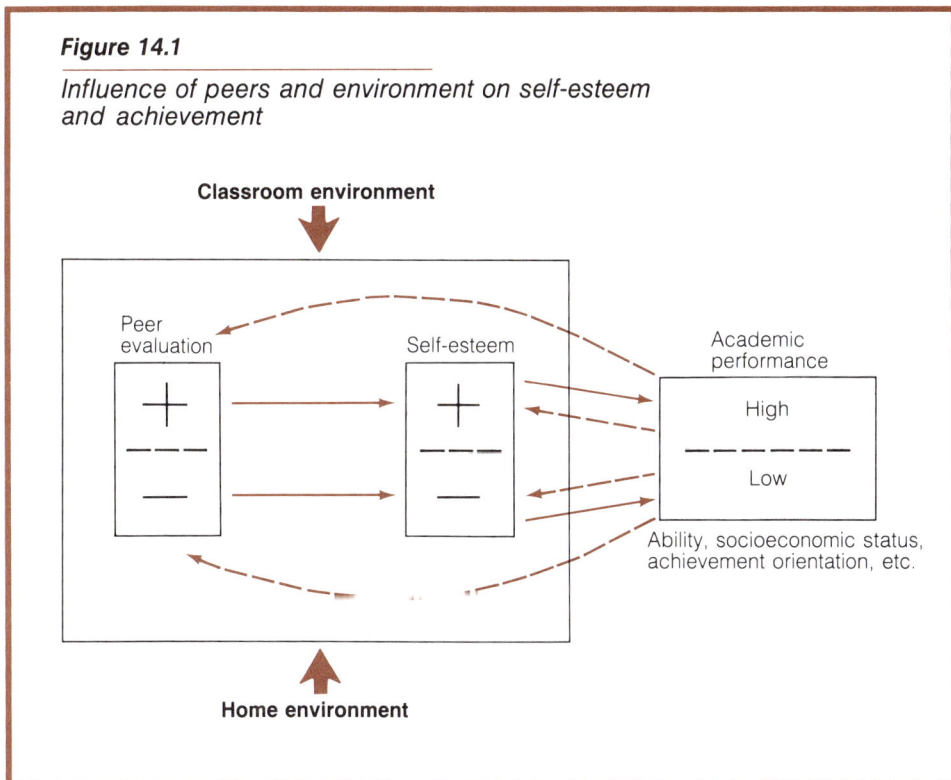

Figure 14.1

Influence of peers and environment on self-esteem and achievement

based in part on peer evaluations, the more confidence they have in their ability, and the higher their performance expectations will be. These expectations, coupled with ability and background characteristics, affect the students' levels of performance. The dotted lines indicate a reverse causal influence: the better or worse students perform, the more strongly will their peers' opinions of them be reinforced. These assessments will in turn be conveyed back to the students, whose self-concepts will be reinforced or perhaps adjusted accordingly.

This interaction among peers is also affected by other socialization agents. The support and encouragement (or lack of it) students find at home are major determinants of self-esteem, and so is the environment created by the teacher in the classroom. Some instructors provide a classroom climate which nurtures cooperation and minimizes competition; others may emphasize independence and downplay group activities and mutual support (see Chapter 13). More will be said about classroom organization in a later section of this chapter.

Because so much importance is attached to academic performance in defining a student's status and the student role is a central one for most children, being able to meet the demands and expectations of peers and teachers is instrumental to a child's sense of well-being. Children's opinions of themselves and the perceived expectations and opinions of others are key determinants of both educational aspirations and expectations. Aspirations are usually congruent with those of others with similar ability levels, so in classrooms where students are grouped by achievement it is not surprising that the students have similar expectations of their own possibilities. Although research has found little direct effect of tracking on achievement, there is good reason to believe that when ability grouping takes ascriptive characteristics into account it may have important *indirect* influences on performance. A child's self-concept may be strengthened or lowered depending on classroom peers and the manner in which their influence is mediated by the teacher's control of the classroom environment.

STUDENT STATUS IN ACADEMIC AND NONACADEMIC GROUPS

In the same way each individual enjoys a status in a community of friends and neighbors, so does each student in a school have a certain status. *Status* is a relative position in a system of social ranking. The attribution of status to an individual is a complex process which is determined by weighing and analyzing the collection of positions the person occupies. One of the principal functions of the school is to produce meaningful learning through the instructional process, which would seem to dictate that rewards are to be distributed according to level of academic performance. Thus demonstrated scholastic ability ought to be the primary determinant of social rank in the school. However, because of the many dimensions of status, this is not always the case. A student's status in a classroom is determined not only by academic performance but by how well the student performs in the roles of friend, student leader, classroom organizer, and athlete, among others.

Students who excel as athletes, for example, are often popular with their classmates. Especially if they are endowed with good looks, athletes are important figures in an adolescent's emerging awareness that psychological rewards can come from various sources. The success of athletes also helps create a common status for the school body as a whole. Victories in games help to generate a *collective* sense of self-worth and identification for all those in the school.

An individual student may be regarded as a failure in the role of scholar but still be accorded status for performing successfully in other school capacities or roles. It is unfortunate that school boards often restrict or eliminate nonacademic activities when it is necessary to cut budgets. Aside from the educational function these activities perform, the roles they create for students may provide a low achiever with a means of developing a positive self-concept and demonstrating some type of role competence. Because students are evaluated and rewarded on the basis of their academic performance, less able students are constantly confronted with evidence of their inferiority. Noncurriculum-related groups, organizations, and activities provide opportunities for students to engage in roles other than those that are based strictly on cognitive ability. Despite the constant challenges to their self-worth, students with poor classroom performance are able to capitalize on success in their nonacademic student roles and thus to bolster their self-image and enhance their status as members of the school mini society.

The determinants of status, especially in a student culture, are transitory and developmentally related. Considerable deference might be paid by peers to a second-grade girl who had the fanciest schoolbag or to the "toughest" boy in the class. A senior in high school who carried a book bag (or at least the wrong kind) would be greeted with friendly hoots of derision by peers, and the class "tough guy" might be scorned by all but a close circle of friends—the primary group. Fifteen years ago, few high school students would be caught riding their bicycles to school; ten years ago you were odd if you did not. The allocation of nonacademic status, which is determined by the students, is subject to the changing whims and currents of school life. But the determinants of academic status, which are in the hands of the school officials, remain relatively constant, and grades persist as a scarce but sought-after commodity.

All student roles are not equally valued in the school, and a given role may not be valued in the same way by a cross section of students. Among better students, grades carry relatively more merit in establishing overall status. Likewise, ability in the dramatic arts is valued more by students who participate in such activities.

A teacher who pays careful attention to group processes and reward structures may find that recognition of the nonacademic successes of certain students helps to promote their academic achievement. The nature of the teacher's role and the bureaucratic structure of the school can work against such a complex, personal assessment of student roles.

THE CLASSROOM AS A BUREAUCRATIC ORGANIZATION

In order for any organization to function effectively, the goals of the system must be clear and relatively stable over time. The conduct of individuals engaged in the pursuit of these objectives also must be regulated and constrained so that it remains within the bounds of prescribed behavior. Educational institutions are no exception. As we noted in Chapter 13, schools are essentially nonvoluntary institutions, that is, students must attend them, whether or not they want to. Because of this, and because the academic motivations and social predispositions of students are so varied, a great deal of effort must be expended by teachers and administrators to control behavior within the framework of a stable, effective instructional process and patterns of organizational activity.

THE AUTHORITY STRUCTURE

One reason schools were characterized as bureaucratic organizations in Chapter 13 is that they maintain rigid, top-down authority structures—from principals, through teachers, to students. The basis of teachers' authority and status in their institutionally prescribed roles was also described in that chapter. Because of their voluntary commitment to the organization, however, teachers have relatively free movement within the class and the school. That is, they are personally free, within limits, to leave the school or a classroom and to change activities or techniques as their purpose or mood determines.

For some teachers and many students, however, the classroom society too often resembles Jonathan Kozol's (1975) description of his own schooling: "I just think of it as a time when all of us, teachers and pupils— for some reason that we never would be told—had been condemned to live in prison" (p. xii). For the most part, he said, the students sat alone and did the work they were told to do. The resemblances between school and prison are striking in many schools: The grounds are enclosed by fences and patrolled by "guards," there are periodic locker checks, passes must be presented when leaving and reentering the classroom, access to corridors and certain parts of the building complex is restricted during designated periods, and hallways and cafeterias are supervised. The rite of passage through the school system is marked by the award of a certificate at the conclusion of the preordained "sentence"—12 years! To comply with these highly regulated procedures, students must discover what types of role behaviors are legitimate. They must learn to conform with organizational norms by observing the expectations of teachers, administrators, and other school personnel.

Unlike most formal organizations, the goals of schools usually are not specific and clearly articulated but rather vague and ambiguous. Although the explicit charge to the school is to develop and promote learning, this objective can take a variety of forms and dimensions, depending on the particular value emphasis incorporated into the definition. Not only are the goals of formal schooling difficult to define, but criteria for their accomplishment are equally difficult to establish. Because it is nearly impossible to specify how day-to-day achievement (however that is measured) is related to the long-term objectives of the school (however having arrived at that end is measured), it is difficult to pinpoint what types of student and teacher behaviors will contribute most to "success."

STUDENT COMPETITION
FOR CLASS REWARDS

Schools are organized so that those in power provide information, evaluation, and asessments to those lowest on the bureaucratic totem poll—the students. As a result, the students may have to struggle for scarce resources—namely, grades—even though it may be difficult for them to perceive how the effort to get the grades is related to their own vague career objectives. When it is unclear how mastery of the material relates to future social or economic position, it is small wonder that students study for the sake of exams rather than for future benefits, especially when the pursuit of such goals depends on incremental, often imperceptible advances in learning.

The competition for grades is not as straightforward as it may seem. The allocation of reward implies that some sort of an evaluation of role performance must take place. Supposedly standardized, and therefore completely objective, evaluations of students nevertheless vary by how the appraisal is conducted, the conditions under which they are made, the criteria involved, and the degree of completeness (Jackson, 1968).

No two teachers instruct in the same way. Some are painstaking when it comes to spelling and grammar, others are very lax. Some demand prompt assignments, others are more flexible. Students are under tremendous pressure to sort out a teacher's expectations and to discover which rules of the "academic game" have been modified by the instructor (McMillan, 1980). Mr. Quintero, the Spanish teacher, had a very rough day with his students last week and was in a foul mood when he graded his students' weekly essays. This week, all is well and so the same students average a letter grade higher on their essays for the same quality work. What kind of puzzlement must go through his students' minds? Mrs. Judkins, the fifth-grade teacher, had a busy weekend with relatives visiting from out of town, so Monday morning she merely checked off her students' homework assignments, rather than scoring them as is her custom. The following week she is appalled at how little effort her students put into their assignments, and they are shocked when their papers are returned covered with red slashes!

Success in school is measured primarily by achievement, and teachers have the principal responsibility for measuring performance, as we will show in Part IV. The power incumbent in their role in the organizational structure and their control over rewards and punishments (see Chapter 13) enables teachers to elicit behavior which students might not normally engage in willingly. Few tenth-graders are keen to read *Macbeth*, for example, but most of them will comply with a teacher's instructions to do so because they realize that if they do not they may get a poor mark in English class.

Although the subject and perhaps even the mark or grade earned may not be important to a student, the perception that good grades are held in high regard by parents or peers can lead the student to push to achieve them. But the power of the teacher and the importance of grades also may not be enough of an inducement to encourage a particular student to concentrate on a given task. Although academic performance is a key part of the individual's role as a student, conflicting pressures may be exerted by the requirements of her or his other roles. Marge has an exam tomorrow, for example, but all of her friends are going roller-skating tonight. She knows that if she uses the excuse of studying for her test, her friends will tease her unmercifully for putting studies before friends. She decides to go skating.

THE SCHOOL REGIME

Schools have a relatively stable, unchanging format. The activities which go on in them are for the most part repeated on a day-to-day basis in terms of the sequence in which they are presented and the form in which they are conducted. Classes begin and end at the same time each day, and one subject follows another with regularity and consistency. Adults also are tied to schedules, but most of their daily regimes have a certain flexibility. With the exception of workers on assembly lines whose activ-

Student leaders can gain status among their peers by making light of the rules and regulations prescribed for the school regime by authorities.

ities are controlled by automated machinery, most people can take breaks or change the focus of activities with only a general regard to time. Few executives divide their day into 45- or 50-minute blocks allocated to specific tasks, with no concern for bringing their work to completion, for example.

In the rigid day-to-day schedule of school activities, teachers' directions like, "Close your readers now, class, and take out your mathematics books" can be expected, as we noted in Chapter 13. Transitions from one activity to the next are abrupt and frequently without logic or recourse. A student still engaged in the plot of a story is asked to focus attention on dividers, multiplicands, and remainders. When, as a result, students are resentful, agitated, or lost in reverie, it is difficult to engage them in the instructional process. Their disinterest may be due less to the material than to the process and form of the instruction. No matter how enthusiastic students may be about the subject matter, a traditionally ritualistic, cyclical process is essentially boring.

Schools, like other bureaucratic organizations, are also characterized by a set of prescribed rules and procedures. These rules, which theoretically are established to ensure smooth, efficient operation, apply without exception to all members of the organization. Thus the norms of behavior and proper conduct established by the school ought to apply equally to students at all grade levels and with any level of ability. In reality, however, it is very difficult to always interpret and enforce rules with regularity and impartiality. Ambiguous rules are subject to individual interpretation. The more specific the rules are, the easier they are to apply uniformly.

THE TEACHER'S PARADOX AND THE
US AGAINST THEM ALLIANCE

Bureaucracies develop rules of operation and conduct which emphasize the common interests of their members. The behaviors they are designed to elicit are perceived as being most useful in accomplishing the goals of the organization. But schools, unlike most bureaucracies, require both collective activities in the classroom and attention to the *needs of individual students* in order to realize their goals. Learning is an individual process, even though it takes place in a collective setting. The organization of the classroom and the methods of evaluation demand equal treatment of students, regardless of their abilities and behaviors. The accomplishment of school goals and objectives, however, is contingent on recognition of individual differences and response to students' strengths and weaknesses.

Teachers thus must establish a universalistic climate of regularity and uniformity in the classroom while attending to the particularistic needs of their pupils (see Chapter 13). The struggle to resolve this teacher's paradox is constant. Students are quick to note shortcomings or irregularity in the application of rules and will try to exploit discrepancies in teachers' treatment when they can.

Because of the hierarchical authority structure of the school, and because students have a common objective of trying to secure the relatively scarce rewards the system has to offer, an "us against them" (students versus teachers) alliance can emerge. Students may gain more status from peers by circumventing the rules of the organization than they could earn from the keepers of the system for following them. The respect of others in school can be obtained in a variety of ways which are not directly related to academic performance. Students who consistently encounter failure in their learning efforts particularly are apt to conclude that they can gain little status or recognition by accepting the school's criteria of merit, and other activities and behaviors may be more rewarding to them—causing class disruptions, skipping classes, being tardy, and so on. A student who cannot gain status in the eyes of the teacher may be able to do so in the eyes of peers. Successful circumvention or exploitation of the school system can be rewarded by both positive and negative recognition from others. If carried to an extreme, however, this type of status recognition can lead to deviant conduct or complete repudiation of society's established norms.

The accomplished teacher is aware of the competing needs for status and recognition that students have in their pursuit of academic achievement. When the incentives of the organization cease to be important to the student, and when nonacademic roles emphasize forms of status and recognition that are not related to academic achievement, the academic tasks associated with the role of being a student lose their importance. As a result the tendency to drop out of school increases, particularly in the adolescent years (see Chapter 4).

INDIVIDUALS AND GROUPS

Everyone belongs to at least one primary group, as defined in a preceding section, and many people hold simultaneous memberships in five or six of them (Mills, 1967). In the classroom the principal primary groups are self-selected school friendship groups based on mutual attraction. These peer groups are comprised of same-sex members in later childhood and include both sexes in adolescence, as we noted in Chapter 4. They are consistently evolving social units—as the interests of the members change, so does the composition of the membership. Such informal, noninstitutional groups do not have clearly stated standards of exclusion. Unlike formal groups which have explicit criteria of membership, such as ability groups, personal friendship groups have vague boundaries, and membership rarely is officially noted.

Figure 14.2 illustrates a typical pattern of classroom friendship alliances, a concept which was introduced in Chapter 13. The first layer at the base of the pyramid contains the group core, or all students in the class. This layer is partitioned into permeable divisions (indicated by dotted lines) which divide the class into subgroups. The larger the group core is, the more subgroups there will be. On average, subgroups have five to seven student members. Each of these is headed by an understood but rarely designated leader. Without the support of these constituencies and their leaders, the teacher will not be able to maintain control from the top of the pyramid. Notice that the boundary demarcating subgroup

Figure 14.2

Friendship alliances in the classroom hierarchy

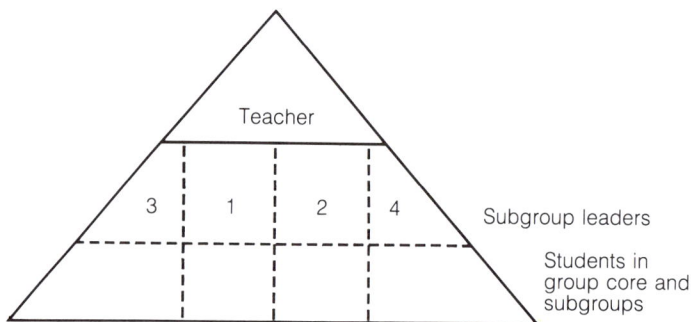

leaders from the teacher is impermeable, to indicate that the power and authority vested in the teacher by the definition of the role allows for only guarded fraternization with students.

Figure 14.2 also illustrates that some subgroups have more affinity with one another than others do: Subgroups 1 and 2 are congruent, indicating closer interests than those shared by 3 and 4, 1 and 4, or 2 and 3. Groups 1 and 2 also have greater contact with the teacher than groups 3 and 4, so they can offer more support to the maintenance of the teacher's position.

Membership in nonstructured school friendship groups may be influenced by assignment to ability groups. But membership in a friendship group rarely serves to legitimize status in an ability group, where status is accorded on the basis of academic achievement.

Classroom teachers must be aware of the various membership affiliations and patterns of status allocation which can be present. They must walk a fine line between maintaining authority and control and violating student norms which define the limits of deference that are acceptable to the group (see Box B).

In order to reconcile the bureaucratic need to treat students as an aggregate group with the instructional process need to address the individual requirements of students, teachers must find ways of directing group and subgroup membership to achieve individual and group goals. Activities can be structured in such a way that at times cooperative goals and means of achieving them are emphasized, while at other times competitive or individualistic learning situations are created. The advantages of presenting students with a variety of goal structures and learning environments were described in Chapter 11.

Shared confidences are a basis for classroom friendship alliances. These informal groups are headed by recognized but usually undesignated leaders.

CLASSROOM GOAL STRUCTURES AND GROUP PROCESSES

Goal structures in the classroom are of three principal types—cooperative, competitive, and individualistic (see Chapter 11). These goal structures characterize the learning environment and determine the most appropriate type of group processes for the class.

Cooperative or shared membership goals can be of two sorts. Some tasks require an *additive group structure,* in which the product of the group

BOX B   *Who's in charge here?*

The harrowing experiences many years ago of a very young novice teacher were recounted by Willard Waller. This instructor, dubbed Mr. J., began teaching at Central High School one February in the early 1930s, a week after the second semester had started. The principal thoughtlessly assigned him to a large third-period study hall composed of boys. The week before this study hall had been monitored by a substitute, with whom the boys had taken great liberties.

Mr. J. began to try to establish quiet and order by calling the roll and asking all the boys to be seated and to devote their time to schoolwork. But the breakdown in discipline that had occurred the preceding week, coupled with Mr. J.'s extremely youthful appearance and his obvious lack of experience in managing a classroom, conspired to make the boys uncontrollable.

When Mr. J. stood on one side of the room to try to quell discipline problems, the boys on the other side would act up. If he shifted his ground, the boys on the previously patrolled side of the study hall would misbehave. The boys began to realize that Mr. J. could not enforce control of them, and their behavior became increasingly boisterous and disorganized. The second day was worse than the first.

By the third day Mr. J. had a cold and fever which he felt contributed to his inability to improve the situation and his impending downfall. The boys began to knock inkwells on the floor; wherever Mr. J. went, the

represents the total effort of *all* the members—a tug of war contest, a bake sale, and even a competitive team spelling bee are examples. The success of the group is in part, but not entirely, dependent on the successful performance of a group task by all the members. Other cooperative tasks require a *conjunctive group structure*—they depend on the separate contributions of all the individual members of the group. In these groups the proficiency of the group is contingent on the capabilities of the least able member. Mountain climbing, for example, relies on a group effort in which the failure of any one of the team members substantially reduces the probability of success for the other members. In the classroom context, cooperative group projects such as team presentations on a given topic, in which each member of the group has an individual responsibility and for which the group will be assigned a common grade, is an example of a conjunctive group arrangement.

misdeeds occurred in some other part of the large room. He never could identify the culprits, but with the passage of time, inkwells were no longer being knocked from the desks. They were being hurled. One or two boys suffered mild injuries.

On the fifth morning Mr. J. could stand it no longer. He announced that while he himself had no quarrel with any of the students, if they wanted one with him, he was prepared to fight them outside. This was greeted with a hailstorm of thrown inkwells, and the situation became frighteningly dangerous. One boy had to be sent to the nurse for treatment of a cut over his eye. Finally a student, angry at Mr. J. for his failure to control the situation, ran from the room, announcing that he could stand it no longer. A dozen more boys ran for the door, which Mr. J. attempted to block. Then, suddenly, the entire host of students charged the door. Mr. J. fell away from it and watched as all his young charges dashed into the corridor. He was left only with a sense of relief that at last it was over.

Although this young teacher tried valiantly to remind the students of their responsibility to study and to follow the rules of the school, he was the one, in the final analysis, who was held accountable for the riotous conditions in the study hall.

Source: Willard Waller, *The Sociology of Teaching* (New York: John Wiley & Son, 1932), pp. 164–167.

In *competitive* classroom tasks, students can obtain goals only at the expense or failure of others. In grading on a curve there is no fixed criterion of achievement, and some students must fall to the bottom of the grade distribution. In a competitive situation, successful performance is relative to the work of others and is not tied to an absolute standard of achievement.

The third kind of group structure is based solely on *individual* effort and merit. Obtaining a goal is unrelated to the achievement of other students. For example, the memorization of the valences of elements on the periodic chart is an either-or situation—the student either knows the proper valences or does not. Mastery of this type of material is independent of the success of others in the group. Individualistic goals and processes are usually assessed on the basis of explicit evaluation criteria.

No single goal structure or group process is necessarily correlated with student achievement. Certain subjects and specific tasks may be more suited to a particular type of group process than another, but the issue of which classroom climate contributes most to academic achievement is an enduring one, as was noted in Chapter 11. Students also vary in their ability to adjust to each of these means of achieving goals. Some students excel in competitive settings and others do better in cooperative group structures. Regardless of the form the group activity takes, however, all students are engaged in an individualistic contest for grades.

There is evidence that more learning takes place when students are deliberately matched to their preferences for certain types of learning processes in appropriately structured classrooms. What may be a traumatic, unproductive learning arrangement for one student may be exactly the type another will prosper in. Indeed, it may be that grouping students according to type of learning environment is a much more productive form of classroom organization than grouping on the basis of ability.

THE RELATION OF GROUP STRUCTURE TO ACHIEVEMENT

Around the turn of the century a noted psychologist, N. Triplett, conducted an experiment on almost 2,000 bicyclists. In the first part of the experiment the cyclists were asked to ride as fast as they could in a race against a clock. In the second part the same cyclists were asked to race the same distance, this time in competition with other riders. The results of the experiment clearly demonstrated that performance was dramatically increased in head-to-head competition. Similar experiments have been done with children on tasks such as winding fishing reels. In most of these group versus individual contests, the participants performed better when competing with one another than when they worked independently. But whether or not it can be concluded from these findings that higher rates of learning are more likely in competitive group situations than in cooperative or individualistic ones is a complicated question involving the costs and benefits of a psychological nature associated with each approach.

The learning behavior of a group is influenced by the distribution of cognitive and noncognitive characteristics of the various learners. Research has indicated that cooperative group attitudes make it more likely that the members of the group will share their sentiments and ideas with each other and the teacher (Johnson & Ahlgren, 1976). As the leader of a cooperative group, the teacher may influence patterns of interaction by the extent to which authority over the group members is invoked. There is also some indication that groups headed by a nonauthoritative leader and characterized by a relatively open, interactive atmosphere produce higher achievement among members than groups in which the leadership is absolute and concentrated in the hands of a single figure. Thus there is empirical support for the proposition that, at least in some classes, when teachers utilize democratic group decisions as the basis for control and administration they can expect higher student performance than when classroom climates are more closed and highly structured. Student members of democratic groups are also more likely to express a sense of satisfaction with the group structure and process.

One of the difficulties in ascribing higher levels of achievement to the cooperative structure of groups is that due to the nature of the task, performance may be improved because more people are working on it, not because of the processes at work within the group. As we noted in Chapter 11, each type of goal structure and learning environment has positive and negative consequences, and under certain circumstances each may be preferable. The effects of group organization and processes on performance are still being studied. Nevertheless, gifted students may help others master the material, and well-motivated students may spur less industrious colleagues to greater effort when they are all engaged in a cooperative task.

CLASSROOM CONTROL AND STUDENT INTERACTIONS

One of the tasks of the instructor is to marshal students' diverse interests and backgrounds to accomplish common tasks (see Chapter 13). But working toward a common objective does not mean that students must all think alike or respond in the same way to issues presented in the classroom. Exploring the interpretations and opinions of others, as in the critical thinking described in Chapter 10, allows students to appraise and evaluate their own thinking. Debate, controversy, and passionate (but rational) dialogue may not only stimulate critical thinking but also may generate a greater number of diverse ideas than would be possible in an isolated, individualistic learning environment.

There is a danger, however, that controversy and debate which are not kept in check by reason, courtesy, and forebearance will result in a destructive learning environment. The extent to which students are willing to put forth their ideas, to challenge those of others, and to accept rebuttal depends on how well the teacher as leader of the group maintains an open, inviting classroom climate.

If the learning environment fosters a sense of security among the students, and if their self-concepts permit challenges to their ideas, and if they feel that debate will help accomplish their objectives, controversy will be valued and freely engaged in. The teacher must artfully encourage discussion while preventing the polarization of students' attitudes and opinions. The more mixed the students' backgrounds, the more is controversy likely to be generated, but at the same time, the greater is the likelihood of irreparable conflict (Torrance, 1961). Heterogeneity in student groups is an asset, however, "when there are varied functions to perform in the group, when group members have the social skills needed to exchange and utilize information, and when expertise relevant to the group's task is present in the group," according to Johnson (1980).

EFFECTS OF GROUP SIZE

The typical American classroom contains anywhere from 20 to 40 pupils. When the instructional process must utilize groups this large, it is difficult for the teacher to recognize how well individual students are mastering the material. Various ways of dividing the classroom into smaller working groups have been described in this chapter, but the ideal working size of such subgroups has not been considered. Subgrouping may facilitate social interactions among members, but groups which are too small or too large or too heterogeneous also can restrict them.

In groups which are too small, discussion may be restricted and easily affected by ideological cleavages and personality disputes. As the size of a group increases, however, more individuals have to share a limited amount of time. Consequently, when groups pass a certain point in size, the law of diminishing returns begins to apply to the collective strength of the group. Also, as the group becomes larger and more heterogeneous, it is increasingly difficult for individuals to make their ideas clear to all members of the group. With increasing size also come the needs for more organization and stricter procedures for the maintenance of order. More intricate and more numerous rules are required for more participants in an activity, and as the administrative tasks of the group increase, less time is left to devote to its objectives.

Analyses of interactions in groups have indicated that most conversations take place with individuals who are very near to one another, if not adjacent. In a study done a number of years ago, researchers discovered that regardless of the size of the group, over 50 percent of the talking is usually between only two people. In groups with eight or fewer members, over 60 percent of the talking is done by only two people (Stephan & Mischler, 1952).

Such findings have implications for the organization of groups for learning in schools. A number of interviews of students in classrooms have examined the relationship between group size and psychological comfort. For purposes of promoting discussion and interpersonal exchange, five-person groups appear to be the ideal size. The larger the class or group size, the more students feel under the pressure of scrutiny by others, and consequently the more reluctant they are to speak. Students in large discussion sections also report less group satisfaction and feelings of involvement. Students in small groups have been found to be more willing to take on heavier work assignments and to commit great time and effort to the success of a collective undertaking. Studies in other settings indicate that the motivational level of group members declines in direct proportion to increase in group size, however.

In sum, although students differ considerably in their response to group structure, small, semicompetitive groupings appear most likely to facilitate the completion of objectives. Groups of this size also foster a high degree of personal satisfaction among the members.

CHAPTER 14 IN RETROSPECT

Students are members of a number of formal or informal and voluntary or involuntary school groups, as well as having certain unchangeable ascriptive memberships such as race, sex, or social class. In their group associations they may be guided by the need for affiliation and by either intrinsic or extrinsic motives. Their place in the social system of the school is defined by their membership affiliations and the status these confer on the individual.

Students are assigned to specific school classes in order to facilitate the instructional process and ensure an orderly sequence of learning. The rationale for student placement is varied, however. In most school systems, students are assigned to classrooms which are structured to bring those of comparable academic ability together. This is called tracking, in which placement in groups is on the basis of prior educational performance and teacher recommendations, but a student's ascriptive characteristics also can influence the composition of ability groups. Since success in school is measured to a large extent by grades, status is largely a function of academic ability. Tracking indirectly reinforces a student's status, whether it be low or high, because it physically and psychologically differentiates between low and high achievers.

Tracking may be more than an indication of academic potential, however. Research has demonstrated that some students from low-income and minority families begin schooling poorly prepared, both emotionally and academically, for the structure and discipline required in the average classroom. At a very early age, they may be placed in low-ability streams, even though their learning difficulties are more social than cognitive in origin.

Each of us has a number of roles and identities which are central to our concept of self. We form primary group relationships with others who share similar role orientations and values. Our self-concepts are determined by direct and indirect comparisons of ourselves with others and by analyzing what we feel to be our peers' assessments of us. Our self-appraisals are important in helping us define realistic goals and in fostering the motivation and enthusiasm to accomplish them. There appears to be no clear-cut relationship between homogeneous ability grouping and academic performance, but evidence supports the fact that higher ability groups of students may have greater access to educational resources than lower ability groups.

The nonacademic memberships of students which also determine status, such as athletic teams and clubs, are important to the maintenance of a positive self-concept, especially for pupils who are subject to academic failure. It is important for the teacher to recognize the saliency and strength of such groupings and to incorporate them into the instructional goals and processes.

Classroom activities can be structured so that goals are cooperative, competitive, or individualistic in nature. Although simple behavioral tasks appear to be accomplished more quickly in competitive situations, the impact of each group structure on learning is dependent on the specific nature of the task and the attitude of the individual learner. Thus it is impossible to prescribe an ideal group arrangement for instructional purposes. Small groups of five or so students seem to be best suited for classroom discussion. Increasing the size of the group also increases group tensions and the effort required to administer the group.

A successful teacher must be able to create a classroom climate which fosters debate but minimizes antagonism; generates cooperation but encourages individualism; stimulates criticism and eliminates dogmatism. In a setting such as the classroom, where student roles are multifaceted, backgrounds are diverse, and uncertainty is common, developing a classroom climate which is tuned to both the cognitive and social needs of students is a complex, often frustrating, but also rewarding task.

QUESTIONS FOR DISCUSSION

1. The "Who am I?" exercise is an interesting way to take stock of yourself. On a piece of paper list 10 words or phrases you would use to answer the question, in their order of importance to you. Ask a friend or a parent to do the same and then discuss the similarities and differences in your lists. Can you account for them?

2. Think back to a class you had in your high school days or reflect on one you have had recently which was particularly enjoyable. What was there about the class organization or membership which made it especially rewarding?

3. In this chapter a lot was said about the merits and problems associated with tracking in schools. Have you ever been in a tracked classroom? Do you think the experience enhanced or stifled your motivation to achieve? What about your fellow classmates? What about your peers in the "other" track?

4. In one section of this chapter we raised the question of the ideal class size for learning. What size classes do you prefer to be a member of? Why do you feel less comfortable in other types of situations? What could the instructor do to increase the appeal of the other class types for you?

5. Instructors frequently find that when students evaluate them at the end of the semester, some class members complain that the course was too structured, and others in the same class indicate that it was not structured enough. Take a poll of your classmates to see how many of them prefer each teaching style. Are their opinions related in any way that you can tell to their personalities or social background? Can you find any patterns in their preferences?

6. All bureaucratic organizations, including schools, have rules and regulations. Think back to your elementary or high school days. Were there any regulations that particularly bothered you? Can you think of any that you felt may have interfered with your learning or which may have dampened your enthusiasm for schooling?

Introductory Level

Jackson, Philip. *Life in Classrooms.* New York: Holt, Rinehart & Winston, 1968.

This easy-to-read text provides an excellent description of the routine and sometimes frustrating structure of activities in an elementary classroom.

Brookover, Wilbur, and Erickson, Edsel. *Sociology of Education.* Homewood, Ill.: Dorsey Press, 1975.

Chapters 11–13 introduce the reader to the interesting but complex study of self-concept. The authors focus on the specific relationships of self-concept of ability to academic achievement.

John, D. W. *The Social Psychology of Education.* New York: Holt, Rinehart & Winston, 1970.

This text offers a good review and in some cases elaboration of the general principles in this chapter and throughout the book.

**READINGS
FOR
REFLECTION**

Boocock, Saranne. *Sociology of Education: An Introduction.* Boston: Houghton Mifflin Co., 1980.

This book affords an excellent overview of the major topical areas in the field. Chapters 8 and 9 focus on classroom roles and relationships and the class as a social system. The reader will be struck by the strongly converging interests of sociologists and psychologists in the study of what goes on in classrooms.

Advanced Level

Persell, Caroline Hodges. *Education and Inequality.* New York: Free Press, 1977.

Chapters 6–8 deal with tracking and the origins and consequences of teacher expectations for pupils.

Bowles, Samuel, and Gintis, Herbert. *Schooling in Capitalist America.* New York: Basic Books, 1976.

This critical attack on the structure of American schooling argues that patterns of recruitment, tracking, and instruction induce in students a social-psychological acceptance of the status quo.

McMillan, James (Ed.). *The Social Psychology of School Learning.* New York: Academic Press, 1980.

Newman, Ruth. *Groups in Schools.* New York: Simon & Schuster, 1974.

REFERENCES

Boocock, Saranne. *Sociology of Education.* Boston: Houghton Mifflin Co., 1980.

Drews, Elizabeth. *Student Abilities, Grouping Patterns and Classroom Interaction.* Cooperative Research Program, Office of Education, DHEW, ED 002679. Washington, D.C.: U.S. Government Printing Office, 1962.

Findley, Warren, and Bryan, Miriam. *Ability Grouping: 1970—I. Common Practices in the Use of Tests for Grouping Students in Public Schools.* ED 948382. Athens: Center for Educational Improvement, University of Georgia, 1971.

Hargreaves, David. *Social Relations in a Secondary School.* London: Routledge & Kegan Paul, 1967.

Hegns, Barbara. Social selection and stratification within schools. *American Journal of Sociology,* 1974, *79,* 1434–1451.

Jackson, Brian. *Streaming: An Education System in Miniature.* London: Routledge & Kegan Paul, 1964.

Jackson, Philip. *Life in Classrooms.* New York: Holt, Rinehart & Winston, 1968.

Johnson, David W. Group processes: Influence of student-student interactions on school outcomes. In James H. McMillan (Ed.), *Social Psychology of School Learning*. New York: Academic Press, 1980.

Johnson, David W., and Ahlgren, Andrew. Relationships between student attitudes about cooperation and competition and attitudes towards schooling. *Journal of Educational Psychology*, 1976, *68*, 92–102.

Kozol, Jonathan. *The Night Is Dark and I Am Far from Home*. Boston: Houghton Mifflin Co., 1975.

Lortie, Dan. *School Teacher*. Chicago: University of Chicago Press, 1976.

McMillan, James (Ed.). *The Social Psychology of School Learning*. New York: Academic Press, 1980.

Mills, Theodore M. *The Sociology of Small Groups*. Englewood Cliffs, N.J.: Prentice Hall, 1967.

Persell, Caroline Hodges. *Education and Inequality*. New York: Free Press, 1977.

Rist, Ray. *The Urban School: A Factory for Failure*. Cambridge, Mass.: M.I.T. Press, 1973.

Stephan, Frederick F., and Mischler, Elliot G. The distribution of participation in small groups: An exponential approximation. *American Sociological Review*, 1952, *17*, 598–608.

Torrance, E. Paul. Can grouping control social stress in creative activity? *Elementary School Journal*, 1961, *62*, 139–145.

Educational Measurement and Evaluation

Part IV is a fitting conclusion to this text because it embraces all three dimensions of the instructional process and all the factors in it. It describes how to measure and evaluate student achievement, teacher competency, and school program and policy effectiveness. These various types of evaluation are concerned with the instruction provided to individual learners (the first dimension) and to learners in groups (the second dimension), as well as with the relations between the instruction and the external environment (the third dimension). In all three dimensions feedback of the evaluation results provides the vital link between the instruction and the learner or the environment.

The first three chapters in this part describe classroom measurement and evaluation of both individual students and class groups. Guidance is given in using the two principal types of educational evaluation—teacher-made tests and assignments (Chapter 16) and standardized tests (Chapter 17). The final chapter enters the third dimension to consider the influence of the public and social and economic forces on the instructional process. Efforts to evaluate teachers, programs, and schools and to assess national trends in achievement scores reflect the need for the schools to be accountable to the community for their processes and products.

Principles of Classroom Measurement and Evaluation

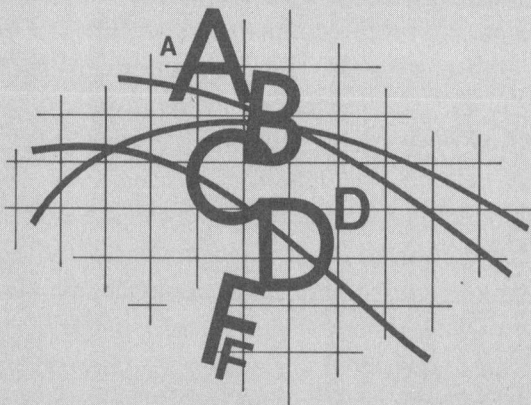

Scientific principles of measurement and evaluation are applied in the classroom in order to provide an objective basis for judging the progress of students' learning, the effectiveness of teachers' methods, and the functional effects of school programs and policies.

Teachers must make evaluative judgments about their students' learning and their own teaching. They use this information to assign grades to students, to strengthen or revise their teaching methods, and to advise students and their parents about educational procedures.

Students must know how to make accurate judgments about their own knowledge and skills. They use this information to guide their studying, to decide which courses and teachers to choose, to settle on an occupation or a major in college, to determine whether to continue their education or to drop out, and so on.

Others also need a sound basis for making educational decisions. School administrators need accurate information on student achievement which they can use as a basis for decisions about the placement of students in appropriate classes or courses, curriculum content, the achievement standing of their schools compared to others, and salaries and tenure for teachers. Parents make judgments about their children's knowledge and skills and the quality of schools and kinds of teachers being provided in their community.

These are all examples of educational evaluations: the formation of educational judgments of value that lead to action. These judgments are most useful when they are based on concrete evidence of student achievement that has been accumulated in a scientific manner. Teachers must know what type of data to gather for educational evaluations, how to construct or use instruments like tests and assignments to produce accurate results, and how to use these results as a basis for making and reporting evaluations.

There are several methods teachers can use to arrive at judgments of their students' abilities and academic achievements. They may simply watch the students in various situations and use these observations as a basis for their judgments. They may evaluate students' answers to questions asked during lessons and discussions. They may discuss various students with other teachers and with the students' parents.

But these informal evaluation processes have no scientific basis. Teachers' expectancies about certain students, as described in Chapter 9, can distort their perceptions of these students' potential for academic achievement. The teachers may therefore inadvertently allow student characteristics that are not relevant to achievement to cloud their evaluations. In the *halo effect*, students who are good in one area or who are attractive and well behaved in school are evaluated highly in all school areas because the instructor's overall perception of those students is

Test results can be the basis for important decisions by students such as these high school seniors. The school's evaluations of their academic achievement may help them to settle on an occupation or a college major or to determine whether to continue in school or drop out.

positive. For example, a quiet child may receive a higher grade than an active child because the quiet one follows directions and never disrupts the class. An opposite *pitchfork effect* also occurs. For example, a student with an abrasive personality may receive a lower evaluation than a student with a pleasant one, even though both students actually achieve at the same level.

Teachers therefore must have ways to conduct formal, objective evaluations of student learning, based on systematic procedures for measuring a sample of some area of the students' achievement behaviors. Systematic observation and carefully constructed tests, either teacher-made or standardized, and various kinds of assignments usually are the basis for these evaluations.

The tests, assignments, and systematic observations used by teachers are all forms of measurement which utilize a common set of principles and concepts. We will introduce these principles and concepts in this chapter and then explain them in more detail and apply them to typical school situations in the other chapters in this part. Principles relevant to teacher-constructed tests and assignments are detailed in Chapter 16; those relevant to standardized tests in Chapter 17; and those related to the function of evaluation and accountability in schools in Chapter 18. A few concepts also were introduced in Chapter 6, Intelligence and Education.

BASIC ELEMENTS OF CLASSROOM EVALUATION

The principles underlying evaluation of classroom teaching and learning are concerned with such variables as the selection of a valid and reliable sample of learning behavior, the function and use of general and specific educational objectives, norm referencing and criterion referencing as standards of comparison, the relative merits of teacher-made and standardized tests, and methods for achieving objective observational measures.

SAMPLING STUDENTS' LEARNING BEHAVIORS

Whatever the technique or instrument used in classroom evaluation, they all serve the same purpose: to provide a method for determining a quantitative measure of a student's score on some sample of a certain learning behavior. If the teacher wants to test the class on the ability to multiply one three-digit number by another, for example, it is not possible, or even reasonable, to give a test with one multiplication item for each possible pair of three-digit numbers. Instead, the teacher has to use a *sample* of multiplication problems. If a school district wants to give a standardized arithmetic test to all of its elementary pupils, the test selected will consist of a sample of arithmetic problems and skills.

The selection of the sample of items to be used in testing students' learning is very important. The sample must be systematic, and the resulting score must be accurate. In measurement terms, the instrument should have reliability and validity, concepts which will be discussed in the next main section of this chapter.

USE OF OBJECTIVES AS A BASIS FOR TEACHING AND MEASUREMENT

All instruction is designed to accomplish certain objectives. Some teachers' objectives are vague and implicit, but teaching and the accompanying evaluation are easier for both teachers and students if the instructional objectives are definitely specified and clearly and openly understood.

Figure 15.1

*General objective and goal and specific objectives for
a high school social science unit on television watching*

General objective: When the students have completed this unit, they will be critical viewers, rather than passive watchers, of television.

General goal: When the students have completed this unit, they will be able to judge the appropriateness of cartoons and educational shows for preschool-aged children.

Specific objectives: After viewing a 30-minute series of cartoons and a 30-minute educational show, the students will be able to:

1. Report the proportion of commercial time in each show.

2. Analyze the selling techniques used in the commercials.

3. Count the number of violent occurrences in each show.

4. Report the number of prosocial episodes in each show.

5. Report the number of positive, neutral, and negative outcomes to the violent and prosocial episodes in each show.

6. Discuss three things that preschool-aged children could learn from each show.

7. Evaluate and discuss the appropriateness of each show for young children.

Suppose a high school social science teacher decides to teach a unit on the effects of TV watching on children (see Figure 15.1). The teacher's overall or general objective for the unit is to teach students about the role of TV in the lives of U.S. children, so they will learn to be critical watchers rather than passive viewers. But this objective is not specific enough to give much direction to the actual instruction, so the teacher constructs a series of long-term, general goals by breaking down the general objective. One outcome of the unit, therefore, should be that the students are able to judge the appropriateness of cartoons and shows for preschool-aged children. The teacher then writes a series of short-term specific objectives to guide the teaching to accomplish this goal. Specific objectives are very useful to the teacher in planning instruction, making assignments, and writing tests.

Several standardized schedules of objectives have been constructed to help teachers direct the instructional process and measure the learning outcomes. Two of the best known classification schemes were devised by Benjamin Bloom and associates to measure the cognitive and affective domains, which are similar but not identical to the cognitive-intellectual and social-emotional developmental domains in the typology described in Part I. Bloom's taxonomies of educational objectives outline the possible levels of learning and behavior with respect to content areas in these domains.

The cognitive domain (Bloom et al., 1956) is the one involved in most school learning (see Box A). In ascending order, the taxonomy goes from knowledge, which is the easiest level of learning and is in the major class called remembering, through comprehension, application, analysis, synthesis, and evaluation, in the major class called thinking. The levels of thinking involve more advanced thought processes than memorization, the only skill in the knowledge level. Basic knowledge in any subject matter area, such as multiplication tables in arithmetic, must be memorized and available for recall in the long-term memory, or cognitive structure (see Chapter 7). But observational research has shown that teaching and measurement in all areas seldom go beyond the knowledge level (Good & Brophy, 1973).

A taxonomy such as Bloom's is useful in teaching and measuring outcomes at the learning levels a teacher considers important, based on the development of the students in the class and the material to be covered. An example of how the taxonomy is applied in constructing a table of specifications for a teacher-made test is given in Chapter 16, on teacher-made tests and assignments.

STANDARDS OF COMPARISON: NORM- AND CRITERION-REFERENCED MEASUREMENT

A student's academic achievement can be measured by comparison to a norm—the achievements of comparable students—or comparison to a criterion—a certain standard of performance. Whether achievement in a class will be measured with norm-referenced or criterion-referenced techniques, or a combination of the two, depends on the decisions of teachers, administrators, and boards of education.

In *norm-referenced measurement,* the teacher wants to see how well each student achieves in comparison to other students: in that class; in all of the classes in that grade level within the school, within the school district, or within the state; or in some other norm group. In *criterion-referenced measurement*, the teacher examines each student's achievement in relation to a standard, perhaps the percentage of items on a test that the student correctly answers. Criterion-referenced measurement is often used with the instructional methods called teaching for mastery (see Chapter 12) and contract teaching (see Chapter 16). Both norm- and criterion-referenced measurement are discussed further in Chapters 16 and 17 on teacher-made and standardized tests.

A verbal guide to cognitive skills:
From recall to evaluate

Benjamin Bloom's Taxonomy of Educational Objectives in the cognitive domain includes two major classes—remembering and thinking—and six levels of learning and behaving arranged in a hierarchy or sequence from least to most difficult. Cognitive skills must be measured in order to evaluate student progress at these levels.

Teachers have found that certain verbs are most appropriate in writing objectives to guide the instructional process, assignments to develop the skills, and tests to measure them. The table below lists the verbs that are used most often to direct students' learning activities at each of the six levels. These terms are not mutually exclusive, however, and they can be used to measure learning at other levels as well.

Major Class	Level of Learning and Behaving	Verbs Used in Stating Objectives, Assignments, and Test Questions
Remembering	1. Knowledge—recalling material	Recall, define, list, name
	2. Comprehension— understanding the meaning of material	Explain, summarize, interpret, translate
	3. Application—using information in specific situations	Compute, relate, solve, apply, classify (when given the rule)
Thinking	4. Analysis—breaking a whole into its parts	Estimate, diagram, order, analyze, classify (when not given the rule)
	5. Synthesis—arranging parts into a whole	Construct, develop, combine, synthesize, integrate
	6. Evaluation—judging the value of something	Criticize, compare, judge, evaluate

Source: Norman E. Gronlund, *Constructing Achievement Tests,* 2nd ed.
(Englewood Cliffs, N.J.: Prentice-Hall, 1977).

CHARACTERISTICS OF TEACHER-MADE AND STANDARDIZED TESTS

Testing is one of the most common forms of formal evaluation used in schools. There are many different categories of tests, but one broad, universally used system divides them into two classes: teacher-made and standardized.

Teacher-made tests, constructed by classroom teachers, should be achievement tests designed to measure students' knowledge and skills in a school-relevant content area. The tests should represent what the teachers have been teaching, which may vary from what other local teachers teach who are covering the same material at the same level. Teachers may share test questions or occasionally whole tests, or they may use questions given in manuals or other information accompanying the instructional materials. These tests are administered and scored according to the teachers' own judgment, and they may compare students' performance to each other (norm referencing) or to a standard (criterion referencing). Teacher-made tests are compared to standardized achievement tests in Table 15.1.

Standardized tests have several identifying characteristics. They are purchased from a commercial test publisher and have been written by a group of experts to provide a set of questions that sample the content and skills generally agreed upon as representing the current levels of learning in a subject matter area across the nation. Everyone who takes these tests has the same opportunity to answer an appropriate set of questions in the same time limit under similar conditions. All standardized tests are scored in objective ways, and most are norm referenced.

There are four principal types of standardized tests:

1. Achievement tests, which measure a student's learned skills and knowledge in an academic area.
2. Aptitude tests, which measure a student's potential in various areas.
3. Diagnostic tests, which identify a student's specific problems in basic academic areas such as reading or mathematics.
4. Noncognitive tests, which measure aspects of behavior other than school learning and thinking.

These categories will be discussed fully in Chapter 17, with emphasis on standardized intelligence and achievement tests.

OBSERVATIONAL MEASURES OF PROCESSES AND PRODUCTS

Many kinds of school learning can be evaluated through the use of paper-and-pencil tests, but many other kinds of skills and knowledge cannot.

Table 15.1

*Comparison of teacher-made and standardized
achievement tests*

Aspect	Teacher-Made Achievement Tests	Standardized Achievement Tests
Purposes and uses	Measurement of performance in relation to the teacher's own objectives; local comparisons to other students and occasionally to other classes	Measurement of performance in relation to nationally recognized curriculum objectives; local, state, and/or national comparisons with other students, classes, schools, and districts
Constructed by	Teacher, sometimes with the help of other teachers or from questions accompanying curricular materials; procedures vary from careful to careless; generally no item trial	Groups of experts following careful procedures, including a trial of the items
Construction time and cost	A few minutes to several hours; no monetary outlay	Three to five years; thousands of dollars
Coverage	Specific to that classroom	Broad and systematic; represents national concerns
Administration	According to the teacher's judgment	According to explicit directions
Test format	Any types of items and answers	Precise, objective items requiring short, objective answers
Scoring	Objective or subjective, according to the teacher's judgment	Objective and mechanical
Scores	Usually number correct, perhaps with percent correct (criterion-referenced) or percentile (norm-referenced) scores	Usually norm referenced; may be criterion-related information available
Norm group	One or a few classrooms	Various ones available, both local and national

In these cases, teachers must devise methods for systematic observation of either products (such as a piece of pottery created by a student in an art class) or the procedures used to produce the end result (such as the steps followed by a student in a chemistry experiment). The instruments used for such evaluations often take the form of checklists or rating scales. Like paper-and-pencil tests and assignments, each instrument should be an objective measure of the student's knowledge and skills which yields one or more scores that indicate the quality of the student's work.

CONCEPTS TO ENSURE ACCURATE CLASSROOM MEASURING INSTRUMENTS

Many people, including parents, teachers, and students, think that scores on school instruments are precise, and each score indicates exactly what the student knows and can do. In reality, every score consists of two parts: a true score, which is an exact measurement of the person's skills, and an error score. We can never know precisely the value of each of these two parts, even though we do know the value of the overall score.

The error part of the score should be as small as possible, regardless of the measuring instrument being used, so that the overall score is a good estimate of the true score. Two integral measurement qualities that influence the true and error parts of the score are *validity* and *reliability*. These concepts are compared in Table 15.2 for teacher-made and standardized tests.

VALIDITY

The validity of a measuring instrument is the extent to which the instrument measures what it is supposed to measure. An instrument with high validity succeeds in this, while one with low validity does not.

Table 15.2

Comparison of the reliabilities and validities of teacher-made and standardized tests

	Teacher-made Achievement Tests	Standardized Achievement Tests
Validity		
Content	Varies greatly; depends on the construction procedures	High nationally; local validity must be determined by the user
Construct	Usually unimportant; generally unknown	Usually high
Criterion related	Usually unimportant; generally unknown	Usually unimportant; moderately high, when relevant
Reliability		
Internal consistency	Varies greatly; generally unknown	Uniformly high, often above 0.90
Stability	Usually unimportant; generally unknown	Generally high
Equivalence	Usually unimportant; generally unknown	Generally very high
Standard error	Usually unknown	Usually small

A teacher-made classroom test to measure students' skills in adding together pairs of two-digit numbers has high validity if it actually measures achievement in that area of addition. This test would not be a valid measure of the students' knowledge about the capitals of the states or even their skills in adding together pairs of three-digit numbers.

There are three types of validity: content, construct, and criterion related. Although all three are important for some kinds of measuring instruments, content validity is the most important type for teacher-made instruments, as well as for standardized achievement tests.

An instrument has *content validity* if it adequately samples the content areas and skills that it is supposed to be testing. This can be evaluated by examining the match between the content and skills involved in the area being tested and those measured by the instrument. A high degree of match is an indication of high content validity.

A second type of validity, *construct validity,* is not usually considered as very important in relation to teacher-made instruments, but it is significant for standardized tests. An instrument has construct validity if it measures the construct that it is supposed to measure. Construct validity is determined by examining the scores on the instrument to see if they vary in the same ways that scores on other accepted measures of the construct vary and, with changing conditions, if they vary as the accepted theories about the construct suggest. For example, the construct validity of a new test of intelligence for children is investigated by relating the scores on that test to those of the same children on either the Stanford-Binet or the WISC-R, the two accepted intelligence tests for children (see Chapter 6). Scores on the new test would also be compared to scores on other types of measures related to intelligence, including measures like achievement test scores, since according to theory more intelligent children are generally higher achievers. The stability of the scores of children as they grow older also might be tracked, since a person's intelligence is supposed to be quite stable after age six. Other comparisons could be made by relating the scores on the new test to other changes suggested by theories of intelligence.

The third type, *criterion-related validity,* is important for any measure that is used for selection purposes: for entry into higher education, jobs, promotions, treatment, special classes or tutoring, and so on. Standardized tests generally are used for such selection purposes. The criterion-related validity of such a test is an indication of how closely a person's test score is related to an independent measure of the person's success in that experience. Companies that use tests as a basis for selecting or promoting employees must be able to show that their tests have criterion-related validity, using an accepted measure of job success, to avoid charges of discrimination.

Content, construct, and criterion-related validity are related to the characteristics of the instruments and the purposes for which they are used. All three types also are strongly influenced by the characteristics of the people who take the tests. Certain skills are required to even complete most measuring instruments. Many paper-and-pencil teacher-made assignments and tests, as well as standardized tests, require the test taker to read and follow directions, read questions, and write out answers on paper or select and mark them on an answer sheet. If these skills are not part of the skills that the instrument is supposed to measure, and if the test takers do *not* possess them, then the instrument has low content validity for that group of people.

Thus an instrument can have low overall validity, have high validity for one purpose but not for others, or have high validity for use with one group of people but not for use with other groups. The three types of validity and their relationships to the instrument, the people who take the instrument, and the purposes for which it is used are discussed more fully in relation to teacher-made tests and assignments and to standardized tests in the following two chapters. Regardless of these validity considerations, an instrument cannot be valid unless it is reliable (see Box B).

RELIABILITY

Reliability means consistency in school-related instruments, as it does with any type of measurement. The three aspects of reliability listed in Table 15.2 are internal consistency, stability, and equivalence.

Internal consistency is the aspect of reliability that is most important for teacher-made instruments and for standardized tests. An instrument with high internal consistency is one in which the instrument taker responds to each item in a similar way. For tests, this means that students who answer one item correctly also tend to answer correctly most of the other items, while those who answer the item incorrectly also tend to miss the other items. Each item on the test helps in measuring the material covered by the test; the items fit together to form a cohesive whole.

A second type of reliability is called *stability*, or test-retest reliability. This refers to the consistency of scores when an instrument is retaken by the same people a short time later. Tests designed to measure constructs such as ability, personality, and interests must produce stable scores, because these constructs are considered stable for moderate amounts of time, generally several years. Stability is less important in achievement tests, since growth in academic achievement is a goal of education (Mehrens & Lehmann, 1978). Even so, achievement tests scores should be relatively stable across short time spans.

BOX B   *Would your bathroom scale lie to you?*

The two principal criteria for judging the scientific accuracy of a measurement instrument are validity and reliability. Both are important, but reliability is essential. A measure can be reliable (consistent) without being valid (a true measure), but it cannot be valid if it is unreliable. George Bohrnstedt and David Knoke give the following example in a book on statistics for social science:

> A bathroom scale, for example, is both *reliable and valid* if on a given morning you get on it several times and it records your weight the same each time, and if the weight it records is accurate. The scale is *reliable and invalid* if it records your weight the same each time you get on it but it consistently indicates you weigh five pounds below your true weight. And if the scale indicates a different weight each time you get on it, it is not only *unreliable* but clearly *invalid* as well. It cannot be valid if it indicates a different weight each time you step on it, because it does not accurately measure the concept (your weight) it is intended to measure.

Source: George W. Bohrnstedt and David Knoke, *Statistics for Social Data Analysis* (Itasca, Ill.: F. E. Peacock Publishers, 1982), p. 14.

The third type of reliability is called *equivalence*. Many standardized tests have two or more versions. These forms are equivalent if the scores people receive on one form are very similar to the scores they receive on the others if they complete all forms. Since teachers generally do not write two versions of their tests and assignments, this aspect of reliability is not important for most teacher-constructed instruments.

Reliability values range from 0 to +1. A reliability of 0 means that the instrument has no reliability at all; a score from such an instrument is meaningless because it is all error. A reliability of +1 means that the instrument has perfect reliability; a score is the person's true score with no error. These extreme reliabilities are actually never found, however.

Even the best instrument does not have perfect reliability. Test takers change between testings. They learn something vicariously that helps them on one testing and then they promptly forget it on the next testing, or they are highly motivated at one time and not at another. People change even during a test; they may be so tired by the end of a testing session that they do not read the questions carefully, or they fill in the answer sheets incorrectly even though they know the correct answers.

The testing situation itself may contribute to unreliability. For example, a fire drill in the middle of a test results in a lower reliability because students have the opportunity to share answers and, if the test is timed, the timing becomes confused. If people rather than machines score the tests, they also can make scoring errors.

In general, reliabilities of about 0.85 or higher are needed for decision making about individuals, and those of about 0.65 or higher are needed for group decisions or comparisons. A test used in group decisions can be less reliable because the measurements of a group of people combined into averages tend to eliminate errors due to unreliability (Mehrens & Lehmann, 1978). For example, if one person's score is higher than it should be, based on the person's actual knowledge and skill, another's is probably lower, and they cancel each other in the mean score. A test must be very accurate when its score is used to make decisions about one individual because the error in that score is not balanced by the errors in others' scores.

The internal consistency reliabilities of standardized measures tend to be quite high, often in the 0.90s. Those on teacher-made instruments, however, vary from very low to very high, with an average of about 0.60 (Diederich, 1973).

STANDARD ERROR

Suppose students could retake the same test or do the same assignment over and over without learning anything that would increase their scores. This, of course, really could not happen. But if it did, each student's scores would vary, due to the unreliability of the instrument. In fact, if the instrument were retaken enough times, a student's scores would be normally distributed (bell-shaped in a diagram, like the IQ score distributions shown in Figure 6.4 in Chapter 6). The student's true, or errorless, score would fall somewhere within this set of scores.

Because tests and assignments are only given once at any point in a student's schooling, it is not impossible to determine each student's true score exactly. Teachers can use the standard error to set up error bands around each person's obtained score, however, and the true score usually falls within these bands. The standard error of a measure is essentially the average distance an obtained score is from the true score.

The standard errors associated with standardized tests are reported in the manuals for these tests. If the error bands set up by a teacher include scores located between +1 and −1 standard error around the obtained score, the student's true score will be in that range about 68 percent of the time. Thus the 68 percent confidence band assures the teacher of being correct over two thirds of the time, which normally is quite adequate. A teacher who wants to be even more certain could set the bands between $+2$ and -2 standard errors around the obtained score, which would assure that the student's true score would be in that range 95 percent of the time. Bands of three standard errors can even be set, but the result usually is so large that it is not useful. Chapter 17, on standardized tests, gives the reliabilities and standard errors on the Iowa Tests of Basic Skills, a popular standardized achievement test.

Teachers generally do not know the standard errors associated with the instruments they construct. There are guidelines for writing them, however, that can help assure the reliability and validity of the instruments. These are presented in the following chapter.

CHAPTER 15 IN RETROSPECT

Educational evaluation requires concrete evidence of student achievement that has been accumulated in a scientific manner. The results are used by teachers to measure their students' academic progress and to judge the effectiveness of the instruction, by students to appraise their own knowledge and skills, and by administrators and community representatives as a basis for decision making about the schools.

Formal evaluations of students' learning may take the form of assignments and tests, either teacher made or standardized, or of systematic observation using instruments like rating scales and checklists to measure processes and products. All these methods involve measuring a sample of relevant academic knowledge and skills, and they all should be based on specific instructional objectives. A taxonomy like Bloom's is very useful for both planning and evaluating instruction. Academic achievement can be measured by comparison to a norm or a criterion.

Teacher-made instruments should measure only achievement. Standardized tests whose results may be relevant and useful to teachers include achievement, aptitude, diagnostic, and noncognitive tests.

Good measuring instruments possess both high reliability and validity. A highly reliable instrument is one that is highly consistent. For achievement tests, both teacher-constructed and standardized, internal consistency is the most important aspect of reliability. For certain types of standardized tests, stability and equivalence are important too. But no matter how reliable an instrument is, it must be valid to be of any use in schools.

A valid instrument is one that measures what it purports to measure. Content validity is the most important type for achievement tests: Does the instrument adequately sample the skills and content in the purported achievement area? Construct- and criterion-related validity are important for some standardized tests too.

Every score contains two parts—one that represents the student's actual knowledge and skills and a second part that is error. The standard error is a measure of the amount of error in a score. Instruments with high reliability and validity have small standard errors. Although teachers usually do not know the standard error associated with their own instruments, the standard errors of standardized test scores are readily available in test manuals. They can be used to set up confidence bands around each student's obtained score.

The measurement concepts presented in this chapter are discussed and applied to teacher-constructed instruments, standardized tests, and school-related evaluations in the following three chapters. At the end of these chapters there are questions for discussion and suggestions for further reading on these topics.

REFERENCES

Bloom, B. S., Englehart, M. B., Furst, E. J., Hill, W. H., and Krathwohl, D. R. *Taxonomy of Educational Objectives: The Classification of Education Goals. Handbook I: Cognitive Domain.* New York: Longmans Green, 1956.

Diederich, Paul B. *Short-cut Statistics for Teacher-made Tests.* Princeton, N.J.: Educational Testing Service, 1973.

Good, Thomas L., and Brophy, Jere E. *Looking in Classrooms.* New York: Harper & Row, 1973.

Mehrens, William A., and Lehmann, Irvin J. *Measurement and Evaluation in Education and Psychology.* 2nd ed. New York: Holt, Rinehart & Winston, 1978.

Evaluation with Teacher-Made Tests and Assignments

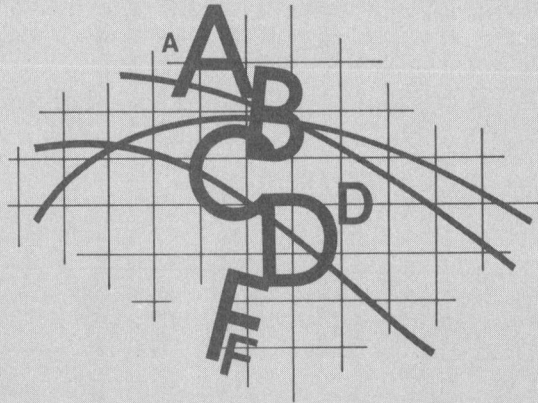

In order to determine what their students are learning, teachers are most likely to use questions to elicit the information they need. They use questions for many other purposes, too, of course, such as to make a bridge from one topic to another or to focus the attention of a student who seems to be wool-gathering. But when questions are incorporated in teacher-made tests and assignments, they provide formal measures of student learning.

This chapter explains how teachers can construct valid and reliable tests and other evaluation instruments, such as projects, homework problems, and term papers. Validity, reliability, and other basic concepts of measurement and the principles of educational evaluation were introduced in the preceding chapter. Since tests are the most common way to measure school learning and to assign grades, they will be emphasized, but much of the discussion of how to construct, use, and evaluate tests is generalizable to other forms of teacher-made measuring instruments.

Tests that are developed by classroom teachers should be tied to one or more of the teacher's objectives of instruction (see Chapter 15). The results of tests are used to evaluate how well the students are achieving these objectives. They also provide feedback to the teacher about the adequacy of the curriculum and the instruction students are receiving, as was shown in the instructional process model in Chapter 1. Scores on tests and assignments not only comprise important data about how well students are doing, they also help the teacher understand the strengths and weaknesses of the instructional program. This provides a basis for modification of the instructional objectives and the design of the instruction.

The technical ideas and skills that are important to the development of good classroom tests and assignments introduced in this chapter are simple enough to be understood by those who need to apply them. Teachers who understand the significant role of tests and assignments in the instructional process should also be willing to invest the time and effort that are required to produce valid, reliable classroom measurement instruments.

PLANNING TESTS
AND ASSIGNMENTS

The same planning that goes into the design of classroom instruction lays the groundwork for testing the effectiveness of the instructional process. A test should not be filled with surprises for students but should táp both the content and the intellectual or other skills the instruction was designed to teach. A test that requires performance from students in knowledge or skills that have not been taught to them cannot be valid. Consequently, it cannot assist the teacher in analyzing the curriculum or the instructional program or in evaluating student achievement.

A practical device teachers can use in designing classroom tests is to construct a table of specifications which reflects both the content that has been taught and the kinds of learning and behaving that the students are to master. A useful guide in constructing such a table is a taxonomy of educational objectives in the cognitive domain such as the one by Benjamin Bloom described in Chapter 15 (Bloom et al., 1956). The example of a table of specifications given in Table 16.1 was designed for a test to cover the social studies unit at the high school level on television viewing which was described in the preceding chapter. The teacher's general objective was to teach the students about the effects of TV on U.S. children and help them become critical rather than passive viewers. To construct the table of specifications, the teacher analyzed the kinds of content dealt with in the five-week unit. Specific objectives for the unit, such as those listed in Figure 15.1 in Chapter 15, are helpful in this task.

The rows in Table 16.1 show the content divided into four areas: values, positive and negative effects on children, ways to influence the content of TV shows, and appropriateness of various TV programs for

Table 16.1

Table of specifications for a teacher-made test about
the effects of television viewing on children

Content Area	Percentage of Test Points Covered in Learning Behavior Area*				Percent of Total Points in Content Areas
	Knowledge and Comprehension	Application	Analysis and Synthesis	Evaluation	
Values presented in TV shows	0	5%	10%	10%	25%
Positive and negative effects on children	5%	10	10	20	45
Ways to influence the content of shows	0	5	5	0	10
Appropriateness of shows for children	0	0	0	20	20
Percentage of total test points in behavior areas	5%	20%	25%	50%	100%

*See Bloom's Taxonomy of Educational Objectives for the cognitive domain in Box A in Chapter 15.

children. As the last column on the right shows, these were not equally treated in the unit. For each learning behavior measured, more instructional time and effort were devoted to positive and negative effects on children than to the other topics, and discussions of how the content of programs could be influenced were relatively brief.

Similarly, different cognitive behaviors were expected from students for the several content areas. The unit stressed the evaluation of television programs, so the greatest weight was for test items in that behavior category. Application and analysis of the information were also evaluated. The possession of basic information (knowledge and comprehension) was not heavily stressed, or it was measured in some other fashion as with a criterion-referenced quiz. The last row in the table shows these differences.

The percentages in the cells of the table (the combinations of rows and columns) indicate the emphasis on the test for the combination of each content and cognitive behavior area. Thus, for example, 10 percent of the items on the test should represent the evaluation of values presented on television programs; if the test contains 50 points, 5 of them should reflect this content-behavior mix.

A thoughtfully designed table of specifications for a test helps to assure the test's content validity. In practice many teachers rarely, if ever, draw up such tables, preferring to rely on their memories of what was covered in class or to use the textbook coverage to estimate what should be examined by the test. Given the fallibility of human memory and the wide supplementary materials for instruction, a test's content validity may suffer drastically if the teacher depends on either of these in constructing classroom tests.

MEASURING ACHIEVEMENT WITH PAPER-AND-PENCIL TESTS

Paper-and-pencil tests are used to measure a great deal of learning that takes place in the classroom. The teacher's usual procedure is to select the type or types of items to be used, write the test, making it as reliable and valid as possible, prepare the students for the test, and then administer it.

SELECTING TYPES OF ITEMS

One way to classify the various types of questions or items used in paper-and-pencil tests uses four basic categories: selection items, completion and short-answer items, essay questions, and problem questions. Table 16.2 gives a summary and comparison of these four types.

Table 16.2

Teacher-made item and test characteristics

Characteristic	Selection Items	Completion and Short-Answer Items	Essay Items	Problem Items
First use for students	Early elementary school	Preschool	Middle elementary school	Preschool
Learning behavior levels covered*	Knowledge, comprehension, application for true-false and matching; all, especially knowledge, comprehension, application for multiple-choice.	Knowledge, comprehension, application	All, especially analysis, synthesis, and evaluation	All, especially application, analysis, synthesis, and evaluation
Aspect(s) of student's thinking involved	Only the end product	Only the product	Process and product, ability to present and organize	Process and product, ability to present and organize
Aids for test-wise students	Guessing, cues in items	Some bluffing	Bluffing and writing skills	Some bluffing and organization skills
Responses	Chosen from provided alternatives	One or a few student-constructed words	Extensive student-constructed written answer	Brief to extensive student-constructed solution
Item preparation	Difficult, time-consuming	Relatively easy	Relatively easy	Relatively difficult
Number of items	Many	Many	Few	Few
Objectivity of scoring	Objective	Relatively objective, some judgment	Reader's judgment	Semiobjective, some reader's judgment
Ease of scoring	Easy, rapid	Relatively easy, rapid	Difficult, time-consuming	Relatively difficult, time-consuming
Reliability	High	High	Low	Moderate
Validity	High	High	Low	Low

*See Bloom's Taxonomy of Educational Objectives for the cognitive domain in Box A in Chapter 15.

Source: Based on a similar table developed by Charles D. Hopkins and Richard L. Antes, *Classroom Testing: Construction* (Itasca, Ill.: F. E. Peacock Publishers, 1979).

The types of questions or items chosen for use in tests are related to the reliability of the resulting tests. For a test to be *internally consistent* (see Chapter 15), that is, to measure a set of common objectives, it must contain enough questions or points to measure adequately the learning behaviors and content taught in the unit. Generally, a test or assignment must contain at least 20 points to be reliable. Tests consisting of some types of items—essays, for example—often contain fewer points than tests of other types, such as multiple choice, and so they are less reliable.

Selection Items

Selection items require students to select the correct response from several given with the question. There are three basic kinds of selection questions: matching, true-false, and multiple choice.

Matching-Item Questions   Matching items present two sets of information; the student is to pair the word or words from each set that go together in some way. Teachers often use matching items to measure knowledge at the recall, comprehension, and application levels (see Box A in Chapter 15). An application-level matching item from a quiz on the TV-watching unit is given in Figure 16.1.

Figure 16.1

Example of a matching item for the TV-watching unit test

Directions: For each of the TV examples related to learning in column 1, match the letter of the learning term describing it in column 2. Each learning term may be used once, twice, or not at all.

Column 1
Example from TV Related to Learning

Column 2
Learning Terms

_G_ 1. Brad watches the Cookie Monster on Sesame Street stuff cookies in his mouth. That night, at dinner, Brad stuffs food in his mouth.

_H_ 2. The food that Brad stuffs in his mouth is french fries, not cookies.

_C_ 3. Brad's parents take the french fries away from Brad because of his behavior

_F_ 4. Because Hona saw a person on TV sent to jail for stealing, Hona decides never to steal.

_D_ 5. On TV, a woman gives Jim $5 because he returned the wallet she had dropped. Lena watches this show.

A. Direct positive reinforcement

B. Direct negative reinforcement

C. Direct punishment

D. Vicarious positive reinforcement

E. Vicarious negative reinforcement

F. Vicarious punishment

G. Modeling

H. Generalization

When using matching items, teachers should be sure to give students directions on the type of relationship to be used in the matching process. Usually there are five to eight items in each list, because more items require much more reading time before the task can be undertaken. Since testwise students use elimination to aid them in the matching process, the second list often includes some items that are never correct matches and others that can be used more than once. Matching items should be arranged so that each question is complete on one page and students do not have to flip back and forth among the test pages. A summary of guidelines to assist teachers in writing matching questions is given later in Box A, which lists guidelines for writing each of the four basic types of items on paper-and-pencil tests.

True-False Items   A true-false item presents a statement, and the student indicates whether it is true or false. Like matching items, true-false questions generally are used to measure learning behavior at the remembering, comprehension, and application levels (see Box A in Chapter 15). Comprehension examples from a test over the TV unit might include:

Some TV shows for children are value free.   True   False
Children can learn specific behaviors by
    watching TV.   True   False

Teachers who write successful true-false items meet several criteria. They only include one idea in each question—an important one from the unit covered which is essentially either true or false. They write simple, short items because complex, lengthy statements may measure reading ability as much as they do achievement. When possible, they write questions as positive statements; when they have to use negative words, they draw attention by underlining them.

Good true-false item writers also minimize the cues they give to students which could help them answer the questions correctly without knowing the material. These include clue words such as *always* or *often*; items with the words *always* or *never* usually are false, while those using *usually* or *often* generally are true. They use synonymns or alternate language rather than words taken directly from the text or lessons (except for technical vocabulary), so students cannot answer the items correctly with just word recognition. Since true statements often require more qualifications than false ones do, true questions tend to be longer, so good test writers try to make the true and false statements approximately the same length. They also include about the same number of true and false items.

A summary of guidelines to use in writing true-false test items is given in Box A. Even when teachers follow these guidelines, there are certain disadvantages to this type of question. It is very difficult to write good items because almost nothing is completely true or false. And students who guess the answer to a question have a 50-50 chance of being right; a student could guess throughout a test and still receive credit for half of the items.

Multiple-Choice Items   The kind of selection item that is most frequently used in classroom tests is the multiple-choice question. This type includes a stem that presents the basis of the question and a set of three, four, or five options that the students use to select their responses. In the usual form, one of the options is correct and the remainder, called *distractors,* are incorrect. A good test writer can construct multiple-choice questions that measure all levels of learning behavior, but they most often apply to knowledge, comprehension, or application. Examples of comprehension-level and application-level multiple-choice questions that might be included in a test on the TV-watching unit are given in Figure 16.2.

Figure 16.2

Examples of multiple-choice questions for the TV-watching unit test

COMPREHENSION-LEVEL QUESTION

According to Bandura's theory and studies of aggression,

a. A child has to be rewarded in order to learn a specific aggressive response.

b. A child has to be frustrated in order to be aggressive, because aggression is the natural outcome of frustration.

c. A child can learn an aggressive action through observational learning.

d. A child can learn an aggressive action through observational learning, but reinforcement influences whether or not the action is performed.

e. A combination of frustration and the observation of a model's aggression is necessary before a child will imitate that model's actions.

APPLICATION-LEVEL QUESTION

Children are most likely to behave calmly after watching

a. Just about any show, since television has a calming effect on the viewer.

b. Mr. Rogers, a low-key program designed to familiarize children with everyday living activities.

c. Star Trek, a series where the crew of a starship encounters life-threatening experiences in space.

d. The Roadrunner, a cartoon show filled with hectic chases and violent antics.

e. The evening national news.

Writing good multiple-choice items takes skill and practice (see Box A for a summary of writing guidelines). Each question should present one meaningful, important problem. The stem can be in the form of an incomplete sentence, with the options finishing the sentence, or it can present a question, with the options providing possible answers. As with true-false items, negative words should be avoided whenever possible and underlined if they are used. The best multiple-choice items include four or five options in each question to aid the test's reliability, but teachers settle for fewer options if they cannot make all of them plausible. Use of the answers "all of the above" and "none of the above" should be avoided. Each question should contain only one correct or best answer, and they should never be "trick questions." Good items do not repeat words or phrases from the text in the options, but they may include them in the stem of the question.

Care must be taken to avoid giving clues on these questions to testwise students. Because longer options often are the correct ones, all the options in a question should be about the same length. All the options also must be grammatically parallel to the stem; if the stem is singular and two of the options are plural, for example, a testwise student would not choose either of those two. The position of the correct option within the questions should be varied; as clever students quickly discover, many multiple-choice questions have option c as the correct answer. As with other types of items, synonyms should be used instead of the language of the text.

Advantages and Disadvantages of Using Selection Items Experience has shown that selection items work well for some testing. All three kinds of selection items can be used to measure recall, comprehension, and application, and multiple-choice questions can be used to measure higher levels of behavior. Tests using these types of items have content validity if they contain enough items to cover the content and the learning behavior levels adequately. Since the tests would be long, they also would be quite reliable. Scoring is easy and rapid, so teachers are able to give ongoing feedback to students. Because the scoring is objective, with the number correct given for each student, selection items are also considered to be objective. These types of items, especially true-false, can be used with students at all levels, from the first grades in elementary school.

Teachers also find disadvantages to the use of selection items. Most of the items of this type found in the teachers' guides are written at the recall and comprehension levels, and it is almost impossible to write true-false or matching questions at any level higher than application. Teachers can, and do, write higher-level multiple-choice items, but these take a great deal of time to construct, often over 20 minutes for each question. Because of this, most teachers write multiple-choice questions only over

For students taking paper-and-pencil tests, the clarity of the questions and their relevance to what the class has studied are vital considerations.

units that they will teach repeatedly. In addition, since students merely choose their responses to these questions and do not construct them, only the results of their thinking are shown, not the process. Selection questions also encourage students to guess when they do not know the correct answers.

Completion and Short-Answer Items

In completion test items, the student is given a sentence with a missing word (or words) and is told to fill in the blanks with the correct response. An application example from the TV-watching unit test is:

> When children see a person hit another on TV and then the children hit their friends, the TV people are serving as   (models) .

An item which presents a question and asks the student to answer it with a word, phrase, or a few sentences is called a short-answer item. The above completion item in short-answer form is:

> What is the term that describes someone's behavior that is later imitated by another person who sees it?   (modeling) .

These types of items can be readily used in any subject area, especially to measure how well material is remembered. Science and mathematics teachers use them often. Short-answer questions can also be used to measure some of the other lower thinking levels, but they are harder to write than those that measure at the recall level. Short-answer items, particularly, may be similar to essay items. Guides for writing these types of questions are given in Box A.

There are several advantages to these types of items. A teacher can ask many of them on a test, which can raise both the reliability and the validity of the test. They are relatively easy to write and to score, and students use little guessing in answering them. These types of items can be used at all educational levels; even preschool-aged children can answer them when they are asked verbally.

There are also disadvantages. Completion and short-answer items mostly measure learning behavior at the lower levels. Since the students' responses are not completely structured by the test items, scoring often requires the scorer's judgment, which makes these items somewhat less reliable than selection items. Even though students do not guess on them they do try to bluff. They have a little freedom in responding, but the responses are so short that the teacher only knows the result of the student's thinking, not the process behind it, as in selection items.

Essay Items

In essay items, the teacher presents a question and the student must write a complete answer to it. Guidelines for writing, using, and scoring these types of questions are given in Box A.

As teachers gain experience in writing, giving, and scoring tests, they recognize the advantages of essay items. This kind of question can easily be written to measure learning at any level. Since students construct their own answers, teachers can follow their thought processes as well as evaluate their written responses. Essay items also provide a measure of each student's ability to organize and present ideas. They can be used from middle elementary school on, or as soon as students learn to write.

But the essay form of question also has disadvantages. Since essay tests contain only a few questions, they cannot cover all of the desired content-behavior areas (see Table 16.1), and therefore they lack content validity and reliability is lower. Moreover, the teacher's score for each answer is based on judgment, and others might evaluate the responses differently. Because the scoring is subjective, essay items may also be considered to be subjective, which also lowers reliability. Students with good writing skills usually score higher than other students, even when both know about the same, because their responses "read" better and they are able to bluff more effectively. Scoring of essay questions can be difficult and extremely time-consuming, so there generally is a delay in returning the

---

Figure 16.3

---

*Poor and improved forms of an essay question on the
TV-watching unit test*

Poor form: Read the following description of a children's TV show. How can you
determine if this show is appropriate for viewing by preschool-aged children?
(10 points)

Improved form: Read the following description of a children's TV show. Describe
how you should determine if this show is appropriate for viewing by preschool-aged
children. Include in your discussion:

a. A list of the negative behaviors, like violence, and the positive behaviors, like
helpfulness, found in the show. (2 points)

b. A description of the outcomes to each of the positive and negative behaviors
found in the show. (3 points)

c. Three "lessons" that young children might learn from watching this show.
(3 points)

d. Your conclusion about the appropriateness of this show for young children.
(2 points)

---

tests and obtaining feedback from students. Another disadvantage is
that beginning teachers may write questions that are so general their
students cannot tell exactly what they are to discuss.

There are several ways to overcome these disadvantages. One way is
to write each question in a very specific fashion. In the sample essay
item for a test on the TV-watching unit in Figure 16.3, the poorly stated
form is too general. The improved form lets students know what to
discuss and how much time and emphasis to devote to each part. Thus
teachers need to give substantial time and thought to writing essay questions. By increasing the number of essay questions on a test, they can
improve its reliability and validity. More items calling for short essay
answers of about one-half page are preferable to a few items requiring
longer answers of two or more pages. Since the other item types can
easily be used to measure recall, comprehension, and application, most
teachers use essays to measure the higher levels of learning behavior
such as analysis, synthesis, and evaluation.

As with the other types of items, teachers should try to use terms and
language which vary from those used in the instruction. Students should
have no options in choosing which questions to answer, because students'
performance cannot be compared if they answer different questions.

Scoring Essay Questions   Since the scoring of essay items is generally
difficult and subjective, many teachers outline the answer they want for

each question in advance and use it as a model to compare to students' answers. Teachers, as we noted in Chapters 9 and 14, form unintentional, and sometimes unconscious, judgments about which students know the material and which ones do not. They like students who smile at them during class, since smiling is an indication of liking and attending. They dislike students who doze during class and obviously cannot learn the material while sleeping. To be certain that their attitudes do not influence their essay test grading, most teachers use blind scoring, for which students put their names on the backs of their papers. As the course continues, however, teachers learn to recognize most of their students' handwriting and even their typewriting styles. The use of model answers lets teachers remain fairly objective.

All of the responses to one essay item should be scored before going on to others, and all of the answers to each question should be graded in one sitting. There are two main ways to score essay-type answers, both of which are very time-consuming. In the *point-score method*, the teacher decides how many points will be given for each part of the answer (as illustrated in Figure 16.3) and assigns points to each student's answer as it is read. A student's test score is the sum of the points the student received on all items in the test.

In the *sorting method* of scoring, the teacher reads each answer and sorts it into a pile which represents the teacher's judgment of the grade it merits. For the final grade on the entire test the teacher averages the grades on all of the questions or weights them if some are more important than others. The students should have the weighting information (the number of points per answer) while they are taking the test.

Regardless of which scoring method is used, the reliability of the grading is improved if the teacher rechecks the scoring by ordering the papers from high to low on each question and going through them again to be certain that the scores are accurate. Students usually appreciate written comments that provide them with positive, as well as negative, feedback on their answers.

Problem Items

Problem items present a situation involving a problem that students are to solve. In the elementary grades, these are called *story problems*. This question type is useful in content areas where the process used in arriving at an answer is as important as the answer itself. These areas include mathematics, the sciences, and business and vocational courses. An application-level example from a physics test is:

> One car is traveling east on a road at 50 mph. A second car is traveling west on the same road at 55 mph. If the cars start their trips 300 miles apart, how long will it take them to meet?

Problem items have several advantages. They can measure all levels of learning behavior and are especially useful for measuring the skills of application, analysis, synthesis, and evaluation. Students at all levels of educational development, from preschool through postgraduate classes, can do appropriately written problems. Since the answers are completely generated by students, little guessing is involved, and the teacher can evaluate the students' process in answering the question as well as their proposed solutions. This information is extremely useful in diagnosing students' weaknesses.

The disadvantages to problem items are related to those for essay tests. A test which consists exclusively of problem items usually includes only a few questions, which makes it difficult to sample the content area and so has low content validity. Since there may be more than one correct solution to a problem, and since errors students make early in their solutions will compound and create errors throughout the remainder of the answer, scoring is only semiobjective. It has to be mediated by the scorer's judgment, and the result is often only moderate test reliability. Some students will bluff when they do not know a solution, so students with good organization skills may receive higher scores. Teachers find it relatively difficult to write and score problem items, and it takes a great deal of time to do both well.

There are several ways to minimize these disadvantages. Guidelines for writing and scoring problem items are given in Box A. Teachers should give themselves plenty of time to write and score these tests and make certain that each problem is unique, distinctively stated, and specifies what students are to do. The use of several shorter problems increases validity and reliability. Teachers should decide before the test how to handle arithmetic and other cumulative errors and let the students know how this will be done. As with essay questions they can work out model answers, assign points to the various parts of the solutions, and use the point-score method of grading. Problem items are usually used only for measuring content and learning behavior areas that cannot be measured easily with other types of items.

CONSTRUCTING TEACHER-MADE TESTS

As the preceding survey of the various types of teacher-made test items indicates, there is no one best type of test or item. Nevertheless, some general guidelines, in addition to those for specific types of questions summarized in Box A, can help teachers write good tests.

Test writing is easier if items or questions are drafted as the teacher initially presents the instruction to students. The items can then be rewritten into final form on note cards, one to a card, and kept in a test

BOX A   *Guidelines for writing test items*

The four types of items used in paper-and-pencil classroom tests and assignments require the teacher to apply different types of writing and scoring skills in their construction. The guidelines presented here are designed to help teachers write selection, completion and short-answer, essay, and problem items and use them effectively to measure the outcomes of the instructional process.

SELECTION TEST ITEMS— MATCHING, TRUE-FALSE, AND MULTIPLE-CHOICE

Matching-Item Questions

1. Each question includes directions to the student indicating the type of relationship to be used in the matching process.
2. Each question generally includes five to eight items.
3. The two lists in each question often contain different numbers of items, and some of the items in the second list can be used more than once or not at all.
4. An entire matching-item question appears on one page of the test.

True-False Questions

1. Each question contains one important idea that is basically true or false.
2. Items are simple and short rather than long and complex.
3. Questions are worded positively, whenever possible; negative words are underlined.
4. To avoid giving cues to testwise students:
   a. Words like *always*, *never*, *usually*, and *often* are avoided.
   b. True and false statements are about the same length.
   c. True and false statements are used in about equal numbers.
   d. Statements use alternate language or synonyms rather than words taken directly from the instruction or the text where possible.

Multiple-Choice Questions

1. Each question contains one meaningful, important problem.
2. Questions usually do *not* include
   a. Negative words.
   b. The options "all of the above" or "none of the above."
3. Each question includes four or five options, and each one is plausible.
4. Each item contains only one correct or best answer.
5. Items are never "trick questions."
6. Words or phrases are not repeated in the options but are included in the stem.
7. To avoid giving cues to students:
   a. All options within a question are of about the same length.
   b. All options are grammatically parallel to the stem.
   c. The correct answer is randomly positioned in items throughout the test.
   d. The questions and options use synonyms rather than direct quotations from the text or instruction material.

COMPLETION AND SHORT-ANSWER ITEMS

1. Each item contains only one important point.
2. Items are stated in different words than those used in the text or instruction.
3. Generally, the same amount of space is provided for each answer.

(continued)

(BOX A *continued*)

ESSAY ITEMS

1. Each essay question is written in a specific form which provides a framework for student answers and specific point values or weights for each part of the answer.
2. Several shorter essay questions make a more reliable and more valid test than a few longer questions.
3. Essay questions measure the higher levels of learning behaviors (analysis, synthesis, and evaluation) that cannot be measured easily with more objective item types.
4. Essay questions express new ideas, not familiar issues that can be answered with memorization.
5. No options among essay questions are allowed; all students answer each question to ensure the answers are comparable.
6. For the teacher's own information, an answer to each question is outlined before the test is given, and that model is used in scoring the papers.
7. Essays are scored blindly using the point-score method, the sorting method, or a combination.
8. In scoring, teachers write comments, both positive and negative, on students' papers.

PROBLEM ITEMS

1. Each problem item clearly states what the answer should contain and the worth of each part of the answer.
2. Several shorter problems provide more reliable and more valid tests than a few longer problems.
3. Problem items measure higher levels of learning behavior: application, analysis, synthesis, and evaluation.
4. Items are expressed in distinctive language or present original situations so memorization is not stressed.
5. The teacher outlines a sample answer to each problem and uses it as a model in scoring the papers. Provisions must also be made for handling arithmetic and other cumulative errors.
6. Problems are scored using the point-score method.

file. This makes it simple to rearrange the items and to see what additional types need to be written to cover other content and learning behavior areas. Other good sources of potential test items are other teachers' test item files and texts or manuals with test questions. These must be carefully examined to be certain that they have content validity for a particular course or classroom, however, and such items often must be rewritten.

Use of a table of specifications, as was shown in Table 16.1, in writing tests helps ensure their content validity. The most valid and reliable types of items to use to test student performance at various learning levels were indicated in Table 16.2. The more subjective essay and problem question types should be used when the content or learning behavior cannot be measured adequately with the more objective selection, completion, or short-answer question types. To increase reliability and validity, tests should include at least 20 points, and 30 or more is better. For preschool and early elementary school children, many short tests, or other methods of evaluation such as projects, assignments, and performance measures, are appropriate.

Test items should be arranged in a logical order, with all items relating to a single topic placed together so students do not have to switch topics continually in their thinking. Within each topic, the items should be arranged from easy to difficult. A very easy first item can help relax students, and the remainder of their test performance will be a truer indication of their current level of understanding.

Good tests measure power, not speed, except when speed is a factor in the content area. Work rate should be based on a student's working style and personality, as well as learning. With adult learners it is especially important to test their power rather than their speed. Adults' rates of learning start to slow down in the late teens and continue to decrease with age, as we noted in Chapter 6.

PREPARATION AND ADMINISTRATION

Tests always should be discussed in advance with students. The teacher should indicate the content areas and behavior levels the test will cover and the number of items or points in each area. Some teachers give students copies of their test table of specifications to use in studying for taking a test.

Ideally, teachers should administer their own tests. Even adults feel more secure and relaxed when the person who has been teaching the course writes and administers the test on the content. If this is not possible, students should be told in advance who will give it. When the teacher is not there to answer questions and deal with problems during the exam, scoring should be more flexible.

Directions should be given for each type of item used as the questions appear on the test. Many students, even in college, either do not or cannot read directions accurately, so instructors should give the directions verbally even when they are written out on the test. Students should also have guidelines about the time and effort to be spent on each part of the test.

Motivational aspects of the testing situation can affect performance as much as the students' ability or knowledge, as we noted in Chapter 11. Research has shown that reducing the anxiety and pressure of the situation improves test performance, particularly for disadvantaged children. Hill (1980) suggests that time pressures should be relaxed where possible, students should be informed in advance of the difficulty of a test and learn cognitive strategies to prepare for it, and practice should be allowed with the mechanics of the test in a relaxed setting.

EVALUATING PROCESSES AND PRODUCTS

A large part of school learning can be measured with paper-and-pencil tests administered in the classroom. Some kinds of skills and knowledge cannot be evaluated this way, however. These include performance in vocational courses such as car mechanics, secretarial skills, or accounting; laboratory sciences; second languages; physical education; and art and music. In these cases it often is necessary to evaluate students' end products or results, such as a laboratory report, term paper, homework problem, or relief map; or the processes or procedures followed in producing results, such as the stance taken in batting a baseball.

The most critical aspect of this type of evaluation is setting up the standards or criteria to be applied. These must be based on professional knowledge and judgment about what is important in the process, product, or both. Instructors' manuals, teacher-training textbooks on methods, and other teachers can suggest sets of evaluation criteria and recommend methods for measuring how well the process or product fits the standards. Processes and products may be evaluated both for general efficiency, such as typing speed, and for accuracy, such as the number of errors made.

Procedures generally are more difficult to evaluate than products are. They can be evaluated through direct observation as the process occurs or delayed observation of the recorded action. The latter is much simpler and more reliable. Evaluating a tennis score, for example, is easier if it has been recorded on videotape and so can be replayed a number of times, even at a slower speed. This technique is extensively used with athletes to evaluate their performances, to help them isolate strengths and weaknesses, and to improve their deficiencies. The result or product also can be inspected for evidence relating to process. Generally, good results come from good procedures; a tennis serve that lands out of bounds indicates that something was wrong with the service.

Products generally are more important than the procedures used to create them, however. For many types of products, such as homework problems, term papers, and reports, the evaluation methods can be similar to those used with problem and essay test items. Products which are problems or papers can be compared to models written by the teacher and scored using the point-score or sorting method.

Figure 16.4

Rating scale for evaluating science fair projects

Directions: After examining a display and talking to the student who constructed it, rate each of the following aspects. Use a scale from 1 to 7.

1	2	3	4	5	6	7
Poor			Moderate			Excellent

After rating all aspects, sum your scores.

Display number _____

Student's name _____

Aspect	Rating	Total
Appearance of display		
Clear presentation of content	_____	
Logical organization	_____	
Attractiveness	_____	
		_____
Content of display		
Originality	_____	
Thoroughness	_____	
Use of the scientific method	_____	
		_____
Student performance		
Knowledge of background area	_____	
Understanding of methods used	_____	
Skill in handling questions from a judge	_____	
		_____
Grand total		**_____**

CHECKLISTS AND RATING SCALES

Checklists and rating scales are the evaluation instruments most commonly used for certain types of assignments. These instruments should be designed to measure specific qualities in the procedure or product, in order to ensure reliability and validity and to avoid involving the teacher's expectations about a student's performance. Measuring specific qualities and judging all assignments against the same criteria contribute to the reliability of the teacher's judgments.

Checklists are useful in measuring whether or not the process or product contains all of the elements deemed important by the teacher. For example, a biology teacher might use a checklist to evaluate students' drawings of laboratory animals. The checklist could list all the essential animal parts, in the teacher's judgment. To evaluate each drawing, the teacher would go through the checklist and check off each part of the animal that the student included in the drawing. The student's score would be the number of check marks.

Rating scales require the teacher to judge various qualities in a student's process or product. Judges at a science fair might use the rating scale shown in Figure 16.4, for example, to evaluate each student's display. It calls for rating three aspects of the display—appearance, content, and the student's knowledge—and characteristics of each one. The major aspects can be weighted so that some count for more than others do. The student's final score is the sum of all of the ratings. A similar rating scale could be used with any type of project that consists of a display.

NORM- AND CRITERION-REFERENCED CLASSROOM MEASUREMENT

From the middle elementary level on up, most teacher-made measurement is norm referenced; that is, as we noted in Chapter 15, one student's achievement is compared to that of other students. Both general and specific objectives can be used in norm-referenced instruction, and all types of test items can be used to measure it. Norm-referenced tests should contain items that vary in difficulty from moderately easy to moderately hard, and no student should receive a perfect score. Because of these two characteristics, coupled with content validity, students' scores are spread out, and accurate comparisons among students are possible.

The object of criterion-referenced measurement is to determine what each student knows or doesn't know in comparison to a certain standard. Most criterion-referenced classroom testing with teacher-made tests is meant to accompany teaching for mastery programs. In this type of teaching, which was described in Chapter 12, the subject matter is broken down into a set of specific objectives which are generally concerned with the learning behavior levels of knowledge, comprehension, and application. These levels can be measured with selection, short-answer, completion, or problem items, but essay items are usually not used on criterion-referenced tests. Test results are often scored as passing (meeting the criterion) or not passing, with the cutoff based on correct answers to some percentage of the questions, frequently 85 or 90. Students who do not meet the criterion restudy the material and then take a related test. With a successful teaching program, most students eventually pass a test on the material.

Criterion-referenced measurement is also used with *contract teaching*, in which each student and the teacher specify in a contract exactly how the student will show that she or he has reached the desired competency level. The students must satisfy a set achievement goal on tests or projects or fulfill the contract in some other manner.

An example of a comprehension-level multiple-choice question from a criterion-referenced vocabulary quiz on the TV-watching unit is:

When a child sees a model on TV being rewarded, this is called

a. direct reinforcement
b. vicarious reinforcement
c. modeling

Criterion-referenced measurement often works better than norm-referenced measurement in the preschool or early elementary school and with many types of exceptional students. From middle elementary school on up, the teacher (within the guidelines set by the school) can choose whether to use norm- or criterion-referenced measurement or a combination of the two. The introductory material in most subject matter areas, such as definitions and methodologies, can easily be tested with criterion-referenced items. This type of testing is especially useful when the teacher is working on basic content and skill acquisition, as in arithmetic, spelling, and reading.

TEACHER-MADE TEST SCORES AND SCORE DISTRIBUTIONS

Merely listing the scores attained by various students on a test or assignment will not tell the teacher much about the students' learning behaviors. The scores in Table 16.3, for example, represent the total number of points that each student in a high school social science class answered correctly, or the students' raw scores, on a 50-point test on the TV-watching unit described in Chapter 15 and referred to above. Discovering anything from this table other than an individual's raw score

Table 16.3

Raw score (number correct) for each student on a 50-point test for the TV-watching unit

Tom	41	Michelle	41	Juanita	41	Steve	34
Robert	50	Mary Ann	41	Paz	43	Geronimo	39
Candace	28	Jenny	37	Gail	34	Harold	41
Carole	42	Juan	47	Judy	50	Marcia	47
Russ	42	William	35	Lamar	33		
Jim	34	Jean	47	Lorna	29		
Gary	30	Ricardo	40	Bernadette	40		

Table 16.4

Number correct for each student on the test for the TV-watching unit (raw scores arranged in descending order)

Judy	50	Russ	42	Bernadette	40	Lamar	33
Robert	50	Michelle	41	Geronimo	39	Gary	30
Juan	47	Juanita	41	Jenny	37	Lorna	29
Marcia	47	Harold	41	William	35	Candace	28
Jean	47	Mary Ann	41	Steve	34		
Paz	43	Tom	41	Jim	34		
Carole	42	Ricardo	40	Gail	34		

is difficult, however. The table is just a list of numbers, with no organization except by name.

The simplest way to organize the raw scores from any test or assignment is to list them from highest to lowest (or lowest to highest), as in Table 16.4. This table makes it clear that Judy and Robert received the top scores of 50, while Candace received the bottom score of 28.

FREQUENCY DISTRIBUTIONS

To get a group picture of the class's achievement on the TV-watching unit test, the teacher can tally the number of times a particular raw score was made by class members. To construct such a frequency distribution, the class scores are reordered by listing all possible scores from high to low (or vice versa) and then recording the number of students who received each test score. Table 16.5 represents the frequency distribution for this test; it shows, for example, that two students in the class received a score of 42, without identifying the students. Now the teacher can look at the frequency distribution and quickly determine the top and bottom scores, as well as some of the other test characteristics. Since most students received fairly high scores, it can be assumed that the test was relatively easy, for example.

On the basis of this distribution, the students' raw scores can be graphed as in Figure 16.5. Such a diagram shows the distribution in a visual way that is easy for parents and students to understand. Knowing how others have performed on an assignment or test lets students judge how easy or hard the task was and helps them evaluate their own scores.

MEASURES OF CENTRAL TENDENCY

In order to use the frequency distribution of raw scores in grading class members (see Chapter 18), the teacher must determine where the "middle" of the scores falls. Such measures are called *measures of central ten-*

Table 16.5

Frequency distribution of raw scores of students on the TV-watching unit test

Test Score	Frequency
50	2
49	0
48	0
47	3
46	0
45	0
44	0
43	1
42	2
41	5
40	2
39	1
38	0
37	1
36	0
35	1
34	3
33	1
32	0
31	0
30	1
29	1
28	1
	25

Figure 16.5

Plot of test score distribution for the TV-watching unit test

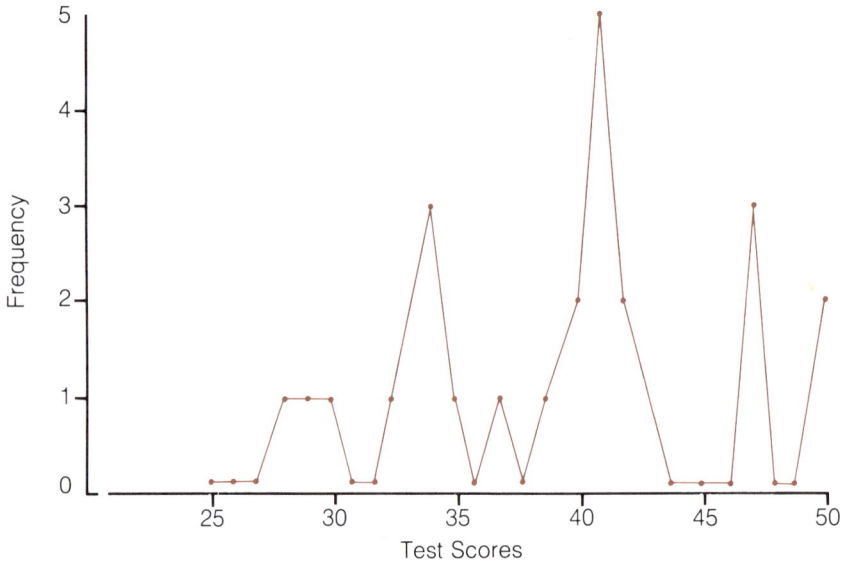

dency. The measures of this type used most frequently by teachers are
the mean and the median.*

Mean

The mean is the measure that is used most often on teacher-made assignments. It is just the average score, equal to the sum of all of the
scores divided by the number of scores:

$$\text{Mean} = \frac{\text{Sum of all scores}}{\text{Number of scores}}$$

A method of computing the mean from a frequency distribution is
shown in Table 16.6. The problem in computing the mean is how to
sum the scores, since each possible score is listed only once in the frequency distribution. For example, three people received scores of 47;
that means that 47 must be added in three times (47 × 3 = 141). To

---

*The mode, which is the most frequently occurring score in a distribution, is a
third measure of central tendency. It is rarely used in either teacher-made tests
and assignments or in standardized tests.

Table 16.6

*Computation of mean score for students
taking the TV-watching unit test*

Test Score	Frequency	Frequency × Test Score
50	2	100
47	3	141
43	1	43
42	2	84
41	5	205
40	2	80
39	1	39
37	1	37
35	1	35
34	3	102
33	1	33
30	1	30
29	1	29
28	1	28
Totals	25	986

Mean = Sum of all scores/Number of scores
　　　 = Sum of frequency × score column/Sum of frequency column
　　　 = 986/25
　　　 = 39.44

show these computations another column labeled "Frequency × Test Score" is added to the frequency distribution. The numbers in this column are summed, and the total is divided by the sum from the frequency column to obtain the mean. In this example, the sum of the frequency times test score column, 986, is divided by 25, the sum of the frequency column. The result is 39.44 (rounded to two decimal places), which is the mean for the test.

Median

The median is the score that splits the class scores in half. There are several statistical formulas for calculating an exact median score. Medians may be reported on standardized tests, but teachers usually do not calculate the median for their own tests and assignments.

MEASURES OF VARIABILITY

Computation of the mean for the TV-watching test shows that the mean, or middle of the test score distribution, is 39.44. The three students who received scores of 47 thus know that they are about seven and one-half points above the mean score. But they also want to know if 47 is a good score in relation to the rest of the class. This is especially true if the test results will be used for norm-referenced grading.

The characteristic of a set of scores that gives this information is its variability. Measures of variability show how much the scores vary, or the extent to which they are dispersed or spread out. The measures of variability most often used by teachers are the range and the standard deviation.

Range

The easiest measure of variability, which unfortunately is a very rough measure, is the range. The range is often given by indicating the bottom and the top scores:

$$\text{Range} = \text{Bottom score, Top score}$$

In the TV-watching unit test, this would be 50, 28.

Sometimes the range is defined as the difference between the highest and lowest scores. In this example this would be $50 - 28 = 22$.

The range may also be defined as:

$$\text{Range} = \text{Highest score} - \text{Lowest score} + 1$$

This definition indicates the actual number of possible points between the high and low scores—in the example, 23. Any of these definitions is acceptable.

If the students who got the scores of 47 on the TV-watching unit test know that the range is from 28 to 50, they also know that they are closer to the highest score than to the average one. If the range were from 36 to 65, for example, they would know that they are closer to the average student's performance.

Standard Deviation

The best measure of variability is the standard deviation, or the average distance that the test scores vary from the mean. To find it, the difference between each test score and the mean test score is squared. These squared differences are then summed, and the total is divided by the number of students who took the test, minus one. The square root of that number is then calculated. The formula for calculating the standard deviation (SD) is:

$$\text{SD} = \sqrt{\frac{\Sigma\,(\text{Score} - \text{Mean})^2}{N - 1}}$$

The standard deviation on this test is 6.19, rounded to two decimal places.

Writing, administering, and scoring teacher-made tests are among the teacher's most demanding tasks. Test scores must be organized to provide a picture of how well the students are achieving class objectives, as well as to point to the strengths and weaknesses in the instructional process.

Since the standard deviation is rather difficult to calculate, most teachers do not compute it. Many calculators will calculate the standard deviation automatically.

While the mean indicates the average score on a test or assignment, the standard deviation indicates the average variability in a set of scores. One standard deviation unit is the average distance in raw scores that any score is from the mean score. A large standard deviation indicates wide variability in scores, while a small one indicates that all scores are quite close together. If the standard deviation is squared, the result is called the *variance*.

PERCENTILE AND PERCENT-CORRECT SCORES

There are two easy ways to convert students' number-correct or raw scores to other forms which can increase their understanding of how well they have performed. The percentile score is the percentage of students who scored below a particular student's raw score. This score is norm referenced; it shows how well each student did in relation to the rest of the class. The *percent-correct* score is the percentage of test items answered correctly by a student. This score is criterion referenced; it shows how well the student did in relation to the assignment. Either or both of these scores can be included in a frequency distribution by adding new columns to the table.

Percentile Scores

A percentile score, also called a percentile rank or centile score, represents the percentage of *people* who scored below a certain raw score. (Percentile scores may also be defined as the percentage of people with scores *at or below* a specific raw score.) The formula is:

$$\text{Percentile score} = \frac{\text{No. of people who scored below a raw score}}{\text{Sum of the frequency column}} \times 100$$

Table 16.7 shows all of the percentile scores for the students taking the TV-watching unit test. Two students had the top scores of 50. Adding up the numbers in the frequency column below that score would show that 23 students scored lower. To convert to a percentage score, this

---

Table 16.7

Percentile and percent-correct scores for the TV-watching unit test

Test Score	Frequency	Percentile Score	Percent-Correct Score
50	2	92	100
47	3	80	94
43	1	76	86
42	2	68	84
41	5	48	82
40	2	40	80
39	1	36	78
37	1	32	74
35	1	28	70
34	3	16	68
33	1	12	66
30	1	8	60
29	1	4	58
28	1	0	56
	25		

proportion score is multiplied by 100. Thus, a raw score of 50 correct is equivalent to a percentile score of 92 (23/25 × 100). Similarly, three students received scores of 34, and four students scored lower. So a raw score of 34 correct is equivalent to a percentile score of 16 (4/25 × 100).

Percentile scores on teacher-made assignments and tests are used primarily for grading on the curve, which will be discussed in Chapter 18.

Percent-Correct Scores

A percent-correct score shows what percentage of the assignment or test a student correctly answered. The formula is:

$$\text{Percent-correct score} = \frac{100 \times \text{No. of items correct}}{\text{Total No. of items}}$$

On the TV-watching unit test, two students got 40 items correct. Since there were a total of 50 points on the test, a raw score of 40 is equivalent to 80 percent (40/50 × 100) correct. Table 16.7 also shows the percent-correct scores on this test.

Percentile and percent-correct scores are completely different and almost always result in different numbers. As Table 16.7 shows, the three students who had raw scores of 34 had percentile scores of 16 and percent-correct scores of 68. On this exam, none of the percentile scores matched the corresponding percent-correct scores.

PROVIDING FEEDBACK ON TEST AND ASSIGNMENT SCORES

Feedback on test and assignment scores operates both ways in the instructional process—it provides information to students on how their work is being evaluated, and it gives the teacher an indication of how successful the instruction has been.

Students should always see their papers after they have been marked with the number correct and the various scores used in the evaluation. A student's test scores are a private matter between the teacher and the students and sometimes their parents, and individuals' scores should not be publicly identified. All students should know the distribution of the scores and the grading scale, however, to the extent that they can understand them. They also should know the mean and the range of scores where this knowledge is useful.

A general review of the assignment or test with the class is a helpful learning process for both students and teacher. Students' comments often indicate parts of the material that they do not understand, or items that are ambiguous or contain cues and could be improved.

TEST EVALUATION

Tests generally are given in a specified time frame and setting which allows little interaction between the teacher and the students. To evaluate a test, therefore, it is necessary to evaluate each item. This analysis provides information on which items should be used again, which ones need to be changed, and which should be discarded. It also helps identify weak areas in instruction.

Item analysis for norm-referenced tests is discussed briefly here. More information, including procedures for using item analysis for criterion-referenced tests, can be found in the suggested readings section at the end of the chapter.

ITEM ANALYSIS FOR
NORM-REFERENCED TESTS

The easiest way to begin an item analysis of a test is to select the test papers of the high-achieving students, those who scored in about the top one third of the class, and those of the low-achieving students, those who scored in about the bottom one third. These two groups of papers are used to calculate two measures for each item: the ease index and the discrimination index.

The Ease Index

The ease index for an item indicates how easy it was for the students who took the test. It is equal to the proportion of high and low achievers who answered the item correctly. The formula is:

$$\text{Ease index} = \frac{\text{No. in the high and low groups who answered item correctly}}{\text{No. in the high and low groups who tried to answer item}}$$

The ease index is used as an estimate of the proportion of students in the class who answered the item correctly.

The range of the ease index is from 0.00 (very difficult; no one in the two groups answered it correctly) to +1.00 (very easy; everyone in both groups answered it correctly). What constitutes a good value for the ease index varies with the type of item. As we have noted, in the various types there are differential effects of guessing. Good ease indexes for each type fall around the middle of the "not correct from guessing" range. Generally, for true-false and multiple-choice items, the ease index should be between 0.50 and 0.80. For completion, short-answer, problem, and essay items, it should be between 0.25 and 0.75. When questions are within these ranges, the reliability of the test is increased.

The Discrimination Index

A discrimination index indicates how well each item in a test discriminates between the high and low achievers on the test. A norm-referenced test is used to define the high and low achievers, and the discrimination index for each item indicates how well it contributes to this function. This index is equal to the proportion of high achievers who answered an item correctly, minus the proportion of low achievers who did so. The formula is:

$$\text{Discrimination index} = \frac{\text{No. in high group correct}}{\text{No. in high group who tried}} - \frac{\text{No. in low group correct}}{\text{No. in low group who tried}}$$

The range of discrimination indexes is from $+1.00$ (perfect discrimination) through 0.00 (no discrimination) to -1.00 (opposite discrimination). For maximum test reliability, all norm-referenced items should have discrimination indexes over $+0.20$. Items with indexes over $+0.40$ are excellent discriminators, while items under $+0.20$ should be rewritten or discarded.

To evaluate distractors, which are wrong answers in selection items, a discrimination index should be formed for each one. Comparatively more of the students in the low group select these answers, so good distractors ought to have negative discrimination indexes. Distractors that have either zero or positive discrimination indexes should be rewritten or replaced.

Using the Ease and Discrimination Indexes

The ease and discrimination indexes for an item are related. Items that are too easy cannot discriminate well because almost everyone, both high and low achievers, can answer them correctly. Items that are too difficult also cannot discriminate well because almost everyone gets them wrong. The teacher can alter the discrimination indexes of items by making those that are too difficult, as determined by the ease index, easier or making those that are too easy harder. In selection items, another way to improve the discrimination indexes is by replacing poor distractors. Both of these techniques also increase test reliability, and so they increase test validity.

The ease and discrimination indexes should be added to the information on the teacher's test item file cards, as described in the section on constructing teacher-made tests. Then, when it is necessary to write a test again over the same material, the item analysis information is readily available.

TEST AND ASSIGNMENT ACCURACY

The accuracy of a teacher-made test or assignment is related to its reliability and validity. These measurement concepts were defined in Chapter 15.

Test Reliability

Reliable teacher-made tests and assignments provide consistent measurements. Internal consistency, the most important form of reliability for teacher-made instruments, is an indication of how well they hang together or how similar the items are in measuring common objectives. Most students who do well on the test as a whole should do well on each item in it, and most students who do poorly on the test should do poorly on each item.

Although most teachers do not calculate the internal consistency of the tests they construct, the discrimination and ease indexes for the items are an indication of how consistent the test is. For internal consistency, the ease indexes should fall within the proper ranges for the various item types, and most items should have discrimination indexes of about +0.20. In addition, the test should contain at least 20 points to ensure its internal consistency.

The internal consistencies of teacher-made tests vary greatly, from very low to very high, with an average of about 0.60. This has been identified as the lowest acceptable reliability for a teacher-made test (Diederich, 1973). It is not very high, but if teachers use many different tests and assignments in grading, the resultant grades can be good indications of each student's achievement (see Chapter 18). If item analysis indicates that a test has low internal consistency, however, the teacher should consider omitting it from grading decisions.

Content Validity

A teacher-made test or assignment that has content validity measures the content and learning behavior levels that were taught in the unit. Teachers do not usually calculate the content validity of their tests, but the use of a thoughtfully constructed table of specifications in writing a test (as described in the first section of this chapter) helps ensure its content validity.

Teacher-made tests and assignments must be reliable to be valid (see Box B in Chapter 15). They cannot measure the material they are supposed to unless they measure it consistently. An assignment or test can be reliable without being valid for the purpose for which it is used, however. A test of addition may give the same scores time after time, and so be reliable, but those scores will not tell the teacher what the students know about vowels.

CHAPTER 16 IN RETROSPECT

The fundamentals of writing, scoring, interpreting, and evaluating teacher-made tests and assignments may initially seem complex, but the process is quite logical—and it works. Repeated use in the classroom of the appropriate procedures can make them almost automatic, and the resulting instruments will be accurate and fair. As preparation for writing tests and assignments teachers should develop a table of specifications to ensure coverage of the desired content and learning behavior levels and provide content validity. They may need to design instruments to measure processes and products or paper-and-pencil tests which require students to select or write responses to questions. For complete, accurate results, at most educational levels both types of measurement should be used.

Four different types of items can be used in paper-and-pencil tests. Selection items include matching, multiple-choice, and true-false questions. In matching questions, students match each item in one list with an item from another list. In multiple-choice items, they select their responses from a set of options, and in true-false items, they mark each answer true or false. In short-answer and completion items, students write an answer that consists of one or a few words. For essay items students construct an answer that may be brief or extensive, and for problem items they develop and present a solution. Each of these item types has advantages and disadvantages; a teacher should use the most valid and reliable type possible for the testing of selected content areas and learning behavior levels.

When teachers are concerned with comparing each student with other students, norm-referenced teaching and measurement are used; when they want to compare each student to a given standard, criterion-referenced teaching and measurement are appropriate.

To evaluate results of teacher-made tests and assignments, the results should be displayed in a frequency distribution. The mean, which shows where the middle of the test scores falls, and the range, which shows how variable the test scores are, should be calculated. Students' scores can indicate how many items they answered correctly, their percent-correct scores, or their percentile scores. The percent-correct score is a criterion-referenced measure which compares a student's score to the maximum possible score on the test, while the percentile score is a norm-referenced measure which compares the student's performance to that of the rest of the students taking the test.

To evaluate the worth of each test item, item-analysis techniques are used. The ease and discrimination indexes identify good or poor items and point out trouble areas in the instructional process. They help determine test reliability and content validity and thus contribute to the accuracy of teacher-made tests and assignments.

1. List the four major types of test questions from most to least reliable and justify your order. Then list them from most to least valid and justify your order.
2. Discuss the factors, in addition to differences in learning, that affect students' test scores. Include factors related to the students themselves, the type of test items used, the quality of the test, and scoring.
3. The following test scores were made on a 25-item test you administered to your class:

   11, 10, 14, 15, 16, 15, 14, 4, 5, 25, 9, 24, 19, 21, 20, 15, 10, 11, 21, 20, 17, 18, 19, 15, 12, 20, 11, 14, 16, 19

   a. Create a frequency distribution for this set of scores.
   b. Calculate the mean and the range.
   c. Plot the distribution.
   d. Find the percent-correct and the percentile scores for each raw score. JoAnne's raw score is 12. Explain the meaning of this student's percent-correct and percentile scores to her parents.
   e. Is this test easy, hard, or of moderate difficulty? How do you know?
4. Analyze each of the following test items from the television-watching unit described in the chapter. For each item, include the ease index, a discrimination index for each response, an evaluation of each item, and ways to improve the item, if the item needs improvement.

	No. of high achievers who gave this response (out of 8)	No. of low achievers who gave this response (out of 8)
A. Multiple-choice		
According to Bandura's theory and studies of aggression,		
(1) A child has to be rewarded in order to learn a specific aggressive response.	0	1
(2) A child has to be frustrated in order to be aggressive, because aggression is the natural outcome of frustration.	0	3
(3) A child will act aggressively just as a consequence of observational learning.	2	0

	No. of high achievers who gave this response (out of 8)	No. of low achievers who gave this response (out of 8)
*(4) A child can learn an aggressive action through observational learning, but reinforcement influences whether or not the action is performed.	6	1
(5) A combination of frustration and the observation of a model's aggression is necessary before a child will imitate that model's actions.	0	1
No. in each group who tried the item	8	6

B. True-False

Some TV shows for children are value free.

True	0	0
*False	8	8
No. in each group who tried the item	8	8

C. Part of an essay item

Discuss three "lessons" that young children might learn from watching this show. Desired responses:

(1) People who break the law initially get what they want.	0	0
(2) People who break the law eventually go to jail.	6	6
(3) Police help people who are in trouble.	4	6
No. in each group who tried the item	7	7

* = Correct response.

5. Can tests and other forms of evaluation in the classroom serve as part of the learning process, as well as for evaluation purposes? Discuss.

6. Suppose you see the following scene. A high school student holding a test paper comes up to the teacher and starts shouting, "I studied for this test over 20 hours, and I still got a C. It just isn't fair. The test didn't ask me anything I learned." Could this student's point be valid? Why or why not?

7. What is wrong in each of the following test items? There may be more than one problem in each item.

   (1) As a general rule, children should not be allowed to watch much television. True or false?

   (2) Bandura's first name is
   1. James   2. Alfred   3. Albert   4. Thomas   5. Ray

   (3) Television was invented in _____.

   (4) After watching a violent television show, a child who is not reinforced won't behave aggressively. True or false?

   (5) According to Bloom's taxonomy, a question that asks students to use information in a specific situation is an example of an _____ question.

   1. knowledge   2. comprehension   3. application
   4. analysis   5. synthesis

   (6) Children learn aggressive actions from watching TV and perform these actions principally when they are frustrated. True or false?

READINGS FOR REFLECTION

Introductory Level

Diederich, Paul B. *Short-Cut Statistics for Teacher-Made Tests.* Princeton, N.J.: Educational Testing Service, 1964.

This short booklet was written by an ex-Latin teacher who did not want to spend the time necessary to measure his test results with the "real" formulas developed by statistics and measurement experts. He developed short-cuts for doing item analysis and finding standard deviations, standard errors, reliabilities, and correlations. The user needs only to be able to count and do arithmetic (his 8th-grade child could do all the math).

Hopkins, Charles D., and Antes, Richard L. *Classroom Testing: Construction.* Itasca, Ill.: F. E. Peacock Publishers, 1979.

Gronlund, Norman E. *Constructing Achievement Tests.* Englewood Cliffs, N.J.: Prentice-Hall, 1977.

These two paperbacks, written for pre- and in-service teachers, cover in detail how to write paper-and-pencil tests, how to write the various kinds of items, how to construct and use performance tests, reliability and validity issues, and score interpretations.

Advanced Level

Hopkins, Charles D., and Antes, Richard L. *Classroom Measurement and Evaluation.* Itasca, Ill.: F. E. Peacock Publishers, 1978.

Mehrens, William A., and Lehmann, Irvin J. *Measurement and Evaluation in Education and Psychology.* 2nd ed. New York: Holt, Rinehart & Winston, 1978.

These two textbooks written for courses in tests and measurement are especially useful and readable. Both include in-depth treatment of writing tests, types of test items (including performance tests), reliability, validity, and norm- and criterion-referenced measurement. Both also have glossaries of technical terms. Hopkins and Antes's book has a chapter on writing classroom objectives.

REFERENCES

Bloom, B. S., Engelhart, M. B., Furst, E. J., Hill, W. H., and Krathwohl, D. R. *Taxonomy of Educational Objectives: The Classification of Educational Goals. Handbook I: Cognitive Domain.* New York: Longmans Green, 1956.

Diederich, Paul. *Short-Cut Statistics for Teacher-Made Tests.* Princeton, N.J.: Educational Testing Service, 1973.

Hill, Kennedy T. Motivation, evaluation, and educational testing policy. In Leslie J. Fyans (Ed.), *Achievement Motivation.* New York: Plenum Press, 1980.

Use of Standardized Tests in the School

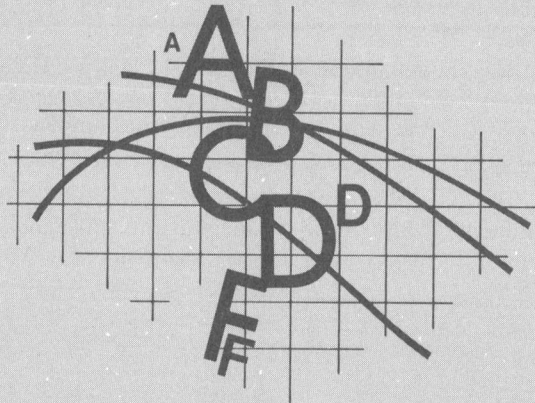

It has been estimated that over one million standardized tests are given in U.S. schools each school day. Moreover, people are faced with standardized tests throughout their lives, not only in schools but in careers, in the military, and so on. The results are used in a variety of ways: Students use them to make personal decisions, such as whether or not to apply for admission to a certain university; educational institutions use them to make decisions about program effectiveness, such as whether or not a new reading program works better in helping students learn to read than the traditional program. If standardized tests are used correctly, the test results are valid for these and similar purposes.

Nevertheless, standardized tests of all kinds are under fire from various segments of society. There has been legislation regarding standardized tests, such as the Family Education Rights and Privacy Act passed by Congress in 1974. This gives adult students and parents of students who are not yet adults access to student records from any school or agency that receives federal funds. Included are standardized test results and any interpretation of the scores placed in a student's file. The use of intelligence tests and other standardized evaluation instruments has been legally tested, particularly in regard to their influence on equal opportunities in education and employment.

THE NATURE OF STANDARDIZED TESTS

The standardized test results teachers use most often come from two basic types of tests: achievement and intelligence. In this country standardized tests generally are produced by commercial test publishers and are written by groups of experts. Most tests used in schools are designed to measure intellectual potential or skills and subject matter that have been identified as representative of the content areas and learning behavior levels treated by the instructional process in most areas of the country. Most standardized tests are norm referenced, and administration and scoring procedures are standardized and objective.

The principles of administering and scoring standardized intelligence tests will be described in this chapter in relation to the Wechsler Intelligence Scale for Children—Revised (WISC-R), and, to a lesser extent, the Stanford-Binet Intelligence Scale, both of which were discussed in Chapter 6. The Iowa Tests of Basic Skills (ITBS), an elementary school achievement test battery, is used as an example of an achievement test. According to the *Teacher's Guide* (1979), this test battery was designed and written by professionals in the college of education at the University of Iowa, with the help of consultants from various educational levels. It

Figure 17.1

Subtests in the 1978 multilevel battery of the Iowa Tests of Basic Skills

Vocabulary*	Work-study skills
Reading comprehension*	Visual material
Language skills	Reference material
Spelling*	Mathematics skills
Capitalization	Concepts*
Punctuation	Problem solving*
Usage	Computation*

Note: Science and social studies skills subtests are available also, but these are not part of the multilevel battery.
*These six subtests make up the basic battery of the ITBS.

is produced and sold by the Riverside Publishing Company, a Houghton Mifflin subsidiary. The 1978 revision of the full multilevel battery covers grades 3 through 9 and includes 11 tests in five basic skill areas: vocabulary, reading comprehension, language, work-study, and mathematics (see Figure 17.1). The tests have two equivalent forms to improve test reliability, as will be explained later. All of the questions are multiple choice. Students are given four hours and four minutes of working time to complete a test, according to explicit directions provided for the teacher-administrator and the students. Generally, the test is norm referenced; the majority of scores are obtained by comparing each student's performance to that of a group of comparable students. The teacher also can determine criterion-referenced information as to which objectives a student has and has not met.

QUESTION-AND-ANSWER FORMATS

Standardized tests differ in how items are arranged in test booklets and on answer sheets. In some tests students fill in answers in the test booklets, while in others they use separate answer sheets. Marking in the test booklet is expensive for the school, since the booklet cannot be reused.

All standardized tests include directions to be given by the teacher and samples to be done with the teacher's guidance. Item and answer formats similar to those used in several standardized tests are shown in Box A, which also points out potential problems that the requirements for answering may cause. To make the test results as valid as possible, teachers must instruct students in how to use a test format accurately and quickly. This does not mean the actual content of the test should be taught, but lessons in how to use the format that tests knowledge of content and how to use the answer sheet can be given shortly before administering a test.

CLASSIFICATION OF STANDARDIZED TESTS

There are several ways to group standardized tests. One of the most useful and frequently used typologies is the four-category classification introduced in Chapter 15, which includes the following types of tests:

1. Aptitude—measures potential in, for example, intellectual, scholastic, mechanical, or musical skills.
2. Diagnostic—tests the performance of major skills involved in the learning of an academic content area such as reading or mathematics and so identifies specific problems in that learning.
3. Noncognitive—measures areas that are not primarily related to thinking and learning, such as personality, attitudes, and interests.
4. Achievement—measures learned skills and knowledge in academic content areas such as reading and science.

Standardized Aptitude Tests

Aptitude tests are used to measure a person's potential in a specific area. They are designed to indicate how much generally available information or which skills a student possesses, not what specific information or skills the student has learned in formal settings such as schools or private lessons. Intelligence tests, for example, are supposed to measure people's basic intellectual potential, that is, how readily they can and do learn. The College Board Scholastic Aptitude Test, commonly known as the SAT, is designed to measure a person's potential for college work. (Trends over the last 30 or so years as measured by the SAT are discussed in Chapter 18.) Aptitude tests such as these are usually administered by someone other than the classroom teacher, such as school psychologists or psychometrists, although the teacher can administer group intelligence tests with some preparation.

Standardized Diagnostic Tests

Diagnostic tests are built to identify a student's specific problems in a content area or learning behavior by testing her or his knowledge and skills in that area. Good diagnostic tests are based on an analysis of the instructional process in terms of single-component knowledge and skill areas which can be tested. The test results indicate which components the students have and have not mastered. In this sense, diagnostic tests are criterion referenced. They generally yield several scores, often be-

BOX A *Types of question-and-answer formats in standardized achievement tests*

1. Vocabulary test, grades 1½–2, horizontal answer format.

   Directions (dictated orally): Fill in the circle under the word that names the picture.

   heart ○   hurt ○   hear ○   hit ○

   Potential problems:
   1. Students must be able to follow horizontally; which many at this age level are not able to do.
   2. Students must fill in the circle under the answer; they may instead circle the answer itself.

2. Mathematics tests, grades 1½–2, combined horizontal and vertical answer format.

   Directions (dictated orally): Fill in the circle next to the answer to the problem.

   $$\begin{array}{r} 10 \\ -\ 3 \\ \hline \end{array}$$

   0 ○   7 ○
   3 ○   10 ○

   Potential problems:
   1. Students may be used to seeing answers under, not next to, the problem.
   2. Students must fill in the circle closest to the desired answer; they may instead fill in the other circle on the same horizontal line.

3. Mathematics test, grades 2½–4, vertical answer format.

   Directions: Fill in the space next to the answer you select.

   $36 - \underline{\ \ \ } = 17$

   ▯ 29
   ▯ 19
   ▯ 57
   ▯ NG
   ▯ DK

   Potential problem:
   Students must remember that "NG" stands for "not given" and "DK" stands for "don't know."

4. Reading test, grades 4–5½, answer blanks in test booklet but located on the right-hand side of the page.

   Directions: Decide which of the numbered words below each item fits best in the blank. Look at the answer space to the right. Fill in the circle that has the same number as your chosen answer.

   Enormous means _____13_____ .

   13.　　1. quite small　　　　　　　1　2　3　4
   　　　　2. very large　　　13.　⬚　⬚　⬚　⬚
   　　　　3. enough
   　　　　4. large

   Potential problem:
   The number of the item is repeated three times. The student must read the question numbered 13, find the answer from the ones labeled 13, remember the number of the option picked, and mark it next to the answer space numbered 13.

5. Language test, grades 4–9, separate answer sheet.

   Directions: Read the paragraph below. Select the option to each item that makes the sentence grammatically correct. Find the item number on your answer sheet. Fill in the space that has the same letter as the option you choose.

   Alicon and Melinda were sisters.

   They had a disagreement ⎰A. between⎱ themselves.
   　　　　　　　　　　　　　⎱B. among ⎰
   　　　　　　　　　　　　　　32

   Potential problem:
   The student must remember the option letter chosen, find the number 32 on the separate answer sheet, and mark the remembered option.

tween 6 and 25, each identifying achievement in a single important component of the learning area covered by the test (e.g., word pronunciation in a reading diagnostic test). These tests generally contain more items than most standardized ability and achievement tests because they must cover many of the essential skills needed for achievement in the area measured by the test.

Once a student's strengths and weaknesses have been identified, the teacher can develop an individualized plan to work on the weak skills and so improve the student's achievement in that area. These tests only identify the problems, however, not why they exist. Diagnostic tests should be administered only to students who are having trouble in the content area, as indicated by their class work and by their scores on standardized achievement tests; they should not be given to whole classes.

Diagnostic tests are available primarily for elementary-school students in arithmetic and reading, although some tests measure students' skills and knowledge through the high school level. Because reading often is a major cause of school problems, the greatest number of diagnostic tests are in this area. The Stanford Diagnostic Reading Test, with four levels ranging from the sixth month of first grade through the first year past high school, measures skills in vocabulary, phonetic analysis, and reading comprehension. At the upper grades it also covers skimming, scanning, and reading rate. Other diagnostic reading tests may measure these skills and knowledge or others such as visual discrimination, auditory discrimination, and motor skills. Although some diagnostic tests are paper-and-pencil tests, most are individually administered. This type of person-to-person administration yields a great deal of information about a student's problems. Diagnostic tests generally take a great deal of practice to administer correctly, and they usually are administered by a trained examiner.

Standardized Noncognitive Tests

Noncognitive tests measure areas other than those primarily involved in the cognitive processes of thinking and learning. These include personality, interests, and attitudes. The term *noncognitive* is misleading, however; the areas measured by these tests do have cognitive components.

These tests generally are given by psychologists and psychometrists. Results may be reported back to classroom teachers to help them deal more effectively with students who are tested. Information on students' interests is useful for intrinsic motivation (see Chapter 11), and attitude testing results can be applied in values education (see Chapter 9).

Standardized Achievement Tests

Achievement tests are the most common form of standardized test given in the public schools. They are designed to measure what students have learned in school and not their potential for learning, as aptitude tests do.

Single-content achievement tests measure an individual's skill and knowledge in one academic area, such as social studies or mathematics. *Achievement test batteries* are sets of tests that measure performance in several content areas. Several different batteries are commonly used in schools throughout the United States. In addition to the ITBS, other frequently used primary and early secondary batteries are the Stanford Achievement Test, Comprehensive Tests of Basic Skills, Metropolitan Achievement Tests, California Achievement Tests, Iowa Tests of Educational Development, and Tests of Academic Progress, to name a few. Each battery has a set of sequential tests for use at different grade or achievement levels. It is up to school personnel to determine which single-content test or battery best tests the results of their instructional process; that is, they must evaluate the content validity of each test for their school.

From early elementary school up through eighth or ninth grade, achievement batteries are frequently used to obtain a broad picture of each student's performance. These tests can answer questions about how a student compares to others locally or nationally; how a student is progressing from year to year; what a student's academic strengths and weaknesses are; where a student belongs in relation to grade placement; and how one class, school, or district compares with another and with national norms.

If the results from the battery indicate that more thorough information is needed on a few students in specific content areas, these students may then be given selected single-subject achievement tests. These tests are longer and take more time to administer, since they sample an area more thoroughly than the corresponding subtest of an achievement battery. If battery results indicate poor achievement for a student in a basic content area, the teacher may request that the student take a diagnostic test in that area.

In secondary school, single-subject tests are used as frequently as batteries are. The objectives in many high schools and the programs of the students vary too much to make the results of general achievement very useful.

Comparison of Standardized Aptitude and Achievement Tests

Many standardized aptitude tests ask some of the same kinds of questions that standardized achievement tests do. Both types of tests measure acquired behavior, but aptitude tests have more general coverage, while the content of achievement tests more closely matches the material covered directly in school. Achievement tests measure learning of school material that is quite recent, while aptitude tests measure general learning and development that occurs throughout life, both in and out of school. Aptitude tests are designed for use in predicting future behavior, such as how well a student can be expected to do in school, while achievement tests are used to relate to the present, that is, what knowledge and skills the student has now. Basically, then, the two types of tests differ in regard to the author's intent in designing them and how closely the tests match formal school learning (Mehrens & Lehmann, 1978).

As we noted at the beginning of this section, intelligence and achievement tests are the principal types of standardized tests used in schools. Together they can measure the entire range of a student's aptitude and achievement in all the cognitive tasks, skills, and processes. Noncognitive skills tests, which are used much less often, are the only major tests not encompassed in these two types. Intelligence tests are a type of aptitude test, and achievement tests may also be used as diagnostic tests. The format and use of standardized intelligence and achievement tests are described in the following sections.

STANDARDIZED INTELLIGENCE TESTS: FORMAT AND USE

Standardized psychometric intelligence tests are by far the most frequently administered tests of intellectual aptitude or ability. These tests, as described in Chapter 6, are constructed by experts in the field to sample learning and behaviors that are generally agreed upon as representing the construct of intelligence. The tests give every student the same opportunities to respond to an appropriate subset of questions and tasks in the same time limit under similar conditions, and the answers are scored objectively. Much of the content of IQ tests comes from the mainstream middle- or upper-class culture of the United States, however, as we noted in Chapter 6. Efforts to ensure the "culture fairness" of standardized IQ tests are described at the end of this section.

Generally, the relationship between learners' scores on intelligence tests and their scores on general achievement tests is quite high, especially when the achievement tests cover content areas that require verbal knowledge and skills (Siegler & Richards, in press). On the average, both sets of scores tend to place a student at about the same cognitive level. In fact, after age five, an IQ score is the best predictor available of future educational progress and attainment (Jensen, 1980). Even so, there is a great deal of variability in achievement that cannot be predicted from IQ scores.

The types of items and skills included in psychometric intelligence tests have changed very little since the first editions of the Stanford-Binet and the Wechsler tests (see Chapter 6). This is due to the way new intelligence tests are validated and existing ones are revised. In the Stanford-Binet, for example, new items are included in a revision if performance on them is related to performance on the existing version of the test, and if the item difficulty decreases as student age increases. This means that only intellectual skills that vary with age and that already are represented on the test are included in the Stanford-Binet revisions. New items are included in revisions of the Wechsler tests if performance on them is related to performance on other measures of intelligence, such as the Stanford-Binet.

The Stanford-Binet and Wechsler tests also serve as the criteria against which new intelligence tests are validated. Thus, new intelligence tests must contain items that measure skills present in the Stanford-Binet and Wechsler tests. Even though many people feel that creativity, for example, is an important part of intelligence, creativity items are not included in most intelligence tests primarily because they were not included in the original versions of the Stanford-Binet and Wechsler tests (Siegler & Richards, in press).

Most current intelligence tests are norm referenced; that is, each person's intelligence is determined by comparing her or his score with those of a preselected, rather large group of people called the *norm group.* The norm group for the WISC-R consisted of 2,200 children, with 100 girls and 100 boys at each of 11 age groups. In addition to the age and sex criteria, the children were selected by race (in the same proportions as found in the 1970 national census), geographic region of the country, occupation of the head of household, and urban-rural residence (Wechsler, 1974). Other intelligence test norm groups have been chosen according to similar characteristics.

To find a student's score on an intelligence test, the number of points the student answered correctly on the test is first summed to yield a raw score. Each standardized intelligence test provides a table of the scores attained by members of the norm group, grouped by age. This is called the *norm table* or *conversion table.* The student's score is compared to the table, and the score associated with the student's age is read from it.

If the IQ scores for the norm group are graphed, they closely follow a normal distribution (as in the IQ score distributions in Figure 6.4 in Chapter 6). Figure 17.2 is a graph of the theoretical distribution for the WISC-R scores. The mean IQ score on this and the other Wechsler tests identified in Chapter 6, as well as the mean score on the Stanford-Binet, is 100. Therefore a person with a raw score of 100 on a standardized IQ test is exactly average in measured intelligence.

Figure 17.2

Theoretical distribution of IQ scores for WISC-R

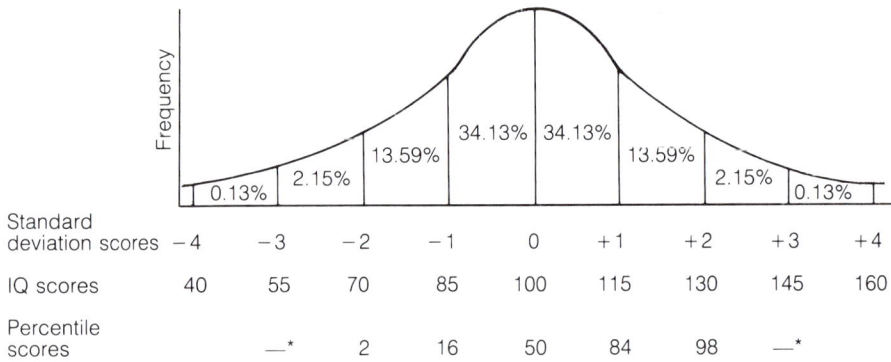

Standard deviation scores	−4	−3	−2	−1	0	+1	+2	+3	+4
IQ scores	40	55	70	85	100	115	130	145	160
Percentile scores		—*	2	16	50	84	98	—*	

*There are no 0 or 100 percentile scores.

Source: Data from David Wechsler, *Manual for the Wechsler Intelligence Scale for Children—Revised* (New York: Psychological Corporation, 1974).

RANGE AND STANDARD DEVIATION IN IQ TEST SCORES

As with teacher-made tests (see Chapter 16), the *range* of IQ scores on an intelligence test indicates how much they can vary. The lowest score is about 40 and the highest is about 160 on all Wechsler tests. Occasionally a person scores higher or lower, but not very often—much less than 1 time in 1,000.

But the range is a very rough measure of variability. A more precise and helpful measure is the *standard deviation,* which was described in Chapter 16 as the average distance that the test scores vary from the mean. The range given is from 4 standard deviations above the mean (+4) to 4 standard deviations below (−4). The standard deviation of the WISC-R is 15 IQ points. So the lowest score shown in Figure 17.2 is 40 [100 − (4 × 15)], while the highest is 160 [100 + (4 × 15)].

As scores, IQs are particularly useful because they are *standard scores;* that is, the scores in the frequency distribution for the norm group are transformed by subtracting the mean for each outcome and dividing by the standard deviation.* Any standard score can be converted into a percentile score, as described in Chapter 16. In IQ tests, *percentile scores*

*The formula for deriving standard scores (symbolized z scores) is given in Chapter 18.

indicate the percentage of people with IQ scores lower than the corresponding standard score. They are easily found with a table which lists the converted scores, but a general knowledge about their relationship to the standard score helps in understanding IQ measurements.

On the WISC-R normal IQ curve shown in Figure 17.2, 68 percent of the people have IQ scores between 115, which is +1 standard deviation (100 + 15), and 85, which is −1 standard deviation. And 95 percent have scores between 130, which is +2 standard deviations [100 + (2 × 15)], and 70, which is −2 standard deviations [100 − (2 × 15)]. Scores between 145 and 55 are made by 99.7 percent of the people, and virtually everyone has scores between 160 and 40, the lowest and highest scores.

Qualitative classifications, such as those for the WICS-R given in Table 17.1, often are attached to these scores. (Although the lowest category in Table 17.1 has a derogatory label, this classification is used frequently.) The Stanford-Binet classifications are quite similar. Thus a student whose IQ score on the WISC-R is 125 would be classified as superior in intelligence in relation to his or her peers.

VALIDITY FOR IQ TESTS

Two of the three types of validity described in Chapter 15 have primary importance for intelligence tests: criterion-related and construct validity. Suppose IQ scores are used to select children for participation in an educational program for the gifted. The IQ test used has *criterion-related validity* for selection purposes if the children's IQ scores are strongly

---

Table 17.1

Wechsler's qualitative classification of IQ scores

IQ Range	Classification	Percentage of Norm-Group Children in Category*
130 and higher	Very superior	2.3%
120–129	Superior	7.4
110–119	High average (Bright)	16.5
90–109	Average	49.4
80– 89	Low average (Dull)	16.2
70– 79	Borderline	6.0
69 and lower	Mentally defective	2.2

*These percentages are quite close to the theoretical percentages associated with a perfect normal curve.
Source: Data from David Wechsler, *Manual for the Wechsler Intelligence Scale for Children—Revised* (New York: Psychological Corporation, 1974).

related to their scores on some measure of success in the program. The idea of criterion-related validity may be clear, but it is often hard to determine because agreement on an acceptable criterion measure can be difficult to reach. Intelligence tests can have criterion-related validity for some purposes and not for others.

Construct validity is concerned with the construct of intelligence as defined by accepted theories (such as those discussed in Chapter 6) and by scores on accepted intelligence tests. Theories of intelligence suggest, for example, that intelligence should be related to age, at least through adolescence (i.e., older children are more intelligent than younger ones in an absolute sense), and to school achievement (i.e., more intelligent children have higher potential for learning and so should have higher achievement). Items for the Stanford-Binet test accordingly were selected so that, with increasing age, higher proportions of the norm sample could answer the items correctly. Therefore older children answer more items correctly on the Stanford-Binet than younger children do, which bears out the age-intelligence relationship. The Stanford-Binet score also shows moderate to high relationships of intelligence with achievement in school and on standardized achievement tests, which supports the learning potential–achievement relationship suggested in the accepted theories of intelligence.

When the Stanford-Binet test was initially developed, there was no accepted measure of the construct of intelligence. By the time the Wechsler tests were developed, however, the Stanford-Binet was the accepted measure of intelligence. Scores on the Wechsler tests therefore were related to scores on the Stanford-Binet; the relationship is high. Also, as in the Stanford-Binet, scores on the Wechsler tests match the age-intelligence and the learning potential–achievement relationships in the theories of intelligence. The Wechsler tests are considered to have construct validity because their scores are strongly related to scores on the Stanford-Binet, an accepted measure of the intelligence construct, and they match patterns suggested in the major theories of intelligence. Currently, the Stanford-Binet and the Wechsler tests serve as the criteria against which the construct validity of new intelligence tests is determined.

Content validity is not a concern with IQ tests, since intelligence is not a content area. It is relevant to the goal of achieving culture-fair IQ tests, however.

RELIABILITY FOR IQ TESTS

The three aspects of test reliability identified in Chapter 15 apply to different aspects of the consistency of measurement provided by an IQ test. *Stability,* or test-retest reliability, indicates how much IQ scores change when two testings are separated in time. Theoretically IQ is a fairly

Culture fair intelligence tests would use language and experiences which are common to children in both the mainstream and minority cultures. Such tests are constructed to improve their validity for all students who may take them.

stable trait, at least for those older than five or six, and so IQ scores should remain about the same from one testing to another, provided the tests are not spaced too far apart. IQ scores from the well-accepted intelligence tests are quite stable.

For IQ tests to have *internal consistency*, each item should contribute positively to the total IQ score. *Equivalence* between forms is not a concern with individually administered intelligence tests, which generally have only one form. It is relevant, however, in group-administered intelligence tests, which often have more than one form.

STANDARD ERROR FOR IQ SCORES

Each IQ score contains some error due to temporary differences in the people taking the test, in those scoring it, and in the environment in which it is taken. The standard error of a score is a measure of that error, as we noted in Chapter 15.

The standard errors on the WISC-R vary according to the subtest and the age level of the children taking it. For the global IQ score, they range from 2.90 to 3.41 IQ points, with a mean of 3.19. Using the standard error, chances are that 68 percent of the time a person with a measured IQ of 115 has a true IQ score between 118.19, which is 1 standard error above the measured score (115 + 3.19), and 111.81, 1 standard error below the score (115 − 3.19). With repeated testings, 95 percent of the time the score will be between 121.38, 2 standard errors above the measured score, and 108.62, 2 standard errors below it; or it is 95 percent certain that the true score is between 109 and 121. The 99 percent confidence level (3 standard errors) is between 124.57 and 105.43. Teachers generally are satisfied with being 68 percent certain, which means looking at a band of scores ranging from 1 standard error above the score to 1 standard error below it.

GROUP-ADMINISTERED IQ TESTS

Group-administered intelligence tests are more efficient to use than individual tests because they can be administered to a number of people at the same time and therefore they require less time and money. They can be given by a classroom teacher with some preparation, but they do not provide as much information as individual intelligence tests do. A tester can gain a great deal of diagnostic information from watching and listening as a student takes an individual test. Group administered tests depend heavily on reading achievement, and their scores are influenced by test-taking skills. They should not be used with children under the age of six or with people who lack reading skills. If IQ scores are to be used in important classroom decisions, such as placement in special classes or courses of study, individually administered intelligence tests should be used.

CULTURE-FAIR IQ TESTS

The intelligence tests most frequently used in this country have been charged with being biased in favor of students from the middle- and upper-class mainstream culture, as we noted earlier. If children from the majority culture have more chances of being exposed in their daily living to the content and processes used in intelligence tests than those from minority cultures do, the validity of the tests is open to question. Some intelligence test authors, such as Wechsler (1974), have changed their tests in response to this criticism, but achieving culture-fair instruments is a long, slow process. Other researchers and theorists, such as Jensen (1980), deny that the tests are biased, at least for blacks.

The Davis-Eels Test of General Intelligence or Problem-Solving Ability and the Cattell Culture-Fair Intelligence Test are examples of attempts to use either test content that is readily available to everyone in all cultures or nonsense material with which no one is familiar, regardless of cultural background. Tests developed from Piaget's theory are often considered culture fair, or at least culture reduced, because they aim at discovering how people think, not what they think. The outcome, however, generally has been that these tests do not eliminate, or even reduce, differences in IQ scores among races or social classes (Eysenck & Fulker, 1979; Jensen, 1980; Mehrens & Lehmann, 1978). Moreover, they do not predict school success as well as the traditional intelligence tests do. This should be expected, since many school systems are designed for majority-culture children, just as the traditional intelligence tests are. In fact, for minority children, traditional intelligence tests may be fairer than *achievement* tests because intelligence tests do not depend as heavily on the specific content taught in a school (Scarr, 1979).

Even a quick perusal of traditional intelligence tests shows that some of the language and examples would be more accessible to students from the mainstream culture. The language includes such terms as child labor laws, marriage license, and summer camp.

STANDARDIZED ACHIEVEMENT TESTS: FORMAT AND USE

The process used in the construction of norm-referenced standardized achievement or diagnostic tests is similar to that used by classroom teachers in writing their own tests. The goal is the same: to develop an achievement test with maximum appropriate content and skills coverage that is

BOX B   *Steps in the construction of standardized achievement tests*

1. The test publishing company decides on general test characteristics, including purposes, content areas, grade levels, item format, and length.
2. Testing and curriculum experts analyze relevant sources of information in the content areas and develop a table of specifications.
3. Test item specialists write items from this table.
4. Items are reviewed and edited.
5. Items are assembled into a test and field-tested.
6. Results are item analyzed; items are revised or discarded as needed, and the accepted items are assembled into the final test.
7. The battery is administered to the norm group. Norm tables are developed, and initial studies of reliability and validity are started.
8. The test manual is written.
9. The test is published and made available for use.

highly reliable and valid and that can be administered to students in a short time. For standardized achievement tests, however, the process is much more precise. It is done on a very large scale involving many people, costs many thousands of dollars, and usually takes three to five years to complete.

All norm-referenced standardized achievement tests are constructed according to the same general process, with some minor variations from test to test. A summary of this process is given in Box B. First, the test publishing company determines the general characteristics of the test: its purposes and content areas, the grade levels to be covered, types of items to be included, and approximate length. This aspect of test development for the 1978 revision of the ITBS was easy because the company adopted the purposes and formats used in the previous version of the battery. The general purpose of this test is to "provide for comprehensive and continuous measurement of growth in the fundamental skills: vocabulary, reading, the mechanics of writing, methods of study, and mathematics" (*Teacher's Guide*, 1979, p. 3).

Experts in testing and curriculum development, including classroom teachers, then analyze texts, instructional programs, and other sources of information in the content areas to be included in the test. They develop a table of specifications for the test based on a series of objectives and skill levels that include those most frequently found in these sources. In developing and writing the ITBS, educators from a college of education and other consultants examined texts, guides to curriculum, and relevant research and other literature to locate content and skills. This resulted in 208 skills objectives, which were grouped into 61 major categories. The mathematics concepts subtest has six major categories of objectives, for example. One of the seven skills objectives under the objective category of "Whole Numbers" is "Fundamental Operations: Number Facts." Similarly, the capitalization subtest has seven major categories, and one of the six skills objectives under the "Place Names" category is "Names of Countries and Continents."

Using this table, specialists write the test items, generally in multiple-choice form. They usually write about twice as many items as will eventually be included in the finished battery, to allow for the elimination of some items after initial testing. The ITBS staff actually wrote four times as many questions as the 1,141 items that were utilized in the final version of the six levels of the test. In its final form on the ITBS, the reading comprehension subtest covers three major categories of objectives, with 16 skill objectives. For level 11, Form 8, which is one of the two equivalent forms of the test, there are six questions that measure the skills objective concerning the student's application ability: "to apply information through generalization or prediction" (*Teacher's Guide*, 1979). An example of a question which was designed to measure this objective following a three-paragraph story about sailors and scurvy is:

> What can a person do to keep from getting scurvy?
> 1. Drink plenty of milk.
> 2. Get plenty of exercise.
> 3. Not go on long sea voyages.
> 4. Eat plenty of fresh fruits and vegetables.
>
> (Iowa Tests of Basic Skills, 1978, p. 15)

The test items then are reviewed and edited. The ITBS *Preliminary Technical Summary* (1979) reported that the review was completed by staff members as well as consultants of both sexes from five ethnic groups. These people reviewed for clarity and accuracy as well as for possible sexual and ethnic biases. Changes in the items were made accordingly.

After the items are put into a testing format, they are field-tested through administration to a pilot group of students at the appropriate grade levels. This testing generally involves several hundred students at each grade or age level in several schools located in different areas. The ITBS was field-tested with over 300,000 students, and at least 200 students responded to each question. The results from the field-testing are item analyzed, using guidelines similar to the ease and discrimination indexes for teacher-made tests which were presented in Chapter 16. Items that fall outside the acceptable ranges for these indexes are either discarded or rewritten, and the final version of the test is assembled.

The resulting test is given to large groups of students across the nation, selected to provide a variety of geographical locations, sex, ethnicity, and social class. These groups of students serve as the norm groups for the test. Norm tables developed from this testing give the norm group's average scores for use in interpreting test results with other students who take the test. Several different norm tables may be developed to reflect different geographical locations or characteristics of the students. At about the same time, reliability and validity studies using the test are started. The final version of the ITBS was administered in the fall to about 18,000 students at each grade level, chosen by region, size of school district, family income, and education, to obtain fall norms. In the spring, a subsample of this group retook the test to obtain spring norms. Different tables are available for the total norm group, for each of the five geographical regions in the country, for private schools, and for large city schools.

After the norms are established the test manual is written. It includes the test purposes, a description of the test construction, norm tables, instructions for administration, statistical considerations of reliability and validity, and potential uses. The ITBS manual not only gives all this information, it also has suggestions for how teachers can develop students' skills in the various objectives measured by the test. It describes what the test scores mean and how to use the test results in both norm-referenced and criterion-referenced ways. The manual also explains how the test battery can be used in a more individual testing program, either in nongraded situations or where some students in a classroom are much different in achievement than other students.

Criterion-referenced standardized achievement tests are developed using a similar process. In this case, however, the table of specifications is geared to mastery of objectives and skills. The items are analyzed using criterion-referenced methods, usually related to the percentage of students who pass each item.

SELECTING A NORM-REFERENCED STANDARDIZED ACHIEVEMENT TEST

The selection of a standardized achievement test for use in a school is of interest to numerous groups and individuals—administrators, parents, representatives of the public, and classroom teachers. All should be represented in the selection process, in which questions such as those given in Box C are considered.

BOX C *Questions to be considered in*
selecting a standardized achievement test

---

1. Is the test really needed to provide a basis for educational decision making or evaluation?
2. Statistical considerations
   a. Is the test reliable?
   b. Is the test valid?
3. Practical considerations
   a. Is the test easy to administer?
   b. Are there two or more equivalent forms at each testing level?
   c. Is it fast and easy to score?
   d. Are the scores readily interpretable?
   e. Are tables from appropriate norm groups available?
   f. How expensive is the test?
   g. Are the test booklets reusable?

The most important preliminary in selecting a test is deciding whether it should be given. If the test results will not assist in decision making or evaluation, the test should not be used. One reason for using these tests is to provide students, parents, teachers, school administrators, boards of education, state legislators, and taxpayers with information about the achievement of individuals, classes, schools, and school districts. From the ITBS results for a fifth-grade class, for example, the teacher can tell how well any student is achieving in reading comprehension as compared to the other fifth-grade students in the state. The results also can be used to assist in evaluation of the effectiveness of various institutional procedures and instructional programs; those financed in part by the state or the U.S. Department of Education may require this.

Once the decision is reached that a standardized achievement test is needed, the most important considerations are the reliability and validity of the test to be used.

STANDARDIZED ACHIEVEMENT TEST VALIDITY

As with teacher-made tests and assignments, the most important type of validity for standardized achievement and diagnostic tests is *content validity:* Does the test adequately sample the content and skills it is testing?

Because of the way these types of standardized tests are constructed, the majority of them do have content validity for an academic area as seen from a national perspective. But for each group that uses a test, its content validity for that group's purposes must be established. The test must be examined to determine if the content and learning behaviors covered match those taught in each classroom being tested. If the match is high, 75–80 percent or better, the test has content validity for those classrooms.

In the spelling subtest of the ITBS, for example, students must recognize whether or not a word is misspelled. This is much different than actually spelling words correctly, which is the learning process used in many classrooms. Students in these classrooms may achieve differently on the ITBS spelling subtest than they do on classroom spelling tests and assignments. For these students, the behavior level tested by this subtest does not match that taught in their classrooms, and the content validity of the ITBS spelling subtest is therefore lower.

There is evidence that the ITBS also has *construct validity* because it accurately measures achievement in the basic skills, which is a general psychological and educational construct. The four major content area scores on the ITBS (reading comprehension, language skills, work-study skills, and mathematics skills), plus the composite score, are quite strongly related, and the ITBS scores for a sample of eighth- and ninth-graders from the norm group related well to their scores on another standardized achievement test, the Tests of Achievement and Proficiency. The ITBS achievement scores are also fairly stable across time, with a pattern of stability for up to three years, and quite strongly related to high school grades (*Preliminary Technical Summary*, 1979). Thus, like all of the major standardized achievement tests on the market in the United States, the ITBS has high construct validity.

Criterion-related validity is only important for tests used to select people for special opportunities, often related to education, social treatment, or jobs. This type of validity is concerned with how closely the test scores match other measures of success in these opportunities. Since the ITBS, like most standardized achievement tests, is not used for selection purposes, the manual does not give information on the test's criterion-related validity. Standardized *aptitude* tests, however, often are used for selection purposes. The College Board Scholastic Aptitude Test (SAT), for example, is one of the major bases for college admission. It has criterion-related validity if students' SAT scores are strongly related to their subsequent college performance, as measured by grade-point averages, graduation, or any other accepted measure of college success. Scholastic aptitude test results in general are moderately related to success in college.

Table 17.2

*Reliabilities and grade-equivalent score characteristics
for the fifth-grade ITBS*

	Vocabulary	**Reading**	**Language Total**	**Work-Study Total**	**Mathematics Total**	**Composite**
Reliability (external consistency)	0.93	0.92	0.96	0.93	0.94	0.98
Grade-equivalent score						
Mean	5.15	5.24	5.29	5.19	5.22	5.24
Standard deviation	1.58	1.60	1.60	1.46	1.13	1.34
Standard error	0.43	0.46	0.33	0.40	0.28	0.17

Source: Data from *Preliminary Technical Summary*, 2nd ed. (Iowa City, Iowa: Riverside Publishing Co., 1979).

In selecting an achievement test, the principal concern is with choosing a test with high content validity for the students in a particular classroom. If the norm groups and the group to be tested are dissimilar, the validity of the test for the classroom group is lowered. No standardized test can be valid, however, unless it is reliable.

STANDARDIZED ACHIEVEMENT TEST RELIABILITY

All three kinds of reliability (see Chapter 15) are important in standardized tests, and they should be reported in the test manual accompanying an achievement or diagnostic test. The most important aspect of reliability for standardized achievement tests is *internal consistency,* which is related to item discrimination.*

The internal consistency reliabilities for level 11 of the ITBS, given in the first row of Table 17.2, are very high, as is true for most stan-

---

* Internal consistency also is important in aptitude tests and in some noncognitive tests such as those that measure personality characteristics (Mehrens & Lehmann, 1978). Reliabilities on most standardized noncognitive tests are generally lower because experts disagree on the content of areas like personality, and these areas are more difficult to measure.

dardized achievement and aptitude tests. They range from 0.84 to 0.93 on individual subtests and from 0.92 to 0.96 on main-area scores, with 0.98 on the composite score. Individual subtest reliabilities are lower than the others because they are based on fewer items. The language total, for example, includes items from all four language subtests, so it has a higher reliability than any individual subtest. Likewise, the composite score is based on all of the items in the test and so is the most reliable. Overall, reliabilities for all levels of the ITBS vary from 0.89 to 0.96 for main-area scores and from 0.97 to 0.98 on composite scores (*Preliminary Technical Summary,* 1979).

Equivalence is an important aspect of reliability for achievement tests (as with aptitude tests) if the students will be measured at two different times using equivalent forms, as when the effects of an instructional program are measured with an achievement test. Since the two or more forms are different samples of behaviors from the same content area, and since both are designed to measure knowledge and skills in that area, high equivalence is a necessity. The ITBS has two equivalent forms. They were developed concurrently through methods designed to assure their equivalence, and so their raw scores, and all scores developed from them, have been equated.

While *stability* is important in aptitude tests and in noncognitive tests such as interest measures, it has less bearing on achievement tests. The construct of achievement includes the notion of stability across short time spans, however. The ITBS scores show at least a limited pattern of stability, as we have noted.

STANDARD ERROR IN ACHIEVEMENT TEST SCORES

Table 17.2 also gives the means, standard deviations, and standard errors (a measure of test accuracy) for a score called the grade equivalent, which is often used with standardized achievement tests. *Grade-equivalent scores* are reported as a number representing the grade in school followed by a decimal point or a dash and a number representing the number of months within that grade, ranging from 0 to 9. To find the grade-equivalent score, the teacher looks up the raw score in a conversion table. (Table 17.3 in the next section is an example of part of a conversion table.) The resulting grade-equivalent score indicates that the average child in the norm group obtained that same raw score during a specific month in a specific grade.

Robbie, for example, took the fifth-grade level of the ITBS during the fall and received a raw reading score of 40, which (according to Table 17.3) yields a grade-equivalent score of 7.2. This means that Robbie's reading score is the same as the mean score obtained on the fifth-grade test by those students in the national norm sample who were in the second month of the seventh grade, a score well above the national average. As Table 17.2 shows, the grade-equivalent mean for the fifth-grade reading subtest is 5.24, which is about two and one-half months into fifth grade. It is to be expected that the means for all of the subtests would be about in that range, since the test was normed on fifth-graders during the fall.

Table 17.2 also shows that the standard error for the reading subtest is 0.46, which is four and six-tenths months. Robbie's teacher used this standard error to examine her score, as explained in the section on intelligence tests. The teacher was 68 percent certain that Robbie's true score was between 6.74 (7.20 − 0.46) and 7.66 (7.20 + 0.46), or about 6.7 and 7.7. That is, if she retook the test several times without learning anything between testings (which of course is not very likely), 68 percent of the time her test scores would be between these scores. Using 2 standard errors, the teacher also could be 95 percent certain that Robbie's score would be between 6.28 [7.20 − (2 × 0.46)] and 8.12 [7.20 + (2 × 0.46)].

Even though the ITBS, like most standardized achievement tests, is very accurate, the error associated with any student's score is sizable. Therefore this teacher was satisfied with the 68 percent confidence level, or knowing that Robbie's true score was likely to be between 6.7 and 7.7. Although taking account of the error did not change the interpretation of Robbie's performance, it could do so for many students who are just above or below the mean score. In the case of the reading comprehension subtest, any student in fifth grade whose grade-equivalent score is between 4.8 and 5.7 is reading at the fifth-grade level, because of the error associated with the scores. As the certainty gets higher, from 68 to 95 percent, the range within which the true scores falls also gets larger. The test user has to balance these two aspects when using the standard error; most teachers are satisfied with the 68 percent level.

In choosing a standardized achievement test, therefore, a test with high reliability and low standard error is preferred. This means that the test scores will be as close to the true scores as possible.

PRACTICAL CONSIDERATIONS

The statistical considerations described above should be used to make an initial selection of several appropriate standardized achievement tests, but the final selection is based on more practical considerations. For one thing, the test should be easy to administer. It should have clear, complete directions, fit into the time frame of the school, and be easy for students to take. The ITBS directions are very clear and easy to understand, but the test can be difficult to give to certain students. Since all achievement levels of the test are in one test booklet, students taking different levels start and stop at different places. Pupils in a class who have low language achievement, for example, will begin and end the language subtest at different places in the test booklet than the rest of the class does. All pupils therefore must be carefully supervised to be certain that they are answering the appropriate questions.

The ITBS actually takes five hours to give, four hours and four minutes of working time and 56 minutes for directions, questions, rest breaks, and so on. Many schools administer it in four sessions on four different days. Some teachers complain that this disrupts their schedules for half of each day for almost a week. The test also could be given in eight sessions on four days, which would be worse from the teachers' point of view, or in four sessions in two days, which would be very tiring for students.

The test should have two or more equivalent forms at each level, as the ITBS has, to use when the test is given at different times or in evaluating a program when the test must be given twice, before and after the program is used. It also should be fast and easy to score and interpret, or it should be possible to send the tests to the test publisher for machine scoring. However the tests are scored, teachers, administrators, parents, and students all must be able to understand what the scores mean. The ITBS *Teacher's Guide* (1979) includes a good section on the meaning of test scores and how to interpret them to students and parents.

Data from appropriate norm groups must be available in order to compare and interpret test scores. Test publishers make data on different norm groups available for comparison. The ITBS has fall and spring national norms, as well as norms for each of the five sections of the country, for private schools, and for large city schools. It also has midyear norms, but these were estimated statistically from the fall and spring norms and so are not as accurate as if they had been collected through actual testing. Test publishers also will develop local norms at a school's request.

For schools today cost is an important consideration in the initial purchase and reuse of a standardized test. If the test has separate answer sheets, as the ITBS does, the test booklets can be used again; the only additional cost is for answer sheets and for scoring if desired. If the students write on the test booklets, the whole test has to be replaced each time it is used. Balanced against the cost of new booklets is the appropriateness of the answer sheet for the students, however. Many early elementary students as well as other special groups have trouble using them, so writing on the test booklets makes a more valid test for these students. For most students a lesson or two on how to mark answer sheets reduces confusion and thus improves the precision of the test scores when separate answer sheets are used.

SOURCES OF INFORMATION ABOUT STANDARDIZED TESTS

A realistic appraisal of standardized achievement tests requires concrete evidence of how well a test satisfies the statistical and practical considerations described in this section. The various sources of information on standardized tests also can be used in selecting intelligence tests and other types of cognitive and noncognitive standardized instruments.

A good source of information about standardized tests is the catalogs test publishers provide free of charge. On request, publishers will also provide specimens of tests and copies of the test manuals for examination. Since the manual is written for the test publisher, who wants to sell the test, it is important to check other sources too.

The most comprehensive source of information about standardized tests is *The Mental Measurements Yearbooks* edited by Oscar K. Buros; the most recent is the eighth (1978). *Tests in Print,* also edited by Buros, is the master index for the yearbooks, which have been published every six or seven years. In addition to factual information about standardized tests, such as their uses, reliability and validity, and construction, they also include test reviews written for the yearbooks and partial reviews that have appeared in journals. For widely used standardized tests, one review may positively evaluate the test while another is more critical.

Other sources include testing bureaus and divisions at universities and colleges; bulletins published by many of the major testing corporations, such as the Educational Testing Service (also known as ETS); journals such as *Educational and Psychological Measurement;* and test evaluations of standardized tests done by the Center for the Study of Evaluation at UCLA.

ADMINISTERING AND SCORING STANDARDIZED TESTS

Achievement tests are more likely to be administered by classroom teachers than the other types of standardized tests. Individual intelligence and aptitude tests, diagnostic tests, and noncognitive instruments are usually administered by the school psychologist or psychometrist or some other type of trained examiner. Nevertheless the classroom teacher must understand how all standardized tests are scored in order to be able to interpret the scores for students, parents, administrators, and other interested parties.

The first rule in administering standardized tests is to follow the directions exactly. Otherwise the resulting scores will not be interpretable, since when the norm group scores were collected the standardized procedures presented in the directions were followed. The ITBS mathematics computation subtest, for example, gives students 20 minutes of working time. If one class is given 25 minutes, the students' scores will be higher, not because they are better at computations but just because they had extra time.

Teachers who are to administer a standardized test should go over it well in advance to make certain that they understand how to give it and they have the materials they will need. According to the *Teacher's Guide* for the ITBS, teachers need soft-lead pencils, test booklets, answer sheets, scratch paper, and a timepiece with a second hand or, preferably, a stopwatch.

Students also need to be prepared. They should know when the test is to be given and how to use the test booklet and answer sheets. Such preparation can markedly reduce students' anxiety and concern about being tested. Various achievement tests differ in the arrangement of items in the test booklet and on the answer sheets (see Box A above). To make the test results as accurate as possible, teachers should instruct students in how to use the format accurately and quickly. They can develop practice materials similar but not identical to actual test content to help students gain experience and confidence. This type of preparation is especially important with younger students, special students, and those who do not read well. The ITBS can provide practice tests to help students learn the test-taking skills they need for this test.

STANDARDIZED TEST SCORES

Most completed standardized tests can be either sent back to the publisher for scoring or hand scored, generally by the classroom teacher. Test publishers provide stencils or scoring keys that are easy to use in hand scoring. The teacher first obtains the number correct, or the raw score, for each student. These scores do not mean much themselves, so a conversion table such as Table 17.3 is used to convert the raw score to one of a number of commonly used scores. When the tests are machine scored by the publisher, the results are reported in any of these converted scores. Most converted scores have been normalized; that is, they have been statistically adjusted so they follow a normal distribution, as shown in Figure 17.3. The vertical axis shows the frequency for each score, while the horizontal axis gives data on four types of converted scores: standard deviation units, and percentile, stanine, and grade-equivalent scores.

Table 17.3

*Portion of a conversion table for the
fifth-grade ITBS reading comprehension subtest,
fall norms, Form 7*

Raw Score	Grade-Equivalent Score	Percentile Score	Stanine Score
	4.3	30	
18	4.4	33	
	4.5	35	4
19	4.6	37	
20	4.7	40	
21	4.8	42	
	4.9	44	
22	5.0	46	
23	5.1	48	5
24	5.2	50	
	5.3	53	
25	5.4	55	
26	5.5	57	
27	5.6	59	
28	5.7	61	
29	5.8	63	
	5.9	66	
30	6.0	68	6
31	6.1	70	
32	6.2	72	
33	6.3	74	
34	6.4	75	
35	6.5	77	
36	6.6	79	
	6.7	81	
37	6.8	82	7
38	6.9	84	
39	7.0	85	
	7.1	86	
40	7.2	88	
41	7.3	89	
	7.4	90	
42	7.5	91	
43	7.6	92	8
	7.7	93	
44	7.8	94	
45	8.0	95	

Source: Adapted from *Teacher's Guide, the Iowa Tests of Basic
Skills,* Form 7/8 (Iowa City, Iowa: Riverside Publishing Co., 1979).

Figure 17.3

Relationship of scores commonly used with standardized tests

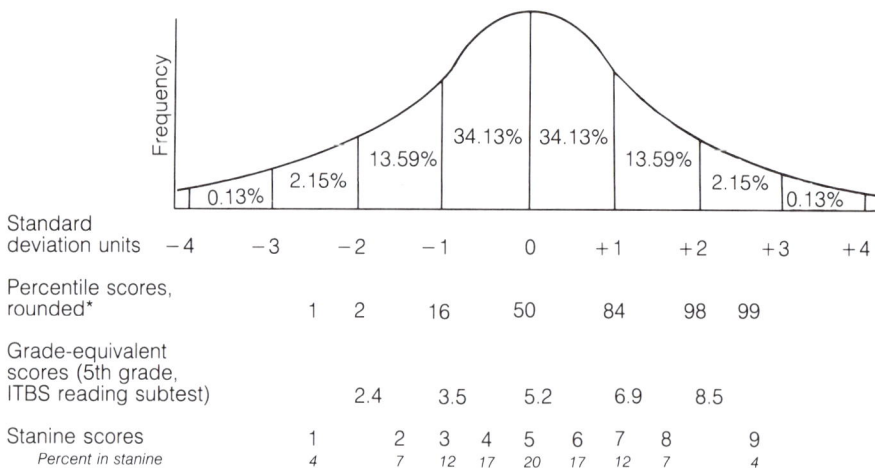

Standard deviation units	-4	-3	-2	-1	0	$+1$	$+2$	$+3$	$+4$	

Percentile scores, rounded*

| | 1 | 2 | 16 | 50 | 84 | 98 | 99 | |

Grade-equivalent scores (5th grade, ITBS reading subtest)

| | 2.4 | 3.5 | 5.2 | 6.9 | 8.5 | |

Stanine scores

| | 1 | 2 | 3 | 4 | 5 | 6 | 7 | 8 | 9 | |
| *Percent in stanine* | | 4 | 7 | 12 | 17 | 20 | 17 | 12 | 7 | 4 |

*There are no 0 or 100 percentile scores.

Standard Deviation Units

The first row of scores in Figure 17.3 merely marks off the score axis in standard deviation units. As we noted in Chapter 16 in relation to teacher-made tests, the standard deviation unit indicates the average distance that scores vary from the mean score. These units are equally spaced: The distance between $+2$ and $+3$ units is the same as the distance between -3 and -2 units, or that between 0 and $+1$ units. Each standard deviation unit has the same precision and so the same standard error. The manual for a standardized test or other accompanying publication should report the mean and standard deviation for each subtest, for the total test score, and for any other composite or converted scores.

Percentile Scores

One of the scores most commonly reported on standardized tests is the percentile, or percentile rank, score. As with teacher-made tests, a percentile score indicates the percentage of the norm group who received raw scores lower than a particular raw score. Ted, for example, has a raw score of 38 on the fifth-grade reading subtest in the fall. The conversion table (see Table 17.3) indicates that this is equivalent to a percentile of 84, which means that Ted's raw score surpasses those of 84 percent of the fifth-graders in the national norm sample. The conclusion about Ted's reading skills is that he is well above the national average.

There is no 100th percentile in a conversion table because no one can have a score better than all of the norm group. Generally at least one person in that group answers every question on a subtest correctly. No one is given a 0 percentile score either. As Figure 17.3 indicates, almost everyone's score in a norm group falls between 4 standard deviations above the mean ($+4$) and 4 standard deviations below the mean (-4). In fact, due to the shape of the normal distribution, over half of the scores (68.26%) cluster around the middle of the distribution, between $+1$ and -1 standard deviations. There are very few scores at either extreme: 0.13% at the high end, above $+3$ standard deviations, and 0.13% at the low end, -3 standard deviations.

The major problem with percentile scores is due to these characteristics. The percentile scores in Figure 17.3 are not equally spaced, as the standard deviation units are. The distance between the 50th and 60th percentiles, for example, would be much smaller than that between the 80th and 90th, and that distance would be smaller than the distance between the 90th and 99th. This means that it is much easier for a percentile score to be changed on retest when the score is in the middle of the distribution, near the mean, rather than at either end. Suppose Suza, a fifth-grader like Ted, retakes the ITBS reading subtest. If she got a raw score of 23 the first time, Table 17.3 indicates that her percentile score would be 48, which is close to the middle percentile score of 50. The second time, if she gets a raw score of 25, or gains two raw-score points, her percentile would be 55. In this case, her score is raised seven percentile points, for a change of two raw-score points. But if Suza got a raw score of 43 the first time, giving a percentile score of 92 (which is close to the top score of 99), and if she retook the subtest and got a raw score of 45, again changing it by two raw-score points, her percentile score would be 95. This time the score would change only three percentile points for the change of two raw-score points. This means that the percentile ranks in the middle of the distribution are not as stable as they are at the extremes; that is, the middle percentile scores have higher standard errors associated with them than the extremes. Therefore teachers and others cannot be as confident about middle scores.

The main advantage to percentile scores is that they are easy to explain. People are used to percentages in life and can easily relate to percentile scores.

Grade-Equivalent Scores

Grade-equivalent scores (introduced in the preceding section) are one of the most frequently used types of scores on standardized tests, especially in elementary and early secondary schools. The grade-equivalent scores for the fifth-grade ITBS reading subtest, Form 7, are given in the third row of Figure 17.3. To obtain this score, the test publishers administered each grade level of the test to a selected norm group of students in several consecutive grades. The grade-equivalent score indicates the average raw score earned by students in the norm group at a specific month in a specific grade. A student's grade-equivalent score is determined by matching her or his raw score to the month and grade in which this score was earned by the average student in the norm group.

According to Table 17.3, Ted's raw score of 38 gives him a grade-equivalent score of 6.9 on the reading subtest, indicating that his raw score is the same as the mean score of the norm group of students who were in the ninth month of sixth grade when they took the fifth-grade test. This does *not* mean that Ted is capable of doing sixth-grade work, since the test he took was designed for fifth-graders. It only indicates that he scored higher than the majority of fifth-graders in the norm group.

The interpretation problem is the biggest disadvantage of grade-equivalent scores. Parents and students can be confused about these scores because they do not mean what they appear to mean. Despite their frequent use, therefore, many testing authorities recommend against their use. If they are used, they should be discussed with parents and students in conjunction with other scores.

Stanine Scores

The score that is used more frequently with standardized achievement tests is called the stanine score. As the last row in Figure 17.3 shows, stanine scores range from 1 to 9, with a mean of 5. They are *normalized* scores, which means each includes that percentage of the total number of cases that corresponds to the area of the normal curve under which they lie. For example, stanine 5 straddles the mean, accounting for the cases that lie ± 0.25 standard deviations from it. This turns out to include about 20 percent of all cases under the normal curve. Other stanine scores are read in the same fashion, except for stanines 1 and 9. Each of these accounts for all of the cases at the extreme ends of the distribution (lying beyond approximately 1.75 standard deviations above and below the mean), and each contains 4 percent of the total scores.

Thus each stanine represents a band of scores. This is the major advantage of stanines; they indicate that a student's score really does have some error in it and so is not exactly precise. Table 17.3 shows that Ted's stanine score in reading is 7, again above average. Unlike percentile scores, where a small change in a raw score may markedly alter the student's percentile score, stanine scores tend to be the same for many pupils who earn quite different raw scores, especially at the extreme ends of the distribution.

COMPARING TYPES OF SCORES

One reason there are different kinds of test scores is that test publishers and writers, as well as teachers and other test users, suggest new scores to correct the faults they find with established scores. All of the scores we have discussed have advantages and disadvantages, some of which have already been mentioned. To compare these various types of scores we will use Figure 17.3 and Table 17.4, which gives the scores on the various ITBS subtests earned by Ted, the imaginary student in the examples in this section.

Table 17.4 shows that Ted's highest subtest raw score is in the language total, and his lowest score is in vocabulary. This does not mean that Ted performs best in language but worst in vocabulary, however, because the vocabulary test only has 39 possible points, while the language test has 130. So we have to convert Ted's raw scores to give an accurate picture of his strengths and weaknesses.

The percentiles and the grade-equivalent scores appear to be easiest to use. Both of these scores indicate that language is Ted's best subtest and mathematics is his worst. The stanine scores support mathematics as his lowest score but indicate similar performance in vocabulary, reading, and language. To determine which interpretation is more accurate, we must refer to Table 17.2, which gives standard errors for the grade-equivalent scores on the subtests of the fifth-grade ITBS. When error bands are tacked onto the grade-equivalent scores for each subtest, the 68 percent confidence band (plus or minus 1 standard error) for reading is completely contained in the band for language. Vocabulary and reading overlap somewhat, while vocabulary and language overlap very little. Similarly, the percentile scores for reading and language are quite close, while the score for vocabulary is slightly lower. So it is most accurate to say that Ted performs about equally well in reading and language and

Table 17.4

Hypothetical scores for a student on the fifth-grade ITBS, Form 7

	Vocabulary	Reading	Language Total	Work-Study Total	Mathematics Total	Composite
Raw score	31	38	97	48	44	258
Stanine score	7	7	7	6	5	6
Percentile score	79	84	86	60	40	74
Grade-equivalent score	6.5	6.9	7.2	5.6	4.8	6.2
68% confidence band for grade-equivalent score	6.1 to 6.9	6.4 to 7.4	6.9 to 7.5	5.2 to 6.0	4.5 to 5.1	6.0 to 6.4

Figure 17.4

Profile of a student's hypothetical ITBS scores

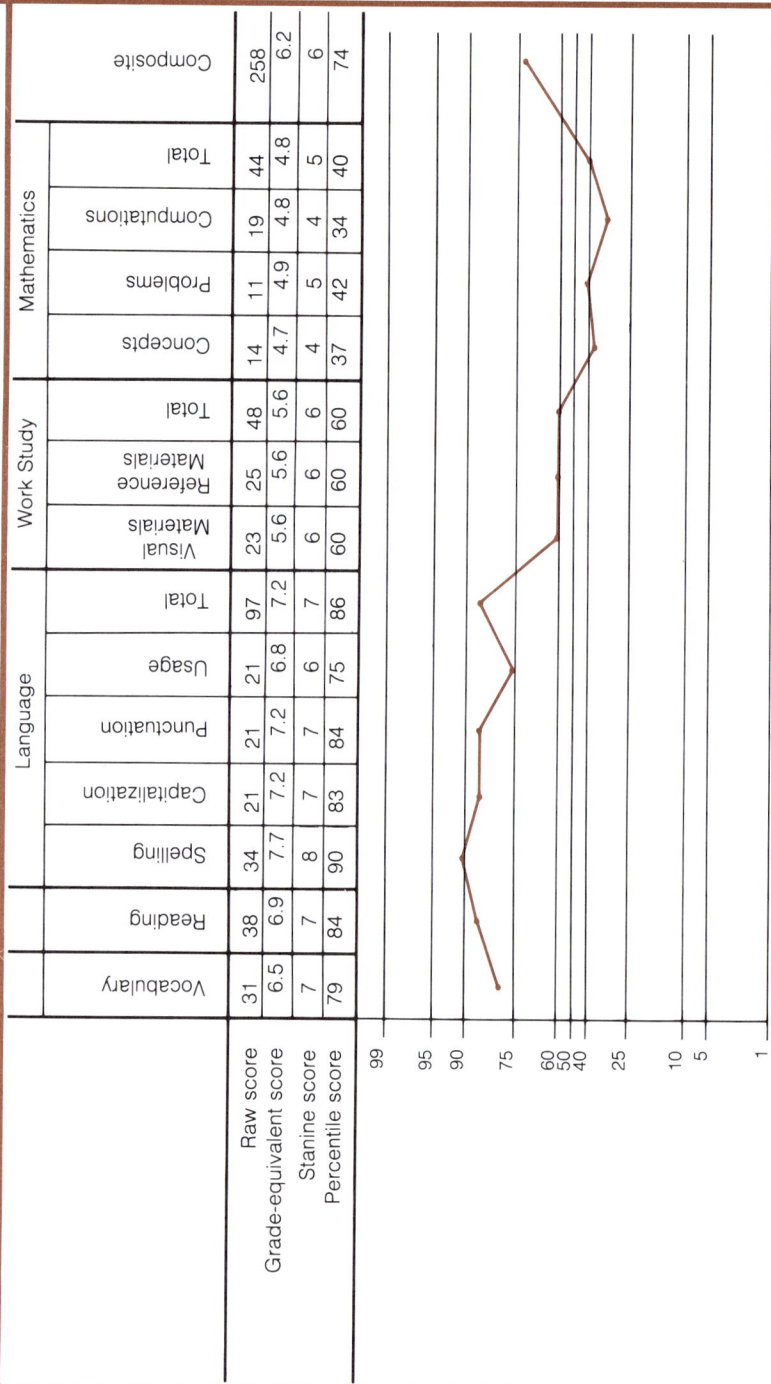

		Raw score	Grade-equivalent score	Stanine score	Percentile score
	Vocabulary	31	6.5	7	79
	Reading	38	6.9	7	84
	Spelling	34	7.7	8	90
Language	Capitalization	21	7.2	7	83
Language	Punctuation	21	7.2	7	84
Language	Usage	21	6.8	6	75
Language	Total	97	7.2	7	86
Work Study	Visual Materials	23	5.6	6	60
Work Study	Reference Materials	25	5.6	6	60
Work Study	Total	48	5.6	6	60
Mathematics	Concepts	14	4.7	4	37
Mathematics	Problems	11	4.9	5	42
Mathematics	Computations	19	4.8	4	34
Mathematics	Total	44	4.8	5	40
	Composite	258	6.2	6	74

Note: ITBS student profiles usually do not report raw or stanine scores.

After administering and scoring standardized tests, the school psychologist or the classroom teacher must provide feedback on the results to individual students and their parents. For evaluation purposes, the raw score for each student is converted to various types of scores.

slightly less well in vocabulary. Relative to the norm group, Ted's stanine scores indicate that he is about average in everything except mathematics, in which he is average.

So stanines, used in conjunction with percentile scores, probably give the most accurate and useful information to the teacher. With stanines, Ted's teacher could make direct comparisons between Ted's scores on tests that have different possible numbers correct and that have different means and standard deviations. Ted's performance on each subtest could also be related to the norm. Percentile scores are slightly more accurate than stanines, but stanines help keep teachers from ascribing too much precision to the percentile scores.

FEEDBACK ON TEST RESULTS

Students should receive notice of their test results, preferably in the form of a test profile which lists the scores and graphs them. This type of visual presentation is a good way to show a student's relative strengths and weaknesses. Complete profiles can generally be ordered from the test publisher when they score the tests, or teachers can create their own quite simply. Figure 17.4 represents a profile of Ted's ITBS scores created by his teacher; student profiles prepared by the test publisher usually do not give the raw and stanine scores.

Other forms of reporting also may be available. For the ITBS, the teacher receives a "list report" which gives each student's grade-equivalent and percentile scores on each subtest, as well as the grade-equivalent means of the whole class on each subtest. The publisher also makes available a "pupil item response record" for each student who takes the test. This report groups the items according to the skill objectives they measure and indicates which objectives a student has passed or failed. A similar record for the whole class also can be obtained. Other types of records of ITBS results are available, but most involve additional expense for the school.

CHAPTER 17 IN RETROSPECT

Most of the standardized tests teachers use in the classroom are of two basic types which are concerned with measuring cognitive learning. Intelligence tests are a type of aptitude test; they measure a student's potential for future academic achievement. Achievement tests, the type most widely used in schools, measure how well content and skills in academic areas have been learned. Two other types of standardized tests are also used in the schools. Diagnostic tests measure a student's performance in the major content and learning behavior areas in order to identify specific problems. Noncognitive tests measure personal attributes in areas such as personality, interests, and attitudes; they are the only type that is not concerned with academic performance.

Standardized psychometric intelligence tests, which are constructed by experts to sample learning and behaviors that are generally agreed to represent the construct of intelligence, are the most frequently administered type of test of intellectual aptitude or ability. After age five, an IQ score is the best predictor available of future educational performance, though there is a great deal of variability in achievement that cannot be predicted from IQ scores. Most intelligence tests are norm referenced; each student's IQ score is determined by comparing her or his score on the test with those of a norm group in a conversion table.

The validity of an IQ test is related to culture fairness, or the use of content, language, and question-and-answer formats that all students have an equal chance to respond to correctly. Criterion-related validity is important for IQ tests that are to be used for selection purposes (as in grouping of students in classrooms), and construct validity is concerned with the accepted definition of the construct of intelligence.

Standardized achievement tests have great potential for classroom use. They are constructed in a manner similar to that used by conscientious teachers in constructing their own classroom tests and are designed to measure skills and knowledge that are considered important from a national perspective.

In selecting a standardized achievement test, school personnel need to consider three groups of criteria: need, statistical considerations, and practical considerations. If test results will *not* assist in educational evaluation and decision making, no test should be selected. If such a test is needed, however, statistical considerations are of major importance. A standardized achievement test must have content and construct validity. All major standardized achievement tests have construct validity, but each school or district must decide if a test has content validity for its own programs. Also, a test may be valid for some purposes and for some students and not for others. Reliability, especially internal consistency, is also important; without it a test cannot be valid. Practical considerations in the decision include ease of administration, existence of equivalent forms of the test, ease and speed of scoring, score interpretation, availability of appropriate norm groups, and cost of the test. Sources of information about standardized tests include the test manuals and bulletins produced by the test publishers, Buros's *Mental Measurements Yearbooks*, journals, test evaluations done by the Center for the Study of Evaluation, and college and university testing bureaus.

There are several types of test scores. A percentile rank score indicates the percentage of students in the norm group who scored below each raw score. Stanine scores, which range from 1 to 9, represent a band of raw scores including the percentage of the total number of norm group scores that correspond to nine areas of the normal curve. A grade-equivalent score represents the grade level (year and month) of the norm group who received that average raw score. All test scores contain error due to unreliability, so each student's score should be represented by and interpreted as a band of scores rather than a single one.

Standardized tests are most useful in the classroom if teachers examine them for content validity in relation to their instructional programs and use their students' scores and patterns of responses as one source of information in student guidance and the development of individual educational plans. They also can use the overall results to alter their general instructional plans to correct any deficiencies they might find in their classes as a whole.

QUESTIONS FOR DISCUSSION

1. What aspects must school personnel consider in determining if a norm-referenced standardized achievement test is valid for use in their school?
2. What are the differences between aptitude, achievement, and diagnostic tests? Include characteristics related to author's intent, specificity of material covered, match to school learning, and length.

3. Consider the relevant aspects of test reliability and validity in each of the following situations. What procedures could be used to obtain valid, reliable measurement in each case? Be specific about what type(s) of reliability and validity each is concerned with and how they could be ensured.

   a. While Magen was taking a timed standardized achievement test, the school received a bomb scare, and her building was evacuated for three hours in the middle of the test.

   b. A company decided to try out a test to use in hiring salespeople. They administered it to current salespeople and looked at the relationship of the test scores to the amount of product each one sold. The relationship was very small.

   c. A school adopted a revolutionary new program to teach mathematics. After one year in operation, school personnel examined the students' math-related standardized achievement test scores and compared them to the prior year's scores in math. They found no differences. Does this mean that the program is not working?

   d. Dan took a standardized achievement test, moved to a new town, and retook the same test three weeks later at his new school. His two scores were not similar.

   e. Children educated in Europe often do poorly on U.S. objective standardized tests.

   f. A school on a rural Indian reservation used an achievement test battery that did not have norms for American Indians.

4. Mara is in the fifth grade. When she took the ITBS with the rest of her class in October, her reading comprehension raw score was 22.

   a. Using the conversion table in the text (Table 17.3), find her grade-equivalent score, percentile score, and stanine score.

   b. Set up 68 and 95 percent confidence bands around her grade-equivalent scores.

   c. Explain what each score indicates about Mara's reading achievement. Characterize Mara's reading achievement.

READINGS FOR REFLECTION

Introductory Level

Hopkins, Charles D., and Antes, Richard L. *Classroom Testing: Administration, Scoring, and Score Interpretation.* Itasca, Ill.: F. E. Peacock Publishers, 1979.

This paperback discusses standardized test administration, scoring standardized tests (by hand and by machine), various types of test scores, criterion-referenced testing and scoring, and score interpretation.

Lyman, Howard B. *Test Scores and What They Mean*. 3rd ed. Englewood Cliffs, N.J.: Prentice-Hall, 1978.

This paperback discusses ethical issues and new developments related to standardized testing; various classes of standardized tests; and test reliability, validity, and useability. It presents frequency distributions and graphs; measures of central tendency and variability, correlation, and standard error; and many different kinds of converted scores.

Advanced Level

Mehrens, William A., and Lehmann, Irvin J. *Measurement and Evaluation in Education and Psychology*. 2nd ed. New York: Holt, Rinehart & Winston, 1978.

This extensive treatment of standardized tests uses actual standardized tests and examples and identifies them by name. It has a partial list of test publishers.

REFERENCES

Buros, Oscar K. (Ed.). *The Eighth Mental Measurements Yearbook*. Highland Park, N.J.: Gryphon Press, 1978.

Diederich, Paul P. *Short-Cut Statistics for Teacher-Made Tests*. Princeton, N.J.: Educational Testing Service, 1973.

Eysenck, Hans J., and Fulker, D. W. *The Structure and Measurement of Intelligence*. Berlin: Springer-Verlag, 1979.

The Iowa Tests of Basic Skills, Forms 7/8. Iowa City, Iowa: Riverside Publishing Co., 1978.

Jensen, Arthur R. *Bias in Mental Testing*. New York: Free Press, 1980.

Mehrens, William A., and Lehmann, Irvin J. *Measurement and Evaluation in Education and Psychology*. 2nd ed. New York: Holt, Rinehart & Winston, 1978.

Preliminary Technical Summary. 2nd ed. Iowa City, Iowa: Riverside Publishing Co., 1979.

Scarr, Sandra. *Heritability and Educational Policy: Genetic and Environmental Effects on IQ, Aptitude, and Achievement*. Address presented at the annual meeting of the American Psychological Association, New York, 1979.

Siegler, Robert S., and Richards, D. Dean. The development of intelligence. In Robert J. Sternberg (Ed.), *Handbook of Intelligence Research*. Cambridge, England: Cambridge University Press, in press.

Teacher's Guide, The Iowa Tests of Basic Skills. Forms 7/8. Iowa City, Iowa: Riverside Publishing Co., 1979.

Wechsler, David. *Manual for the Wechsler Intelligence Scale for Children—Revised*. New York: Psychological Corporation, 1974.

School Evaluations and Accountability

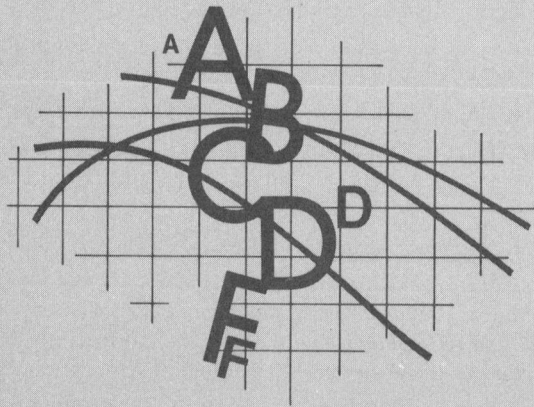

Educational evaluation, as we defined the term in the first chapter in Part IV, is the formation of judgments of value, based on concrete evidence, that are intended to lead to action in some aspect of education. Teachers need to be knowledgeable about this evaluation effort, particularly those aspects that affect their work with students or their role position. They must know how to use various marking systems and how to interpret standardized test scores, for example, since this is how they evaluate their students' achievement or ability. They also must know how teachers are evaluated, because this affects their careers in education. While schoolwide and nationwide evaluations usually are planned and supervised by professionals who are trained in evaluation and research, not by local school personnel, the results of these evaluations also concern the teacher. They may be the reason elementary teachers must learn to use a new reading program the school decides to implement to improve achievement in this content area, or why they must devise an answer for a parent group which demands an explanation for why reading achievement is declining and wants to know what the school plans to do about it.

THE NATURE OF EDUCATIONAL EVALUATION

Evaluation of educational programs or personnel and student achievement or ability can be categorized as either formative or summative. *Summative evaluation,* which is done at the end of a program or project, indicates an overall judgment about the program or the people in it and generally includes recommendations for action. It could be expressed, for example, as the grade a student receives at the end of the semester, indicating the teacher's evaluation of the student's achievement and recommendations for the future, or it could be a school's decision to continue to use a new method of teaching science, based on increased student achievement.

Formative evaluation is conducted during the instructional program or project and is used to make changes in it as it progresses. This is the type of evaluation teachers use when they give a series of quizzes and tests during the semester and use the results to modify the instructional process. The teachers who use a new science method might give quizzes to measure student achievement and have students fill out rating scales to see what types of material they like, and then alter their use of the material accordingly. In formative evaluations, the information collected is used as a basis for changing behavior.

Some evaluation may be both formative and summative. A college student's course grade is summative in the sense that it marks achievement in the whole course, but if the course is an introductory one for a major field of study, the grade can be used in a formative way as an indication of progress in an academic program.

Various measuring instruments are used as a basis for evaluation. Tests and assignments are the commonest form, both those constructed by teachers (see Chapter 16) and the standardized tests prepared by educational publishers (see Chapter 17). Other types are used in evaluating processes and products, as we noted in Chapter 16. Observation scales, for example, can be used to measure what people actually do, such as the percentage of higher-level questions a teacher asks during class discussions. Rating scales are used to measure people's perceptions, such as how an instructor's students rate a mathematics course in regard to its difficulty and relevance to their program of study. Rating scales are also used to evaluate performance, such as the physical education teacher's rating of the form of a student's tennis serve. Once these measures are taken, they must be used to make the needed judgments and decisions.

An aspect of educational evaluation that is receiving increasing attention is accountability, or the obligation to account to others for actions and results. As Gronlund (1974) puts it, to be accountable is to be answerable. If school personnel are to be accountable to the communities they serve, they must let the public know their objectives, how well the objectives are being met, and the cost of meeting them. They also must accept the responsibility for the results (Mehrens & Lehmann, 1978).

At the local level, educational evaluations can be conducted of learners' achievement, teachers' performance, or the effectiveness of instructional programs and materials. Wolf (1979) has identified eight general groups of educational evaluation models and 20 specific models or frameworks. A general framework for an implementation plan encompassing both evaluation and accountability might include the seven steps given in Box A.

ACCOUNTABILITY IN EDUCATION

The issue of accountability in education arose in the late 1960s and early 1970s, largely because efforts to assure equality of educational outcomes and opportunities had preoccupied educational thought as an aspect of the civil rights movement. That concern remains today, but pressures for accountability have become more insistent as enrollments have declined nationwide and support for the public schools has been limited by economic and social conditions.

BOX A   *A framework for implementing educational evaluation and accountability*

1. Setting broad, reasonable goals for what the learner, teacher, material, or program is to accomplish.
2. Stating objectives that meet these goals in measurable terms and developing and implementing a plan to accomplish the objectives.
3. Assessing initial performance levels of the learners or teachers.
4. Collecting formative evaluation information during the implementation of the activities that have been designed to meet the goals and objectives, and altering the activities to reflect needed changes as they are identified by the evaluation.
5. Collecting summative data to determine if the objectives and goals have been met and making decisions based on the summative evaluation.
6. Disseminating these data and decisions, along with cost information, to the people who are involved with and paying for the educational activities.
7. Accepting feedback and taking responsibility for the results of the activities and the evaluation findings.

There are very few school districts in the nation which are expanding their enrollments or the size of their teaching staffs. On the contrary, the *Wall Street Journal* for August 17, 1982, reported that the American Federation of Teachers union was predicting teacher layoffs would rise 21 percent over the preceding year, to a record 55,500, and the National Education Association was estimating there would be 50,000 layoffs. As reductions in force have become common, teachers have had to learn to live with the prospect of being "riffed." Decisions as to which teachers will not have their contracts renewed are an intensely personal and practical aspect of educational accountability.

Traditionally when a school district has had the difficult task of reducing the size of a teaching force, it has approached the problem with procedures similar to those used by labor unions, at various levels of government, and in other employment situations. In such cases it often

Decisions that profoundly affect the daily lives and careers of teachers are made by community school boards, which represent the many invisible visitors present in the nation's classrooms.

is either impossible to discriminate among employees on the basis of their competence and performance, or there is resistance to making and acting on such differences. Minor reductions of teaching staff can be accomplished through attrition if enough teachers resign or retire and leave positions available for those who wish to remain. If deeper cuts have to be made, beginning teachers and others who have not been awarded tenure are dismissed. By the 1980s many school districts had passed through these two stages and were confronting the question of which tenured teachers should stay and which should go. Since tenure makes seniority inapplicable, some other evaluation criteria must be applied.

There are no simple, clear-cut solutions to such difficult matters. In the profession of education conceptual models and empirical data that can provide equitable evaluative bases for such decisions are desperately needed. An example of such a model is Dyer's (1970) school effectiveness indexes (SEI), which use a variety of data to estimate how well comparable teachers (such as those who teach at the same level or in the same subject area) succeed with specific groups of students (such as low achievers or the gifted). The aptitude and prior achievement of students in a school, environmental or context variables, and levels of current achievement are all considered. The Dyer model and others can be used to supply objective data about the effects of specific teachers and schools on children's achievement, but many of the accountability judgments that must be made are independent of the competency or demonstrated ability of specific teachers.

One example is related to the current widespread shortage of teachers of science and mathematics. Despite media reports that many of the teachers in these areas have had minimum or substandard preparation for the content they are teaching, when reductions in the teaching force are necessary it is unlikely that these teachers will be affected. One reason is that most college graduates who have the training to be competent teachers in science and mathematics departments of junior and senior high schools instead accept entry positions in industry that pay them twice what they could expect to earn as beginning classroom teachers. If the enrollment in Latin classes sinks close to zero, though, the teacher will no doubt be dismissed, no matter how competent he or she may be.

Thus the issue of accountability can become inextricably mixed with matters of national educational and social policy. The "invisible visitors" to the teacher's classroom which inhabit the third dimension of the instructional model introduced in Chapter 1 are more numerous and more powerful than may be recognized. Decisions that profoundly affect the daily lives and careers of teachers often are made by persons representing forces that are well beyond their control.

PLACING THE RESPONSIBILITY

While the trend to accountability in education has been clearly established, determining just who is accountable for what in the schools is open to question. Normally people are not held accountable for events over which they have no control, and the various groups in a school do not exercise complete control over one another. Teachers, for example, are not in complete control of students' behaviors, and the students cannot be held responsible for school policies. The responsibility of everyone involved in education should extend only to those outcomes that they can actually affect by their actions (Barro, 1970).

Students are accountable for their school attendance and for their own behavior. They must try to learn the material presented and behave and interact in appropriate ways at school. Both of these types of action contribute to achievement and to a good school climate.

Parents are responsible for ensuring that their children attend school and for supporting the school's policies and practices or trying to change those with which they disagree. A Southwestern state even has a law that allows prosecution of parents on a charge of educational neglect if their children are consistently truant. Most of the children whose parents have been taken to court on this charge have since attended school much more regularly.

Teachers are accountable for planning and presenting reasonable, appropriate lessons, evaluating their students' progress and the effectiveness of their teaching, using this information in positive ways, and setting and enforcing rules that contribute to a classroom climate that is conducive to learning. As representatives of the school in the community they have a public relations role and the responsibility to convey positive impressions. Teachers also are accountable for their own professional development, which means taking additional courses and seminars to upgrade their knowledge and skills, as well as working individually and with others on their teaching and their own learning.

School administrators are responsible for the overall quality of the programs and the climate in their schools, and also for their own professional development. School boards are responsible for the overall quality of the schools in their districts and for their own policies and actions as governmental groups. All citizens also have a responsibility to maintain an informed interest in the education of the country's children.

POTENTIAL OUTCOMES OF ACCOUNTABILITY

Evaluation is an anticipated outcome whenever a person or group sets out to accomplish a goal, although the evaluation may be informal or vague. Because taxpayers who support public schools and parents who pay for private schools are holding the schools accountable for their actions, school evaluation results must be formally and publicly stated.

The results of evaluation and accountability are not always welcome, as when students receive lower marks than they expect. But efforts to produce explicit, measurable evaluation results often have positive outcomes. When public accountability is of concern, the schools become better at specifying and evaluating educational objectives. They spend more time looking at how their programs affect the students, that is, examining the relationship between what their students are like when they enter, how the school affects them while they are there, and what they are like when they leave. Accountability often results in better management of both personnel and finances. Good evaluation procedures produce information that is needed for valid decision making about the strengths and weaknesses within the school and what to do to remove the weaknesses. The public also becomes better informed about what the schools are doing and why (Mehrens & Lehmann, 1978).

How teachers and the schools do their jobs is a concern of the community, and the public should have an input in educational decisions. People's favorable or unfavorable perceptions of schools and teachers (as discussed in Chapter 13) will affect the future of the nation's educational institutions. Moreover, accountability and evaluation are most useful if representatives of all concerned groups are involved in their planning. When the resulting information is relevant and acceptable to everyone, it is more likely to be used in positive ways.

EVALUATION OF STUDENTS

Evaluation of students has been a part of formal education since schooling began. The results are needed by many people, including the students. Formative evaluation helps them determine from day to day what they know and what they do not, which skills they have and which need more work. Summative evaluation is useful in long-term occupational and educational decisions, such as whether or not to take certain advanced courses. Students usually are not experienced enough to evaluate themselves. Unless they have been extensively involved in using the skills and knowledge, they are too inexperienced to know which ones they need.

Knowledge of students' competencies is also useful to teachers, counselors, and other educational personnel. It helps them advise students, as well as to evaluate their own work and the instructional processes and curricula used with the students.

Evaluative information about secondary school students is particularly useful to prospective employers. Students are protected by law so their records cannot be made available to employers without their written consent, but if the information is voluntarily given a prospective employer can quickly learn how much basic or vocational education students have had and how successful they were. If this information isn't available to employers, they must base their hiring decisions on some substitute, such as the "impressions" they receive during an interview or tests of their own. In these cases the samples of information obtained are likely to be brief and not highly reliable.

Student evaluations are also needed by colleges, universities, and technical-vocational and other educational institutions to assist their entrance and placement decisions. Since the best predictor of future performance is similar past performance, for most colleges and universities the best predictors are high school grades, in conjunction with standardized scholastic aptitude test scores. The relative worth of these two sources may vary, depending on the student's ethnicity and social class, but both are important and valid when used properly.

Parents need the information to help them understand their children's development and advise them on educational matters. Parents are the principal influence on students' decisions about academic achievement and future educational and vocational plans, as we noted in Chapter 4.

GRADING TESTS AND ASSIGNMENTS

The two major sources of information on academic evaluation of students are standardized test results, which were described in Chapter 17, and the grades teachers assign to students' work. Criticism of grading is widespread, but it usually is directed at how the grading is used, not to the idea or construct of grades. If grades are to be accurate measures of student's work, the grades students receive must be valid. And in order to give valid grades, teachers need several different kinds of measures of knowledge and skills, such as classroom tests, homework, and projects.

There are two approaches to assigning grades: The teacher can either grade students on their performance relative to that of their classmates or use an absolute scale of some kind. The two approaches also can be combined, using relative marking on some achievement measures and absolute marking on others. Teachers can modify the grading scale in any logical manner, taking into account the difficulty of the course and the general achievement level of the students.

In *relative marking,* as in norm-referenced testing, each student's achievement is compared with that of other students. Probably the most widely known method of relative marking is *grading on the curve,* or deviation grading. Traditionally, the middle 38 percent of students receives grades of C, 24 percent receives Bs and another 24 percent Ds, while the highest 7 percent receives As and the lowest 7 percent Fs. Often the teacher adjusts these percentages to avoid penalizing or overrewarding individual students; the traditional scale is used mostly in undergraduate college courses and rarely at any other educational level. It is appropriate only in classes that are large and are *not* tracked by ability levels.

Another type of relative marking uses the visual or *eyeballing* method. Here the teacher examines the score distribution and awards grades according to natural breaks in the distribution.

All of the relative marking methods depend on the achievement of the class as a whole. For example, a student with a score of 50 percent of the items correct might receive an A if the class as a whole scored low on the test or an F if the class scored high.

Absolute grading, in contrast, compares a student's achievement to an absolute standard, not to that of other people. This type of grading generally is applied in one of two ways. In the *percent-correct system,* the teacher adopts a test score that represents the base for each letter grade and another that represents its ceiling. One frequently used scale is: 90–100 percent correct, A; 80–89 percent correct, B; 70–79 percent correct, C; 60–69 percent, D; and 0–59 percent correct, F.

As an alternative the teacher might adopt a *pass-fail system.* A cutting score is selected and all of the scores that fall below this score are "failures" and those above it are "passes." For instance, if the cutting score is 65 percent correct, a student with a score of 70 percent would simply be given a *pass,* and a student whose score is 64 percent would be given a grade of *fail.* Pass-fail is similar to the mastery level used with the learning for mastery model of teaching.

Grading scales have different effects on students. Relative scales encourage competition and discourage cooperation because the students are competing against each other in a norm-referenced manner. Absolute scales encourage cooperation because everyone is competing against a criterion-referenced standard. In fact, it may encourage students to help each other too much, by actually copying homework or passing on test information.

A comparison of how test scores on a teacher-made test would be graded using the four types of grading systems described above is given in Table 18.1. The scores are arranged in a frequency distribution from

Table 18.1

Marks given on a teacher-made test using four different grading systems

| Test Score | Frequency | Relative Marking | | | Absolute Marking | | |
| | | Grading on the Curve | | | Percent Correct | | |
		Percentile Score	Grade	Visual	Percent Correct	Grade	Pass-Fail (criterion: 65%)
50	2	92	A*	A	100	A	P
49	0						
48	0						
47	3	80	B	A*	94	A	P
46	0						
45	0						
44	0						
43	1	76	B	B	86	B	P
42	2	68	B*	B	84	B	P
41	5	48	C	B	82	B	P
40	2	40	C	B	80	B	P
39	1	36	C	B	78	C	P
38	0						
37	1	32	C	B*	74	C	P
36	0						
35	1	28	D	C	70	C	P
34	3	16	D	C	68	D*	P
33	1	12	D	C	66	D	P
32	0						
31	0						
30	1	8	D*	D	60	D*	F
29	1	4	F	D	58	F	F
28	1	0	F	D	56	F	F

*These marks could have been assigned differently.

high to low, as described in Chapter 16 on teacher-made tests. The percentile score used in grading on the curve and the percent-correct score are also described in Chapter 16.

The scores in Table 18.1 could also have come from an evaluation of the processes and products involved in learning skills and knowledge in ways that cannot be measured with paper-and-pencil tests. The measures used to evaluate these processes and products, such as the rating scales and checklists described in Chapter 16, also result in a number score for each student. The scores in Table 18.1 and their corresponding grades therefore could have come from a rating scale used to evaluate a science project or a checklist used to evaluate a drawing, for example.

COURSE AND SEMESTER GRADING

Most teachers use the same marking system for the entire grading period that they use in grading individual learning tasks, such as assignments and tests. In this case, however, they must decide how to combine marks from several types of assignments into one grade.

Teachers must first decide how much each task is worth in the whole grade. A teacher might decide to weight test scores as 50 percent of the final grade, homework scores as 15 percent, and a project as 35 percent, for example. Three tests were given in this course, and the ranges of the scores varied widely in these tests. If the teacher adds the scores from all three together, the test with the biggest range will influence the total test grades the most.

The most accurate statistical method for handling the variability in scores on different tasks for a student is to convert the score on each task to a z score.* A teacher would need to know the standard deviation of the scores on each assignment in order to do this, however, and this takes some time to calculate unless a calculator that does it automatically is available. Generally, however, these variations are not large enough to cause a real problem. Most teachers find a mean score for each type of assignment, multiply that mean by the weight given to that type, and sum the results. Grades are then assigned to these totals.

Table 18.2 shows how a teacher might apply this method to the scores of two students, Juanita and Tom, throughout a grading period. Juanita's mean test score, for example, was 32.00, and the tests were allotted 50 percent of the credit for the grading period. To find the weighted

---

*To convert a student's raw score to a standard or z score, the mean of the frequency distribution of scores is subtracted from the raw score, and the result is divided by the standard deviation of the scores. The formula is:

$$z = \frac{\text{Raw score} - \text{Mean of raw scores}}{\text{Standard deviation of raw scores}}$$

Table 18.2

Teacher's method of computing total scores for grading period for two students

Tests (50%)

	1	2	3	Sum	Mean	Weighted Mean
Juanita	45	41	10	96	32.00	16.00
Tom	24	41	50	115	38.67	19.33

Homework (15%)

	1	2	3	4	Sum	Mean	Weighted Mean
Juanita	6	9	8	7	30	7.50	1.13
Tom	5	10	2	5	22	5.50	0.83

Project (35%)

	Score	Weighted Score	Total Weighted Score for Period
Juanita	40	14.00	31.13
Tom	35	12.25	32.41

mean for Juanita, the teacher multiplied the mean of 32.00 by the weight of 50 percent (0.50), which equalled 16.00. This procedure was repeated for Juanita's homework mean ($7.50 \times 0.15 = 1.13$). Only one project was assigned, so Juanita's project score (40) was multiplied by the project weight (.035) to find the weighted project score (14.00). Then the teacher added the three weighted scores together to obtain Juanita's total score for the grading period ($16.00 + 1.13 + 14.00 = 31.13$). This procedure was repeated for each student, and the teacher then assigned grades to the total scores.

The weighting scales used can encourage students to adopt different study strategies. If the work at the end of the term is weighted more heavily than that at the start, students study more at the end. When tests are cumulative, students continue to work on all the material throughout the grading period, which aids retention. In the example, the teacher's scale would lead students to put very little effort into homework, since its weight is so low. Most of the students' efforts would be directed to studying for the tests, and a moderate amount would be spent on their projects. These effects do not occur unless students have been informed of the basis for their grades early in the marking period, however.

A student's grades are a private matter between the teacher and the student (and sometimes the parents), but students should know the grade scale and weighting system that will be used before they start the work in a course. Teachers' explanations of report cards also make them a more effective means of providing feedback to students and parents.

CHOOSING A MARKING SYSTEM

Although an individual's grades are a private matter between the teacher and the learner (and sometimes parents or guardians), the grading scale and weighting system should be announced before any work is started. The choice of a marking scale and a weighting system is an individual decision to be made by each teacher. It usually is based on the difficulty of the course, the general achievement level of the class, and the teacher's course objectives. Teachers who instruct the same kinds of students and classes should collaborate and pick systems that are mutually agreeable, and their decisions should reflect the overall grading philosophy of the school.

Setting absolute criteria for grading is easier for teachers who have had experience working with the material, testing, and students. The relative methods of marking depend entirely on the general achievement of the class, however. Students in advanced classes or classes with higher achieving students may be frustrated when they do not receive good grades even though their absolute achievement is high. Students in classes with lower achieving classmates may not be challenged to achieve because they only have to do better than most of their peers to receive good grades.

ASSIGNING AND REPORTING GRADES

Grades should be based only on the student's achievement; other characteristics should not enter the picture. Suppose a teacher decides to grade solely on the amount of improvement students exhibit from the beginning to the end of a course. If this is announced to the students, as it should be, the best strategy for the students to use would be to purposely do poorly at the beginning of the course and finish it with high achievement. This would mean very little studying at the beginning and a great deal at the end. In this system, a student could fail at the start of the class but receive an overall grade of A by getting As at the end, while a student with mostly As but a B on the last test might be given a B for the course.

If characteristics other than achievement are allowed to contribute to grades, the grades will lack validity. Grades must always be used to measure the same aspect of behavior, such as achievement, or marks from different teachers will mean different things and will be impossible to interpret. To ensure validity, grades should never be based on variables such as social class, ethnicity, race, or personality characteristics. Who can say, for example, if children who are quiet and compliant or those who are loud and assertive are better students? Some teachers like one type, some the other, and some like both. The effects of teachers' expectancies on grading and on student performance and behaviors have been described earlier (see especially Chapters 9 and 11).

Once the basic marking scale, based only on achievement, is determined, minor adjustments to individual students' grades can be made through the use of other criteria, including extra-credit work, improvement, and so on. This technique is especially effective for students on the borderline between two grades. Other characteristics the teacher considers important can be evaluated with additional marks, clearly labeled, or other mechanisms such as written comments or rating scales.

Figure 18.1

Example of a report card used at the high school level

MIDDLETOWN SCHOOL DISTRICT / School: Ronstadt High School

			1st period Days absent	tardy	2nd period Days absent	tardy
Graduation Credits	Home Room	Student No.				
25	108	38754	12	4	18	8

Subject	1st Quarter G E C			2nd Quarter G E C			Semester I Grade
English	B	2	2	B	2	2	B
World geography	C	3	2	C−	3	3	C−
Algebra	D	3	3	D−	3	3	D−
Shop	A	1	1	A	1	1	A
Biology	D	3	3	D−	3	3	D−

School Year 1983-84

Grade Point Averages

Accum.	Semester	Current
3.00	2.20	2.20

To the parent(s) of

Harry Harrison
1357 Alameda Way
Middletown, VT 03123

Grade (G)
A   outstanding
B   superior
C   average
D   below average
F   failure
    credit
I   incomplete
WP withdraw passing
WF withdraw failing
H   honors

Effort (E)
1   superior
2   satisfactory
3   unsatisfactory

Conduct (C)
1   outstanding
2   satisfactory
3   unsatisfactory

These characteristics might include improvement, effort, and work habits, for example.

Course or grading period grades are formally reported to the student and often to the parents, and they are kept in the student's permanent school file. Figure 18.1 shows a report card for a high school student whose marks for each course include a grade (G), which is an evaluation of achievement; a mark for effort (E); and a mark for conduct (C). Figure 18.2 reproduces the mathematics portion of a report card for a seventh-grade student which splits each course into subskills and behavioral goals and reports the student's effort on each, as well as an overall grade for each grading period. On this report card, the initial E stands for "excellent," S for "satisfactory," and NI for "needs improvement." The school's failure to explain its key, as in this example, makes the parents' task of interpreting their children's schoolwork unnecessarily difficult and perplexing.

Figure 18.2

Example of a report card used at the middle school level

Student: Carly Shaw
Yearly Average: B

Mathematics	I-E	I-S	I-NI	II-E	II-S	II-NI	III-E	III-S	III-NI	IV-E	IV-S	IV-NI
Grade	B			B+			B+			B−		
Effort	X			X			X			X		
Skills												
Whole numbers												
Computation	X											
Properties	X											
Problem solving												
Numbers and Numeration	X											
Number Theory		X		X								
Fractions												
Computations				X								
Concepts and notation				X								
Problem solving					X							
Decimals												
Computation							X					
Concepts and notation							X					
Problem solving							X					
Ratio and Proportion												
Computation										X		
Concepts and notation										X		
Problem solving										X		
Percent												
Computation							X					
Concepts and notation							X					
Problem solving							X					
Integers												
Computation												
Concepts and notation												
Problem solving												
Geometry												
Concepts and notation	X											
Problem solving	X											
Number Phrases and Sentences												
Equations and Inequalities												
Graphing												
Other Topics: Special Math	B											

Teacher Comments

I

II

III

IV Missing
8 papers

Behavioral Goals	I-S	I-NI	II-S	II-NI	III-S	III-NI	IV-S	IV-NI
Has materials at hand	X		X		X			X
Follows directions	X		X			X		X
Is courteous to others	X		X			X		X
Uses class time profitably	X		X			X		X
Works independently	X		X		X			X
Cooperates willingly	X		X			X		X
Listens while others speak	X		X			X		X
Is neat and accurate	X		X		X		X	

USES OF STANDARDIZED TEST RESULTS

Standardized test results, as we noted in Chapter 17, are used in the schools to evaluate student achievement, ability, or aptitude. Standardized achievement tests can be used to compare a student's achievement in various academic areas to average achievement in a number of norm groups, including comparable students in the school district, in the state, and in the nation. They can be used to examine a student's relative strengths and weaknesses in the areas measured and to chart academic growth from year to year, as well as to place new students in classes appropriate to their achievement levels.

Standardized intelligence and aptitude tests can be used to evaluate student potential for intellectual progress and more advanced academic work. They also can measure a student's chances for successfully completing college and provide career guidance.

EVALUATION OF TEACHERS

Ever since the first teacher taught the first learners, teachers have been informally evaluated. One student will say to friends, "Try not to get in Miss Jones's English section; she's tough and grades too hard." Or a parent will say to the principal, "I don't like Mr. Thomas. He just lets his students wander around the room instead of making them stay in their seats where they belong."

As the accountability trend has spread from the program evaluations required by federal legislation to the state or local level, there has been an increasing acceptance of formal teacher evaluation. Though school costs have increased significantly, the expenditures have not always been matched by a better product in the form of student learning. Some unsatisfactory aspects of student achievement and scholastic aptitude which became evident in the mid 1960s are still prevalent.

Local demands for school accountability are often translated into state legislation which requires the evaluation of school personnel, particularly teachers (Borich, 1977). One problem with this effort is the resistance of teachers to being evaluated. The major difficulty, however, is to construct measures of teacher effectiveness that are valid and that examine the complex roles and activities of teaching in a comprehensive way.

TEACHER RATING BY ADMINISTRATORS

While school administrators may say that the reason for teacher evaluation is to improve teaching performance, the information obtained is

Table 18.3

*General categories in teacher evaluation instruments
used in public school districts of New Mexico*

Category	Percent of Total Items in Instruments
Teaching role	28%
Administrator/manager role	14
Social role	12
Professional role	7
Organizational membership role	7
Personal characteristics	30
Student outcomes	1
Other	Less than 1%

Source: Data from Carolyn J. Wood and Paul A. Pohland, *Principal as Evaluator*, paper presented at the annual meeting of the American Educational Research Association, San Francisco, 1979.

basically used for administrative purposes. According to analysis of teacher evaluation information obtained in 1978 from 363 schools across the United States, this information serves two purposes: improving teacher performance, mentioned about one fifth of the time; and administration, including staffing and compensation decisions, mentioned about four fifths of the time (Wood & Pohland, 1979). When teacher evaluation instruments from the majority of school districts in the state of New Mexico were examined, the results were comparable, as shown in Table 18.3. Overall, the items in these evaluation instruments focus on the teachers more than on their teaching and require the evaluator to make subjective judgments about teachers and their environments.

These same general categories have been used in teacher rating scale instruments since the early 1900s, and the evaluation has been conducted primarily by principals and superintendents. This is still the major trend used for the summative evaluation of teachers, though most evaluating experts conclude that this type of evaluation is not very valid (Coleman, 1973). That is, the ratings do not correlate highly with student achievement or with other estimates of teacher effectiveness. Other forms of teacher evaluation that have been used include student ratings, systematic observation, peer ratings, self-ratings, and performance tests of teaching (McNeil & Popham, 1977), pupil achievement on standardized tests (Mehrens & Lehmann, 1978), and microteaching (Borich, 1977).

TEACHER RATING BY STUDENTS

Evaluation of teachers by their students has been used primarily at the college and university level for summative evaluation purposes. Some of these procedures would be helpful at the middle school and secondary school levels, however, if the maturity of the students is taken into account. This type of evaluation is typically by means of rating scales, most of which have common elements: They ask students for ratings related to the instructor's skill in teaching and communicating, content and structure of the course, student-instructor interaction, challenge offered, evaluation mechanisms used, student outcomes in terms of what has been learned, and overall satisfaction with the course or the teacher or both.

As this type of evaluation has gained recognition at the postsecondary level, there has been some concern for its reliability and validity. Research has shown that, in general, students are reliable raters; they are consistent in their ratings of individual teachers, and their ratings are stable across time (Marsh, Overall, & Kesler, 1979; Rotem & Glasman, 1979; Overall & Marsh, 1980). Validity is a different matter. Ratings by students are valid as indicators of student satisfaction with teachers (Rotem & Glasman, 1979). But most administrators use these ratings as measures of how well students learn the materials in the courses.

Groups of students tend to concur on the comparative effectiveness of individual teachers. In one study student ratings agreed with those of faculty who indicated which courses were taught "most" and "least" effectively (Marsh, Overall, & Kesler, 1979). In another, student ratings of the instructors who taught their courses agreed with judgments by graduating seniors in relation to which faculty were "most" and "least" outstanding (Marsh, 1977). However, according to Rotem and Glasman (1979), faculty concerns that student ratings do not accurately reflect learning, defined by performance on a final exam, are somewhat justified. Students are only moderately accurate in this regard.

Research has found that factors other than the actual quality of the teaching, such as class size, course content, and class level of the students, do affect students' ratings of teachers. In higher education, students' ratings can be considered only one moderately accurate source of information for use in summative evaluation. There are few other commonly used mechanisms for evaluating teachers at this level, however.

Outcomes of Student Evaluation

One of the outcomes of the use of student evaluation is that faculty members may behave in classes in ways that they feel will help them gain high ratings, even though the techniques may not make them better teachers. One example is the use of lenient grading scales; there are moderate positive relationships among several aspects of students' ratings of teachers and the students' final examination scores (Frey, Leonard, & Beatty, 1975), even when their initial abilities and interest levels are equated (Marsh & Overall, 1980), as well as their final grades in these courses (Peterson & Cooper, 1980).

Midterm student evaluations can give valuable formative evaluation information for instructors to use in modifying their instruction. This use of evaluation can be done with formal rating scales, as with summative evaluation, or it can be more informal, such as a discussion of what the students like and do not like and their suggestions for change. The input from formative evaluation can help instructors change their behavior and course content during the course, thus benefiting the current group of students. Summative evaluation can only be used to change the course for the next group.

Ratings of teachers by students do not show what a teacher actually does in the classroom, only what students think of the teacher. The evaluation method that comes closest to revealing actual classroom behavior is observation.

CLASSROOM OBSERVATION OF TEACHERS

Traditionally, when supervisory personnel observe teachers their evaluations are based on an overall judgment of the quality of the teaching. Such informal evaluations have very questionable validity and reliability, however, and recent efforts have been directed to making observation a more formalized method of measurement. There are now more than 100 observation scales for use in educational settings. *Mirrors for Behavior* (Simon & Boyer, 1970), for example, contains observation scales that measure many areas of classroom interaction, including cognitive, emotional, and classroom management aspects. Different scales can be used to measure the cognitive level of questions asked of the class, which sex is called on most frequently, how much positive and negative feedback the teacher gives, and so on. Observers must be trained to use these scales reliably and validly.

Observational research in the classroom has provided several general conclusions about teacher-student interactions (Good & Brophy, 1973). Most teachers talk more than students in class discussions, even when the discussions are supposed to be student centered, for example. And most questions asked by teachers, in class as well as on homework and tests, require students to use the lowest cognitive levels of rote memory and comprehension.

Classroom observation is an effective way to identify how teachers behave in their classrooms. Most teachers do not have accurate perceptions of their classroom behaviors, and when observation is used as a formative evaluation measure it can help teachers bring their behaviors into line with their objectives. But there is very little firm evidence on the relationships between teacher behavior, or knowledge for that matter, and student learning. Until more information about these relationships is available, observation results should not be used for absolute, summative evaluation purposes. There is a use for systematic, frequent observation, however, in evaluating teachers by the extent of the match between what they say they want to do and what they actually do in class.

EVALUATING TEACHERS BY PUPIL ACHIEVEMENT ON STANDARDIZED TESTS

Another method that is used to evaluate teachers is to examine their students' scores on standardized achievement tests. Teachers whose classes score low on the tests are evaluated negatively; those whose classes score high are regarded positively. This procedure often gives a biased evaluation of a teacher's competencies, because more goes into a student's achievement than the teacher's teaching. When students' test results are the criteria an excellent teacher with a poor class can appear to be ineffective, and an indifferent teacher can be made to look good by achievement-oriented students. To counter this effect, school administrators are examining the amount of achievement gain students experience with a teacher compared to their gains in the previous year. When this procedure is repeated for three or four years, it may be possible to determine the impact of a particular teacher on students' academic achievement.

EVALUATING HOW TO EVALUATE TEACHERS

There is little agreement among researchers, theoreticians, administrators, students, and teachers on how teachers should be evaluated. The evaluation should involve several methods of measurement (such as classroom observations and ratings by learners, colleagues, superiors, and self) and several types of criteria (such as student achievement and teacher's knowledge and teaching skills). It should be done on the basis of shared concepts between the teacher and the evaluator about what aspects of school-related activities will be examined.

The biggest problem with teacher evaluation is that so little is known about the relationship between teacher behavior and learner outcomes (Borich, 1977). Basically, this means that all current measures of teaching effectiveness are of unknown validity in relation to student achievement.

EVALUATION OF SCHOOLS
AND SCHOOL DISTRICTS

Although most educational evaluation is concerned with students and teachers, schools and school districts also need to be evaluated, for several purposes. Accountability to the public requires some measure of the effectiveness of the instructional process, and most federal and state mandated educational programs specify formal evaluations. Secondary schools require accreditation if their graduates are to be admitted to higher education, and some states provide for formal measures to assure all schools meet a certain standard.

The most common way to judge the merits of a school or school district involves a systematic, standardized achievement testing program that covers student learning from kindergarten through high school (see Chapter 17). In this case the school or school district is evaluated on the basis of the average results of students' standardized achievement tests, in the same way the student is evaluated as described earlier in this chapter. As a measure of the effectiveness of the instructional process, class achievements can be examined in relation to various norm groups, for changes over time, and in relation to how well objectives have been met.

Overall school achievement by grade level also can be compared to that of various local, state, and national norm groups. A measure of the effectiveness of the Chicago public school system, for example, is the gradual improvement in class reading scores on the ITBS reported in the spring of 1982, although most students still lagged behind their national counterparts in this respect. Such comparisons have political implications, and they are also useful to the school district because they provide a basis for changes in school policies and instructional plans. A school might discover, for example, that the upper grades, on the average, are high in reading comprehension compared to local norms, average compared to state norms, and below average nationally. The school then might investigate new reading programs for the upper elementary grades that would improve the students' reading comprehension scores in relation to national norms.

NATIONAL AND INTERNATIONAL
ASSESSMENTS OF ACHIEVEMENT

Standardized test results provide the only real source of information on national trends in achievement by U.S. students. One very important national evaluation effort is that of the National Assessment of Educational Progress (NAEP), which was started in the mid 1960s. The purpose of this survey is to measure the educational attainments of students who are 9, 13, and 17 years old and adults in ten learning areas: mathematics, reading, social studies, writing, music, literature, citizenship, art, career and occupational development, and science. Different areas are examined each year and all are periodically reassessed, so changes in these areas can be charted across the years. Reading achievement, for example, has been measured three times: in 1970–1971, in 1974–1975, and in 1979–1980 (see Box B).

The tests for the NAEP are constructed in much the same manner as any other standardized achievement test. They are administered to groups of people who vary systematically in age, sex, and ethnicity as well as region of the country, type of community (advantaged-urban, disadvantaged-urban, rural, other), and size of community in which they live. Due to careful sampling, the results can be generalized to similar groups of people (e.g., all nine-year-olds) across the country. The resulting information is used to make meaningful comparisons between these groups of people, as well as to examine changes across time. Results are reported as percentages of groups who answered correctly.

NAEP publishes papers summarizing their findings in all of the areas measured. They also report the objectives on which their tests are based, items measuring these objectives, and information about how the samples are designed and the results are analyzed (NAEP Publications, 1981).

Other sources for national achievement information are the standardized testing programs described in Chapter 17. Although they are not explicitly developed to chart trends, these tests are given yearly, and most test publishers do examine trends. Students who take these tests are asked to report demographic information, such as sex, ethnicity, and so on, so group comparisons can be made.

TRENDS IN ACHIEVEMENT SCORES

According to the NAEP reading results, coupled with those from other standardized achievement tests, the reading scores of early and middle elementary school children have increased since the 1960s. This may be due, at least in part, to reading programs developed with federal funds which stress basic reading skills such as word recognition. Reading scores for middle school and high school students generally have not changed or have declined, however, and the decline is especially apparent for above-average students (Harnischfeger & Wiley, 1977). Achievement tests at these levels generally measure high-level skills such as vocabulary and reading comprehension.

Average scores on many achievement and scholastic aptitude tests were maintained or increased until the mid 1960s, but they later declined in middle schools and high schools ("Verbal Average Falls," 1980; CEEB, 1977). The initial increase is generally attributed to the increased em-

BOX B   *The rise and fall of reading achievement*

An example of the trends in school achievement uncovered in the National Assessment of Educational Progress is the changes in reading performance reported in *Three National Assessments of Reading: Changes in Performance, 1970–1980*. Skill areas covered were literal comprehension, inferential comprehension, and reference. Results of this evaluation included the following findings for 9-, 13-, and 17-year-old students:

1. Significantly more nine-year-olds read better in all three skills areas at the third assessment (1979–1980) than at the first (1970–1971). Most of the increase was due to great improvements by students in the lowest and next-to-lowest quarters in reading achievement; students in the top half did not improve significantly. Black nine-year-olds improved more than any other group. Other groups who improved significantly included nine-year-olds who live in the Southeast, whose schools are in rural communities, and whose schools are in disadvantaged urban communities.

2. Thirteen-year-olds remained about the same in reading achievement, although they showed a small but significant increase in the literal comprehension skill area. Students in the lowest and next-lowest quarters improved significantly in achievement, while those in the top quarter decreased significantly. The only group who improved significantly was blacks.

3. Seventeen-year-olds' achievement remained about the same, except that significantly fewer answered the inferential comprehension questions correctly at the third assessment, compared to the first assessment. This decline was due to a loss in students in the top quarter of achievers. No group improved significantly, and students who reported that at least one of their parents had graduated from high school and those who indicated that a parent had some post-high school education decreased significantly in reading skills.

4. Girls at all three age levels at all three assessments read better than boys did, but the gap between the sexes was narrowing.

5. Students at all age levels showed high comprehension of basic material.

Source: National Assessment of Educational Progress, *Three National Assessments of Reading: Changes in Performance, 1970–1980*, Reading Report No. 11-R-01 (Denver, Colo.: Education Commission of the States, April 1981).

phasis on mathematics, science, and technical education which was mobilized as a response to the Russians' early lead in space exploration when they launched Sputnik, the first technological satellite to orbit the earth, in 1957 (Munday, 1976).

While the decline in average scores was quite small each year, it accumulated to an alarming size. One measure is the results of the Scholastic Aptitude Test (SAT), which is taken by many college-bound juniors and seniors to evaluate their potential for college work. Many colleges and universities require it, or a similar test called the American College Testing Assessment Program (ACT), for entrance. The SAT has a potential score range from 200 to 800, and scores are adjusted so they have the same meaning as when the test was first given in the early 1950s. The verbal average or mean score in 1951–1952 was 476, and it stayed at about that level until 1963–1964, when it started decreasing. It continued to decrease consistently; the mean score in 1979–1980 was 424, a significant change of about 0.5 standard deviation. The mathematics mean also decreased, but not as drastically. Whereas in 1951–1952, the mean was 494; in 1962–1963, it was 502; and in 1979–1980, it was 466, representing a significant decline of about 0.33 standard deviation.

The downward trend leveled off in 1980–1981, and by 1981–1982 it had been reversed slightly; the combined verbal and mathematics scores were up by a total of three points compared to the preceding two years. Out of a perfect 800 score, the nationwide average on the verbal section was 426 (compared to 424 in 1979–1980 and 1980–1981), and on the mathematics section it was 467 (compared to 466).

In 1977 the College Entrance Examination Board and the Educational Testing Service, publishers of the SAT, issued the report of a panel that had been assembled to study the decline in SAT scores. Two possible reasons for the decline were identified. First, from about 1963 to 1970, the characteristics of the students who took the SAT changed. The proportion of students who might be expected, on the basis of personal characteristics, to score lower on one or both portions of the SAT increased during that period as more students from lower socioeconomic homes, more minority students, and more women were taking the test. Second, during that period, the dropout rate in high schools decreased. One third of the students dropped out before graduation in 1964, and only one fourth did so in 1970. In 1964, also, one third of high school graduates went on to college, and a full half went on in 1970.

So, in the latter half of the 1960s, educational opportunity was expanding. According to the CEEB (1977) report, this shift in the composition of the test takers could account for between two thirds and three fourths of the drop in SAT scores from the mid 1960s to 1970. During this time, the scores of the top group of test takers did not decrease but remained high. After 1970, the composition of test takers continued to change somewhat, but not as much as it had in the preceding years.

Only one fourth of the continued decline in scores after 1970 could be attributed to the change in test takers, the CEEB found. At this point, every group's scores were declining, including the top scorers (those who went on to highly selective colleges and universities) and students in all regions of the country.

The CEEB (1977) report attributed the remainder of the decline in scores to five factors. First it noted school changes, with less emphasis being placed on general and required courses that usually include critical reading and writing. This change resulted in declining proportions of students in English, foreign language, mathematics, and natural science classes (Harnischfeger & Wiley, 1977).

Second, the CEEB (1977) found, there was "clearly observable evidence of diminished seriousness of purpose and attention to mastery of skills and knowledge in the learning process as it proceeds in the schools, the home, and the society generally." Changes have included higher school grades without higher achievement, called grade inflation (Munday, 1976); more absenteeism (Harnischfeger & Wiley, 1977); less homework; the lowering of entrance requirements for college admission; and use of texts and other curricular materials which require lower levels of skills and knowledge.

Third, students were learning more through viewing and listening than through reading, according to the CEEB report. By age 16, most students have watched 10,000–15,000 hours of television. This may be why middle school and high school scores have actually declined, though elementary school scores have increased. Most children now know numbers and letters when they enter school because they have watched educational television shows.

Fourth, family roles have changed, as divorce has become more common and both parents often work outside the home. This leaves less time and opportunity for parents to teach their children.

Fifth, the CEEB report suggests, achievement motivation appears to have declined. It is now easier to gain admission to colleges and universities, so students may be putting less effort into preparing for college entrance. Grade inflation and the generally lower requirements for promotion from grade to grade may reinforce students for less effort. Some subjects, such as mathematics, are stereotyped as "male" in character, so girls have comparatively less motivation to excel in them.

Even with these changes since the 1950s and 1960s, the academic achievement of U.S. students is generally very good. There is no question that students can read better today than they did in the 1940s. Almost all meet at least the minimum standards for basic reading literacy (Farr, 1977).

In the United States, the great majority of the population is educated, and the best students achieve as highly as the best students in other countries do. In international comparisons, the top 9 percent of U.S.

seniors scored better in the reading comprehension test than similar groups of seniors from all other participating countries, and they performed as well as seniors from five other countries on the mathematics test. Moreover, in 1976, 75 percent of U.S. students of appropriate ages were attending high school; in European countries attendance varied from a low of 9 percent (West Germany) to a high of 45 percent (Sweden), with most European countries averaging about 20 percent (Wolf, 1979).

THE BACK TO BASICS CONTROVERSY

Despite the record, the negative changes in achievement are the ones that have been publicized by the communications media. One outcome of the bad press, coupled with the rising costs of education, is a push for education to get "back to basics." This generally means more emphasis on the "3 Rs" of reading, writing, and mathematics and the traditional methods of education, and less emphasis on electives and educational innovations.

The advisory panel that studied the decline in SAT scores made three general recommendations in its report (CEEB, 1977). One was to restore the emphasis on "critical reading and careful writing." A second suggestion was to vary educational processes and methods to deal with the greater individual differences among students as more different types continued on in school. The panel deplored the trend to lower standards to cope with this diversity. The third suggestion was for the responsible use of television with children.

All three of these CEEB suggestions, to be effective, would have to involve parents and other adults as well as educators. The advisory panel certainly did not see the decrease in achievement among middle school and high school students as being "caused" by the schools. Rather, it was presented as a result of the social climate in this country. Their suggestions called for a stronger emphasis on basic subject matter and perhaps less on electives, but they also recommended use of a greater variety of educational methods.

Many advocates of "back to basics" would eliminate most educational innovations, but there is no evidence that innovations are related either positively or negatively to achievement. A study for the American Institutes for Research involving 30,000 students in grades 1 through 9 in 13 school districts found no relationship between student achievement and educational innovations such as experimental teaching methods or open classrooms (cited in CEEB, 1977). Many experts attribute at least part of the increased reading achievement of early elementary school students to new reading programs and materials (NAEP, 1981).

Moreover, elementary school children obviously have learned the basics of reading (NAEP, 1981); their test scores are the highest they have ever been (Farr, 1977). In fact, Farr speculates that emphasis on basics in reading, such as word recognition skills, in early elementary school could result in a deemphasis on the conceptual teaching of reading. And it is conceptual reading skills that are measured by achievement tests at the high school level.

Many different solutions to this complex problem have been proposed. Without doubt, one thing the classroom teacher should do is to help and encourage students to acquire advanced verbal and quantitative skills. These skills not only form the basis for entrance into the most sought-after careers in this country, they also help citizens accomplish, accurately and quickly, many of the tasks required for daily living.

CHAPTER 18 IN RETROSPECT

Educational evaluations are being increasingly recognized as having a legitimate role in education. They are a logical terminus of the instructional process, but they are not the end of it. Through feedback, evaluation results constantly provide necessary information to students, teachers, administrators, and the general public.

Formative evaluation, conducted during the implementation of a course, program, or project; summative evaluation, conducted at its conclusion; and accountability are evaluative aspects of education which are increasingly affecting teachers' lives. The most familiar aspect is their own evaluations of students, either through the grades they give or the decisions they make based on students' standardized test scores. Grades can be relative, as in grading on the curve, in which each student's achievement is compared to that of others, as it is in norm-referenced testing. Or grades can be absolute, such as percent-correct and pass-fail grades, in which each student's achievement is compared to a standard, as it is in criterion-referenced testing. Marking scales also can be devised which combine relative and absolute grades. The advantages and disadvantages of different types of scales, as well as the school's philosophy, should be considered in choosing a marking scale. Grades always should be based on achievement, however. Other potentially important characteristics, such as effort, can be reported through other means. Standardized achievement test results can be used to evaluate a student's achievement in comparison to norm groups, to determine relative strengths and weaknesses across content areas, and to measure growth from year to year.

Other types of measures are used to evaluate teachers. These include ratings by administrators and supervisors, ratings by students, systematic observation of teachers' classroom behaviors, and the students' standardized achievement test scores. All of these methods *may* be valid, depending on the teacher, the purpose of the evaluation, and the use of the method. Several measures of different types should be used, and the evaluation should be based on concepts about teaching that the evaluator and the teacher share.

Schools and school districts, as well as students and teachers, also must be evaluated. The existence of a good standardized testing plan covering all grade levels is a necessary part of evaluation at this level. Comparisons of achievement by grade level within the school and the district can provide useful information for the evaluation of policies, priorities, and instructional programs. Changes in achievement over time can also be tracked. School districts should monitor the accomplishment of objectives for all classes at the same grade level, ensure a consistent and logical approach to marking, and determine the public's perceptions of the schools.

Nationally, several aspects of achievement, as measured by standardized tests, have declined since the mid 1960s, although reading achievement scores in the elementary schools have been increasing. Generally, reading literacy in high school is high. The National Assessment of Educational Progress as well as other standardized test results have charted these changes in educational achievement across time. They also allow comparisons between groups of people based on demographic characteristics such as sex or ethnicity. The reasons given for the decline in scores include changes in the composition of the test takers; changes in schools; changes in homes, including increased television viewing; and declining achievement motivation. Internationally, the top U.S. high school seniors continue to achieve well in reading and mathematics, as they do in other content areas, compared to students in other countries.

**QUESTIONS
FOR
DISCUSSION**

1. Examine Table 18.1. How could the grades that are marked with asterisks be assigned differently? How would you, as a teacher, choose between the two possible grades in each case?

2. It is the end of the grading period, and a sixth-grade teacher needs to find each person's total score for science before she assigns grades. She gave them three tests (worth 30 percent) and seven homework assignments (worth 35 percent) and had them do two projects (worth 35 percent).

   a. Discuss her value system about which type of work is most important. Do you agree with her for this grade level?

b. Assuming that the students knew about this scale all semester, what study strategies should they have used if they want good grades?

c. Here are two of her students' scores. Find their total scores.

	Tests			Assignments							Projects	
	1	2	3	1	2	3	4	5	6	7	1	2
Mike	20	15	22	6	8	9	8	9	9	9	30	29
Madeline	25	26	24	7	6	5	6	5	6	6	35	34

3. Discuss each of the following grade situations:

a. Assume that the courses in the school where you teach are sectioned for ability (i.e., one section for high-ability students, one for average, and one for low). Is it "fair" to grade each section on its own curve? Or is it fair to grade the students on one curve for all three classes? Why or why not? How would you grade these classes?

b. Suppose Sally took a science achievement test, and she received a percentile score of 85. She is doing average work in your science class. Should you give her a D because she is not working up to her ability? Explain.

c. You gave a pretest at the start of the semester. Sue answered 25 percent of the questions correctly, while Sam answered 65 percent correctly. At the end of the semester on the final, Sue answered 65 percent correctly, while Sam answered 85 percent correctly. Should you give Sue a higher grade than Sam, since Sue improved more? Why or why not?

4. College-level teacher rating scales often include the following aspects: instructor's skill in teaching and communicating (clarity, enthusiasm); content and structure of the course (organization); student-instructor interaction (student contact); challenge to the student (difficulty); evaluation (tests); and student outcomes (amount learned). Which of these aspects of college teaching do you think are most and least important? Do your choices match those of your classmates? Do you always agree with other students about which teachers are the best and the worst? How do you decide what ratings to give your instructors?

5. Do you agree with the five factors selected by the College Board's advisory panel as being responsible for the declining aspects of achievement? Are there other factors they have missed? Are the declines worth worrying about? How would a "back to basics" approach help or hinder? What, if anything, do you think should be done?

Introductory Level

Gronlund, Norman E. *Improving Marking and Reporting in Classroom Instruction.* New York: Macmillan Co., 1974.

This short paperback discusses many ways of marking and preparing marks, including letter grades, pass-fail, checklists of objectives, letters to parents, report cards, and parent-teacher conferences. It also suggests methods for relative and absolute marking, a checklist for evaluating marking and reporting systems, and a sample parent-teacher conference guide.

Gronlund, Norman E. *Determining Accountability for Classroom Instruction.* New York: Macmillan Co., 1974.

This companion paperback discusses the nature of educational accountability and problems associated with it. It tells how to develop instructional objectives, use tests in accountability, and evaluate classroom instruction and teachers. Included is a checklist for evaluating a school accountability program.

Advanced Level

Mehrens, William A., and Lehmann, Irvin J. *Measurement and Evaluation in Education and Psychology.* 2nd ed. New York: Holt, Rinehart & Winston, 1978.

This book has an interesting section entitled "Evaluation: Its Disclosure and the Public" which discusses marking, interpreting standardized test scores results, school accountability, evaluating programs and schools, public concerns about evaluation (especially invasion of privacy and test fairness to minority students), and future trends in evaluation.

Hopkins, Charles D., and Antes, Richard L. *Classroom Measurement and Evaluation.* Itasca, Ill.: F. E. Peacock Publishers, 1978.

This testing and measurement text has chapters on the role of evaluation in education, classroom observation of students' learning behaviors, and screening for learning disabilities.

Borich, Gary D. (Ed.). *The Appraisal of Teaching: Concepts and Process.* Reading, Mass.: Addison-Wesley Publishing Co., 1977.

Part I, written by Borich, discusses the framework and concepts involved in defining and measuring teacher competencies and performance. The remainder of the book is selected readings which examine the relationship between teachers' behaviors, knowledge, and skills and students' learning; teacher evaluation; performance appraisal techniques; and how to develop valid teacher evaluation systems.

> *On Further Examination: Report of the Advisory Board on the Scholastic Aptitude Test Score Decline.* Princeton, N.J.: College Board Publications, 1977.

This very readable and interesting booklet discusses the SAT score decline, speculates as to its causes, and suggests how to remedy it and the decline in other achievement scores in this country.

> National Assessment of Educational Progress. *Three National Assessments of Reading: Changes in Performance, 1970–1980.* Reading Report No. 11-R-01. Denver, Colo.: Education Commission of the States, April 1981.

This booklet presents the changes that have occurred in students' reading skills from 1970 to 1980 in the areas of literal and inferential comprehension and reference skills as measured by the NAEP assessments.

REFERENCES

Barro, Stephen M. An approach to developing accountability measures for the public schools. *Phi Delta Kappan,* 1970, *52*(4), 196–205.

Borich, Gary D. (Ed.). *The Appraisal of Teaching: Concepts and Process.* Reading, Mass.: Addison-Wesley Publishing Co., 1977.

Coleman, Peter. The improvement of aggregate teaching effectiveness in a school district. *Educational Administration Quarterly,* 1973, *9*(3), 28–45.

College Entrance Examination Board. *On Further Examination: Report of the Advisory Panel on the Scholastic Aptitude Test Score Decline.* Princeton, N.J.: College Board of Publications, 1977.

Dyer, Henry S. Toward objective criteria of professional accountability in the schools of New York City. *Phi Delta Kappan,* 1970, *52*, 206–211.

Farr, Roger. Is Johnny's/Mary's reading getting worse? *Educational Leadership,* April 1977, pp. 521–527.

Frey, Peter W., Leonard, Dale W., and Beatty, William W. Student ratings of instruction: Validation research. *American Educational Research Journal,* 1975, *12*(4), 435–444.

Good, Thomas L., and Brophy, Jere E. *Looking in Classrooms.* New York: Harper & Row, 1973.

Gronlund, Norman E. *Determining Accountability for Classroom Instruction.* New York: Macmillan Co., 1974.

Harnischfeger, Annegret, and Wiley, David E. *The Decline of Achievement Test Scores: Evidence, Causes, and Consequences.* ERIC TM Report 59, February 1977.

Marsh, Herbert W. The validity of students' evaluations: Classroom evaluations of instructors independently nominated as best and worst teachers by graduating seniors. *American Educational Research Journal,* 1977, *14*(4), 441–447.

Marsh, Herbert W., and Overall, J. U. Validity of students' evaluations of teaching effectiveness: Cognitive and affective criteria. *Journal of Educational Psychology,* 1980, *72*(4), 468–475.

Marsh, Herbert W., Overall, Jesse U., IV, and Kesler, Steven P. Class size, students' evaluations, and instructional effectiveness. *American Educational Research Journal,* 1979, *16*(1), 57–70.

McNeil, John D., and Popham, W. James. A critique of widely used criteria in assessing teacher competency. In Gary D. Borich, *The Appraisal of Teaching: Concepts and Process.* Reading, Mass.: Addison-Wesley Publishing Co., 1977.

Mehrens, William A., and Lehmann, Irvin J. *Measurement and Evaluation in Education and Psychology.* 2nd ed. New York: Holt, Rinehart & Winston, 1978.

Munday, Leo A. *Declining Admissions Test Scores.* ACT Research Report No. 71. Iowa City, Iowa: American College Testing Program, February 1976.

National Assessment of Educational Progress Publications. Denver, Colo.: Education Commission of the States, March 1981.

Overall, J. U., and Marsh, Herbert W. Student's evaluations of instruction: A longitudinal study of their stability. *Journal of Educational Psychology,* 1980, *72*(3), 321–325.

Peterson, Christopher, and Cooper, Sloan. Teacher evaluation by graded and ungraded students. *Journal of Educational Psychology,* 1980, *72*(5), 682–685.

Rotem, Arie, and Glasman, Naftaly S. On the effectiveness of students' evaluative feedback to university instructors. *Review of Educational Research,* 1979, *49*(3), 497–511.

Simon, A., and Boyer, E. G. (Eds.). *Mirrors for Behavior: An Anthology for Observation Instruments.* Philadelphia: Research for Better Schools, 1970.

Verbal average falls to 424, Math to 466 as decline in SAT scores persists for 13th year. *Chronicle of Higher Education,* October 1980, p. 4.

Wolf, Richard M. *Evaluation in Education: Foundations of Competency Assessment and Program Review.* New York: Praeger Publishers, 1979.

Wood, Carolyn J., and Pohland, Paul A. *Principal as Evaluator.* Paper presented at the annual meeting of the American Educational Research Association, San Francisco, 1979.

Index

Name Index

Subject Index